AMERICA'S
CONSTITUTION

AMERICA'S CONSTITUTION

A Biography

AKHIL REED AMAR

RANDOM HOUSE ⚜ NEW YORK

Published in the United States by Random House, an imprint of
The Random House Publishing Group, a division of Random House, Inc., New York.

RANDOM HOUSE and colophon are registered trademarks of Random House, Inc.

LIBRARY OF CONGRESS CATALOGING-IN-PUBLICATION DATA
Amar, Akhil Reed.
America's constitution: a biography / Akhil Reed Amar.
p.   cm.
Includes bibliographical references and index.
ISBN 1-4000-6262-4 (hardcover)
1. Constitutional history—United States. I. Title.
KF4541.A87 2005
342.7302'9—dc22   2004061464

Printed in the United States of America on acid-free paper

Random House website address: www.atrandom.com

8 9

Book design by Mary A. Wirth

For Vinita, of course,
and for our children—Vik, Kara, and Sara.
May they and their generation continue to enjoy the blessings of liberty.

Contents

Preface

AMERICA'S CONSTITUTION BECKONS—a New World Acropolis open to all. Ordained in the name of the American people, repeatedly amended by them and for them, the document also addresses itself to them. It does its work in strikingly clean prose (as law goes) and with notable brevity. Its full text, including amendments, runs less than eight thousand words, a half hour's read for the earnest citizen. The document's style thus invites us to explore its substance, to visit and regularly revisit America's legal city on a hill.

Most citizens have declined the invitation. Many could probably recite at length from some favorite poem, song, speech, or scripture, yet few could quote by heart even a single paragraph of the supreme law of our land, one of the most important texts in world history. Lawyers, politicians, journalists, and opinion leaders converse fluently about legal dictums and doctrines that appear nowhere in the Constitution itself while slighting many intriguing words and concepts that do appear in the document. For instance, we rarely stop to think about what lay beneath the Constitution's promise of a "more perfect Union," or why the Founders required presidents to be at least thirty-five years old, or how the Fourteenth Amendment built upon earlier bans on "Titles of Nobility" when it made everyone "born" in America a "citizen[]." University professors who teach constitutional law often neglect to assign the document itself. The running joke is that reading the thing would only confuse students. The joke captures an important truth. Without background materials placing the Constitution in context, a modern reader may miss much of its meaning and richness.

This book seeks to reacquaint twenty-first-century Americans with the written Constitution. In the pages that follow, I invite readers to join me on an interpretive journey through the document, from its first words to its last clause. Along the way, we shall explore not merely what the Constitution says, but also how and why it says these things. How did various provisions at the Founding intermesh to form larger patterns of meaning and structures of decision making? How did later generations of constitutional Amenders reconfigure the system? Why did the Founders and Amenders act as they did? What lessons did they deduce from the distant past and from their own experiences? Which historically available models did they copy, and which plausible alternatives did they overlook or reject? What immediate problems were they trying to solve? Which long-range threats and possibilities did they espy on the horizon, and which future developments did they fail to foresee? What material and ideological resources did they command, and what practical constraints did they confront? How and why did their political opponents take issue with them? Who got to participate in the various decisions to ordain and, later, amend America's supreme law?

The Constitution has given rise to a remarkable range of interpretations over the years. In the chapters that follow I offer my own take: This book is an *opinionated* biography of the document. For example, while I try to say at least something in passing about every paragraph of the document, I pay special attention to those aspects of the Constitution that are, in my view, particularly significant or generally misunderstood. Because readers deserve to be told about other views, this book's endnotes identify contrasting perspectives (and also, where appropriate, furnish additional elaboration). In a brief Postscript, I summarize the main areas where my method and substance are, for better or worse, distinctive. For convenience, this book's Appendix contains the complete text of the Constitution, keyed to the corresponding pages of my narrative.

OUR STORY BEGINS—where else?—at the beginning, with the Constitution's opening sentence, conventionally known as the Preamble. This sentence bids us to ponder basic questions about our Constitution and our country. How democratic was the Constitution of 1787–88? Did it bind Americans into an indivisible nation? If so, why?

America's
Constitution

Chapter 1

IN THE

BEGINNING

The Pennsylvania Packet, *and Daily Advertiser.*

[Price Four-Pence.]   WEDNESDAY, September 19, 1787.   [No. 2690.]

WE, the People of the United States, in order to form a more perfect Union, establish Justice, insure domestic Tranquility, provide for the common Defence, promote the General Welfare, and secure the Blessings of Liberty to Ourselves and our Posterity, do ordain and establish this Constitution for the United States of America.

The Pennsylvania Packet, and Daily Advertiser (September 19, 1787).
When, after a summer of closed meetings in Philadelphia, America's leading statesmen went public with their proposed Constitution on September 17, 1787, newspapers rushed to print the proposal in its entirety. In several printings, the dramatic words of the Preamble appeared in particularly large type.

*I*T STARTED WITH A BANG. Ordinary citizens would govern themselves across a continent and over the centuries, under rules that the populace would ratify and could revise. By uniting previously independent states into a vast and indivisible nation, New World republicans would keep Old World monarchs at a distance and thus make democracy work on a scale never before dreamed possible.

"We . . . do"

With simple words placed in the document's most prominent location, the Preamble laid the foundation for all that followed. "We the People of the United States, . . . do ordain and establish this Constitution . . ."

These words did more than promise popular self-government. They also embodied and enacted it. Like the phrases "I do" in an exchange of wedding vows and "I accept" in a contract, the Preamble's words actually performed the very thing they described. Thus the Founders' "Constitution" was not merely a text but a deed—a *constituting*. We the People *do* ordain. In the late 1780s, this was the most democratic deed the world had ever seen.

Behind this act of ordainment and establishment stood countless ordinary American voters who gave their consent to the Constitution via specially elected ratifying conventions held in the thirteen states beginning in late 1787. Until these ratifications took place, the Constitution's words were a mere proposal—the text of a contract yet to be accepted, the script of a wedding still to be performed.

The proposal itself had emerged from a special conclave held in Philadelphia during the summer of 1787. Twelve state governments—all except Rhode Island's—had tapped several dozen leading public servants and private citizens to meet in Philadelphia and ponder possible revisions of the Articles of Confederation, the interstate compact that Americans had formed during the Revolutionary War. After deliberating behind closed doors for months, the Philadelphia conferees unveiled their joint proposal in mid-September in a document signed by thirty-nine of the continent's most eminent men, including George Washington, Benjamin Franklin, James Wilson, Roger Sherman, James Madison, Alexander Hamilton, Gouverneur Morris, John Rutledge, and Nathaniel Gorham.

When these notables put their names on the page, they put their reputations on the line.

An enormous task of political persuasion lay ahead. Several of the leaders who had come to Philadelphia had quit the conclave in disgust, and others who had stayed to the end had refused to endorse the final script. Such men—John Lansing, Robert Yates, Luther Martin, John Francis Mercer, Edmund Randolph, George Mason, and Elbridge Gerry—could be expected to oppose ratification and to urge their political allies to do the same. No one could be certain how the American people would ultimately respond to the competing appeals. Prior to 1787, only two states, Massachusetts and New Hampshire, had ever brought proposed state constitutions before the people to be voted up or down in some special way. The combined track record from this pair of states was sobering: two successful popular ratifications out of six total attempts.

In the end, the federal Constitution proposed by Washington and company would barely squeak through. By its own terms, the document would go into effect only if ratified by specially elected conventions in at least nine states, and even then only states that said yes would be bound. In late 1787 and early 1788, supporters of the Constitution won relatively easy ratifications in Delaware, Pennsylvania, New Jersey, Georgia, and Connecticut. Massachusetts joined their ranks in February 1788, saying "we do" only after weeks of debate and by a close vote, 187 to 168. Then came lopsided yes votes in Maryland and South Carolina, bringing the total to eight ratifications, one shy of the mark. Even so, in mid-June 1788, a full nine months after the publication of the Philadelphia proposal, the Constitution was still struggling to be born, and its fate remained uncertain. Organized opposition ran strong in all the places that had yet to say yes, which included three of America's largest and most influential states. At last, on June 21, tiny New Hampshire became the decisive ninth state by the margin of 57 to 47. A few days later, before news from the North had arrived, Virginia voted her approval, 89 to 79.

All eyes then turned to New York, where Anti-Federalists initially held a commanding lead inside the convention. Without the acquiescence of this key state, could the new Constitution really work as planned? On the other hand, was New York truly willing to say no and go it alone now that her neighbors had agreed to form a new, more perfect union among themselves? In late July, the state ultimately said yes by a vote of 30 to 27. A switch of only a couple of votes would have reversed the outcome. Meanwhile, the last two states, North Carolina and Rhode Island, refused to ratify in 1788. They would ultimately join the new union in late 1789 and mid-1790, respectively—well after George Washington took office as president of the new (eleven!) United States.

Although the ratification votes in the several states did not occur by direct statewide referenda, the various ratifying conventions did aim to represent "the People" in a particularly emphatic way—more directly than ordinary legislatures. Taking their cue from the Preamble's bold "We the People" language, several states waived standard voting restrictions and allowed a uniquely broad class of citizens to vote for ratification-convention delegates. For instance, New York temporarily set aside its usual property qualifications and, for the first time in its history, invited all free adult male citizens to vote.[1] Also, states generally allowed an especially broad group of Americans to serve as ratifying-convention delegates. Among the many states that ordinarily required upper-house lawmakers to meet higher property qualifications than lower-house members, none held convention delegates to the higher standard, and most exempted delegates even from the lower. All told, eight states elected convention delegates under special rules that were more populist and less property-focused than normal, and two others followed standing rules that let virtually all taxpaying adult male citizens vote. No state employed special election rules that were more property-based or less populist than normal.[2]

In the extraordinarily extended and inclusive ratification process envisioned by the Preamble, Americans regularly found themselves discussing the Preamble itself. At Philadelphia, the earliest draft of the Preamble had come from the quill of Pennsylvania's James Wilson,[3] and it was Wilson who took the lead in explaining the Preamble's principles in a series of early and influential ratification speeches. Pennsylvania Anti-Federalists complained that the Philadelphia notables had overreached in proposing an entirely new Constitution rather than a mere modification of the existing Articles of Confederation. In response, Wilson—America's leading lawyer and one of only six men to have signed both the Declaration of Independence and the Constitution—stressed the significance of popular ratification. "This Constitution, proposed by [the Philadelphia draftsmen], claims no more than a production of the same nature would claim, flowing from a private pen. It is laid before the citizens of the United States, unfettered by restraint. . . . By their *fiat,* it will become of value and authority; without it, it will never receive the character of authenticity and power."[4] James Madison agreed, as he made clear in a mid-January 1788 New York newspaper essay today known as *The Federalist* No. 40—one of a long series of columns that he wrote in partnership with

Alexander Hamilton and John Jay under the shared pen name "Publius." According to Madison/Publius, the Philadelphia draftsmen had merely "proposed a Constitution which is to be of no more consequence than the paper on which it is written, unless it be stamped with the approbation of those to whom it is addressed. [The proposal] was to be submitted *to the people themselves,* [and] the disapprobation of this supreme authority would destroy it forever; its approbation blot out antecedent errors and irregularities." Leading Federalists across the continent reiterated the point in similar language.[5]

With the word *fiat,* Wilson gently called to mind the opening lines of Genesis. In the beginning, God said, *fiat lux,* and—behold!—there was light. So, too, when the American people (Publius's "supreme authority") said, "We do ordain and establish," that very statement would do the deed. "Let there be a Constitution"—and there would be one. As the ultimate sovereign of all had once made man in his own image, so now the temporal sovereign of America, the people themselves, would make a constitution in their own image.[6]

All this was breathtakingly novel. In 1787, democratic self-government existed almost nowhere on earth. Kings, emperors, czars, princes, sultans, moguls, feudal lords, and tribal chiefs held sway across the globe. Even England featured a limited monarchy and an entrenched aristocracy alongside a House of Commons that rested on a restricted and uneven electoral base. The vaunted English Constitution that American colonists had grown up admiring prior to the struggle for independence was an imprecise hodgepodge of institutions, enactments, cases, usages, maxims, procedures, and principles that had accreted and evolved over many centuries. This Constitution had never been reduced to a single composite writing and voted on by the British people or even by Parliament.

The ancient world had seen small-scale democracies in various Greek city-states and pre-imperial Rome, but none of these had been founded in fully democratic fashion. In the most famous cases, one man—a celebrated lawgiver such as Athens's Solon or Sparta's Lycurgus—had unilaterally ordained his countrymen's constitution. Before the American Revolution, no people had ever explicitly voted on their own written constitution.[7]

Nor did the Revolution itself immediately inaugurate popular ordainments and establishments. True, the 1776 Declaration of Independence proclaimed the "self-evident" truth that "Governments are instituted among Men, deriving their just Powers from the Consent of the Governed." The document went on to assert that "whenever any Form of Government becomes destructive of [its legitimate] Ends, it is the Right of the People to alter and abolish it, and to institute new Government." Yet the Declaration only imperfectly acted out its bold script. Its fifty-six acclaimed signers never put the document to any sort of popular vote.

Between April and July 1776, countless similar declarations issued from assorted towns, counties, parishes, informal assemblies, grand juries, militia units, and legislatures across America.[8] By then, however, the colonies were already under military attack, and conditions often made it impossible to achieve inclusive deliberation or scrupulous tabulation. Many patriots saw Crown loyalists in their midst not as fellow citizens free to vote their honest judgment with impunity, but rather as traitors deserving tar and feathers, or worse. (Virtually no arch-loyalist went on to become a particularly noteworthy political leader in independent America. By contrast, many who would vigorously oppose the Constitution in 1787–88—such as Maryland's Samuel Chase and Luther Martin, Virginia's Patrick Henry and James Monroe, and New York's George Clinton and John Lansing—moved on to illustrious post-ratification careers.)[9]

Shortly before and after the Declaration of Independence, new state governments began to take shape, filling the void created by the ouster of George III. None of the state constitutions ordained in the first months of the Revolution was voted on by the electorate or by a specially elected ratifying convention of the people. In many states, sitting legislatures or closely analogous Revolutionary entities declared themselves solons and promulgated or revised constitutions on their own authority, sometimes without even waiting for new elections that might have given their constituents more say in the matter, or at least advance notice of their specific constitutional intentions.[10]

In late 1777, patriot leaders in the Continental Congress proposed a set of Articles of Confederation to govern relations among the thirteen states. This document was then sent out to be ratified by the thirteen state legislatures, none of which asked the citizens themselves to vote in any special way on the matter.

Things began to change as the Revolution wore on. In 1780, Massachusetts enacted a new state constitution that had come directly before the voters assembled in their respective townships and won their approval. In 1784, New Hampshire did the same. These local dress rehearsals (for so they seem in retrospect) set the stage for the Preamble's great act of continental popular sovereignty in the late 1780s.[11]

As Benjamin Franklin and other Americans had achieved famous advances in the natural sciences—in Franklin's case, the invention of bifocals, the lightning rod, and the Franklin stove—so with the Constitution America could boast a breakthrough in political science. Never before had so many ordinary people been invited to deliberate and vote on the supreme law under which they and their posterity would be governed. James Wilson fairly burst with pride in an oration delivered in Philadelphia to some twenty thousand merrymakers gathered for a grand parade on July 4, 1788. By that date, enough Americans had said "We do" so as to guarantee that the Constitution would go into effect (at least in ten states—the document was still pending in the other three). The "spectacle, which we are assembled to celebrate," Wilson declared, was "the most dignified one that has yet appeared on our globe," namely, a

> people free and enlightened, establishing and ratifying a system of government, which they have previously considered, examined, and approved! ...
>
> ... You have heard of Sparta, of Athens, and of Rome; you have heard of their admired constitutions, and of their high-prized freedom.... But did they, in all their pomp and pride of liberty, ever furnish, to the astonished world, an exhibition similar to that which we now contemplate? Were their constitutions framed by those, who were appointed for that purpose, by the people? After they were framed, were they submitted to the consideration of the people? Had the people an opportunity of expressing their sentiments concerning them? Were they to stand or fall by the people's approving or rejecting vote?[12]

The great deed was done. The people had taken center stage and enacted their own supreme law.

FROM ANOTHER ANGLE, the drama was just beginning. Preamble-style popular sovereignty was an ongoing principle. No liberty was more central than the people's liberty to govern themselves under rules of their own choice;[13] and the Preamble promised to secure this and other "Blessings of Liberty" not just to the Founding generation, but also, emphatically, to "our Posterity."

As Wilson explained in Pennsylvania's ratification debates, the people's right to "ordain and establish" logically implied their equal right "to repeal and annul." The people "retain the right of recalling what they part with.... WE [the people] reserve the right to do what we please." Leading Federalists in sister states echoed this exposition. North Carolina's James Iredell, who would one day sit on the Supreme Court alongside

Wilson, reminded his listeners that in America "our governments have been clearly created by the people themselves. The same authority that created can destroy; and the people may undoubtedly change the government." Not content to leave the matter implicit, Virginia ratified the Constitution on the express understanding that "the powers granted under the Constitution, being derived from the people of the United States, may be resumed by them, whensoever the same shall be perverted to their injury or oppression."[14]

Similar ideas surfaced in New York. Writing as Publius in *The Federalist* No. 84, Alexander Hamilton explained that "here, in strictness, the people . . . retain everything [and] have no need of particular reservations. 'WE THE PEOPLE . . . , to secure the blessings of liberty to ourselves and our posterity, do *ordain* and *establish* this Constitution . . . . ' Here is a [clear] recognition of popular rights." By "popular rights" Publius meant rights of the people qua sovereign, including their right to revise what they had created. Following Virginia's lead, New York used its ratification instrument to underscore its understanding of the Preamble's principles: "All power is originally vested in, and consequently derived from, the people. . . . The powers of government may be reassumed by the people whensoever it shall become necessary to their happiness."[15]

These assorted speeches, essays, and ratification texts emphasizing the "popular rights" that "the people" "retain" and "reserve" and may "resume" and "reassume" exemplified what the First Congress had centrally in mind in 1789 when it proposed certain amendments as part of a general bill of rights. With its last three words proudly paralleling the Preamble's first three, the sentence that eventually became the Ninth Amendment declared rights implicitly "retained by the people," such as their right to alter what they had ordained. Similarly, the Tenth Amendment declared powers "reserved . . . to the people," and the First Amendment guaranteed "the right of the people peaceably to assemble" in constitutional conventions and elsewhere. In all these places, the phrase "the people" gestured back to the Constitution's first and most prominent use of these words in the Preamble.[16]

In the First Congress, lawmakers pointed not just to the Preamble's words but also to its more immediate "practical" effect concerning the right to amend.[17] By ordaining the federal Constitution, Americans had in practice altered their state constitutions and abolished the Articles of Confederation. For example, most state constitutions in place before 1787 had given state legislatures power to issue paper money and emit bills of credit.[18] The federal Constitution abrogated these and other powers by fastening a new regulatory framework upon state governments.[19] In deed as well as word, the Preamble stood for ongoing popular sovereignty—the people's right to change their mind as events unfolded.

Even more dramatically, the Preamble by its very deed implicitly affirmed that the people's right to amend ultimately required only a simple majority vote, at least within a state. In Massachusetts, a two-thirds vote of the electorate had been required to launch the 1780 state constitution; and the document had provided for an amendment process to begin in 1795 if endorsed by "two-thirds of the qualified voters . . . who shall assemble and vote." Yet the federal Constitution drafted at Philadelphia proposed to modify this state constitution well before 1795, and to do so by a mere majority of a specially elected Massachusetts convention, which in the end voted 187 to 168 for the new legal order—far short of two-thirds, and not by a direct tally of all the qualified voters. Even so, once this vote occurred, Massachusetts Anti-Federalists immediately acquiesced, acknowledging that the people had truly spoken, albeit not in the precise manner that had been set out in 1780. In essence, Bay Staters in 1788 reconceptualized their earlier amendment clause as merely one way, rather than the only way, by which the sovereign people might alter their government.[20] Ratification of the federal Constitution broke similar new ground in several of Massachusetts's sister states, where analogous state constitutional issues arose.

Preamble-style ratification also broke new ground by establishing that the people's right to alter government did not require proof of past tyranny. When the Declaration of Independence trumpeted "the Right of the People to alter or abolish" governments, it had limited this right (as had the influential English philosopher John Locke)[21] to situations in which governments had grossly abused their powers—"whenever any Form of Government bec[ame] destructive" of its legitimate ends. The longest section of the Declaration aimed precisely to detail the insufferable "Evils," the "long Train of Abuses and Usurpations, pursuing invariably the same Object, evinc[ing] a design to reduce [Americans] under absolute Despotism." Such a clear pattern of "repeated Injuries and Usurpations, all having in direct Object the Establishment of an absolute Tyranny" justified a people in exercising their right to change government, even if the consequence would be all-out war against the king.

By the late 1780s, Americans had toppled the old order of George III, and the right to alter could now operate far more freely. Unlike the Declaration, the Constitution did not purport to show—because it did not *need* to show—that the regime it was amending was tyrannical. The people could properly amend whenever they deemed the status quo outdated or imperfect. If reformers proposed a change, ballots rather than bullets would decide the contest. In contrast to Old World monarchs, New World public servants would accept the people's constitutional verdict without waging war on them.

Americans understood this transformation even as they were doing the transforming and marveling at their own handiwork. "The people may change the constitutions whenever and however they please," explained Wilson. "It is a power paramount to every constitution, inalienable in its nature."[22] By their very act of assembling in ratifying conventions to debate the Philadelphia plan, the people were making these words flesh. "Under the practical influence of this great truth, we are now sitting and deliberating, and under its operation, we can sit as calmly and deliberate as coolly, in order to change a constitution, as a legislature can sit and deliberate under the power of a constitution, in order to alter or amend a law."[23]

Outside Pennsylvania, other Federalists followed Wilson's cue. North Carolina's Iredell contrasted "other countries," where the people could rightfully change their government only if the king either consented or acted tyrannically (and thus forfeited his right to rule), with America, where "the people may undoubtedly change the government, not because it is ill exercised, but because they conceive another form will be more conducive to their welfare." In New York, Publius likewise pushed beyond the Declaration in championing "the right of the people to alter or abolish the established Constitution, whenever they find it inconsistent with their happiness."[24]

In going a step beyond the Declaration, the Preamble also went several steps beyond ancient republics and the British constitution. In seventeenth- and eighteenth-century England, constitutional reformers often claimed, with varying degrees of accuracy and sincerity, that they were merely restoring good old rules unearthed from a hallowed past rather than minting entirely new rules for a modern era. Shrouding their founding moments in myth and superstition, ancient Greek republics had been even less open to progressive alteration. Solon had stipulated that his constitution for Athens could not be amended for a hundred years, and Lycurgus had contrived to render his Spartan constitution wholly unamendable.[25] Contrasting the Preamble with these models from antiquity, Madison/Publius in *The Federalist* No. 38 took pride in the remarkable "improvement made by America on the ancient [Greek] mode of preparing and establishing regular plans of government."[26]

AMERICA'S FOUNDING GAVE the world more democracy than the planet had thus far witnessed. Yet many modern Americans, both lawyers and laity, have missed this basic fact. Some mock the Founding Fathers as rich white men who staged a reactionary coup, while others laud the framers as dedicated traditionalists rather than democratic revolutionaries. A prominent modern canard is that the very word "democracy" was anathema to the Founding generation.[27] When today's scholars quote the framers on how America's Constitution broke with ancient Greek practices, the standard quotation comes not from Wilson's July 4 oration or Madison's similar *Federalist* No. 38, but rather from a passage in Madison's *Federalist* No. 63 that is brandished to prove that the framers were *less* democratic than the ancients, and proudly so: "The true distinction between [ancient democracies] and the American governments, lies *in the total exclusion of the people, in their collective capacity,* from any share in the *latter.* . . . The distinction . . . must be admitted to leave a most advantageous superiority in favor of the United States."

This conventional account misreads both Madison and the Constitution. True, Madison did harbor strong anxieties about the ability of a large mass of people to meet together to legislate. In another unfavorable comment on Greek-style democracy, he observed in *The Federalist* No. 55 that in "all very numerous assemblies, of whatever character[s] composed, passion never fails to wrest the sceptre from reason. Had every Athenian citizen been a Socrates, every Athenian assembly would still have been a mob." However, Madison was not an antidemocrat scoffing at the limited capacities of ordinary folk, but rather a republican proceduralist pondering how best to structure lawmaking institutions. Even if every citizen *were* a philosopher king, how could a legislature function if composed of "six or seven thousand" (Madison's hypothetical) all clamoring to be heard?

In his view, thousands of people could not have immediately and equally participated in the countless specific decisions implicated in drafting a proposed Constitution in Philadelphia, clause by clause. On the other hand, the issue of ratifying a completed, 4,500-word proposal was a simpler one more fit for democratic judgment. Should the document be approved, yes or no? Thus Madison and the other Philadelphia drafters proposed that their handiwork come before the American people, organized in specially elected statewide conventions. These conventions would be deliberative forums facilitating extended democratic discussion. Large-scale direct referenda would have prevented the ultimate ratification votes from benefiting from detailed presentation of competing arguments on issues large and small. In each state, the convention debate process might properly take several weeks. Would it be fair to ask every voter in America to drop everything for so long a period? Wouldn't it make more sense to ask ordinary voters to read the document on their own, discuss it with friends, and then deputize persons they most trusted to think like themselves to attend a special convention on their behalf? Such specially deputized delegates could then act as ordinary voters themselves would have done had they been present to hear all the extended analysis pro and con.

Nevertheless, the decision to ratify the Constitution via conventions rather than by direct popular votes did risk introducing distortions into the Founding process. Convention delegates might be systematically malapportioned, giving some regions within a state far more than their fair share of influence; delegates might betray the explicit or implicit instructions of ordinary voters; and so on. We shall revisit these possible distortions later in our story, after we have had occasion to examine more general issues of apportionment and representation in Revolutionary America. For now, let us simply note that conventions offered the promise of democratic deliberation that direct statewide popular votes would have lacked.

Similarly, as Madison and other Federalists saw the matter, judicial decisions should not occur via mass society-wide votes of guilty or innocent, liable or not liable, and in this sense *The Federalist* No. 63 correctly observed that the Constitution excluded the people *"in their collective capacity"* from day-to-day judicial governance in America. Yet clusters of ordinary citizens—juries—would indeed make crucial decisions after hearing presentations from different sides. Though far smaller than Greek juries (some five hundred jurors had sat in judgment of Socrates), American grand juries, criminal petit juries, and civil juries would enable ordinary Americans to participate directly and daily in American government.

In fact, the Constitution infused some form of democracy into each of its seven main Articles. Echoing the Preamble's first three words, Article I promised that all members of the new House of Representatives would be elected directly "by the People." No constitutional property qualifications would limit eligibility to vote for or serve in Congress; nor could Congress add any qualifications by statute. Also, Article I prohibited both state and federal governments from creating hereditary government positions via titles of nobility. Under Articles II and III, the presidency and federal judgeships would be open to men of merit regardless of wealth or lineage.

Government servants in all three branches would receive government salaries, lest the right to hold office or public trust be restricted to the independently wealthy. Military hierarchies would answer to democratically elected leaders, not vice versa. Juries of ordinary people would counterbalance professional judges in the judicial branch, as militias of ordinary people would check professional armies in the executive branch. Article IV guaranteed every state a "Republican Form of Government"—that is, a government ultimately derived from the people, as opposed to an aristocracy or monarchy. (The word "republican" came from the same etymological roots—*publica, poplicus*—as the pivotal Preamble word "people," whose Greek counterpart, *demos,* in turn underlay the word "democracy.") If ordinary legislatures clogged necessary reforms, Article V enabled Americans to bypass these legislatures with specially elected conventions to propose and ratify new constitutional rules. Article VI banned Old World religious hierarchies from formally entrenching themselves in the federal government or excluding adherents of competitor religions from federal service. Finally, Article VII specified how the Preamble's ordainment and establishment would take place.

The Federalist reflected these populist themes from start to finish. The first paragraph of Publius's first essay reminded ordinary citizens that "you are called upon to deliberate on a new Constitution" and by an "election" set a new example in world history. The last paragraph of his last essay reiterated the point. "The establishment of a Constitution, in time of profound peace, by the voluntary consent of a whole people, is a prodigy." Between these bookend paragraphs, Publius repeatedly extolled and elaborated the Preamble's enactment of popular sovereignty.[28] Indeed, in *The Federalist* No. 39, Madison/Publius wrote that the "first question" to be asked about the Constitution as a whole was whether "the government be strictly republican"—essentially, "a government which derives all its powers directly or indirectly from the great body of the people," as opposed to an aristocracy or monarchy. Why was *this* the first question? Because "no other form would be reconcilable with the genius of the people of America [and] the fundamental principles of the Revolution." Throughout the rest of *The Federalist,* Publius linked this idea of republicanism to the Constitution's defining characteristics—its extensive geographic and demographic reach; the interior design of each of its three main branches; its limits on state governments; and so on.[29] Similarly, in both his opening and concluding speeches before the Pennsylvania ratifying convention, Wilson pronounced the Constitution "purely democratical," and in yet another speech he boasted that "the DEMOCRATIC principle is carried into every part of the government."[30]

Although some modern readers have tried to stress property protection rather than popular sovereignty as the Constitution's bedrock idea, the words "private property" did not appear in the Preamble, or anywhere in the document for that matter. The word "property" itself surfaced only once, and this in an Article IV clause referring to *government* property. Above and beyond the Constitution's plain text, its clear commitment to people over property shone through in its direct act: As we have seen, the Founders generally set aside ordinary property qualifications in administering the special elections for ratification-convention delegates.

The Founders' decisions to waive these property rules in the special elections of 1787–88 built upon conceptual and practical foundations laid by several states when framing their state constitutions. In 1776, Pennsylvania militiamen who were unable to meet the property threshold for electing colonial legislators nevertheless voted for delegates to a special constitutional convention, which then drafted and promulgated (without any ratifying vote by the electorate) a remarkably democratic state constitution. By historian Pauline Maier's estimate, Pennsylvania's "constitutional convention [was] chosen under rules that expanded the electorate by as much as 50 to 90 percent." Several years later, the framing and ratification of the Massachusetts Constitution featured even more direct participation by otherwise ineligible propertyless men. In essence, the Massachusetts experience drove a wedge between property qualifications for ordinary legislative elections—qualifications that the document raised compared to colonial rules still in operation in the late 1770s—and property qualifications for adopting the new constitution itself, qualifications that the new constitution eliminated altogether. Thus, the very document adding new property qualifications for ordinary elections was framed by a convention elected by all adult freemen regardless of property, and was then directly submitted to these freemen for ratification. (All freemen were also eligible to serve as delegates at the convention that drafted the proposed constitution.) *Constitutional* elections, the Massachusetts experience seemed to suggest, were different from ordinary elections and should rest on the broadest popular foundation. In neighboring New Hampshire, the state constitution of 1784 and its three previous unsuccessful incarnations were submitted to an expansive electorate that included all taxpaying New Hampshiremen—an electorate the state legislature in its implementing legislation referred to as "the People" with a capital P.[31]

Pennsylvania, Massachusetts, and New Hampshire were the three states whose constitution-ordaining procedures, going well beyond simple promulgation by the sitting legislature or its equivalent, most closely foreshadowed what the Preamble would call for at the federal level in 1787.[32] At Philadelphia, Massachusetts's Nathaniel Gorham explicitly drew upon his state's experience when he declared that "many of the ablest men are excluded from the [state] Legislatures, but may be elected into a Convention." For example, men "of the Clergy" were formally barred from serving in most state legislatures and elsewhere could not serve unless they owned real estate in their own names. Yet Gorham believed that such ordinarily ineligible men had proved "valuable in the formation & establishment" of the Massachusetts Constitution, and that the federal Constitution should likewise be ordained by conventions that would waive ordinary eligibility rules. Fellow Bay Stater Rufus King agreed, and predicted that such conventions would "draw[] forth the best men in the States." Along with the inclusive ordainment experiences in Pennsylvania and New Hampshire, the high-profile Massachusetts precedent thus pointed those who drafted and implemented the Preamble toward the widest imaginable participation rules for the continental ordainment process.[33]

THE WIDEST RULES imaginable in the eighteenth century, of course. From a twenty-first-century perspective, the idea that the Constitution was truly established by "the People" might seem a bad joke. What about slaves and freeborn women?

The question is particularly pointed in modern America because it reflects more than some purely subjective or theoretical definition of democracy. Rather, the sensibility underlying the question is itself a constitutional sensibility, informed by the very vision of democracy embodied in the United States Constitution. The Constitution *as amended,* that is. Later generations of the American people have surged through the Preamble's portal and widened its gate. Like constitutions, amendments are not just words but deeds—flesh-and-blood struggles to redeem America's promise while making amends for some of the sins of our fathers.

In both word and deed, America's amendments have included many of the groups initially excluded at the Founding. In the wake of the Civil War, We the People abolished slavery in the Thirteenth Amendment, promised equal citizenship to all Americans in the Fourteenth Amendment, and extended the vote to black men in the Fifteenth Amendment. A half-century later, We guaranteed the right of woman suffrage in the

Nineteenth Amendment, and during a still later civil-rights movement, We freed the federal election process from poll taxes and secured the vote for young adults in the Twenty-fourth and Twenty-sixth Amendments, respectively. No amendment has ever cut back on prior voting rights or rights of equal inclusion. (If this be Whiggism, Americans should make the most of it.)

Previously excluded groups have played leading roles in the amendment process itself, even as amendments have promised these groups additional political rights. Black voters, already enfranchised in many states, propelled the federal Fifteenth Amendment forward; women voters helped birth the Nineteenth; and the poor and the young spearheaded movements to secure their own constitutionally protected suffrage. Through these dramatic acts and texts of amendment, We the People of later eras have breathed new life into the Preamble's old prose.

WHICH BRINGS US BACK to the Constitution as it looked in the eighteenth century. It's worth remembering that the Founding generation had fought a revolution against one of the world's most powerful monarchies, and that the most staunchly conservative elements of colonial society had fled America during the 1760s and 1770s. True, the act of constitution fell far short of universal suffrage as modern Americans understand the idea, but where had anything close to universal suffrage ever existed prior to 1787? Ancient democracies had excluded women and slaves. In classic republican theory, the rights of collective self-government stood shoulder to shoulder with the responsibilities of collective self-defense.[34] As a rule, women did not serve in the military; neither should they vote, the argument went. According to eighteenth-century political theory, their interests in both war and politics would find representation through their fathers, brothers, husbands, and sons. Slaves—widely viewed not as part of "the People" but rather as aliens who in war might be more likely to aid the enemy than to defend the polity—were even more obvious candidates for disenfranchisement.[35] Also, in a time of widespread voice voting in public, married women and slaves could hardly have voted their own minds, knowing that their husbands and masters retained broad powers of physical chastisement over them.

It is scarcely surprising, then, that no Revolutionary-era state witnessed expansive woman suffrage (although New Jersey apparently did allow a few propertied widows to vote)[36] or that no regime either before or after the Revolution ever gave the vote to slaves (as distinct from ex-slaves). In failing to immediately enfranchise slaves or freeborn women in its own ratification process, the Constitution was not backsliding. It was simply not leaping forward.

And yet . . . in important ways the document did worsen the plight of those most cruelly denied the blessings of liberty. Slavery was the original sin in the New World garden, and the Constitution did more to feed the serpent than to crush it.

During the 1770s, soaring rhetoric of liberty and earnest debate about the sources of legitimate authority pulled many Americans toward abolition. The world's first antislavery society was born in Philadelphia in 1775. By 1787, Massachusetts judges and juries, reflecting the evolving practices and norms in their local environment, had effectively outlawed slavery in the Bay State. Elsewhere, systems of gradual emancipation began to emerge, aiming to put slavery on what Lincoln would later call a path of "ultimate extinction." In 1780, Pennsylvania enacted a law under which all children born to slave mothers after the enactment date would be released from service on their twenty-eighth birthdays. Connecticut and Rhode Island passed similar laws in the early 1780s, and several other Northern states would join the crusade over the next two decades. In 1784, the Confederation Congress came close to prohibiting slavery in Western lands after 1800, and in 1787 it barred slavery in the Northwest Territory. By 1788, the ten most northerly states had effectively banned further importation of African slaves, North Carolina had imposed a tax on slave imports, and even South Carolina had temporarily suspended its participation in this transatlantic traffic.[37]

In sharp contrast, nothing in the original Constitution aimed to eliminate slavery, even in the long run. No clause in the Constitution declared that "slavery shall cease to exist by July 4, 1876, and Congress shall have power to legislate toward this end." Although many slave children were the flesh-and-blood offspring of the men who ordained and established the Constitution, the blessings of liberty were hardly secured to *this* posterity, or to the millions of other slave children yet unborn.

In fact, many of the Constitution's clauses specially accommodated or actually strengthened slavery, although the word itself appeared nowhere in the document. Article I temporarily barred Congress from using its otherwise plenary power over immigration and international trade to end the importation of African and Caribbean slaves. Not until 1808 would Congress be permitted to stop the inflow of slave ships; even then, Congress would be under no obligation to act. Another clause of Article I, regulating congressional apportionment, gave states perverse incentives to maintain and even expand slavery. If a state freed its slaves and the freed-men then moved away, the state might actually lose House seats; conversely, if it imported or bred more slaves, it could increase its congressional clout. Article II likewise handed slave states extra seats in the electoral college, giving the South a sizable head start in presidential elections. Presidents inclined toward slavery could in turn be expected to nominate proslavery Article III judges. Article IV obliged free states to send fugitive slaves back to slavery, in contravention of background choice-of-law rules and general principles of comity. That Article also imposed no immediate or long-run constitutional restrictions on slaveholding in federal territory. Article V gave the international slave trade temporary immunity from constitutional amendment, in seeming violation of the people's inalienable right to amend at any time, and came close to handing slave states an absolute veto over all future constitutional modifications under that Article.

In the near term, such compromises made possible a continental union of North and South that provided bountiful benefits to freeborn Americans. But in the long run, the Founders' failure to put slavery on a path of ultimate extinction would lead to massive military conflict on American soil—the very sort of conflict whose avoidance was, as we shall now see, literally the primary purpose of the Constitution of 1788.

"form a more perfect Union"

"We the People *of the United States* . . ." United how? When? Few questions have cast a longer shadow across American history. Jefferson Davis had one set of answers, Abraham Lincoln another. And the war came.

In word and deed, the Constitution yielded its own answers to these epic questions. The very process by which Americans in thirteen distinct states ordained the Constitution in the late 1780s and early 1790s confirmed that they were not a single indissolubly united people prior to the act of ordainment. But that act, along with key words in the Preamble and companion language later in the document, put all concerned on fair notice: After ordainment, Americans from consenting states would indeed "form a more perfect Union" that prohibited unilateral exit. Thus, the establishment of "this Constitution" was not just the world's most democratic moment, but also, in a manner of speaking, the world's largest corporate merger.

To put that merger in context, we must recall how the New World took shape in the seventeenth and early eighteenth centuries. British North America grew up not as one continental legal entity but rather as juridically separate colonies founded over a span of many decades. Each colony had its own unique legal charter or other founding instrument—its proto-constitution—and its own laws, governmental institutions, and customary usages. The precise location of the geographic and jurisdictional lines dividing the provinces sometimes blurred or shifted over the years. Nevertheless, it was clear during the century before 1776 that, say, Massachusetts, Maryland, and Virginia were three quite distinct political societies—tied to a common Crown, but as legally separate from one another as India and Ireland.[38]

The thirteen colonies that ultimately revolted were not the only British outposts in the new continent. As of 1763, these thirteen were nestled between the British West Indies and Floridas to the south, British Nova Scotia to the northeast, and British Quebec to the northwest. Prior to 1776, it was hardly foreordained that these thirteen, and only these thirteen, would eventually unite to form a single legal entity. To be sure, as children of the same Mother England living in adjoining lands far from their parent country, the British North American provinces had much in common, culturally, ethnically, and geostrategically. In the years following the French and Indian War, England began to pay increasing and often unwanted attention to her American brood, adopting a series of stern measures applicable or potentially applicable to all, and thereby driving many of them closer together in resistance. In 1774, representatives of twelve colonies from New England through the Carolinas met in Philadelphia as part of a Continental Congress, which was structured as a kind of international conclave, with each colonial delegation voting as an equal unit. The Congress ended with a public message to Quebec urging it to send delegates to a second Congress to begin in May 1775, and private letters to the colonies of St. John's, Nova Scotia, Georgia, East Florida, and West Florida asking them to stand together with the twelve in boycotting British goods.[39] None of these invitees came in May, but Georgia showed up later. Ultimately, in July 1776, thirteen colonies declared themselves independent of the British Crown and the British Empire.

But did they remain independent of one another? The Declaration of Independence was issued in the name of "the Representatives of the united States of America, in general Congress," but exactly how were these long-distinct states "united"? Were they more legally "united" than, say, the modern United Nations? Was the word "united" part of the name of a new indivisible nation, or simply an adjective describing thirteen states, acting in unanimous coordination?

In the pivotal sentence of the famous hand-signed 1776 parchment, the word "united" appeared in lowercase, describing the plural and capitalized noun, "States."[40] In the banner stretching across the top, the various fonts and capitalizations also could be read to suggest an alliance more than an indivisible nation:

The unanimous Declaration of the thirteen united States of America

The only place where the Declaration capitalized the adjective so as to make it look like part of a legal name was in a phrase describing "these United Colonies," but strictly speaking, as *British colonies* the thirteen had never been united as a distinct continental entity.[41] Twice the Declaration proclaimed the thirteen to be "Free and Independent States"—perhaps implying by its plural noun, though never quite stating, that the thirteen were independent even of one another, save as they chose to coordinate their actions.[42] When the Connecticut assembly met for its regular session in the fall of 1776, it quoted Congress's "Free and Independent States" language, resolved to "approve of the Declaration of Independence published by said Congress," and then further resolved "that *this Colony* is and of right ought to be *a* free and independent *State.*"[43]

The very act of the declaration, and the structure of the body doing the declaring, seemed to confirm the qualified independence of each state. Each colony in the Congress voted as a unit—the colonies were unanimous in July 1776, but not the individual delegates, whose individual votes were never tallied across different colonies. Each delegation routinely obeyed "instructions" issued by its home colony; and in the formal decision to declare independence, each delegation acted on the specific instruction or authorization of its home regime.[44] Unlike the newly emerging state legislatures, each of which claimed a right to bind all within the state, patriot and loyalist alike, the Declaration did not purport to bind any state or colony absent its consent. Quebec, Nova Scotia, and the Floridas, for instance, were left out.

The legislative history behind the Declaration is also suggestive. In mid-May 1776, the Congress styled its most important statement yet not as an "order" or "instruction," but as a "recommend[ation]" that individual colonies adopt new governments wherever the old Crown-linked regimes had lapsed. Three weeks later, delegates from several colonies remained unwilling to vote for independence and reminded the others that Congress had no right to bind any dissenting province, "the colonies being as yet perfectly independent of each other." If independence were prematurely agreed to by the others, these unready delegates threatened to "retire"—that is, quit Congress—and warned that "possibly their colonies might secede from the Union." In response, delegates from colonies eager for immediate independence openly conceded that each colony remained free to stay in the budding alliance or to secede from it.[45]

Over the next few weeks, however, wavering colonies moved toward independence, and the alliance held firm. Events were rushing forward furiously. American patriots were already locked in armed combat with British regulars, and George III had recently dispatched a massive assault force—some thirty thousand men—to crush all rebellion. In the grim words of the Declaration, the king "is at this Time, transporting large Armies of foreign Mercenaries to compleat the Works of Death, Desolation, and Tyranny, already begun." Practically speaking, once a colony formally declared its independence from the Crown, there could be no going back. Without a sizable cadre of colonies willing to plunge ahead together, military and diplomatic prospects looked bleak. If some colonies strayed too far ahead of the rest politically, the vanguard would become a tempting military target. Indeed, if any foot-dragging colony ultimately sided with Britain, it could provide staging grounds for the king's soldiers, who would be aided by local loyalists controlling the levers of colonial government.[46] Better, then, for each colony to stay in tight formation with the others than to break ranks. Thus, the thirteen colonies took care to synchronize their decisions as they headed uncertainly toward independence. Yet mere synchronization hardly meant that the thirteen necessarily became one indivisible nation in July 1776. (No one thinks that the tight synchronization of the D-Day invasion somehow united Britain, America, and Canada as one indivisible nation in June 1944.)

Clearly, the thirteen states were "united" in unanimously declaring independence and pledging to fight together.[47] This unanimity, however, said little about the general legal authority of the Continental Congress in any future situation in which the newly independent states might strongly disagree among themselves, or where one or more states might seek to leave the alliance after independence had been won. Nor did the Declaration's text commit the thirteen states to anything other than independence. Fairly construed, the Declaration and other decisions made in Congress did call upon the thirteen to hang together during the campaign for independence. Beyond this, much of the future relationship among the states—or put differently, between the individual states and the continental collectivity—had yet to be hammered out.

For instance, how would future nonunanimous rules be made? By simple majority vote, or something more? Would some issues require more consensus than others? Would each state count equally, or would more populous states have more votes?[48] If the latter, would slaves count, and if so, how much? How would the burdens of raising men and materiel be allocated among the several states? By what procedures would disputes between states be resolved? If a state found itself unhappy with its partners after independence had been won, under what conditions, if any, could it withdraw from its sister states and go its own way?

WELL BEFORE IT ADOPTED the Declaration, the Continental Congress understood that such questions had to be addressed in some future legal instrument that each new state would need to ratify. On June 7, 1776, when Richard Henry Lee, seconded by John Adams, famously moved the magic words "*Resolved,* That these United Colonies are, and of right ought to be, free and independent States," he concluded his motion with a proposal "that a plan of confederation be prepared and transmitted to the respective Colonies for their consideration and approbation." Four days later—weeks before it finally approved the Lee-Adams independence language—the Congress voted to appoint a committee "to prepare and digest the form of a confederation to be entered into between these colonies."[49]

When such a plan ultimately emerged from the post-independence Congress, it underscored in word and deed the sovereignty of each individual state. The opening passages of the Articles of Confederation variously described the arrangement among the states as a "confederacy," a "confederation," and a "firm league of friendship with each other" in which "each state retains its sovereignty, freedom, and independence." Legally, the words "confederacy," "confederation," and "league" all connoted the same thing: The "United States" would be an alliance, a multilateral treaty of sovereign nation-states.[50] Moreover, the word "retains" strongly suggested that each state was already sovereign and had been so since independence. So, too, the words "freedom, and independence" echoed the Lee-Adams motion and Jefferson's Declaration itself while making it clear, as the earlier language had not, that *each* state was "free and independent."[51] The 1780 Massachusetts Constitution further reinforced the point in a clause that reworked the language of the Articles: "The people *of this commonwealth* have the sole and exclusive right of governing themselves, as a free, sovereign, and independent state."[52] The New Hampshire Constitution of 1784 featured a virtually identical clause.[53]

The act of confederation confirmed the text of Confederation. The

Articles did not formally go into effect until ratified by each and every state. Thus, no state was bound absent its own consent. Historian Jack Rakove has observed that during debates over the drafting of the proposed Articles—debates after the Declaration of Independence—"threats of disunion flowed freely. James Wilson warned that Pennsylvania would never confederate if Virginia clung to its western claims. The Virginia delegates replied that . . . their constituents would never accept a confederation that required their sacrifice." South Carolina's Thomas Lynch, Jr., sternly advised his fellow congressmen on July 30, 1776, that "if it is debated, whether . . . slaves are [our] property, there is an end of the confederation."[54] If independence in early July had given birth to one indivisible nation rather than thirteen sovereign states working together, how could so many of the Declaration's signers speak so freely of quitting the union? Why was each state's consent even necessary to formally activate the Articles?

The Articles further provided that any subsequent amendment would require the states' unanimous approval—the hallmark of a multilateral treaty regime based on the sovereignty of each state, as opposed to a national regime founded on a truly national people. If the people retained an inalienable right to amend, why should an overwhelming majority of Americans be thwarted simply because a single state—perhaps a tiny one—refused?[55] The obvious answer was that both before and after ratifying the Articles, the people of each state—and not the people of America as a whole—were sovereign. A state populace would no more be bound by confederate amendments agreed to in sister states than it would be obliged to obey laws enacted in Geneva or Amsterdam. As Philadelphia delegate William Paterson (who would one day serve on the U.S. Supreme Court) explained these defining traits of the Articles, "This is the nature of all treaties. What is unanimously done, must be unanimously undone."[56]

The Confederation's provisions governing daily relations among the states further reinforced its basic structure as a multilateral treaty. Each state would appoint a delegation of up to seven members, with each delegation casting a single state vote regardless of the delegation's overall size or the state's underlying population. Delegates would receive their pay from state governments, which could alter salaries at will to keep delegates in line. State governments also routinely instructed their delegations on how to vote, and retained the right to "recall" and replace their ambassadorial delegates "at any time."[57]

Given the clarity of the Confederation's foundational premise of state sovereignty, its classic international architecture, and its self-description as a "league," how could so many Americans in ensuing eras—Lincoln most famously—have denied that individual states were sovereign prior to 1787? Partly by mistakenly reading later history back into an earlier period. The Constitution itself set a trap for the unwary by using old legal words in new legal ways without clear warning. Just as the word "Congress" under the Constitution described a different and more powerful institution than did the word "Congress" under the Articles,[58] so the phrase "United States" in the Constitution meant something different and much stronger than did the same syllables in the earlier document. It is only a happy coincidence that the same thirteen "United States" from the Declaration and the Articles became the first thirteen "United States" in the Constitution. We must remember that when George Washington took office, North Carolina and Rhode Island were not part of the "United States" as the Constitution used the term. Thus the Preamble spoke precisely of its purpose to *"form"* a new—more perfect—union rather than simply "continue" or "improve" the old union.

Further confusion about the pre-1787 location of sovereignty has arisen because later readers have often misunderstood what sovereignty did and did not mean to late-eighteenth-century American lawyers. Sovereign states under traditional legal principles were free to enter multilateral treaties, leagues, federations, and confederations without surrendering their ultimate sovereignty. In the words of Swiss jurist Emmerich de Vattel, whose *Law of Nations* was widely read and cited in Revolutionary America, "Several sovereign and independent states may unite themselves together by a *perpetual confederacy,* without each in particular ceasing to be a perfect state. They will form together a federal republic: the deliberations in common will offer no violence to the sovereignty of each member." In his influential *Second Treatise,* Locke had offered a similar account of the ongoing sovereignty of governments merely "in league" with one another, who had not combined "to make one body politic." William Blackstone's *Commentaries* also affirmed the continuing sovereignty of nation-states that merely joined together in "foederate alliance."[59] Hence, the mere fact that each of the thirteen states agreed to what the Articles called a "perpetual" "union" in no way negated each state's continuing sovereign status.

Nor was each state's ultimate legal sovereignty undermined by the fact that Congress—basing its authority initially on the Declaration and de facto alliance and later on the formal Articles—acted and spoke on behalf of the individual states in diplomatic dealings with foreign powers.[60] Classic leagues of sovereign states, such as the eighteenth-century Dutch and Swiss confederacies, often coordinated the military and diplomatic affairs of the individual member states. Vis-à-vis the rest of the world, the thirteen American states could act as a unit, so long as their league held together and each state consented to be represented by Congress. Yet this apparent external unity while the Confederation continued intact said little about whether and how a formally "sovereign" state might one day lawfully exit the league.[61]

What, then, *did* each state's ultimate "sovereignty" mean, and how was a "confederation" or "league" any different than a single sovereign nation-state? Within the interior of daily arrangements, a very strong confederacy might well approximate a decentralized nation-state. A confederacy might give important powers, including all powers over foreign affairs, to its common council, while a nation might leave many issues to be decided by local subunits. But at crucial junctures of system creation, amendment, and abolition, the differences could be dramatic. A *confederacy* essentially rested on the ongoing voluntary participation of its sovereign member states. Each sovereign member of a classic confederacy was free not to join at the moment of creation, typically free to refuse to accede to any later proposed amendment, and ultimately free to leave if, in its good-faith judgment, the core purposes of the confederation were going unfulfilled. Based on the Latin *foedus* (meaning treaty or covenant) and its cognate *fides* (faith), a traditional "confederated" union ultimately depended on the good faith and voluntary compliance of member states.[62] Thus the precise language of the Articles' closing clause—in which the delegates of sovereign states agreed to "solemnly plight and engage the faith of our respective constituents"—confirmed the basic structure announced in the document's opening words.

Alas, plighted faith did not always translate into actual performance. Although on paper the Congress under the Articles enjoyed some important powers, it had no effective means of carrying them out. It could not directly tax individuals or legislate upon them; it had no explicit "legislative" or "governmental" power to make binding "law" enforceable in state courts; it lacked broad authority to set up its own general courts; and it could raise troops and money only by "requisitioning" contributions from each state. On paper, such requisitions were "binding." In practice, they were mere requests. As one wag put it, Congress "may declare every thing, but do nothing." By 1787, the Confederation was in shambles. Various states failed to honor requisitions, enacted laws violating duly ratified treaties, waged unauthorized local wars against Indian tribes, and maintained standing armies without congressional permission—all in plain contravention of the Articles.[63]

America needed a new system. But how to launch it?

THE ANSWER LAY in the Preamble's matching bookend, Article VII. The Preamble began the proposed Constitution; Article VII ended it. The Preamble said that Americans would "establish this Constitution"; Article VII said *how* we would "Establish[] this Constitution." The Preamble said this deed would be done by "the People"; Article VII clarified that the people would act via specially elected "Conventions." The Preamble invoked the people of "the United States"; Article VII defined what that phrase meant both before and after the act of constitution. The Preamble consisted of a single sentence; so did Article VII. The conspicuous complementarity of these two sentences suggests that they might sensibly have been placed side by side, but the Philadelphia architects preferred instead to erect them at opposite ends of the grand edifice so that both the document's front portal and rear portico would project the message of popular sovereignty, American style.

According to Article VII, "The Ratification of the Conventions of nine States, shall be sufficient for the Establishment of this Constitution between the States so ratifying the Same."

The last seven words clinch the case for the sovereignty of each state prior to 1787. The very act of constitution itself began with the premise that each state prior to ratification was free and independent—free to decide for itself whether to "form a more perfect Union" with its sister states or instead go its own way. No state could be bound by the new plan unless it chose that fate for itself; hence Rhode Island and North Carolina found themselves outside the *new* United States when George Washington took his oath of office on April 30, 1789.

Thus, the text of the Constitution did not say, and the act of constitution did not do, something like the following: "Because the United States is [sic] already one sovereign and indivisible nation, the ratification of nine states shall suffice to establish this Constitution in all thirteen United States." Instead, the text and act of constitution envisioned a possible dissolution of the old union, with nine or more states going one way while a minority of free and independent sovereign states veered off. In effect, the very act of constitution amounted to a mass secession from the old, confederated united states.

The prospect that some subset of states might secede from the Confederation and reunite under a new Constitution came into view in the opening days of the Philadelphia drafting convention, when Wilson floated the idea that the Constitution could be ratified on the footing of a "partial union, with a door open for the accession of the rest" of the states at some later time. Wilson meant to remind smaller states of the precariousness of their position in the event they were left behind. Small-state men like Paterson were quick to call the bluff. Alluding to "the hint thrown out heretofore by Mr. Wilson of the necessity to which the large States might be reduced of confederating among themselves, by a refusal of the others to concur," Paterson welcomed them to "unite if they please, but let them remember that they have no authority to compel the others to unite." Long after the large-state/small-state wrangling had ended, the point of legal principle remained. In Wilson's words: "As the Constitution stands, the States only which ratify can be bound."[64]

But how could such a secession and partial reunion be squared with the Articles of Confederation? The closing section of that document provided that "the Articles of this Confederation shall be inviolably observed by every state, and the union shall be perpetual; nor shall any alteration at any time hereafter be made in any of them; unless such alteration be agreed to in a Congress of the United States, and be afterwards confirmed by the legislatures of every state." If the proposed Constitution were an amendment of the Articles (an amendment of the form, "Delete everything thus far and replace it as follows . . ."), then how could only nine states suffice? Alternatively, if the proposed Constitution were a flat repudiation of the Articles, then how could nine or more ratifying states justify abandoning their supposedly "perpetual" union with the remaining states?[65]

A strong realpolitik answer was that sovereign states sometimes broke their pledges in order to safeguard their vital interests.[66] If repudiation of the Articles would violate the niceties of international law, so be it. The very violation of the Articles implicit in the Constitution's ratification by a supermajority of nine or more states would only prove that the Confederation was a failed experiment.

A more legalistic answer was that the material breaches of promised state performance under the Articles gave each compacting party—each state—a right to rescind the agreement under general principles of contractual and international law. Blackstone's influential *Commentaries* had noted that in the case of a nonconfederate, "incorporate union" such as the 1707 union of England and Scotland (the very kind of more perfect union that, as we shall see, the Constitution would later propose) no rescission option existed: "The two contracting states are totally annihilated [qua sovereign states], without any power of revival; and a third arises from their conjunction, in which all the rights of sovereignty . . . must necessarily reside." But in the case of a simple "foederate alliance"—that is, a mere confederation or league of sovereign states—an infringement of fundamental conditions "would certainly rescind the compact."[67]

Nor did the language in the Articles of Confederation that "the union shall be perpetual" doom this legal analysis. This language was itself yoked to a mandate that the Articles "shall be inviolably observed by every state." Under standard principles of international law, each of these yoked mandates was a condition of the other. When inviolable observation lapsed, so did the obligation of perpetual union. Indeed, international law principles helped explain why perpetuity and inviolability were so pointedly paired. As the influential jurist Vattel made clear, "Treaties contain promises that are perfect and reciprocal. If one of the allies fails in his engagements, the other may . . . disengage himself from his promises, and . . . break the treaty."[68] Thus, the legalistic argument went, the decisive fact about the Confederation was that it was a self-described league, a multilateral treaty. The word "perpetual" merely specified what kind of league it would be: the firmest of leagues, but a league nonetheless.

When pressed, leading Federalists at times resorted to this legalist defense of the act of constitution as embodied in Article VII. Having privately penned the breached-treaty argument in the months before Philadelphia,[69] Madison repeatedly advanced this claim in the closed-door deliberations. "As far as the articles of Union were to be considered as a Treaty only of a particular sort, among the Governments of Independent States," the writings of various "Expositors of the law of Nations" clearly suggested that "a breach of any one article, by any one party, leaves all the other parties at liberty, to consider the whole [compact] as dissolved."[70] Several months later, Madison/Publius went public with the idea in *The Federalist* No. 43:

> A compact between independent sovereigns, founded on ordinary acts of legislative authority, can pretend to no higher validity than a league or treaty between the parties. It is an established doctrine on the subject of treaties, that all the articles are mutually conditions of each other; that a breach of any one article is a breach of the whole treaty; and that a breach, committed by either of the parties, absolves the others, and authorizes them, if they please, to pronounce the compact violated and

void. Should it unhappily be necessary to appeal to these delicate truths for a justification for dispensing with the consent of particular States to a dissolution of the federal pact, will not the complaining parties find it a difficult task to answer the MULTIPLIED and IMPORTANT infractions with which they may be confronted?

Other leading Federalists, including South Carolina's Charles Cotesworth Pinckney (who had studied law at Oxford under Blackstone himself) and North Carolina's James Iredell (a future justice), mustered similar public defenses of Article VII in their home states.[71]

For sound rhetorical reasons, the Federalists tended to whisper this legalistic defense rather than shout it from the rooftops.[72] Few friends of the Constitution were as forthright on the issue as Madison/Publius, who himself put the point as softly as possible—calling the question "very delicate," prefacing his exposition with a capitalized "PERHAPS," and admitting that he raised the breached-treaty defense "unhappily." A breached treaty was voidable, not void ab initio. A state had a right to withdraw, but it also had a right to stay and demand full performance. Even if it was legally permissible, was withdrawal wise? What if the Constitution failed to win the assent of nine states? Even a tottering alliance might be better than none, and Madison was not the kind of man to pull down his only shelter, however ramshackle, before fitting up his new abode. Hence his closing comment: "The time has been when it was incumbent on us all to veil the ideas which this paragraph exhibits."

Conclusively establishing the requisite breaches would have required lots of ugly finger-pointing—hardly the kind of thing conducive to launching a new nation in the spirit of harmony. Any direct references to specific state violations of the Articles risked causing offense to particular persons or states that the Federalists were seeking to woo.[73] As a rule, the best Federalist strategy was to blame everything on the tiny, ill-governed, and obstreperous state of Rhode Island, which had first thwarted needed reforms of the Confederation and then boycotted the Philadelphia Convention. Additionally, the precise details of any ultimate breached-treaty defense would depend on which state or states might choose to both reject the Constitution and then complain about the dissolution of the old confederacy, and also on how the new union treated the new outsider(s)—yet another exceptionally delicate set of issues (which Madison explicitly ducked in *The Federalist* No. 43). The states abandoning the old confederacy would be on firmest ground if the nonratifying complainant itself had ranked among the league's most flagrant laggards. In the midst of the ratification process, however, no one could know which states, if any, might ultimately refuse to ratify.

This uncertainty was one of the reasons that the Preamble spoke generally of "the United States" rather than listing the thirteen states seriatim, as Wilson had done in his first draft.[74] Such a list would have unwisely counted thirteen ratifications by name before any had materialized—and in a section of the document whose special visibility might prove particularly embarrassing if one or more states failed to say yes.

THE PROMINENCE OF THE PREAMBLE also made it a perfect place to renounce the basic structure of the Articles. Although states would enter the Constitution as true sovereigns, they would not remain so after ratification. The formation of a *"more perfect* Union" would itself end each state's sovereign status and would prohibit future unilateral secession, in plain contrast to the decidedly less-than-perfect union under the Articles. True, the Preamble did not expressly proclaim that its new, more perfect union would be "perpetual"—and for good reason: Why borrow a word from the Articles of Confederation that did not quite mean what it said in that document, a word that was being thrust aside by the very act of constitution itself? Thus, the Constitution signaled its decisive break with the Articles' regime of state sovereignty and false federal perpetuity in other ways.

One notable Preamble word marking the metamorphosis was "Constitution." Not a "league," however firm; not a "confederacy" or a "confederation"; not a compact among "sovereign" states—all these high-profile and legally freighted words from the Articles were conspicuously absent from the Preamble and every other operative part of the Constitution. The new text proposed a fundamentally different legal framework. Henceforth America would have a written "Constitution" deriving from a continental people, unmistakably styled after earlier state prototypes, like the Massachusetts Constitution of 1780. As these state constitutions, exalted texts in confederate America, had exemplified state-based popular sovereignty under the Articles, so now a new United States Constitution—the new supreme law of the land—would shape a new continental nation whose sovereign would be a truly continental people. Lest there be any doubt, later parts of the document precisely defined the status of *"this Constitution,"* a self-referential phrase that appeared several more times—

most importantly in Articles V and VI (the only places where the phrase popped up more than once) and in Article VII, the Preamble's matching bookend. [75]

Article VI specified how "this Constitution," once ratified, would stack up against current and future state constitutions. For example, what should happen if the people of South Carolina, having adopted "this Constitution" in 1788, reconvened at some later time to amend their state constitution, and in that convention adopted an amendment purporting to repudiate the federal Constitution in whole or in part? In a subsequent lawsuit, which law would a state judge be obliged to follow? If the people of South Carolina were sovereign, the answer would plainly be the state constitution as amended. The sovereign people's right to alter or abolish their government at any time would remain a core attribute of their sovereignty, and their judicial agents—state judges—would be bound to enforce their will and judgment even if their amendment might be alleged by other sovereigns to violate an earlier treaty under international law. Yet the Article VI supremacy clause explicitly compelled even state judges to disregard the attempted amendment—a rule plainly inconsistent with the post-ratification sovereignty of the people of each state: *"This Constitution . . . shall be the supreme Law of the Land; and the Judges in every State shall be bound thereby, any Thing in the Constitution or Laws of any State to the Contrary notwithstanding."*[76]

Surrounding Article VI and reinforcing its plain meaning, Articles VII and V conspicuously contrasted the rules for constitutional ratification with the rules for subsequent constitutional amendment—a contrast that made it plain that the new Constitution spelled the end of state sovereignty for all states that might choose to join. As of mid-July 1788, ten states had ratified the Constitution, thereby guaranteeing that the document would go into effect in those states under Article VII. New Yorkers had yet to ratify, and Article VII made it clear that the people of that state were a distinct sovereign entity free to vote down the new Constitution and ignore it. Yet Article V put New Yorkers on clear notice: If they chose to ratify the Constitution in convention, they would lose their freedom to disregard *subsequent* constitutional proposals agreed to by conventions of three-fourths of the states, whose ratifications would suffice to make future amendments "valid to all Intents and Purposes, as Part of this Constitution" even in nonratifying states. Nowhere was the Constitution's break with the Articles of Confederation and all other purely confederate regimes more dramatic. Simply put, Article VII recognized the sovereign right (or at least the sovereign power) of different states in a flawed confederacy to go their separate ways; but Articles V and VI extinguished the right and power of unilateral secession for each state populace that joined the Constitution's new, more perfect union, thereby merging itself into the continental sovereignty of the American people.[77]

Anti-Federalists across the continent got the message and sounded the alarm. In Massachusetts, Samuel Nasson pointed to the Preamble as proof that the Constitution would effect a "perfect consolidation of the whole Union" that would "destroy" the Bay State's status as "a sovereign and independent" entity. The influential *Federal Farmer* warned that when a state populace "shall adopt the proposed constitution, it will be their *last* and supreme act" qua sovereign. New York's *Brutus* complained that the Constitution would not be "a compact" among states but rather would create a "union of the people of the United States considered" as "one great body politic." Pennsylvania Anti-Federalists put forth a similar reading of the Preamble. Meanwhile, Maryland's Luther Martin advised his audience of the strongly nationalist logic of the Constitution's treason clause, which made allegiance to the United States paramount over allegiance to a single state in the event of armed conflict between the two.[78]

Patrick Henry, true to form, was the bluntest of all as he led the charge against the Constitution in Virginia. "The fate . . . of America may depend on this. . . . Have they made a proposal of a compact between the states? If they had, this would be a confederation. It is otherwise most clearly a consolidated government. The question turns, sir, on that poor little thing—the expression, We, the *people*, instead of the *states*, of America." If "the states be not the agents of this compact, it must be one great, consolidated, national government, of the people of all the states." This difference, Henry warned, would profoundly limit the rights of future Virginians to act on their own. "Suppose the people of Virginia should wish to alter their government; can a majority of them do it? No; because they are connected with other men, or, in other words, consolidated with other states. . . . This government is not a Virginian, but an American government." Because the American Revolution of 1776—in which he had played no small part—had ultimately made Virginia free and independent, the proposed Constitution was "a resolution as radical as that which separated us from Great Britain."[79]

In response, the Federalists refined their critics' terminology while confirming that the new union would indeed be indivisible. The Constitution, Federalists stressed, hardly annihilated the states or melted thirteen peoples into one mass for all purposes. State lines would continue to configure the politico-legal map, and state governments would continue to wield important powers. In fact, states would form the basic building blocks of the new government. State borders and state-law electoral quali-fications would shape the House of Representatives; state legislatures would elect a Senate in which each state would have equal weight; state-chosen electors would ballot for president; a Senate sensitive to states' rights would confirm federal judges; each state's borders and republican form of government would be guaranteed; and states could help propose and ratify federal constitutional amendments. Thus the new Constitution was not wholly national but partly federal, argued the Constitution's sup-porters, who cleverly called themselves "Federalists" rather than "Nation-alists."

But on the fateful question of whether states would continue to be truly sovereign, with rights of unilateral exit, the Federalists agreed that the Anti-Federalists had not exaggerated. The difference of opinion on this question was not over what the document meant, but over whether the impermissibility of future secession was reason to commend or con-demn the proposed "more perfect Union." Madison at Philadelphia stressed that one of the essential differences between a *"league"* and a *"Constitution"* was that the latter would prevent subunits from unilaterally bolting when-ever they became dissatisfied.[80]

Madison here appeared to build on Blackstone's account of the indis-soluble union of England and Scotland in 1707, a union that furnished a high-profile paradigm for what the Philadelphia framers were proposing in 1787. Draftsman Gouverneur Morris, who put the finishing stylistic touches on the Preamble, used language strongly resembling, and perhaps consciously borrowed from, the British union. The phrase "*a more perfect Union,*" blended language from the official 1707 enactment, which spoke of "rendring the *union* of the two kingdoms *more* intire and compleat," with language from Queen Anne's July 1, 1706, letter to the Scotch Parlia-ment, which spoke of "an entire and *perfect union*."[81] This language from Queen Anne appeared verbatim in *The Federalist* No. 5, as Publius (here, John Jay—later America's first chief justice) explained exactly what kind of new, more perfect union was now being proposed to Americans. A few essays later, Hamilton/Publius in *The Federalist* No. 11 spoke of the need for a "strict and indissoluble" union. More generally, the entire opening section of *The Federalist* urged Americans to emulate the British by per-manently unifying their landmass for military and geostrategic reasons.

Federalists from north to south sang from the same hymnal. Pennsyl-vania's Wilson contrasted traditional "confederacies" that historically "have all fallen to pieces" with the proposed Constitution, in which "the bonds of our union" would be "indissolubly strong." North Carolina's Governor Samuel Johnston declared that "the Constitution must be the supreme law of the land; otherwise, it would be in the power of any one state to counteract the other states, and withdraw itself from the Union." Both Wilson and Johnston had emigrated from Scotland, and their visions of the proposed American union doubtless drew upon their intimate understanding of the British union that England and Scotland had achieved some four score years earlier. In Virginia, the distinguished legal scholar George Wythe forcefully explained what was at stake, blending language from the Declaration (which he had signed in 1776) and the Preamble. "To perpetuate the blessings of freedom, happiness, and independence," Americans must form "a firm, indissoluble union of the states" and thereby avoid "the extreme danger of dissolving the Union."[82]

Even more striking than what the Constitution's friends said is what they did *not* say. No leading Federalist ever publicly sought to win over states' rightists by conceding that a state could unilaterally nullify or secede in the event it later became dissatisfied. The Federalists' silence here was deafening, given how reassuring to states' rightists such a response would have been in all the places where the Philadelphia proposal hung precariously in the balance. Responding to the fears voiced by Anti-Federalist "men of little faith," Federalists stressed many specific protections, including bicameralism, separation of powers, enumerated powers, refinements in representation, the amendment process, and the states' status as building blocks in the national government. But never did Federalists float the right of an individual state to secede or nullify. Never did they say, "Give the new plan a try, and if you don't like it, your state may always leave."

Alongside what various people said and did not say in constitutional debates, we must attend to what the American people themselves did and did not do in the act of constitution itself. No state convention, in its ratification instrument, purported to reserve the right of its state populace to unilateral secession. Notably, Virginia's convention spoke of the right of the people of the United States, not the people of Virginia, to reassume power through future acts of popular sovereignty. Nor did any state convention impose any condition on its act of ratification.[83]

The secession question arose most dramatically in the New York ratification convention, where Anti-Federalists held a strong majority when discussion began. At one point, Federalist Alexander Hamilton despairingly described "our chance of success here" as "infinitely slender." After extensive debate, and upon receiving word that New Hampshire and Virginia had recently ratified the Constitution as the decisive ninth and tenth states—thus ensuring that the Constitution would go into effect in these ten states—Anti-Federalist leaders proposed a compromise under which the convention would ratify the Constitution "upon condition" that the new Congress make way for certain constitutional amendments. With the ultimate prospects for New York ratification still in grave doubt, the offer tantalized Hamilton and his allies, but in the end they refused to take the bait. Instead, the Federalists insisted on replacing the words "upon condition" with language expressing the convention's "full confidence" that Congress would take up the suggested amendments—a factual expectation rather than a binding legal condition. The convention then beat back a proposal from Anti-Federalist John Lansing that "there should be reserved to the state of New York a right to withdraw herself from the Union after a certain number of years, unless the amendments proposed" were taken up.[84] In this sharply focused debate, no one supposed that the Constitution already contained a general right of state secession. Had such a right been thought to exist, Lansing's proposal would have *limited* it (to "a certain number of years" and a small set of triggers) and thus states' rightists should have opposed Lansing, while continentalists should have favored him.

In actual fact, the exact opposite occurred. At the risk of alienating swing voters and losing on the ultimate ratification vote, New York's Federalists rose up to oppose the Lansing compromise. In doing so, they made clear to all observers—both in New York itself and in the many other places across the continent where men were following the New York contest with interest—that the Constitution did not permit unilateral state secession. In a letter to Hamilton, Madison had emphasized that "the Constitution requires an adoption *in toto,* and *for ever.* It has been so adopted by the other States" (including Madison's own Virginia). Hamilton read the letter aloud to the Convention and then added his own words. The "terms of the constitution import a perpetual compact between the different states. . . . The [Article VI] oath to be taken stands in the way" of any subsequent right of unilateral secession. According to the contemporaneous account published in New York's *Daily Advertiser,* both Hamilton and his fellow delegate John Jay insisted that "a reservation of a right to withdraw . . . was inconsistent with the Constitution, and was *no ratification.*"[85]

THUS, IN THE GREAT DEBATE of the 1860s, both Jefferson Davis and Abraham Lincoln got some things right and some things wrong, but Lincoln was right when it counted. Contrary to what Lincoln said, it is doubtful that a new, indivisible nation—as opposed to thirteen nation-states in a classic confederacy—sprang into existence in July 1776, four score and seven years before the battle of Gettysburg. In fairness to Lincoln, perhaps we should say that vis-à-vis the rest of the world, a new (confederate) nation was born in 1776. But the United States did not become an *indivisible* nation prohibiting unilateral state secession—the crux of the Gettysburg contest—until 1788. Lincoln also stumbled in claiming that none of the thirteen original states had ever been truly sovereign. If the issue were somehow unclear from 1776 to 1788, surely "sovereign" is the right word to describe North Carolina and Rhode Island in April 1789. The burning question in the 1860s, however, was not whether states had ever been sovereign in a strong sense, but whether they still were. Texas had undeniably been a sovereign Lone Star republic in the years before statehood, but did she retain that status after joining the union? On that question, Lincoln properly insisted that the Constitution's more perfect union did not permit unilateral secession. Even though Jefferson Davis rightly read his namesake's Declaration, he wrongly read his country's Constitution. The fact that a new union was lawfully formed in the 1780s by secession from the old confederacy did not mean that a new confederacy could be lawfully formed in the 1860s by secession from the old union.[86]

Chief Justice John Marshall had lived through the Revolution and the Founding, and thus was less likely than later interpreters to conflate the two events, either by arguing, as would Lincoln, that the Revolution had already made America one indivisible nation or by claiming, as would Davis, that the Founding had carried forward the confederate essence of the failed Articles. Writing in 1824, exactly midway between the fall of the Articles of Confederation and the rise of a second self-described American Confederacy, Marshall summarized the issue nicely. "Reference has been made to the political situation of [the] States, anterior to [the Constitution's] formation. It has been said, that they were sovereign, were completely independent, and were connected with each other only by a league. This is true. But, when these allied sovereigns converted their league into a government, when they converted their Congress of Ambassadors, deputed to deliberate on their common concerns, and to recommend measures of general utility, into a Legislature, empowered to enact laws on the most interesting subjects, the whole character in which the States appear, underwent a change."[87]

"Justice, . . . Tranquility, . . . defence, . . . Welfare, . . . Liberty"

It remains to ask why. Why did Anti-Federalists fight so hard to keep a confederacy, and voice such fear of the new, more perfect union? Why, on the other hand, did the Federalists insist on so radical a change of fundamental legal structure?

Anti-Federalists in this debate stood as traditionalists steeped in the American custom of provincial self-government. These men also drew upon world history, which furnished no model of a genuinely democratic regime stretching across a continental expanse. In response, Federalist reformers put forth a novel theory of extended republics and unfolded a compelling set of insights about geostrategy and liberty, insights that explained what the Anti-Federalist reading of world history had overlooked.

The Anti-Federalist commitment to local self-government had deep roots in the American experience. Pilgrims had compacted among themselves while still on the *Mayflower,* and Virginians were already electing delegates to a House of Burgesses in the 1620s. By 1640, eight colonies had assemblies in place.[88] No similar assemblies ever met at the continental level in colonial America, and the elected body that did claim authority to legislate continentally—the British Parliament—was an assembly that no colonist had ever voted for or in.[89] Not that colonists really wanted direct representation in Parliament.[90] A small number of Americans amid a sea of British legislators would likely be consistently outvoted. Moreover, these few colonial representatives would not personally know the vast majority of the voters whom they would allegedly be representing. Even if they started off with sound instincts, they might easily lose a sense of connection with their constituents when living in a grand imperial city an ocean away, rubbing elbows with English aristocrats and haughty diplomats from undemocratic lands. If they mutated into Londoners, such representatives might ultimately become part of the problem rather than the solution. Colonial legislators, by contrast, knew their voters by name, met only hours away, and regularly returned to mingle with their constituents and to live under the laws they had passed.

When continental congresses began to meet in the mid-1770s, colonial assemblies or their Revolutionary equivalents generally picked congressmen and retained the power to instruct or recall them at will, a pattern that continued after independence. Much of the democratic action in confederate America took place within each state, usually featuring an annual election to the state legislature as the main event. In Connecticut and Rhode Island, patriots simply carried on under their old colonial charters—which had enabled locals to select all government officials without English intervention—after cleansing these documents of all reference to the Crown. These colonial legislatures thus became state legislatures with no break in continuity. In other states, new constitutions were needed to fill the craters that opened up when independence destroyed the authority of royal and proprietary appointees—typically governors, judges, and executive councilors who often doubled as upper-house legislators. Most states preserved the essence of their colonial assemblies—sometimes renaming them, sometimes broadening the electorates that picked them, often expanding their size, but in general featuring strong institutional continuity between the old colonial assemblies and the new state legislatures.[91] Colonial laws generally remained in force in the states unless and until superseded.

Thus, even as it cast out the king and underwent more change than did Connecticut or Rhode Island, a state such as Virginia carried forward many of her colonial laws and institutions. But for Virginia to indissolubly yoke herself to these Northern colonies and others, in a new continental nation where Virginians would be vastly outnumbered by non-Virginians (as indeed each state would be outnumbered by the rest), and where a newfangled continental legislature could legislate coercively—that was quite a different thing.[92] Virginia and New England, after all, had different climates and cultures. No democracy in world history had ever spanned so vast a range encompassing such diverse weather zones, dominant sects, labor systems, and local temperaments. The widely admired French writer Montesquieu was commonly read as suggesting it could not be done. If an imperial Parliament with formal representation of the colonists would not have worked—because of geographic distance between representatives and represented, and deep cleavages of interest and circumstance between British voters and American voters—how could an analogous continental legislature work in America? How were the thousand miles and culture gap separating New Hampshire from Georgia decisively different than the three thousand miles and culture gap separating both from Britain?

The confederation solution of the early 1780s was precisely *not* to create any unprecedented continental parliament, but rather to rely on good old local legislatures, which would send ambassadorial delegations to an inter-sovereign Congress. In 1787, however, Washington, Madison, Wilson, and company were audaciously proposing to raise up an entirely new continental government with its own bicameral legislature (whose lower branch would be chosen directly by ordinary voters), independent executive, and life-tenured judiciary. In short, America was now being offered something akin to the Massachusetts Constitution of 1780—*on a continental scale.*[93]

Traditionalist jaws dropped in disbelief. "The Scheme is itself totally novel. There is no parallel to it to be found," worried states' rightist John Lansing at Philadelphia. Luther Martin agreed, excoriating the general plan as "without example and without precedent." Neither man signed the final Philadelphia proposal, and each worked furiously to defeat its ratification in his home state. Their reactions and those of countless other Anti-Federalists confirmed that Americans in 1776 had not somehow abandoned the primacy of the states in the blink of an eye. Any plan to form an indivisible continental nation and thereby relocate ultimate authority away from individual states with century-deep roots needed to win the consent of the governed in a well-focused continental conversation. No extended conversation about indivisible nationhood had occurred in 1776, but the Federalists were inviting such a dialogue in 1787. To win this great debate, Federalists first and foremost had to answer the traditionalist critique articulated by men like Lansing, Martin, and the Anti-Federalist essayist "Centinel," who urged skepticism of all "innovation in government."[94]

In the closing sentences of *The Federalist* No. 14, Madison/Publius did not fight the innovator label, but instead wore it proudly:

> My fellow-citizens, . . . Hearken not to the voice which petulantly tells you that the form of government recommended for your adoption is a novelty in the political world; that it has never yet had a place in the theories of the wildest projectors; that it rashly attempts what it is impossible to accomplish. . . . Why is the experiment of an extended republic to be rejected, merely because it may comprise what is new? . . . Numerous innovations [have already been] displayed on the American theatre, in favor of private rights and public happiness. [America's leaders] accomplished a revolution which has no parallel in the annals of human society. They reared the fabrics of governments which have no model on the face of the globe. . . . If they erred most in the structure of the Union, . . . this is the work which has been new modelled by the act of your [Philadelphia] convention, and it is that act on which you are now to deliberate and to decide.

With his last words, Madison/Publius looped back to Hamilton/Publius's first sentence in *The Federalist* No. 1 (". . . you are called upon to deliberate . . ."), thus rhetorically closing the circle of *The Federalist*'s extended opening argument. In this opening section, Publius aimed to explain to skeptics why an altogether novel continental constitution was urgently required.

MODERN AMERICANS OF ALL STRIPES—lawyers, historians, political scientists, and general readers—have missed the central argument of these early *Federalist* essays. *The Federalist* No. 10 is taught everywhere, while the rest of the Publius's early exposition goes unassigned and unappreciated. Bristling with insights, No. 10 indeed has something for everyone today—an explicit reference to property rights and class conflict, a celebration of demographic and religious diversity, a sophisticated account of interest groups and electoral dynamics, and a prophetic sketch of the federal government's eventual role in protecting minority rights. But however interesting No. 10 may be to modern readers, scholars have shown that this essay and its ideas had remarkably little impact on Madison's contemporaries.[95]

On reflection, it is not hard to see why. Madison speculated that an elected continental legislature, the likes of which had never before been seen in world history, would in theory be more likely to protect the liberties of its own citizens—especially minorities—than the colonial and state legislatures that had been in place for over a century. In hindsight, modern readers may find that Madison was right, and brilliantly so, but in 1787 it was a hard idea to sell. Madison hypothesized that large congressional districts would yield better representatives with wider reputations and sounder judgment than the folk of modest stature more likely to prevail in small electoral districts. Traditionalist critics could easily reverse Madison's normative spin: The new government's representatives would be too far removed, both geographically and socially, from the concerns of ordinary farmers, artisans, and shopkeepers.

If Madison's argument had persuaded large numbers of his fellow Americans, they should have supported reforms at the state level to shrink the number of state legislators, increase the size of state legislative districts, and eliminate the right of constituents to instruct state representatives. Additionally, large states like Virginia and North Carolina should have sought to grow even larger by retaining control over interior sections rather than allowing them to break off to form new states like Kentucky and Tennessee. Also, the Bill of Rights proposed by the First Congress should have aimed to protect minority rights against states in light of

Madison's concerns—expressed on the floor of the House as well as in No. 10—that these were the governments most likely to succumb to the tyranny of the majority.[96] At least in the near term, history did not move in Madison's direction on any of these issues.

The very fact that Madison's novel ideas appeared in the *tenth* essay should tip us off. These reflections came too late in Publius's overall argument to constitute the primary reasons for a dramatic restructuring of America. The points most likely to persuade skeptics and fence-sitters needed to, and did, come earlier, in *The Federalist* Nos. 2 through 8, with further reinforcement from *The Federalist* essays immediately following No. 10. In 1787–88, *The Federalist* Nos. 1–6 and 8–9 were reprinted more often than any of Publius's other essays.[97]

Madison's was fundamentally an internal argument about democracy and demography. In essence, he asked readers to consider whether, if one were trying to make self-government work on some island nation removed from the rest of the world, it would be better to have a low-population and relatively homogeneous island (the orthodox view) or a high-population and modestly heterogeneous island (Madison's theory). But the bulk of early *Federalist* essays focused less on internal arguments about democracy than external arguments about defense, less on demography within a republic than on geography at its borders. The central argument for a dramatically different and more perfect union was not that it would protect Virginians from the Virginia legislature, but rather that it would protect Virginia from foreign nations and sister states, and in turn protect these sisters from Virginia. The question was not so much whether to pick a big or a small island nation, but how to create an island nation in the first place—a nation where foreign powers would be far removed and where internal borders would be demilitarized.

Individual and collective liberty, common defense and domestic tranquility, justice between men and between regions, economic prosperity and general welfare—all these Preamble goals, Publius argued in his opening essays, required America to merge thirteen separate states into one indivisible island nation. By creating an "insular" condition in America, the proposed Constitution would guarantee Americans the rights of Englishmen, and more, by replicating—indeed, surpassing—the geostrategic niche of Englishmen.

As Publius saw the world, most of continental Europe groaned in chains under absolutist tyrants and feudal overlords. Yet Britain was relatively free because of its "insular situation, and a powerful marine, guarding it in a great measure against the possibility of foreign invasion." So long as Britannia maintained a strong navy and ruled the waves—remember the Armada!—she would not need a large domestic standing army. A navy was a relatively defensive instrument that could not easily be turned upon Englishmen to impose domestic tyranny. Blackstone's *Commentaries* had in fact described the navy as Britain's "greatest defence and ornament: . . . its ancient and natural strength; the floating bulwark of the island; an army, from which, however strong and powerful, no danger can ever be apprehended to liberty."[98]

But large standing armies were another story—the story of tyranny. Regimes on the European continent, Publius argued, required such armies to defend their land borders against invasion. Because "most other BORDERING nations [are] always . . . either involved in disputes and war, or live in the constant apprehension of them," a single ambitious regime bent on military adventurism could force all nearby nations to build up their armies to deter and, if necessary, repel invasion. Unlike navies, armies could be and were easily used not just to thwart invaders, but also to crush individual freedom and collective self-government. With the threat of military crackdowns stifling political freedom and a brooding military presence overshadowing the entire society, "the military state becomes elevated above the civil" and liberty suffers.[99] In short, land borders begot arms races that begot large standing armies that begot domestic tyranny.

Americans, Publius argued, must avoid continental Europe's fate by permanently unifying their New World landmass, as Britons had earlier permanently unified their island. When England, Wales, and Scotland were separate kingdoms, military competition between them invited invasion and foreign intrigue, triggering a heightened domestic militarization that threatened liberty. The indivisible union of England and Scotland at the outset of the eighteenth century gave island residents more room to breathe free.[100]

Publius thus urged that 1787 America emulate 1707 Britain by forming its own more perfect, "strict and indissoluble" union.[101] What were the alternatives? The existing Articles of Confederation were unworkable yet virtually impossible to amend, given the high bar of state unanimity. With a little luck and a lot of help from the French navy, America had won her most recent war, but her prospects for the next big one, whenever and however it might arise, appeared uncertain at best. Experience had proved that the individual states could not be trusted to provide their fair share of American soldiers and the money to pay them, and could not even be trusted to honor America's treaties with foreign powers. Without dramatic revision, the confederation could not fulfill its most basic purpose, which the Articles described as securing the several states' "common defense, . . . Liberties, . . . and general welfare" against "all force offered to, or attacks made upon them, or any of them" by hostile powers. To perpetuate the Articles' feeble regime would invite increased European military adventurism in North America and would leave Americans ill equipped to resist.[102]

If the Constitution were not ratified, Publius warned, some sort of "dismemberment of the union" would likely follow. Suppose Americans were to scrap the confederation in favor of thirteen separate land-bordering nations, each free to arm itself without limit. Each nation-state might well raise an army, ostensibly to protect itself against Indians or Europeans, but also perhaps to awe its neighbors. America would then recreate continental Europe—borders, armies, dictators, chains, and all. To opt instead for a system of three or four regional confederacies would not be much better, especially in light of the tremendous conflict that would likely arise among them concerning control of Western territory. "Territorial disputes have at all times been found one of the most fertile sources of hostility among nations. . . . This cause would exist among us in full force. We have a vast tract of unsettled territory." Already, some of the states had come close to blows in land disputes.[103]

If, however, an *unum* could be forged from *pluribus,* America would resemble Britain. The Atlantic Ocean would become a pacific ocean in all but name—an English Channel times fifty, a vast moat that would protect America against replication of, and subjugation by, the militarism of the European continental powers. Under a new national Constitution, America could rely primarily on a navy. Along with other federal organs, the navy could be directly financed by new federal imposts, duties, and other taxes imposed on individuals from every region—individuals who would be directly represented in the Congress that would set general tax rates and approve the overall defense budget. This new and readily enforceable revenue system would cure the collective-action problems that had doomed the Articles' requisition regime, which lacked strong mechanisms to sanction shirking states. (State self-interest alone had failed to guarantee adequate financial support; continental defense was a classic shared good whose benefits radiated beyond the contributing states.) To be sure, the new nation might require a small army to fortify the South against Spain, the West against Indians, and the North against Canada. Yet none of these land-bordering regimes could overawe the United (with a capital U) States, or provide any future president with a pretext to create a dangerously large standing army.[104]

Unless, of course, one of the land-bordering regimes received strong support from the Old Powers in Europe. Thus, Publius argued, Americans must discourage European monarchs from strengthening their footholds in the New World. And constitutionally "*United* States" would be more likely to blunt European adventurism, disabling the Old Powers from playing off state against state in classic divide-and-conquer fashion. Ominously, under the Articles, individual states had already failed to honor certain parts of America's 1783 peace treaty with Britain, which in turn had yet to live up to its promise to relinquish its forts in the American Northwest.[105] (The shirking states did not bear the full cost of their defaults, which put sister states at risk by giving Britain a pretext for further North American interventions.)

Also, separate states acting individually or in multiple confederacies would find it harder to pry trade concessions from Europe than would a continental nation acting as a unit, with extra bargaining power and the enforcement muscle to back up any threatened retaliatory tariff or boycott. Without a strong union, a single state might undercut its neighbors' tariffs, import the lion's share of foreign goods, and then wink as smugglers sneaked the goods into adjoining states, overland or by boat. Pro-tariff states would find it hard to stop such intracontinental smuggling without hordes of expensive and liberty-threatening internal border guards.[106]

The flip side of a common front against Europe would be increased intercourse between Americans themselves in a demilitarized interstate free-trade zone. Separate New World nation-states or confederacies might squabble over unfair intra-American trading practices and retaliatory tariffs, and Publius warned that disputes such as these ranked high among the classic causes of war. By contrast, free and fair trade across state lines under a national Constitution would redirect citizens' energies into commercial and social intercourse that would strengthen ties among Americans from different regions. In *The Federalist* No. 2, Jay/Publius described America as "one connected . . . country" in which a "succession of navigable waters forms a kind of chain round its borders, as if to bind it together; while the most noble rivers in the world, running at convenient distances, present [Americans] with highways for the easy communication of friendly aids, and the mutual transportation and exchange of their various commodities." Jay/Publius gilded this ode to increased interstate social and commercial interaction with fraternal imagery borrowed from Shakespeare's account of Agincourt, scene of England's great military triumph against a continental power: America's "band of brethren, united to each other by the strongest ties, should never be split into a number of unsocial, jealous, and alien sovereignties."[107]

Free intra-American trade would also encourage a domestic shipping industry and make America a "nursery of seamen," argued Publius. In times of war or international crisis, America's commercial fleet could be converted into an American navy through letters of marque and reprisal— governmental commissions authorizing private ships to engage and raid the enemy. The synergy would also work the other way, as an incipient navy would protect America's commercial navigation from European and piratical attack.[108]

Finally, expanding the geographic sphere of government by bringing thirteen states under a single continental canopy would economize on the total amount of money needed for military defense and other core functions. A larger landmass would generate a lower overall perimeter-to-area ratio, and a strong union would reduce the need to spend money to guard intracontinental borders between states.[109] Most important of all, the very strength of a united America would eliminate the need for a large standing army in peacetime. The result would be enormous peace dividends in both dollars and democracy.

This, in a nutshell, was Publius's first and most elaborate response to the traditionalist critique. Though Jay and Hamilton took the lead in unfolding it in the early *Federalist* essays, Madison himself had earlier outlined the argument at Philadelphia,[110] and as Publius he nicely distilled it in the opening words of *The Federalist* No. 14 and further embellished it in *The Federalist* No. 41. Hamilton, too, returned to these themes when summarizing the Constitution's virtues in his final essay, *The Federalist* No. 85. Among the six chief "securities to republican government, to liberty and to property, to be derived from the adoption of the [Philadelphia] plan," two were as follows: "the diminution of the opportunities to foreign intrigue, which the dissolution of the Confederacy would invite and facilitate" and "the prevention of extensive military establishments, which could not fail to grow out of wars between the States in a disunited situation."

OTHER LEADING FEDERALISTS shared Publius's geostrategic vision. Wilson harmonized with it in his opening and concluding words in the Pennsylvania debates; Oliver Ellsworth (another Philadelphia delegate, later to become America's chief justice) reprised it at the outset of his remarks in

Connecticut's convention; and Virginia's Governor Edmund Randolph made it a central theme of several of his speeches urging ratification.[111] Randolph's support was particularly important, coming as it did from the governor of America's oldest, most expansive, and most populous state, a state whose geographic centrality made it practically indispensable.[112] In September 1787, delegate Randolph had declined to sign the Constitution when given the chance at Philadelphia. But after two of Virginia's land-bordering neighbors, Pennsylvania and Maryland, voted to join the new union, Randolph repeatedly emphasized that fact in explaining why he now deemed Virginia's quick ratification essential. In language that would resound in the remarks of other Virginia Federalists,[113] Randolph hammered home the analogy between the British Union of 1707 and the new American union being proposed. Virginia, he insisted, would face un-acceptable military and commercial risks should she stay out of the new union while her border-states were in.

Publius's geostrategic argument also made good sense to George Washington, who as a surveyor and general instinctively grasped geography and military strategy better than abstract philosophy. In 1796, President Washington would devote major portions of his Farewell Address to the implications of Publian geostrategy;[114] and later presidents would push Publius's geostrategic vision even further with the Louisiana Purchase, the Monroe Doctrine, and Manifest Destiny.

Most important in 1787–88, the geostrategic argument gave moderates and traditionalists an account of the newfangled union that did not require them to disown their state legislatures. The argument's logic enabled ordinary Americans to ratify not because they distrusted their own democratic state lawmakers—men of middling rank like themselves, men who lived nearby and seemed to understand their daily problems—but rather because they needed to rein in *other states'* legislatures. The less specific the Federalists were about which particular states were the worst shirkers under the Confederation, the better. Each state could tell itself that its sisters were the chief offenders, and everyone could blame tiny Rhode Island most of all.

Moderate Americans could also appreciate the need to consider novel continental arrangements to guard against foreign invasion. In an effort to shield America's northwest flank, the Continental Congress of 1774 had crafted an open appeal to "Friends and fellow-subjects" in the largely French-speaking and Catholic British province of Quebec, which American colonists feared as a possible staging ground for King George's troops. The 1774 letter urged the Canadian Quebecois to "join us in our righteous contest, [and] make common cause with us."[115] Later, the Articles of Confederation provided for Canada's automatic admission into the confederation upon her proper application. (All other prospective candidates for admission would be screened on a case-by-case basis.) Large legal and cultural differences separated the Quebecois from their southern neighbors. The two sides had, after all, fought against each other in the previous decade's French and Indian War. Quebec, as a civil-law province, failed to honor many of the traditional rights of Englishmen, such as trial by jury. Yet during the Revolution, American patriots rushed to make common cause with neighbors who lacked the common law. Geography trumped tradition.

The very idea of a possible Canadian-American alliance conjured up images of Switzerland, a classic confederation of local cantons. The 1774 open appeal to Quebec explicitly pointed to the Swiss as proof that "difference of religion" between the Canadians and the Americans posed no insuperable obstacle to a firm alliance. "The Swiss Cantons . . . [are] composed of Roman Catholic and Protestant States, living in the utmost concord and peace with one another, and thereby enabled . . . to defy and defeat every tyrant that has invaded them."[116] Thirteen years later, leading Anti-Federalists repeatedly invoked the Swiss model. If a purely confederated system could keep the peace among the Swiss and also keep them free from outside invasion, why wouldn't the same be true of America?[117]

The Federalists' short answer was that America was no Switzerland. Geographically, commercially, and strategically, America was far more like Britain. Landlocked, the Swiss had no coastline to defend against a foreign fleet or to exploit for commercial advantage, and thus no need for a navy or for a centralized system to avoid local shirking to fund naval operations. Mountains and rugged terrain guarded individual Swiss cantons not only from foreigners, but also to a considerable extent from one another. Switzerland was not interlaced by large navigable rivers and broad highways. The cantons lacked a common coin and common troops. The Swiss had no vast unsettled territory as a possible ground of contention. In an extended analysis in *The Federalist* No. 19 (coauthored by Hamilton and Madison), Publius argued that the Swiss were held together by "the peculiarity of their topograph[y]" and many other features that distinguished them from Americans. In Connecticut, Ellsworth added that the Swiss "have nothing to tempt an invasion. Till lately, they had neither commerce nor manufactures. They were merely a set of herdsmen." More ominously, Publius concluded his analysis of the Swiss by observing that relations among the cantons had not always been as harmonious as the

1774 letter to Quebec had suggested. Religious disputes had in fact "kindled violent and bloody contests" that had virtually "severed the league," with Protestant cantons and Catholic cantons having then proceeded to form "opposite alliances with foreign powers."[118]

For the Federalists, Switzerland was a cautionary tale of the dangers and limits of purely confederated systems. Allied regimes did not always stay allied. If the precise facts about Switzerland and Old World diplomacy were perhaps contestable—leading Anti-Federalists vigorously challenged the Federalists' account—the New World offered more immediate illustrations. According to the colonists' 1774 overture to Quebec, the previous decade's hostilities between Quebec and her southern neighbors should not stand in the way of a new alliance between former foes. Yesterday's "brave enemies" might become today's "hearty friends."[119] If so, wasn't it also possible that today's hearty friends might become tomorrow's brave enemies? If Americans from different regions were willing to forget that they fought against the Quebecois in the French and Indian War, might they someday also forget that they fought alongside each other—a "band of brethren," as Jay would have it—in the Revolutionary War? Hence the need to transform an imperfectly perpetual league into a more perfect union, an indivisible nation designed to bind Americans of different regions together and thus prevent the parts from ever warring against one another or against the whole.

This general geostrategic vision informed much of the antebellum Constitution's overall structure and many of its specific words, such as its ban on standing appropriations for armies (but not navies) in Article I, section 8; its rules about state troops in Article I, section 10; its elaborate protections of the militia in Article I and the Second Amendment; its skepticism of "soldiers" (but not "sailors") in the Third Amendment; its particular rules for a muscular civilian president in Article II; its contemplation of westward expansion and the admission of new states in Article IV; its Article IV guarantees of each state's boundaries against invasion and each state's democracy against military despotism; and its pointed Article VI language describing the Constitution as the law of *"the Land."*

THE LAND, INDEED, LOOMED LARGE for Lincoln in the 1860s. Early in his First Inaugural, he put particular emphasis on the Preamble's purpose, *"to form a more perfect Union."* Moments later, in language that he repeated verbatim in his Second Annual Message to Congress, he explained that "physically speaking, we cannot separate. We cannot remove our respective sections from each other, nor build an impassable wall between them. A husband and wife may be divorced, and go out of the presence, and beyond the reach of each other; but the different parts of our country cannot do this. They cannot but remain face to face; and intercourse, either amicable or hostile, must continue between them. Is it possible then to make that intercourse more advantageous, or more satisfactory, *after* separation than *before*? Can aliens make treaties easier than friends can make laws? Can treaties be more faithfully enforced between aliens, than laws can among friends?" If these words called to mind parts of Jay's *Federalist* No. 2, so did the following section of Lincoln's Second Message:

> The great interior region [of America] has no sea-coast, touches no ocean anywhere. As part of one nation, its people now find, and may forever find, their way to Europe by New York, to South America and Africa by New Orleans, and to Asia by San Francisco. But separate our common country into two nations, as designed by the present rebellion, and every man of this great interior region is thereby cut off from some one or more of these outlets, not, perhaps, by a physical barrier, but by embarrassing and onerous trade regulations.
>
> . . . These outlets, east, west, and south, are indispensable to the well-being of the people inhabiting, and to inhabit, this vast interior region. [These outlets] of right, belong to [the American] people, and to their successors forever. True to themselves, they will not ask *where* a line of separation shall be, but will vow, rather, that there shall be no such line.

Like the Founders, Lincoln worried about militarily defensible borders and the need to prevent the emergence of two powerful and hostile regimes, side by side, generating an arms race or a trade war that might lead to the permanent militarization or impoverishment of the continent. From the Founding to the outbreak of the Civil War, the United States flourished as a remarkable free-trade and demilitarized zone.* As Lincoln saw it, those Americans in any given state who disliked Union policies

---

*Still later generations of Americans have continued to benefit from the peace- and trade-dividends created by the Constitution's more perfect union. Though many nations suffered massive devastation in their own backyards during World War II, America's wide oceanic moats kept the forty-eight states safe. Only Pearl Harbor and certain parts of Alaska came under serious attack. Before the tragedy of September 11, 2001, the last time foreign enemies wreaked havoc in the heartland was during the War of 1812. Not until after World War II would Americans feel obliged to field a large standing army in peacetime, and even then most American soldiers would be stationed overseas.

were free to leave, but they had no right to take the land with them, or to impose their secessionist preferences on their pro-Union neighbors both within their states and beyond. All Americans had invested in Fort Sumter and had a stake in the Mississippi River, and no single state or region could unilaterally take its land or waters and go home.

America *as a whole,* however, might decide to divide. Neither Lincoln nor his Federalist predecessors meant to prevent *national* reconsideration when they insisted that the more perfect union must be "indivisible" or "indissoluble." Lincoln elsewhere hinted at several ways that a national alteration of borders might properly occur, via constitutional amendments (perhaps informed by nonbinding referenda or national conventions), federal statutes and treaties, and regular presidential elections.[120] The right of the entire American people to rethink national boundaries was part of the continental people's inalienable right to alter or abolish; and Lincoln, as a proud pupil of the Preamble, emphatically affirmed government of, by, and for the people.

Thus what we the American people did in 1788, we were free to undo in 1861, and are free to undo today, for that matter. But the Preamble's words and underlying vision gave earlier generations—and continue to give Americans in the twenty-first century—strong reasons to embrace union as liberty's best hope.

Chapter 2

NEW RULES
FOR A
NEW WORLD

EARLIEST KNOWN PHOTOGRAPH OF THE UNITED STATES CAPITOL (1846).
A large building to accommodate a large legislature and the viewing public.

$\mathcal{T}$HE CONSTITUTION'S FIRST ARTICLE flowed naturally from the document's first sentence. "The People," in word and in deed, figured prominently in Article I following their dramatic debut in the Preamble, and much of the Article redeemed the Preamble's promise of deliberative democracy on a continental scale. Yet just as the Preamble excluded those in bondage from the blessings of liberty, so Article I made large compromises at slaves' expense.

"Congress"

Even as Article I began by borrowing the name of confederate America's central organ—"Congress"—it promised a quite different institution: "All legislative Powers herein granted shall be vested in a Congress of the United States, which shall consist of a Senate and House of Representatives."[1]

The old Congress could not point to any words in the Articles of Confederation expressly granting it "legislative" authority or describing its edicts as judicially enforceable "law." The new Congress, by contrast, would openly wield "legislative Powers"—a point reiterated by later constitutional language affirming Congress's power to "make all Laws" within its designated domain and exalting Congress's proper commands as "the supreme Law of the Land," enforceable in all American courts.

The old Congress stood as America's preeminent continental body. The new Congress would stand as merely the first of three continental branches. Thus Article I vested Congress with only "legislative Powers" as opposed to "executive Power" vested by Article II in an independent president and "judicial Power" vested by Article III in independent federal courts. The old Congress had acted less as a legislature than as an executive council, conducting foreign affairs and wielding many powers that the Crown had exercised in the old empire.[2] The new Congress, as a true legislature, would be shorn of classic executive functions, though its Senate would continue to play a role alongside the new president in making treaties and appointments.

The old Congress possessed only powers "expressly" conferred by the Articles. The new Congress would enjoy powers "herein granted," both in explicit terms and by fair implication. Also, the new Congress, unlike the old, could point to specific words in its authorizing document empowering it to tax individuals, to regulate interstate and international commerce, to impose a national currency, to directly raise a national army, to create sweeping civilian law-enforcement agencies, to regulate federal territory, and to guarantee the republicanism of each state.

The old unicameral Congress was a creature of state legislatures. The new bicameral Congress would enjoy considerably more independence. A wholly new institution, the "House of Representatives," would directly represent the people as distinct from state governments. Even the upper house, in which each state would count equally and members would be chosen by state legislatures as in the old Congress, would differ from its predecessor in key ways. This new "Senate" would bear a classical title suggesting independent judgment rather than slavish subordination to the dictates of state legislatures, who would lose their formal authority to recall their federal delegates.[3] Old congressmen were paid by states, but new congressmen would be paid by the central government. Old congressmen had short leashes—one-year terms. New congressmen would have freer rein—two years in the House, and six years in the Senate. Old congressmen could not seek perpetual reelection; lest they become overly attached to the union, they could spend no more than three of any consecutive six years in Congress. New congressmen could stand for reelection time and again without limit.[4] As a classic assemblage of ambassadors, the old Congress lacked power to sanction wayward members, remove them for gross misconduct, or even compel their attendance. The new Congress would wield all these powers, as befitted a genuine legislature. The old Congress voted state by state, as diplomatic delegations. The new Congress would vote member by member, as individual lawmakers. In sum, the old Congress consisted of states' men; the new Congress would consist of statesmen.

THESE VARIOUS MODIFICATIONS—making Congress a true legislature and only a legislature, expanding its regulatory sphere, splitting it in two, and reducing its dependence on state legislatures—interlocked. Precisely because the new Congress could make enforceable law operating directly on individuals, it posed a vastly greater risk to liberty than had its predecessor. The new Congress's wider scope and its increased independence from states only compounded the danger. As the Philadelphia drafters explained in an official letter accompanying their proposed Constitution, "the impropriety of delegating such extensive trust to one [unicameral, undifferentiated] body of men is evident."[5] Hence the need to introduce into the federal system the same devices that some state constitutions—especially the Massachusetts Constitution of 1780—had used to limit the powers of their respective state legislatures: separation of powers and bicameralism.

As Federalists eventually came to see the matter, early Revolutionary constitutions had created grossly imbalanced regimes. Before the Revolution, the Crown and landed proprietors had typically picked provincial executive and judicial officers and even upper-branch legislators. Thus colonial lower houses claimed to—and did—represent the people in a way the other parts of colonial government did not, a pattern that continued even after the Revolution ousted all remnants of imperial authority. Large lower houses gave men of middling rank opportunities to win election in their neighborhoods, even if they could never aspire to be state governors or senators—or law-trained judges, for that matter.[6] Men with only modest property holdings could vote and run for state assemblies even as other government institutions sat behind higher property barriers. Lower houses of state legislatures thus saw themselves as uniquely democratic and tended to dominate early state governments. In two states, Pennsylvania and Georgia, no counterbalancing upper house even existed. Legislatures regularly appointed executive and judicial officers, including governors in most states. In only two states did the governor enjoy a qualified veto power (in Massachusetts on his own, in New York as one member of a judge-dominated council).

Federalists in the late 1780s surveyed the scene with dismay. Skewed state constitutions, they believed, were enabling state legislatures to run amok. Writing as Publius, Madison quoted his old friend Jefferson on the Virginia experience: "All the powers of government, legislative, executive, and judiciary, result to the legislative body. The concentrating [of] these in the same hands is precisely the definition of despotic government." In seemingly democratic Pennsylvania—with its unicameral legislature, puny president, and weak executive council—a similar pathology prevailed, according to Madison. "It appears that the [state] constitution had been flagrantly violated by the legislature in a variety of important instances." Hamilton/Publius sharpened the point, condemning state legislatures' efforts to "exert an imperious control over the other departments" and acidly noting that "the representatives of the people, in a popular assembly, seem sometimes to fancy that they are the people themselves."[7]

The constitutional solution—first promoted at the state level in places such as Massachusetts and then copied by the architects of the new central government—was to give the executive and judicial branches more powers and increased independence from the legislature, which had to be split in two. In Virginia, Jefferson had urged that "the powers of government should be so divided and balanced among several bodies of magistracy, as that no one could transcend their legal limits, without being effectually checked and restrained by the others." To this, Madison added that "it is not possible to give to each department an equal power of self-defense. In republican government, the legislative authority necessarily predominates. The remedy for this inconveniency is to divide the legislature into different branches."[8]

The precise line of analysis in these passages went beyond the general insight that diffusion of power among competing branches would tend to promote liberty. Jefferson and Madison aimed to structure government power so as to promote compliance with the specific legal rights and rules established by the underlying state or federal constitution itself. Thus Jefferson spoke of enforcing the "legal limits" on each part of government, and Madison claimed that the federal Constitution's very structure would maintain the rules "laid down in the Constitution," would keep the branches in their constitutionally "proper" places, and would thus safeguard "public rights" and "the rights of the people" against improper "encroachments."[9]

Modern Americans associate enforcement of the Constitution with the doctrine of judicial review, under which judges refuse to enforce federal statutes that they deem inconsistent with the supreme law of the Constitution. At the Founding, however, the Constitution integrated several enforcement devices in its general system of separated powers. Broadly speaking, the Constitution enabled and in some cases obliged each of the three main departments—indeed, each half of the legislature and perhaps each half of the judiciary—to thwart schemes that it, and it alone, deemed unconstitutional. If House members judged a proposed bill unconstitutional, their oaths to uphold the Constitution would generally require them to vote no and thereby prevent the bill from ever becoming law—even if the Senate, the president, and the judiciary would likely endorse, or had already endorsed, the bill's constitutionality. Symmetrically, the Senate was expected to prevent enactment if a bill offended *its* distinct constitutional sensibility. The president also had a right and responsibility to veto bills that violated *his* understanding of the Constitution.[10] Beyond the veto, a president might refuse to enforce a statute that in his view contravened the higher law of the Constitution itself. If the law created criminal sanctions, a principled presidential refusal to prosecute violators would as a rule be unreviewable in court, as would a presidential decision to pardon anyone convicted or facing possible conviction under the law. Also, grand juries could refuse to indict whenever they doubted a criminal statute's constitutionality. Trial juries, widely viewed as the lower half of a bicameral judiciary, likewise had the power (and perhaps even the right and duty) to acquit with finality in such cases, even if the bench had already adjudged the law to be constitutionally sound. Within this larger context, judicial review was less a unique attribute of judges than a symmetric counterpart to the constitutional negatives enjoyed by coordinate branches.*

Although many modern Americans have been taught that the Constitution's intricate machinery of multiple decision points was designed to minimize the number of federal laws, savvy eighteenth-century Americans understood that a bicameral legislature might well produce more statutes than would a unicameral body. True, whenever the House preferred one set of bills and the Senate another, the dispute might end in legislative stalemate, with nothing passing and each house checking the other's enthusiasms. Alternatively, things might end in a legislative orgy in which all the bills passed in a giant logroll: "We will vote for your bills if you vote for ours." A similar point applied to the president's veto. A clever executive could wield his veto pen either as a shield to preserve the status quo or as a spur to goad a balky legislature into action. With pen in hand, an executive could tell legislators to give him his pet bills or else he would block theirs. Such horse-trading had commonly occurred during the colo-

---

*Americans resolved their first constitutional crisis by deploying several of these nonjudicial enforcement devices. In 1798, Congress enacted and President Adams signed a temporary Sedition Act making it a federal crime to criticize Congress or the president. The Virginia and Kentucky legislatures promptly adopted resolutions condemning the act as unconstitutional. When the administration began prosecuting its vociferous critics, federal judges brushed aside persuasive constitutional objections raised by defense lawyers and also prevented the defense from appealing to the constitutional sensibilities of trial jurors. These rulings hardly ended the constitutional controversy. Led by Thomas Jefferson, opponents of the 1798 Act sharpened the election of 1800 into a referendum of sorts on the statute. The opponents won sweeping victories in House and Senate elections, and Jefferson himself (with help from the three-fifths clause) bested Adams in the contest for the presidency. The new president pardoned all those previously convicted under the act, and the new Congress refused to reenact the temporary statute after it expired. The House of Representatives then proceeded to impeach Associate Justice Samuel Chase for alleged misconduct in one of the sedition trials and for other alleged misbehavior. Chase narrowly escaped conviction and removal in his Senate trial. The heroes of this Sedition Act saga were not federal judges, but the post-1800 House, Senate, and president, as prompted by state legislatures and the American electorate in 1800. Jurymen, too, might have played more heroic roles in the constitutional drama but for controversial bench rulings pushing these decision makers offstage.

nial era. Benjamin Franklin, whose loyalist son, William, had served as the royal governor of New Jersey from 1763 to 1776, put the point bluntly at Philadelphia: "The negative of the [colonial] Governor [of Pennsylvania] was constantly made use of to extort money. No good law whatever could be passed without a private bargain with him. An increase of his salary, or some donation, was always made a condition." Madison similarly elaborated the ability of one house in a bicameral system both to "obstruct" the other's favorite measures and to "extort" the other's consent for its own favorite projects. All this makes clear that the Constitution's complex system of multiple decision nodes was not designed simply to clog all bills regardless of subject matter.[11]

Nor would such a goal have been sensible. Between 1763 and 1776, American patriots had repeatedly urged Parliament to speedily *enact* certain laws—most obviously, laws repealing repressive legislation, such as the Stamp Act, the Townshend Duties, and the Coercive Acts. Similarly, various provisions of Article I made clear that public liberty would sometimes require the affirmative adoption of a federal law—like the first census law, without which the constitutionally mandated reapportionment could not take place. Had the Constitution disfavored all statutes, it could have required that every federal law expire after a certain period. But it did no such thing, outside a narrow category of laws dealing with standing armies.[12]

Instead, the Constitution structured an ingenious system of constitutional checks and choke points designed to minimize the likelihood that an *arguably unconstitutional* federal law would pass and take effect. If constitutional interpreters outside the legislature deemed a statute unconstitutional, they could—via executive pardons and nonenforcement, grand-jury refusals to indict, judicial review, jury acquittals, and the like—render the statute a virtual dead letter and thereby restore a libertarian baseline for most practical purposes. With the slate in effect wiped clean, the issue could then return to Congress for reconsideration, with each branch retaining its ordinary power to thwart any new assault on constitutional rights. De facto statutory slate-cleaning would roughly approximate the effect of a mandatory expiration date, but only for laws deemed unconstitutional outside the legislature, not all laws generally.[13]

Two main springs would drive this ingenious Constitution-protecting machinery. First, government officials in each branch would swear oaths to abide by the Constitution. Among men punctilious about their personal reputations, such oaths would discourage—by making *dishonorable*—any legislative logrolls involving proposals that either house deemed unconstitutional. When such proposals came before the legislature, the final bill would need to satisfy the constitutional scruples of each branch, with the standard effectively set by whichever house had the more punctilious view of the constitutional issue. So, too, if the president were asked to put his own name on every proposed bill, his sense of personal honor would prevent him from signing on to a project that he found to violate his personal pledge to "preserve, protect, and defend the Constitution."[14]

If, over time, the American people retained their attachment to the document they had ordained and established (and, later, amended), then the document's general popularity would provide a second incentive mechanism for government officials to keep faith with it. Even if a particular proposal commanded broad popular support, if the skeptical branch could voice its resistance in constitutional language that resonated with the voters, it might be emboldened to stand its ground. Ultimately, both enforcement devices, constitutional oaths and constitutional popularity, presupposed that the Constitution spoke not merely to federal judges, but rather to all branches and ultimately to the people themselves.

SEPARATION OF POWERS would also embody the rule of law. Congress would be obliged to define in advance, via generally applicable statutes, which misdeeds deserved punishment. Because branches independent of Congress would ultimately apply these laws—perhaps even against congressmen or their friends—legislators would have strong incentives to define punishable misconduct with precision and moderation, thereby benefiting all citizens, whether friends of Congress or not. All persons seeking to obey the law and avoid punishment would be able to learn what their legal duties were. For his part, the president could prosecute only those who ran afoul of legislatively defined standards; if he overstepped, judges and juries independent of both him and the legislature would dismiss the prosecution, with the public monitoring all involved. The judiciary, though often aware of how its rulings would immediately affect the named parties before it, would be required to follow the laws as laid down by a separate branch and to treat like cases alike regardless of party identity. Through this three-branch structure—textually reinforced by clauses barring sitting legislators from executive and judicial posts, limiting the scope of congressional impeachments, and banning ex post facto laws and bills of attainder—America hoped to rise above a personalized "rule of men." No single branch could heap punishment on someone merely because it disliked him or his clan, as might be possible in a world where one all-powerful entity legislated expansive mush words that it then applied lightly to its friends and harshly against its foes. In theory, Congress could never be sure who might ultimately benefit or suffer from its general and prospective rules, and other branches would be obliged to follow general laws framed in advance of the dispute.

The reality would prove somewhat messier, especially when government acted outside the criminal-law context. When ladling out benefits rather than imposing penalties, legislators had more discretion to separate known friends from known enemies. Also, even when formally acting via general and prospective laws, Congress could sometimes be sure who would benefit or suffer. Conversely, executives and judges could play favorites whenever laws were less than crystalline. Nevertheless, the general system marked an advance over the more primitive and personalized forms of authority that governed most of the planet in 1788.

Separation of powers also facilitated a certain degree of specialization of labor, enabling each branch to concentrate on a different function and thereby operate more efficiently. And because each government entity would be selected in a different way by a different constituency, ultimate government policy would reflect multiple indices of popular sentiment. Although no single electoral sampling would capture all of the public's will and judgment, different branches chosen at different times through different voting rules might together produce a more accurate and more stable composite sketch of deliberate public opinion. Americans would not risk losing everything whenever they acted unwisely on a single election day. Only over a series of elections and selections would public policy change decisively.[15]

"Representatives ... chosen ... by the People"

The Preamble promised Americans more direct democratic participation in ordaining their supreme law than anyone had ever seen on a continental scale. Echoing the Preamble's invocation of "the People," Article I promised something similar for ordinary lawmaking: The House of Representatives would be elected biennially "by the People of the several States."

The new House offered several democratic improvements on the old Confederation Congress. Confederation delegates were selected "in such manner as the legislature of each state shall direct." Except in Connecticut and Rhode Island, where statewide voters weighed in, state legislatures themselves did all the choosing.[16] Not only were Confederation delegates mere "representatives of representatives,"[17] but in most states the legislators picking these delegates were themselves required to meet higher property qualifications than those applicable to ordinary voters.[18] In sharp contrast, members of the new House would be directly elected by the voters themselves—more precisely, by all those eligible to vote for "the most numerous Branch of the State Legislature." This was the broadest franchise operating in the states, as opposed to more restricted electorates for various state upper houses and governorships.[19]

In theory, the Constitution could have gone further, prescribing a uniform rule of free-male-citizen suffrage, or something close, for federal elections. But such a standard would have gone beyond the prevailing practice in all thirteen states. Even the strikingly inclusive Pennsylvania Constitution limited voting to taxpayers. A universal suffrage rule would also have raised enforcement questions if any state balked. Without a veritable army of federal election bureaucrats, could a uniform system be implemented? Would the public accept a large federal bureau of elections only a decade after the Declaration had scolded King George for "erect[ing] a multitude of New Offices and sen[ding] hither Swarms of Officers"?[20]

The state franchise rules incorporated into Article I included a much higher proportion of citizens than did voting rules in English elections. Several Revolutionary state constitutions had lowered the property requirements traditionally used in colonial elections; and even those states that retained the old rules, or substituted something similar, in practice saw many more adult free male citizens voting than did England. America boasted vast tracts of land ripe for the taking and a youthful economy with countless paths to economic advancement. Most freemen who wanted land could get some or otherwise amass enough personal property to meet the states' liberal voting rules—and thus the new Congress's as well. Along this democratic dimension, America's House of Representatives far surpassed its Atlantic counterpart and imperial predecessor, England's House of Commons.[21]

Because representatives would derive their authority directly from the people, Americans could confidently entrust the new Congress with authority to legislate directly upon the citizenry. The old Confederation Congress members had not personally faced the voters and thus could claim no democratic mandate to lay burdens on them. In Revolutionary America, it was a small step from the rallying cry "No taxation without representation!" to the notion of no citizen taxation without citizen representation. Thus, the old Congress had been limited to requisitioning (with uneven success) the state legislatures that it represented.

If the new Congress's voter-qualification rules were liberal by the standards of the eighteenth century, its legislative membership rules were even more so. Nowhere did the Constitution require House members to meet any property threshold, and the document also barred both Congress and states from adding statutory property qualifications—or any other qualifications, for that matter—to Article I's short list of age, residency, and citizenship requirements.[22] Along this democratic dimension, America's House of Representatives towered far above England's House of Commons, where only men with vast estates could sit, and the old Congress as well.[23] Under the Articles, two states—New Hampshire and Maryland—had formally imposed high property qualifications on their congressional delegates, and other states were free to follow suit.[24] The new House rules were also miles ahead of existing state practice. A man of merit and repute who owned little or no property—say, a minister, schoolmaster, or war hero—could serve as a federal representative even though eleven states would have barred him from their own lower houses.[25]

The federal Senate also opened its doors to the unpropertied, thereby breaking with the membership practices of every state upper house in America.[26] Remarkably, a man could serve as a United States senator even if he did not own enough property to *vote* for his state senate, or his state assembly for that matter. In this respect, America's republican Senate stood as a rebuke not only to England's aristocratic House of Lords, but also to states such as Maryland and South Carolina, where only men of considerable wealth could join the upper-house club.

The new federal Constitution could easily have required House and Senate members to meet the property-qualification rules for the corresponding house of their respective states, but it did no such thing. Nor did the Constitution apportion its upper house according to wealth, as did both the Massachusetts and New Hampshire state constitutions. (A third state, South Carolina, apportioned both houses with reference to taxable property as well as white population.)[27] In 1787, only one state—unicameral Pennsylvania—declined to impose property restrictions on lawmakers. On this issue, the federal Constitution positioned itself on the democratic frontier.

Behind closed doors at Philadelphia, several draftsmen had leaned toward a far more propertied and less democratic regime. Gouverneur Morris openly advocated a Senate limited to men of "great personal property" and animated by "the aristocratic spirit." Though often at odds with Morris, George Mason also argued for property qualifications for congressmen in general and senators in particular. South Carolina's Pierce

Butler and John Rutledge repeatedly contended that congressional apportionment should track wealth alongside population, and notable delegates from other states were quick to agree. Madison himself sympathized with these men and smiled on states that privileged property in their upper houses.[28]

In the end, more democratic proposals prevailed. Midway through the Convention, Morris moved to "restrain the right of suffrage" for House elections to those who owned freehold estates. Although some delegates, including Madison, had kind words for Morris's motion, only Delaware ultimately supported it, while seven states stood opposed. America's "common people" and "lower class," Franklin reminded his colleagues, had fought nobly in the Revolutionary War. If such men had enough "virtue & public spirit" to fight for America, shouldn't they be allowed to vote in America? If excluded from the suffrage, might such men shed their remarkable patriotism? Mason—himself a father of nine—declared that the franchise (as distinct from the right to *serve* in Congress) should extend to "every man having evidence of attachment to & permanent common interest with Society," such as a "Father of a Family," regardless of his estate or lack thereof. Wilson observed that it would be "hard & disagreeable" to exclude those who voted in state elections from comparable federal elections. Ellsworth gave Wilson's point a decisive twist: "The people will not readily subscribe to the Natl. Constitution, if it should subject them to be disfranchised."[29]

Ellsworth's insight, variations of which surfaced in the comments of many other delegates, worked on two levels. First, the people might literally refuse to "subscribe" to the Constitution, and might instead reject the Philadelphia plan in the upcoming special ratification elections, just as voters in Massachusetts and New Hampshire had rejected four of the six state constitutions presented to them in the previous decade. Second, even if ratifiers were to accept the Philadelphia plan, the Constitution and the Congress would need the ongoing goodwill of the people thereafter. Any constriction of the franchise would jeopardize that goodwill.

Ellsworth's words remind us that the small knot of men drafting secretly in Philadelphia understood full well that the American people would have the last word on the ultimate fate of the American Constitution. The uniquely democratic act of ratification that the drafters were envisioning and the uncertain prospects of their plan in the months ahead shaped every major debate at Philadelphia and often gave a decided advantage to more democratically defensible ideas. Thus the Preamble exerted gravitational pull over all that followed, both in the text and over time. The drafters' need to win one extraordinarily democratic round of elections in the late 1780s disposed them to democratize subsequent Articles and subsequent elections.[30]

The Philadelphia debate over congressional membership rules followed a similar pattern. By a vote of seven states to three, the drafters rejected a proposal empowering Congress to establish membership qualifications. One telling objection was that incumbents might manipulate these rules so as to entrench themselves in office. Parliament, Madison reminded his colleagues, had notoriously abused its powers to regulate the qualifications of voters and members. If such self-dealing laws were allowed, a republic could sink into "an aristocracy or oligarchy." Also, Congress might find it hard to fashion uniform rules applicable to members from rich and poor states alike. Had these been the only problems, however, they could have been solved by a simple requirement that each federal lawmaker meet whatever property qualification his home state imposed for membership in the comparable branch of state government—a policy that would mirror the strategy used to define the federal suffrage in House elections. John Rutledge in fact floated this suggestion, but the democratic tide ran hard against him.[31]

Franklin argued that the "Constitution will be much read and attended to in Europe," and "a great partiality to the rich . . . will not only hurt us in the esteem of the most liberal and enlightened men there, but discourage the common people from removing to this Country." As had Ellsworth, Franklin thus reminded his colleagues that the ultimate success of the document—and of the American experiment more generally—would depend on the broad popular verdict outside Philadelphia. While Ellsworth had spoken of America's masses voting with their hands and hearts, Franklin called attention to Europe's masses voting with their feet.[32]

When the secret conclave ended and friends of the Constitution had to defend the document before the American people and the world, leading Federalists stressed the republican principles underlying the Article I rules of voter and candidate eligibility. Noting in *The Federalist* No. 52 that the "definition of the right of suffrage is very justly regarded as a fundamental article of republican government," Madison/Publius praised the document for securing this right from legislative manipulation, and also for opening the doors of congressional membership to "merit of every description, whether native or adoptive, whether young or old, and without regard to poverty or wealth, or to any particular profession of religious faith." A few days later, in *The Federalist* No. 57, Madison reiterated the point with uncharacteristic flourish: "Who are to be the electors of the federal representatives? Not the rich, more than the poor; not the learned, more than the ignorant; not the haughty heirs of distinguished names, more than the humble sons of obscure and unpropitious fortune. The electors are to be the great body of the People of the United States. . . .Who are to be the objects of popular choice? Every citizen whose merit may recommend him to the esteem and confidence of his country. No qualification of wealth, of birth, of religious faith, or of civil profession is permitted to fetter the judgment or disappoint the inclination of the people."

While *The Federalist* spoke most directly to the citizens of New York (where the essays first appeared seriatim in newspapers before coming out in two hardcover volumes published in the spring of 1788), similar expositions occurred across America. In Pennsylvania, Wilson bragged that Article I "secures, in the strongest manner, the right of suffrage" because it piggybacked on state rules that themselves had to conform to "a republican form of government." Addressing the Maryland House of Delegates, Philadelphia drafter James McHenry reported that some at Philadelphia had urged a freehold requirement for federal voters to avoid "all the Disorders of a Democracy." McHenry then proceeded to summarize the populist counterargument of "the Venerable Franklin." In Massachusetts, Anti-Federalists actually criticized the Constitution for omitting property qualifications for congressmen, prompting Federalist Theodore Sedgwick to condemn the objections as "anti-democratical" and to chide his opponents for their "wish to exclude from the federal government a *good* man, because he was not a *rich* one." Rufus King, a leading Philadelphia draftsman, also chimed in: "He never knew that *property* was an index to abilities. We often see men, who, though destitute of property, are superior in knowledge and rectitude." Virginia's George Nicholas probably had *The Federalist* No. 52 in hand as he paraphrased its prose and commended the Constitution for its refusal to exclude "men of eminent abilities" from Congress merely because they lacked landed property. Later in the debate, Madison proudly contrasted Parliamentary rules requiring a county member to have land worth £600 annually with the Philadelphia plan, under which "any citizen may be elected."[33]

THE MEMBERSHIP REQUIREMENTS that Article I did impose— citizenship, residency, and age—received less attention in ratification debates, yet these, too, embodied republican principles. Although aliens owing allegiance to foreign nations and foreign lords could not properly lead America, the House would welcome naturalized citizens after their seventh year of citizenship, as would the Senate after their ninth. This openness kept faith with Franklin's dream of luring Europe's best to America's shores even as it broke sharply with England's 1701 Act of Settlement, which forbade naturalized subjects from serving in Parliament.

Several Philadelphia draftsmen argued vigorously, if unsuccessfully, for even broader immigrant eligibility. Randolph and Wilson (himself a native of Scotland) urged reducing the House waiting period from seven years to four, and Hamilton (born in the West Indies) proposed abolishing the waiting period altogether: "Persons in Europe of moderate fortunes will be fond of coming here when they will be on a level with the first Citizens." Madison seconded the motion and linked the idea of "liberal[]" eligibility to republicanism. "He wished to invite foreigners of merit & republican principles among us. America was indebted to emigration for her settlement & Prosperity." Wilson spoke with special passion on the immigrant issue, "mentioning the circumstance of his not being a native, and the possibility, if the ideas of some gentlemen should be pursued, of his being incapacitated from holding a place under the very Constitution which he had shared in the trust of making." As he saw it, any extended or permanent ineligibility would impose a "degrading discrimination" upon nonnative Americans, who would thereby suffer "discouragement & mortification." Yet Wilson and his allies were willing to live with the short immigrant waiting periods in the final Philadelphia plan. In the first congressional election cycle under their new Constitution, the American people were quick to exercise the ample freedom of choice guaranteed them by Article I, sending nine naturalized citizens to the House and Senate. Four of the nine had been among the document's signers at Philadelphia.[34]

Article I's state-residency rule also squared with republican principles, and in fact aimed to prevent wealthy candidates from gaming the system. As Mason explained: "If residence be not required, Rich men of neighbouring States, may employ with success the means of corruption in some particular district and thereby get into the public Councils after having failed in their own State. This is the practice in the boroughs of England."[35]

Article I's age limits—requiring representatives to be at least twenty-five years old and senators thirty—would likewise tend to limit the rich and highborn more than the poor and middling classes. Who other than the "haughty heirs of distinguished names" would be famous enough at a tender age to win a seat in the continental House or Senate?[36] Without a minimum-age rule, voters and legislatures in each state might be tempted to send the state's favorite son, such as the governor's scion, to Congress as young as possible. Such a youngster could then begin to make contacts that would give him—and derivatively, his state—a head start in future contests for federal honors, such as congressional leadership positions, cabinet posts, judgeships, and even the presidency itself. If each state chose such a strategy, an unrepublican race to the bottom might ensue, with family-name recognition elbowing out the actual accomplishments of older candidates. In England, William Pitt the younger, whose father and namesake had led the British ministry in the mid-1760s, entered Parliament in 1781 at the age of twenty-one. In 1783, this twenty-four-year-old favorite son himself became prime minister, a post that he continued to hold in Britain even as Americans deliberated over the different constitutional rules that would govern their side of the Atlantic.

As the New World's new system played out in its early years, Congress did in fact operate as a springboard to further federal honors. Four of the first dozen men to reach the Senate before their thirty-third birthdays went on either to win the presidency itself (James Monroe and Andrew Jackson) or to become the electoral-college runner-up (De Witt Clinton and Henry Clay, the latter twice). Fifteen of America's sixteen antebellum presidents came to office with congressional experience. Several of these men were indeed state favorite sons in a rather literal sense: One was a president's heir and namesake, and three were the children of governors. Yet by the time they reached Congress, each of these sons had an extensive political track record of his own, thanks to Article I's age rules. Thus, John Quincy Adams had already distinguished himself as a leading American diplomat, William Henry Harrison had won acclaim as a territorial governor and war hero, John Tyler had served for many years in state government, and Franklin Pierce had led his state legislature. (No state constitution required its lower-house members to meet any special age limits beyond those for voters generally.)[37]

Cumulative data from the new Congress's first decade provide further evidence that Article I's age rules probably did tend to dampen intergenerational aristocracy. While 40 percent of the Senate's youngest cohort (ages thirty to thirty-four) boasted fathers, fathers-in-law, or uncles of extraordinary political distinction, less than 15 percent of the rest had comparable political pedigrees. On the House side, men who arrived young (under age thirty-two) were three times as likely as other representatives to claim close family ties to high-placed elder statesmen. Tennessee even sent a twenty-two-year-old to the House in flagrant violation of the Con-

stitution's rules. Young William Charles Cole Claiborne was indeed a favorite son—or at least a favorite nephew. His uncle Thomas Claiborne
was already serving in Congress as a Virginia representative.[38]

Lest Congress try to create an exclusive club by blackballing lowborn
men or others who did not fit in socially, Article I also required a special
two-thirds supermajority before either house could expel a member. This
rule, too, broke with English tradition: Parliament could and did expel
members by simple majority vote. In the 1760s, Parliament had notoriously abused this power in the case of the flamboyant John Wilkes, who
became a hero to American patriots in the Revolution. Parliament's recent
misconduct strongly influenced the drafting of Article I. In order to protect a future Wilkes—adored by his constituents but disdained by legislative barons—the Constitution made it difficult for Congress to oust a duly
elected member.[39]

ANOTHER PARLIAMENTARY ABUSE concerned a common electioneering
practice that Edmund Morgan has provocatively subsumed within the
category of "bribery." Members of Commons regularly won their seats by
"offering to pay for some civic benefit: paving the streets, erecting a town
hall or school or market, paying the town's public debt or its bill for poor
relief."[40] Such a system disadvantaged both less wealthy candidates who
could not match their rivals' bids and less wealthy districts that could ill
afford to spurn bribes. In colonial America, a similar if subtler form of
bribery occurred whenever a candidate agreed to serve without pay. In
England, this precise form of bribery was unavailing; before 1911, Parliament members as a rule served without pay. Yet this lack of Parliamentary
compensation only reinforced the reality that the House of Commons was
hardly a house of common folk. Only gentlemen of independent wealth
could afford to serve without pay. Legislative membership in England
was not a democratic vocation, but rather a genteel avocation. The same
was true generally, if less dramatically, of legislative service in colonial and
Revolutionary America.[41]

Against this backdrop, Article I's explicit provision that members of
both houses would draw salaries from the national treasury powerfully
democratized the right to serve in government. Historian Gordon Wood
has labeled this little-noted aspect of Article I "radical for the age."[42]
Although many state legislatures voted themselves compensation,[43] they
typically did so in the face of state constitutions that made no express provision for legislative salaries or even for reimbursement of out-of-pocket

travel expenses. Only three state constitutions explicitly provided for legislative payment of any sort, two of which (Massachusetts and New
Hampshire) spoke of reimbursing the travel expenses of lower-house
members while saying nothing about the upper house.[44] As for wages
above and beyond expenses, New Hampshire explicitly saddled each
township with the obligation to pay its own delegates, and Massachusetts
did so by tradition. Such a system encouraged poorer towns to favor
wealthy delegates willing to forego salary—a modest form of bribery, perhaps, but bribery nonetheless.[45] A similar vice infected the Articles of
Confederation, in which each state maintained its own delegates.

The federal Constitution's payment rules, by contrast, enabled men of
modest means to serve and spared poorer states the temptation to pick a
wealthier candidate willing to sit without salary. The cost of each congressman's salary would be spread nationwide rather than imposed on the
voters of his home state. Here, too, Article I's modern vision placed it
on the cutting edge of late-eighteenth-century democracy, alongside the
Pennsylvania Constitution of 1776, the only state charter that openly
promised "wages" from the "state treasury" to all lawmakers.[46]

An avowedly egalitarian ideology fueled this part of Article I. At
Philadelphia, Mason championed a proposal for "liberal compensation"
from the national treasury. The "parsimony" of some states under the confederation had weakened the old Congress, where the question in some
places was not "who were most fit to be chosen, but who were most willing to serve." Randolph argued that congressmen must "certainly" be paid
because, unlike aristocratic England with its peers and old wealth, young
America lacked "sufficient fortunes to induce gentlemen to attend for
nothing." Hugh Williamson opposed these egalitarian arguments with a
crass appeal to class and regional interests. Envisioning "the prospect of
new States to the Westward," which were likely to be "poor" and with "different interest[s] from the old States," Williamson "did not think therefore
that the [old States] ought to pay the expences of men who would be employed in thwarting their measures & interests." These remarks drew a
sharp rebuke from Madison. "If the Western States hereafter arising
should be admitted into the Union, they ought to be considered as equals &
as brethren. . . . Provisions should be made as would invite the most capable and respectable characters into the service." Thus the delegates pointedly rejected the aristocratic arguments of Charles Cotesworth Pinckney
and Gouverneur Morris, who favored an unpaid Senate in which "the
wealthy alone" and "none but" the "rich" could afford to serve.[47]

During the ratification debates, while some Anti-Federalists worried that Congress might milk the salary system, others fretted that Congress might set compensation levels too low in order to drive poor men out. (Roger Sherman had raised a similar concern at Philadelphia.) In Virginia, Madison deemed this danger "remote" and noted that voters could counter such a ruse by replacing aristocratic schemers with challengers committed to fair compensation. Thus, the Congress would remain open to "those who have the most merit and least wealth."[48]

Payment of congressmen via salaries set by congressmen raised the specter of legislative self-dealing, with lawmakers engaged in the "indecent" (to Madison) activity of putting "their hands into the public purse for the sake of their own pockets."[49] But payment by states would have raised real problems of bribery and inequality, and it would also have rendered the new national legislature overly dependent on state governments. Nor could the Constitution itself easily fix congressional salaries for all time, given the prospect of unpredictable swings in the future cost of living. The better and more egalitarian solution was to give the choice to Congress, whose members would feel obliged to explain their salary votes to their constituents. To prevent politically unaccountable lame-duck congressmen from voting themselves bonuses on their way out, the First Congress would ultimately propose a constitutional amendment delaying any salary change until after an election had intervened. Through this amendment (whose interesting ratification experience we shall consider elsewhere in our story), the people of the nation would ultimately have the last word on congressional salaries—a fittingly democratic procedure to implement the ideal of democratic public service.

ALLOWING CONGRESSMEN TO DETERMINE their own salaries was one thing; allowing them to determine the timing of their own elections, in British parliamentary fashion, was quite another. In Stuart England, the timing of parliamentary elections had fluctuated wildly as kings and Commons struggled for supremacy. From 1629 to 1640, Charles I ruled with no Parliament, after which the aptly named Long Parliament held its ground for thirteen years without returning to the voters. With the Restoration of 1660, another Parliament sat for almost two decades under Charles II, followed by three quick Parliaments that the king dissolved in rapid succession in 1680–81. After the Glorious Revolution of 1688–89, Parliament gained the upper hand, and the English Bill of Rights of 1689 declared that "parliaments ought to be held frequently." The rub was that "frequently" meant whatever Parliament said it meant. In 1694, Parliament promised triennial elections, but in 1716 it ignored that promise, voted its current members an extra four years in power, and pledged (unenforceably) to hold septennial elections thereafter.

Georgian America followed the pattern set in Stuart England. As royal governors confronted colonial assemblies across the continent, election timing seesawed furiously. In most royal colonies, Crown-appointed governors could prorogue and dissolve assemblies at will, with "no minimum frequency for convoking difficult Assemblies and no maximum duration for retaining pliant ones."[50] In 1767, the Crown issued instructions to royal governors to veto (with no possibility of override) any colonial bill aiming to fix the meeting and duration of assemblies.[51] The 1776 Declaration thundered against the royal abuse of the veto generally, and specifically condemned the Crown for "dissolv[ing] Representative houses repeatedly & continually" and for "refus[ing] for a long time after such dissolutions to cause others to be elected." In response to such abuses, Revolutionary state constitutions specified regular times for elections and eliminated executive dissolution power.[52]

The federal Constitution reinforced the reformist movement in favor of fixed and frequent elections. Article I mandated that every two years, like clockwork, all House members and one-third of the Senate would come before the electorate. This simple rule solved three potential legislative abuses. First, it imposed an outside limit on the time period between elections. No such absolute limit existed in the unwritten English Constitution. If a past Parliament, without prior notice to the voters, could lurch from three to seven years, only self-restraint seemed to prevent a future Parliament from moving to ten or twenty years. Second, Article I guaranteed that federal elections would in fact occur more frequently than the parliamentary elections promised by the 1716 Septennial Act. Every House member would face his constituents every second year, and even members of America's upper house would serve shorter terms than members of Britain's lower house. Third, while Parliament enjoyed discretion to hold early elections whenever such acceleration might favor the dominant legislative faction or incumbents generally, Congress would have no comparable power to manipulate election timing. Elections would be held at unchangeable intervals, let the political chips fall where they may.

Revolutionary state constitutions had gone even further in guaranteeing frequent elections. Two states held elections for the lower house twice a year, ten others ran annual elections, and only one—South Carolina—gave lower-house members two-year terms. Although several state upper houses featured multiyear terms, none exceeded five years. Against this backdrop, the Constitution's longer electoral intervals gave critics pause, but Federalists mounted a powerful defense. Because of the vast distances that congressmen would need to traverse between House and home, annual elections would have required members to spend too much time coming and going and too little time mastering the issues. Compared to state legislators crafting local laws in light of local conditions familiar to resident lawmakers, continental legislators would need extra time to study the circumstances of other states in a diverse and far-flung union. The responsibility of Congress—especially the Senate—for foreign affairs also counseled longer terms to enable lawmakers to learn about other nations and maintain a stable stance toward them. Although elections would occur only biannually, Article I, section 4 obliged Congress to meet at least once a year, and unlike Stuart kings and colonial governors, the American president would have no power to dissolve the legislature at whim.[53]

In response to Anti-Federalists who pointed out that congressmen under the Articles were elected annually, Federalists identified important differences between the old and the new systems. Under the Articles, state legislatures customarily reelected delegates until the three-year term limits began to bite. Confederation delegates had little need to return home to electioneer, and they typically communicated with their masters in writing. Under the Constitution's system of popular election, representatives would ordinarily be expected to face their neighbors in person, and this political reality reinforced the travel-time argument for longer terms.[54] Thus Federalists could and did offer persuasive reasons for their proposed congressional calendar.

"The Number of Representatives"

Other numbers in Article I were harder to defend. The first House would consist of sixty-five members (if all thirteen states ratified) and nothing in the text required subsequent Houses to be any larger. Although Article I provided that the House should not "exceed" one representative per thirty thousand constituents, its only minimal mandate was that each state have at least one member. Virginia's Patrick Henry boggled at this "strange[] language. . . . Let our [population] numbers be ever so great, this immense continent may, by this artful expression, be reduced to have but thirteen representatives."[55]

Even if Americans could rest assured that the federal legislature would never shrink—and as we shall see, it never did—the new Congress started out disturbingly small. True, it would be no smaller than the old

Congress. Sixty-five representatives plus twenty-six senators would equal ninety-one total congressmen—exactly the maximum size of Congress under the Articles if each of the thirteen states chose to send a full seven-man delegation.[56] In fact, most sessions of the old Congress in the 1780s fell far below this number. A state needed only two delegates to cast its vote, and every extra body imposed added travel burdens on delegates and additional maintenance costs on states. For much of the decade, Congress had limped along without a quorum or with barely enough states in the room to transact vital business.[57] During the Confederation's final five years, all thirteen states showed up for only eight of the more than one thousand days on which Congress met. Less than half of the sessions saw nine or more states in the room.[58] (All important decisions under the Articles required the concurrence of nine states.)

With its per-capita voting rules, its national payment of members, its formal authority to compel members to show up, and its broad power to make binding law, the new Congress was structured to yield a much higher attendance rate.[59] Still, the very vastness of Congress's new law-making powers argued for an even bigger House that would give Americans across the continent confidence in the genuine representativeness of the new "Representatives."

At the state level, the Revolution had triggered dramatic increases in the size of many a lower house.*[60] Several Revolutionary state legislatures dwarfed the new Congress in absolute numbers, to say nothing of the ratio of lawmakers to constituents. The Massachusetts House of Representatives alone boasted five times as many members, and the Virginia House of Delegates almost thrice as many, as the House that would represent the entire nation.[61] Only two states, New Jersey and Delaware, had lower houses with fewer than sixty-five members.[62] Overall, some 1,500 assemblymen legislated for the thirteen states respectively, whereas the Philadelphia plan envisioned that less than one-twentieth of that number would legislate for the thirteen states collectively.[63] At a glance, even Parliament seemed better, with a House of Commons that weighed in at 558 members—more than eight times the size of America's new House, and with about three times as many lawmakers per free citizen.

---

*These increases marked the new state constitutions as distinctly more democratic than their colonial precursors, even in states that did not dramatically widen the suffrage in the 1770s. The Constitution itself reflected the perceived linkage between legislative size and democracy by describing each state's lower house (as distinct from its senatorial counterpart) not as the house with the wider suffrage base or the more frequent elections or the more inclusive eligibility rules, but rather as the "*most numerous* Branch" of the state legislature.

No aspect of the federal Constitution provoked more trenchant criticism than House size.[64] The Anti-Federalists' anxiety about this one little number inspired much of their distrust of the Philadelphia plan as a whole. These "men of little faith" feared that members of an overly select House would become targets for bribery and corruption, whether at the hands of a dishonest president, a wealthy manipulator, or a foreign power. If even a handful of congressmen turned out to be crooked, the intrigues of such a junto might carry the day in a small assembly. A larger assembly would have been that much harder to bribe.[65] Anti-Federalists also doubted the adequacy of the specific anticorruption rules of Article I, section 6, which sought to prevent presidents from seducing congressmen with government sinecures, as English kings had notoriously bought off members of Parliament with offers of special place and preferment.

The low ratio of members to constituents compounded Anti-Federalist doubts about the document's democratic bona fides. Despite Congress's theoretical openness to all aspirants, Anti-Federalists worried that in practice the House would be closed to men of modest fortune and station, howsoever virtuous and well respected by their neighbors. Only lordly men with wide geographic reputations and fat purses would be able to win elections in the extended geographic districts necessitated by a small House. Such large districts, spanning both town and country, would likely give the inside track to city leaders and money men—lawyers, bankers, wealthy merchants, and their ilk. Compared to scattered country farmers, city men could more easily caucus to coordinate their votes behind a single candidate and could use the press more effectively to publicize their preferences.[66] A larger House would have permitted more districts—some for cities and others for rural areas.

A small House thus raised large questions: If the great mass of politically active citizens could never realistically aspire to serve in a small Congress, and if most men might not even know their congressman personally, would high-toned congressmen be able to sympathize with the concerns of ordinary folk? In turn, would congressmen enjoy the necessary confidence of their constituents? Or would federal lawmakers instead feel obliged to rule through force and fear via a vicious cycle of standing armies and heavy taxes?[67]

The elitist cast of the lower house, Anti-Federalists warned, would stamp the basic character of the government as a whole. Codifying Whig theory and republican ideology, the Delaware and Maryland constitutions of 1776 had proclaimed that the very "foundation" of "all free government" was "the right in the people to participate in the Legislature." In both Britain and colonial America, the lower house had been conceptualized as democracy's cornerstone—the main "democratical" element of a mixed constitution whose upper house represented the aristocratic element and whose executive branch embodied the monarchy. By eliminating all property qualifications for Senate membership, and for the presidency and the judiciary as well, the Philadelphia plan promised to democratize traditionally aristocratic positions, but would its select House aristocratize the traditionally democratic assembly? So small a House seemed ill structured to actualize the right of ordinary people to "*participate* in the legislature" as envisioned by republican and Whig ideology. A mere sixty-five men drawn from a vast continent would likely fall far short of John Adams's famous ideal that an assembly "should be in miniature an exact portrait of the people at large. It should think, feel, reason, and act like them." Though chosen "by the People" according to the dictates of Article I, would such representatives truly be *of* the people? *For* them?[68]

Madison and other Federalists did indeed envision a House composed of enlightened lawmakers with extensive geographic reputations and the ability to rise above ill-informed popular prejudices when the need arose. Such enlightened statesmen would give the new republic more stability and wisdom in its dealings with foreign nations, and would add needed gravitas to domestic politics as well. The trick was to structure the new House so as to attract America's best and brightest, the kind of men who had stepped forward to lead America in the mid-1770s, as opposed to the lesser figures who seemed all too common in politics a decade later.[69] The Philadelphia Convention itself had attracted some of the continent's greatest statesmen to draft a new plan of government. By proposing that the new House be a select body of true distinction, these drafters aimed to lure other great men onto the public stage. As the new system would play out in its first electoral cycle, nine Philadelphia framers would serve as representatives in the first House, and another eleven would serve in the Senate.[70]

Yet Madison and his allies also understood that proper republican representation required strong bonds of sympathy and confidence linking legislators and constituents. At Philadelphia, Madison had urged doubling the size of the initial House to 130 members. A 65-member House (with a quorum of 33, of which 17 would constitute a majority) "would not possess enough of the confidence of the people, and wd. be too sparsely taken from the people, to bring with them all the local information which would be frequently wanted." Moreover, any "unpopular[ity]" that might be occasioned by the increased expense of a larger House would be "overbalanced by its effect on the hopes of a greater number of the popular Candidates" who could realistically aspire to a seat in Congress. Several days before the delegates presented their plan to the public, Hamilton declared "with great earnestness and anxiety" that it was "essential that the popular branch . . . should be on a broad foundation. . . . The House of Representatives was on so narrow a scale as to be really dangerous, and to warrant a jealousy in the people for their liberties." In these remarks, we see once again how the brooding specter of the people's ultimate judgment out-of-doors hovered over the Philadelphia draftsmen indoors. These draftsmen also knew that their personal political prospects—for example, their odds of serving in the First Congress—would ultimately depend on their popularity with the broader American electorate. In short, the framers hoped for a double ratification—first of their collective proposal, and then of their individual aspirations.[71]

Initially, Hamilton's plea for a larger House failed at Philadelphia by a vote of six states to five. Concerns about increased travel burdens— a larger House would oblige more of each state's leading men to leave home—evidently proved decisive. Every state from Pennsylvania through North Carolina supported the increase, while every state farther north and south of center opposed it.[72] There the matter stood until the Convention's last day, when George Washington dramatically intervened. Departing from his presiding practice of keeping silent on all substantive questions under discussion, he urged the delegates to reconsider the issue of House size. "It was," he said, "much to be desired that the objections to the plan recommended might be made as few as possible— The smallness of the proportion of Representatives had been considered by many members of the Convention, an insufficient security for the rights & interests of the people." The delegates knew how to take a hint; they promptly agreed to a last-minute change allowing the House to grow at a quicker rate after the first census. The parchment, which had already been prepared for the signing ceremony, was hastily revised by substituting a maximum of one representative for every "thirty" thousand constituents instead of "forty," as had initially been proposed.[73] (The parchment smudge remains visible today.)

Thirty-nine delegates proceeded to add their names,[74] while three others pointedly declined to do so. One of the non-signers, George Mason, promptly published a brief catalogue of his "Objections." High on this list was his claim that the House had "not the substance but the shadow only of representation," though he admitted that "this objection has been in some degree lessened" by the last-minute "amendment" and "erasure" backed by Washington. Other Anti-Federalists soon joined Mason in complaining about House size. Madison, Hamilton, and Washington had indeed been prophetic in identifying a constitutional sore spot.[75]

IN RESPONSE TO THEIR CRITICS, Federalists nimbly pivoted and promised to expand the House posthaste. The number sixty-five, they explained, was simply a stopgap that would quickly yield to a much larger number. Devoting four consecutive essays to the topic of House size—a testament to its significance—Madison/Publius began and ended by assuring his readers that within three years a continental census would be taken and the House would total at least one hundred members. Future population increases would in time bring the House to four hundred members, Publius predicted. Pennsylvania's Thomas McKean proclaimed that the House "will be increased" in "three years' time," and in Massachusetts, Philadelphia delegate Caleb Strong declared that Congress would expand "very soon." Parroting Publius verbatim, Virginia's George Nicholas assured his fellow ratifiers that after the first enumeration, there would be one Representative for every thirty thousand constituents. "I take it for granted that the number . . . will be increased . . . to one hundred representatives . . . [and] that the number of representatives will be proportioned to the highest number we are entitled to." Hamilton likewise stuck to the party line in the New York convention: "One representative for every thirty thousand inhabitants is fixed as the standard of increase. . . In three years, [the House] would exceed one hundred."[76]

Anti-Federalists countered by emphasizing that nothing in Article I guaranteed such an increase.[77] One representative for thirty thousand constituents defined the maximum House size, not its minimum. Nonetheless, after the first census the new House did indeed balloon from 65 to 105 members and then swelled to 142 over the next decade. Though the Constitution's *text* did not compel this increase (even after the erasure and rewrite), the Constitution's *act* did, for all practical purposes. In the demanding public regimen required to ordain the Constitution, the American people made clear via emphatic Anti-Federalist criticisms and explicit Federalist concessions that the House had to expand as fast as possible until it reached three figures. Here too, the Preamble's exceptionally democratic process pulled later events into a more democratic orbit.

In the New York ratifying debate, Hamilton observed that "if the general voice of the people be for an increase, it undoubtedly must take place." Hamilton suggested that in the first congressional elections, a demand for a larger House "will be the standing instruction to [congres-sional] delegates."[78] In fact, the people did not wait that long to make their "general voice" known: Five state ratifying conventions explicitly ap-pended proposals to secure a larger House to their formal instruments of ratification, and no state convention opposed the suggestion.[79] When the First Congress met, it proposed twelve constitutional amendments, the first of which began as follows: "After the first enumeration required by the first article of the Constitution, there shall be one Representative for every thirty thousand, until the number shall amount to one hun-dred."[80] Ten states promptly ratified the proposed amendment—one state shy of the eleven (out of fourteen—Vermont joined the union in early 1791) needed under Article V to make the amendment part of the Con-stitution. Even without the formal amendment, by 1793 the Congress had largely achieved the Amendment's immediate target, and the Federalists' ratification-debate promise, of a hundred-man House based on a ratio of roughly thirty thousand to one.[81] The people had spoken, and Congress obeyed.

Congress also obeyed the people's demand for open access to the leg-islative sessions themselves. The text of the Constitution said nothing about a public gallery, though it did say that a mere fifth of each house could compel a roll-call vote, and that each house must publish its general journal "from time to time" after excising items requiring secrecy. The Articles of Confederation had demanded slightly more openness, giving every delegate the power to force a recorded vote, specifying monthly publication of the journal, and allowing excision only in matters of na-tional security. The Articles, however, had not required that Congress allow public spectators, and in practice the Confederation Congress never did so, even after the war ended and all military and diplomatic justifica-tion for secret meetings evaporated.

Traditionally, Parliament had also met behind closed doors and in fact had treated unauthorized publication of its proceedings as a breach of privilege. In the 1770s, this regime began to break down, and Parliament largely abandoned its practice of excluding public observers. Colonial leg-islatures had also customarily met in secret prior to the 1760s, but then began to let the people in as Revolutionary politics heated up and patriot leaders sought to mobilize mass support. Reflecting this populist trend, Pennsylvania's 1776 Constitution promised that "the doors of the house . . . shall be and remain open for the admission of all persons who behave de-cently, except only when the welfare of this state may require the doors to be shut." New York's 1777 constitution similarly promised open doors in both assembly and senate sessions.[82]

Textually, the federal Constitution lagged behind this vanguard. The republican spirit was faintly discernable in the etymology and ideology of the Article I, section 5 requirement that Congress "publish" its journal— that is, make its proceedings available to the American *public*.[83] Companion language in section 9 required that "a regular Statement and Account of the Receipts and Expenditures of all public Money shall be published from time to time." Also, per-capita voting in both houses made it somewhat easier for the public to hold statesmen personally accountable than had been the case under the Articles, in which each state had voted as a unit.[84]

If we view the Constitution of 1787–88 not merely as a text but as a deed, a more populist picture emerges. The extraordinary conventions of 1787–88, and the spirited public discourse they prompted, enabled Americans across the continent to voice strong doubts about whether the new people's house would truly be the people's house. Heeding these strong messages, and hoping to maintain the confidence of the ordinary voters who had selected them and who could send them packing in two years, House members opened their doors from the start. Though most Americans across the vast continent could never dream of attending sessions in person, newspapers in the national seat could cover the open proceedings with ease, and their published accounts in turn could be republished elsewhere, thus widening the lines of communication between the representatives and the voters back home. Slower to heed the new spirit of democracy, senators at first tried to cloak themselves in the old Congress's tradition of secrecy. In the mid-1790s, however, the Senate moved into the sunshine and once there found it impossible to move back—just as the House, once it hit a hundred members, never fell below that magic number.[85]

For some Anti-Federalists in 1787–88, however, even a promised hundred-member House meeting in open sessions seemed too cozy when compared to the larger groups of lawmakers in Parliament and several state legislatures. In response, Federalists argued that, unlike state assemblies addressing a multitude of acutely local problems, Congress would focus on laws of continental and international sweep that required less familiarity with every neighborhood.[86] Parliament had both local and national responsibilities, so in theory it, too, needed more local members than would Congress. Federalists also pointed out that in practice most members of Parliament did not even live in the districts that sent them. More than half of its 558 members came from "rotten" or "pocket" boroughs where almost no one lived. Only the other half could boast election by any sizable number of actual voters. In truth, Parliament thus had roughly 250 elected lawmakers for 8 to 9 million free Britons, compared to a promised 100 House members for 3 million free Americans.[87]

"actual Enumeration"

Even the Commons' non-rotten members—many of them nonresident, and virtually all of them enormously propertied men chosen only by propertied voters—came from a crazy quilt of districts of widely varying population. This archaic patchwork left several of late-eighteenth-century Britain's largest populous areas, such as Manchester and Birmingham, scandalously underrepresented. Apart from the admission of forty-five new members from Scotland in 1707, Parliament did not reapportion itself at any time in the eighteenth century despite tumultuous demographic changes wrought by the industrial revolution. Over the centuries, Parliament had never once authorized a comprehensive enumeration.

By contrast, the Constitution promised an enumeration as soon as possible—within the new government's first three years—followed by a fresh count every decade in perpetuity. This enumeration would in turn feed into a precise constitutional apportionment formula based solely on population. Future congressmen would thus be prevented from openly basing apportionment on wealth, or devising some other sly formula to entrench themselves against demographic shifts in the outside world. Like clockwork, a decennial census would map Americans on the move, and the face of the people's House would regularly adjust to mirror the people's changing shape.

This system marked a notable advance over general practice in the several states. Prior to the Revolution, no automatic census had operated in the American colonies. Unlike Parliament, most colonial assemblies scrambled to accommodate population shifts, adding new seats as established population centers blossomed and new regions opened up.[88] Yet no colony enjoyed anything close to a precisely proportionate representation; in most places, corporate units—cities, towns, counties, and the like—constituted the basic building blocks of representation, without a fine-grained formula attentive to the precise population within each unit. In 1767, the Crown instructed all royal governors to use their absolute vetoes to block further increases in assembly size, prompting the Declaration of Independence to rail against the king's refusal to "Accommodat[e] large

Districts of the People, unless those people would relinquish the Right of Representation, a Right inestimable to them, and formidable to Tyrants only."[89]

Revolutionary state constitutions generally moved toward proportionality, but they typically fell far below this ideal. Most states continued to give equal weight to local units of highly unequal population. Only half of the state constitutions prescribed general rules for reapportionment, and even these documents tended to use vague or clumsy formulas. Massachusetts and New Hampshire each required the assembly to swell with every underlying population increase, thereby ensuring that the legislature would eventually bloat to unwieldy dimensions. Upper-house apportionment would track taxable wealth as opposed to population, with no fixed timetable for reapportionment. South Carolina—already the most malapportioned state—adopted a mushy clause explicitly basing apportionment on both wealth and white population without specifying how the two factors should be weighted. Lawmakers thus retained broad discretion to choose whatever formula best entrenched the largely rotten status quo.[90]

Most democratic of all were the Pennsylvania Constitution of 1776 and the New York Constitution of 1777, the only two Revolution-era documents promising to allocate all future legislative seats solely on the basis of population, as measured by periodic enumerations. Pennsylvania's constitution announced that "representation in proportion to the number of taxable inhabitants is the only principle which can at all times secure liberty, and make the voice of a majority of the people the law of the land; therefore the general assembly" was obliged to conduct a septennial census and reallocate assembly seats "in proportion to the number of taxables." (Despite this ringing pronouncement, the document neglected to apply the proportionality principle to two oddly constructed "councils," which wielded various executive and constitution-amending powers.) In New York, a census would likewise take place every seven years, followed by mandatory reapportionment to ensure that representation numbers in both the assembly and senate "shall forever remain . . . justly proportioned to the number of electors" in each underlying county and district.[91]

Compared to general English and American practice circa 1787, the Constitution's apportionment system looked rather republican and rationalistic. Building directly on the Pennsylvania and New York models, the House promised ongoing proportionate representation in a fast-moving nation. By contrast, the Senate perpetuated the equality of states that prevailed in the Confederation Congress—an obvious compromise of the proportionality principle, but no worse than the status quo ante. Nor did state equality dramatically skew American politics, at least at the Founding. In 1787, the Senate's overrepresentations and underrepresentations tended to cancel out, randomly cutting across America's main geographic and ideological fault lines.[92] In Britain, by contrast, Parliament's malapportionment systematically underrepresented a major region (the North) and a distinctive set of interests (urban, industrial). Avoiding the whiff of plutocracy detectable in various state upper houses apportioned by wealth, the Senate roughly resembled regimes in several states that gave equal weight to counties of widely different size.

Several factors conspired at Philadelphia to produce a precisely proportioned House. The very novelty of the House of Representatives offered a clean slate on which to draft. In individual states, any rationalistic reapportionment proposal had to overcome established usages and entrenched interests of incumbent lawmakers and the localities they represented. No comparably entrenched federal apportionment system existed. The equality of states under the Continental and Confederation Congresses had not been a true system of legislative apportionment; nonlegislative nonapportionment would be a more accurate description. In any event, that system had proved itself enough of a failure so as to invite a wholly new template for the new House. Few would be in a strong position to object when the initial House allocation of the sixty-five members among the thirteen states—an avowedly temporary allotment that plainly sprang from guesswork and horse-trading—quickly yielded to a more accurate allocation. Although many Philadelphia draftsmen sympathized with the notion that representation should track wealth alongside population, any wealth measure would have been hard to specify in a simple formula good for all time. Giving incumbent congressmen wide discretion over reapportionment would have invited legislative self-entrenchment. Perhaps large and well-established state legislatures could be trusted with such discretion, but a smaller and untested Congress could not. Ironically, healthy distrust of the new legislature led to more trusty rules for its composition.

Strong regional rivalries also argued for clean apportionment rules that would resist legislative legerdemain. Draftsmen worried that if one region ever achieved a congressional majority, it might abuse any discretion it enjoyed to perpetuate its control even if population began to shift elsewhere. Several framers voiced egalitarian arguments on behalf of future generations likely to populate the West. Mason insisted that new Western states "be treated as equals, and subjected to no degrading discriminations." Mason aimed these remarks at Gouverneur Morris, who had urged that the Atlantic states constitutionally guarantee themselves a perpetual majority of House seats, regardless of future westward migration. Morris doubted that the backcountry would ever produce its share of wealth or "enlightened" political leaders, even if this region might one day boast a majority of citizens. "The Busy haunts of men not the remote wilderness, was the proper School of political Talents. If the Western people get the power into their hands they will ruin the Atlantic interests." Madison punctured this ode to oligarchy by exposing its similarity to English corruption and ossification: Did Americans really want to replicate the rotten borough system? "With regard to the Western States," Madison "was clear & firm in opinion that no unfavorable distinctions were admissible either in point of justice or policy." Critiquing Morris's added argument that the apportionment formula openly include wealth, Wilson declared that the "majority of people wherever found"—whether in "the interior Country" or elsewhere—ought to govern the minority in all questions. Wilson "could not agree that property was the sole or the primary object of Govert. & Society. The cultivation & improvement of the human mind was the most noble object" and "this object, as well as . . . other personal rights," argued for population as "the natural & precise measure of Representation."[93]

The result of these deliberations was a clever combination of New World gears and gadgets. Less than twenty years after the famous American clock maker David Rittenhouse unveiled his mechanical "orrery" modeling the precise dimensions of the solar system in motion, the Philadelphia delegates offered their own constitutional clockwork designed to make the American House replicate in miniature the movements of the American people in macro. The proposed machinery of regular elections, regular enumerations, and regular reapportionments based solely on population exemplified eighteenth-century American innovation at its best.

"three fifths"

And also at its worst.

Let's begin with two tiny puzzles posed by the Article I command that "Representatives and direct Taxes shall be apportioned among the several States . . . by adding to the whole Number of free Persons . . . three fifths of all other Persons." First, although this language specified the apportionment formula "*among* the several states," it failed to specify the formula *within* each state. Under Article I, section 4, state legislatures would enjoy broad latitude over the "Manner of holding Elections for . . . Representatives," subject to congressional override. What if a state legislature, perhaps tracking its own internal malapportionment, chose to divide the state into congressional districts of highly unequal population? During the ratification debates, several leading Federalists assured listeners that Congress could use its section 4 override authority to cure such malapportionments, but the Federalists generally refrained from asserting that Congress would be constitutionally obliged to act, or that if Congress failed to do so, federal courts would require equal districts.[94]

Why, we might wonder, did Article I pay so much attention to interstate apportionment and so little to intrastate districting? At Philadelphia, leading delegates declared that a legislature should be "the most exact transcript of the whole Society" and that "the true principle of Representation" merely "substituted" a smaller body to stand in for "the inconvenient meeting of the people themselves."[95] In the absence of a clear constitutional rule barring grossly unequal congressional districts within each state, the document offered inadequate assurance that Congress would indeed be a faithful "transcript" and "substitute[]." More was needed to prevent state and federal incumbents from blessing intrastate apportionment plans defined by overrepresented rotten boroughs and underrepresented Manchesters.

A second small puzzle: Why did Article I peg the number of representatives to the underlying number of *persons,* instead of to the number of eligible *voters,* à la New York? If representation merely substituted for an unwieldy meeting of all the voters in the flesh, why shouldn't the representatives mirror the distribution of the voters themselves? Applied across the several states, such a voter-based formula would have had an additional, democracy-promoting aspect, spurring states to expand their electorates and thereby gain additional congressional seats.

These two small puzzles, centering on the seemingly innocent words "among" and "Persons," quickly spiral out to the most vicious words of the apportionment clause: "adding . . . three fifths of all other Persons." "Other" persons here meant *other than free* persons—that is, slaves. Thus, the more slaves a given state's master class bred or bought, the more seats the state could claim in Congress, for every decade in perpetuity.

The Philadelphia draftsmen camouflaged this ugly point as best they could, euphemistically avoiding the S-word and simultaneously introducing the T-word—taxes—into the equation[96] ("Representatives *and direct Taxes* shall be apportioned . . ."). All this protective coloring would have been wasted had the Constitution pegged apportionment to the number of voters, with a glaringly inconsistent add-on for nonvoting slaves. Also, any constitutional formula for intrastate congressional apportionment would have needed to specify how slaves should count. Any number other than three-fifths would have smacked of hypocrisy; but an intrastate three-fifths formula would have obliged even reform-minded Southerners to give special credit to slave-belts within their home states. (The intrastate issue had not arisen under the Articles. Southern congressmen were picked at large by state legislatures, whose apportionment generally derived from inertia and county equality rather than any precise population-based formula.)

The full import of the camouflaged clause eluded many readers in the late 1780s. In the wake of two decades of debate about taxation burdens under the empire and confederation, many Founding-era Americans confronting the clause focused more on taxation than on representation. Some Northern critics grumbled that three-fifths should have been five-fifths so as to oblige the South to pay more taxes, without noticing that five-fifths would have also enabled the South to claim more House seats.

Modern laypersons and law students confronting the words "three fifths" for the first time often suffer from a similar confusion, recoiling at the idea of valuing slaves at less than 100 percent. This initial reaction misses the point. The clause did not aim to apportion how much a slave was a person as opposed to a chattel. Had this been the question, the antislavery answer in the 1780s would have been to value slaves fully: five-fifths. Yet in the context of House apportionment, a five-fifths formula would not have freed a single slave, or endowed any bondsman with more rights of personhood against his master or the world. Five-fifths would simply have given slave states even more voting power vis-à-vis free states. The precise Article I question concerned Congress's proportions, not the slaves'. The principled antislavery answer to this question in 1787 was that *for legislative apportionment purposes,* slaves should be valued not at five-fifths, or even three-fifths, but rather zero-fifths.

So argued slavery's bluntest critics at Philadelphia, including Morris, Paterson, King, Jonathan Dayton, and Elbridge Gerry.[97] Morris also opposed the general idea of a fixed apportionment formula that would bind all future Congresses. In urging more flexible language, Morris doubtless hoped that Congress would use its discretion to count wealth alongside population and thus shore up Eastern financial interests against the westward flow of migration. Yet to plot Morris's gambit only along the East-West/rich-poor axis is to miss its second, North-South/free-slave dimension. Morris's proposal openly aimed to give Northern-dominated

Congresses in the near future leeway to count slaves at some ratio less than three-fifths. Several of the harshest criticisms of Morris came, unsurprisingly, from Southerners seeking more solid guarantees for slaveholders in future apportionments. In 1787, most observers expected American settlers to pour more quickly into the Southwest than the Northwest. The appeals of men such as Mason and Madison on behalf of their Western brethren thus had a dark side. It is worth remembering that over the course of their lifetimes, these two Virginians owned more than one hundred slaves apiece, and that neither man freed his slaves upon his death.

In any event, the Constitution as drafted and ratified committed the new nation to perpetually credit slavery in the apportionment process. Confronting this harsh constitutional calculus, some antebellum antislavery leaders sought to construe three-fifths as a moral victory of sorts. On this view, anything less than five-fifths was an acknowledgment that slavery was constitutionally disfavored. The document's pointed refusal to use the S-word in the apportionment formula and elsewhere further evidenced the document's implicit antislavery stance, in the eyes of these apologists. Some theorists went so far as to claim that the Article I formula actually encouraged abolition: A state that freed its slaves could increase its share of the House by counting its blacks at five-fifths, thus avoiding the two-fifths slavery penalty.[98]

This clever argument blinked the fact that states with large slave populations were hardly inclined to free slaves while encouraging freedmen to remain within the state as valued citizens. Dreams and schemes of colonization accompanied most serious proposals for widespread abolition. If emigration followed emancipation, a state would not rise from three- to five-fifths, but rather would sink to zero-fifths as freedmen moved out. Contrary to apologists' rosy mathematics, a slave state would thus likely wield less congressional clout after emancipation.[99]

Once we envision the possibility of black bodies crossing borders, the extreme viciousness of the three-fifths clause comes violently into view. The more slaves the Deep South could import from the African continent—innocents born in freedom and kidnapped across an ocean to be sold on auction blocks—the more seats it would earn in the American Congress. Morris painted in vivid colors at Philadelphia: "The inhabitant of Georgia and S.C. who goes to the Coast of Africa, and in defiance of the most sacred laws of humanity tears away his fellow creatures from their dearest connections & damns them to the most cruel bondages, shall have more votes in a Govt. instituted for protection of the rights of mankind, than the Citizen of Pa. or N. Jersey who views with a laudable horror, so nefarious a practice. . . . Domestic slavery is the most prominent feature in the aristocratic countenance of the proposed Constitution." During the ratification process, several leading Anti-Federalists condemned the three-fifths clause in similarly scathing terms.[100]

To make matters worse, despite the new Congress's general Article I, section 8 power over international commerce, section 9 barred Congress from ending the international slave trade before 1808. By that time, the Deep South hoped to have enough extra muscle in Congress, based on white migration and slave importation, to thwart any possible antislavery constitutional amendments and perhaps even to weaken any proposed ban on further slave importation. Unlike every other clause in the entire Constitution, the 1808 date itself was exempt from constitutional amendment under Article V. Each of the two main Article I numbers accommodating slavery—three-fifths and 1808—was bad enough, but together they threatened to interlock in a vicious proslavery cycle. As events actually unfolded, however, the Deep South imported far fewer slaves in the 1790s than had been expected in the late 1780s. A 1791 slave revolt in the French colony of St. Domingue (modern-day Haiti) made American slave masters wary of foreign-born blacks, who might bring with them a memory of freedom and an appetite for insurrection.

The numbers from the 1790 census illustrate the practical effect of the three-fifths clause in its early years. New Hampshire's 140,000 free citizens entitled it to four seats in the expanded House, compared to six seats for South Carolina's 140,000 free citizens and 100,000 slaves. Connecticut boasted 20,000 more free citizens than Maryland but won one less seat because Maryland got to count its 100,000 bondsmen. Although slaveless Massachusetts had a significantly larger free population than did Virginia, the Old Dominion got five more seats, thanks to her nearly 300,000 slaves.[101]

WITH THESE NUMBERS in view and the interlocking effect of the 1808 clause in mind, let us now consider the argument that the Constitution was essentially neutral on the topic of slavery, an argument famously advanced by the eminent historian Don E. Fehrenbacher. "As a matter of political theory," wrote Fehrenbacher, "it made just as much sense in 1787 to base allocation [of legislative power] on the whole population, including slaves, women, children" and other nonvoters. If one started from that whole-population baseline, the three-fifths clause looked like a penalty, not a bonus, giving slave regions less than their baseline entitlement, not more. Whether three-fifths was a proslavery bonus or an antislavery penalty depended on whether one saw *free* population or *total* population as the proper baseline. According to Fehrenbacher, neither baseline was "intrinsically sounder" than the other.[102]

But as a matter of basic political theory circa 1787, one perspective surely *was* intrinsically sounder. Let's imagine two jurisdictions with equal numbers of voters but unequal numbers of total free persons. Should the jurisdiction with many more free women and children get the same number of seats, or more? Had the issue arisen between two of its counties, New York would have counted only voters. By contrast, Pennsylvania, Massachusetts, and New Hampshire apportioned based on a variant of free population rather than qualified electors. Neither perspective might seem intrinsically sounder. So far, so good for Fehrenbacher.

The basic argument for apportionment based on free population rather than voters was that in 1787, voters could with a straight face claim to virtually represent the interests of the larger free population—their minor children; their mothers, daughters, wives, and sisters; their unpropertied adult sons and brothers; and so on. But masters did not as a rule claim to virtually represent the best interests of their slaves. Masters, after all, claimed the right to maim and sell slaves at will, and to doom their yet unborn posterity to perpetual bondage. If this could count as virtual representation, anything could.

By 1787, the American Revolution had already established, for American patriots at least, that some claims of virtual representation flunked the straight-face, let-facts-be-submitted-to-a-candid-world test. If, because of serious conflicts of interest and circumstance, Parliament could not plausibly claim to represent Americans, surely masters could not plausibly claim to represent slaves. If George III had no right to speak for Americans after he sought to deny them their "unalienable Rights" of "Life, Liberty, and the Pursuit of Happiness," to "reduce them under absolute Despotism," and to deprive them of jury trials and legal protection, surely slaveholders had no right to speak for their slaves.

The candid 1787 argument for counting slaves was not that masters sincerely *represented* them but that masters, rightly or wrongly, *owned* them. They were property, and property, many openly argued, deserved representation alongside population. On this account, however, the interests to be represented were not the slaves', but the masters'. With this claim, Southerners decisively distinguished slaves from free dependents, categories that Fehrenbacher inexplicably conflated.

Though candid, the Southern property argument was neither neutral

nor democratic. As antislavery men repeated time and again at Philadelphia and throughout the ratification debates, Article I treated slavery as
preferred property. Animal chattel didn't count, land didn't count, buildings didn't count, jewels didn't count, securities didn't count, specie didn't
count—only slave property would count. In Morris's biting words at Philadelphia, "The Houses in this City . . . are worth more than all the wretched
slaves which cover the rice swamps of South Carolina." Southerners, too,
in moments of frankness, conceded that they were seeking a special break.
When trying to sell the Constitution to his constituents, South Carolinian
Charles Cotesworth Pinckney reminded his audience that "the Eastern
States . . . allowed us a representation for a species of property which they
have not among them."[103]

Although any attempt to assess nonslave forms of wealth would have
raised difficult valuation issues, counting only slave property permanently
skewed apportionments and spawned perverse incentives. Southern governments would be rewarded for promoting slaveholding vis-à-vis other
forms of property acquisition. The extreme vice of such a system snaps
into focus when we notice that in 1787 no *slave* state counted slaves as preferred property for state apportionment. Even South Carolina promised
to count all "taxable property," not just slaves.

More generally, it is fair to ask why property should have been counted
at all in the federal apportionment formula. Nowhere else did the federal
Constitution concede so much political power to property per se. True,
voters for the House had to meet modest state-law property thresholds in
most places, but the man who owned fifty times the minimal property
threshold would get exactly the same single vote as the man who barely
cleared the bar. By contrast, the three-fifths clause gave a state extra credit
for each new unit of slave property it could breed, buy, or steal. Among the
states, only rotten South Carolina openly included property as an ingredient of lower-house apportionment. Under the Articles of Confederation,
wealthy states faced higher requisitions, but were not thereby entitled to
more votes in Congress.

Beyond the pure property argument, slave masters tried to bend Revolutionary slogans about taxation and representation to their advantage.
If there should be no taxation without representation, masters asked,
shouldn't direct representation be proportioned to direct taxation? If the
Constitution allotted direct taxes among the states according to population, counting slaves at three-fifths, why shouldn't it use the same ratio in
allotting direct representatives?

One obvious answer was that "direct Taxes" in the Constitution was a term of art that did not begin to count all the taxes that Congress could and likely would impose on individuals. The big money would likely flow—and after 1789 did in fact flow—from federal levies on imports, yet these levies fell outside the ambit of the three-fifths clause. Indeed, by capping pre-1808 federal taxes at ten dollars per imported slave, Article I gave slave importers a special twenty-year *exemption* from the plenary taxation power that Congress would enjoy over all other imports. Thus, even if one assumed, more plutocratically than democratically, that representation should mirror tax revenues rather than the number of voters or free citizens, Article I's apportionment bore no real relationship to the actual amount of taxes likely to be contributed by slave states and free states respectively.

The best justification for the three-fifths clause sounded in neither republican principle nor Revolutionary ideology, but raw politics. Southerners sought credible assurances that their interests would receive adequate protection in a newfangled indivisible union likely to be dominated, at least initially, by legislators from regions with non-Southern interests and cultures. Although a few slaves were scattered across states as far north as New Hampshire, more than 90 percent lived in the five states south of the Mason-Dixon Line. Assuming universal ratification, the South would initially be outnumbered eight to five in the Senate. Yet new states like Kentucky and Tennessee might soon join the union, as might New England's Vermont. If Delaware, with a 15 percent slave population, leaned toward its Southern neighbors, the slaveholding region would have approximate parity in the Senate.

In terms of free population, however, this region found itself outnumbered by a rough margin of three to two—a ratio that would not change much no matter which way tiny Delaware leaned, and regardless of whether trans-Appalachian Southerners called themselves Virginians and North Carolinians or Kentuckians and Tennesseans. By counting slaves at three-fifths, the Constitution gave the South something closer to parity in the early House. In the Congress that convened in 1793—the first Congress based on the first census—the South had forty-seven seats compared to the North's fifty-eight. Without the three-fifths clause, which gave Southerners partial credit for their 650,000 slaves, they would have lost a net thirteen seats, thus placing them at a substantial disadvantage—thirty-three to fifty-seven—in the House.[104]

In the near term, the three-fifths clause thus aimed to inspire Southern confidence in, and ease Southern concern about, a new kind of union in which men from vastly different cultures and climates would meet in a continental legislature of unprecedented geographic scope. Also, what the three-fifths ratio lacked in principle, it made up for in familiarity. Under the Articles, states were supposed to contribute to confederate coffers according to the respective value of their land and buildings. Assessing these values proved difficult, and in 1783 the Confederation Congress proposed an amendment to the Articles using population as a wealth proxy, and valuing slaves at three-fifths to correspond to their rough productivity vis-à-vis free laborers. Though failing to win ratification in all thirteen states, the 1783 proposal made the three-fifths number—widely referred to as "the federal ratio"—a familiar basis for compromise, a focal point for slavery-related negotiations in the late 1780s.

Focal, but nonetheless inapt. Critics of slavery, after all, wanted slaves rated high for tax purposes and low for representation purposes. Slogans aside, this was hardly a hypocritical stance, for in truth taxation and representation implicated different root concerns. If the question was how wealthy a state was, and how much it could be fairly asked to pay in taxes, three-fifths might be a fair proxy of labor productivity. But in Article I, the issue was not really the fig leaf of direct taxes (though the leaf did in fact fool many Northern ratifiers as a result of the prominence of the tax/requisition debate under the confederation). Rather, the real Article I issue concerned how legislative seats needed to be allocated so as to ease the South's anxieties about its initial minority status in the new House.

THE THREE-FIFTHS CLAUSE offered one solution. But in 1787 there may have existed at least one other plausible solution that could have satisfied both slavery interests and antislavery intuitions. Imagine, for example, that Gouverneur Morris had proposed that slaves should count for *four*-fifths in the first decennial census in 1790, three-fifths in 1800, two-fifths in 1810, one-fifth in 1820, and zero-fifths thereafter. Such a sliding-scale approach would have addressed the South's concerns about its immediate prospects as a legislative minority while ensuring a gradual transition away from a rotten ratio, with plenty of time for slaveholders to make adjustments. Because most Southerners expected their region's population to grow much faster than the North's,[105] they could have anticipated that their rising share of free citizens within the union would tend to offset the effect of the declining rate at which they could count slaves.

The precise details of the sliding-scale numbers, of course, could have been subject to negotiation between Northern and Southern delegates. Details aside, the sliding scale's broad outline—more representation of slavery regions in 1787 in exchange for less in the future—would have brought the Philadelphia plan into harmony with various gradual anti-slavery systems that had begun to operate in several states in the 1780s, and that would continue to receive strong support, even in some parts of the South, well into the nineteenth century. For example, as late as 1832, Virginia's leaders seriously debated proposals for gradual emancipation.[106]

Alas, a declining-scale alternative to the three-fifths clause never came clearly into focus at Philadelphia. Morris lacked the extraordinary intellectual discipline and political acuity of a Madison; and Madison himself showed little interest in bending his great mind toward formulating a credible ultimate-extinction strategy. What Morris did propose was to give Congress vast discretion over future apportionments. With this as the only real competitor to the three-fifths clause, the Philadelphia delegates unsurprisingly chose three-fifths. Morris's gambit offered the South no guarantee that an initial Northern majority would refrain from an immediate and wrenching transition to an apportionment system based solely on free population. Nor did Morris allay concerns that a future Congress might manipulate the apportionment formula so as to entrench itself or otherwise privilege property over population. Nowhere did the Morris gambit even guarantee that slaves would count for less as the decades progressed. A declining-ratio approach would have avoided these glaring defects while putting the slavery-bonus system on a gradual but sure path to elimination.

A declining ratio would not have guaranteed that slavery itself would die on a date certain, but it would have meant that slaveholding regions would eventually stop getting extra House seats as rewards for their peculiar institution. As of 1830—or whatever other target date the delegates ultimately might have agreed upon—a state would never have received more seats simply because it allowed its master class to own human flesh. Thereafter, slave states might indeed have hoped to increase their clout in Congress by freeing slaves, so long as any freedmen chose to remain. Compared to the three-fifths clause, a declining ratio might have given the South extra seats immediately while soothing the North with a clearer expression of an ultimate-extinction constitutional telos—a win-win for both regions, blending short-term politics with long-term principles.

Although no one at Philadelphia floated the specific idea of declining slave ratios in the context of the three-fifths debate, the general concept of a declining ratio undoubtedly lay within the imaginative grasp of the Founding generation. On the topic of congressional size, the various formulas proposed in the ratification debates and by the First Congress explicitly featured sliding scales, with a strict ratio of one representative for every thirty thousand in the near term, until Congress reached one hundred or two hundred members, after which lower ratios kicked in. A declining ratio of sorts was also implicit in the other key slavery-related numerical clause in Article I, which allowed only a temporary accommodation to the Deep South and anticipated a date certain—1808—when transatlantic slave importation could be prohibited. Had Article I required rather than merely permitted an end to the slave trade in 1808, the analogy would have been tighter still. To ensure that the Deep South would not use the guaranteed window between 1788 and 1808 to hoard African-born slaves and thereby increase its apportionment, a superior Article I system might also have counted only American-born slaves.

THE RADICAL VICE of Article I as drafted and ratified was that it gave slaveholding regions extra clout in every election as far as the eye could see—a political gift that kept giving. And growing. Unconstrained by any explicit intrastate equality norm in Article I, and emboldened by the federal ratio, many slave states in the antebellum era skewed their congressional-district maps in favor of slaveholding regions within the state. Thus the House not only leaned south, but also within coastal slave states bent east, toward tidewater plantations that grabbed more than their fair share of seats. After the 1820 census, Virginia carved itself into twenty-two House districts, one of which encompassed Richmond in the plantation belt and another of which surrounded Wheeling on the state's northwestern rim. Although the Richmond district had less than half the Wheeling district's free population—16,000 compared to 42,000—each sent one member to the House. In effect, Richmond's master class got full (five-fifths) credit for their 25,000 slaves, as compared to 2,000 slaves in the Wheeling region. Overall, the fifteen Virginia districts with the highest percentage of slaves averaged only 25,000 free folk compared to an average 37,000 in the other districts, all in the west. Meanwhile, North Carolina opted for a pair of high-slaveholding districts averaging only 24,000 free persons, five moderate-slaveholding districts averaging 33,000 free persons, and six low-slaveholding western districts averaging 38,000 free persons. South Carolina's numbers looked even worse. Other large differentials distorted the House maps in other states and in other decades. The very foundation of the Constitution's first branch was tilted and rotten.[107]

And not just the first branch. The Article II electoral college sat atop the Article I base: The electors who picked the president would be apportioned according to the number of seats a state had in the House and Senate. In turn, presidents would nominate cabinet heads, Supreme Court justices, and other Article III judges. Even state legislatures began to mimic the Article I model. In 1798, Georgia decided to use three-fifths as the apportionment ratio for its own state house, thereby giving plantation belts extra credit within the state. Thus one inapt borrowing begot another. In the years following the Missouri Compromise, Virginia reformers' plans for reapportionment based on white population were defeated by opponents who argued that such plans would undermine the case for three-fifths at the federal level.[108] Then came new apportionment rules in Louisiana, Florida, Maryland, and North Carolina, all of which started to count slaves at three-fifths or more in one or both houses of their legislatures, even though no slave state had done so prior to 1787.[109] In turn, these slavery-skewed state legislatures chose the men who would represent these states in the U.S. Senate. By the 1840s, the corrosive effects of the three-fifths clause had seeped into every branch of the federal government.[110]

All this proslavery malapportionment—an expanding rot at the base of America's system of representation—helps explain the proslavery tilt of antebellum American law and politics, as exemplified by the infamous 1857 *Dred Scott* case. And with this proslavery tilt in mind, we are now in a position to reconsider Fehrenbacher. However slanted toward slaveholders the original Constitution may have been, it offered little support for Chief Justice Roger Taney's extremist *Dred Scott* opinion, which claimed that Congress was constitutionally required to allow slavery in the territories. As the author of a classic study of *Dred Scott,* Fehrenbacher took pains to acquit the document of Taney's reckless reading, and was thus inclined to emphasize—and perhaps overstate—the basic point that the framers did not intend the document to be radically proslavery. "The few concessions to slavery in the text," wrote Fehrenbacher, were "more like eddies in a stream than part of the current. Moreover, the concessions were offset by a stylistic tone of repugnance for the institution."[111]

What Fehrenbacher overlooked is that the document's neutral and antislavery features—its refusal to use the S-word, for instance—unsurprisingly turned out over the next seventy years to be weak pieties and parchment barriers compared to the perverse structures of permanent power that the document authorized in the three-fifths clause. If, as Fehrenbacher has shown, men like Taney badly misread the document three generations after its ratification, such men were in a position to matter because the document itself created a vicious apportionment structure that helped put them in power.

Chapter 3

CONGRESSIONAL POWERS

THE UNITED STATES SENATE, A.D. 1850.

Senator Henry Clay addressing his colleagues (including Daniel Webster and John C. Calhoun) under the watchful gaze of the gallery. Congressional freedom of speech as guaranteed by Article I, section 6.

*I*F THE THREE-FIFTHS CLAUSE endowed one form of private property with too much public power, several other Article I clauses—especially the provisions concerning congressional privileges—struck a better balance between private rights and the public good. In general, the closing sections of Article I carried forward the main themes of its opening sections and of the Preamble. Americans would run a continental republic designed to keep foreign powers at bay, aggressive states in line, America's military under control, and slave masters on board.

"Speech"

Article I, section 6 "privileged" senators and representatives from certain kinds of "Arrest during their Attendance" in Congress. The privilege applied only to various civil cases, still prevalent in the eighteenth century, in which a litigant sought the physical arrest of a defendant. (No congressional privilege would exist in cases of "Treason, Felony and Breach of the Peace"—a catchall English-law term of art effectively covering all crimes.)[1] Without the privilege, a single private civil litigant, perhaps by design, might undo the voters' verdict by keeping their man off the floor. As Jefferson explained in his famed *Manual of Parliamentary Practice,* "When a representative is withdrawn from his seat by summons, the 30,000 people whom he represents lose their voice in debate and vote." The private privilege thus served a public purpose. In the name of democracy, a sitting congressman could claim temporary immunity and oblige his would-be civil arrester to wait until the legislative session had ended. If a lawmaker abused this privilege, the voters could punish him at the next election. To put legislators from distant states on equal footing with those living near the national seat, the privilege would apply to lawmakers traveling to and from Congress.[2]

A crucial companion privilege in Article I, section 6 shielded congressmen from being "questioned" outside Congress for any "Speech or Debate in either House." As with the arrest clause, this privilege had roots in the language of the Articles of Confederation and, deeper still, in English practice. According to the English Bill of Rights of 1689, "the freedom of speech, and debates or proceedings in parliament, ought not to be impeached or questioned in any court or place out of parliament." The

Revolutionary-era constitutions of Massachusetts, New Hampshire, and Vermont featured roughly similar language affirming legislative freedom of speech.[3]

The core privilege in both England and America aimed to ensure that legislatures remained forums for robust political discourse. Parliament—from the French *parler*—functioned as a privileged parley place, a special speech spot. Neither the executive nor the judiciary could punish a lawmaker for any floor speech. Here, too, a private right vindicated the larger public interest, as James Wilson emphasized in 1791: "In order to enable and encourage a representative of the publick to discharge his publick trust with firmness and success, it is indispensably necessary, that he should enjoy the fullest liberty of speech, and that he should be protected from the resentment of every one, however powerful, to whom the exercise of that liberty may occasion offence."[4]

In America, this privilege also implicated issues of federalism. Congressional debaters could claim absolute immunity from state civil and criminal libel actions, just as state lawmakers speaking in their assemblies could fend off federal libel suits. In the late 1790s, this immunity for state legislative speech, rooted in colonial traditions and implicit in the Constitution's general structure, emboldened Virginia and Kentucky legislators to condemn federal lawmakers at a time when many other would-be critics kept mum for fear of federal prosecution under the 1798 Sedition Act.

Even as it built upon English antecedents, the Constitution broke new ground by giving lawmakers less power to censor and citizens more power to criticize than did England. English law fortified freedom of speech inside Parliament but left freedom of speech outside Parliament rather vulnerable. In fact, outsiders who criticized Parliament could find themselves accused of violating the privileges of Parliament itself. Thus, eighteenth-century Parliaments regularly visited contempt sanctions on common speakers and printers who had the effrontery to criticize or "question" Parliament, in violation (as Parliament saw the matter) of the 1689 command that "proceedings in Parliament" simply could not be "questioned" by outsiders.[5]

In sharp contrast, nothing in the Article I speech clause, rightly read, allowed Congress to punish ordinary Americans who spoke out against Congress. Nor did any other clause of the Constitution authorize Congress to censor opposition speech—a point stressed by Federalists from North to South in the ratification debates.[6] Anti-Federalists demanded express language affirming this and other limitations on Congress, and guaranteeing various rights of the people. To mollify these skeptics and woo North Carolina and Rhode Island—which had yet to join the new union—the First Congress codified Federalist reassurances in a proposed constitutional amendment safeguarding citizen speech rights alongside freedom of religion, press, petition, and assembly. (Thus we see again how the exceptionally democratic process of constitutional ordainment propelled still further republican reforms and refinements.) Originally numbered third on a slate of twelve proposed amendments, the speech language eventually became the First Amendment when it won ratification in the states in 1791, along with initial amendments Four through Twelve.

Elsewhere in our story, we shall study these first ten amendments—America's Bill of Rights—in some detail. At this point, however, it is useful to keep the First Amendment speech clause in mind alongside its older sibling, the Article I speech clause. Underlying both clauses lay profound, if not altogether English, ideas about the nature of popular self-government. In England, Parliament was legally sovereign and socially superior. For an ordinary Englishman to criticize Parliament was, in a way, impudent. Perhaps there was thus a certain (classist) logic when Parliament held such a critic in "contempt"—*le mot juste*. But in America, where the people themselves were sovereign, by what right could government punish members of the sovereign citizenry who spoke out against Congress? America's first premise of popular sovereignty decisively separated it from England, as Madison briefly noted in the First Congress when introducing an amendment that would guarantee ordinary citizens a freedom of speech and debate akin to what congressmen enjoyed under Article I. In 1794, Madison sharpened the point: "If we advert to the nature of Republican Government, we shall find that the censorial power is in the people over the Government, and not in the Government over the people." In America, if not in England, the people were truly the sovereign masters, and government officials were merely servants who could indeed be scolded.[7]

In 1798, in violation of all that the Constitution's supporters had said and written in 1787–89, Congress passed a federal Sedition Act that punished Americans for criticizing Congress. Though congressmen calling themselves "Federalists" backed the act, very few of these men had been Federalist leaders a decade before, when the American people ordained the Constitution and added a Bill of Rights. Madison, who *was* a preeminent Founding Federalist, not to mention the sponsor of the speech amendment, joined forces with Jefferson to crusade against the oppressive act.

While Jefferson emphasized that Congress lacked any enumerated federal power to enact censorship laws—an argument that implied that state libel law could fill the breach—Madison went further, calling attention to the deep logic of popular sovereignty and the "essential difference between the British Government and the American constitutions." Whereas Parliament was "omnipotent," in America "the people, not the government, possess the absolute sovereignty." American elections depended on "the equal freedom" of "examining and discussing [the] merits and demerits of the candidates respectively."[8] Unless challengers enjoyed a freedom of speech roughly comparable to that of incumbent congressmen, the election debate would not be "equal," Madison argued. If incumbents were free to attack challengers in speeches inside Congress and elsewhere, challengers must be comparably free to criticize incumbents in speeches outside Congress. The Amendment I free-speech clause thus complemented the Article I free-speech clause so as to guarantee America's true sovereign—the people—the same broad right of political discourse traditionally enjoyed in England by the sovereign Parliament.

Although this Madisonian reading of American speech law became judicial orthodoxy only in the twentieth century,[9] even supporters of the Sedition Act positioned themselves far ahead of contemporaneous English law. The 1798 Act made truth an absolute defense. Granted, this was insufficient protection because certain biting criticisms were legally presumed false, and because truth could not always be affirmatively proved in court, especially where critical commentary blended fact and opinion. Yet English law did not even recognize truth as a defense until the 1840s. At the time of America's Founding, English law held that the truth of a libel actually compounded its harm by lowering the libel target's reputation and in effect depriving him of his property. The greater the social standing of the target and the greater the truth of the insult, the greater the legal harm.

On top of all this, the hereditary nature of the House of Lords and the steep property qualifications for Commons combined with parliamentary privilege so as to give special speech rights to the upper class not enjoyed by the mass of commoners. The lords also enjoyed immunity from civil arrest whether or not Parliament was in session.[10] English speech law thus routinely subordinated the liberty and equality of the many to the dignity and property of a privileged few. American speech law championed wider notions of freedom and democracy in the paired speech clauses of Article I and Amendment I.

"among the several States"

The longest section of the Constitution's longest Article aimed to enumerate the main powers of Congress and thereby resolve hard questions of federalism, separation of powers, and rights. Some of the powers not given to Congress would reside with the states; others would be wielded by the president and federal courts; and still others simply lay beyond the proper scope of all government and were thus reserved to the people.

The federalism issue, in its previous incarnations, had torn the British Empire apart in the mid-1770s and had bedeviled America's first efforts at continental coordination in the mid-1780s. Prior to 1763, a rough working arrangement had emerged within the empire, whereby each provincial American assembly decided matters of taxation and internal affairs while London regulated trade among different parts of the whole and promulgated general foreign policy. In most colonies, a resident governor appointed in England could irreversibly veto all assembly bills, which could also be set aside by the British Privy Council. Then came the 1765 Stamp Act, the 1767 Townshend Duties, the 1773 Tea Act, and the 1774 Coercive Acts, by which Parliament asserted authority to saddle the colonists with newfangled internal taxes, other revenue-seeking duties, and a variety of intrusive internal regulations. Outraged, some advanced American thinkers in the mid-1760s laid the intellectual groundwork for complete American independence from Parliament. Under their sweeping theory, provincial assemblies and Parliament simply shared a common king, and Parliament itself had no direct authority over the provinces. Most American patriots before 1775 took a more moderate position. Essentially, moderates proposed to constitutionalize an early version of federalism by codifying the working arrangement that had prevailed before 1763: Provincial assemblies should retain power over internal matters and taxes while Parliament and the king could continue to manage imperial trade, continental defense, and foreign affairs.[11]

British authorities countered American moderates' proposals with the absolutist logic of parliamentary sovereignty. Sovereignty implied legal omnipotence—plenary power over all colonial matters, whether external or internal. In the words of Britain's Declaratory Act of 1766, Parliament "hath, and of right ought to have, full power and authority to make laws and statutes of sufficient force and validity to bind the colonies and people of America . . . *in all cases whatsoever.*"[12]

In response, Americans ultimately declared their independence not just from the old empire but also from old ideas of sovereignty. Led by

Wilson, American legal theorists in the 1780s conceptually relocated sovereignty from Parliament to the people themselves, and thereby fashioned an intellectual framework facilitating the constitutionalization of federalism, separation of powers, and limited government. In this new framework, no single government entity had, or of right ought to have, all power. Sovereignty originated and remained with the people, who could parcel out and reclaim discrete chunks of power as they saw fit. Thus, the people could divide power howsoever they chose between their state and continental officers, or among different branches within the continental government. Or they could choose to withhold some powers from all governments.

The challenge confronting America in 1787 was to avoid both a dangerously strong central regime (Parliament) and a dangerously weak one (the Confederation Congress). Between these two extremes, two visions of national power emerged at Philadelphia. The first, which ultimately prevailed, aimed to vest Congress with ample authority over interstate and international affairs for the geostrategic reasons soon to be elaborated in the early *Federalist* essays. The second, unsuccessfully championed by Madison, sought to add to these powers a general federal veto of state laws, in keeping with the more ambitious vision of union on display in *The Federalist* No. 10.

MOST OF THE POWERS that Article I, section 8 conferred on Congress flowed naturally from the geostrategic vision of union distilled in the Preamble. Thus, section 8 began by echoing the Preamble almost verbatim, in language affirming the need to "Provide for the common Defence and general Welfare." (Similar phraseology had also appeared in the Articles of Confederation.) Section 8's opening clause minced no words in affirming that, precisely in order to promote these goals of continental security and prosperity, the new Congress would be empowered to impose a broad range of "Taxes, Duties, Imposts and Excises." The old Confederation had notoriously lacked power to impose such taxes, and national defense and prosperity had visibly suffered. State governments had often failed to provide the funds that the Confederation demanded of them. For example, in 1781 Congress requisitioned states for some $8 million for the following year but received less than half a million. Without a strong revenue stream, vital federal functions were withering. Lacking a powerful army and navy, Americans in 1787 found themselves at the mercy of monarchs and pirates. Also, with no power to impose continental tariffs on foreign imports, the Confederation had little leverage in prying open foreign markets for American exports.[13]

Thus, only a decade after they revolted against imperial taxes, Americans were being asked to authorize a sweeping regime of continental taxes, with the decisive difference that these new taxes would be decided on by public servants chosen by the American people themselves—taxation *with* representation. Elsewhere, Article I required that all revenue bills originate in the House of Representatives, a rule with little bite because the Senate would enjoy unlimited power to propose amendments.

Section 8's opening clause went on to link federal taxation to the payment of national "Debts"—most obviously war debts. The vast bulk of preexisting continental debt came from the Revolutionary War, and congressional power to "borrow Money on the credit of the United States," as authorized by section 8's next sentence, surely contemplated the possibility of future wars. Without the ability first to borrow money from abroad when war threatened and then to pay back the loans on time—lest lending nations treat nonpayment as grounds for their own wars[14]—America would become a tempting target for European empires lusting after dominion.

Next came words giving Congress power "to regulate Commerce with foreign Nations, and among the several States, and with the Indian Tribes." Modern lawyers and judges typically refer to these words as the "commerce clause," and today's Supreme Court has moved toward reading the paragraph as applicable only to economic interactions.[15] But "commerce" also had in 1787, and retains even now, a broader meaning referring to all forms of intercourse in the affairs of life, whether or not narrowly economic or mediated by explicit markets. Bolingbroke's famous mid-eighteenth-century tract, *The Idea of a Patriot King,* spoke of the "free and easy commerce of social life," and other contemporary texts referred to "domestic animals which have the greatest Commerce with mankind" and "our Lord's commerce with his disciples."[16] Structurally, the broader reading of "Commerce" in this clause would seem to make better sense of the framers' general goals by enabling Congress to regulate *all* interactions (and altercations) with foreign nations and Indian tribes—interactions that, if improperly handled by a single state acting on its own, might lead to needless wars or otherwise compromise the interests of sister states. Draft language at Philadelphia had in fact empowered Congress "to regulate affairs with the Indians," but the word "affairs" dropped out when the delegates opted to fold the Indian clause into the general interstate and international "Commerce" provision.[17] Without a broad reading of "Commerce" in this clause, it is not entirely clear whence the federal government would derive its needed power to deal with noneconomic international incidents—or for that matter to address the entire range of vexing nonmercantile interactions and altercations that might arise among states.[18]

Under a broad reading, if a given problem genuinely spilled across state or national lines, Congress could act. Conversely, a problem would not truly be *"with"* foreign regimes or *"among"* the states, so long as it remained wholly internal to each affected state, with no spillover. On this view, legal clarity might be advanced if lawyers and judges began referring to these words not as "the commerce clause," but rather as "the international-and-interstate clause" or the "with-and-among clause."*[19]

The rest of section 8 continued in the same geostrategic spirit. Six separate paragraphs—a cluster that we shall consider in more detail presently—addressed interrelated issues of war, armies, navies, and militias. Two other paragraphs authorized Congress to naturalize immigrants from foreign lands and to punish criminals who menaced ships on the high seas or violated the law of nations. Most of these proposed federal powers had traditionally fallen outside the purview of individual colonial governments prior to 1763. Congress here inherited the mantle of British imperial authority.

Several other clauses aimed to further harmonize relations between the states, in keeping with the expansive vision sketched out in Jay/Publius's *Federalist* No. 2. Uniform bankruptcy rules would stabilize interstate lending practices and spur a national market in negotiable instruments, just as continental standards for copyrights and patents would create a broad New World market for authors and inventors. Standard weights and measures, federal post offices and post roads, a continental money supply alongside uniform regulations of foreign currency—all these would help knit far-flung Americans together, economically and socially.

---

*Federal power over genuinely interstate and international affairs lay at the heart of the plan approved by the Philadelphia delegates. According to the Convention's general instructions to the midsummer Committee of Detail, which took upon itself the task of translating these instructions into the specific enumerations of Article I, Congress was to enjoy authority to "legislate in all Cases for the general Interests of the Union, and also in those Cases to which the States are separately incompetent, or in which the Harmony of the United States may be interrupted by the Exercise of individual Legislation." *Farrand's Records,* 2:131–32. It also bears notice that the First Congress enacted a statute regulating noneconomic interactions and altercations—"intercourse"—with Indians; see An Act to regulate trade and intercourse with the Indian tribes, July 22, 1790, 1 Stat. 137. Section 5 of this act dealt with crimes—whether economic or not—committed by Americans on Indian lands.

Largely omitted from this list of congressional powers was the authority to intervene to protect a citizen from the folly or injustice of his own state legislature. Prior to 1776, royal and proprietary governors and the Privy Council had typically claimed the absolute right to block bills passed by colonial assemblies, but by 1787 only Massachusetts and New York had opted for any sort of gubernatorial veto, and even in these two states the veto could be overridden by a two-thirds vote of each house. Madison and other Federalists decried the absence of executive vetoes in most state governments and took pride in building a nonabsolute presidential veto, à la Massachusetts, into the structure of federal lawmaking. Madison also tried, unsuccessfully, to revise the basic structure of *state* lawmaking by giving Congress the same wide-ranging power to veto state laws that imperial governors and privy counselors had wielded in the colonial era.

As Madison saw it, state governments lacked sufficient ballast, and a general congressional "negative" over all new state laws would enable continental representatives of greater wisdom and reputation to prevent ill-considered or oppressive state laws from taking effect. When Charles Pinckney proposed such a negative at Philadelphia, arguing that "under the British Govt, the negative of the Crown had been found beneficial," Madison warmly seconded the motion. While Pinckney and other supporters emphasized how this proposed veto would protect the interests of the nation and of citizens of sister states, Madison went further. A congressional veto would also prevent state assemblies from "oppress[ing] the weaker party within their respective jurisdictions." In a similar spirit, Wilson argued that "we have seen the Legislatures in our own Country deprive the citizen of Life, of Liberty, & property [and] we have seen Attainders, Banishments, & Confiscations."[20]

Yet most delegates at Philadelphia remained unpersuaded that Congress should enjoy sweeping authority to protect a citizen from his own state legislature, a legislature that in most cases had roots more than a century deep. Hugh Williamson spoke for many in opposing a general power of Congress "that might restrain the States from regulating their internal police."[21] Ultimately, although the Constitution proposed to protect a key cluster of internal matters from state abuse under Article I, section 10, these guarantees of individual rights against one's own state would largely be enforced by state and federal courts, not directly by Congress. While Madison had faith that wise federal lawmakers operating over an extended geographic sphere would be more trustworthy and protective of minority rights than would state lawmakers—a vision he later elaborated in his

Federalist No. 10—his fellow drafters did not fully share this vision, and repeatedly refused to give Congress the sweeping veto that Madison craved.

"necessary and proper"

The delegates did vest Congress with sweeping power of a different sort in the final clause of section 8. Anti-Federalists fretted about the threat to states' rights posed by words empowering Congress "to make all Laws which shall be necessary and proper for carrying into Execution the foregoing Powers." In response, Federalists repeatedly explained that these words did not constitute some free-floating grant of near-plenary power. Rather, the clause merely clarified that the rest of Article I, section 8 should be read at face value. While the Articles of Confederation had proclaimed that Congress had only the powers "expressly" granted by that document, Article I pointedly avoided this stingy word. The new Congress would thus have all powers expressly listed in the document and also anything that followed by fair, commonsensical implication.[22]

In the most famous case ever to construe the necessary-and-proper clause, Chief Justice John Marshall, writing thirty years after the Founding, in fact placed primary reliance on the other clauses of section 8 to uphold a broad view of federal legislative authority. As Marshall saw it, congressional power to create a national bank flowed from various early enumerations, and the last words of section 8 added little or nothing to the affirmative case. Reading the document through a geostrategic prism, Marshall emphasized the national need for an army able to defend a "vast republic, from the Saint Croix to the Gulph of Mexico, from the Atlantic to the Pacific." Because a national bank with branches across the continent might help in paying soldiers on-site and on time, Marshall (who had spent the winter of 1777–78 encamped at Valley Forge) held that such a bank fell within Article I's enumerations concerning "the great powers to lay and collect taxes; to borrow money; to regulate commerce; to declare and conduct a war; and to raise and support armies and navies."[23]

In truth, the real sweep of section 8's final clause extended not downward over states but sideways against other branches of the federal government. Congress would have broad authority to pass laws "carrying into Execution . . . all other Powers vested by this Constitution in the Government of the United States, or in any Department or Officer thereof." Here the Constitution's text made explicit what otherwise might have been a disputable reading of the document's organizing schema: Congress stood first among equals, with wide power to structure the second-mentioned executive and third-mentioned judicial branches. Thus Congress would decide how many cabinet departments would fill the executive branch; how these cabinet departments would be shaped and bounded; how many justices would compose the Supreme Court; where and when the Court would sit; what substantive laws and procedures would apply to federal admiralty cases; and a multitude of similarly weighty organizational issues.*[24]

Other language of Article I, section 8 likewise operated more horizontally than vertically, reinforcing Congress's primacy among the three federal branches. The English Crown had historically created courts by royal prerogative, and had notably exercised this power in America by establishing certain juryless chancery courts and vice-admiralty tribunals that many colonists came to detest.[25] But now Congress would be the branch to "constitute" inferior courts by deciding how many courts there should be, where they should sit, how they should be organized, what sorts of cases they should hear, what rules of procedure and evidence they should follow, and so on. (The president would nominate the judges to these courts, subject to Senate confirmation.) The monarch had also enjoyed various powers over naturalization, weights and measures, patents, copyrights, and coins that, as we have seen, Article I vested in the legislative branch.[26]

Article I's seat-of-government clause implicated yet another aspect of separation of powers. By British tradition, the king could summon Parliament to meet at a place of his choosing. Royal governors claimed similar powers over colonial assemblies. According to historian Allan Nevins, South Carolina's governor in the early 1770s had "fatuously called a session of the legislature at an inconvenient, unhealthy spot, Beaufort, hoping the stubborn Charleston members would not attend."[27] Jefferson's Declaration of Independence had condemned George III for "call[ing] together legislative bodies at places unusual, uncomfortable, and distant from the depository of their public records, for the sole purpose of fatiguing them into compliance with his measures." Against this backdrop, Article I made clear that Congress, not the president, would decide where to sit and

---

*Though Article I did not explicitly enumerate the point, it also implicitedly gave each house of Congress broad powers of investigation and oversight—powers that had historically been exercised by parliaments and legislatures on both sides of the Atlantic and that were necessary and proper adjuncts to Congress's enumerated powers to enact legislation, appropriate funds, conduct impeachments, and propose constitutional amendments. (We shall consider Congress's impeachment role in Chapter 5, and its amendment powers in Chapter 8.)

where to locate the permanent national capital—a "District" forming "the Seat of the Government." Earlier language of Article I made clear that any decision to move the legislative meeting place during any particular congressional session would require the concurrence of both legislative houses.

Broad congressional authority over other branches raised the problem of pretext. For instance, what if Congress tried to twist its power to constitute tribunals or regulate the Supreme Court into a general right to dictate how federal judges should rule on the merits in constitutional cases? Similar concerns about pretext arose in the domains of federalism and rights. Although Congress lacked general power to tell a state where to locate its state capital—and was affirmatively barred by section 4 from dictating where a state legislature could meet when "chusing" its federal Senators— what if Congress prohibited all imports into any state that refused to plant its statehouse where Congress preferred? What if Congress tried to target opposition newspapers by imposing a tax on these papers and only these papers, or withholding copyright protection from them, or prohibiting them from being shipped across state lines?

The general problem of pretext had vexed American colonists in the years before independence. Moderate patriots had conceded that Parliament might properly regulate trade among different parts of the Empire but had contested Parliament's authority to impose taxes—even when such taxes appeared in sheep's clothing, as with the 1767 Townshend Duties that took the form of trade regulations but were plainly aimed at raising revenue. To discourage analogously pretextual use of congressional power, section 8 employed three main strategies. First, the framers at times tried to specify the purpose of a particular power. Patents and copyrights could not be given merely to reward political allies, but only "to promote the Progress of Science and useful Arts."

A second strategy denied Congress the power to play favorites among states in various contexts. Unlike Parliament, which had privileged Englishmen in England at the expense of Englishmen in America, Congress should pursue only the "common" defense and "general" welfare. All duties, imposts, and excises were to be "uniform" throughout the United States. Federal naturalization and bankruptcy laws should likewise be "uniform," and a national seat would lie outside the formal jurisdiction of any member state. Later language in Article I, in section 9, demanded federal neutrality among ports in different states.

A third and still more global safeguard came from the language at the end of section 8 confirming its general spirit: Only laws that were truly "proper" to permissible federal ends would be allowed. For example, the object of censoring its critics was, for sound republican reasons, not entrusted to the government. Thus any pretextual use of the tax power to single out opposition newspapers would not be constitutionally "proper." As John Marshall would reiterate in 1819, Congress could not "under the pretext of executing its power, pass laws for the accomplishment of objects not entrusted to the government." Congressional statutes, wrote Marshall, had to comport with the "spirit" as well as the "letter" of section 8 enumerations.[28]

WHICH BRINGS US TO one area where power was conspicuously absent in both letter and spirit: abolition in the several states. Nothing in the section 8 list gave Congress general authority to end slavery, even in the long run; and no one at Philadelphia floated such a proposal. (Madison's preferred negative would have operated only to restrain new state laws, but would not have enabled Congress to undo state slave codes already on the books.) Addressing his fellow slave masters in the Virginia ratifying convention, Madison spoke bluntly: "No power is given to the general government to interpose with respect to the property in slaves now held by the states"—a point forcefully reiterated by Edmund Randolph, who noted that even the slavery-obsessed South Carolinians at Philadelphia had been satisfied on that count.[29] In the Palmetto State itself, another Philadelphia delegate, Charles Cotesworth Pinckney, had already publicly assured his audience that "the general government can never emancipate [our Negroes], for no such authority is granted." James Iredell later offered similar assurances to North Carolinians. Federal lawmakers confirmed this understanding in a report printed by the first House of Representatives in March 1790, which declared that "Congress have no authority to interfere in the emancipation of slaves, or in the treatment of them within any of the States." Though the report made no mention of Congress's power to regulate or prohibit interstate commerce in slaves, even an expansive view of this power left the vast majority of in-state slaves beyond the reach of would-be federal abolitionists.[30]

In early 1861, a lame-duck Congress hoping to avert a civil war went so far as to vote for Ohio's Representative Thomas Corwin's plan to add a new (thirteenth) amendment to the Constitution that would explicitly and irrevocably (!) disclaim congressional power "to abolish or interfere, within any State, with the domestic institutions thereof, including that of persons held to labor or service by the laws of said State."[31] In his First Inaugural

Address, Lincoln tentatively endorsed this solution. "Holding such a provision to now be implied constitutional law, I have no objection to its being made express."

This proposed thirteenth amendment failed to appease Southern extremists, who worried that Lincoln would use his executive authority to appoint antislavery territorial governors, and that his congressional allies would use their plenary power over the territories to prevent slavery's further expansion. A more immediate threat to slavery in the states came from Lincoln's anticipated use of federal patronage power to build an antislavery party in Dixie, and his apparent desire to allow abolitionist literature—which had long been excluded from the federal mail—to circulate freely. Yet the very modesty of such likely Lincolnian measures serves to highlight how little direct authority the federal government had, circa 1861, to uproot slavery in the states.

When the South spurned the proposed Corwin Amendment, an epic military struggle ensued, forging a chain of events that ultimately led Congress in 1865 to propose a diametrically opposed thirteenth amendment, whose provisions we shall study later. At present, let us merely note that the nation's ultimate constitutional fate in the 1860s pivoted on the alignment of American military power—an alignment that had been shaped by several critical section 8 paragraphs. To these key paragraphs we now turn.

"Armies, ... Navy; ... Militia"

The Constitution dramatically expanded the central government's military powers while fashioning several safeguards to deter and if necessary overcome abuse of these powers.

Under the Articles of Confederation, Congress could raise troops only by "requisition[ing]" each state for its proportionate "quota" of men determined by white population. Each state legislature retained the power to "raise, ... cloath, arm and equip" its troops, and to appoint all regimental officers "of or under the rank of colonel." To raise the funds to pay for these men and materiel, Congress once again had to rely on state governmental compliance with a quota system, this time based on wealth. The requisition system failed miserably and came perilously close to handing victory to the British in the Revolutionary War. With inadequate mechanisms to enforce states' obligations, many states held back, hoarding resources for local defense despite more urgent need for them elsewhere on the continent. The challenge facing America in the late 1780s, then, was to find a way to strengthen its military structure against foreign foes without imperiling domestic liberty.

Breaking with the old requisition system, the new Constitution empowered the central government to raise its own army and navy without state intervention, to impose taxes and duties on individuals to pay for these armed forces, and to appoint all professional military officers. The Constitution also went beyond the Articles by authorizing the continental government to nationalize state militias in order to "execute the Laws of the Union, suppress Insurrections and repel Invasions." Should any state succumb to a military dictator, menace its neighbors, or proclaim itself independent, the union thus had authority to intervene with military force, relying on militiamen from sister states as well as loyal militiamen from the insurrectionist state, in addition to the union's own professional troops.

The awesomeness of these new military powers, and their evident susceptibility to abuse if not properly constrained, prompted the framers to balance military power more carefully *within* the national government. In England, the king had the power to both declare war and command troops. He could also unilaterally issue letters of marque and reprisal, authorizing private ships to engage in limited military assaults. Under the Confederation, all of these powers resided, at least on paper, in a single unicameral body. By contrast, the Constitution split these powers between legislature and executive, empowering Congress to declare war and authorize the issuance of letters of marque and reprisal, while making the president the military commander in chief with implied authority to use force if necessary to push back a sudden invasion or put down a violent insurrection.* Similarly, Congress could lay down "Rules for the Government and Regulation" of military forces, but the president would execute these rules. Congress could authorize army appropriations, but the president would superintend actual disbursements. Congress could provide rules for nationalizing state militias, but the president would command these men whenever they were called into service. Congress, via its power to spend and regulate, would have the last word on the basic structure of the officer force, but the president would nominate individual officers, subject to Senate confirmation.

The Constitution also enabled the voters themselves to check the mili-

---

*The Philadelphia draftsmen used the phrase "declare War" rather than "make war" so as to empower the president to act unilaterally to "repel sudden attacks." *Farrand's Records,* 2:318–19 (Madison and Gerry). See also U.S. Const. art. I sect. 10, para. 3 (generally prohibiting states from "engag[ing] in War" without congressional consent, but making an exception if a state is "actually invaded, or in such imminent Danger as will not admit of delay").

tary via a special sunset rule for military funding: "No Appropriation of [army] Money . . . shall be for a longer Term than two Years." For all other purposes—even navies—Congress could authorize standing appropriations that would keep funds flowing until a later Congress repealed the initial appropriation law. Had these ordinary appropriation rules applied to the army, whenever one careless or corrupt Congress created a standing appropriation for the military, a permanent army might stand its ground even after it lost the support of the House of Representatives, so long as it stayed enough in the good graces of the Senate or the president to block repeal. Precisely to prevent this scenario, section 8 required army—and only army—appropriations to run a stricter gauntlet. No standing appropriations would be permitted for standing armies. Every army appropriation would automatically dry up after two years, and only a fresh vote in each new term of Congress could keep the money flowing. Thus the people's House could unilaterally stop a standing army in its tracks simply by refusing to fund it; and even if the new House favored reauthorization, the Senate would still need to agree, as would the president (absent a veto override).

The particular two-year cutoff meshed perfectly with the gears of the Constitution's electoral clock, which would bring the entire House membership before the American electorate every two years.[32] If the people did not want to continue the army, they could simply vote for a new House, which could then just say no—or more precisely, refuse to say yes—and thereby oblige the standing army to fold its tents. America would never be more than two years away from presumptive demilitarization. Even if ten consecutive Congresses overwhelmingly supported a standing army, the eleventh House—and by extension, the American electorate at the eleventh election—could bring the money and the men to a halt.[33]

Federalism offered another check against national military despotism. Despite the union's vastly increased practical power—including the power to quell insurrections, secessions, and coups at the state level—states would not be defenseless. For sound geostrategic reasons, the Constitution did prevent states from keeping foreign mercenaries or any other body of permanent professional "Troops . . . in time of Peace" without "the Consent of Congress." But local militias composed of state citizens serving part-time fell outside this prohibition. Indeed, the Constitution expressly charged states with "the Appointment of the Officers, and the Authority of training the Militia according to the discipline prescribed by Congress." While these militias, which would later figure prominently in the Second Amendment, were ultimately subject to nationalization in times of emergency, their loyalties were likely to be local. State governments would train these men, equip them, and appoint their officers. If central authorities tried to use a national standing army to suspend the Constitution and subjugate the people, state militias could spring into action, much as colonial governments had mobilized military resistance to George III in the mid-1770s.

In a pair of *Federalist* essays penned separately by Hamilton and Madison, Publius elaborated the argument that, in the highly improbable scenario of a national military despotism run amok, states could ride to the rescue. In a wholly national regime lacking independent state governments, "if the persons entrusted with supreme power become usurpers, the different parcels, subdivisions, or districts of which it consists, having no distinct government in each, can take no regular measures for defense. The citizens must rush tumultuously to arms, without concert, without system, without resource." But in the United States, a very different scenario could unfold. Should tyrannous national leaders attempt a military coup d'état, "the State governments, with the people on their side, would be able to repel the danger. . . . [The standing army] would be opposed [by] a militia amounting to near half a million of citizens with arms in their hands, officered by men chosen from among themselves, fighting for their common liberties, and united and conducted by governments possessing their affections and confidence. . . . Local governments . . . could collect the national will and direct the national force."[34] The chief advantage of this latent force was that it would probably never be put to the test. The very existence of small but expandable militias organized by state governments could deter a large professional standing army organized by the national government from acting abusively—much as a would-be monopolist must take into account not only current competitors but also others poised to enter the market if prices rise too high.

By balancing military power between two levels of government, the American people would in theory retain greater control over both. The national government could put down any local coup or insurrection menacing the republican government of a single state or region, but any scheme of national tyranny could be thwarted by an alliance of local militias led by state governments, in the spirit of 1776. Thus, wrote Hamilton/ Publius, "the people, without exaggeration, may be said to be entirely the masters of their own fate. Power being almost always the rival of power, the general government will at all times stand ready to check the usurpations of the state governments, and these will have the same disposition towards the general government. The people, by throwing themselves into either scale, will infallibly make it preponderate. If their rights are invaded by either, they can make use of the other as the instrument of redress."[35]

To be clear: Publius did not argue for a general right of state militias, or anyone else, to engage in armed resistance merely because they sincerely believed that national authorities were acting unwisely or even unconstitutionally. Ordinarily, the people's remedies for allegedly improper or unconstitutional conduct would be political and legal—speeches, petitions, assemblies, elections, and lawsuits—with the ultimate decisions over good-faith disagreements to be rendered by the nation's duly constituted civilian authorities in Congress, the executive branch, and federal courts. The scenario painted by Publius as the occasion for militia opposition was, by hypothesis, anything but ordinary. Rather, it was the extraordinary case of an attempted national coup. No political or legal remedies would exist in this situation. Presumably, national courts would have been shut down or, at best, their judgments would be unenforceable. Ballot boxes would be shut (or stuffed), critics muzzled (or worse). Whatever law existed would be martial law, enforced only by gun and sword. In such an extreme scenario of open usurpation—and only in such a scenario—the sole practicable remedy left to the people would involve recourse to arms.

Of course, this was hardly the situation faced by secessionists in early 1861. The national political channels remained open: Lincoln had won the presidency fairly and promised to hold honest elections on schedule—as he would in fact later do. So, too, the national courts in 1861 remained open. (If anything, the Taney Court stood as a shameless apologist for Southern interests.) Nor had the national military taken aggressive steps to threaten civilians. On the contrary, Southern insurrectionists struck first in attacking Fort Sumter. Confederate moderates defended secession by asserting that each state's people retained the right to decide for themselves whether the federal compact had been breached, regardless of what the federal courts, Congress as a whole, a duly elected president, or the voters of other states sincerely believed. Other Confederates went even further, resting secession not on claims of federal wrongdoing, but rather on the sovereign right of each state populace to alter its government at any time for any reason—to withdraw from the Constitution as a nation might withdraw from a treaty it no longer deemed suitable. Both Confederate theories rested on a view of state sovereignty plainly inconsistent with the federal Constitution as explained by its supporters and understood by its skeptics in the great ratification debates of the late 1780s.

Later, we shall see how the Civil War experience gave birth to a transformed vision of the national army and the state militias, and how this transformed vision in turn enabled the Reconstruction Amendments to become the law of the land. The modern American Constitution properly respects the federal army more and celebrates state militias less than did the Founders' Constitution. The Founders had seen the dangers of imperial redcoats at close range—close enough to see the whites of the soldiers' eyes—but modern America stands on the shoulders of a later central army dressed in blue. It is largely due to state militias that the South was able to wage and almost win an unjustified and unconstitutional war of secession; and it is largely thanks to U. S. Grant's central army that the Reconstruction Amendments were fairly adopted in a process that included Southern Unionists and Southern blacks.

Yet in its early years, the Founding vision served Americans—white Americans, at least—rather well. The federal government faced extra hurdles whenever it sought to authorize standing armies, and the president's military powers were counterbalanced both horizontally by Congress and vertically by states. The result of all this, and of America's unique geostrategic insulation from Old World armies, was that for much of her history, America lived free from a large standing army on home soil. Especially in the critical early years of the new republic, the absence of an imposing military structure helped Americans establish a strong tradition of civilian supremacy and military subordination. Other New World regimes south of the border have been haunted by the specters of military coups and crackdowns, while the United States has not. This freedom from fear of our own military—a freedom so pervasive that it seems as invisible as the air we breathe and as vast as the continent itself—ranks among our greatest blessings of liberty.

"No ... No ... No"

The concluding language of Article I enumerated specific prohibitions on federal and state power. Some of these specifics merely elaborated rules and principles implicit elsewhere in the document. Other language went further, and laid the conceptual foundations for what would later become the Bill of Rights and the Reconstruction Amendments.

Section 9 began its list of constitutional don'ts by guaranteeing that willing states (read: the Carolinas and Georgia)[36] could continue to import foreign slaves until 1808 (and forever count them under the three-fifths clause), despite Congress's otherwise plenary power to bar or tax foreign imports. The Deep South thus had a twenty-year window through which to hoard more slaves, with all the protections of a strong national government behind the importers and none of the risks of national prohibition to which all other importers were subject. With this special exemption, the Constitution risked a huge expansion of American slaveholding and blinked the horrors of the international slave trade, with its fresh enslavements of freeborn Africans and its hellish middle passage across the Atlantic. As part of the proslavery package, other language in section 9 forbade Congress from taxing domestic slavery out of existence via head taxes ("Capitation") on slaves, and also forbade any congressional taxes on "Articles exported from any State." Though formally applicable to all exported goods produced by all sorts of laborers, this rule primarily aimed to insulate the fruits of Southern slave labor—such as tobacco, rice, and indigo—from federal taxation.[37]

In the Virginia ratifying debates, Madison defended the 1808 clause as a short-term concession to bolster long-term defense. "The [Deep] Southern States would not have entered into the Union of America without the temporary permission of that trade; and if they were excluded from the Union, the consequences might be dreadful to them and to us. . . . Great as the evil [of the international slave trade] is, a dismemberment of the Union would be worse. If those states should disunite from the other states for not indulging them in the temporary continuance of this traffic, they might solicit and obtain aid from foreign powers." Northerner Oliver Ellsworth had said much the same thing at Philadelphia, warning that without this clause, "he was afraid we should lose two States, with such others as may be disposed to stand aloof," with the result that America might "fly into a variety of shapes & directions, and most probably into several confederations and not without bloodshed."[38]

Other provisions of sections 9 and 10 reflected national-security and geostrategic concerns even more directly, in keeping with the vision sketched out in the early *Federalist* essays. No federal officer would be allowed, without congressional consent, to accept any gift from foreign governments or potentates. Individual states would be barred from making treaties with foreign powers or making trouble for foreign ships; and no state, without congressional consent, would be allowed to "keep Troops, or Ships of War in time of Peace" or engage in any war of aggression. Most of these provisions had antecedents in the Articles of Confederation.

By 1787, many Americans understood that a president backed by a continental army of hirelings and a nationalized militia might at times be necessary to protect against invasions and insurrections.[39] Nevertheless, the very thought of such vast power at the command of one man inspired dread; Revolutionary Americans had seen firsthand just how much havoc a large mercenary force could wreak upon civilians. Thus, section 9 piled additional military safeguards atop the ones provided in section 8. Reinforcing the special two-year limit on military spending, section 9 forbade the executive from dipping into the treasury on his own initiative, in the absence of a proper "Appropriation[] made by Law." Another section 9 clause, sounding in both federalism and separation of powers, guaranteed that "the Privilege of the Writ of Habeas Corpus shall not be suspended, unless when in Cases of Rebellion or Invasion the public Safety may require it." In the absence of any such extreme circumstance, courts would remain open to hear all challenges to the lawfulness of executive detentions.

These courts would include state tribunals, unless Congress chose to create federal courts with exclusive jurisdiction to hear federal habeas cases. As a practical and constitutional matter, the Supreme Court could hear only a very limited set of cases while sitting in its original (trial) jurisdiction. Stationary in the national seat, the high court would mostly hear appeals from cases arising elsewhere. Any widespread executive effort to detain persons illegally could be countered only by courts scattered throughout the land. Since the Constitution nowhere required the creation of federal trial courts in the hinterlands, the crucial trial courts might well be state courts of general jurisdiction, armed with traditional common-law powers, including authority to issue writs of habeas corpus. Under this Great Writ, judges could scrutinize bodily detentions and order the release of persons deemed to be unlawfully confined.

It was this preexisting state/common-law writ that section 9 protected against undue suspension, thus confirming that state governments, via their courts, could help to prevent federal lawlessness—precisely as Hamilton/ Publius had explained in a related context when he declared that if the federal government invaded the people's rights, Americans could turn to states as "instrument[s] of redress."[40] Any state judge issuing a habeas writ against a lawless president would not be defying but rather enforcing the Constitution's supremacy clause, which of course made the Constitution itself the supreme law—supreme even over a contrary presidential edict. However, a president in such a scenario would likely contend that he had been acting within the scope of the suspension clause in particular and the Constitution more generally. Ultimately, federal judges would have the right to decide these federal legal issues on appeal, by dint of their Article III authority to review all state court decisions arising under the Constitution. State trial courts would be the first word but not the last word in this judicial conversation.

Nothing in the habeas clause, however, specified whether suspension required prior congressional approval. In 1861, Lincoln powerfully argued that the logic of events might at times demand temporary unilateral presidential action. Congress might not be in session when rebels attacked or invaders landed (as it was not when Fort Sumter came under unprovoked bombardment), and the rebellion or invasion might physically prevent Congress from assembling when summoned. As America's chief officer, always on deck and oath-bound to keep the constitutional ship afloat, a president could properly suspend habeas and take other emergency actions so long as he received legislative authorization as soon as Congress could be safely convened.

Or so Lincoln argued in defense of a wide range of military measures he undertook before Congress could meet in July 1861. In his view, the placement of the nonsuspension clause in Congress's Article I rather than the president's Article II did not impliedly require *prior* congressional approval. Rather, the Article I location of the clause simply confirmed that *ultimately* the decision was Congress's. The president could merely act temporarily, as Congress's faithful on-duty servant maintaining the pre-rebellion status quo precisely in order to preserve Congress's options. Even Lincoln's sensible claim of temporary-suspension power went beyond the traditional authority of British monarchs—a point stressed by Chief Justice Taney, speaking only for himself, in an 1861 in-chambers habeas ruling that sharply challenged Lincoln's suspension policy. Taney's ringing rhetoric slighted the fact that presidents were subject to constitutional checks—most important, front-end election and the ultimate threat of impeachment—that rendered them more trustworthy than hereditary kings. In response, Lincoln proceeded to disregard Taney's solo ruling, thereby challenging Taney's very jurisdiction over the matter. Jurisdictional technicalities aside, Lincoln insisted that his suspension of the writ was necessary to safeguard the very existence of the Union, its Constitution, and the great mass of other laws that he had sworn to uphold.[41]

In addition to the clauses addressing military threats from home and abroad, other provisions of sections 9 and 10 aimed at ending incipient economic warfare among the states and related forms of interstate exploitation. To prevent New York City and Philadelphia (to take two notorious examples) from unfairly taxing unrepresented out-of-staters sending or receiving goods through these ports, states and localities would generally be banned from unilaterally imposing revenue-seeking duties on imports and exports. The ban would also avoid state competition with, or frustration of, federal import duties and tariff policies. On the opposite side of the ledger, New York City, Philadelphia, and other financial centers would benefit from section 10 rules barring states from inflating currency or otherwise abrogating creditors' rights under preexisting contracts. Through these rules, the Constitution prevented agrarian states from catering to the mass of in-state debtors at the expense of out-of-state creditors and banks.[42] Under the Confederation, several states had used debt-relief laws to impose a tax of sorts on unrepresented citizens of sister states and, even worse, foreign creditors. Unless such shortsighted state policies could be stopped, foreign lenders might well urge their home governments to retaliate economically, diplomatically, or militarily, and thereby put all America at risk.

BUT SECTION 10's RULES proscribing states from "coin[ing] Money; emit[ting] Bills of Credit; mak[ing] any Thing but gold and silver Coin a Tender in Payment of Debts; [and] pass[ing] any . . . Law impairing the Obligation of Contracts" drove even deeper. In both letter and spirit, they worked not merely to prevent state legislatures from exploiting citizens of sister states and foreigners, but also to prevent state lawmakers from ganging up on a minority of their own citizens—in-state creditors, to be specific.[43] These were the document's most distinctively Madisonian provisions, reflecting his prediction that a Congress brimming with enlightened continental statesmen would be wiser and juster than state legislatures apt to be populated by small-minded and shortsighted demagogues. In keeping with this vision of differential trustworthiness, the document gave Congress explicit authority to coin money and relieve insolvent debtors via federal bankruptcy laws that could apply even when all the creditors came from the debtor's state. Nowhere did the document specify the precise gold or silver content of *federal* coinage or prohibit, say, federal copper coins—or federal paper money or bills of credit for that matter. All these were rather pointed omissions, given that the Confederation Congress had issued paper currency by the bushel to keep America afloat during the Revolutionary War.

As with Madison's unsuccessful proposed congressional negative on state laws, the section 10 cluster of economic provisions aimed to give the new continental government authority that had once been wielded by the old empire: In 1764, Parliament had imposed a general ban on colonial laws that made paper money or bills of credit legal tender. But this Currency Act had provoked broad resentment among agrarian interests across the colonies, and even Parliament had never imposed a sweeping ban on all impairments of existing contracts. Unsurprisingly, the section 10 economic clauses—and the contracts clause in particular—sparked fierce criticism from Anti-Federalists during the ratification debates. At a theoretical level, the contracts clause represented an unprecedented continental intrusion into a traditionally "internal" local matter. Skeptics and traditionalists could accept the need for continental rules concerning genuinely interstate and international affairs, but here the federal Constitution would in some cases insinuate itself between a state and its own citizens. As a practical matter, the clause fueled the strong suspicion aroused by a too-small House—and by the very eminence of the Philadelphia draftsmen themselves—that the proposed Constitution was at heart an aristocratic scheme favoring nabobs and grandees, despite its remarkable array of populist provisions. In a private letter to Jefferson penned after eleven states had ratified, Madison confided that "the articles relating to Treaties [which gave the federal government power to protect the interests of British creditors against American debtors], to paper money, and to contracts, created more enemies than all the errors in the System positive & negative put together."[44]

IT REMAINS TO CONSIDER three other section 10 provisions that further limited states in matters of internal governance: "No State shall . . . pass any Bill of Attainder, ex post facto Law, . . . or grant any Title of Nobility." These provisions, too, reflected distrust of unbridled state assemblies, but distrust on these three topics applied against Congress as well. Section 9 made clear that "No Bill of Attainder or ex post facto Law shall be passed" by Congress, and that "No Title of Nobility shall be granted by the United States." With this short list of don'ts protecting individual liberty and republican equality against Congress and the states, the Constitution offered, in miniature, a stylistic and conceptual template for the later Bill of Rights and Reconstruction Amendments.

The bans on attainders and ex post facto laws had deep roots in rule-of-law ideology. As we have seen, the basic tripartite structure of the federal government reflected a strong commitment to the ideal that legislation, at least if punitive, should be general and prospective. Otherwise, a legislature could simply impose penalties upon political opponents by name, and no one, howsoever virtuous his conduct, would be safe. The ban on bills of attainder prohibited one specific type of abuse, under which a legislature purported to name a particular individual and pronounce him or her guilty of a capital offense. The English Parliament had passed many such bills—perhaps most notoriously in 1641, when it legislatively decreed death for Thomas Wentworth, the Earl of Strafford, an influential Crown advisor. In the federal Constitution, the spirit animating the ban on bills of attainder extended to all laws heaping scorn or punishment upon specifically named individuals.[45] The companion ban on ex post facto laws—retroactive statutes making conduct that was innocent when committed criminally punishable—aimed at preventing a similar legislative abuse. In the absence of the companion ban, a legislature seeking to target a specific victim could simply reverse engineer an attainder by substituting a precise description of the victim's past (and wholly innocent) conduct for his proper name. The gross injustice of such legislative trickery bordering on lawlessness prompted the Federalists to ban all such practices, state as well as federal. Prior to this universalization, roughly half of the state constitutions had explicitly condemned ex post facto laws and/or restricted bills of attainder.[46]

If attainders and ex post facto laws warped proper rules of dishonor and punishment, titles of nobility warped republican principles of honor and reward.[47] Citizens of the New World deserved to be judged on the basis of their behavior, not their birth status. In a national government deriving its authority from the people and opening itself to all candidates (at least among adult male citizens), Congress had no "proper" power to create hereditary posts. As the attainder and ex-post-facto clauses buttressed separation of powers and the rule of law, so the nobility clauses reinforced America's basic republican structure.

Article I's two antinobility clauses grew directly out of the Articles of Confederation, which had barred both the United States and individual states from conferring aristocratic titles. Nowhere else had the Confederation so directly regulated states' internal governance. This early antiaristocracy language thus attests to the depth of Revolutionary Americans' commitment to maintain a New World order free from the oppressive weight of the Old World order. Prior to 1776, very few English noblemen had crossed the water to lord over the colonists, and most Americans wanted to keep things that way. In the mid-1780s, veteran Revolutionary army officers (as distinct from common soldiers) formed a private military honor society, the Order of the Cincinnati, and proceeded to make the organization hereditary, with memberships to be handed down from fathers to eldest sons. Republican purists were quick to condemn this proto-peerage. As Sam Adams saw the matter, the organization was "as rapid a Stride towards an hereditary Military Nobility as was ever made in so short a Time."[48]

In two widely separated *Federalist* essays, Madison and Hamilton explicitly linked the nobility clauses to the Constitution's general republican ethos. According to Madison, the "most decisive" proof "of the republican complexion of this system . . . [is] found in its absolute prohibition of titles of nobility, both under the federal and the State governments; and in its express guaranty of the republican form to each of the latter." Hamilton concurred: The "prohibition of titles of nobility . . . may truly be denominated the corner-stone of republican government; for so long as they are excluded, there can never be serious danger that the government will be any other than that of the people."[49]

In theory, the bans on state bills of attainder, ex post facto laws, and titles of nobility, along with the Article IV republican-government clause, could have had radical implications for freedom and equality in America. Were not slaves in effect punished simply for who they were at birth in defiance of the anti-attainder ideal? Was not South Carolina, a land of light-skinned lords and dark-skinned serfs, in violation of the spirit of the antinobility clause? The candid answer to such questions was that the Constitution's general structure, when read closely, evinced indifference (at best) to the liberty and equality claims of slaves. Essentially, the document excluded such men, women, and children, born and unborn, from "the People" whose general welfare the Preamble pledged to promote.

Yet even if bondsmen lay beyond the Constitution's protective compass, free blacks could make a strong textual and historical case for equal inclusion. Not one word of the document, and virtually nothing in its surrounding enactment history, suggested that free blacks should be subordinated to free whites. Alas, throughout the antebellum era, free blacks were stigmatized and stained by laws, state and federal, that punished them for who they were and allowed whites to lord over them.

Though antebellum officialdom showed little interest in deploying the letter and spirit of sections 9 and 10 on behalf of free colored persons, these sections fed the legal imaginations of other nineteenth-century Americans more committed to liberty and justice for all. If section 9 could secure the federal "Privilege" of habeas corpus against a powerful president, perhaps a new amendment might broaden this and other federal "Privileges" against powerful state officers. What one generation had done to protect the bodily liberty of free whites against military despotism, another generation might redo to safeguard the bodily liberty of freed blacks against forced labor. If the Constitution needed to go further in reining in states than section 10 had gone, perhaps a new amendment could reiterate the "No State shall" language of section 10 while expanding the scope of its prohibitions. If the bans on state impairments of contracts could be used to help powerful creditors, perhaps other language might protect less powerful constituencies at even greater risk of state demagoguery and injustice. If, as the paper-money issue revealed, Congress could sometimes be trusted when state legislatures could not, perhaps a new amendment should give Congress explicit authority, alongside the federal judiciary, to enforce state compliance with the dictates of fairness.

As will become clearer when we focus on the Reconstruction Amendments, mid-nineteenth-century reformers did indeed creatively adapt some of the words and concepts of sections 9 and 10 to end abuses that leaped onto the national stage in the antebellum and Civil War eras. When Americans turned to the long-overdue task of righting the worst wrongs of their founding fathers and grandfathers, several aspects of sections 9 and 10 would give them a good place to start.

Chapter 4

AMERICA'S
FIRST OFFICER

THE WASHINGTON FAMILY (1789–1796).
The president, his wife, Martha, his two adopted step-grandchildren (Eleanor Parke Custis and George Washington Parke Custis), and a liveried servant (probably William Lee—a slave later freed). A rising sun in the background, but no rising son in the picture.

ARTICLE II OBLIGED THE FOUNDERS to venture deep into uncharted territory. The young continent needed a president who would be far more than a legislative presiding officer, a state governor, or a prime minister, but far less than a king. Nothing quite like this new office had ever existed. Nevertheless, as Americans in 1787 tried to envision a republican head of state who could protect them against old King George without becoming a new King George, they did have a particular George in mind.

"President"

In the middle of the Philadelphia Convention, during the deliberations of a five-man Committee of Detail, delegates began calling their proposed legislature the "Congress" and their proposed executive the "President."[1] Despite many differences between the old (confederate) Congress and the new (constitutional) one, two basic features of the old body would live on in the new Senate: equal representation of states and selection by state legislatures. The Constitution's "President," however, bore absolutely no resemblance to the "president" under the Articles of Confederation. That Confederation officer was simply the delegate "appoint[ed] . . . to preside" in Congress for no more than a year in any three-year stretch. His position was largely honorary, with no powers of appointment or veto, no official military command or direct superintendence of executive departments, no personal authority to negotiate or block treaties, no explicit authorization to receive ambassadors, no pardon power, no fixed term of office or perpetual reeligibility, no continental electoral mandate beyond Congress, no immunity from home-state instruction or recall, and no guaranteed national salary. The new president would enjoy all these powers and privileges, and more.

Under the Confederation, the president needed to be a sitting member of Congress. Under the Constitution, the president would head his own independent branch. Indeed, Article I, section 6 barred a sitting president from serving in Congress (as it barred all other executive and judicial officers from sitting in the legislature). Thus, the old president merely presided in Congress, while the new president would preside over

America generally, as reflected in his very title: "President *of the United States of America.*"

While the new Congress would go in and out of session, America itself would always be in session, as would the nation's new presiding officer. Under the old Articles, various recesses and quorum failures of the Confederation Congress had compromised America's ability to conduct foreign affairs.[2] In response, the Constitution created a presidency that, officially, would never sleep. By contrast, the speakership of the House of Representatives would automatically lapse every two years, along with the House that created it. In 1855–56, a regularly scheduled congressional adjournment would combine with political wrangling by incoming representatives so as to leave the House without a speaker for a full eleven months. In 1859–60, the pattern would repeat itself. But during these months and the many other intervals when America had no House speaker, she would always have a "President" vested with "executive Power." When one "Term of four Years" ended, another would begin without a moment's gap. If a president died, resigned, was removed, or became disabled, Article II provided for immediate substitution of a vice president. If in turn something happened to that officer, further immediate substitutions would take place (in contrast to the temporary vacancy periods that might occur for individual House and Senate seats under the rules of Article I).[3] Other Article II clauses authorized the president to act as a stopgap during legislative recesses by making temporary appointments to executive and judicial vacancies and by calling one or both houses of Congress into emergency session when events warranted. These clauses plainly presupposed the essential continuity of presidential power.

In his first months in office—March to July 1861—President Lincoln would rely on this characteristic of executive power to justify his quick military moves to suppress Southern insurrectionists, moves that he made without obtaining prior congressional approval. (The old Congress's term had expired on the eve of his inauguration, and the new Congress was not due to meet until December, a full nine months later. On April 15, two days after the fall of Fort Sumter, the president summoned congressmen to assemble in special session on July 4, five months ahead of schedule.)[4] As America's presiding officer, Lincoln believed that he was permitted and indeed obliged to preserve the Union intact unless properly authorized to do otherwise by Congress or the American people. Lincoln also made clear that some of his unilateral emergency measures would require Congress's explicit blessing once that body could be convened. Otherwise, these measures would eventually lapse, and in some cases the president and subordinates who had carried them out might be subject to legal sanction, including impeachment.[5] As it turned out, Congress generally voted to validate Lincoln's actions.[6]

Lincoln's structural vision can be recast into a simple textual argument: The opening words of Article II vested America's president with the "executive Power," a power encompassing the right and duty to protect the United States as an ongoing venture. While later specific clauses of Article II clarified and qualified this opening grant of power in a variety of ways,[7] these additional clauses did not purport to exhaustively list all presidential powers. Rather, the first words of Article II themselves vested the president with a residuum of general authority to preserve, protect, and defend the republic in emergencies—unilaterally, if need arose and Congress happened to be out of town.[8]

Although only a few state executives circa 1787 could point to comparably sweeping vesting clauses in their state constitutions,[9] the federal Constitution envisioned even the weakest state executive as a continuous entity, unlike a typical state legislature. Article I authorized "the Executive" of each state to fill any temporary vacancy in the federal Senate until his state legislature met, and also to issue a writ of election whenever a federal House vacancy needed filling. Article IV empowered state executives to act unilaterally in requesting federal assistance whenever "domestic Violence" erupted and state lawmakers "cannot be convened." Continuity was thus seen as a core attribute of executive power in all the states, even as these executive branches widely differed in other respects.[10]

In 1787, ten states referred to their chief executives as "governors," while three preferred the word "president."[11] Pennsylvania's "president" was notorious for being the weakest of the thirteen, a legislatively chosen officer who did little more than preside over an executive council making group decisions. The "presidents" of Delaware and New Hampshire enjoyed slightly more power than that, but far less than America's most muscular state executive, the "governor" of Massachusetts. Directly elected by statewide voters, this "governor" could veto all legislative bills (subject to a two-thirds legislative override), pardon convicts (with the advice of a council), and appoint judges and other important officials (as long as the council concurred). John Adams, the draftsman who conceived this powerful officer and styled him a "governor," would later, in a debate about executive titles, underscore the weakness of the word "president" by observing that "there were presidents of fire companies and of a cricket club."[12]

Against this backdrop of weak state "presidents" and occasionally stronger state "governors," early drafts of the Philadelphia Committee of Detail unsurprisingly referred to a federal "Governor." So why did the drafters eventually substitute the weaker word?

Although the documentary sources yield no definitive answer, several hypotheses are worth mulling over. Perhaps, having opted for the familiar Confederation word "Congress" to describe the new proposed legislature, delegates decided that it made sense to borrow the matching Confederation word "president," despite the enormous differences between the pre-1787 and post-1787 versions of this office. If the word's tame associations tended to bathe the Constitution's proposed executive in an unthreatening and emphatically republican light, so much the better for the document's ratification prospects, delegates may have reasoned.

Or perhaps South Carolina's John Rutledge, a pivotal figure on the pivotal committee, pushed for the word "president" for personal reasons. Rutledge himself had served from 1776 to 1778 as South Carolina's first (and only) elected "president" and then from 1779 to 1782 as its first elected "governor" after the state changed the designation of its chief executive. Going against the grain of usage elsewhere in America, the Palmetto State's 1776 constitution initially gave its "president" veto power over all laws, but the 1778 replacement constitution denied such power to the newly named "governor." When presented with this proposed constitutional change, President Rutledge refused to sign the 1778 document into law and chose instead to resign, only to return to office the following year with a new title and less power.[13] In light of this experience, Rutledge may have had a nostalgic preference for the P-word over the G-word.[14]

More likely, the Philadelphia delegates, both on and off the committee, were consciously or subconsciously influenced by the fact that George Washington was the presiding officer—the unanimously chosen "president"—of the Philadelphia Convention itself. There, Washington's role was mainly honorific. "President Washington" had no veto at Philadelphia, no extra vote in Virginia's delegation, and no power to appoint the members of any particular committee. Yet his presence filled the room. His ultimate willingness to come out of retirement to attend the Convention had signaled the importance of the conclave. Even before the Convention commenced, the mere possibility that Washington might once again ride to the aid of America had inspired the states to commission their best men and in turn encouraged most of these men to accept their commissions. Everyone at Philadelphia understood that Washington's name alongside Franklin's on the bottom of the proposed Constitution might be the key to ratification. If America's most revered figures vouched for the new document, this fact alone might persuade doubters to give the experiment a try.

Every man at Philadelphia also understood, as did later ratifiers, that Washington would likely serve as America's first president. What better way to remind fence-sitters of Washington's place in the document's past and future than to use the very label for the chief executive that everyone knew Washington had worn in the Convention itself? A yes vote would poetically enable "President Washington" to continue as "President Washington." Or to put the point in a less coldly calculating way, the Philadelphia delegates in the end probably chose the P-word simply because by midsummer they had grown accustomed to calling George Washington "Mr. President."

THE ISSUE OF EXECUTIVE TITLES resurfaced early in the First Congress. During a three-week span in the spring of 1789, federal lawmakers spent considerable time and energy debating the proper form of address for the nation's new chief. A Senate committee proposed "His Highness, the President of the United States of America, and Protector of their Liberties," and the Senate as a whole leaned toward the proposal. (This was the specific context in which John Adams—himself the "President of the Senate" and its tie breaker—pointed out the commonness of the word "president" and urged lawmakers to adorn it with additional words of grandeur.) Critics in both houses sounded republican alarm bells. Insisting that Congress could not "alter, add to, or diminish" the simpler title contained in Article II itself, Pennsylvania Senator William Maclay laid particular stress on the Article I ban on federal titles of nobility. According to Maclay, "the appellations and terms given to nobility in the Old World" were "contraband language" in America. South Carolina Representative Thomas Tudor Tucker worried that a fancy title squinted toward a "crown and hereditary succession." When the dust had settled, the words "His Highness, the . . . Protector" lay abandoned, largely at the insistence of the lower house.[15]

The intensity and extensiveness of this debate might at first puzzle modern Americans. "What's in a name?" we might wonder.[16] The simple answer is that many who had risked their lives against King George III strove to preserve the New World order from even the slightest hint of creeping monarchy and aristocracy. In Maclay's words, "We have lately had a hard struggle for our liberty against kingly authority [and] everything related to that species of government is odious to the people." The new Constitution, in Maclay's eyes, was wholly antiaristocratic and anti-monarchical, as evidenced by its guarantee of "a Republican Form of Government" to "every State" and its several antinobility clauses, including a provision banning federal officeholders (absent special congressional permission) from accepting even nominal "titles" from any Old World "foreign state, king, or prince." Thus, the very text of the Constitution itself proved that titles mattered, leading Maclay to insist that Congress stick to the document's own simple and republican description of America's chief executive.[17]

Maclay went on to observe that Anti-Federalists had recently worried aloud that the new regime might by degrees give rise to a "kingly government and all the trappings and splendor of royalty." All the more reason, then, for Congress to resist anything that might look like "the first step of the ladder in the ascent to royalty." Tucker reminded the lower house that one of the Constitution's "warmest advocates, one of the framers of it, (Mr. Wilson, of Pennsylvania,) has recommended it by calling it a pure democracy. Does this look like a democracy, when one of the first acts of the two branches of the Legislature is to confer titles? Surely not." The bottom of the slippery slope seemed all too clear to Tucker: "a high title, an embroidered robe, a princely equipage, and, finally, a crown and hereditary succession."[18]

Representative Madison found such claims overwrought. "I believe a President of the United States, clothed with all the powers given in the constitution, would not be a dangerous person to the liberties of America, if you were to load him with all the titles of Europe or Asia." Nevertheless, Madison ultimately sided with the republicans. "I am not afraid of titles, because I fear the danger of any power they could confer, but I am against them because they are not very reconcilable with the nature of our Government or the genius of the people. . . . Instead of increasing, they diminish the true dignity and importance of a republic."[19]

In this fascinating debate, all involved appeared to have the highest personal regard for Washington, whom Maclay in his diary described as "the greatest man in the world." Indeed, Maclay, Madison, and others argued that pompous Old World titles would actually degrade America's first man by lumping him together with Europe's "sons and daughters of crown heads" and with Asia's "Grand Turk." As we shall see, this debate in the First Congress was hardly the first or last time that open anxieties about "princes of the blood" and "hereditary succession" hovered above the Founding generation's deliberations on the presidency in general and Washington in particular.[20]

"four Years"

The new-minted American president towered over his state counterparts. In 1787, eleven states declined to give their chief executives any veto power over legislatively approved bills, and a twelfth (New York) merely allowed the governor to sit as one member of a judge-dominated council collectively wielding a defeasible veto. By contrast, the federal Constitution empowered the president to veto any bill he chose, thus single-handedly nullifying the judgment of a Congress structured to comprise the continent's most eminent statesmen. (Although a two-thirds vote in each house could override the president, such votes would prove rare in antebellum America. Not until 1866 would Congress surmount a veto of an important bill.)[21] While most state chief executives owed their jobs to the legislatures that directly chose them, America's president could win and keep office independently of Congress. The typical state chief executive had to contend with an executive council chosen by others. The president would handpick cabinet department heads, each of whom would answer to him personally, with no formal power vested in the cabinet as a group. Even the muscular Massachusetts governor could not measure up to America's president, who would control a military force of continental sweep and would serve as America's head of state, with personal authority to treat with foreign princes. Indeed, no treaty whatsoever could take effect unless the president assented.

As if all that were not enough, the president would automatically serve for four straight years—double the tenure of federal House members—and could seek perpetual reelection. In sharp contrast, ten states, including Massachusetts, set the chief executive's term at only one year. Among this group, Northern states commonly permitted perpetual reelection, while Southern states either forbade reelection altogether or limited governors to three consecutive terms. Among the three nonannual states, none had an executive term of office longer than three years, and only one (New York) allowed immediate reelection.[22]

Modern eyes tend to glide past the Article II words "four Years" and other basic dimensions of presidential power. What could be more common than a quadrennial chief executive elected independently of the legislature and wielding a qualified veto power? Nowadays, almost every state governor answers to this description.[23] But this clear modern pattern marks a complete inversion of state practice at the Founding—which leaves us with some obvious questions: Why did the Philadelphia drafters propose an executive term of office and a cluster of executive powers so very different from contemporary state practice? And why did the states eventually embrace the Philadelphia executive model for their governors?

Part of the answer may be found in the desired balance of power between legislature and executive. Federalists admired Massachusetts's regime of bicameralism and presentment, and recoiled from Pennsylvania's unicameral and virtually headless system. As they saw the matter, a lower house often had good instincts but needed to be counterbalanced. A select upper house and an independent executive branch armed with a qualified veto would likely attract men of recognized learning and distinction. With larger reputations at stake, such men would hesitate to join any unwise or unjust scheme. By contrast, the sheer numbers in a lower house would tend to dilute a sense of individual responsibility among representatives.[24]

To balance the legislature, the executive needed a term of office calibrated to counterpoise the weight of the legislators' temporal mandate. In Massachusetts, an annually elected governor might be able to hold his own against an annually elected lower house and an annually elected senate, but the federal executive would face House members with two-year terms and senators with six-year positions. To approximate the legislative-executive balance that Massachusetts had struck, America's president would need a term four times longer than his Bay State counterpart because he would confront federal lawmakers with comparably long terms.

This domestic-balance explanation makes sense of, and draws support from, the broad history of legislative and gubernatorial terms of office across the centuries. The typical American governor's term has increased from one year in 1787 to four years today in a way that rather precisely tracks similar increases in average legislative terms. At the Founding, eight states elected all legislators on a yearly or half-yearly basis, and each of these eight set one-year terms for their chief executives. South Carolina elected legislators biannually and did the same for governors; Delaware picked its senators and executives triennially; and in New York, quadrennially elected senators offset triennial governors.[25] Nowadays, the typical state counterbalances two-year legislators in the lower house and four-year lawmakers in the upper house with a four-year governor. In New Hampshire and Vermont, the only two states where governors are currently elected biannually, so are all state legislators.[26]

The more general story here is thus the move away from annual elections across the board, a move that reflects the maturation and consolidation of American democracy. In the shadow of wildly irregular and permissibly infrequent colonial elections under the British Empire, American revolutionaries in most states understandably rushed to codify the popular maxim that "where annual elections end, tyranny begins." Eventually, the track record of the few nonannual states and the federal government itself proved that yearly rituals were not needed to ward off oppression. At some point, less frequent elections could actually improve democracy by focusing public attention during energized election seasons. (If annual elections were always better than biannual ones, would semiannual elections be better still? Monthly elections?) Once regular fixed-calendar elections became settled American practice, the path was clear for gradual amendment at the state-constitutional level moving toward longer terms.

Interestingly enough, this sweeping process of state constitutional revision began in 1787–88 with wide-ranging public debates about executive power and election timing prompted by the Philadelphia plan. Once approved in extraordinarily democratic meetings up and down the continent, the federal Constitution itself offered a visible and validated template for states to copy. Thus, the federal Preamble process, in which Americans in every region said "We do," propelled a populist bandwagon in support of more executive power and longer executive terms at the state level.

Before the Philadelphia Convention, the state-executive bandwagon had moved forward in fits and starts but had yet to hit full speed. In 1777, New York created an independently elected governor with a three-year renewable term and a seat on a veto council, but the following year South Carolina notably abolished its executive veto. In 1780, the people of Massachusetts voted to create a strong governor, but in 1781 the people in neighboring New Hampshire voted against just such a creature and in 1784 ultimately opted for a far weaker presiding officer. Then came the ratification of the federal Constitution in 1788, after which the state-executive bandwagon visibly accelerated.

Most dramatic was the experience in Pennsylvania, whose 1776 constitution had given its legislatively dependent and annually elected "president" little power in his own right. Flush with victory in the federal constitutional context, Pennsylvania Federalists pushed for a special convention to revise the state system. The result was a new constitution promulgated in 1790 and bearing a striking resemblance to the fledgling federal Constitution. Following a one-sentence Preamble—"We, the people of the Commonwealth of Pennsylvania, ordain and establish this constitution for its government"—the new document proceeded in Article I to vest legislative powers in a house of representatives and a senate. (This bicameral regime broke sharply with the unicameral system that Pennsylvanians had long lived under, first as a colony and then as a state under the constitution of 1776.) Representatives would be elected annually, senators quadrennially. All bills would come before "the governor" for his signature or veto, subject to a two-thirds override. Article II opened with words vesting this new-minted governor with "supreme executive power" and then provided that he would be elected by statewide voters, would enjoy a three-year term of office, and could stand twice for reelection. In a flash, America's weakest state executive became its strongest, with an independent electoral base, a Massachusetts-style veto pen, and a New York–style term of office.

Pennsylvania did not stand alone. In 1789, Georgia gave its governor a veto pen, and Kentucky and New Hampshire did the same for their governors in 1792.[27] (As we have seen, New Hampshire voters had vetoed the veto only a decade earlier.) Kentucky's independently elected and re-eligible governor also became the first state chief executive entitled to a four-year term. All told, of the eight states adopting a new constitution or revising an old one in the decade after 1788, four gave their executives a qualified veto power and a fifth (Vermont) gave its governor and council a suspensive veto allowing them to block a bill until the next legislative session; six embraced independent election; and six gave the executive a term of at least two years.[28]

And so it would go in ensuing decades as new states joined the union and old states amended their early constitutions. The 1787–88 ratification process did not give Americans the option to vote separately on the provisions of Article II, or on any other specific parts of the document. The ultimate question was a holistic and binary one: yes or no to the Constitution as a package. Thus, it cannot be said that ratifying Americans gave any special blessing to Article II. Yet over the next two centuries, Americans everywhere chose to sculpt governors in the president's image, giving repeated, if implicit, votes of confidence to Article II's basic vision.

SO FAR, OUR STORY of executive power has focused on the executive-legislative balance, an issue relevant at both the state and federal levels of government. This story has drawn upon ideas that should be familiar to modern students of the most frequently assigned *Federalist* essays— Nos. 10 and 51—which identified defects in state governments circa 1787 and proposed remedies that included legislative bicameralism and enhanced executive power. Alongside this story, let us now consider an interpenetrating set of foreign-policy concerns, which induced many Americans in the late 1780s to accept a strong American president regardless of their views about individual state governments and state governors.

A muscular president was needed not merely to check Congress, but also to check foreign monarchs. On the first official day of the Philadelphia Convention, the central role of the federal executive in military and national-security matters was foreshadowed when the delegates unanimously elected a general as their leader and soon thereafter began calling him "Mr. President."[29] George Washington was widely seen as the man most likely to head the new government on the drawing board at Philadelphia precisely because he had already proved that he could protect Americans against a foreign tyrant without becoming a tyrant himself. When the Revolutionary War had ended, the general had disbanded his troops and surrendered his sword to Congress, in a gesture that had astounded a world long used to seeing commanders from Caesar to Cromwell usurp power rather than relinquish it. (Napoléon would soon follow in these Old World footsteps.)

In the years between General Washington's initial retirement to Mount Vernon in 1783 and his eventual decision to attend the Philadelphia Convention in 1787, unfolding world events raised large questions about whether the Articles of Confederation could secure their most essential purpose—"common defence"—without drastic revision. In a world dominated by powerful monarchies, could a cluster of fledgling democracies with limited military muscle survive and flourish? Britain had yet to abandon its military outposts on American soil as promised, retaining five forts within the borders of New York alone and thereby blocking free access to the lucrative fur trade and complicating American relations with Indian tribes in the region. British-controlled Canada loomed to the north, while Spain claimed vast lands to the west and south. Although France had helped Americans win the Revolution—just barely—could Americans count on the French monarchy in all future situations? Didn't France have interests of her own that might diverge from America's? Hadn't Louis XVI been driven more by a hatred of the British than a love of the Americans? By 1787, British and French trade barriers had closed various European and West Indian ports to American goods and American ships, Barbary pirates were preying on Americans in the Mediterranean, and Spain had closed the Mississippi River to trans-Appalachian American farmers seeking to float their goods to market. Americans were not yet masters of their hemisphere and might yet again be called upon to take up arms to protect their hard-won liberties and promote their vital interests.[30]

To solve these problems, the Articles would need to be drastically revised or, more likely, simply abandoned. (The Articles could not be revised unless all states agreed, yet Rhode Island had blocked previous proposed remedies and refused even to send delegates to Philadelphia.) The union must be empowered to raise armies directly, to pay soldiers with its own funds derived from its own taxes, to regulate international trade and navigation, and to enforce state compliance with treaties. All these new powers would require the creation of a truly representative continental legislature with a democratic mandate to act directly upon individuals. To safeguard domestic liberty, such a powerful new legislature needed a powerful new executive to keep it in check. (So ran the domestic-balance argument.)[31]

A powerful executive would also be invaluable internationally in coordinating America's defense and trade policies vis-à-vis the rest of the world. Thus, when Philadelphia delegates early on debated whether to vest executive power in one man or three, Elbridge Gerry strongly opposed an executive branch troika as "extremely inconvenient . . . particularly in military matters, whether relating to the militia, an army, or a navy. It would be a general with three heads."[32] Perhaps this metaphor brought pained smiles to the lips of Washington and other Revolutionary War veterans in the room, for these men knew firsthand how the absence of a strongly unified military-command structure had indeed compromised America's military effectiveness in the fight against Britain.[33] With Gerry's words fresh in mind, the delegates opted for a one-man executive, and later that day voted to give this officer a defeasible veto over all bills. Other major aspects of Article II—the president's power over treaties, his quadrennial term of office, his perpetual reeligibility, and his electoral independence from Congress—took shape only in the Convention's final weeks.

During the ratification period, leading Federalists invoked foreign-policy concerns alongside domestic-balance arguments to sell the American people on the basic Article II package—a president with a four-year renewable term, an independent electoral base, and a veto pen. A short term of one or two years would have made it difficult for a president to master world issues and pursue long-term international strategies. Just as a one-year president would have had a hard time domestically counterbalancing two-year representatives and six-year senators, so he would have been no match internationally for lifetime foreign princes and professional European diplomats. And as The Federalist No. 72 put the point, America's very "political existence" might depend on having the right man at the helm in an international crisis or war. Hence the unwisdom of excluding an incumbent president from being reelected at a critical moment.[34] If, however, a president were allowed to stand for reelection, he needed to be allowed to make his case to a body of electors independent of Congress. Otherwise, he might hesitate to check congressmen when needed, fearing their reprisals on reelection day.

Thus foreign-policy concerns argued for a substantial and renewable term, which in turn argued for an independent electoral base to solidify the veto power; and to complete the circle, the veto would enhance a president's ability to represent and protect America abroad. Using his pen as a shield, he could thwart unwise measures that might offend foreign nations or injure foreign nationals. Using his pen as a sword, he could offer to add his signature to various legislative measures in exchange for congressional yes votes on treaties and related legislation that he deemed vital to national security. (Federalists understandably tiptoed around this foreseeable vote-trading scenario, which invited unflattering images and comparisons.) Unlike individual senators and representatives, whose need to be reelected locally might incline them to slight the broader national interest, a president would be a continental figure with a continental mandate to safeguard the nation as a whole.[35]

The debates in the First Congress about Washington's title further illustrate the foreign-policy aspects of the Founders' presidency. Supporters of a grand title aimed to give Washington additional heft not merely at home but also abroad. Against whom was Washington to be the "Protector of [American] Liberties"? Against Congress? This would be an odd admission from Congress itself. The obvious answer was that Washington would protect Americans against King George and other foreign powers, just as he had done in the Revolution.

After Washington's departure, Americans for the next two generations invariably chose men with extraordinary military or foreign-policy experience to fill his chair. Having spent nearly a decade representing the United States in France, the Netherlands, and England, John Adams had more diplomatic background than any other living American, with the possible exception of John Jay. Five of the next seven presidents—Jefferson, Madison, James Monroe, John Quincy Adams, and Martin Van Buren—had served previously as secretaries of state. The remaining pair—Generals Andrew Jackson and William Henry Harrison—had shown in the War of 1812 that they, too, could stand up against the British. Not until the mid-1840s, when America's position in its own hemisphere and the world was far more secure than in 1787, would the American people elect a president, James K. Polk, who lacked high military or diplomatic experience. Or to see the point from a different angle, note that prior to the Civil War one out of every two men to serve as secretary of state for a full term would later become president.[36] The pattern of presidential generals and diplomats prevailed for almost the entire first century of constitutional government: Of the seven elected presidents after Polk (up through James A. Garfield, who took office in 1881), five had served as combat generals, and a sixth had headed the State Department.[37] The seventh was Abraham Lincoln.

HAVING BEGUN BY TRYING to account for a presidential term of office that seemed long when compared to a typical state governor's, we might now wonder why the term wasn't made even longer. Domestically, why did it make sense to have a president with a shorter term than a senator's? Internationally, would a president with a mere four-year term be able to hold his own against kings in power for life?

Part of the answer is that anything longer than four years would have been hard to sell to an American populace haunted by the specter of tyranny. Although individual senators would have six-year terms, one bad senator could do infinitely less damage than one bad president—a fact that invited a shorter presidential leash. (In Maryland and Virginia, senators served five-year and four-year terms respectively, yet governors were trusted with only one-year terms.) Also, the Senate's staggered structure meant that a third of the body would be replenished every two years. In any individual state, no more than four years would ever elapse between senatorial elections.

Six-year terms for individual senators would give these lawmakers not only enough heft to resist unwise or unjust House measures (the domestic-balance argument), but also enough time to learn about world affairs, a point strongly emphasized by Publius and other leading Federalists.[38] In early deliberations at Philadelphia, Wilson had argued for nine-year Senate terms: "Every nation may be regarded in two relations 1 to its own citizens. 2 to foreign nations. It is therefore not only liable to anarchy & tyranny within but has wars to avoid & treaties to obtain from abroad. The Senate will probably be the depositary of the powers concerning the latter objects. It ought therefore to be made respectable in the eyes of foreign nations. The true reason why G. Britain has not yet listened to a commercial treaty with us has been, because she had no confidence in the stability or efficacy of our Government."[39]

Although some of the arguments for long Senate terms also applied to the executive branch, the president would at the time of his initial election already be a continental personage with a broad enough reputation and background to win support far beyond his home state. Presumably, a new president would need less time to learn about the continent and the world than would a new senator, who may have never ventured beyond his home state.[40] Indeed, the shorter presidential term itself created incentives for Americans to choose presidents with strong military and diplomatic credentials.

More generally, the overall structure of a biennial House, quadrennial presidency, and sexennial Senate gave each institution a unique electoral time horizon to accompany its unique electoral base. As a result, each of the three institutions had political incentives to see issues from its own angle, to ponder problems the other two might miss. The presidency and the Senate would be more independent of each other (and each would be more independent of the House) if each had its own election cycle.[41]

Compared to monarchs for life, a four-year president might look downright paltry. Yet the very size of the gap between America's new head of state and his European counterparts attested to Article II's republican bona fides. Elected by fellow citizens, subject to potential impeachment, and coming before the nation for reelection at fixed and frequent (by *international* standards) intervals, American presidents would be utterly unlike European kings, who inherited crowns from their fathers, served until death, and then handed power to their sons. Hamilton/Publius's repetition and italicization evidenced both the Federalists' pride in their new-modeled officer and their awareness of the Anti-Federalists' anxieties that needed to be eased: "[The president] is to be elected for *four* years; and is to be re-eligible as often as the people of the United States shall think him worthy of their confidence. In these circumstances there is a total dissimilitude between *him* and a king of Great Britain, who is an *hereditary* monarch, possessing a crown as a patrimony descendible to his heirs forever. . . . The President of the United States would be an officer elected by the people for *four* years; the king of Great Britain is a perpetual and *hereditary* prince."[42]

Once the Federalists persuaded Americans to sign on the dotted line, later events would flesh out exactly what the italicized *four* years meant in the real world. In practice, would Article II amount to life tenure, with incumbents perpetually reelected unless they somehow disgraced themselves?[43] Would incumbents in fact surrender power when outvoted? Would elections really be held on schedule in times of war or crisis?

Washington set a striking example for his successors when in 1796 he declined to stand for reelection at the end of his second term, even though he would have been a shoo-in. A republic should be bigger than any one man, and one way to establish this principle was for the republic's first man to step aside and make room for other leaders. This was not a lesson firmly established in America before Washington's resignation. In many a state that permitted perpetual reelection of its chief executive, the state's leading man had held the spotlight until the end. Massachusetts' first governor, John Hancock, stayed in power from 1780 to 1785, then stepped down for health-related reasons, only to return to serve from 1787 until 1793, when he died in office; Connecticut's first governor, Jonathan Trumbull, served from 1769 to 1784, when he left a year before his death; and New Jersey's first governor, William Livingston, remained in office from 1776 until his death in 1790. New York's first governor, George Clinton, held office for almost two decades, from 1777 to 1795, before stepping down. Clinton would later return to the governorship for yet another three-year term (his seventh), and would eventually die in office as vice president of the United States. Against this backdrop of governors seeking perpetual reelection or electoral advancement, Washington's 1796 announcement helped redefine the meaning of "four Years." In effect, Washington added an unwritten gloss to these words, encouraging his successors to consider retirement if and when they reached the end of their second quadrennial term.[44]

Washington's successor, Adams, gave the country and the world another striking example of restraint when he ultimately left office on schedule after losing the bitter election of 1800–01. In turn, Adams's successor, Jefferson, dramatized his own restraint by announcing in his second term that he would not seek a third. Invoking "the sound precedent set by an illustrious predecessor" (Washington), Jefferson declared that without a norm of timely resignation, the presidency, though "nominally four years, will in fact become for life, and history shows how easily that degenerates into an inheritance."[45] With a pair of two-term precedents (and presidents) now in the history books, Jefferson's immediate successors, Madison and Monroe, each followed suit by declining to serve beyond eight years. Thus was a tradition born.

A half-century later, in the middle of a great civil war, Lincoln presided over a fair election on schedule in 1864, even though for much of the campaign he had expected to lose this contest, and its result threatened to unravel everything that he had done in office. Twice in his First Inaugural Address, at a time when he could hardly be sure that the voters would allow him to give a second one, Lincoln had pointedly quoted the Article II words "four Years" and urged those Americans who disliked him to simply wait the allotted time and register their views in the next presidential election. In his words, the American people "have wisely . . . provided for the return of [power] to their own hands at very short intervals. While the people retain their virtue, and vigilance, no administration, by any extreme of wickedness or folly, can very seriously injure the government, in the short space of four years."

The republican restraint evident in the text of "four Years" and these early glosses was not simply radical by eighteenth- and nineteenth-century standards. It remains radical in the modern world. During World War II, the British Parliament suspended its standing rules requiring at least one election every five years and held no general elections between 1935 and 1945. Ordinary Britons never voted for Churchill as their wartime leader. As Churchill himself noted in a speech before Commons in late 1944, "No one under the age of thirty has ever cast a vote at a General Election, or even at a by-election."[46] Though extraordinary circumstances were obviously at work, the fact remains that incumbent English lawmakers agreed to perpetuate themselves in power beyond the promised end of their terms—as incumbent Parliament members had done in 1716, when they abrogated the Triennial Act and voted themselves another four years with no chance for the voters to say no, and as parliamentary incumbents had also done during World War I. By contrast, Americans held regular elections precisely on schedule throughout the Great Depression and World War II.

It is also worth noting that during this period, for the first and only time in America's history, a president went beyond the eight years that had sufficed for George Washington. Later in our story, we shall consider the amendment adopted in the wake of Franklin Roosevelt's unprecedented stint, but for now one final aspect of Washington's 1796 decision to step down deserves our attention. Thanks to this decision, America's George set precedents not only as her first president, but also as her first ex-president. Here, too, America broke new ground compared to European monarchies, where to be an ex–head of state meant death or exile. Hamilton/Publius had worried aloud in *The Federalist* No. 72 that any limit on presidential reeligibility might endanger "the peace of the community, or the stability of the government," with "half a dozen" ex-presidents "wandering among the people like discontented ghosts, and sighing for a place which they were destined never more to possess."

Washington's conduct in his final retirement showed that a republic need not fear its ex-leaders—men on the out-side of their final "four Years." As he had embodied republican restraint as general and as president, so he largely controlled himself as ex-president, thereby helping to give birth to the now-familiar role of the elder statesman, available to help the sitting president when asked, yet otherwise content to be a private citizen leading by example.[47] Perhaps Washington's greatest act as ex-president came at the very end, in the closing hours of the eighteenth century, when he provided in his last will and testament for the ultimate emancipation of all the slaves he owned in his own right. It was a poignant, if terse, reminder to his country of the redemptive work that remained to be done and of the sacrifices that propertied men should be prepared to make in order to achieve that redemption. Washington's last act was only one small and private step in the long road toward slavery's ultimate extinction. But it was a step in the right direction, away from an institution that was a pervasive presence in Washington's world—and as we shall now see, a discernable presence even in the electoral-college system underlying Article II itself.

"a Number of Electors"

The standard electoral-college stories fed to modern students by their teachers and textbooks come in two versions, neither of which fully satisfies.[48] The stodgy version portrays the framers' intricate presidential-election system as a clever contraption counterbalancing large and small states—an Article II analogue of the famed Connecticut Compromise underlying Article I. The edgy version presents Article II's electoral scheme as proof that the framers abhorred democracy. Each account raises more questions than it answers.

As some tell the story, Article II structured an almost bicameral election process in which large states would predictably dominate the qualifying heat but small states would likely have the advantage in the final round. Initially, each state would choose, in whatever manner it saw fit, a number of presidential electors equal to the number of its congressmen—House members plus senators. While no state, however small, would ever fall below a three-elector minimum (to match its guaranteed one House member and two senators), the most populous states would name the most electors. Meeting in their respective states on a day set by Congress, electors would ballot for president. But if no presidential candidate received an absolute majority of electoral votes in this qualifying heat, the presidential race would continue into a second round. There, the House of Representatives, acting under a special one-state, one-vote rule, would choose among the top five candidates. The framers expected, the story goes, that after George Washington passed from the scene, electors would typically scatter their votes across a wide range of candidates, thus making round two the decisive event. According to George Mason, in a remark at Philadelphia relied upon by many a modern storyteller, "nineteen times in twenty" the electors would likely fail to generate a first-round majority winner.[49]

If Article II's main goal was to boost candidates from small states, the framers failed miserably. Over the centuries, only three small-state men have ever been elected president—Louisiana's Zachary Taylor, New Hampshire's Franklin Pierce, and Arkansas's Bill Clinton.[50] As the system has in fact operated, nineteen out of every twenty elections, on average, have been decided in the first heat. Only twice has this initial heat failed to generate a winner, and on both occasions the House ended up choosing the finalist from the largest eligible state—Virginia in 1800–01 and Massachusetts in 1824–25.[51] As national presidential parties began to congeal in the 1790s and later hardened into permanent features of the political landscape, the broad dispersion of electoral votes anticipated by Mason never occurred. Instead, elaborate preelection coordination via party caucuses and conventions typically narrowed the field to two leading presidential candidates, one of whom almost always emerged with an absolute majority of first-heat electoral votes.[52] Also, state winner-take-all systems for selecting electors—systems that became the norm by 1800—have worked to enhance the importance of populous states, offsetting the initial head start that small states have enjoyed via the three-elector minimum.

If the original elector system had been chiefly designed to aid small states, its inadequacies were already plainly visible within its first dozen years of operation. Yet the Twelfth Amendment, adopted in the afterglow of this early experience, did little to protect small states even as it modified the elector system in other ways. In fact, this amendment (which we shall study in more detail later) weakened the influence of small states by decreasing the likelihood of House involvement in a second round and by restricting the number of candidates amongst which the House would choose. Most stodgy storytellers never remind their audience that the electoral-college framework in place today is not the one cobbled together in Philadelphia in 1787 but a rather different one fashioned after the election of 1800–01 and adopted as the Twelfth Amendment (with later amendments working still further modifications). Were such storytellers to include this reminder, their apologetic accounts of the Philadelphia framework would invite obvious questions: If the framers' presidential-election machine was so good, why did it jam up so soon and require retooling? If the 1787 system was primarily designed to protect small states, why did the 1804 system forsake this goal? Once that goal lay abandoned, why didn't the Twelfth Amendment's framers simply embrace direct popular election of the president?

The state-balance story also fails to illuminate essential aspects of presidential elections *before* the Twelfth Amendment. For example, everyone in 1789 knew that Washington would be the first president. The state-balance story might prompt us to ask whether Washington's vice president came from a counterbalancing state. Indeed he did—but the *way* he did snaps into focus only if we ignore the stodgy story's emphasis on state size and attend instead to state geography.

John Adams's Massachusetts ranked second among the states in total population—hardly an apt small-state counterbalance to Washington's Virginia, which ranked first. But geographically, Northerner Adams did counterbalance Southerner Washington. Tellingly, in each of the four contests governed by the original elector system, Americans opted for presidential–vice presidential pairs balanced by geography, not state size: Virginia-Massachusetts in 1789 and 1792, Massachusetts-Virginia in 1796, and Virginia–New York in 1800–01. (Had the Federalists prevailed in 1800–01, as they almost did, the balance would have been Massachusetts–South Carolina.) In each of these early elections, both winning candidates hailed from large states. Also, in the two exciting elections after Washington's departure, the electoral fault lines ran not between big states and small ones, but rather between North and South.[53]

None of this came as a surprise to Madison, who had repeatedly stressed behind closed doors at Philadelphia that "the great division of interests in the U. States . . . did not lie between the large & small States: it lay between the Northern & Southern," in part because of their different climates but "principally from . . . their having or not having slaves." The real issue for Madison, then, was not how to count small states but how to count slaves. For Congress, Madison toyed with the idea that one house could be apportioned "according to the number of free inhabitants only" and the other house according to total population, "counting the slaves as if free"—i.e., at five-fifths. Although this specific suggestion went nowhere, the three-fifths clause of Article I ultimately struck an analogous compromise, as we have seen.[54]

Which raises the question: How did Article II count slaves? The stodgy story elides the matter, focusing abstractly on "large" states and

"small" ones without highlighting underlying issues of slavery and suffrage. Was New York larger than North Carolina because it had more
free persons, or smaller because it had fewer total persons, counting slaves
"as if free"? What if a "large" state had a "small" eligible electorate because of high property qualifications?

THESE ARE PRECISELY the kinds of questions that the other standard narrative about the Philadelphia electoral system, which purports to focus on
issues of democratic participation, should ask. Alas, this story also ob-
scures and oversimplifies, depicting Article II's elaborate electoral machinery merely as a reflection of the framers' basic contempt of democracy
and their willingness to do anything to avoid direct popular elections.
Here, too, George Mason is often trotted out as the star witness: "It would
be as unnatural to refer the choice of a proper character for chief Magistrate to the people, as it would, to refer a trial of colours to a blind man."[55]

The notion that the framers disdained democracy runs counter to
much of the data we have seen thus far—an extraordinarily democratic
constitutional-ratification process; the direct election of House members; a
broad suffrage for House elections; national salaries for all lawmakers;
fixed elections and regular reapportionments; and a complete absence of
federal property qualifications. If Federalists truly loathed democracy,
why did Article II permit states to choose electors by direct popular vote—
as a substantial number of states did from the very beginning?[56] Why did
so many Federalists favor direct election of governors within individual
states even as they resisted direct national election of presidents?

Geography is surely part of the answer. Many eighteenth-century
Americans spent their entire lives within their home states and had only
limited direct knowledge of men from other parts of the continent. An ordinary voter might well have enough information to choose the best leader
from his town or county or even state, but how would he know which
continental character would be best to run the country? This in fact was
Mason's main point: "The extent of the Country renders it impossible that
the people can have the requisite capacity to judge of the respective pretensions of the Candidates." As in his "nineteen times in twenty" prediction,
Mason here failed to anticipate the emergence of national presidential parties that would link each major continental candidate to a broad slate of
regional and state politicians who might in turn vouch for their party
leader's vision and credentials. Once such parties developed, an ordinary
voter would not be a "blind man" and could well decide what he thought

of a presidential candidate's "colours." At Philadelphia, Abraham Baldwin predicted that "increasing [interstate] intercourse" would increase the visibility of national politicians, and Wilson concurred: "Continental Characters will multiply as we more & more coalesce."[57]

As soon as Washington stepped aside and informal national parties began to fill the political vacuum, presidential politics in the contests of 1796 and 1800 migrated toward broad citizen participation. Ordinary Americans who had never been directly involved in picking the Confederation's paltry presidents, or any other Confederation officials for that matter, made their voices heard and their votes count in energetic electoral spectacles conducted on a truly continental scale. In the wake of all this, the Twelfth Amendment knowingly facilitated national parties and thereby further encouraged mass participation in presidential politics.

To assess Article II's democratic bona fides, we must ask whether such unprecedented mass mobilizations of ordinary Americans were beginning to occur in spite of the federal Constitution or because of it. Regardless of what individual delegates at Philadelphia may have specifically intended, if the structure of Article II pulled America toward a populist presidency, the Constitution should be deemed pro-democracy. (So, too, it must be deemed proslavery, even if many delegates underestimated the foreseeable effects of the words "three fifths.")

By creating a vastly stronger central government headed by a vastly stronger president, the Constitution realigned political vectors in every state and fixed the gaze of both future leaders and future voters on America's new leading man. Essentially, the Philadelphia framers built a grand continental stage that attracted—indeed, created—continental political actors and a continental mass audience. True, the Constitution did not require direct democratic involvement by ordinary voters in the presidential selection process; but neither did the document prohibit voter participation. While Article I mandated direct election of House members and vested state legislatures with the choice of senators, Article II charted a middle path, allowing each state to decide for itself whether to let the voters or the legislators (or some third party) pick the electors. In practice, this formal agnosticism bent toward democracy: Once some states began to give their voters a direct say in the choice of electors—as happened from the beginning—it would prove hard in the long run for other states to withhold this privilege from their own voters. By 1804, most states let voters pick electors, and after 1828, only one state—South Carolina—continued to resist the democratic tide.[58]

The episodic nature of the elector system, featuring ad hoc officials chosen only once in four years for a single discrete purpose, opened up new pathways for political participation outside the channels of ordinary state and congressional elections. With each state allowed to name "a Number of Electors" identical to the number of its congressmen, it might have seemed only natural to permit states to name their congressmen individually or ex officio as electors. Yet the Constitution forbade these choices and also barred all federal executive and judicial officers from serving as electors. Instead, the document invited a broad range of other political actors, including amateurs, to serve as one-shot electors.

Breaking sharply with practice in the states and in England, Article II invited men from all classes to serve as electors and, indeed, to seek the presidency itself. Apart from Pennsylvania, which barely had a chief executive in 1787, every state's constitution imposed property qualifications on those voting and/or running for executive office. In Massachusetts, anyone with a freehold estate of £100 could serve in the General Assembly, while a governor had to own a freehold worth ten times that amount. Maryland required the governor to have real and personal property worth £5,000—more than 150 times the amount demanded of voters for the lower house—and South Carolina set the gubernatorial bar at a freehold estate worth £10,000 in currency, clear of debt.[59] In England, a royal head of state possessing untold riches picked prime ministers from the House of Commons, itself a highly propertied club. (The modern Westminster model, in which Parliament picks its own leader with minimal monarchial involvement, still lay in the future.)

As the American system would unfold over the nineteenth and twentieth centuries, roughly one quarter of her presidents would rise from genuinely humble origins. Lincoln received only a year of formal education in his entire life and grew up in a household that owned a mere handful of books. Several American presidents, including Ulysses S. Grant, would enter office with only modest net assets. In slighting Article II's extraordinary openness to men from all classes, the standard antidemocracy story misses much of the egalitarian drama of that Article and of the American presidency as it has in fact played out.

Behind closed doors, South Carolina's delegates at Philadelphia had voiced strong support for constitutionally fixed property qualifications for the president. At one point, Charles Pinckney floated the figure of $100,000 (the equivalent of nearly $2 million in today's economy). In the end, the Convention overwhelmingly rejected Pinckney's approach. Anything that made the president look like a king would diminish the document's popularity in the wide-open ratification elections ahead. Even

South Carolina's Rutledge, who favored property qualifications, noted the danger of "displeasing the people" with high barriers to high office. In Article II, as in Article I, the looming Preamble process of popular ratification thus pulled the Philadelphia plan toward increased democracy.[60]

In that ratification process, leading Federalists explained how the rules of electoral eligibility would promote democracy by discouraging corruption and self-dealing. English monarchs had traditionally manipulated members of Commons via patronage and financial preferment that at times amounted to rank bribery. By contrast, Article II excluded from the body of first-round electors anyone who, in the language of *The Federalist* No. 68, "might be suspected of too great devotion to the President in office"—namely, federal officeholders (some of whom were likely to have been appointed by the incumbent) and federal congressmen (some of whom might have needed the incumbent's signature for their salary bills or other pet projects). These eligibility rules thus aimed to create a level playing field between executive incumbents and challengers. Highlighting arguments that had earlier been sketched by Wilson, *The Federalist* explained how Article II would also make it impossible for any sinister operative to bribe electors, whose identities would not be known long in advance of their balloting, and who would meet in many separate states on the same day. A standing body of known congressmen or officers would have been easier targets for would-be bribers, both foreign and domestic. Hamilton/Publius laid particular emphasis on the corruption threat posed by "foreign powers," a threat made vivid by the manner in which Russia, Prussia, and Austria had managed to meddle in the election of Polish kings.[61]

In addition, Wilson and *The Federalist* emphasized that a system of independent electors would free the president from undue dependence on the Congress, in contrast to the many states where legislators directly chose governors. Both the anticorruption and the antidependence arguments stressed the rules of the qualifying heat, implicitly challenging Mason's closed-door prediction that "nineteen times in twenty" contests would ultimately be decided in Congress itself. In trying to persuade Pennsylvanians and New Yorkers, Wilson and Hamilton had little reason to portray the presidency as tilted in favor of small states.

Instead, leading Federalists in leading states highlighted the populism of Article II. Wilson declared that "the choice of [the president] is brought as nearly home to the people as is practicable. With the approbation of the state legislatures, the people may elect with only one remove."[62] *The Federalist* No. 68 went a step further, repeatedly speaking of popular selection of electors as if it were a constitutional command or a foreordained conclusion[63] (and mentioning the possibility of a final round in Congress in a single passing sentence). In Virginia, Madison likewise asserted that, under Article II, "the people choose the electors."[64]

At Philadelphia, Wilson had advocated direct national election of the president. In the ratification process, he briefly alluded to this possibility, noting that New York and New England picked governors by direct popular vote. But, said he, "it was the opinion of a great majority in [the Philadelphia] Convention, that the thing was impracticable; other embarrassments presented themselves"—a point echoed by Madison in Virginia. "Perhaps it [would] be impracticable to elect [the president] by the immediate suffrages of the people." Just what were these impracticalities and embarrassments? If electors would limit corruption and undue executive dependence on the legislature, wouldn't direct national election have done so as well?[65]

Though neither Wilson nor Madison nor Publius offered detailed public answers to these questions, three main factors—information barriers, federalism, and slavery—doomed direct presidential election in 1787. We have already glimpsed the information problem: Ordinary voters might not know enough to evaluate presidential candidates from faraway states. Interstate networks of communication and political coordination were not an established fact in 1787—in part because no continental office of any significance existed. As a continental political system took root in future years, sturdy interstate networks might eventually splay out, and a system of ad hoc presidential electors would smoothly accommodate the possibly uneven growth of such networks. In those states and years in which ordinary voters felt ill equipped to judge for themselves, they could choose to give broad discretion to trusted local notables "most likely to possess the information and discernment requisite."[66] In other states and other years in which voters felt that they knew enough to evaluate the leading candidates, and especially to assess the track record of an incumbent president, they could choose electors pledged to their preferred candidate, with electors operating as instructed agents rather than independent actors.

Interstate informational networks were not the only requisite direct-election structure absent in 1787. No sturdy national administrative apparatus existed, either. This was the federalism dilemma: A direct national election would be hard to administer before an extensive national government existed to administer it. In a system of direct election, any state that boosted its turnout would have more clout in the final tally. Without an elaborate regime of federal voting monitors in every precinct, could vote fraud be prevented? Suppose a state decided to inflate its vote totals by reducing its voting age by a year? By five years? What if a state enfranchised its women, thereby doubling its vote total in the national tally? Direct national election would have required a matrix of constitutional and/or congressional rules defining eligible electorates, just as individual states with direct election of governors had rules and regimes in place limiting localities.

When confronting similar issues in both the Preamble and Article I, the Philadelphia delegates ultimately opted to piggyback onto state-law systems and thus avoid direct national legislation and administration. With its grand language of ordainment by "the People," the Preamble invited the broadest realistically imaginable suffrage for ratification, but the precise implementation of that ideal rested with individual state governments that prescribed and administered specific rules for their respective ratifying conventions. Similarly, Article I tied federal House elections to state suffrage rules and pegged House apportionment to the number of a state's inhabitants rather than the number of its voters. Had the Philadelphia plan used the voter metric (as did New York for state apportionment purposes), the document would have created incentives for a state to win more House seats by expanding its franchise; and in turn this foreseeable dynamic would have required a more detailed federal regulatory framework. As actually drafted, Article I avoided the thicket—as did Article II. Whether a given state had a broad or narrow franchise was irrelevant to the number of House seats or electors it could claim.

THIS BRINGS US TO the biggest democratic defect of Article II, a factor that is too rarely featured in standard electoral-college stories: slavery.[67] Early on at Philadelphia, Wilson made the case for direct national election of America's first man. Admitting that some might think it "chimerical," in theory "he was for an election by the people. Experience, particularly in N. York & Massts, shewed that an election of the first magistrate by the people at large, was both a convenient & successful mode." In a pair of later speeches, Gouverneur Morris embellished the idea. Invoking the state governorships in New York and Connecticut, Morris declared that the federal executive "ought to be elected by the people at large, by the freeholders of the Country," who would be the best judge of the executive's policies, as they "will know, will see, [and] will feel the effects of them." Looking ahead to the ratification process, Morris added that popular election combined with short terms of office would render the Philadelphia plan "extremely palatable to the people." Rufus King of Massachusetts chimed in that he was "much disposed to think" that in picking America's chief executive "the people at large would chuse wisely," whereupon Wilson "perceived with pleasure that the idea was gaining ground, of an election mediately or immediately by the people."[68]

Enter James Madison, who chose this precise moment to spell out in unmistakably clear terms a vital difference between a direct ("immediate") election and a system mediated by specially chosen electors: Southern slaves would not count in any direct-election system but could be factored into an electoral-college system. Although "the people at large was in his opinion the fittest" body to choose the federal executive, "there was one difficulty however of a serious nature attending an immediate choice by the people. The right of suffrage was much more diffusive [i.e., extensive] in the Northern than the Southern States; and the latter could have no influence in the election on the score of the Negroes. The substitution of electors obviated this difficulty and seemed on the whole to be liable to the fewest objections."[69] A week later, Madison returned to the point, noting the "disproportion of qualified voters in the N. & S. States, and the disadvantages which [direct national election] would throw on the latter." As a self-described "individual from the S. States," Madison nevertheless pronounced himself "willing to make the sacrifice" in favor of direct election—in part because he anticipated that the South's free population would grow at a faster rate than the North's and that its franchise would broaden over time, and in part because "local considerations must give way to the general interest."[70]

No other Southerner answered Madison's call for regional sacrifice. After his mathematical exposition, making explicit what previous speakers had at most hinted at, direct election was doomed. Even before Madison's intervention, leading Southerners such as Charles Pinckney, Hugh Williamson, and George Mason had spoken against a direct national vote. They were not the only ones—Northerner Roger Sherman, for example, was also an early critic. Nevertheless, it is worth noting that the two most vocal proponents of direct election, Wilson and Morris, came from the free state of Pennsylvania, which boasted a hefty, fast-growing population and imposed virtually no property qualifications on its voters. In any system of direct election, such a state would loom large—a point cryptically alluded to by North Carolina's Williamson after multiple speeches by the Pennsylvanians: "The people will be sure to vote for some man in their own State, and the largest State will be sure to succede. This will not be Virg[inia] however. Her slaves will have no suffrage."[71]

But Virginia would indeed emerge as the big winner under an electoral-college system giving slave states three-fifths credit for their bondsmen. Under America's first census and apportionment, Virginia would receive six more House seats, and thus six more electors, than Pennsylvania, although the two commonwealths at that point had roughly comparable free populations. After the next census, Virginia got 20 percent more electors than did Pennsylvania, even as the Old Dominion had 10 percent fewer free citizens and far fewer eligible voters. For thirty-two of the presidency's first thirty-six years, a (slaveholding, plantation-owning) Virginian would occupy the nation's highest office.

Throughout the antebellum era, pro-Southern candidates—either Southerners themselves or "Northern men with Southern principles"— would enjoy a large head start in presidential races by dint of the three-fifths clause as incorporated into the elector system. Pro-Southern presidents in turn meant pro-Southern cabinets. According to Professor Fehrenbacher's eye-opening tally, "no prominent antislavery leader was appointed to high federal [executive] office before Lincoln's administration" yet "no southerner was too extreme in his proslavery views to be ineligible for such an honor."[72]

Slavery not only illuminates the rules of Article II, but also casts light on related issues of antebellum state practice. We have seen that in the decade after the federal Constitution's ratification, six of the eight states with new or revised state constitutions embraced direct election of governors. The only two that did not were the two most southerly, South Carolina and Georgia. In 1824, these two and their Deep South neighbor Louisiana were among the vanishing minority of states—six out of twenty-four—that still declined to let voters choose presidential electors. By 1860, South Carolina stood as the only state that refused to allow its citizens to directly elect the governor and also as the only state that refused to let its voters directly choose presidential electors. What might explain this pattern in the Southern heartland? In a word, slavery. South Carolina's legislature was grossly malapportioned to favor its plantation belt. Georgia, though less egregious, also gave plantation districts more seats than their numbers of voters would have warranted; starting in 1798, the state explicitly counted blacks at three-fifths in apportioning state house seats. In these states, legislative election of electors and governors amplified the influence of plantation regions in the federal and state executive-selection processes. Had South Carolina embraced statewide elections of electors or governors on a one-person, one-vote basis, this would have meant less power for the state's plantations, just as direct national elections of the president would have meant less power for the nation's plantations.[73]

Article II thus accommodated slavery doubly (as did Article I). First, at the *interstate* level, the Constitution allowed all slave states to inflate their electoral-college (and House) allocations via the three-fifths clause. Second, at the *intrastate* level, the Constitution's formal agnosticism about state methods for choosing electors (and House members) allowed slavery-skewed state legislators broad discretion to give slaveholding regions within a state more than their fair share of electoral-college (and congressional) clout.

"thirty five Years"

By this point in our story, a clear picture is beginning to emerge concerning the relationship between the late-eighteenth-century Constitution and early-nineteenth-century America. Many modern students have been taught that the Founders' Constitution was neither pro-democracy nor proslavery. Yet America in the age of Alexis de Tocqueville and Andrew Jackson was both, it is widely admitted. How did a supposedly aristocratic and antislavery document yield such a democratic and proslavery regime?

The best answer is that the basic structure of the original Constitution was more Jacksonian than standard stories suggest—more welcoming of mass democracy, more open to lowborn and unpropertied (white) men, more proslavery and pro-Southern, and also, as we shall see in later chapters, more pro-Western and territorially expansionist. The modern suspicion that the Philadelphia plan was at heart an elitist scheme to prop up the haves and hem in the have-nots needs revising, as does the complacent view that the Constitution was essentially neutral on slavery or even anti-slavery in spirit. The abiding heart and spirit of the document lay in the structure of its rules for political participation and political power, and these rules were, as we have seen, generally populist yet also proslavery.

The structure of Article II's rules of presidential eligibility furnishes further evidence of the Constitution's populism and liberality, slavery aside. Let's begin by considering the clause excluding candidates "who shall not have attained to the Age of thirty five Years."

At first, it might seem that any limitation whatsoever on the choices of the electorate could never be described as democratic or egalitarian. (From this perspective, it is worth noting how few eligibility rules Article II actually imposed—a handful of modest requirements limited to age, residence, and citizenship.) But from another angle, the age limit also liberated, promoting a broader democratic culture of republican merit and equal opportunity.

In which foreseeable scenarios, after all, might someone less than thirty-five years old command enough continental popularity to win the presidency, but for the bar of Article II? Perhaps a dashing young military hero might one day charm the nation. To the extent that the Article II age clause required young men in uniform to prove themselves more generally, the clause meshed with many other constitutional rules limiting the professional military.

The more likely scenario underlying the age clause involved favorite sons—young men who sprang from famous fathers but had yet to show their own true colors. Instead of being evaluated based on their individual merits and vices, as revealed by a long track record of personal accomplishment and failure, such favorite sons would unfairly benefit from their high birth status and distinguished family name, thus retarding the growth of a truly republican society equally open to meritorious men of humble and middling origin.

Madison's notes contain nothing directly bearing on the drafting history of this clause, and it generated only modest commentary during the ratification period (making it no different from many other important constitutional clauses). What evidence does exist, however, strongly supports an egalitarian reading of the seemingly bland words "thirty five Years"—words that had no counterpart in English law or state constitutions.*

Anti-Federalist critics worried that American presidents would come to resemble British kings. As the *Federal Farmer* put the point, "When a man shall get the chair, who may be re-elected, from time to time, for life, his greatest object will be to keep it; to gain friends and votes, at any rate [i.e., price]; to associate some favourite son with himself, to take the office after him: whenever he shall have any prospect of continuing the office in himself and family, he will spare no artifice, no address, and no exertions. . . ."[74] Anticipating and answering just such anxieties about hereditary succession and "favourite son[s]," Federalists deployed the Article II age clause in a strongly egalitarian fashion. Tench Coxe argued that while Britain's king "is hereditary, and may be an ideot, a knave, or a tyrant by nature," America's president "cannot be an ideot, [and] probably not a

---

*Only one state had a special age limit for governors, and that state—North Carolina—set the bar at thirty years of age.

knave or tyrant, for those whom nature makes so discover [i.e., reveal] it before the age of thirty-five, until which period he cannot be elected."[75] According to another Federalist pamphlet, a president would be highly unlikely to mutate into a "hereditary sovereign" because no American citizen would have "a fortune sufficiently large" or an official "salary . . . []adequate . . . to the purpose of gaining [i.e., bribing] adherents, or of supporting a military force. . . . Besides, the Constitution has provided, that no person shall be eligible to the office, who is not thirty-five years old; and in the course of nature very few fathers leave a son who has arrived to that age."[76]

By their actions in early presidential elections, the American people showed themselves acutely aware of issues of dynastic succession. Part of the reason that George Washington was "first in war, first in peace, and first in the hearts of his countrymen" was that his countrymen knew that he lacked dynastic ambitions. He became father of his country because he was not father of any potential princely successors. He sired no heirs, and his only stepson died in 1781. American republicans could breathe easier knowing that their first general and first president would not try to create a throne and a crown to pass on to some namesake (George II?). Interestingly, the man many contemporaries kept the closest watch on was Alexander Hamilton, himself fatherless, who at times played the role of the good son Washington never had, first as Washington's aide-de-camp during the Revolution and later as his leading cabinet minister.

Of the first five presidents, only one had any (acknowledged) sons.[77] That one was John Adams, whose heir John Quincy Adams did indeed become president—but only in his mid-fifties after a distinguished political career in his own right. A Phi Beta Kappa graduate of Harvard and later a Harvard professor; an accomplished diplomat fluent in several languages, with decades of experience in foreign affairs, including a successful eight-year stint as secretary of state under a president not closely associated with his father—here was a man with extraordinary credentials of his own. Moreover, John Quincy's entrance onto the presidential stage occurred a quarter-century after his father's exit. In 1801, when his father left office, he was not even old enough to run, thanks to the thirty-five-years clause.*

Washington himself understood the dynasty dynamic. In the first

---

*In light of primogeniture and related practices in early America, it is worth noting that none of the first seven presidents had an older brother who ever reached the age of presidential eligibility. Five were eldest sons, Washington's two older half-brothers died in their early thirties, and Jackson's two elder brothers died in their teens.

draft of his First Inaugural Address, he wrote that "Divine Providence hath not seen fit, that my blood should be transmitted or my name perpetuated by the endearing, though sometimes seducing channel of immediate offspring. I have no child for whom I could wish to make a provision—no family to build in greatness upon my Country's ruins. . . . [No] earthly consideration beyond the hope of rendering some little service to our parent Country . . . could have persuaded me to accept this appointment."[78]

When, seven years later, this childless man announced his retirement, dynastic concerns burst into open view as Americans turned their eyes to other Founding Fathers. One Boston paper warned that Adams, if elected, would work to install his *well born* sons as "the Seigneurs or Lords of this country," while Jefferson, with "daughters only," could be trusted. In Pennsylvania, a widely circulated campaign sheet labeled Adams "an avowed monarchist" who "says . . . that some men should be born Kings, and some men should be born Nobles." The broadside went on to stress that "Adams has Sons who might aim to succeed their father. Jefferson, like Washington, has no Son."[79]

In many colonies, political power had regularly flowed through dynastic channels. According to Gordon Wood, it was commonplace in provincial America for fathers to resign their government positions in favor of their sons. Wood has also reported that in the half-century before independence, more than 70 percent of the representatives elected to New Jersey's assembly had family ties to earlier representatives. A similar pattern prevailed in South Carolina.[80] John Adams observed that "every village in New England" had positions that, although filled by "the freest election of the people" nevertheless "generally descended from generation to generation, in three or four families at most."[81] Adams might well have said the same thing about some appointive offices, at least in his home colony. For several months in 1771, two of five justices on Massachusetts's highest court were the sons of previous justices, and yet a third was the younger brother of a previous chief justice. In turn, one of the sons would soon be followed on the court by his own son. All told, nine of the ten men appointed to the court between 1746 and 1772 had relatives who had served or would serve on the court.[82]

In response, Revolutionary state constitutions condemned the idea of automatic hereditary government service. According to the Virginia Bill of Rights, "the offices of magistrate, legislator, or judge" ought not "be hereditary."[83] Maryland's and North Carolina's constitutions condemned "hereditary honours," "emoluments," and "privileges,"[84] and New Hampshire's constitution declared that "no office or place whatsoever in government, shall be hereditary—the abilities and integrity requisite in all, not being transmissible to posterity or relations."[85] Perhaps the most emphatic language came from the pen of John Adams himself, as lead draftsman of the Massachusetts Constitution of 1780: "[Public service] being in nature neither hereditary, nor transmissible to children, or descendants, or relations by blood, the idea of a man born a magistrate, law-giver, or judge, is absurd and unnatural."[86]

Such state constitutional language prohibited government from creating formally hereditary positions of government power but did nothing to address the special advantages favoring the well born in democratic elections. Article II's age clause went a step further, creating a clean and easily enforceable rule leveling the playing field somewhat, obliging favorite sons to bide their time and show their stuff and giving other men a chance to show theirs. Article II did not go so far as to bar capable sons from entering the family business of politics—and with good reason. An absolute prohibition on father-son succession would have eerily resembled the odious old English practice of punishing the children of certain disfavored politicians via "corruption of blood."[87] An absolute bar on favorite sons would also have permanently denied the republic the option of picking someone who might well be the ablest, most distinguished person, such as a mature John Quincy Adams.

The Article II age clause fit snugly into a larger egalitarian pattern. Just as Article II required presidents to be thirty-five years old, so Article I required House members to be twenty-five and senators thirty—graduated rules that gave lower-born men a chance to outshine famous favorite sons.[88] (The Article I age clauses additionally addressed possible concerns about an interstate scramble for future federal honors—concerns inapplicable to a continentally elected president.)

The presence or absence of literal favorite sons also illuminates how the Article II phrase, "four Years," played out in the early republic. The *Federal Farmer* had worried that presidents might seek continued reelection until their sons could succeed them. But beginning with Washington, many early presidents permanently stepped aside after a term or two. Might these men have been less willing to yield to other leaders (and families) had there been literal favorite sons yearning to fill their fathers' shoes?[89] Interestingly enough, none of the first seven presidents who ultimately declined to seek reelection had a biological son and heir. Not until Rutherford B. Hayes, in the early 1880s, would such a father ever permanently walk away from power rather than seek another term. Before Hayes, five of the six childless presidents had simply walked away, as had both of the presidents with only daughters, but none of the ten presidents with sons had followed this lead. Rather, every one of the ten either died in office or finally quit the presidential scene only after losing a bid for more years in power.[90]

"a natural born Citizen"

Early America's evident concerns about presidential dynasties also lurked beneath Article II's most questionable eligibility rule: its requirement that a president be a "natural born Citizen"—that is, a citizen at the time of his birth.[91] By generally prohibiting immigrants-turned-citizens from the presidency, Article II limited both the electorate's choice set and the career options of would-be candidates. Though seemingly illiberal on this point, the Constitution in fact represented a considerable liberalization of eighteenth-century English practice. Under England's famous 1701 Act of Settlement, naturalized foreigners could never serve in the Privy Council or Parliament, or enjoy any office or place of trust, either civil or military. By contrast, the Constitution opened virtually all federal positions—the Congress, the judiciary, the cabinet, and the military—to naturalized citizens. In fact, immigrant Americans would account for roughly one-tenth of the membership of the First Congress, a third of the first Supreme Court, four of the nation's first six secretaries of the treasury, and one of its first three secretaries of war.[92] Only the presidency and vice presidency were reserved for birth-citizens.

Even this reservation would not apply so as to exclude any immigrants who were already American citizens in 1787, men who had proved their loyalty by coming to or remaining in America during the Revolution. Seven of the thirty-nine Philadelphia signers were themselves foreign-born,[93] and during the ratification process, countless naturalized Americans voted on equal terms with their natural-born fellow citizens. If we view the Constitution in deed as well as word, the specific bar of Article II would seem a relatively narrow exception proving the general rule of openness to immigrant Americans.

Why did the Founders create even this narrow exception? If we imagine a poor boy coming to America and rising through the political system by dint of his own sweat and virtue only to find himself barred at the top, the natural-born rule surely looks antiegalitarian. In 1787, however, the more salient scenario involved the possibility that a foreign earl or duke might cross the Atlantic with immense wealth and a vast retinue, and then use his European riches to buy friends on a scale that no home-grown citizen could match. No such grandee had yet reached America's shores. Thus it made republican sense to extend eligibility to existing foreign-born citizens, yet it also made sense to anticipate all the ways that European aristocracy might one day try to pervert American democracy. Out of an abundance of caution—paranoia, perhaps—the framing generation barred not only European-style titles of nobility, but also European noblemen themselves (along with all other future immigrants) from America's most powerful and dangerous office.

Modern historians have uncovered evidence suggesting that several months before the Philadelphia Convention, Confederation President (and later Philadelphia delegate) Nathaniel Gorham had, via Baron Frederick von Steuben, written to Prince Henry of Prussia, brother of Frederick the Great, to inquire whether the prince might consider coming to America to serve as a constitutional monarch.[94] Though few in 1787 knew of this feeler (if it in fact existed), the summerlong secret sessions in Philadelphia did fuel rampant speculation out of doors that the delegates were working to fasten a monarchy upon America. According to historian Max Farrand, "The common form of the rumor was that the Bishop of Osnaburgh, the second son of George III, was to be invited to become King of the United States."[95] To counter such speculation, some delegates anonymously planted a newspaper item in mid-August, a month before the curtain of official silence was lifted: "Tho' we cannot, affirmatively, tell you what we are doing, we can, negatively, tell you what we are not doing—we never once thought of a king."[96] In early September, the Convention added the natural-born clause, a provision that, while overinclusive, would surely lay to rest public anxieties about foreign monarchs.[97]

These anxieties had been fed by England's 1701 Act, which inclined early Americans to associate the very idea of a foreign-born head of state with the larger issue of monarchical government. Though England banned foreigners from all other posts, it imposed no natural-born requirement on the head of state himself. In fact, the 1701 Act explicitly contemplated foreign-born future monarchs—the German House of Hanover, in particular. By 1787 this continental royal family had produced three English kings named George, only the third of whom had been born in England itself. Article II's natural-born language squarely rejected the 1701 idea of future foreign-born heads of state, in no small part because many republicans had come to link the idea (perhaps more sociologically than logically) with hereditary succession and foreign intrigue. Foreign-born princes might be good enough to rule in the Old World but should be kept out of the New World order—or at least the New World presidency.

HAVING CONSIDERED THE CATEGORIES of candidates that the Constitution barred from the presidency, we should also consider the categories that it did *not* bar. Article II not only omitted property qualifications for would-be presidents, but also pointedly avoided religious prerequisites or disqualifications. Article VI broadened the principle beyond the presidency and phrased it in emphatic language: "no religious Test shall ever be required as a Qualification to *any* Office or public Trust under the United States."

This formal openness to men of any religion or no religion ran well ahead of contemporary Anglo-American practice. Britain's Act of Settlement required that all future English monarchs join in Anglican communion. As of 1787, eleven American states—nine in their state constitutions, no less—imposed religious qualifications on government officials, and no state constitution explicitly barred religious tests for public servants.[98] Article VI thus broke new ground, as did early American practice under Article II. Thanks to the broad power they enjoyed under the liberal eligibility rules of the Constitution, early American electors were free to choose, and did in fact freely choose, presidents of various denominations and even some men with no explicit religious affiliation, such as Jefferson and Lincoln.

Shortly after Americans ratified the federal Constitution, the state constitutional pattern began to change. Among the original states that revised their constitutions in the decade after 1788, all but one moved toward increased religious openness. Three states eliminated all constitutional language requiring religious tests, and a fourth significantly narrowed the scope of religious exclusion.[99] Delaware moved all the way from requiring belief in the Holy Trinity in 1776 to a flat prohibition on all religious tests in 1792. The influence of the federal Constitution was obvious on the face of the 1792 document, which tracked the Article VI religious-test clause virtually verbatim. Here, too, the federal Preamble process helped propel the state bandwagon toward modernity.

"Death, Resignation or Inability"

In the sentence immediately following the presidential-eligibility clause, Article II pointedly rejected other aspects of England's Act of Settlement as well. In the event of the English monarch's death or abdication, the 1701 Act prescribed a line of hereditary succession that, as with most hereditary systems, might conceivably vest supreme executive power in a child, a knave, or a fool. By contrast, in the event of presidential "Removal" via conviction in an impeachment court, or presidential "Death, Resignation or Inability," presidential power would flow to a vice president whom Americans had already endorsed as a continental statesman of exceptional stature. Under the Philadelphia plan, the runner-up in the presidential race automatically became vice president. In its early years, when this plan operated as foreseen, it generated vice presidents of undeniable eminence—men who would in fact later win election to the presidency itself, John Adams and Thomas Jefferson.

Aside from the effects of the three-fifths clause, which influenced the vice presidency no less than the presidency itself, the selection rules for the Constitution's second-highest office marked an evident democratic improvement on American colonial practice. In royal and proprietary colonies, lieutenant or deputy governors customarily enjoyed no more democratic legitimacy than governors themselves. Both sets of officers were picked by English monarchs or aristocrats rather than chosen by the people or their representatives.

Whether the vice-presidential selection system represented an advance over the best systems devised by state constitutions in the decade after independence was more doubtful. In most states, lieutenant governors hardly mattered because governors themselves had few real powers and no independent electoral base. In Massachusetts and New York, where statewide voters picked powerful governors, the electorate chose lieutenant governors by separate ballot. By contrast, Article II did not allow federal electors to vote separately for vice president. Instead, electors had to cast two presidential ballots, at least one of which had to go to an out-of-state candidate. The idea behind this intricate double-ballot system was to generate support for continental candidates. Many framers fretted that if given only one vote, each elector would likely support his home state's leading candidate at the expense of candidates with broader national appeal. Double balloting promised to cure this problem by inducing each elector to give one vote to a local candidate and the other vote to a more national figure. Ideally, second votes would settle on men who might be everyone's second choice—broadly acceptable leaders of wide geographic repute. To discourage electors from warping the system by wasting their out-of-state votes on frivolous candidates—thereby reverting to a fractured contest among local favorites—the framers provided that the runner-up in the presidential race would serve as vice president. Not only would this runner-up stand a proverbial heartbeat away from the presidency itself, but he would also preside over the Senate and break its tie votes. The nation's first vice president would end up tipping the Senate balance on twenty separate occasions.[100] Electors thus had good reason to take their out-of-state votes seriously.

As the system took root, no artificial boost to national candidates proved necessary. The very power of the presidency and the emergence of a stronger national government and national party structure themselves attracted and created continental candidates. Once national coalitions began to organize around the presidency, any state that clung to a local favorite lacking national appeal did so at the expense of making itself irrelevant to the real race. The emergence of presidential parties, however, made double balloting problematic. If all party electors supported the party's top two candidates for office, these men would end up in a tie (as did Jefferson and Burr in 1800–01), thus throwing the contest into the House, which might be controlled (as indeed it was in the Jefferson-Burr affair) by the other party. If, instead, a few party electors strategically diverted votes from their second-choice candidate so as to avoid a tie, they would open a window for the other party's top candidate to come in second overall and thus become vice president, as happened in 1796. Even if the American electorate preferred a unitary party ticket, the quirks of the double-ballot system might conspire to place a sworn political foe of the president a heartbeat away from supreme power. Such a system was hardly a model of political stability and might even encourage assassinations. Thus, once presidential parties began to take shape, the Twelfth Amendment eliminated double balloting in favor of separate elections of presidents and vice presidents, à la Massachusetts and New York.

OTHER ASPECTS OF the Article II succession system represented distinct improvements on English law and state practice. England not only allowed the Crown to descend to a known mental incompetent, but also had no stable system in place for withdrawing power from a once-competent monarch who later lost his wits. Massachusetts permitted lieutenant governors to take over in the event of gubernatorial deaths or absences from the chair, and New York provided for transfers of power in cases of death, resignation, removal from office, absence from the state, and impeachment. Neither state constitution explicitly addressed mental-disability scenarios.[101]

The more carefully drawn Article II expressly provided for power transfers in cases of presidential "Inability"—presumably covering mental infirmities as well as physical breakdowns, hostage situations, and all other contingencies in which a president might be unable to perform his duties. Although Article II declined to specify exactly what might constitute "Inability," how it should be determined, or by whom, the general language of the Article I necessary-and-proper clause invited Congress to enact legislation regulating the executive department on these issues.

Alas, Congress never accepted the invitation even as various arguable inabilities arose from time to time over the next two centuries. Ultimately, in the shadow of President John F. Kennedy's assassination, America ratified the Twenty-fifth Amendment, which built on Article II's foundations and erected a relatively comprehensive framework governing myriad succession contingencies. We shall study this amendment in our final chapter. For now, let us merely note that the core Article II idea of transferring executive power in the event of executive inability drew strength from both republican principles and national-security practicalities. As a matter of principle, no man had a private right to rule in a manner that disserved the larger public interest. If a president could no longer do his job, it should go to someone who could. Thus, the inability clause was a concrete application of abstract statements in several state constitutions to the effect that perquisites of government power should exist only "in consideration of public services."[102] As a matter of practicality, an unfit president with an extensive term and weighty responsibilities for national defense could, by both commissions and omissions, imperil his fellow citizens infinitely more than could an incompetent state governor or a single incompetent federal lawmaker.

Similar considerations induced the Philadelphia framers to anticipate scenarios involving the "Removal, Death, Resignation or Inability, both of the President and Vice President." When both men were permanently unavailable, Article II invited a special off-year national election to fill the remainder of the missing president's term. In the meantime, an "Officer" designated by Congress would act as interim president.

Article II did not flamboyantly draw attention to the accelerated election contingency. The bland text merely said that an interim president would yield when "the [presidential or vice-presidential] Disability be removed, or a President shall be elected." Both drafters and ratifiers nevertheless understood that this terse clause authorized Congress to provide for early elections. At Philadelphia, a preliminary version of the clause had proposed that in the event of double death/removal/resignation, an officer designated by law would act as president "until the time of electing a President shall arrive." Madison objected that this wording "would prevent a supply of the vacancy by an intermediate election of the President"—that is, an election "at other than the fixed [quadrennial] periods." He thus offered as a substitute the bland words that now appear at the end of the clause, a substitute that the Convention promptly accepted although some delegates noted the difficulties that a special election might entail.[103] In the Virginia ratification debates, when Mason complained that "there is no provision for a speedy election of another President, when the former is dead or removed," Madison responded that "when the President and Vice President die, the election of another President will immediately take place."[104]

This overstated the case; Congress could provide for such an election but was not obliged to do so. Late in any four-year term, a special election might not be worth the trouble, given the impending regular election. Yet merely by inviting special elections, the Constitution evidenced its commitment to an unprecedented level of democracy. No state constitution provided for accelerated recourse to the voters in a comparable situation. The unique special-election option in Article II also reflected the distinctive actuarial risks attending a four-year presidential term and the awkwardness of allowing an entire nation to be led for long periods by an interim officer lacking a strong personal mandate.

Four years after Madison's remarks in Virginia, Congress adopted a presidential-succession law that provided for an automatic special presidential election whenever a double disaster occurred within the first two and a half years of a presidential term. However, Madison sharply criticized the other key feature of the 1792 law, which designated the Senate president pro tempore (and if he were unavailable, the speaker of the House) as the interim chief executive in double-vacancy situations.*[105]

Madison had a good point. True, Article II empowered Congress to regulate double-vacancy situations "by Law"—that is, by a statute presumably enacted in advance of any tragedy and presented to a fit president for his signature or veto. But the Constitution explicitly provided that Congress should declare *what Officer* shall then act as President, and such *Officer* shall act accordingly" until the disability ended or a new president won election. What exactly did "Officer" mean in this context? An early Philadelphia draft had specified that Congress must choose an "officer *of the United States.*" A style committee later shortened the clause with no ap-

---

*Article I, section 3 provided that ordinarily, the vice president would preside over the Senate, but it went on to allow senators to elect a temporary chair—a Senate "President pro tempore"— to fill in when the vice president was absent.

parent intention of changing its meaning.[106] The Senate president pro tempore and House speaker might be "officer[s]" of their respective houses, but could just any "officer" satisfy the succession clause? Could Congress pick a state "officer," or a local sheriff—or the president of a private cricket club, for that matter?

Surely, Senate and House leaders were not "officer[s] of the United States"—a constitutional term of art reserved for members of the executive and judicial branches. In fact, the Article I, section 6 incompatibility clause made emphatically clear that no sitting congressman could simultaneously "hold[] any Office under the United States." Whereas English monarchs had seduced members of Commons with plum appointments and commissions, American-style separation of powers demanded that any congressman accepting a federal executive or judicial "Office" immediately resign from the legislature. A companion anticorruption clause forbade any congressman from accepting a federal executive or judicial office that had been created, or whose salary had been increased, on his legislative watch.[107]

In Madison's view, the letter and spirit of these Article I provisions argued against allowing a legislative leader to act as interim president. The instant such a lawmaker became acting president, he would thereby "hold[]" an "Office under the United States" and thus be obliged by the incompatibility clause to quit Congress. This point was not only textually explicit but structurally essential: No man could be entrusted, even temporarily, with authority to preside over both the legislature and the executive simultaneously. This was the precise thrust of Article I, section 3, which pointedly relieved the vice president of his ordinary duties as Senate presiding officer whenever he was called upon to "exercise the Office of President." Similar logic would require the immediate resignation of a Senate president pro tempore or a speaker of the House acting as interim president. Yet once he resigned, the ex–legislative leader would no longer even be a congressional "officer." In what sense would he continue to meet the succession clause's "officer" requirement? In effect, the ex-leader would have pulled the rug out from under his own feet.

No such problem would arise if Congress instead designated an executive "officer"—say, the secretary of state—to act as interim president. Such a secretary could formally continue to hold his cabinet office while temporarily performing the duties of the presidency. No constitutional clause or principle barred a man from discharging two *executive branch* offices. In fact, executive deputies often filled in temporarily for their chiefs. (In Madison's own later presidential administration, James Monroe for a time would act as both secretary of war and secretary of state.)[108] Thus, Madison believed that the succession clause should be implemented by devolving interim presidential power on some cabinet officer who had been handpicked by the very president whose vacancy he would fill, and who would likely be intimately familiar with whatever executive policy issues might be pending when the double vacancy happened to arise. In turn, such an officer could choose to hand off many of his cabinet chores to an undersecretary within the department. Madison buttressed this argument by stressing Article II's slightly stilted syntax, which authorized Congress to declare "*what* Officer," as opposed to "*which* Officer," would act as interim president. The word "what" focused more on the post than the person, suggesting an ex officio augmentation of power to some specified government position.[109]

Even if a congressional leader might somehow resign from Congress without thereby disqualifying himself, resignation would surely raise serious problems in cases of temporary disability, as opposed to permanent vacancies occasioned by death, removal, or resignation. What would happen when the president (and/or vice president) recovered? The ex-lawmaker would have no legislative seat to reclaim automatically; indeed, a successor congressman might have been chosen in the interim. Such issues would not arise if a cabinet officer stepped up for his boss and then stepped down when the disability had subsided.[110]

But *what* cabinet position should be designated vice-vice president, ex officio? There was the rub in 1792. Secretary of State Jefferson naturally thought that his office ranked first, while Treasury Secretary Hamilton had different ideas. Madison himself noted that "there [was] much delicacy in the matter," prompting Congress to throw up its hands and put forward its own leaders.[111]

This hardly ended the matter. Since 1792, the American people have ratified no fewer than three constitutional amendments—the Twelfth, the Twentieth, and the Twenty-fifth—modifying the relevant constitutional rules and principles. Also, Congress has twice revised the statutory framework for double-vacancy succession. In 1886, Congress moved in Madison's direction, eliminating legislative leaders from the line of succession and placing the secretary of state first in line after the vice president. In 1947, Congress put legislative chieftains back at the top of the list (this time with the House leader ahead of his Senate counterpart) and omitted any plan for off-year presidential elections. As we shall see in our final chapter, this 1947 statute, which is still on the books, not only disregards

Madison's vision, but also runs counter to the spirit of the Twenty-fifth Amendment, which postdates the statute.[112]

The 1947 rules have never been put to the supreme test of actual operation. Nor did either predecessor statute ever result in a statutory succession. While the nation has witnessed many presidential and vice-presidential deaths, resignations, and disabilities, the two top offices have never lain vacant simultaneously. Although America has not always been smart, at least she has been lucky—so far.

Chapter 5

PRESIDENTIAL
POWERS

KING ANDREW THE FIRST (1833).
President Jackson, with veto message in hand and judicial opinions underfoot. In his eight years in office, Jackson eventually vetoed twelve bills.

$\mathcal{A}$FTER SPECIFYING HOW America would choose her president and who could (and could not) act as first officer, Article II turned to the delicate task of elaborating this officer's rights and responsibilities. While the document reposed a stunning amount of power in one man, it took pains to ensure that America's chief lawmaker/diplomat/general/prosecutor/administrator/et cetera would always remain strongly accountable to his ultimate master: the American people.

"I will . . . defend the Constitution"

In the center of an impersonal legal text setting forth general rules and principles lay a strikingly personal passage revolving around the words "I" and "my"—words that appeared nowhere else in the Constitution. These words should remind us, if we somehow needed reminding, that the presidency was (and for that matter, still is) America's most personal office. Thus, the Preamble's "We . . . do" would be echoed by an "I do," with "our Posterity" safeguarded by "my Ability." What the people had ordained and established, one person would solemnly swear to preserve, protect, and defend. Yet even in this personal passage, we find universal principles at work, namely, religious equality and constitutional supremacy.

Let's begin by reading America's 1789 presidential oath against the backdrop of England's 1689 Act Establishing the Coronation Oath.[1] Protestant trappings suffused the English Crown oath ceremony. By law, the oath had to be administered by an Anglican bishop or archbishop as the monarch placed a hand upon the (Protestant) Bible and then kissed the holy book to complete the event. Article II required none of these religious elements, and by tradition a secular official, the chief justice, has administered the presidential oath. (No chief justice existed in April 1789—Congress had yet to organize the judiciary, and Washington had yet to make his nominations—so New York Chancellor Robert Livingston did the honors in the first inauguration.) Although none of the Revolutionary state constitutions had copied the Crown oath ceremony in its entirety, roughly half had mimicked English practice to the extent of scripting detailed executive oaths featuring the word "God."[2] (In several states, Quakers and other religiously scrupulous persons could opt for a substitute ceremony omitting certain religiously fraught phrases.) By contrast, Article II prescribed a wholly secular presidential oath, which could be either sworn to or "affirm[ed]" (in Quaker fashion, but with no limitation of the affirmation option to Quakers). Emulating the personal example set by George Washington in 1789, presidents over the centuries have chosen to end their oaths with the words, "So help me God." This addition has been an individual religious choice, not a legal command as it was in England and in several states.

The English oath also obliged the monarch to "maintain . . . the Protestant reformed religion established by the law."[3] The American oath contained no such obligation and implicitly obliged just the opposite. By promising to "defend the Constitution" a president was pledging to oppose any attempted federal statutory religious establishment, given that Congress lacked constitutional authority to impose a British-style national religion. The First Amendment's establishment clause later made the implicit point explicit.*

But the difference in the oaths radiated far beyond issues of religious establishment. In England, the Crown promised to govern "according to the statutes in parliament agreed on,"[4] but the president's oath contained no unqualified pledge to abide by every act of Congress. Of course, the president could not just disregard duly enacted statutes whenever he felt like it, nor did he enjoy any general authority to suspend law or dissolve the legislature. Vested by the opening words of Article II with "*executive* Power," he was obviously authorized to *execute* the law, not ignore it. Later language of Article II made clear that his general pledge to "faithfully execute [his] Office" entailed a specific obligation to "take Care that the Laws be faithfully executed." In America, however, "the Laws" included not just congressional enactments, but also the Constitution itself. Thus, Article VI made explicit what the entire structure of the document and its ratification process presupposed: The Constitution was a superior law to an act of Congress, because it came from a superior lawmaker, the American people themselves. Only congressional statutes consistent with

*The American Constitution's repudiation of a British-style establishment represented a check not just on Congress, but also on the president, as Federalist Tench Coxe explained. "The British king is the great bishop or supreme head of an established church, with an immense patronage annexed. In this capacity he commands a number of votes in the house of lords, by creating bishops, who, besides their great incomes, have votes in that assembly, and are judges in the last resort. These prelates have also many honorable and lucrative places to bestow, and thus from their wealth, learning, dignities, powers, and patronage, give a great lustre and an enormous influence to the crown. In America, our president will . . . be without these influencing advantages." "An Examination of the Constitution of the United States (I)" in Ford, *Pamphlets,* 133, 137.

the Constitution—"in Pursuance" of the document, as Article VI put the point—were entitled to be treated as part of the supreme law of the land.

In England, Parliament's enactments were supreme positive law, and a law-abiding monarch thus had to pledge allegiance to them. Such was a bedrock principle of the Glorious Revolution. In America, the bedrock principle was not legislative supremacy but popular sovereignty. The higher law of the Constitution might sometimes allow, and in very clear cases of congressional usurpation might even oblige, a president to stand firm against a congressional statute in order to defend the Constitution itself. Just as judges in certain clear cases might properly disregard laws they deemed unconstitutional, so presidents in some situations might engage in a form of executive review akin to judicial review.

Accustomed as we are to seeing the judiciary—particularly, the Supreme Court—as the sole custodian and unique interpreter of the Constitution, many modern Americans might bridle at the idea that the framers envisioned the president as America's first magistrate, with important and independent authority to construe and defend the Constitution. Yet even Court-centered observers should recall that a president's principled refusal to enforce a law that he in good faith and after careful consideration deemed unconstitutional could often be the vehicle for bringing an issue before the courts. In some situations, were a president to ignore his best constitutional judgment and enforce a statute that he found unconstitutional, he might create facts on the ground that courts would find impossible to undo even if they shared his constitutional objections. Even if the case could otherwise reach the judiciary, a henchman president executing congressional orders that he believed unconstitutional would often be placing an expensive burden of initiating litigation upon an innocent private party rather than upon a powerful (and to the president's mind, offending) legislature.

In other situations, however, a president's refusal to enforce an unconstitutional statute might not be judicially reviewable. No judge, for example, could have obliged President Jefferson to prosecute speakers who had violated the Sedition Act of 1798, an act that Jefferson deemed unconstitutional. The president's greater power to pardon subsumed the lesser power to simply decline prosecution. It is also hard to imagine that anyone would have had standing in court to challenge Jefferson's decision not to wield certain constitutionally troubling deportation powers that had been conferred upon the executive by the Alien Friends Act of 1798.[5] As these actions by Jefferson illustrate, early presidents often saw themselves as defenders of the Constitution regardless of whether judges would be able to weigh in on the issue.

Post-Watergate Americans are often quick to suspect executive insincerity or incompetence in constitutional interpretation; case law generated by federal judges often seems more impartial and professional. Yet at the Founding, presidents were expected to be—and indeed were—magistrates of extraordinary repute. Was President Washington any less constitutionally credible than Chief Justice Jay? Were Adams, Jefferson, and Madison any less so than Rutledge, Ellsworth, and Marshall? Though some presidents might not be law-trained themselves, all presidents would of course have legal advisors to assist them. More profoundly, we must remember that the legal rules in the Constitution—rules that had been ordained and established by the People themselves—aimed to be broadly accessible even to nonlawyers. Prior to the twentieth century, every president save one (Zachary Taylor) referred to the Constitution in his Inaugural Address; most of these addresses included a meditation on the document's meaning. (A strikingly different pattern emerged in the twentieth century.)[6] Whereas Article II vividly specified the president's obligation to "preserve, protect and defend" the Constitution, Article VI used blander language in providing for judicial (and also legislative) oaths "to support this Constitution."[7]

In some ways, early presidents could claim inherent interpretive advantages over judges. Certain constitutional issues were "political questions," off-limits to courts but not to presidents. In a wide range of situations, presidents could take a larger view of constitutional matters, seeing both their narrowly legal aspects and broader dimensions of constitutional statecraft beyond the competence of judges. Judges might not always speak in one coherent voice. (What would happen if the original six-member Supreme Court split three to three?) Also, a single prominent person might well be more publicly accountable for his constitutional conclusions than the comparatively invisible members of a collective court. Presidents would emerge from an electoral process involving ordinary voters and political leaders across the continent, and incumbents would periodically come before the American people for reevaluation. Judges would not. If the Founders' Constitution was essentially a populist document, then the Court's relative electoral insulation did not necessarily argue in its favor as the sole or most preferred constitutional interpreter. The Constitution aimed primarily to restrain not the American people themselves, but rather ordinary government officials in all three branches. In order to keep the legislature in line, other branches needed to be independent of

Congress, yet did not always need to be independent of the citizenry. Similarly, the House and Senate were independent of each other but not independent of the American electorate and political system.

To BOLSTER THE RIGHT SORT of presidential independence, Article II, in a provision immediately preceding the presidential-oath clause, required a fixed presidential salary within each four-year term: Congress could neither add to a sitting president's salary if he proved pliant nor subtract from it if he proved otherwise. (Congress could, however, change the salary for future presidential terms—presumably before anyone could be certain who would be in office when the new law would take effect.) Judicial salaries were also protected from congressional tampering, but less so; lawmakers could never reduce judicial pay but could increase it at will. While an unscrupulous Congress might thus try to tempt judges with winking talk of salary increases as rewards for supine rulings, it would have no such leverage over a president.

In the Pennsylvania ratifying debates, Wilson stressed the salary clauses of Articles II and III in the course of explaining why both the president and the judges could be trusted to defend the Constitution from legislative usurpation. As Wilson saw it, Article II executive review closely tracked Article III judicial review. When an unconstitutional enactment came before the judges, it would be "their duty to pronounce it void," and financially independent judges would, he predicted, do their duty. "In the same manner, the President of the United States could shield himself, and refuse to carry into effect an act that violates the Constitution."[8]

Republican ideology intertwined with separation-of-powers ideas in the Article II salary clause. At Philadelphia, the delegates rejected Franklin's suggestion that a president should serve without pay; and the First Congress disregarded Washington's declared willingness to forego all salary, as he had done during the Revolution. Representative Fisher Ames put the republican point forcefully: "Every man is eligible, by the constitution, to be chosen to this office; but if a competent support is not allowed, the choice will be confined to opulent characters. This is an aristocratic idea, and contravenes the spirit of the constitution." Yielding on the point of republican principle, Washington ultimately signed a bill setting the president's salary at $25,000 and proceeded to draw his salary as appropriated.[9]

But had Article II aimed solely at opening the presidency to all classes, it could have simply specified that Congress shall provide for a "liberal stipend" for the president. Precisely these words appeared in an early Philadelphia draft proposing national compensation for congressmen themselves. Yet this draft used different words in its executive-salary section: The federal executive should receive "a fixed compensation for the services rendered, in which no increase or diminution shall be made so as to affect the Magistracy, existing at the time of the increase or diminution."[10] This separation-of-powers concept found its way into the final version of Article II. Just as the executive should not be able to bribe individual legislators with double salaries or make-work jobs—hence the incompatibility and emoluments clauses of Article I, section 6—so legislators should not be able to bribe the executive with extra pay for extra pliancy. The Article II salary clause also prohibited individual states from greasing a president's palm, and the more general language of Article I, section 9 barred all federal officers, from the president on down, from accepting any "present" or "Emolument" of "any kind whatever" from a foreign government without special congressional consent.

The Article II salary model moved beyond both English and American colonial practice. In England, the issue of the king's "compensation" was steeped in feudal customs concerning Crown revenues and Old World patterns of royal opulence. As the English monarch's negative over parliamentary enactments fell into disuse soon after the Glorious Revolution, kings used their public and private purses to develop alternative techniques to manage Commons, including outright bribery of its members.[11] A rather different dynamic operated in eighteenth-century America. Until 1776, royal and proprietary colonial governors routinely vetoed legislative enactments, with no possibility of override. Lacking any formal say in selecting these governors, colonial lawmakers nevertheless held the purse strings and resisted governors' claims to permanent and fixed salaries.[12] By retaining the power to withhold or reduce a governor's salary, lawmakers believed they might win his signature on bills he might otherwise veto. In effect, the legislature's power of the purse counterbalanced the executive's power of the pen.[13]

The American Revolution initially led most states to eliminate the executive veto altogether while continuing to omit any guarantee of executive salary. Bucking this trend, the Massachusetts Constitution of 1780 armed the governor with both a veto pen (which could be overcome by a two-thirds vote in each house) and a salary shield. According to this precursor of Article II, "As the public good requires that the governor should not be under the undue influence" of the legislature, "he should have an honorable stated salary of a fixed and permanent value" established by "standing laws."[14]

On two of the three pre-1788 occasions when Massachusetts's governor had vetoed bills, he had explicitly claimed that the bills violated the state constitution. (The more recent of these constitutional vetoes, in spring 1787, came in response to a bill that aimed to reduce future gubernatorial salaries.)[15] Similarly, colonial governors had often justified their absolute vetoes as necessary to preserve fundamental principles of the unwritten English Constitution. Against this backdrop, Founding-era Americans expected that, when confronted with a grossly unconstitutional bill that had yet to become law, a president protected from financial reprisal would forthrightly veto the bill and thereby "defend the Constitution." Thus the Constitution's veto, oath, and salary clauses logically intermeshed.

LET US, THEN, turn to consider the veto power more directly. Today, it is conventional to view the veto as primarily a vehicle for expressing a president's policy disagreement with the legislature, with no executive responsibility to veto a bill because of its constitutional flaws: Let the Court decide all that! Founding practice was rather different. In 1792, President Washington explicitly based his first veto on constitutional objections to the congressional-apportionment bill presented to him.[16] The year before, he had chosen to add his signature to a controversial bank bill only after carefully considering and rejecting possible constitutional objections. Altogether, antebellum presidents used their veto pens or veto pockets[17] on roughly fifty occasions—sometimes for pure policy reasons, but more often than not with a veto message explicitly raising constitutional and/or national-security objections, reflecting the president's unique standing as the officer most explicitly charged to "defend the Constitution" against legislative usurpation and foreign threats.[18]

Early practice did not go so far as to oblige the president to veto whenever he deemed any of a bill's provisions unconstitutional. Nor did the Constitution's text or structure impose such an absolutely unyielding obligation. The presentment rules of Article I generally gave a president three options: sign a bill, return it to Congress with his objections, or allow it to become a law without his signature. If the unconstitutional provision of a bill were a mere detail in a large and critical piece of legislation, a president might properly choose the third option, just as an individual legislator might decline to cast a vote on a particular bill or an appellate court might decline to hear a given discretionary appeal. Considerations of collegiality might even induce a president to add his name to a generally sound and desperately needed bill with a minor constitutional flaw, especially if the president deemed the constitutional question a close one in his own mind—much as a modern Supreme Court justice might sometimes join an opinion of the Court that does not perfectly express his individual view on certain minor points. However, as an officer oath-bound to champion the Constitution, the president would also be free to take up his veto pen in defense of the document, in an effort to appeal directly to the American public and to induce Congress to repass the bill without the offending details.

The typical antebellum constitutional veto did not merely anticipate likely judicial invalidation were the dubious bill to become law—for the simple reason that judicial invalidations were highly unlikely in early America. Compared to roughly two dozen constitutional vetoes prior to 1850, we find only one Supreme Court case striking down any part of a duly enacted federal statute. (The case was *Marbury v. Madison,* in which the Marshall Court in 1803 set aside one sentence of the comprehensive Judiciary Act of 1789.) In many of the early veto situations, it was quite clear that the Court would likely uphold as constitutionally permissible the very thing that the president was deeming constitutionally improper.

Part of the reason for this general antebellum pattern of judicial deference is that Supreme Court judicial review sometimes occurred long after a statute had gone into operation, at a time when it would be hard to undo a statute's effects without significant disruption. By contrast, a veto would cleanly prevent a bill from ever taking hold—unless Congress overrode, which never occurred prior to 1845.[19] Thus Chief Justice Marshall began his famous opinion for the Court in the 1819 case of *McCulloch v. Maryland* by observing that the constitutionality of a federal bank had largely been established by longstanding usage beginning in the early 1790s. "This can scarcely be considered as an open question, entirely unprejudiced by the former proceedings of the nation." Constitutional doubts, "if not put at rest by the practice of the government, ought to receive a considerable impression from that practice" and from the "immense property" interests that had crystallized around the bank in obvious reliance on its constitutionality. Marshall also stressed that in 1791 Washington himself—a mind "as pure and as intelligent as this country can boast"—had carefully considered constitutional objections before adding his name to the first bank bill rather than vetoing it. Here again we see evidence—

and in the judiciary, no less—that constitutional judgment was expected to figure prominently in the president's veto decision.[20]

President Jackson appealed to all this, and to other language of *McCulloch*, in vetoing a later bank bill on constitutional grounds, even though the Supreme Court of his day would surely have upheld the bill. Hurling Marshall's words back at him, Jackson noted that presidents in the veto process might take account of certain questions of degree that lay beyond the judicial ken. More broadly, Jackson insisted that

> the Congress, the Executive, and the court must each for itself be guided by its own opinion of the Constitution. Each public officer who takes an oath to support the Constitution, swears that he will support it as he understands it, and not as it is understood by others. It is as much the duty of the House of Representatives, of the Senate, and of the President to decide upon the constitutionality of any bill or resolution which may be presented to them for passage or approval, as it is of the supreme judges, when it may be brought before them for judicial decision. The opinion of the judges has no more authority over Congress than the opinion of Congress has over the judges; and on that point the President is independent of both.[21]

In short, while England explicitly made its king the Defender of the Faith, America explicitly made its president the Defender of the Constitution.

"Commander in Chief"

The Constitution's first two Articles began in different fashion. Article I proclaimed that "all legislative Powers *herein granted* shall be vested" in a bicameral Congress, while Article II declared that *"the executive Power* shall be vested" in the president. Article I's opening clause thus added nothing to the later list of enumerated congressional powers, yet Article II's opening clause itself appeared to vest a general residuum of "executive Power" in the president above and beyond the subsequent roster of enumerated presidential powers. If Article II truly meant what it said, why did it depart from the Article I template? And if Article II's opening clause really did vest the president with some quantum of general executive authority beyond the specific enumerations, what exactly was the purpose of the later list of particular powers?

To answer these questions—which rank among the most frequently debated topics in modern constitutional scholarship[22]—let's begin by recalling the need in 1787 for some flexibility and creativity in the exercise of executive power. Vital national interests might demand urgent reaction to unfolding events at home or abroad, and in ways that might have defied advance specification in a legislative rule. In contrast to the routinized and often cumbersome modes of legislative enactment and judicial adjudication, a faithful executive might sometimes have to improvise to vindicate the spirit of the laws or to keep the ship of state afloat. Unlike Articles I and III—which vested legislative and judicial power in multimember bodies that would switch in and out of session—Article II, as we have seen, revolved around a one-man president always on duty. With this basic structure, the framers aimed to infuse the executive branch with "energy," enabling it to master an unpredictable world by acting speedily where necessary and even secretly where appropriate (for instance, when negotiating sensitive treaties or vetting potential nominees).[23] Complementing this organizational structure, the opening language of Article II gave the president a supple textual mandate to act in various situations that might be impossible to define in advance.

But without a companion catalogue of concrete powers and limitations, the open-ended words at the outset of Article II would have been dangerously indeterminate, failing to exemplify the general sort of executive power America envisioned and to qualify this power in key ways. In particular, the later list of specific presidential do's and don'ts illustrated how an American president would be much less than an English king yet much more than a standard state governor. The list also specified various exceptions to and qualifications of the general grant of executive power in the president and the president alone—much as certain parts of Article I, such as its veto and impeachment provisions, qualified its opening words, which seemed to say that Congress and only Congress would enjoy legislative and only legislative powers.*

Article II, section 2 opened with a cluster of clauses confirming the president's place at the apex of three grand pyramids of national power: military, administrative, and prosecutorial. Unlike England's king, who stood atop comparable pyramids of power across the Atlantic, America's

---

*In effect the veto provisions of Article I, section 7 gave certain legislative powers to the president, and the impeachment provisions of Article I, sections 2 and 3 conferred certain judicial powers upon Congress. Although the veto power appeared textually in Article I, we have examined it primarily in this chapter because of its close relationship to other presidential duties and powers in Article II. For similar reasons, we shall consider various clauses relating to impeachment—clauses that were textually scattered across Articles I and II—later in this chapter.

president would embody a wholly republican, suitably federal, and properly checked chief executive, as made clear by the specific language of this section 2 cluster.

Whereas the British monarch controlled all the island's military forces, the American chief executive would command the various state militias only when they were "called into the actual Service of the United States." Under Article I, section 8, such federalization of the militias could occur only "to execute the Laws of the Union, suppress Insurrections and repel Invasions." Otherwise, state governors would, as we have seen, retain control over their militias—part of a federalism-based balance of military power that had no exact British counterpart.

Article II also gave America's chief executive less administrative authority to demand advice on private and public matters than England's chief executive enjoyed. If George III ordered his royal subjects on the Privy Council to help him manage his personal landholdings, it was the counselors' general obligation to "advise for the King's honour" and to serve their "sovereign lord."[24] George Washington had no comparable power to order his fellow citizens in the cabinet to help him run Mount Vernon; Article II entitled the president to compel cabinet opinions only on public matters "relating to the Duties of their . . . Offices." Nor could Washington oblige constitutionally independent federal judges to give him direct legal advice as he, say, pondered a possible veto on constitutional grounds.[25] By contrast, judges customarily sat on the king's Privy Council. In this respect, the Article II opinions clause widened the separation between the federal executive and judicial branches, breaking with both British tradition and the New York experiment (in which an executive-judicial council wielded a collective veto).

While the British monarch could pardon all criminals, America's president could grant pardons only for federal offenses as opposed to state crimes—a reflection of basic principles of American federalism. Also, English law as a rule assimilated impeachments to other criminal proceedings. The monarch could pardon anyone convicted in the High Court of Parliament (though he lacked power to bar the impeachment trial itself). America's Constitution structured impeachment as a unique system of political accountability sharply distinct from ordinary criminal punishment. Thus Article II pointedly denied the president authority to use his pardon pen to set aside impeachment convictions, while allowing him to spare impeached officials from ordinary federal criminal-law sanctions.

Even as section 2's opening cluster of clauses specified how America's president would wield a less threatening kind of executive power than

Britain's king, the cluster also clarified how the president would enjoy a more robust version of executive power than most state governors. While Article I curtailed the ability of state governments, and thus state governors, to maintain professional troops or warships, Article II made the president the permanent commander in chief of the continental army and navy. The power to direct America's professional troops entailed, at a minimum, authority to deploy these men to repel sudden invasions, even in the absence of prior legislative authorization. During the Civil War, Lincoln repeatedly pointed to his authority as commander in chief to justify his various actions—some of them unilateral, and most of them ultimately blessed by Congress—to suppress what he (rightly) deemed an unconstitutional rebellion against the Constitution itself.[26]

Over the centuries, American presidents have often wielded their commander-in-chief authority even more aggressively, claiming the right to position troops in offensive as well as defensive situations, both at home and abroad, and in situations where the president could not plausibly claim (as did Lincoln) that the Constitution required (as opposed to permitted) these military actions. In principle, Congress has retained the right to challenge presidential authority in these situations by refusing to fund the military, or by enacting "Rules for the Government and Regulation of the land and naval Forces" pursuant to Article I, section 8. But the precise boundary between the power of the purse and the power of the sword, between congressional rules and executive commands, has never been easy to define with perfect precision. One possible guidepost might be that laws *proscribing* certain uses of the military may be easier to justify than laws *prescribing* highly specific uses of armed forces in certain tactical situations: The latter might be thought to cross the line separating the legislation of general rules from the particulars of actual battle command. An alternative view might recognize near-plenary control of Congress to lay down military rules, so long as Congress understands that it is the president and no one else who must ultimately superintend the execution of these military rules.

The president would not merely stand atop America's military, but would also head its civil bureaucracy. Most state constitutions blurred the unique decision-making authority of a single governor by routinely requiring the state chief executive to seek the "advice" or, stricter still, secure the "advice and consent" of a collective council. By emphatic contrast, Article II's opinions clause accented the supremacy of one man over the civilian underlings in his branch. The president would decide for himself whether and when to seek the nonbinding opinions of his individual deputies.[27]

The breadth of the president's pardon power also elevated the federal chief executive above his state counterparts. In almost every state, the governor's pardon authority was sharply restricted by the constitution itself or else subject to legislative override. Even the strong governor of Massachusetts could pardon only with "the advice" of a legislatively chosen council, and then only after conviction. New York's governor also lacked power to pardon before conviction, and in cases of murder and treason, he could merely suspend a sentence until the legislature met to resolve the matter.[28] Article II handed the president a far mightier pardon pen, authorizing him to single-handedly and conclusively pardon at any time after a crime occurred and thereby spare a man from even having to stand trial. As *The Federalist* No. 74 emphasized, this sweeping power in the right hand at the right time might strengthen national security and save lives by inducing desperate offenders to surrender immediately in exchange for guaranteed mercy. "In seasons of insurrection or rebellion, there are often critical moments when a well-timed offer of pardon to the insurgents or rebels may restore the tranquility of the commonwealth." Because the "loss of a week, a day, an hour, may sometimes be fatal," any "dilatory process of convening the legislature" or a council might "let[] slip the golden opportunity."

In this vivid passage, whose script President Washington would closely follow in dissolving the Whiskey Rebellion of 1794, Hamilton deftly interwove several of the threads that defined America's presidency—the sleeplessness and unity of executive power, the president's unique capacity for quick decisive action, and this officer's special role in handling crises that might threaten the national tranquility or even the national existence.[29]

"Advice and Consent"

After clarifying the scope of various powers vested solely in the president, section 2 proceeded to map out two domains where the chief executive would share power with the Congress, especially the Senate. The "Advice and Consent" of the upper house would be required for any treaty that a president might propose or any major nomination that he might make. In England, the monarch embodied British sovereignty internationally and stood as the fountain of official honor domestically. Thus kings claimed unilateral authority to make treaties, create new executive and judicial offices, and name all officers. Article II broke with this model, giving the

Senate a portion of traditionally executive authority—much as Article I gave the president some legislative power via the veto clause. The lower house would also play a decidedly non-English role in appointments, helping to define "by Law" the precise number of executive and judicial slots to be filled. Though America's executive and legislative branches might generally wield different powers and stand on separate electoral bases, the Constitution obliged them to work together on certain joint tasks. To this extent, separation of powers between branches resembled bicameralism within the legislature. In the making of statutes, treaties, and appointments, the Constitution intertwined branches that it elsewhere separated.

Article I statute-making required either the concurrence of all three of America's permanent elective institutions—House, Senate, and president—or strong supermajorities in both legislative houses to overcome an executive veto. Article II treaty-making sidestepped the House of Representatives—the people's house. To offset this democratic deficit, Article II made a president's approval of a treaty indispensable and required the Senate to agree by a decisive two-to-one margin. In this respect, the Constitution resembled the Articles of Confederation, where nine of thirteen state-chosen delegations sufficed to bind America to a treaty. The old Confederation Congress had often acted as a kind of executive council, and although the new Constitution relocated much of this executive power to the president unilaterally,[30] the document retained a part for the Senate—an improved version of the old Confederation Congress—in the treaty-making process. Composed of statesmen chosen for their wisdom by state legislatures, the Senate could check a hasty or corrupt president and guard against proposals that might result in the imprudent creation of international obligations or the needless displacement of state law.

Nor were the treaty-making rules of Article II the Constitution's only protection against bad treaties. In both the Article VI supremacy clause and the document's general structure, statutes made pursuant to Article I might in some ways be thought to have priority over treaties made under Article II. Certain treaties would have little or no domestic effect unless implemented by a statute that would require House approval. For instance, no mere treaty could appropriate federal funds or create a new federal crime. Only Congress as a whole, including the House, could do these things. For similar reasons, although a treaty might suffice to displace state law as part of the "supreme Law of the Land," its power to repeal any and all prior federal statutes might well be doubted.*

---

*We shall return to this nice question in Chapter 8.

Conversely, a strong structural and historical case could be made that certain federal actions might well require a treaty in addition to a federal statute. For example, if the central government sought to cede land—especially land within individual states—to a foreign power, a mere statute of cession, without more, might seem inadequately protective of the extraordinary sectional interests at stake. Arguably, a two-thirds vote of a Senate specially structured to safeguard states' rights, along with the absolute agreement of a continentally elected president entrusted with the defense of the whole union, would also be necessary to effect any such cession. More generally, perhaps a statute-supplementing treaty would be necessary whenever a major international agreement threatened to impose drastically unequal effects upon different regions of the country.

At the Founding, the paradigm case of sectional disparity involved the Mississippi River, whose mouth was controlled by Spain. Seeking to exploit America's extreme weakness under the Articles of Confederation, Spanish negotiators in the mid-1780s had offered the United States special trade concessions in exchange for a temporary American renunciation of the right of free navigation along the Mississippi—a deal that might have benefited certain Eastern interests but would have devastated the trans-Appalachian West.[31] In the shadow of these recent and highly controversial negotiations, leading Federalists repeatedly assured skeptics that the supermajoritarian safeguards of the Article II treaty process would protect regional minorities, thereby implying that in certain regionally divisive contexts, a simple federal statute of cession would not suffice.[32]

More so than ordinary statutes, treaties would be subject to the vicissitudes of international politics. In the event of a treaty partner's breach or collapse, or an executive-branch renegotiation with the partner, a president might act to abrogate or suspend a federal treaty in a way that he could not ordinarily overturn a federal statute. The power to put aside a treaty in such situations plausibly fell within the residuum of "executive Power" vested solely in the president by the opening words of Article II and unqualified by the shared rules of treaty-making set forth later in section 2. By its terms, section 2 simply did not apply to treaty abrogations or to other closely related aspects of foreign policy—treaty negotiations, recognitions of foreign regimes, presidential proclamations, informal agreements between presidents and foreign leaders, and so on—encompassed by the general grant of executive power to the president.[33]

The actual practice of treaty abrogation over the centuries has varied. Sometimes treaties have been superseded by statutes, sometimes by joint action of the president and Senate, and at other times by the president alone.[34] Although America's first treaty abrogation, in 1798, occurred by way of a congressional statute declaring that France had repeatedly breached her treaties with America and pursued a pattern of "predatory violence" against the United States, this statutory pronouncement verged on a declaration of limited war.[35] A congressional declaration (signed by the president) may have been the most appropriate way to process this particular treaty abrogation, but this action did not establish a firm precedent demanding similar statutory action in all future cases of treaty abrogation. Indeed, both Hamilton and Jefferson viewed certain abrogations as wholly executive in nature.[36] Above and beyond whatever powers of abrogation and suspension a president might properly wield, he also enjoyed the power to interpret treaties in the first instance, with American judges often disposed to give decisive weight to his interpretation. Washington's emphatic Neutrality Proclamation of 1793 exemplified this important power, as Hamilton famously explained in an essay penned under the pseudonym "Pacificus."[37]

A president could also unilaterally prevent a potential treaty from ever becoming the law of the land by refusing to negotiate with a given foreign regime, by declining to submit an inchoate treaty to the Senate, or even by deciding not to formally finalize a treaty after the Senate had given its advice and consent. The very word "Advice" reflected the fact that the president, and not the Senate, would have the final, definitive move. In the first major international agreement under the new Constitution, Washington decided to sign off on the Jay Treaty in August 1795 only after weeks of executive deliberation following the Senate's vote of advice and consent. Beginning with this episode, the Senate has claimed the right to propose amendments to a treaty negotiated by the executive branch; any such amendments have required the assent of both the president and America's treaty partner.[38]

Similar rules applied to the appointment of leading executive and judicial officers, the other domain subject to senatorial advice and consent.[39] Here, too, the Constitution obliged the president and the Senate to work together; the need to secure the approval of a separate branch would serve to deter a president from making corrupt or unwise proposals. Unlike treaties, appointments would themselves have no direct impact on domestic or international law; thus, a simple majority of the Senate would suffice to confirm nominees, in contrast to the two-thirds needed for treaty ratification. In appointments, as with treaties, the Senate could say no to what the president proposed but could not compel the president to say yes to the Senate's first choice. Just as a president could refuse to formally ratify a treaty after it won the Senate's consent, so he might decline to commission an officer who survived the confirmation ordeal.

Also, a president retained broad power to unilaterally remove a high-level executive-branch appointee gone sour, much as he could in certain instances unilaterally abrogate a treaty gone bad. The Senate's advice-and-consent function applied to the making of treaties and appointments, but not to their breaking. Instead, the president's general residuum of "executive Power," along with his responsibility to ensure that the laws were being faithfully executed by his deputies, empowered him to remove heads of executive departments—men who answered to him under the section 2 opinions clause and whose legislatively created posts had no fixed terms.

So argued Representative Madison and other supporters of President Washington when the cabinet-removal issue arose early in the First Congress, which in its famous Decision of 1789 bowed to the views of the administration. As Washington saw the matter, executive underlings properly answered to him. "The impossibility that one man should be able to perform all the great business of the State, I take to have been the reason for instituting the great Departments, and appointing officers therein, to *assist* the supreme Magistrate in discharging the duties of *his* trust." Consistent with this understanding, Congress created the first cabinet departments via statutory language designed to concede the president's inherent and unilateral power to remove cabinet heads at will. As Madison explained,

> It is evidently the intention of the constitution, that the first Magistrate should be responsible for the executive department. . . .
>
> The constitution affirms, that the executive power shall be vested in the President. Are there exceptions to this proposition? Yes, there are. The constitution says, that in appointing to office, the Senate shall be associated with the President. . . . Have we a right to extend this exception? I believe not. If the constitution has invested all executive power in the President, . . . the Legislature has no right to diminish or modify his executive authority.
>
> The question now resolves itself into this, Is the power of displacing [removing], an executive power? I conceive that if any power whatsoever is in its nature executive, it is the power of appointing, overseeing, and controlling those who execute the laws.

In keeping with this early understanding, John Adams dismissed Secretary of State Timothy Pickering in 1800 without asking the Senate's permission even though it was in session.[40]

The president's plenary power to remove heads of executive departments who served without term and answered to him under the opinions clause did not necessarily imply the same sweeping authority to remove all lower-ranking officials within executive departments, especially if Congress chose to give such officials fixed terms of office or some other statutory insulation. In general, Article II structured an executive-branch chain of command in which significant policy decisions rendered by lower-ranking officers had to be subject to presidential oversight and countermand,[41] but Congress might properly vest authority over truly technical issues of fact in experts immune from presidential reversal or reprisal. In no case, however, could Congress itself or the Senate in particular directly appoint such officers, or share in whatever removal power might remain in cases of malfeasance (apart from the Congress's power to impeach, and to legislate subject to presidential presentment).

Textually, Article II treated high-level executive and judicial appointments alike, yet Senate practice quickly distinguished between them, giving the president more leeway in choosing his executive deputies. By 1830, the Senate had defeated three Supreme Court nominations—the first in 1795, when it rejected John Rutledge, whom Washington had named to replace John Jay as chief justice—but had yet to turn down any of the much larger number of cabinet candidates.[42] This pattern made structural sense. Cabinet officials were part of the president's branch—secretaries who existed largely to help him carry out his responsibilities and answered directly to him under the opinions clause. A president could closely monitor these men and remove them at will; and no newly elected president would be saddled with his predecessor's picks unless he so chose. Article III judges would be independent officers in a separate branch that emphatically did not answer to the president. Nor could they be removed by him or by a new administration. For these lifetime posts, more Senate scrutiny was appropriate.

Heightened scrutiny was also appropriate in appointments implicating "family connection," as Hamilton/Publius explained in *The Federalist* No. 76. Although Washington never nominated even distant relatives, John Adams raised republican eyebrows when he proposed John Quincy as minister to Prussia. Superbly qualified for the position, young Adams eventually won Senate approval. When President Adams later nominated his son-in-law, William Stephens Smith, to various posts, senators closely reviewed the matter, rejecting Smith for one position and approving him for others.[43]

Although senators would have broad discretion to say no in the confirmation process, the president would enjoy several structural advantages in the foreseeable give-and-take. A presidential nomination would define the agenda, forcing the Senate to consider not merely an abstract ideology but a flesh-and-blood person, with friends and feelings. Even if senators preferred someone else, they could not guarantee that the president would ever propose that person; indeed, senators who sank the president's first choice might face a worse (to them) candidate the next time around. Different senators might be at cross-purposes, making it difficult for the body to speak with one voice, as could the president. (Partially counterbalancing this dynamic, the Senate from its earliest days has tended to give special deference to the views of the two senators from the nominee's home state.)[44] When senators left for home, the president would stay put and could make interim recess appointments ensconcing his men in office, temporarily. The president's sweeping right to remove executive subordinates enabled him to expand various appointment opportunities at will, while the Senate lacked symmetric removal power. Congress by statute might even eliminate the Senate confirmation process in cases of "inferior Officers," who could be directly appointed by their respective superiors—courts, cabinet heads, and the president himself.[45]

Overall, Article II's vesting of such broad appointment and removal power in one man contrasted sharply with most state constitutions, which located far more power in the legislature or some subset thereof, and with the Articles of Confederation, which had vested these personnel decisions in a multimember, quasi-executive proto-Senate.

"as he shall judge necessary"

Article II concluded its roster of specific presidential powers and duties with language authorizing the chief executive to inform Congress periodically of the state of the union and recommend any measures he judged fitting; to convene Congress in emergencies; to receive foreign diplomats; to "take Care that the Laws be faithfully executed"; and to commission all executive and judicial officers. This catalogue of responsibilities envisioned the president as a generalist focused on the big picture. While Congress would enact statutes and courts would decide cases one at a time, the president would oversee the enforcement of *all* the laws at once—a sweeping mandate that invited him to ponder legal patterns in the largest sense and inevitably conferred some discretion on him in defining his enforcement philosophy and priorities. So, too, the president's responsibility to mull the state of the union as a whole and to offer any recommendation that he should "judge necessary and expedient" underscored the breadth of his mandate as the one constitutional officer always in session and presiding over the whole nation.

Ambassadors might arrive at any time, and the president would be there to receive them.* Crises might arise at any moment, and the president would be there to decide whether and when to convene Congress, though he would have no British-style royal power to dissolve or prorogue Congress. Military and civil vacancies would occur around the clock, and the president would be there to superintend the process of commissioning replacements.

Beyond a president's macro-discretion in setting general priorities, many individual statutes were expected to contain significant zones of micro-discretion. Filling in these gaps was a classic executive function, as was the related fact-finding power to determine whether certain statutory conditions had actually been met. Thus, if Congress legislated that in the event of situation X, legal consequence Y should follow, congressmen themselves would as a rule not be the judges of whether X had in fact occurred. Rather, the executive branch would typically make a determination in the first instance, subject to judicial oversight whose precise scope might vary widely, depending on the issue.

DESPITE ITS ELABORATE GESTURES toward specificity and enumeration, Article II left much to be filled in by practice. To clarify that America's chief executive would be much less than an English king and much more than a typical state governor was to say something important, but a vast space separated these two poles. Key questions remained: Just how far did the commander-in-chief power extend? How broadly should the presidential power to receive ambassadors be construed? Was the president's responsibility to "take Care that the Laws be faithfully executed" a narrow ministerial duty or a sweeping font of power? Granted that the residuum of "executive Power" in the opening words of Article II surely encompassed Lincoln's mandate to save the Union and Washington's authority to control his executive-branch deputies, what else fell within the residuum?

---

*By implication, he would also decide which foreign regimes merited his recognition and which did not—a piece of his portfolio that also drew support from his section 2 power to choose his treaty partners and from his general "executive Power" residuum. Early in his second term, Washington asserted broad presidential discretion over this domain, first by recognizing revolutionary France and later by refusing to deal with the presumptuous French minister Citizen Genet.

The evident openness of the text here reflected the framers' genuine uncertainty as they struggled to invent a wholly new sort of executive. Thanks to its gaps and silences, Article II in effect delegated authority to the political branches to negotiate more concrete settlements. Doubtless most Founders looked forward to the leadership of George Washington and expected him to transform a sparse text into actual institutional practice and precedent. Hence the special authority of the settlements and understandings reached during the Washington Administration.[46]

What Article II *did* make emphatically clear from start to finish was that the president would be personally responsible for his branch. Though he would be aided by subordinates in discharging his many and varied functions, the Constitution took pains to disavow the idea of a collective cabinet or directory behind whom he might hide. In the appointments context, the document pointedly repudiated the New York experiment, which united the governor and a number of senators into a council that made appointments by a collective and opaque vote. According to Hamilton/Publius in *The Federalist* No. 70, the New York council had resulted in "scandalous appointments to important offices," but when the public made inquiries, it was almost impossible to apportion blame as individual council members pointed fingers at one another. Following Massachusetts rather than New York, Article II required the president alone to openly nominate his candidates, enabling the public to assess the nominator while the Senate assessed the nominees.[47]

As *The Federalist* No. 70 observed in language distilling earlier statements by Wilson, Madison, Ellsworth, Gouverneur Morris, Charles Pinckney, and others, Article II was structured to prevent a president from claiming, "I was overruled by my council." Unlike state executive councils, a president's cabinet would be composed of men that he himself had nominated, or at least men that he had not removed. In clear contrast to its rules requiring a president to woo the Senate in his nominations and treaties, nowhere did Article II oblige him to seek his executive subordinates' advice, much less their consent.[48] As Iredell explained in urging ratification: "The President will personally have the credit of good, or the censure of bad measures; since, though he may ask advice, he is to use his own judgment in following or rejecting it."[49] The Article II opinions clause invited a president to seek a cabinet officer's opinion only on issues within that officer's "respective" executive department but said nothing to encourage a president to poll his cabinet as a group.

Early presidential practice nevertheless drifted somewhat toward a collective cabinet, yielding to the gravitational pull of widespread state executive-branch practice. Yet even as weak presidents occasionally tried to duck behind strong cabinets, Article II fixed the public eye on the chief executive himself. Legend tells us that Lincoln once submitted a pet proposal to his cabinet and, when met with a unanimous chorus of nays, quipped that "the aye has it." Though too good to be true, the legend captures a deep truth about Article II. James Wilson framed the issue well in 1791:

> The British throne is surrounded by counsellors. With regard to their authority, a profound and mysterious silence is observed. . . . Between power and responsibility, they interpose an impenetrable barrier. . . . Amidst [the ministers'] multitude, and the secrecy, with which business, especially that of a perilous kind, is transacted, it will be often difficult to select the culprits; still more so, to punish them. . . .
>
> In the United States, our first executive magistrate is not obnubilated behind the mysterious obscurity of counsellors. Power is communicated to him with liberality, though with ascertained limitations. To him the provident or improvident use of it is to be ascribed. For the first, he will have and deserve undivided applause. For the last, he will be subject to censure; if necessary, to punishment. He is the dignified, but accountable magistrate of a free and great people.[50]

"Impeachment"

With his blunt references to "culprits" and "punishment," Wilson doubtless meant to remind his audience of one of the Constitution's essential instruments for assuring executive-branch accountability to the American people: the high court of impeachment. Of course, Article II's detailed provisions governing presidential selection and succession aimed at preventing a corrupt or easily corruptible leader from ever reaching the pinnacle of power. Yet even the best of selection systems might occasionally fail and even a well-chosen president might sometimes fall. Thus, the Constitution took care to fashion a peaceful and politically accountable mechanism for removing a president before the end of his fixed term.[51]

By a majority vote, the people's House, acting as a special grand jury, could impeach a president—in effect, indict him—for treason, bribery, or any other "high Crimes [or] Misdemeanors" that made him unfit to serve. (Likewise, the House could impeach any other executive or judicial "Officer[].")* Sitting as both judge and jury deciding law and fact, the Senate would try the impeached defendant. In a case of presidential impeachment, the chief justice would preside over the trial but would have no voice in the verdict. The presence of the chief made double sense, signaling the special gravity of a presidential impeachment and avoiding the conflict of interest that would arise were the trial chaired by the Senate's ordinary presiding officer, the vice president (who stood to gain the presidency in the event of a conviction). If two-thirds of the Senate voted to convict, the defendant would be removed from office, and the Senate could further choose to disqualify him from all future federal office.[52] Anything less than a two-thirds vote would effectively acquit. No appeal from the verdict of the impeachment court would lie to any other tribunal.[53] Its decisions of fact and law were res judicata that could not be undone in separate state or federal court proceedings. Senators could impose only the political punishment of removal and future disqualification. All other possible punishments would be decided in ordinary criminal proceedings that would not be obliged to follow the Senate's findings or verdict.

This system of federal impeachment broke decisively with English impeachment practice. First and foremost, American-style impeachment rendered the president himself accountable for any grave misconduct, while British law had no regularized legal machinery for ousting a bad king. The monarch himself was immune from impeachment and also from ordinary criminal prosecution. In a quasi-feudal system that took the idea of a jury of one's peers seriously, commoners could judge commoners, and lords lords, but who could judge the One who truly had no peers? Although a rump Parliament in the 1640s had purported to try Charles I and then proceeded to execute him, the legality of these actions after the Restoration seemed doubtful to orthodox jurists. In the 1680s, the Glorious Revolution ousted another monarch, with less bloodshed. Yet because James II had fled the throne and the island—and thus arguably abdicated—this episode offered a rather murky precedent for dealing with a bad king who had the bad grace to stay put. The 1689 English Bill of Rights and 1701 Act of Succession provided that no monarch could be a Catholic or marry one, or leave the realm without parliamentary

---

*Congressmen themselves were not, strictly speaking, "Officers," and were thus not impeachable, as the Senate decided in the 1790s in proceedings involving Senator William Blount. Under Article I, section 5, each house was authorized to expel miscreant members upon a two-thirds vote. In this system, unlike impeachment, the House would play no role in ousting senators, and senators would likewise stay out of any effort to unseat House members.

consent—and thus presumably defined these acts as constructive abdications—but specified no procedure for dealing with the myriad other ways in which a future monarch might unfit himself.

In America, by contrast, the head of state could be ousted whenever he committed any "high Crimes [or] Misdemeanors" that warranted his immediate removal. In context, the words "high . . . Misdemeanors" most sensibly meant high misbehavior or high misconduct, whether or not strictly criminal. Under the Articles of Confederation, the states mutually pledged to extradite those charged with any "high misdemeanor," and in that setting the phrase apparently meant only indictable crimes. The Constitution used the phrase in a wholly different context, in which adjudication would occur in a political body lacking general criminal jurisdiction or special criminal-law competence. Early drafts in Philadelphia had provided for impeachment in noncriminal cases of "mal-practice or neglect of duty" and more general "corruption." During the ratification process, leading Federalists hypothesized various noncriminal actions that might rise to the level of high misdemeanors warranting impeachment, such as summoning only friendly senators into special session or "giving false information to the Senate." In the First Congress, Madison contended that if a president abused his removal powers by "wanton removal of meritorious officers" he would be "impeachable . . . for such an act of maladministration."[54] Consistent with these public expositions of the text, House members in the early 1800s impeached a pair of judges for misbehavior on the bench that fell short of criminality. The Senate convicted one (John Pickering) of intoxication and indecency, and acquitted the other (Samuel Chase) of egregious bias and other judicial improprieties.[55]

An impeachment standard transcending criminal-law technicalities made good structural sense. A president who ran off on a frolic in the middle of a national crisis demanding his urgent attention might break no criminal law, yet such gross dereliction of duty imperiling the national security and betraying the national trust might well rise to the level of disqualifying misconduct. (Leaving the Anglican Church or marrying a Catholic, however, would seem very far from impeachable misbehavior under a Constitution that pointedly rejected religious tests; in fact, the impeachment clauses themselves confirmed the document's general religious openness by permitting senators to sit either by "Oath" or by "Affirmation" when hearing impeachment cases.)

The word "high" surely meant what it said in the Article II impeachment clause. Elsewhere the Constitution omitted the word "high" in describing "Treason, Felony and Breach of the Peace" in the Article I arrest clause and "Treason, Felony, or other Crime" in the Article IV extradition clause. But how high was "high"? The Article II clause gave readers some guidance by giving two specific examples of impeachable misconduct: "Treason" and "Bribery." Both were "high" offenses indeed. "Treason"—defined in detail elsewhere in the Constitution—meant waging war against America or betraying her to an enemy power. "Bribery"—secretly bending laws to favor the rich and powerful—involved official corruption of a highly malignant sort, threatening the very soul of a democratic republic committed to equality under law. In the case of a president who did not take bribes but gave them—paying men to vote for him—the bribery would undermine the very legitimacy of the election that brought him to office.

Because reasonable people might often disagree about whether a particular president's misconduct approximated "Bribery" or "Treason" in moral gravity or dangerousness to the republic, the Constitution prescribed not only a linguistic standard but also a legal structure. The House and Senate, comprising America's most distinguished and accountable statesmen, would make the key decisions. Acting under the American people's watchful eye, these leaders would have strong incentives to set the bar at the right level. If they defined virtually anything as a "high" misdemeanor, they and their friends would likely fail the test, which could one day return to haunt them. If, instead, they ignored plain evidence of gross presidential malignance, the apparent political corruption and backscratching might well disgust the voters, who could register popular outrage at the next election.

In making Congress the pivot point, the Constitution structured impeachment as a system of national accountability. Because the president would uniquely represent the American people as a whole, the decision to oust him could come only from representatives of the entire continent. Though the Constitution did not expressly say so, its basic structure afforded a sitting president temporary immunity from ordinary criminal prosecution during his term of office. All other impeachable officers, including vice presidents, cabinet secretaries, and judges, might be tried, convicted, and imprisoned by ordinary courts while still in office. But as Hamilton/Publius passingly implied in *The Federalist* Nos. 69 and 77 and Ellsworth and Adams reiterated in the First Congress,[56] America's president could be arrested and prosecuted only after he left office. Unlike other more fungible or episodic national officers, the president was personally vested with the powers of an entire branch and was expected to preside continuously. Faithful discharge of his national duties might render him extremely unpopular in a particular state or region, making it essential to insulate him from trumped-up local charges aiming to incapacitate him and thereby undo a national election. (Imagine, for example, some clever South Carolina prosecutor seeking to indict Lincoln in the spring of 1861 and demanding that he stand trial in Charleston.) Thus, only the House, a truly national grand jury, could indict, and only the Senate, a national petit jury, could convict, a sitting president. Of course, the people of the nation could also remove a sitting president at regular quadrennial intervals. Once out of office, an ex-president might be criminally tried just like any other citizen.

Here, too, in sharply separating impeachment from ordinary criminal proceedings, the Constitution broke with historic English practice. Although the British monarch was personally immune from impeachment, his aides were not, and as a practical matter monarchs could do little without ministers. By allowing Parliament to impeach a king's "wicked" counselors,[57] English law achieved a measure of executive accountability, but only by criminalizing politics. In order to remove a minister from power, Parliament over the centuries had repeatedly felt itself obliged to try him as a criminal, in a quintessentially criminal process that imposed quintessentially criminal sanctions, including death—though the monarch might mitigate the punishment with his pardon pen.

America's Constitution transformed impeachment into a more precise and proportionate system of political punishment. While the English High Court of Parliament claimed jurisdiction to impeach even private citizens, in America only federal "Officers" would be subject to impeachment. America's impeachment tribunal would itself be politically accountable, structured to permit judgments of statecraft to percolate into the process and thereby enhance the public legitimacy of the verdict. Most important of all, the only punishment that could result from American impeachment would be political punishment—automatic removal from office and possible disqualification to hold future office. All other sanctions were reserved to ordinary criminal courts, state and federal. In England, because impeachment substituted for ordinary criminal prosecution, an impeachment acquittal barred subsequent criminal prosecution. America rejected this rule, and for good reason: It would have encouraged conviction in the impeachment court for any crime, howsoever low and irrelevant to public officeholding, lest an impeachment defendant escape all punishment. Also, as we have seen, the American test of impeachment culpability was broadly political: Was the defendant's misconduct—whether or not technically criminal—so grave as to warrant his removal from office and possible future disqualification?

Though ultimately political, this test required genuine *misconduct;* it was political *punishment,* not simply politics as usual akin to a bland vote of no confidence. Impeachment was a judicialized ritual in which senators sat not as lawmakers, but as judges and jurors. Though as lawmakers they were free to vote against a president's policies merely because they disagreed with him politically, more was required before they might properly vote to impeach or convict him. Thus, no impeachment would be warranted merely because a president in good faith vetoed a bill that Congress favored. The point was implicit in the Constitution's basic structure: Surely it made no sense to say that while a two-thirds vote of each house was needed to override a good-faith veto, a lesser vote would suffice to remove a good-faith vetoer from office. In America's first great presidential-impeachment drama, in 1868, a Senate that would ultimately vote to overrule Andrew Johnson's vetoes a staggering fifteen times out of twenty-one override opportunities (compared to six successful overrides out of thirty-six opportunities for all previous presidents combined) nevertheless acquitted him of the House's impeachment charges.[58]

In offering up a New World impeachment model strikingly different from England's, the Constitution built upon Revolutionary state prototypes—in particular and unsurprisingly the impeachment provisions of New York and Massachusetts. Both states provided that all officers (and only officers) could be tried by an impeachment court and removed and disqualified upon conviction for "mal and corrupt conduct in . . . office[]" (in New York) or "misconduct and mal-administration in . . . office[]" (in Massachusetts). All other sanctions were expressly reserved for ordinary state criminal courts. New York required a two-thirds vote of the lower house to impeach and a two-thirds vote of the upper to convict. Simple majorities sufficed in the Bay State.[59] On this point, the Philadelphia plan split the difference. Perhaps because New York made it harder to trigger an impeachment trial, the state required an impeached governor to hand over power, which he might regain upon acquittal. Neither Massachusetts nor the federal Constitution required an impeached chief executive to step aside before conviction.[60] As did the federal model, these state prototypes rendered their heads of state (and other officers) politically accountable for political misconduct via a political tribunal that could impose only limited political punishments.

Taken as a whole, Article II envisioned the president as an officer who would generally defend the Constitution, but who might at times come to threaten it. Vested with breathtaking power, the president would nonetheless be checked by the House and Senate, as the American people looked on, poised to render ultimate political judgment on all concerned.

Except for the largely ceremonial presence of the chief justice in cases of presidential impeachment, the Article III judiciary would play no adjudicatory part in impeachment dramas. In other constitutional contexts, the third branch was expected to assume a larger role—though not, as we shall now see, a role quite so large as it currently claims for itself.

Chapter 6

JUDGES AND JURIES

JOHN MARSHALL (1808).

As chief justice from 1801 to 1835, Marshall reinvigorated the federal judiciary, which began as the Constitution's weakest branch. America's first chief justice, John Jay, had resigned in 1795 and declined reappointment in 1800 because, in Jay's words, the judiciary lacked "the energy, weight, and dignity which are essential to its affording due support to the national government."[1] In his storied tenure on the bench, Marshall began to change all that.

*M*ODERN CIVICS TEXTBOOKS portray America's Supreme Court as the ultimate interpreter of America's supreme law, first among the branches in the art of constitutional interpretation. The Constitution itself presents a more balanced picture, listing the judicial branch third, pronouncing the justices "supreme" over other judges but not over other branches, and installing juries alongside judges. The Founders surely hoped that the judiciary would do its part to protect the Constitution, but just as surely they knew that much of the document's success, democratically and geostrategically, would depend on men other than life-tenured judges.

"one supreme Court, . . . and . . . inferior Courts"

When leading colonial lawmakers and soldiers spearheaded the drive for independence in 1775–76, few prominent colonial judges stood with them in the vanguard. Although elected patriot leaders did their best to influence the judicial-selection process in the mid-eighteenth century, imperial officials generally retained the right to appoint and remove American judges. In ten of the thirteen colonies, the sitting chief justice or his equivalent ultimately chose George III over George Washington.[2] Connecticut and Rhode Island, where colonists named their own judges, marked the main exceptions to this pattern. Putting aside continental congressmen from this pair of states, only three of the other fifty men who signed the Declaration of Independence had held notable positions on the colonial bench.[3]

In virtually every Revolutionary state constitution, the legislative and executive branches received more overall power and far more textual elaboration than the judiciary. Only in Massachusetts did the constitution feature three separate articles ("chapters") for the three main branches of government. Even this document treated the judiciary last and devoted to it only a fraction of the space spent embellishing the legislature and the executive. No state constitution explicitly authorized courts to disregard duly enacted statutes that the judges deemed unconstitutional.

By 1787, the American judiciary had begun to rise in repute. Patriots now peopled state courts everywhere. Six of the Constitution's thirty-nine signers had already served as prominent state or continental judges and several others were obvious prospects for appointment to the new federal judiciary on the drawing board. As the new system actually took shape, Philadelphia framers received three of the six appointments that Washington made to the Supreme Court in 1789 and filled two of the five Court slots that opened up later in his administration. Washington also tapped two fellow Philadelphians to serve among the first thirteen district court judges in 1789.[4] (By comparison, Philadelphians made up eleven of the twenty-two senators elected in 1789, eight of the initial fifty-nine House members, and two of the first five cabinet officers.)[5]

The Constitution proposed by the drafters gave federal judges more power and independence than their state counterparts commonly enjoyed. Yet even this document listed the judiciary last among the branches. The textual order of the Constitution's first three articles made both conceptual and democratic sense. Laws would first be enacted by the legislature and then implemented by the executive. Only at that point might the judiciary appear, if the executive commenced civil or criminal prosecution or if a private party brought suit claiming some legal violation. Also, in the new Constitution's first months, the budding branches would need to materialize in precise sequence. First, the new Congress would meet to count the ballots cast by presidential electors. Only then could an executive be installed, after which the first two branches could begin structuring the third—deciding the size and shape of the Supreme Court, the contours of the lower federal judiciary, and so on. Once these general decisions were made, the president and Senate would begin appointing individual judges.

This specific 1789 sequence tracked a more general democratic logic in which the institutions mentioned earliest in the document rested on the broadest electoral base, with later-mentioned entities layered atop broader tiers of the democratic pyramid. First came the pyramid's immense foundation, an extraordinary act of constitutional ordainment by "the People" themselves via the Preamble. Then came the next broadest level of popular input, Article I, in which ordinary voters and state legislatures would select congressional public servants. At the next (Article II) tier, voters, state lawmakers, and Congress members would interact to choose the president. In the final stratum (Article III), voters and state legislatures would fade from view as the men they chose for the first two branches made the major choices. Democratically, Congress ranked first among equals, and the life-tenured judiciary—furthest removed from the people and the states—came last.

To see the big picture from a different angle, begin by noting how the

Constitution in various places empowered legislators and executives to pick other legislators and executives. State lawmakers would elect federal senators; each congressional house would choose its own leaders; state legislatures could select presidential electors themselves or let the voters do so; Congress would break electoral-college deadlocks; state governors would tap men to fill temporary Senate vacancies; and presidents would name their cabinet subordinates—unilaterally in cases of temporary vacancies, and with the Senate's approval in other cases. The Constitution also empowered legislators and executives together to select judges, with Congress determining the number and type of judicial slots to be filled by the president and Senate.

Nowhere did the document symmetrically empower judges to name legislators or executives—or even other judges. State legislatures and state governors would help decide who would hold federal positions, but state judges would not. While representatives and senators would choose the House speaker and Senate leader, respectively, federal judges would have no say in the selection of the chief justice; nor would lower federal judges have formal input in selecting Supreme Court associate justices. The Constitution guaranteed the president's rights to hire and fire his cabinet subordinates but failed to guarantee any Supreme Court role in the appointment or removal of lower court judges. While each congressional house could cleanse itself by expelling members who misbehaved, neither the Supreme Court nor the judiciary as a whole enjoyed comparable inherent power to clean the judicial house.[6] Congress could impeach and remove judges, yet judges lacked counterbalancing authority to oust congressmen. In all these ways, implicating the essential power to fill up and empty out the branches, the judiciary was not just last but least.

True, Article III featured a "Court" that it called "supreme," but this adjective hardly meant that the judiciary outranked the legislature and executive. Rather, the word primarily addressed the hierarchy within the judiciary itself, placing America's highest court above any lower federal courts that might be created. Thus each of Article III's first two sentences juxtaposed the "supreme Court" against other "inferior" federal courts, as did earlier language in Article I empowering Congress to "constitute Tribunals inferior to the supreme Court." Yet even this "supreme Court" was given rather few constitutional tools to keep its underlings in line. Apart from its power to reverse or affirm lower court decisions via rulings that all inferior tribunals were honor-bound to follow, the Supreme Court had little inherent power to punish insubordinate deputies or reward loyal ones.[7] While a president typically had several practical ways of disciplining his executive inferiors, the Supreme Court had no automatic authority to change a lower court judge's work assignments, affect his pay, or modify his title. In some ways, Article III judges were almost as independent of one another as they were of other branches.

An early draft from Philadelphia had proposed creating *"one or more* supreme tribunals."[8] Several colonies had structured separate judicial tracks for different types of legal proceedings, and some Revolutionary states continued this pattern. Thus, within a given state, maritime disputes, equity suits, and common-law cases did not always end up in a single common court of last resort.[9] By contrast, the final draft of Article III envisioned "one supreme Court" with simultaneous appellate authority over "Law," "Equity," and "admiralty."* Nevertheless, Congress under the necessary-and-proper clause had considerable power to decide just how unitary this "one . . . Court" would be as a practical matter—for example, whether and when the justices would be obliged to sit in specialized smaller panels, rather than as an en banc collective.

ONCE A CASE REACHED the Supreme Court, no further appeal would lie to any other judicial tribunal. In particular, the president's cabinet would have no right to judicially review and reverse the Court, nor would the House or the Senate. Here, the Constitution broke with prior English and American practice. In England, the House of Lords sat not only as the legislative upper house but also as a general supreme court formally authorized to review judgments of the regular courts of King's Bench, Common Pleas, Exchequer, and so on.[10] Similarly, many American colonies and, later, some states permitted the governor's council (which in some places doubled as the upper legislative chamber) to act as a court of ultimate review. The Articles of Confederation had made "the United States in Congress assembled" the "last resort on appeal" in disputes between states, via a cumbersome process in which the Confederation Congress named individual arbitrators case by case.

The new Constitution structured a stricter separation of powers. As a rule, Congress would wield only "legislative" and not "judicial" power.

---

*In England, common law, equity, and admiralty were three distinct modes of adjudication, each with its own set of precedents and procedures. Juries traditionally sat in common-law suits but not in equity or admiralty cases. England also had ecclesiastical tribunals, in which government-chosen religious officials adjudicated matters of religious law. America's Constitution pointedly made no provision for religious courts, just as it withheld power from Congress to create a national church and it gave the president no power to appoint bishops.

Specific Article I language modified this general principle for a handful of high political matters beyond the ken of Article III courts—impeachments of federal officers, internal legislative disciplinary and expulsion proceedings, and certain controversies concerning contested legislative elections and qualifications. In these unusual situations involving an individual's right to serve as an officer or congressman—where routine interference by Article III courts risked inverting the document's grand democratic pyramid—the Constitution gave legislators power to "try" and "Judge" sundry issues of law and fact. Outside these few specially designated areas, federal adjudication would take place wholly within Article III courts and their state court counterparts.

Whenever a case involved an issue of federal law, the "supreme Court" would indeed stand supreme over state courts. Even if litigation began in a state tribunal, Article III mandated that "all" federal-law cases had to be appealable either to the Supreme Court itself or to one of its lieutenant tribunals among the "inferior" federal courts. As the central government's first line of defense against the excesses of individual states, the new Supreme Court would in a sense occupy an outpost once manned by England's Privy Council. Prior to 1776, the Council had the right to void colonial laws that it deemed contrary to fundamental rights or imperial policy. In all, it nullified over 450 laws in the century before independence.[11]

Yet England's Privy Council had no comparable right to void Parliament's enactments. Nor did regular eighteenth-century English judges claim any right to invalidate such acts. Under the emerging orthodoxy of parliamentary sovereignty, there was an ocean of difference between nullifying provincial laws and striking down parliamentary ones.

Under America's Constitution, founded on principles of popular sovereignty rather than legislative supremacy, the gulf between vertical review of state laws and horizontal review of congressional enactments would not seem quite so unbridgeable. America's judiciary would indeed have the authority to hear claims that Congress had exceeded the powers given to it by the sovereign citizenry. Nonetheless, the early Supreme Court would generally end up deferring to laws that had been approved by America's most distinguished statesmen in the House, Senate, and presidency. Between 1789 and 1850, although the Court would invalidate more than thirty state statutes, it would only once decline to carry out a provision of federal law—and even then the case (*Marbury v. Madison*) would involve a tiny sentence buried in a sprawling statute, a sentence regulating a technical issue of judicial procedure.[12]

State courts enforcing state constitutions in the years between 1776 and 1788 had likewise paid considerable deference to their respective legislatures. In only a handful of cases had any Revolutionary state judge openly refused to enforce a state statute on the grounds that it violated the state constitution, or even claimed the power of judicial review while upholding the state law in question. Spotty judicial reporting practices made it hard for ordinary citizens in the 1780s to know exactly what the judges in these few cases had decided and why.[13] Still, the idea of some sort of judicial review was in the air, even if not firmly on the ground, when the Philadelphia drafters met in the summer of 1787. Behind closed doors, several delegates declared that courts would have the right and even the duty to refuse to enforce congressional statutes that plainly violated the higher law of the Constitution itself. During the public ratification process that followed the secret drafting, Wilson, Publius, and other Federalists, especially in Virginia, explained that judges could and should refuse to enforce federal laws that were, in the words of *The Federalist* No. 78, "contrary to the manifest tenor of the Constitution."

But how "manifest" did a constitutional impropriety have to be so as to justify judicial disregard of a duly enacted congressional statute? Would federal judges void a federal statute if the constitutional issues were fairly debatable, or would they act only if a case involved a particularly egregious violation or an issue that specially related to judicial procedure? Though nothing in Article III's text explicitly addressed this precise point, the Constitution's general structure hinted at a rather modest judicial role.

In tandem with the Article I necessary-and-proper clause, Article III left the Supreme Court's size and shape up to Congress (and the president, via the veto power). While Article I expressly empowered each congressional house to "determine the Rules of its [internal] Proceedings" and authorized the houses jointly to decide when and where to meet, Article III gave the judiciary no comparably broad grant of institutional autonomy. Thus, Congress, not the Court, would have the upper hand in deciding how, when, and where the justices would sit, what rules of procedure they would follow, and so on.[14] Although the Constitution shielded individual judges against politically motivated salary cuts or attempted removals, it left the Court as a whole open to political restructuring. For example, the political branches could detour around an obstinate Court majority by expanding the size of the Court and appointing new justices more likely to defer. Of course, such efforts to pack the Court could fail if American voters opposed the plan—either because of specific agreement with the Court's initial rulings or because the public favored a judiciary with more institutional independence than Article III guaranteed. But these potential political obstacles to Court packing hardly meant that the Constitution designed the Court to be "supreme" over Congress. Rather, these obstacles illustrated how the document made the people supreme over all branches.

Unlike Congress and the president, state governments would have no formal say in determining the Court's general contours or in making the specific decisions about whom to put on it or pull off it. A state whose laws were declared unconstitutional could detour around the existing justices only by convincing the other federal branches that its grievance had merit. The Constitution's structure thus emboldened the Court to vindicate national values against obstreperous states even as it cautioned the justices to avoid undue provocation of Congress.

In fact, Congress had many weapons to wield or at least brandish against the justices, if it so chose. For instance, the legislature enjoyed vast discretion to grant or withhold judicial pay increases, to fund or deny judicial perks and support staff, to reshape the inferior federal judiciary, and even to strip the Court of jurisdiction in many cases. Though the Court might try to resist aggressive congressional tactics, the justices had fewer defensive weapons than did a president, whose fixed four-year salary shielded him against blatant legislative bribery and whose veto pen enabled him to parry any bill that diminished his domain. While judges could disregard a duly enacted law that weakened their branch only if they could with straight faces rule the law unconstitutional, a president could veto a duly presented bill that weakened his branch on that simple ground alone—or indeed for any other reason he saw fit to give.

Against the backdrop of frequent and highly visible gubernatorial vetoes in the colonial era, the Constitution carefully specified the procedures to be followed whenever the president sought to negative a congressional bill. Yet the document failed to specify comparable procedures to be followed when judges sought to void Congress's output—a small but telling sign that the Founders, with little actual experience with judicial review, did not anticipate that the judicial negative would one day surpass the executive negative as a check on Congress. For example, in the case of the veto, the Constitution specified that each presidential negative needed to be accompanied by the executive's "Objections," which would then be immediately entered on the journal of the originating house. The document further required that congressional override votes "shall be determined by yeas and Nays, and the Names of the Persons voting for and against the

Bill shall be entered on the Journal of each House," which had to be published on a regular and timely basis. By contrast, nowhere did the document require each individual justice to give his yea or nay on the constitutionality of a federal statute, or on any other issue. Under the Marshall Court, dissenting justices did indeed sometimes fail to publicly register their disagreement with the Court's ruling. Nor did the Constitution require immediate publication of judicial opinions setting congressional statutes at naught, or even the issuance of written opinions in such momentous cases. In the 1790s, justices routinely delivered oral opinions in the courtroom while offering up no written statement of reasons to the broader public. Timely publication of the justices' reasoning did not reliably occur until the late 1810s.

Even more telling was the Judicial Article's silence on issues of judicial apportionment. The precise apportionment rules for the House, Senate, and presidential electors appeared prominently in the Legislative and Executive Articles. These rules reflected weeks of intense debate and compromise at Philadelphia and generated extensive discussion during the ratification process. Yet the Judicial Article said absolutely nothing about how the large and small states, Northerners and Southerners, Easterners and Westerners, and so on, were to be balanced on the Supreme Court. This gaping silence suggests that the Founding generation envisioned the Court chiefly as an organ enforcing federal statutes and ensuring state compliance with federal norms. Just as it made sense to give the political branches wide discretion to shape the postal service, treasury department, or any other federal agency carrying out congressional policy, so, too, it made sense to allow Congress and the president to contour the federal judiciary as they saw fit. If, conversely, Americans in 1787 conceived of the Court not as a faithful servant of the House, Senate, and president but rather as a muscular overseer regularly striking down federal laws as a fourth chamber of federal lawmaking, then it is hard to explain why the document gave the first three chambers plenary power over the fourth's apportionment.

With no constitutional guidance or constraint, the political branches in antebellum America ultimately structured a Court that leaned south, just as Congress and the presidency themselves tilted in that direction thanks to the three-fifths clause. When not in the capital participating in Supreme Court cases, each justice would be responsible for hearing lower court cases within his assigned geographic "circuit." Antebellum Congresses drew the boundaries of these federal circuits with attention not merely to the underlying litigation population to be served and the caseload to be carried, but also to the number of square miles to be crisscrossed and the condition of the roads to be ridden. With its rural expanses and poor highways, the South won a far larger share of judicial posts than its underlying free population warranted. By the time of the *Dred Scott* case, slave states, with less than one-third of the nation's free population, claimed five of the nine judicial circuits—and thus a clear majority of Supreme Court seats.[15]

In its celebrated Judiciary Act of 1789, the First Congress created a six-man Supreme Court. From a modern perspective that views Court opinions as the unique last word on constitutional meaning—existing on a far higher plane than the constitutional views of congressmen, presidents, jurors, and voters—the number six might seem highly dysfunctional. After all, if the justices tied three to three, the country would lack definitive guidance from its anointed oracle. But at the Founding, an even number was not so odd. The eighteenth-century "supreme Court" was merely the highest judicial tribunal deciding individual cases. In the event of a tie, the status quo would continue. Thus, in an appeal, litigants would live with the result reached by the court below; and if the justices were instead sitting as a trial court, the plaintiff would simply lose his bid for judicial relief. In this eighteenth-century system, each justice would typically offer his own reasoning and speak only for himself, as judges customarily did in England and the states in 1787. No collective Court opinion would presume to be the last word. (Only under Marshall did the Court begin to speak with one voice, and not until the late twentieth century did the Court begin to describe itself as the "ultimate interpreter" of the Constitution.)[16]

Most of the constitutional controversies that flared up in the republic's first dozen years never came before the pre-Marshall Supreme Court. For example, did the president have the unilateral right to remove cabinet officers in whom he had lost confidence? Could the new federal government assume state Revolutionary War debts? Might it create a national bank? In apportioning Congress after a census, what sorts of mathematical rounding practices were permissible? If both the president and vice president died, could Congress name a legislative leader to take over? How and by whom should the Constitution's rules concerning fugitive slaves be enforced? Did the president have unilateral authority to decide whether and when to recognize a given foreign government? Did he have the right to proclaim America's neutrality in a European war? Must the president consult the Senate during the process of negotiating treaties? What part should the House play in assessing and implementing ratified treaties? To what extent could Congress properly interfere with property rights (in particular, preexisting slaveholding) in federal territory south of the Ohio River? Were members of Congress subject to impeachment? Did Congress have proper authority to punish political critics? How should the knotty presidential election of 1800–01 be untied?

Some of these early constitutional controversies presented "political questions" well outside the purview of eighteenth-century federal courts. Others involved lawsuits over which the Supreme Court lacked statutory appellate jurisdiction. Thus, in prosecutions under the Sedition Act of 1798, judiciary acts gave inferior federal courts the last judicial word. Not until the 1890s would Congress give the Supreme Court general appellate power to review federal criminal-law cases tried by lower federal courts. Apart from a few questions involving laws directly regulating judges and their jurisdiction, perhaps the biggest issue to reach the early Court concerned the scope of Congress's power to impose a tax on carriages. In their individual opinions on the matter, the justices unanimously agreed to uphold the constitutional consensus that had been reached by the political branches on this topic.[17]

OVER THE NEXT TWO CENTURIES, several factors would conspire to exalt the Court's absolute and relative positions. In the system's first hundred years, as new states entered the union and Congress periodically redrew circuit lines, the Court's size fluctuated from five to ten members, a fluidity that made Court packing easier to accomplish or at least threaten. But eventually the American frontier closed, circuit riding ended, and the Court's size stabilized at nine. Inertia took hold and certain political levers began to rust up. Even a popular Franklin Roosevelt in the afterglow of a triumphant reelection encountered stiff opposition to his 1937 plan to change the Court's basic size and shape (and thereby pack it with his own appointees).

At the other end of the judicial hierarchy, the mushrooming number of federal statutes on the books has required an ever-increasing number of lower court federal judges to manage all the resulting issues arising under federal law. This vastly broader base of lower court judges has in turn given the high Court that many more "inferior" federal officers to order around, officers who by both constitutional command and professional training have generally seen themselves as the Court's lieutenants. In its earliest judiciary acts, in 1789 and 1790, Congress created fifteen district court judgeships—one for every seven (post-1792) representatives.[18] Today, there are nearly a thousand lower court federal judges, two for every

House member. Thus the ratio of Article III judges to Article I representatives has increased roughly fifteenfold. Each judge today customarily radiates authority over a circle of local intimates—magistrates, masters, law clerks, and so on—through whom the judiciary's informal influence seeps into every corner of the country. For example, top students graduating from elite law schools are far more apt to apprentice by clerking for a federal judge than by interning for a representative or senator. A large federal judicial corps has thus blunted two of the major advantages enjoyed by federal legislators at the Founding: sheer numerousness and personal connectedness to ordinary citizens.[19]

Improved reporting practices have enabled the Court to get its message out, and quickly. Nowadays, in any given case a majority of justices ordinarily sign on to a single "Opinion of the Court," an opinion widely viewed as the last word on the Constitution's meaning. Meanwhile, a partisan and crumbly Congress has often found it hard to speak with one voice, and presidents have come to be seen as party politicians rather than impartial magistrates.

As the Court has asserted more power for itself, the other branches and the citizenry have frequently yielded. At the turn of the twentieth century, Congress gave the Court sweeping power to review lower federal court rulings and greater bureaucratic control over the judiciary as a whole; today, there are no important pockets of federal law over which inferior courts can rule without being subject to direct reversal by the Supreme Court.[20] At the Founding, the prestige-and-power gap between the six Supreme Court justices and the fifteen federal district court judges was much smaller than the gulf that now separates nine justices from the thousand-odd lower federal court judges. For instance, justices no longer routinely sit alongside district judges from their home region. Thus, even as the third branch has risen vis-à-vis the first two, so has the Supreme Court risen vis-à-vis the lower federal bench.[21]

Also, Congress in the early twentieth century gave the Supreme Court vast discretion over its own appellate docket.[22] Today's Court thus has near-plenary authority to define its own agenda, a luxury once possessed only by the political branches. Decades of divided government at the close of both the nineteenth and twentieth centuries have pitted presidents against Congress, enabling the Court to draw more power to itself at minimal risk of political reprisal. After Vietnam and Watergate, much of the public has come to view the judiciary as more honest and competent than the politicians in other branches. Modern presidents and congressmen are far less likely to assert their own constitutional visions than were their antebellum predecessors. For example, in dramatic contrast to the pattern set in the eighteenth and nineteenth centuries, only a handful of twentieth- and twenty-first-century Inaugural Addresses have explicitly meditated upon the Constitution itself, and only a small percentage of recent veto messages have articulated objections based on the president's independent constitutional judgment.[23]

Finally, at the highest level of American lawmaking, the nation has approved one constitutional amendment after another with the increasing expectation that litigants may come to court to define and enforce their constitutional rights, even against Congress. Thus Article III's small-s "supreme Court" has become modern America's capital-S "Supreme Court."

"good Behaviour"

Combining various elements of English law and Revolutionary state practice into a unique pattern, the federal Constitution structured a novel and notable system of judicial selection and tenure.

The new system began with a collaborative judicial appointment process, a process first sketched out by the paper Constitution and then fleshed out by actual practice under George Washington and his successors. As with virtually all other important officers of the United States, federal judges were generally to be nominated by the president and confirmed by the Senate.[24]

This collaborative process aimed to produce judges who embodied republican excellence. During the colonial era, kings had unilaterally named judges in England, and unelected governors had done the same in America. Even when such executives had chosen to honor men of acknowledged merit (perhaps after broad informal consultation), the process nevertheless failed to guarantee the people's elected representatives sufficient input. Whether or not these traditional systems resulted in judicial excellence, they surely were unrepublican. After independence, state legislatures and councils often began to pick judges collectively, with no single leader being obliged to accept responsibility for any given appointment. Similarly, the Articles of Confederation allowed a hydra-headed Congress to choose continental arbitrators and adjudicators. Though tolerably republican, these Revolutionary appointment systems seemed ill suited to maximize judicial excellence. By contrast, each Article III judge would be a man whom the president had personally endorsed, presumably after careful investigation. After all, the nominator's reputation as well as the nominee's would be at stake in the confirmation process, with the Senate free to say yea or nay.

All Article III judgeships would be formally open to all (free) men of merit. While England barred nonnatives from serving as judges, America would welcome naturalized citizens. In fact, three of the first ten men to sit on the Supreme Court and two of the first twenty-five federal district judges were immigrants. At least two early justices, James Wilson and William Paterson, had risen from middling origins. Yet several others—John Jay, John Blair, Jr., William Cushing, James Iredell, Oliver Ellsworth, and Bushrod Washington—were close kin of prominent judges and politicians. Most early justices came from relatively privileged backgrounds, as did the majority of the district judges appointed in 1789.[25]

The Constitution allowed the president and the Senate to consider political and ideological factors in selecting Supreme Court justices and lower court judges, and such variables did in fact figure prominently in early appointments. Every one of the eight men to sit on the Supreme Court before 1796 had been a highly visible Federalist in 1787–88. The first former Anti-Federalist whom Washington named to the Court, Samuel Chase, did not win the president's favor until Chase had shown himself to be a strong post-ratification supporter of the president's administration.[26] Of Washington's sixteen initial nominees to the district bench —all of whom the Senate confirmed but three of whom declined to serve—nine had publicly supported the Constitution in their respective ratifying conventions, and several others had demonstrated their commitment to the Federalist cause in other ways. Conversely, none had voted against the Constitution in state convention.*[27]

---

*Washington's sole Anti-Federalist appointee to the district bench in 1789 was Kentucky's Harry Innes, who had expressed opposition to the proposed Constitution several months before the Virginia ratifying convention met. It is unclear whether Washington knew of this opposition, but he did know that Innes had the strong backing of John Brown, the congressman from Virginia's Kentucky district who himself had vigorously supported ratification. Washington also knew that Innes's younger brother James had delivered a key Federalist speech at the Virginia convention, where young Innes stood out as one of only three (out of fourteen) Kentucky-district delegates to vote yes. (In fact, Washington offered to nominate James as U.S. attorney general, but young Innes declined for personal reasons.)

A note on my terminology in this section and elsewhere in this book: During the Constitution's first decade, political alignments shifted as the great debate between Federalists and Anti-Federalists in 1787–88 gave way to a new competition between Federalists and Republicans in the late 1790s. The "Federalists" of 1787–88 should not be automatically equated with the "Federalists" of 1796 and thereafter. For example, the 1787 Federalist James Madison became a leading Republican in the 1790s; conversely, as mentioned in the text, the old Anti-Federalist Samuel Chase morphed into a prominent Federalist.

After Washington's departure, openly partisan competition heated up in federal legislative and executive races and also in federal judicial politics. John Adams sought to stuff the bench with fellow Federalists; Jefferson, with fellow Republicans. In 1810, ex-president Jefferson counseled his incumbent friend, James Madison, not to appoint Joseph Story to the Court because Story was, in Jefferson's view, "unquestionably a tory" who as a congressman had "deserted" Jefferson on the administration's embargo policies. In the end (after three failed attempts to appoint other men) Madison named Story, who described himself as "a decided member of what was called the republican party, and of course a supporter of the administration of Mr. Jefferson and Mr. Madison," albeit a republican of "independent judgment" and not a "mere slave to the opinions of either [president]."[28] Not until Republican Abraham Lincoln named Democrat Stephen Field would a president openly reach across party lines in a Supreme Court nomination—and when Lincoln did so in 1863, the deepest ideological divide ran not between Republicans and Democrats but between Unionists and Secessionists. (In 1864, Lincoln would run under a "Union Party" banner alongside a War Democrat, Andrew Johnson.)[29]

From its earliest days, the Senate in its confirmation process felt free to consider the same broad range of factors that a president might permissibly consider in his nomination decisions. For example, senators in 1795 voted down John Rutledge for the chief justiceship largely because they doubted his political judgment. The Judicial Article thus provided for an openly political and ideological process of initial appointment. Presidents and senators could not properly extract promises from a judicial nominee but were free to indulge in predictions about how that nominee might rule and to factor such predictions into their appointments calculus.[30]

ONCE A JUDICIAL NOMINEE had successfully run the appointment gauntlet, the Judicial Article promised that he would enjoy an undiminishable salary and tenure during "good Behaviour." These interlocking guarantees counterbalanced the need to shield judges from inflation against the need to shield them from Congress. In the case of a president serving a fixed four-year term, Article II required Congress to cement the executive salary at the outset, with adjustments permitted only for future presidential terms. This rigid Article II system risked unfairness if prices jumped unexpectedly within a single term, but every four years, corrections could be made. Article III required a different approach. Judicial tenure during "good Behaviour" meant indefinite stints stretching out over decades, perhaps. To do justice to the men charged with doing justice, Congress needed authority to increase judicial salaries whenever unforeseeable inflation arose.[31] Yet such authority left the judiciary partially vulnerable to the legislative power of the purse. The power to grant an increase involved the power to withhold an increase, and also the power to dangle an increase.

Nevertheless, Article III gave individual judges more security than was typical in England and America. In Tudor and Stuart times, the monarch could unseat any judge who displeased him. Not for nothing was one prominent English court known as the "King's Bench," for the judiciary largely took shape as an extension of the Crown's authority to do justice to its subjects. After the Glorious Revolution, the 1701 Act of Settlement promised English judges tenure *"quamdiu se bene gesserint"* (Latin for "during good behavior") and further provided that judges should have salaries "ascertained and established"—that is, subject to legislative increase, but not diminution. Yet these words meant somewhat less than met the eye. In the emerging system of parliamentary sovereignty, the monarch could no longer remove judges at will, but Parliament itself could do so when both houses issued an "address" calling for a judicial unseating. Monarchs also retained considerable power to grant, withhold, or dangle judicial pensions and other perks.

Whatever comfort the 1701 Act gave to judges in England, it offered none to judges in America, who continued to be subject to removal at the whim of the executive. At the outset of George III's reign, several colonies tried to insulate judges from unilateral executive removal, but imperial officials vetoed these efforts.[32] Seeking other ways to counterbalance the judiciary's dependence on the executive, many colonial legislatures denied judges fixed salaries. Thus if a colonial judge leaned too far in one direction he could be fired (by the executive) and if he leaned too far in the other direction he could be starved (by the legislature). When England proposed to tip this balance of terror in the early 1770s by giving provincial judges fixed salaries, patriots were outraged. Though judges should be independent of unelected executives, it hardly followed that judges should be equally independent of elected legislatures.

Much as the Glorious Revolution had shifted power over the judiciary from the executive to the legislature, so the American Revolution repeated this shift almost a century later. In 1776, the Declaration of Independence scathed George III for endeavoring to make "judges dependent on his will alone, for the tenure of their offices, and the amount and payment of their salaries." Turning from negation to affirmation, Americans in their initial state constitutions commonly promised judges tenure during "good behaviour."[33] As in England, there was a catch: Most state constitutions with "good behaviour" clauses made clear that legislators could vote to remove judges by "address" even in the absence of adjudicated wrongdoing.[34] Only half the states explicitly guaranteed "fixed" or "permanent" judicial salaries (which legislators might raise but not lower), and none coupled this guarantee with all the other basic features of Article III, namely, executive appointment, life tenure, and the absence of legislative "address."[35]

Article III thus offered the federal judiciary a uniquely protective package. "Good Behaviour" now meant what it said: A federal judge could be ousted from office only if he misbehaved, with adjudication of misbehavior taking place in a judicial forum. Pointedly withholding from Congress any general power to remove a judge by legislative "address," the framers instead told Congress to *adjudicate* a judge's alleged misbehavior while sitting in a judicialized impeachment process. Thus, the House, acting as a grand jury, could impeach any judicial officer—or any executive officer, for that matter—who committed a high crime or misdemeanor, and the Senate, sitting as a court, would proceed to render judgment.

In effect, "good *Behaviour*" and "high . . . *Misdemeanor*[]" defined two sides of the same linguistic coin. The precise wording of Article III confirmed that "Misdemeanor" in Article II was best read to mean misbehavior in a general sense as opposed to a certain kind of technical criminality. In the early republic, the House in fact impeached two federal judges for egregious, but noncriminal, misbehavior. In 1804, the Senate convicted New Hampshire District Judge John Pickering for drunkenness and profanity on the bench; the following year, a majority of senators voted to convict Associate Justice Samuel Chase of judicial impropriety and abusiveness but failed to muster the two-thirds vote required by the Constitution. This supermajority rule, too, offered judges more protection than did England and most states, where simple majorities of impeachment courts sufficed to convict.[36]

Above and beyond impeachment, ordinary criminal courts could entertain prosecutions brought against federal judges, and Congress by law could provide for automatic removal from office upon due conviction. For example, Congress might decide that accepting a bribe was disqualifying misbehavior per se and provide by a generally applicable law that any federal judge convicted of bribery in a criminal court must immediately forfeit his judgeship. In fact, the First Congress did just that in a 1790 bribery statute. This enactment built on foundations laid by several states whose constitutions and/or statutes made clear that "conviction in a court of law" could result in automatic forfeiture of judicial office.[37] Thus, the federal Constitution provided for two distinct removal tracks, one via ordinary criminal conviction and the other via the extraordinary politico-judicial process of impeachment.[38]

In the charged atmosphere following the election of 1800–01, Congress tried to add a third removal track and got away with it. In 1801, a lame-duck (and electorally repudiated) Federalist Congress created a row of new federal judgeships, which President Adams proceeded to pack with Federalists in the closing hours of his administration. Unamused, President Jefferson and his Republican allies in Congress took action in 1802 to oust these judges en masse by simply repealing the 1801 law that had created the judgeships. None of these ousted judges had been adjudged guilty of any misbehavior; and a simple legislative majority had sufficed to enact the repealing statute. In effect, if not in name, this was removal by address. Nevertheless, when the issue reached the Supreme Court in *Stuart v. Laird,* an 1803 companion case to *Marbury v. Madison,* the Court yielded to the new Congress's force majeure and fait accompli.[39]

In this early judicial capitulation, we glimpse yet again the weakness of the early judiciary when confronting a united legislature and executive. Nowadays, *Marbury* is customarily the first case assigned in a law-school course on the Constitution. Most lawyers—indeed, many law professors—have never heard of *Stuart v. Laird.* But in the early nineteenth century, the trivial statutory section that the Court struck down in *Marbury* paled in significance to the prominent provisions that the Court felt obliged to uphold in *Stuart.* For all *Marbury*'s bold notes, John Marshall was sounding his judicial trumpet in retreat.[40]

In a variety of ways, then, judicial tenure during "good Behaviour" did not wholly remove judges from the ebb and flow of larger political currents. Indeed, the very open-endedness of this form of tenure may well have inclined many an early federal judge to think politically about his judicial exit strategy—that is, about a possible political career after his time on the bench and about the optimal political timing of his eventual judicial resignation. For example, neither of America's first two chief justices served for life or anything close to it. Instead, John Jay left the bench after six years to become governor of New York, and Oliver Ellsworth quit after four and a half years, timing his resignation in a manner that guaranteed that fellow Federalist John Adams would name his replacement. Together these two chiefs spent only ten years on the Court and lived for some forty years thereafter. In 1791, Associate Justice John Rutledge left the Court for a government job in his home state, and Associate Justice

William Cushing would likely have followed suit in 1794 had he bested Sam Adams in the contest for the governorship of Massachusetts. In the republic's earliest years, judicial tenure during "good Behaviour" often simply meant "until resignation."

In 1787, this was the only model of judicial independence familiar to most Americans, a model that prevailed in eighteenth-century England and in most of the newly independent states. Only New York had hit upon an alternative approach to judicial independence, featuring a long term with a fixed end date—in New York's case, tenure during good behavior until age sixty.

Today, however, some version of this alternative model prevails in almost every American state and in most other advanced democratic nations.[41] Judges in these regimes typically serve for relatively long fixed stints and/or up to a mandatory retirement age. This alternative model arguably does a superior job of insulating sitting judges from partisan politics. By giving each judge a fixed target date of departure, this model facilitates the emergence of informal norms whereby each judge is expected to either serve out his defined term or give some nonpartisan reason (for example, personal health) for leaving early. By contrast, in a regime of life tenure, unless there exists a strong norm that each judge will in fact serve until death, there is no obvious target date of departure, no fixed and focal baseline against which to measure an "early" resignation. Thus each judge remains freer to design his own individual exit strategy with a finger in the political wind and an eye on the political calendar. Well into the modern era, sitting justices have left the Court for political pastures or have strongly considered doing so.[42] It remains common for a justice to time his resignation so as to advantage the political party that named him to the bench.

Nevertheless, modern judicial exit strategies have been less openly political than one might have predicted based on the early trajectory traced by Rutledge, Cushing, Jay, and Ellsworth. After these men came John Marshall, who profoundly changed the Court simply by staying put, serving for more than three decades, until his death in 1835. (After Jefferson's inauguration, Marshall also avoided open participation in partisan politics of the sort that Jay and Cushing had dabbled in and that Chase had pursued with such clumsy zeal as to provoke impeachment and near-removal.) Just as Washington's unprecedented example helped gloss the phrase "four Years," so Marshall's extraordinary tenure helped redefine the words "good Behaviour." In the Executive Article, "four Years" eventually came to mean no more than eight years, while in the Judicial Article, "good Behaviour" generally came to mean far more than eight years. The combined legacy of the early republic's dominant trendsetters—Washington, Jefferson, Madison, Monroe, and Marshall (Virginians all, interestingly enough)—was that presidents would renounce a norm of de facto life tenure, while judges would embrace it.

"all Cases"

Article III's first section began by vesting all federal courts with "the judicial Power of the United States." Article III's second (and penultimate) section began with complementary language listing nine categories of "Cases" and "Controversies" over which this "judicial Power" would extend. First on the list were "all Cases, in Law and Equity, arising under" federal law; a little later came lawsuits dealing with admiralty and maritime issues, followed by an assortment of suits involving state law—most important, controversies between citizens of different states.

In form and feel—and placement, too—this roster of lawsuits suitable for federal court adjudication resembled the Constitution's earlier rosters describing congressional and presidential powers. Yet these two earlier lists (which appeared in the penultimate sections of Articles I and II) differed in one key way: Article I comprehensively enumerated Congress's legislative powers, whereas Article II merely exemplified and clarified certain aspects of the president's executive power without exhaustively enumerating all its component elements.

In this respect, the judicial-power list resembled the legislative-power list,[43] and for good reason. Federal legislative and judicial power could be exhaustively itemized without grave risk to the republic. When enumerated grants of federal authority ran out, state legislatures with plenary police powers could fill the gaps of federal statutes, and state courts of general jurisdiction could hear any lawsuits that lay beyond the reach of federal courts. By contrast, thirteen state executives—with no international standing, zero diplomatic experience, few if any professional soldiers or warships, and only modest capacity to coordinate among themselves across the miles that separated them—could not always be relied on to save the nation in an hour of crisis. Hence the special need to vest America's president with a residuum of executive power to preserve the Constitution whenever fortune or foes might imperil its very existence.

In another respect, however, the judicial roster resembled its executive counterpart by identifying certain powers that Congress could not take away or give to any other body. Just as the powers vested in the president were his, not Congress's, so the powers vested in the federal judiciary belonged to the third branch, not the first. Congress had no right to snatch the president's pardon pen and hand it to state governors; nor could Congress transfer the final word in federal-law cases from federal courts to state judges. The interlocking language of Article III, sections 1 and 2 demanded that federal judicial power "*shall* be vested" in federal courts and "*shall* extend to *all*" cases arising under federal law.

True, state courts of general jurisdiction could entertain a wide range of federal-law cases—whether the federal issue arose in the plaintiff's complaint, the defendant's answer, or still later in the back-and-forth of litigation. Nevertheless, these state courts could not properly pronounce the last judicial word on federal law. That job was part of "the judicial Power *of the United States*" vested solely in federal courts, and rightly so. No state judge would have been named by the president or confirmed by the Senate; nor would any state judge enjoy federal-constitutional tenure and salary guarantees; nor would a state judge be subject to congressional impeachment in the event of gross misbehavior, or automatic removal from office upon conviction of a federal offense.[44]

While state courts had to be reviewable by some federal tribunal whenever a case hinged on a claim of federal right, that federal tribunal did not need to be the Supreme Court. All other federal courts were also clothed with the judicial power of the United States, and therefore could serve as courts of last resort, with no automatic requirement that their decisions be appealable to the Supreme Court. The Constitution gave Congress broad power to allocate cases within the federal judicial system. For example, Congress was free to decide that in most run-of-the-mill cases, state court decisions should be reviewed by some nearby inferior federal court, and that not every federal case needed to be dragged across a continent for further review by a single Supreme Court. Inferior federal courts could be trusted with the last judicial word because these courts would be staffed by judges selected in the same way, guaranteed the same tenure, and accountable for misconduct in the same manner as Supreme Court justices. Congress's power to shift a given case, or a wide swath of cases, from the Supreme Court to some inferior federal court resembled the power of the political branches to pack the Court or otherwise restructure it. In all these situations, the political branches would decide *which* federal judges would be decisive.

The Constitution did not require Congress to create inferior federal courts. Nevertheless, Congress has always chosen to rely on such courts, and in the new nation's early years these courts played a particularly large role within the federal judiciary. Under the landmark Judiciary Act of 1789, lower federal courts heard and finally resolved virtually all federal criminal cases; no general right of direct appeal to the Supreme Court existed in such cases. On the civil side, early statutes limited the Supreme Court's review over lower federal court judges to cases in which those judges were themselves divided or where great sums of money were involved.

ALTHOUGH THE FIRST JUDICIARY ACT—and indeed all later congressional statutes regulating the judiciary—gave federal courts the last judicial word over all cases arising under federal law,[45] Congress from the beginning pursued a different course concerning other sorts of lawsuits described in Article III. Consider for example what lawyers refer to as "diversity" suits—that is, lawsuits arising between citizens of diverse states. Under the 1789 Act (and all subsequent statutes for that matter), if a citizen of state A were to sue a citizen of state B, alleging small damages in a controversy revolving solely around state-law issues, no federal court could entertain the matter. Yet such a lawsuit surely fell within the federal judicial roster: "The judicial Power shall extend to . . . Controversies . . . between Citizens of different States." Why, then, did the First Congress allow state courts to have the last judicial word over many of these controversies?

Perhaps the answer lay coiled tightly in the intricate and intriguing language of Article III. (For those who wish to solve the textual puzzle for themselves, the key passage is reprinted at the bottom of this page.*) As drafted, the judicial roster contained two textually distinct tiers. In the roster's opening words—the top tier—federal jurisdiction extended to *"all"* cases arising under federal law, to *"all"* cases involving foreign ambassadors and consuls, and to *"all"* admiralty cases. In this top tier, the word "all" popped up again and again. Yet lower down on the roster—the bottom tier—the word "all" suddenly dropped away.

---

*"The judicial Power shall extend to all Cases, in Law and Equity, arising under this Constitution, the Laws of the United States, and Treaties made, or which shall be made, under their Authority;—to all Cases affecting Ambassadors, other public Ministers and Consuls;—to all Cases of admiralty and maritime Jurisdiction;—to Controversies to which the United States shall be a Party;—to Controversies between two or more States;—between a State and Citizens of another State;—between Citizens of different States;—between Citizens of the same State claiming Lands under Grants of different States, and between a State, or the Citizens thereof, and foreign States, Citizens or Subjects." U.S. Const., art. III, sec. 2, para 1.

Why did the Constitution use the word "all" repeatedly but selectively? What meaning, if any, should be attributed to this pattern? On the most straightforward reading, "all" meant just what it said: Federal courts had to be the last word in "all" top-tier cases, but not necessarily all bottom-tier lawsuits. In the bottom tier (including diversity "Controversies . . . between Citizens of different States"), Congress was free to decide, thanks to the necessary-and-proper clause, whether federal courts should hear all of these lawsuits, or some of them, or none of them.[46]

This close textual reading made good structural sense in 1789 and continues to make good sense today. Aside from a handful of cases involving foreign ambassadors (lawsuits whose exceptional international delicacy warranted trials in the Supreme Court itself), the basic difference between the two tiers involved the source of law at issue. Top-tier cases inherently involved matters of federal law. Lower-tier cases did not.

In the top tier, Article III encompassed all claims of federal right—whether the claim derived from the Constitution itself,[47] federal statutes, or federal treaties; and whether the suit sounded in "Law," "Equity," or "admiralty."[48] *Federal* laws would thus be enacted by a *federal* legislature, enforced by a *federal* executive, and ultimately adjudicated by a *federal* judiciary. As Hamilton/Publius explained in *The Federalist* No. 80, "If there are such things as political axioms, the propriety of the judicial power of a government being co-extensive with its legislative, may be ranked among the number."[49]

Bottom-tier controversies were intrinsically different. These disputes might turn solely on state-law issues over which state courts were traditionally seen as authoritative. Federal jurisdiction was nevertheless permissible in bottom-tier situations because some state courts, in applying state law, might betray bias against nonresidents. Thus, in various lawsuits potentially pitting a home-state litigant against an outsider—say, a citizen of a sister state—Congress could choose to open up some federal court whose job would be to apply state substantive law impartially. But Congress could also choose to let state courts decide these state-law cases free from federal judicial oversight. As the new nation began to knit closer together economically and socially, bias against nonresidents might well subside and state courts might prove that they could be trusted to hold the scales of justice evenly between in-staters and outsiders.

Of course, a given lawsuit might simultaneously fall in both the first and second tiers. For instance, a case might pivot on a point of federal law while also arising between citizens of different states. In such situations, federal courts would need to be involved. "All Cases" meant *all* cases.

While drafting records of the Philadelphia Convention confirm that Article III's framers did indeed intend a two-tiered system,[50] none of these secret records were available to the American people when they were asked to ratify the Constitution in 1787–88. Instead, the ratifying generation confronted the bare text of the Article III roster itself—a section bristling with technical legal language that invited a close reading attentive to overarching principles of constitutional structure. Even without the aid of the secret drafting documents, the First Congress designed the 1789 Judiciary Act in a manner that fit snugly within the Judicial Article's basic two-tiered framework.* It probably didn't hurt that this Congress included eight representatives and eleven senators who had served as delegates at Philadelphia.

When questions about the 1789 Act eventually reached the Supreme Court, the justices, in a series of landmark opinions authored by John Marshall and Joseph Story, highlighted the Judicial Article's two-tiered structure. As Story—himself a former congressman, as was Marshall—explained, "congress seem, in a good degree, in the establishment of the present judicial system, to have adopted this distinction" between the two tiers, a distinction which the Court's opinion "brought into view in deference to the legislative opinion, which has so long acted upon, and enforced" it.[51]

Here, too, we see the early judiciary—led by two ex-congressmen—following Congress's cue rather than imperiously dictating to the first branch.

"supreme Court . . . original Jurisdiction"

The most celebrated constitutional-law case ever decided pivoted on one of the Constitution's most recondite provisions. According to John Marshall's opinion for the Court in *Marbury v. Madison,* part of Congress's 1789 Judiciary Act attempted to do what the Judicial Article did not permit—namely, expand the Court's original jurisdiction. Marshall's Court famously proceeded to disregard this part of the act, thereby exercising a

---

*The Act left state courts with exclusive jurisdiction over a huge number of bottom-tier lawsuits—most dramatically, state-law disputes between citizens of different states involving less than $500—but gave federal courts the last judicial word over all claims of federal right. Lower federal courts were left unreviewable over a wide assortment of federal-law cases, but state courts were not; even if a federal-law case in a state tribunal involved the most trifling sum of money, any party claiming a federal right could appeal from state to federal court. Later jurisdictional statutes have followed this 1789 pattern, giving federal courts jurisdiction over all top-tier cases, but nothing close to plenary jurisdiction over lower-tier suits.

power that later Americans would call judicial review. Most constitutional-law casebooks begin with *Marbury* and lavish attention on the topic of judicial review. Few casebooks devote more than a paragraph to the precipitating issue of original jurisdiction.

In listing the cases that federal courts could hear, the judicial roster did nothing to allocate these cases within the federal judiciary, between the Supreme Court and inferior federal courts. Nor did the roster define when the Supreme Court would preside over trials and when it would instead act as an appellate tribunal. Hence the need for Article III's next paragraph, which outlined the Court's original and appellate jurisdiction as follows:

> In all Cases affecting Ambassadors, other public Ministers and Consuls, and those in which a State shall be Party, the supreme Court shall have original Jurisdiction. In all the other Cases before mentioned [in the roster], the supreme Court shall have appellate Jurisdiction, both as to Law and Fact, with such Exceptions, and under such Regulations as the Congress shall make.

This terse paragraph teemed with technical complexities, many of which need not detain us now.[52] But it is worth pondering why the Constitution placed certain *bottom*-tier state-law suits between states and nonresidents in the Court's *original* (trial) jurisdiction. After all, such cases were so insignificant that Congress could have removed them altogether from the federal judiciary as a whole. Why, then, did Article III provide that *if* such lower-tier suits were to be heard by federal courts, they could be brought to the Supreme Court itself for trial?

To answer this question, let's recall that Article III allowed Congress to give federal courts jurisdiction in suits between states and nonresidents because state courts might be biased against outsiders. Yet federal judicial intervention might raise bias problems of its own. Imagine a suit between the state of Massachusetts and a Georgia merchant—involving, say, a business deal gone bad. If the lawsuit involved no issue of federal law, Congress could allow state courts to decide the matter. But if Congress instead opted for federal jurisdiction, just where should the federal trial take place? An inferior federal court sitting in either Massachusetts or Georgia, featuring a local jury and a federal judge who likely came from the forum state, might be seen, especially in the other state, as reflecting federal bias in what was supposed to be an evenhanded venue.

Trial in the Supreme Court itself promised stricter federal impartiality.

Litigation would begin and end in a neutral capital city outside the affected states—a venue metaphorically if not literally equidistant between the states while presumably convenient for all of them. Every state government would have agents in the national seat—most obviously, its senators—who could monitor litigation on the state's behalf, and perhaps argue the state's case themselves. In the early 1780s, Confederation congressmen had appeared as lawyers in each of the three state-versus-state cases that had come before the ad hoc continental tribunals provided for by the Articles of Confederation. A similar litigation pattern would prevail under the new Constitution. For most of the nineteenth century, the Court would meet in the Capitol itself, and congressmen would frequently appear as advocates. Daniel Webster would argue more Court cases (about 170) than any other counsel in history, save one.[53]

Similar considerations of geographic impartiality and convenience help explain why Article III also gave the Supreme Court original jurisdiction over all cases affecting foreign ambassadors, who would customarily live in the national capital. Even in cases involving lesser foreign officials who might reside elsewhere, the Supreme Court's proximity to the president and the State Department made it an apt venue. The justices could easily keep abreast of the executive branch's position on any fast-breaking international development that might bear on such litigation. Trial in America's highest court would also symbolize America's supreme respect for foreign dignitaries.

But could Congress extend the Supreme Court's original jurisdiction to any cases other than those involving states or foreign dignitaries? This was the technical constitutional question to which the Marshall Court answered a resounding no in *Marbury v. Madison*. Marshall's opinion for the Court treated the Article III issue as self-evident. The original-jurisdiction clause, he suggested, would be meaningless unless read as a cap. Yet modern critics have floated facially plausible alternative readings of Article III—arguing, for example, that perhaps the original-jurisdiction clause merely marked a starting point, defining a presumptive amount of Supreme Court trial jurisdiction that Congress might properly augment.[54]

The best reading of Article III supports *Marbury*. While Article III pointedly said that Congress could make "Exceptions" to the Supreme Court's appellate jurisdiction, nowhere did it say that Congress might likewise make "augmentations" to the Court's original jurisdiction. During the ratification debates, several leading Federalists strongly anticipated *Marbury* when they insisted that Article III defined the outer limits of Supreme Court original jurisdiction. Hamilton/Publius repeatedly reassured his readers that the Court's original jurisdiction would "be confined to two classes of causes, and those of a nature rarely to occur." "All other cases" in the roster could be tried by other federal courts but not the Supreme Court, whose original jurisdiction extended "only" to state-party and foreign-diplomat cases, said Publius. In Virginia, ratification-convention president Edmund Pendleton declared that the Constitution "excludes [Supreme Court] original jurisdiction in all other cases" and that "the legislature cannot extend its original jurisdiction, which is limited to these cases only." Later, both Chief Justice Jay and Associate Justice Chase said much the same thing in private correspondence, and no leading figure said otherwise in public. After *Marbury,* none of the critics of John Marshall's opinion—and there were many—challenged his reading of Article III's original-jurisdiction clause.[55]

Why, we might wonder, were early Americans so emphatic and nearly unanimous on the point? Why would *Supreme Court* original jurisdiction differ so decisively from *inferior federal court* original jurisdiction? Or to ask the question a different way, why would Supreme Court *original* jurisdiction be so different from Supreme Court *appellate* jurisdiction?

Once again, the answer was geography. Inferior federal courts would be located in the several states. Trials in these courts would not require all the parties and witnesses to be dragged hundreds of miles to the national capital. Issues of fact and credibility in common-law cases could be decided by jurors who came from the locality where the underlying events had occurred. After trials had taken place in these proper venues, appeals to a faraway Supreme Court could be made without comparable inconvenience. Appeals would enable the high court to review the legal issues involved but would not typically require that all the parties, witnesses, physical evidence, et cetera, be carted to the national seat of government.

All of which leaves us with a final puzzle: Why did the First Congress try to expand the Supreme Court's original jurisdiction, contrary to Article III's letter and spirit? The short answer is that Congress in fact did no such thing. The statutory sentence that the *Marbury* Court flamboyantly refused to enforce did not say what the Court accused it of saying. Rather than adding to the Court's original jurisdiction, the sentence simply provided that if and when the Court already had jurisdiction (whether original or appellate), the justices would be empowered to issue certain technical writs—in particular, writs of prohibition and mandamus.[56]

Thus, in the only pre-1850 case in which the Supreme Court held a federal statute unconstitutional, it did so by faulting Congress for doing what Congress, in truth, never did.[57]

"Trial ... by Jury"

While Article III's cap on Supreme Court original jurisdiction implicitly safeguarded the role of local juries, the next paragraph of Article III did so more explicitly: "The Trial of all Crimes . . . shall be by Jury; and such Trial shall be held in the State where the said Crimes shall have been committed."

These words failed to satisfy Anti-Federalists. Why, these men asked, did Article III guarantee juries in criminal cases but not civil ones? By negative implication, did Article III abolish civil juries in federal court?[58] Whenever a local jury in a state court civil case resolved a certain matter of fact, would a faraway Supreme Court claim a general right to disregard this factual finding on appeal? If not, why did the preceding paragraph of Article III ominously vest the distant Court with "appellate Jurisdiction, both as to Law *and Fact*"?[59] As for federal *criminal* trials, where Article III did indeed promise juries in "all" cases, why did the text say merely that the trial would be held somewhere in the crime-scene *state* without promising that the jury would be drawn from the precise locality—the common-law *vicinage*—where blood had been spilled?[60] And what about the need to provide for grand juries in criminal cases?[61]

These Anti-Federalist questions and criticisms had bite because late-eighteenth-century America placed great faith in her juries, civil and criminal, grand and petit. Before 1776, colonial jurors had stood shoulder to shoulder with colonial assemblymen to defend American self-governance against a formidable alliance of unrepresentative imperial officers and institutions—King George, his ministry, the English Privy Council and its Board of Trade, Parliament, colonial governors, and colonial judiciaries. Few Americans had ever voted for any of these imperial officers or served in any of these imperial institutions. But ordinary colonists could and did vote for colonial assemblies and vote in colonial juries. In the 1760s and 1770s, Americans used these republican strongholds to assail imperial policies and shield patriot practices. In response, British authorities tried to divert as much judicial business as possible away from American juries—toward colonial vice admiralty courts for customs cases and English courts for certain crimes committed by the king's officers in America.

Revolted, Americans revolted. High on their list of reasons, according to the Declaration of Independence, was that the king and Parliament had

aimed to "depriv[e] us, in many Cases, of the Benefits of Trial by Jury";
had claimed a right to "transport[] us beyond Seas to be tried for pretended Offences"; and had sought to shield British murderers who shed
blood on American soil via a regime of "mock Trial" far from the scene of
the crime. Every state constitution after independence contained multiple
guarantees of jury trial. These documents also democratized other parts of
state government whose colonial precursors had been largely or wholly unrepresentative: governorships, executive councils, and judiciaries. Henceforth, all branches of government would represent the people themselves
more or less directly. But jurors would continue to represent the people
more rather than less directly—with lower property qualifications than
for most other forms of government service and no informal requirements
of legal training or professional attainment. Juries were, in a sense, the people themselves, tried-and-true embodiments of late-eighteenth-century
republican ideology.

Thus, when Anti-Federalists accused the Federalists of undermining
the good old jury, this was a charge that mattered, and Federalists loudly
proclaimed their innocence before the American people. Nothing in the
Constitution, Federalists insisted, affirmatively abolished civil juries in federal courts.[62] On the contrary, Federalists predicted—promised, really—
that the First Congress would doubtless provide for civil juries in some
fashion.[63] Yet Federalists publicly defended the Philadelphia delegates'
decision not to constitutionalize a requirement of civil juries in all federal cases.[64] Across the thirteen states, juries sat in most but not all civil
cases. Admiralty, chancery, and probate matters were not universally jury-
triable. Different states defined the precise boundary between jury cases
and nonjury cases in different ways; moreover, the boundary in some
states had shifted over time and might continue to do so. Many of the
civil cases apt to be brought in federal courts would arise under state-law
rules of tort, contract, property, and the like; perhaps these courts should
pay some regard to state procedural rules concerning when juries should
sit. Had Article III imposed a rigid mandate for all federal civil cases in
all states at all times, such inflexibility might, ironically enough, have sym-
bolized disrespect for local diversity—for the very states' rights Anti-
Federalists claimed to embrace.

Federal criminal cases did not pose the same problem, since virtually
all such cases were expected to arise under substantive federal law, not
state law. Here, Article III sensibly laid down a uniform federal rule—a
rule that also tracked the unanimous consensus of American states that
in all serious criminal cases, juries were a must.[65] Nevertheless, different

states had somewhat different rules about the precise region from which the criminal jury should be drawn and how jurors should be summoned. On this vicinage issue, the First Congress could be trusted to fill in the details, Federalists argued. These advocates also claimed that Congress would doubtless provide for federal grand juries, as had state legislatures in jurisdictions that lacked explicit grand-jury language in state constitutions.[66] In fact, language elsewhere in the Constitution—affirming that impeached officials were subject to ordinary criminal "*Indictment,* Trial, Judgment and Punishment"—arguably did implicitly commit the new federal government to a regime of grand-jury indictments for serious federal offenses.

Federalists further predicted/promised that the First Congress would ensure that the Supreme Court would respect factual findings made by local juries, civil and criminal, in both state and inferior federal courts (absent, say, some unusual situation where factual findings were being manipulated to undermine federal rights).[67] But in some types of traditionally nonjury lawsuits—admiralty cases involving captured ships, for example—it might be appropriate to allow the Supreme Court on appeal to review the lower court judge's factual findings as well as his legal conclusions.[68] Thus, Federalists explained, Article III properly extended the Supreme Court's appellate jurisdiction over both "Law and Fact."

How SHOULD WE ASSESS these Federalist arguments? If we read the words of the Constitution strictly or suspiciously, as did the Anti-Federalists, it is hard to ignore the document's gaping holes on the subject of juries. But a different picture emerges if we understand the Constitution not merely as a text but also as an act—a continent-wide ordainment process of contestation and conversation that gave birth to additional promises every bit as binding on the new government as the words of the document itself. From this angle, the Constitution did indeed—thanks in part to the Anti-Federalists—broadly secure jury rights.

Thus the First Congress, in its notable Judiciary Act of 1789, guaranteed that juries would decide the "issues in fact" in "all" non-equity and non-admiralty civil cases tried by inferior federal courts; and also guaranteed that civil juries would sit in "all actions at law against citizens of the United States" tried by the Supreme Court in its original jurisdiction. In addition, the act sharply limited the ability of the Supreme Court, when sitting on appeal, to displace good-faith findings of fact made by state courts. On the criminal side, the act mandated that in all federal capital cases, jurors must come not merely from the state but from the "county where the offence was committed." Though the act oddly made no explicit mention of grand juries, earlier federal criminal statutes did require prosecutors to win indictments from grand juries, and federal judges regularly convened federal grand juries from the start.[69]

What's more, the First Congress proposed a dozen amendments to the Constitution, ten of which ultimately became America's Bill of Rights. One of these amendments (the Fifth) guaranteed federal grand juries and also, via its double-jeopardy clause, barred federal judges from reversing criminal-jury acquittals. Another amendment (the Sixth) provided for criminal juries from "districts" within states; and yet another (the Seventh) safeguarded the right to civil-jury trial in federal courts while also shielding certain factual findings made by state court civil juries.

Although these protections of liberty gestated in the First Congress, they had been conceived by the American people themselves in the very act of constitution. By August 1788—months before Congress would gather and more than a year before it would finally propose its amendments— five of the thirteen ratifying conventions had already made clear, in a series of formal declarations, that Americans wanted more jury safeguards than Article III offered. On this subject—as on many others at the Founding—the People spoke, and Congress obeyed.[70]

IN THE ARTICLE III vesting clause and roster, "shall" and "all" meant what they said. So, too, in the Article III jury-and-venue clause: "The Trial of *all* Crimes, except in Cases of Impeachment, *shall* be by Jury; and such Trial *shall* be held in the State where the said Crimes shall have been committed." Though a criminal defendant might plead guilty and thus avoid trial altogether, any federal defendant who pleaded not guilty and thus went to trial would face a jury—even if he might prefer to be tried by the bench alone. A criminal judge sitting without a criminal jury was simply not a duly constituted federal court capable of trying cases, just as the Senate sitting without the House was not a duly constituted federal legislature capable of enacting statutes. And even if a defendant preferred to be tried outside the crime-scene state—far from the madding crowd or the victim's family—the Judicial Article did not permit judges to operate in such a closet, much as the Legislative Article did not permit congressmen to suspend publication of house journals.

In the twentieth century, the Supreme Court began to disregard the plain meaning of "shall" and "all" in the Article III jury-and-venue clause, treating the issue as merely one concerning the waivable rights of the criminal defendant.[71] But the Founders' jury-and-venue rules had deeper roots. Trials were not just about the rights of the defendant but also about the rights of the community. The people themselves had a right to serve on the jury—to govern through the jury. In effect, each of the three branches of the federal government featured a bicameral balance. In the legislature, members of Congress's lower house—more numerous than senators, more localist, with shorter terms of office and more direct links to the electorate—would counterbalance the members of the upper house. In the executive branch, local citizen militias would counterbalance the central government's professional soldiers, and local citizen grand jurors would counterbalance the central government's professional prosecutors. So, too, within the judiciary, trial jurors would counterbalance trial judges.

Unchecked by a jury, a judge might be tempted—quite literally—to go easy on his wealthy friends. (Permanent magistrates would generally be easier targets to bribe than jurors whose identities would not be known long in advance.)[72] Particularly in cases where government officials had committed crimes against the citizenry, judges acting alone might be overly inclined to favor fellow government officers. Thus Article III promised that local citizens who had felt the brunt of these outrages would not be displaced by judges willing to try the matter on their own, or even by juries remote from the scene of the crime.

Nor did eighteenth-century Americans believe that their commitment to local jury trial would violate the defendant's right to a fair trial. When shots rang out on the streets of Boston on March 5, 1770, leaving five men dead from bullets fired by imperial soldiers, patriots had insisted that fair trials could and should be held in Boston itself, in proceedings that would showcase both community rights *and* defendant rights, republican freedom *and* individual fairness. In fact, most of the Boston Massacre defendants won acquittals on most charges. These verdicts carried special legitimacy precisely because local juries had made the decisions, after open trials that could be easily monitored by the victims' friends and families and Bostonians more generally. When, in the aftermath of these verdicts, Parliament enacted the Administration of Justice Act, which provided for trials back in England for murders committed by imperial officers in America, patriots quickly dubbed the act "intolerable." Indeed, this was the act that the Declaration of Independence derided as offering a "mock Trial"—language all the more striking when we recall that alongside draftsman Thomas Jefferson stood John Adams, who had in fact served as defense counsel in the Massacre trial.

Consistent with the commonplace eighteenth-century analogy between legislative and judicial bicameralism, local juries had to be part of some proceedings—trials, for example—much as the House had to be involved in ordinary lawmaking. At other times, however, judges might properly act on their own. Just as the Senate but not the House would ratify treaties and confirm appointments, so judges but not jurors would, for example, issue warrants and set bail.

Symmetrically, only the House could initiate appropriations bills; and jurors would likewise enjoy certain unique privileges. Only a grand jury, and not a judge, could authorize a criminal indictment. No matter how clear the proof against a man, grand jurors were free to just say no and thereby spare the potential defendant from even having to stand trial (unless prosecutors tried to proceed by "information"—a disfavored process nowhere mentioned in the original Constitution and all but prohibited by the later Fifth Amendment). Even if a grand jury said yes to the prosecution, criminal trial jurors were free to say no—or more precisely, "not guilty"—and no judge could stop or reverse them, no matter how clear (to the judge) the defendant's guilt. In short, eighteenth-century criminal jurors had both the right and power to acquit against the evidence. In a criminal case, no judge could snatch the case from the jury and unilaterally pronounce the defendant guilty; no judge could order jurors to enter a verdict of guilty; no judge could require jurors to make specific factual findings to justify their general verdict of not guilty; nor could any judge overturn the jurors' acquittal, even if it plainly contradicted the facts (as the judge saw them) or other verdicts that the jurors had rendered.

Alongside their right and power to acquit against the evidence, eighteenth-century jurors also claimed the right and power to consider legal as well as factual issues—to judge both law and fact "complicately"—when rendering any general verdict. Founding-era judges might give their legal opinions to the jury, but so might the attorneys in a case, and the jurors could decide for themselves what the law meant in the process of applying it to the facts at hand in a general verdict of guilty or not guilty (in a criminal case) or liable or not liable (in a civil case). Jurors today no longer retain this right to interpret the law, but at the Founding, America's leading lawyers and statesmen commonly accepted it.[73] Indeed, so did the United States Supreme Court itself, in one of its earliest cases, where the court sat in original jurisdiction in a civil case brought by Georgia against a British subject named Brailsford. According to Chief Justice Jay's 1794 instructions to the jury,

Gentlemen, . . . you have . . . a right to take upon yourselves to judge of both . . . the law as well as the fact in controversy. On this, and on every other occasion, however, we have no doubt, you will pay the respect, which is due to the opinion of the court: For, as on the one hand, it is presumed, that juries are the best judges of facts; it is, on the other hand, presumable, that the court are the best judges of law. But still both objects are lawfully, within your power of decision.[74]

In *Georgia v. Brailsford,* Jay spoke these words for a unanimous Court. But in other trials presided over by multiple judges—both in the Supreme Court and in federal circuit courts—judges could and did sometimes disagree amongst themselves. Each judge or justice at the Founding felt free to offer his own views; and in this every-man-for-himself legal universe, the power of each juror to decide for *himself* after considering the various opinions laid before him seemed all the more natural.

BUT IF JURORS, when rendering general verdicts, had the right to follow the law as they understood it, and if the Constitution was the supreme law, then surely—many leaders at the Founding argued—jurors had the right to follow the Constitution as they understood it. Thus, alongside legislative review (in which both the House and Senate weighed the constitutionality of pending legislation), executive review, and judicial review, there was a strong argument at the Founding for jury review, in which jurors might refuse to enforce any law that they deemed unconstitutional. Jury review would not substitute for judicial review but would supplement it. In a criminal case, if *either* judge *or* jury found the underlying criminal statute unconstitutional, the defendant would walk free. The judge could always dismiss the case on constitutional grounds, and symmetrically the jury could irreversibly pronounce the defendant not guilty (since the "law" he had violated was really, in the jurors' eyes, no law). Analogously, no legislative bill could be enacted if either Senate or House deemed it unconstitutional and just said no. Nor could a prosecution take place if either the president or the grand jury had constitutional objections to it. The president could always pardon, even before trial, and the grand jury could simply refuse to indict.

Leading Federalists lent modest support to the idea of jury review. In 1791, Wilson, who in 1787 had openly championed executive review alongside judicial review, declared that "whoever would be obliged to obey a constitutional law, is justified in refusing to obey an unconstitutional act of the legislature." In such "delicate" situations, "every one who is called to act, has a right to judge"—a general formulation that seemed to encompass grand jurors called upon to indict and petit jurors called upon to convict. More emphatic was Massachusetts's Theophilus Parsons, later to become his state's chief justice, who declared in the ratification debates that, via juries, "the people themselves" could thwart congressional acts of "usurpation." Such enactments were "not law," and if any man resisted the government and were prosecuted, "only his fellow-citizens can convict him; they are his jury, and if they pronounce him innocent, not all the powers of Congress can hurt him; and innocent they certainly will pronounce him, if the supposed law he resisted was an act of usurpation." Though perhaps limited to statutes that were not merely unconstitutional but egregiously so—"usurpations"—Parsons's argument plainly envisioned some form of jury review. The Federalist essayist "Aristides" put the point more softly. "Every judge in the union, whether of federal or state appointment, (and some persons would say every jury) will have a right to reject any act, handed to him as a law, which he may conceive repugnant to the constitution."[75]

True, on this view, one constitutionally scrupulous jury might acquit defendant A, while another jury with different views might convict otherwise identical defendant B. But the same point of course applied to judicial review, which was not limited to one Supreme Court but rather reflected a right and power of all courts and could operate even in disputes between private parties where the government was not a litigant.[76] Thus, one constitutionally scrupulous judge might dismiss charges brought against defendant A, while another judge with a different view allowed defendant B to be convicted. Even after the Supreme Court itself had pronounced a statute unconstitutional by refusing to apply it in a given case, the statute would formally remain on the statute books, and a differently composed Court at a later time might come to a different constitutional judgment.

Nor was the average juror's lack of formal law training a decisive argument against jury review in the Founding era. After all, jurors would have the benefit of the legal opinions of judges and lawyers in the courtroom—judges and lawyers who themselves may have received rather informal legal training. (Law schools as we know them today did not exist in eighteenth-century America.) And it bears repeating that even if ordinary jurors lacked understanding of technical lawyers' law, the Constitution embodied a very different, more populist, kind of law—law that had indeed sprung from the people themselves in an extraordinary ratification process.

Yet there was an obvious difference between the countless thousands of ordinary voters, and ratification-convention delegates, across a continent who had ordained and established the Constitution and the twelve men, good and true, from some particular locality who would sit on a typical trial jury (or, for that matter, the twenty-three men who would form a grand jury). Without limits, a sweeping right of jury review might well have given eccentric localities too much power to frustrate—essentially, to nullify—federal laws strongly supported by the national citizenry.

Moreover, both the text and the act of constitution offered only modest support for a broad right of jury review. Civil juries had no automatic entitlement to enter general verdicts, and it was only in the context of general verdicts that, by tradition, juries could judge law (and thus, by implication, judge the Constitution as part of the law). Over the course of the nineteenth century, judges increasingly reined in the powers of civil juries through a variety of technical devices—directed verdicts, special verdicts, demurrers, judgments notwithstanding verdicts—that limited general verdicts.[77] Even on the criminal side, the jury's role eventually shrank to the domain of fact, as antebellum judges asserted a more general monopoly over issues of law in their courtrooms. Jurors could point to no strong statements in constitutional text or the framework Judiciary Act of 1789 that forbade this shrinkage. If anything, the Seventh Amendment highlighted the civil jury's role in deciding issues of "fact," and the Judiciary Act similarly stressed, in both criminal and civil cases, that the "trial of issues [of] *fact*" in all common-law cases would be "by jury."[78]

Having long since lost their Founding-era power to decide law, American juries nevertheless have retained two Founding-era rights that continue to support a limited form of jury review even today. A modern grand jury may decline to indict for any reason it deems proper. By sharing in the president's prosecutorial discretion—which is really the discretion *not* to prosecute—the grand jury would seem to retain the right to decline to indict if it deems the underlying criminal statute constitutionally invalid. Likewise, criminal trial jurors have never lost the right to acquit against the evidence, a right that even today arguably encompasses the authority to acquit for reasons of constitutional scruple.

Or at least, so it has been argued by respectable citizens and scholars. Though twenty-first-century judicial orthodoxy frowns on these claims of constitutional competence, the right of grand juries and trial juries to just say no in certain contexts draws strength from the letter and spirit of the Bill of Rights. As we shall see in more detail later, the Fifth Amendment continues to require grand-jury participation for all serious federal crimes (outside the special context of military justice), and also continues to shield any acquittal rendered by a criminal jury. Jury review today is just a shadow of what it was to our forebears. But it still lives—perhaps.

"Treason"

Article III's concluding section mapped out a miniature Constitution within the Constitution, compressing the document's grand themes into a single paragraph. Words that first appeared at the end of Articles I and II—"Attainder" and "Treason"—came back into view at the end of Article III, this time with more color and precision.

Begin with the Constitution's promise of a more perfect union—an indivisible nation in which no single state or handful of states could secede absent the consent of America as a whole. This idea lay on the surface of the Constitution's opening and closing provisions (the Preamble and Articles V, VI, and VII), and just beneath the surface of Article I's final paragraph, which banned states from unilaterally keeping troops or warships. The Article III treason clause brought the matter to life in strong language. In the event a state made war on the United States, those who fought for the state would be, in a scarlet word, traitors: "Treason against the United States, shall consist . . . in levying War against them, or in adhering to their Enemies, giving them Aid and Comfort."

Anti-Federalist Luther Martin called attention to the issue during the ratification process. In remarks delivered to the Maryland House of Representatives and later expanded into a widely read pamphlet, Martin reported that at Philadelphia, he had proposed an alternatively worded treason clause, which he paraphrased as follows: In a "Civil War" between "any State . . . [and] the General Governmt. . . . no Citizen . . . of the said State should be deemed guilty of Treason, for acting against the General Government, in conformity to the Laws of the State of which he was a member." Yet the Philadelphia delegates had rejected his alternative, said Martin, who thereby reminded Americans that the treason clause as finally worded made no exception for unilateral state secession or civil war. With evident understanding of these words, the American people ratified the document as a whole.[79]

Consider next the treason clause as an exemplification of separation of powers, the rule of law, and open government. While Parliament had often tried Englishmen for treason and put them to death, Congress would have judicial powers only over its own members and federal officers, and punishments in such cases of congressional expulsion and impeachment were sharply limited: Congress could remove a man from power, and even disqualify an officer from future officeholding, but could not touch a hair on his head. Reinforcing this structure, Article III's treason clause confirmed that any truly criminal prosecution for treason would occur in an "open Court" independent of Congress. The explicit reminder that the court would be "open" to the public, in keeping with a long American tradition of open judicial proceedings, complemented Article I's transparency guarantee—its requirement of published legislative journals—and anticipated the Sixth Amendment promise of public trials in all federal criminal cases.

A general commitment to Enlightenment values (slavery aside) pulsated through the Constitution, and this theme also manifested itself in the treason clause. Under England's feudalistic treason rules (eventually abolished in 1834), the Crown could lawfully seize a traitor's homestead from the family members due to inherit it. The traitor's blood was deemed corrupt, and descendants whose property claims flowed through that blood were divested of these claims.[80] By contrast, Article III barred the federal government from imposing any "Corruption of Blood" in treason cases. In the New World, the black mark—the taint, the "attainder"—of a treason conviction was to be individual, not familial. Just as no favorite son should be handed his sire's government post, so no child should be punished for the sins of his father.* [81]

The treason clause also underscored the Constitution's commitment to broad rights of speech and dissent. Treason would consist "only" in levying war or adhering to enemies with aid and comfort—notably, this was the only clause in the entire Constitution that used the word "only." In England, kings and Parliaments had for centuries treated treason law as a political instrument to be expanded or contracted at will. English history was littered with the corpses of men who had been found guilty of various "constructive" treasons—which often meant little more than being in the wrong political place at the wrong political time. In the Pennsylvania ratifying debates, James Wilson related the story of an Englishman who had

---

*Of course, American slavery made a mockery of this Enlightenment ideal. Even if an African warrior who was captured in a "just war" might justifiably be enslaved rather than killed—accepting for a moment all the grotesque fictions this theory invited—how could enslavement of the captive's offspring, born and unborn, be justified? In effect, slavery transformed the master class into hereditary lords while corrupting the blood of all captives.

been convicted of treason simply because he had killed one of the king's hunting stags.[82] More ominously, American Whigs knew that Algernon Sidney and other English martyrs had been executed as traitors for holding political opinions that power-holders sought to crush.

Before the adoption of the Bill of Rights, the treason clause thus formed an important proto–First Amendment, prohibiting any federal treason law that criminalized mere dissent. As men who had first raised their voices in loyal opposition to imperial policies in the 1760s and early 1770s and later waged war against their king—treason under the strictest of definitions—Washington, Franklin, and company knew the difference.

Viewed from yet another angle, Article III's concluding section was not merely a proto–First Amendment, but an entire proto–Bill of Rights, spelling out various procedural privileges of treason defendants that anticipated the broader Fifth and Sixth Amendments, and limitations on Congress's punishment power that foreshadowed the Eighth Amendment. Under Article III, a treason conviction would require either two witnesses testifying to the same overt act or a confession in open court. In specifying certain rights of treason defendants above and beyond those of all other accused persons, the framers borrowed a page from the famous English Treason Trials Act of 1696, which had done much the same thing, though with a different set of specified procedural entitlements. In one particular—its rule that two witnesses testify to the *same* overt act— Article III went beyond the 1696 statute, albeit in a clumsy way. Exactly how much did the two witnesses' testimony need to overlap in order to satisfy the sameness requirement?

Despite the considerable virtues of the treason clause, Anti-Federalists remained skeptical. Substantively, the word "only" offered uncertain protection for political speech. Without an emphatic constitutional guarantee of free expression, couldn't Congress outflank the bulwark of the treason clause simply by devising some other criminal label—say, "sedition"— and criminalizing expression under that new label? (As later events would prove, this was no idle hypothetical.) Even in treason trials, what about other key rights that England protected in its landmark 1696 statute, such as the rights of counsel, compulsory process, and notice of specific criminal allegations? What about the obvious need to provide criminal safeguards in other kinds of criminal prosecution—whether for sedition or forgery or counterfeiting?

During the ratification debates, Federalists ultimately agreed with many of these suggestions for additional protections, which found their way into the formal declarations of three of the four ratifying conventions held in the summer of 1788, in the states where the Federalists faced the stiffest resistance. Virginia, New York, and North Carolina all demanded that Congress move toward a bill of rights that, among other things, would bolster free expression via language far more explicit than anything in the treason clause. These state conventions also called for explicit guarantees of various criminal-procedure entitlements—rights of counsel, confrontation, notice, and compulsory process—beyond what the treason clause had promised. North Carolina, which declined to ratify the Constitution at its summer convention and thus remained outside the new union, went so far as to suggest that it would not say yes until some action had been taken on its suggested amendments.[83] When the First Congress convened in March 1789, it would confront a daunting list of constitutional holes to fill and promises to keep.

Chapter 7

STATES AND TERRITORIES

JOIN, OR DIE. (MAY 9, 1754)

Benjamin Franklin's early argument for American union: North and South must cooperate and the center must hold. Notably, New England here appeared as a unit, Delaware was depicted (by a Pennsylvanian) as part of Pennsylvania, and Georgia had yet to make an impression.

$\mathcal{A}$s each ratifying state pledged vertical allegiance to the United States, it simultaneously promised horizontal fidelity to other states and their citizens. Over a wide spectrum of civil rights, every state vowed to give citizens of sister states the same treatment that it gave its own citizens. Also, states agreed to pay special regard to one another's laws and court decisions. As usual, the devil was in the details: Slave states won important concessions in Article IV. Slavery aside, Article IV envisioned a vast empire of liberty stretching to the Mississippi and perhaps beyond. In the East, established states would buttress one another's republican systems of government. In the West, Americans would people new lands and rear new republics that would ultimately join the union as new states on equal footing with their elder siblings.

"Privileges and Immunities"

The thirteen American entities that united as states in 1776 began their legal lives as widely scattered English colonies, founded as separate feudal domains and corporate business ventures over the course of a century and a half. Virginia, for example, celebrated her hundredth birthday long before Georgia was born.

As English settlements took root, spread out, and eventually began to verge upon other settlements, old boundary lines occasionally moved or gave way to new legal structures. For example, in 1664 the Dutch outpost of New Amsterdam was absorbed into English New York, a colony that in turn ceded lands that would later become parts of New Jersey, Pennsylvania, and Delaware. In 1665 the colony of New Haven joined Connecticut; in 1691 the Plymouth Bay Colony and the province of Maine merged into Massachusetts; and in 1702 East New Jersey and West New Jersey united. For a brief time in the reign of James II, the king tried to revoke and restructure certain charters so as to consolidate all the lands from New Jersey to Maine into one large dominion. The plan fizzled when James fled the throne during the Glorious Revolution of 1688–89. Delaware passed through several stages before achieving the status of an independent colony sometime before the American Revolution, and Vermont had yet to cleanly separate herself from New York when the Revolution broke out.

In the early eighteenth century, neighboring colonies sometimes shared a governor—as did Massachusetts and New Hampshire from 1702 until 1741, New York and New Jersey from 1702 until 1738, and Pennsylvania and Delaware prior to 1776. Yet in general, each colony retained its status as a distinct entity within the British Empire. Mid-eighteenth-century British North America thus formed a partial wheel, with imperial spokes radiating from London to each colony but precious little legal rim binding the colonies directly to one another.[1]

Ever the tinkerer, Benjamin Franklin in 1754 proposed to add a sturdier intercolonial rim. Franklin himself was a continentalist who had been born in one colony (Massachusetts), traveled as a young man to a second (New York) in an unsuccessful job search, and then relocated to a third (Pennsylvania). His 1754 plan, presented to a conclave of colonists meeting in Albany, envisioned the creation of an eleven-state Grand Council that would be elected by colonial assemblies and presided over by a Crown-appointed president-general with an absolute veto. (The plan subsumed Delaware within Pennsylvania and omitted Georgia, whose colonial legislature had yet to meet.) Franklin proposed to vest this council with broad control over Indian affairs, westward expansion, and continental defense, and with the power to levy its own taxes, duties, and imposts in order to finance its ambitious continental operations. Here, as elsewhere, Franklin was far ahead of his time. His imaginary new wheel went nowhere in the 1750s, thanks to colonial legislators who refused to endorse any system that transferred so much authority away from themselves.

Some twenty years later, as America headed toward independence, Franklin drew on his Albany plan in drafting an early version of what eventually became the Articles of Confederation.[2] The Confederation document that ultimately emerged declined to give America's Grand Council—now called Congress—explicit power to regulate the West, make laws, or lay taxes, as had Franklin's 1754 blueprint. However, the Confederation document went beyond Franklin in specifying certain obligations that each state owed to the citizens of its sister states. According to the Confederation's fourth Article,

> The free inhabitants of each of these states, paupers, vagabonds, and fugitives from justice excepted, shall be entitled to all privileges and immunities of free citizens in the several states; and the people of each state shall have free ingress and regress to and from any other state, and shall enjoy therein all the privileges of trade and commerce, subject to the same duties, impositions and restrictions as the inhabitants thereof respectively.

Article IV of the Philadelphia Constitution recast the idea as follows: "The Citizens of each State shall be entitled to all Privileges and Immunities of Citizens in the several States." This new provision marked several improvements upon the old. First, it pruned away excess and confusing verbiage. As Madison/Publius observed in *The Federalist* No. 42, it was hard to fathom why the Confederation text had lurched from "free inhabitants" to "free citizens" to "people" and why it had added language about trade and commerce privileges to the earlier general command encompassing "all privileges and immunities." A similar point applied to the Confederation's specific guarantee of "free ingress and regress" between states. Not only were such rights sheltered by Article IV's more general formulation, but they also found further refuge in the Constitution's overall structure of sister states formed into a more perfect union, and in the negative implications of the Article I interstate-commerce clause: Congress, not states, would generally regulate who and what could cross state lines.

Second, the new Article IV dovetailed with other clauses of the Constitution so as to restrict the ability of a single eccentric state to dictate immigration policy to its sister states. Under the Confederation language, if one state decided to naturalize an alien, all other states were apparently obliged to treat the newcomer as a full-fledged American. By contrast, Article I, section 8 of the Constitution empowered Congress to establish uniform naturalization rules, thereby allowing all states to participate in naturalization decisions that would, via interstate privileges and immunities, potentially affect every state within its own borders.

Third, by eliminating the Confederation's exceptions for "paupers" and "vagabonds," Article IV implicitly extended the promise of interstate citizenship to *all* state citizens, rich and poor alike. (The Confederation had also excepted "fugitives from Justice"—a category that Article IV dealt with in a separate section.) When a young Benjamin Franklin had first come to Pennsylvania in 1723, he had arrived with little more than the clothes on his back. Article IV could easily be read (though the antebellum Court never read it this way) as promising that future penniless Franklins would not be barred at the gates of sister states.[3]

BUT EXACTLY WHO WAS a "Citizen" of any given state? In particular, did women and free blacks count? And exactly what were the "Privileges and Immunities" that a state citizen could claim when venturing into other states?

Article IV was not the first constitutional clause to speak of "Citizens," and one of the document's earlier clauses confirmed that freeborn American women were indeed "Citizens." As we have seen, Article III authorized federal courts to hear lawsuits between "Citizens of different States." From the beginning, federal courts acting under this language decided suits brought by and against women. According to an 1875 Supreme Court case reaffirming that "women have always been considered as citizens the same as men," the law books from 1789 forward teemed with federal diversity suits that presupposed women's status as state citizens, and not a single case contradicted this "uniform[]" understanding.[4] If women were state citizens for Article III purposes, surely the same held true for Article IV, for as Hamilton/Publius explained in *The Federalist* No. 80, these twin citizenship clauses aimed at a common purpose—namely, the prevention of state discrimination against citizens of sister states.[5]

Free blacks were also plainly encompassed by Articles III and IV as originally understood. Several states in 1787 not only openly regarded free blacks as citizens, but also allowed them to vote on equal terms with white men and thereby wield a political privilege that even white women, though citizens, generally lacked. Free blacks had fought at Bunker Hill, and in January 1776 Congress explicitly authorized the reenlistment of "the free negroes who have served faithfully in the army at Cambridge."[6] When Congress later drafted the Articles of Confederation, the language of the interstate-privileges clause made no racial distinction whatsoever, in evident contrast to its class distinctions (excluding "paupers" and "vagabonds") and to language elsewhere in the document, which pegged each state's quota of soldiers to "the number of its *white* inhabitants." Plainly, when the Confederation document meant "white" it said "white." In the interstate-privileges context it purposefully used a different formulation, encompassing "free" inhabitants, both white and black.

South Carolina's leaders took note and took offense. In 1778, while the proposed Articles of Confederation were pending in the several states, Carolina's delegation moved to interject the word "white" into the phrase "free inhabitants." Congress rejected the suggested rewrite by a vote of eight states to two, with one state divided.[7] Later, in its proposed 1783 tax amendment that would have counted slaves at three-fifths, Congress explicitly referred to "white *and other* free citizens and inhabitants, of every age, sex, and condition."[8] Also in 1783, Virginia lawmakers repealed a state law that limited citizenship to whites, replacing it with more universal language guaranteeing "all the rights, privileges, and advantages of citizens" to "all free persons born within the territory of this commonwealth."[9]

When the issue of citizenship resurfaced in the drafting of the Constitution, America's leaders once again eschewed restrictive racial language, thereby extending the protections of Articles III and IV to all citizens, black and white alike. Had the document instead openly excluded non-white citizens from the scope of its guarantees, it might well have provoked strong opposition in some Northern states where, to repeat, free blacks had served as Revolutionary War soldiers and were eligible to vote in ratification-convention elections. Massachusetts voters had in fact overwhelmingly rejected a proposed state constitution in 1778 that contained racially restrictive language. Many townships had sharply condemned this language, and the successful 1780 state constitution had taken care to omit it.[10] Under the federal compromise hammered out at Philadelphia several years after this Massachusetts experience, slave states could keep their slaves, but in exchange they promised that they would duly respect certain rights of free blacks from sister states.

But exactly how much respect was due, and to what sort of rights? Article IV essentially said that whenever a free man or woman (or child, for that matter) ventured into another state, that state had to give him or her the same civil rights that it would give its own citizen in a comparable situation.[11] The simple idea was that in the domain of civil rights—"Privileges and Immunities"—no state should discriminate against a sister-state citizen as such.

Consider a few hypothetical cases illustrating the scope and limits of this principle. If a Virginia citizen went to Massachusetts and insisted on bringing his slaves with him, Massachusetts could indeed punish him if he shackled and beat his slaves on what was, after all, free soil. In prosecuting the Virginian for assault and battery, Massachusetts would be treating him just as it treated its own citizens: *No one* in the Bay State was allowed to hold, restrain, or beat slaves. (Nor did the Article IV fugitive-slave clause apply if a master voluntarily took his slaves across state lines; as we shall soon see, that clause applied only to interstate runaways.) Conversely, if a free black man from Massachusetts went to Virginia, he could be held to whatever rules Virginia applied to its own free black adult males. Out-of-state women would get the civil rights of in-state women; so, too, with children.

Had these basic points been clearly understood by the Supreme Court, perhaps American history in the momentous 1850s and 1860s might have played out very differently. As events actually unfolded, Chief Justice Taney penned a convoluted opinion in the 1857 *Dred Scott* case, declaring that free blacks could never be deemed state citizens under Articles III and IV—even if such persons had been born free and their home states explicitly called them "citizens." According to Taney, the very survival of slave states depended on excluding all blacks from the ambit of Article IV. Otherwise, free blacks from the North could maraud around the South claiming "full" rights as citizens "to keep and carry arms wherever they went."[12] Taney's claims were hard to swallow. Under a proper reading of the Article IV interstate-equality principle, out-of-state free blacks could claim no more than in-state free blacks. If a state could lawfully restrict firearms of its own free black inhabitants, then it could do the same for free blacks from sister states. If, conversely, a slave state were somehow restricted in regulating certain rights of its own free blacks, its real complaint would be with the source of that restriction, whatever it might be, and not with Article IV.[13]

Additionally, the interstate-equality principle at the heart of Article IV had other built-in limits to accommodate legitimate state interests. For example, no state had to extend equal treatment to out-of-staters in the domain of state governance, involving the rights to vote, hold office, serve on juries, and serve in the militia. A Virginian would presumably have a right to leave Virginia indefinitely and become a Massachusetts citizen; but unless and until he made that switch, he could be barred from certain forms of political participation reserved for Massachusetts men. As the idea would come to be phrased in the nineteenth century, Article IV privileges and immunities encompassed fundamental "civil rights" but not "political rights." Also, in doling out certain special benefits—government jobs, perhaps—a state might permissibly advantage its own citizens insofar as these perks lay beyond the spirit of Article IV.

Of course, a state might well choose to give out-of-state citizens more benefits than Article IV required, especially if other states proved willing to reciprocate. In some situations, two or more states might formalize their reciprocity agreements into official interstate compacts to be blessed by Congress, under the provisions of Article I, section 10. Certain regional regimes made particularly good sense if neighboring states shared a common resource (say, a lake or a stream) whose optimal management called for extended cooperation between the affected states. The Philadelphia Convention itself had been prompted by an earlier interstate conference held in 1786 in Annapolis—a conference that, in turn, had sprouted from bilateral efforts between Virginia and Maryland to coordinate their use of the Potomac and Pocomoke Rivers.

Alongside its longwinded discussion of interstate privileges and immunities, the fourth Article of Confederation covered two additional items:

> If any person guilty of, or charged with treason, felony, or other high misdemeanor in any state, shall flee from justice, and be found in any of the United States, he shall, upon demand of the Governor or executive power of the state from which he fled, be delivered up and removed to the state having jurisdiction of his offence.
>
> Full faith and credit shall be given in each of these states to the records, acts and judicial proceedings of the courts and magistrates of every other state.

Both of these provisions, with certain stylistic refinements, found their way into the Constitution's aptly numbered Article IV.

In the Constitution's flight-from-justice clause, the Philadelphia draftsmen replaced the Confederation phrase "high misdemeanor" with the word "crime," thereby avoiding confusion with the Constitution's very different, noncriminal usage of "high . . . Misdemeanor[]" in the impeachment context.[14] The only other notable change here was that Article IV omitted all reference to interstate extradition in cases of those not merely "charged with" crimes but instead already found "guilty of" them. Essentially, criminal convicts were covered by the more general language of the full-faith-and-credit clause, under which each state promised to enforce the "judicial Proceedings of every other State," including its criminal verdicts of guilt.

In noncriminal cases, a similar rule applied. Whenever a court of one state rendered a verdict against a civil litigant, Article IV obliged sister states to give that verdict "Full Faith and Credit." For example, if A had sued B and prevailed in one state court, a sister-state court could not blithely turn around and give judgment to B against A on the same facts. More generally, sister states pledged not merely to avoid undoing one another's verdicts but also to affirmatively enforce them. If a litigant who lost in one state court had assets in another state that were needed to satisfy the initial judgment, Article IV told the second state to cooperate in making those assets available to the judgment creditor.

Despite the seeming simplicity of this core idea, technical complications abounded. Exactly what did "full" faith and credit mean? The same kind of credit that the *first* state court in the underlying litigation would typically give its own judgments or the same kind of credit that the *second* (enforcing) court would normally give to an in-state verdict? What if the first court lacked proper jurisdiction? Further complexities arose from other language in Article IV, which made clear that states owed full faith and credit not only to one another's judicial proceedings but also to one another's legislative "public Acts." If read broadly, this language suggested that each state had to enforce statutes adopted by another state whenever that other state's statutes most sensibly applied to a given transaction.

But which state was that? For example, if two business associates from Massachusetts met in Connecticut to make contracts dealing with their joint business ventures in New York, which state's laws most sensibly applied? If a Virginia master beat his slave in Virginia and then marched him to Massachusetts where the slave died from these abuses, should free-soil law or slave-soil law govern? To deal with the many intricacies of this vexing body of interstate conflicts of law, Article IV went well beyond its Confederation precursor, via new language authorizing Congress to "by general Laws prescribe" rules governing the precise effect of each state's laws and judgments in multistate transactions. Although Congress in 1790 addressed certain technical aspects of full faith and credit,[15] nineteenth-century federal lawmakers did far less to implement this ideal than they might have. In the absence of congressional leadership, the Supreme Court acted sporadically but failed to develop any comprehensive framework. Thus one of the Constitution's most intriguing promises—of truly "full" harmonization of state-law adjudications in state courts—went largely unfulfilled in antebellum America, and indeed, remains unfulfilled even today.[16]

"held to Service or Labour"

While underenforcing one of Article IV's most admirable constitutional provisions, the antebellum Congress and Court overenforced its ugliest clause.

In its entirety, this clause read as follows: "No Person held to Service or Labour in one State, under the Laws thereof, escaping into another, shall, in Consequence of any Law or Regulation therein, be discharged from such Service or Labour, but shall be delivered up on Claim of the Party to whom such Service or Labour may be due."

As with the Constitution's other euphemistic references to slavery, the

Philadelphia delegates detoured around the S-word here. But the harsh reality bled through the words "held" and "escaping": This was a clause about humans in bondage seeking liberation. Though camouflaged by its placement alongside a clause dealing with fugitives from "Justice"— alleged criminals facing presumptively fair trials with the promise of liberty if adjudged innocent of personal wrongdoing—the fugitive-slave clause dealt with pitiable folk whose only alleged crime was their thirst for freedom.

The clause shackled free-soil states in two ways. First, no state could use its domestic antislavery laws to declare a conceded interstate fugitive slave to be a free person, legally "discharged" from all future obligations to serve his or her former master. Second, each state had an affirmative duty to "deliver[] up" the fugitive to his or her master whenever the master made a proper "Claim."

This two-pronged clause gave slave masters pursuing their quarry onto free soil more explicit protection than did the prior regime. The Articles of Confederation imposed no requirement that free states play the part of slave-catchers and gave the Confederation Congress no power to impose such a requirement. Nor did general principles of international law and doctrines of interstate comity circa 1787 oblige free states to render up all slaves, thereby subordinating their own free-soil laws to the slave-laws of other states. Whether, under general legal principles, free states could properly ignore slave-law altogether and legally discharge a fugitive from all obligations to his master was a murkier question.

Analogous issues had long vexed English jurists. With little direct guidance from Parliament, how should English judges balance the general principles of English liberty against the reality of widespread slavery in England's colonies? In their most exuberant moments, some judges and commentators spoke as if England's very soil, water, and air fully emancipated any and all who reached that charmed isle.[17] According to one 1701 dictum from Sir John Holt, chief justice of the King's Bench, "as soon as a negro comes into England, he becomes free: one may be a villein in England, but not a slave." In 1762, another jurist declared that "as soon as a man sets foot on English ground he is free: a negro may maintain an action against his master for ill usage, and may have a *Habeas Corpus* if restrained of his liberty." Three years later, Blackstone's *Commentaries* gushed that the "spirit of liberty is so deeply . . . rooted even in our very soil, that a slave or a negro, the moment he lands in England . . . becomes a freeman," at least with regard to "the protection of the laws."[18]

Yet other pre-1770 English cases and authorities reached rather different conclusions and muddied the waters.[19] Even Blackstone suggested that a slave might still owe "perpetual service" to his master after reaching England.[20] On this view, English law might limit some of the classic incidents of slavery, such as the master's right to inflict savage bodily punishment, but the slave would remain a servant for life—a kinder, gentler (and presumably nonhereditary) form of subordination, akin to an extended eighteenth-century apprenticeship.

Once a colonial slave had reached English soil, would English law allow a master to physically detain the servant and forcibly carry the captive back into the realm of slave-law? In a landmark 1772 case, *Somerset v. Stewart,* Lord Mansfield ordered that such a captive must be unchained. "The black must be discharged" on a writ of habeas corpus, explained Mansfield, because returning a former slave into slavery was an "odious" and "high . . . act of dominion" that free-soil judges should not allow in the absence of a strong local custom or a clear legislative command to that effect.[21]

Fifteen years later and an ocean away, Article IV provided such a command, obliging officials in free states to "deliver[] up" fugitive slaves on request. The clause thus gave slave states an explicit guarantee that they lacked under the background legal rules in place in 1787 America. In trying to sell the Constitution to his fellow slave masters in Virginia, Madison explained that, despite its linguistic indirection, the language governing "service or labour" was "expressly inserted, to enable owners of slaves to reclaim them. This is a better security than any that now exists." Without the clause, free states could not only refuse to "deliver[] up" fleeing slaves but could even formally free them, reported Madison. "At present, if any slave elopes to any of those states where slaves are free, he becomes emancipated by their laws; for the laws of the states are uncharitable to one another in this respect." In the Carolinas, leading Federalists offered similar accounts of Article IV.[22]

YET PERHAPS THE FUGITIVE-SLAVE clause gave slave states less than Madison claimed—or put differently, gave free states more than he conceded. In the absence of this clause, couldn't slave states have used the flight-from-justice provisions of Article IV to get many of their slaves back? That is, wouldn't slave states have begun charging various fugitive slaves with crimes? After all, many runaways could be accused of having stolen the very clothes they wore or the horses they rode—clothes and horses that legally belonged to their masters. And if horse-theft was a crime, so, too, was slave-theft. Wasn't every escaping slave guilty of precisely such theft—by "stealing" himself? Outrageous though such ideas might sound to modern ears, claims rather close to this were indeed made by the antebellum American State Department in urging Canada to extradite various fugitive slaves who had escaped to that country.[23]

Had slave states attempted to cram fugitive slaves into the Article IV flight-from-justice box, would free states have been obliged to send interstate fugitives back to the land of bondage? Though lawyers for the runaways would doubtless have invoked Mansfield's *Somerset* ruling, this case would have offered them only slender support, and slave-state lawyers would have found it easily distinguishable. In *Somerset,* the master, Charles Stewart, had voluntarily brought his slave, James Somerset, onto free soil. By following his master's orders and accompanying him to England, Somerset could hardly have been accused of having thereby violated any slave-soil law against theft. Even had a colony trumped up bogus criminal charges and sought extradition, the Mother Country would have had no duty to comply with such an impudent demand from her legal dependency. But in America, each state, when confronting a criminal-extradition request from a sister state, was indeed bound to comply, thanks to the "flee from Justice" language of Article IV (and its Confederation predecessor).

From this perspective, the fugitive-slave clause itself could be read—if one were so inclined—as striking a balance that was not one-sidedly proslavery. In effect, the fugitive-slave clause obliged slave states to forego the extradition gambit. Since a highly specific constitutional clause addressed the precise issue of fugitive slaves, its detailed terms governed. Any attempt to stretch the flight-from-justice category could plausibly be viewed as an impermissible evasion of the careful limits built into the relevant clause—limits that offered free-soil states something in return for their promise to render up.

What were these limits? First, although a free state had to deliver up escaping slaves, it had no duty to hand over former slaves whose masters had voluntarily brought them onto free soil or otherwise emancipated them. Were a slave state to trump up charges against such a former slave, a free state would be on strong ground in resisting such an effort to outflank the fugitive/non-fugitive compromise built into the fugitive-slave clause itself. Second, while the criminal extradition provision of Article IV required a state to hand over anyone who had been "charged" with a crime, the fugitive-slave clause required more. A state had no duty to render unless a person *in fact* was a runaway slave. Third, and related, in determining whether an alleged fugitive slave was indeed the person the master claimed he was—as opposed to a freeborn black in a case of mistaken identity or an ex-slave who had lawfully won his freedom—a free-soil state would be entitled to use *its own* legal apparatus to determine the key facts. In slave-soil states, blacks were often presumed slaves, with little or no right to testify or otherwise present evidence. But a free state was entitled to give blacks a fair hearing and to presume that all persons on its soil were indeed free until proven otherwise, thus requiring masters to shoulder a substantial evidentiary burden. So long as a free state's judiciary applied the same sort of fact-finding procedures as it might otherwise use in cases involving bodily liberty, the state could not properly be found derelict.

The fugitive-slave clause's most obvious precursor had itself reflected a compromise between free-soil and slave-soil principles. According to the Confederation Congress's Northwest Ordinance of 1787, slavery would be banned from the vast federal territory north and west of the Ohio River and east of the Mississippi, but slave-state masters would have the right to recapture any bondsmen who might escape onto this newly free soil.

Yet this ordinance, adopted in New York City in July, gave fugitives less procedural protection than did Article IV, drafted in Philadelphia a month later.* The ordinance affirmed the common-law right of masters to recapture fugitives on their own, without coming before a magistrate.[24] By contrast, Article IV omitted mention of self-help recaption or reclamation. Instead, it spoke of a fugitive's being "delivered up"—presumably, by agents of the state government itself. After all, these were the agents who were the targets of the "deliver up" command in the flight-from-justice clause; and these were also the agents who were the subjects of the initial words of the fugitive-slave clause, barring legal discharge of a runaway slave via any state "Law or Regulation."

Alas, neither the antebellum Congress nor the antebellum Court proved willing to read Article IV in a restrained or balanced fashion. In 1793, Congress enacted a fugitive-slave law that allowed a slave-catcher to bring an alleged fugitive before a federal judge, who could issue a certifi-

---

*A quick refresher on the Northwest Ordinance: While the Philadelphia delegates were meeting behind closed doors, the Confederation Congress was continuing to meet in New York City. Though members of Congress had no clear idea about what the Philadelphians were planning, the Philadelphians knew about the Northwest Ordinance as soon as it was adopted—in mid-July, a full two months before the end of the federal Convention. Once the Constitution was ratified, the old Confederation Congress went out of business, but the new constitutional Congress quickly embraced the Northwest Ordinance, with minor modifications, in a statute enacted in early 1789.

cate entitling the slave-catcher to carry the fugitive back to the master's state. This process allowed the slave-catcher, if he chose, to cut the free-state government out of the fact-finding loop, a defect made worse by the act's failure to specify the procedures to be followed in federal court if the alleged fugitive contested the slave-catcher's allegations.[25] The statute further reached beyond Article IV in authorizing a slave-catcher to seize alleged fugitives on his own authority before bringing them to court for a determination of their runaway status. The obvious alternative, better fitting Article IV's logic and language, would have obliged a slave-catcher to go first to state authorities and procure their authorization and/or supervision in bringing any alleged runaway to state court.

Where, exactly, did Congress get this power to tip the balance struck by Article IV itself? Had Article IV been silent on the fugitive-slave question, Congress might properly have pointed to the broad text of Article I that empowered it to regulate transactions—"Commerce"—that spilled across state lines. Slaves and slave-hunters running from one state to another plausibly fell within the letter and spirit of this clause. But didn't Article IV itself change the equation? On an issue so uniquely delicate as the balance between free-soil law and slave-soil law, the specific and particular compromise set forth in Article IV arguably displaced the far more general language of Article I. What might have been a "proper" exercise of congressional power in the absence of the fugitive-slave clause perhaps became improper once the specific rules of that clause were taken into account.

To put the point another way: Just as Article I studiously omitted any general congressional power to emancipate bondsmen in slave states, so Article IV pointedly withheld from Congress any general authority to implement the "Service or Labour" clause in free states. The previous section of Article IV expressly empowered Congress to enforce the full-faith-and-credit principle, yet no similar enforcement clause appeared in the fugitive-slave context. Wasn't this a notable omission, and one that free-soil ratifiers were entitled to rely on? Given that any open constitutional reference to a federal fugitive-slave law displacing free-state structures would probably have stiffened opposition to the document in several Northern states—Massachusetts comes first to mind[26]—was it truly proper to read this dubious power into the document after the fact? If Lord Mansfield had been right to ask for a clear legal command before ruling against liberty in *Somerset,* shouldn't the Constitution itself be construed as favoring liberty in the absence of clear language to the contrary?

Thus, had the antebellum Supreme Court been so inclined, it might sensibly have questioned congressional authority to circumvent free-state procedures designed to ensure that free folk on free soil were not erroneously treated as fugitive slaves. But the Taney Court was hardly disposed to favor free law over slave law, as it made clear in a series of fateful rulings that had the effect of encouraging Southern slavocrats to wallow in an increasingly warped and ultimately unacceptable constitutional ideology in the years leading up to the Civil War.

First, in *Prigg v. Pennsylvania*,[27] decided in 1842, the Court held that Article IV authorized sweeping congressional legislation on behalf of slave-catchers. Not a single justice denied that the federal government could create its own slave-catching regime on free soil, wholly or partly displacing the free-state government's own legal apparatus and procedures. A majority of the Court then proceeded to invalidate one particular free state's efforts to protect its free blacks from being kidnapped, even though these efforts squared with the plain meaning of Article IV.

The facts underlying *Prigg* were heartrending. Marylander John Ashmore owned several slaves whom he had allowed to live in virtual freedom but never formally emancipated. One of these, Margaret, married James Morgan, a free black. The couple had several children in Maryland and later, with the apparent acquiescence of Ashmore's heirs, moved to Pennsylvania, where for many years they lived openly as a free family. There, Margaret gave birth to one or more additional children, who under Pennsylvania law were free citizens born on free soil and thus fell far outside the fugitive-slave category. Eventually, Ashmore's heirs decided to claim Margaret as their slave and sent Edward Prigg and others into Pennsylvania to recover their alleged property. The Prigg party dragged Margaret and her children into Maryland, where the blacks were treated as slaves and apparently sold. Pennsylvania prosecuted and convicted Prigg for what it viewed as a grotesque kidnapping. The Supreme Court reversed.

But why? Article IV obliged Pennsylvania to render up a fugitive slave upon a suitable demand. Pennsylvania had not violated this obligation. Prigg had never come before the proper Pennsylvania authorities to prove that Margaret and her children were all fugitive slaves. Surely the state was entitled to satisfy itself that a black person residing openly and peacefully within its borders was indeed a fugitive slave before allowing her to be dragged off in chains to a land where black skin was presumptive evidence of slave status. Had she been heard in Pennsylvania, Margaret might have had several strong legal and factual responses to the assertion that she was a fugitive slave, and at least one of her children would have had an ironclad defense.

Nor did the 1793 Act support the outcome in *Prigg,* even if we assume, for argument's sake, that this act was itself constitutionally valid. The federal act provided a mechanism by which the Prigg party could have gotten a certificate from a federal judge in Pennsylvania, but these body-snatchers had not complied with this procedure, either. Instead, they simply grabbed a woman and her children and then ran for the border. If this was constitutionally protected behavior, as the *Prigg* Court held, it was open season on free blacks everywhere in America.

In the 1849 case of *Jones v. Van Zandt,* the Taney Court returned to the Act of 1793 and unanimously reaffirmed its constitutionality in every respect. The great antislavery lawyer Salmon P. Chase, whom Lincoln would later appoint to replace Taney as chief justice, argued before the Court that the 1793 law not only exceeded Congress's enumerated powers, but also violated several aspects of the Bill of Rights—by authorizing unreasonable bodily seizures (contra the Fourth Amendment), providing inadequate procedural safeguards (contra the Fifth Amendment due-process clause), and neglecting to give the alleged fugitive a free-soil jury (contra the Seventh Amendment).[28] The *Jones* Court brusquely swept aside these objections. When it came to helping slave masters, Congress had virtual carte blanche.

Emboldened by *Prigg* and *Van Zandt,* Congress passed a far more sweeping and oppressive fugitive-slave law as part of an intricate ensemble of statutes commonly referred to as the Compromise of 1850. As in 1793, Congress allowed slave-catchers to sidestep state governments, this time via a veritable army of federal slave-catching commissioners authorized to dragoon ordinary free-soil citizens into slave-catching squads. As bad as this impressment system was for those free whites who conscientiously objected to slavery, the act posed a far worse threat to free blacks—the threat of being falsely adjudged a fugitive slave in a case of mistaken identity or prior manumission. Federal commissioners were told to act in summary proceedings where the slave-catcher had a statutory right to testify, but the alleged fugitive was legislatively barred from testifying in return and had no right of counsel. If this were not enough to skew the proceedings against liberty, the act further provided for a remarkable compensation structure: A commissioner would receive $10 for his trouble if he decided for the slave-catcher but would get only half this amount if he instead released the alleged fugitive. Slave-catchers won 90 percent of the cases tried under these rigged rules.[29]

When the issue reached the justices, in the 1859 case of *Ableman v. Booth,* Taney's opinion for the Court spent exactly one sentence dismissing all constitutional objections to the 1850 Act. Though Anglo-American law had long condemned financially biased decision makers, free blacks apparently had no rights which the Taney Court was bound to respect.[30]

"Territory"

Which brings us back to Taney's lead opinion in *Dred Scott v. Sanford*. In that 1857 case, the chief justice did more than say that blacks, even if free, could never be citizens because at the Founding they "had no rights which the white man was bound to respect." He also claimed that the federal government had no constitutional power to exclude slavery from federal territory.[31]

Yet the Constitution itself said no such thing. Article IV gave Congress sweeping authority to "make *all* needful Rules and Regulations respecting the Territory . . . belonging to the United States." Structurally, this clause endowed Congress with the same plenary power that a state legislature had over state soil and that Congress itself enjoyed under Article I when enacting "exclusive Legislation in *all* Cases" for the national capital city. If a state legislature could abolish slavery on its own soil, so could the federal legislature when regulating *its* soil.

In July 1787 the Confederation Congress had barred slavery from the Northwest Territory, and this bar formed the backdrop against which the Philadelphia delegates drafted, and the American people ratified, the unqualified language of the Article IV territory clause. In Pennsylvania, Wilson assured ratification delegates that the new Congress would honor this aspect of the Northwest Ordinance. He began by predicting that in 1808 Congress would likely end the "reproachful" transatlantic slave trade and thereby lay "the foundation for banishing slavery out of this country" via a "gradual change." He then added that "in the mean time, the new states which are to be formed will be under the control of Congress in this particular, and slaves will never be introduced amongst them."[32] No prominent Southern Federalist during the ratification process contradicted Wilson's early public statements on this issue or otherwise denied congressional power to exclude slavery from federal territory.

When the First Congress convened, it quickly redeemed Wilson's pledge, enacting a statute designed to give "full effect" to the principles of the Northwest Ordinance. Passed in August 1789 as the new nation's eighth public law, the statute tweaked the old ordinance to "adapt" its territorial governance system to the Constitution's apparatus of presidential appointment and removal but left the ordinance's free-soil rules untouched.[33] In 1820, as part of the Missouri Compromise, a later Congress excluded slavery from the Louisiana Purchase territory north of the latitude line 36° 30'. Before adding his signature to this act, Virginian James Monroe polled his cabinet, which included the staunch South Carolinian slavocrat John C. Calhoun and several other leading slave-state politicians. The group unanimously affirmed the free-soil rule's constitutionality.[34]

Taney's argument that Congress lacked power to ban slavery from the territories thus did violence to the Constitution's text, structure, enactment history, and early implementation. Things did not improve for the chief when he recast his bald assertion in the language of due process. True, in exercising its general authority over federal territory and the national capital, Congress had to comply with separation of powers—hence the 1789 Act—and after 1791 it also had to abide by the Bill of Rights. In the territories, as in the states, Congress could not, say, foist financially biased federal magistrates upon inhabitants, for such officers would indeed violate the Fifth Amendment's promise of due process. Taney took this uncontroversial premise and ran with it. "An act of Congress which deprives a citizen of the United States of his liberty or property, merely because he came himself or brought his property into a particular Territory of the United States . . . could hardly be dignified with the name of due process of law."[35]

This was nonsense. Free-soil statutes like the 1789 Northwest Ordinance Act and the 1820 Missouri Compromise Act were textbook examples of due process of law. After all, they had been *duly* enacted in a manner that gave fair notice to everyone—"Don't bring slaves here or else you will lose them"—and that contemplated fair enforcement *procedures,* with judges and juries acting in the standard *legal* way. Exactly what due legal process was missing? The very phrase "due process" derived from English jurisprudence, which famously deprived slave masters of various property rights over slaves whom the masters had chosen to bring onto English soil. This was precisely the principle that American free-soilers sought to apply to federal territory. If free-soil laws were inherent violations of due process of law, then each and every Northern free state was flagrantly violating due process—an outlandish conclusion but one that logically followed from Taney's slavocrat premise. Nor did Taney's opinion look any better if a reader pondered the future rather than the past. If America were one day to bring certain Canadian territories into the union for geostrategic reasons, would Congress be obliged to introduce slavery into these Northern lands? Would the national capital forever need to be a slave jurisdiction? Even if virtually every American state and every other nation in the world eventually abolished slavery on its own? Even if the capital were moved to, say, Boston?

ALAS, THOUGH THE CONSTITUTION nowhere mandated that all federal lands be slave soil, neither did it require that they be free soil. The general expectation, both in Philadelphia and in Southern ratifying conventions, was that slavery would likely spread into the area south of the Ohio River, and that the new Congress would facilitate this process. In keeping with this understanding, the First Congress in 1790 transplanted most of its general rules for the Northwest Territory to a new federal Southwest Territory—whose borders roughly tracked the eventual state of Tennessee—but also promised "that no regulations made or to be made by Congress shall tend to emancipate slaves." This language reiterated the explicit conditions that North Carolina had attached when ceding this land to the union.[36] In 1798, Congress formed a new Mississippi Territory and applied to it the same regulatory regime then in place for the Northwest Territory, with the sole exception of the Northwest's rule banning slavery.[37] Formally, this new territory had not come into federal possession via a state cession stipulating that it be treated as slave soil. Yet for most congressmen, it seemed clear that the federal government should not try to stretch the Northwestern antislavery rules southward. (Perhaps an implicit understanding on this point can be traced to the old Confederation's Northwest Ordinance itself, which, unlike earlier failed Confederation plans, expressly limited itself to the area "northwest of the River Ohio.")[38] Between 1800 and 1805, the federal government exempted two more Southern territories from the Northwest's antislavery rules,[39] and of course in its 1820 compromise, Congress allowed slavery in federal land south of 36° 30' even as it banned slavery in Louisiana Purchase territory north of that line.

In effect, Article IV structured a footrace between free-soilers hoping to move into the Northwest and slave owners aiming to carry their property and culture into the Southwest, with the three-fifths clause giving slave owners a big political head start. America's destiny—whether the new nation would long continue half-slave and half-free, or whether one side would decisively preponderate—would depend on future demographic, diplomatic, military, and economic contingencies that none could predict with certainty in 1787.

In one sense, the framers simply got lucky. Their legacy would have been far darker had American history unfolded differently, as for all they knew it might have. Instead of unfurling due west from its original Atlantic coastline, nineteenth-century America could instead have curled southward into a vast slavocratic empire encompassing much of modern-day Mexico, Central America, Cuba, and the Caribbean, and perhaps even parts of slave-rich Brazil. Had Southern slave masters, with their three-fifths head start, won the early footrace into the Southwest, they could have exerted even more control over American foreign affairs and expansion policy than they ultimately did, and in ways that might have locked in their early lead.[40]

Though this alternative historical path might seem the stuff of bad science fiction, nineteenth-century slavocrats undeniably did push hard for extra elbow room for slavery—successfully in the case of Florida and Texas, unsuccessfully in the case of Cuba. Some Southern slavocrats—whose power was hugely magnified by the three-fifths clause among states and comparable malapportionments within slave states—dreamed even bigger dreams. Mississippi's Senator Albert Gallatin Brown minced no words in 1858: "I want a foothold in Central America . . . because I want to plant slavery there. . . . I want Cuba, . . . Tamaulipas, Potosi, and one or two other Mexican States; and I want them all for the same reason—for the planting or spreading of slavery."[41] In response to such aggressive visions, free-soilers such as David Wilmot and Abraham Lincoln drew a line in the sand: No new slavery in new territories. Southern slavocrats could not accept this cramping of their lifestyle, and in the end it was this dispute over slavery in the territories, as much as anything, that sparked the Civil War.

WAS THERE ANY REALISTIC ALTERNATIVE to Article IV's footrace, had the framers been less complacent that the future would somehow take care of itself or more clairvoyant about the ultimate divisiveness of Article IV's agnostic stance?

One possible rule might have simply constitutionalized and universalized the Northwest Ordinance, permanently prohibiting slavery in all federal territory. Such a rule would have been less unacceptably confining of slave-soil states, and less immediately advantageous to free-soil states, than might first appear. In 1787 most of the Southwest remained in the hands of individual slave states, who had yet to cede these lands to the union.[42] In the face of an alternative Article IV, the Carolinas and Georgia might have simply kept their western backcountry to themselves until a slavery culture had put down deep roots and achieved enough settlers to bypass any period of federal territorial status. These areas could then have moved directly to independent statehood, as would Virginia's district of Kentucky in 1792 and Massachusetts's district of Maine in 1820. Even if Southwestern lands did go through a brief territorial period before ripening into states, à la Tennessee, the Northwest Ordinance model did not seek to uproot preexisting master-slave relations, but only to prevent new slaves from being brought in. (At least, this was the understanding of the ordinance put forth by a committee of the Confederation Congress in 1788, and generally implemented in the Northwest, with the acquiescence of President Washington.)[43] Thus, an Article IV that constitutionalized the Northwest Ordinance would likely have made little difference in what later became the states of Kentucky, Tennessee, Alabama, and Mississippi.

But such a rule might have made a big difference in the far West— a vast trans-Mississippi empire beyond American control in the 1780s, and thus perhaps easier for Southerners to give up, since they did not have it in hand or even fully in sight. An alternative Article IV would have put all on notice in 1787 that free soil was the constitutionally preferred condition in a new nation conceived in liberty. Along with a revised 1808 clause that could have mandated (rather than merely permitted) an eventual ban on the transatlantic slave traffic, the Constitution might thus have promised a freedom-tending future in which ultimately no slaves would cross the Atlantic from the East or traverse the Mississippi to the West.

In 1787, such a plan could probably have garnered significant Southern support. Even leading slave masters, at least in the upper South, saw slavery as an evil. In 1784, Thomas Jefferson proposed that slavery be excluded from *all* Western lands after 1800, a plan that the Confederation Congress failed to pass because of the health-related absence of a single delegate.[44] At Philadelphia, few spoke more bluntly of "the evil of having slaves" than did Virginia's Mason, who blamed the peculiar institution for "discourag[ing] arts & manufactures," dampening the "immigration of Whites," making citizens more vulnerable to wartime sabotage and insurrection, and warping the very souls of masters, each of whom was "born a petty tyrant." More cosmically, slavery brought "the judgment of heaven on a Country. . . . Providence punishes national sins, by national calamities." Yet this very same Mason in the ratification period railed against anything that might precipitate the immediate abolition of slavery in places where it had become entrenched. Mason's specific proposal at Philadelphia was thus "to prevent the *increase* of slavery" by allowing an immediate federal ban on transatlantic importation—in part to prevent the spread of

the evil to "new lands" in the "Western . . . Country." A man like this—
and there were many such men in 1787—might well have accepted an explicit Article IV rule banning slavery from all federal territory as part of a
long-term strategy of containment.[45]

To be sure, even a constitutionalized and universalized Northwest
Ordinance might not have prevented American slavery from expanding
via annexation of new lands where slavery had already implanted itself—
whether Louisiana or Florida or Texas or Cuba or Brazil.* Nor would it
have prevented Northern and Middle states from choosing to reverse their
systems of abolition and/or expand their existing slave regimes, had slavery somehow become more economically viable in cold climes. For example, New York and New Jersey together had more slaves than Georgia in
the late 1780s, and neither Northern state had yet promised gradual manumission. Thus a ban on new slavery in new territories might have needed
additional constitutional supports.

We have already considered one structural alternative that could have
given each state decreasing apportionment credit for its slave population
over time. Another approach, advocated years too late by Philadelphia delegate Rufus King, would have limited the three-fifths bonus to the original
thirteen states.[46] A still more direct and farsighted approach would have expressly empowered Congress to provide for compensated emancipation in
the states, with explicit directions to use the proceeds of Western land sales
to emancipate (and voluntarily resettle) American slaves. In this way, the
West could have been used to bring the North and South closer together.

Elbridge Gerry, a Philadelphia delegate (and Declaration signer) who
opposed the completed Constitution, floated a version of this idea in the
First Congress, and Rufus King publicly revived the concept in the aftermath of the Missouri Compromise. Madison himself privately endorsed a
similar plan in 1819, when he focused directly on the issue of slavery in the

---

*It would not have been sensible to have used Article IV to limit the precise path of future ter-
ritorial development, given the impossibility in 1787 of predicting America's future vital interests, opportunities, adversaries, and allies. In the nineteenth century, it was sometimes suggested
that Article IV itself envisioned only federal governance over the territory that existed in 1787.
Of course, Article IV said nothing of the sort, and for good reason. The Founders understood
that geostrategic considerations might well call for expansion beyond the 1787 footprint. Though
the Constitution nowhere guaranteed—as had the Articles of Confederation—that Canada
could automatically join the union as a new state, nowhere did it prohibit this possibility, or the
related possibility that some Canadian lands might become federal territories before later ma-
turing into statehood. Many farsighted Founders hoped one day to acquire New Orleans. With
the entire trans-Appalachian region draining into the great waters of the Mississippi, whoever
commanded the mouth of that river controlled a key continental choke point. Yet in 1787, New
Orleans lay beyond America's borders.

West; and in the middle of the Civil War Lincoln presented Congress with his own detailed proposal for compensated emancipation via Western land proceeds.[47] Had the Constitution itself provided such a blueprint for federal territory, perhaps it might have transformed America's vast Western lands into an answer to, rather than an aggravation of, the nation's most intractable problem.

"New States may be admitted"

The most extraordinary thing about the Northwest Ordinance of 1787 is simply that it came to pass. After all, in notable contrast to Franklin's failed Albany Plan of 1754, the Articles of Confederation declined to confer any explicit authority on Congress to regulate Western lands. What's more, the document began by emphatically rejecting the idea of any implied congressional powers above and beyond the ones "expressly delegated." As Madison/Publius observed in *The Federalist* No. 38, the Confederation Congress adopted the ordinance "without the least color of constitutional authority."

Madison hastened to add that he did not mean to "censure" the old Congress. "I am sensible they could not have done otherwise. The public interest, the necessity of the case, imposed upon them the task of overleaping their constitutional limits." Like the unconquered summit beckoning mountaineers, the West was simply there, drawing men to it, and no responsible group of planners could ignore its looming presence.

The story of America cannot be told apart from the story of the landmass itself. It was the promise of land that lured many of the first European settlers to the New World and that kept them coming in the ensuing centuries. In a sense, the continent itself structured a giant footrace for real estate between England (and later America), France, and Spain. Among the English-speakers, different views about the disposition of Western land would initially pit colonist against Crown, then "landed" states against "landless" ones, and ultimately North against South.

The colonial battle for the West began soon after Britain bested France in the global Seven Years War and claimed Canada as its prize. Americans dreaming of interior lands received a rude awakening when George III issued a formal 1763 proclamation forbidding his subjects from crossing the crest of the Appalachians and thereby mixing with various Indian tribes whom the king did not (yet) want to confront. Then came the Quebec Act of 1774, which purported to assign the entire region northwest of the Ohio River—territory originally promised to Virginia and several other colonies (with partially overlapping claims)—to the province of Quebec. The act simultaneously created a permanent civil-law government for that province as a whole, with no provision for an elected provincial assembly or local juries. The Declaration of Independence listed this land-and-liberty grab as cause for revolution, condemning the king and Parliament for "abolishing the free system of English laws in a neighboring Province, establishing therein an arbitrary government, and enlarging its boundaries, so as to render it at once an example and fit instrument for introducing the same absolute rule into these Colonies."

Though united in the struggle to wrest the West from England, the thirteen states had conflicting claims to and clashing ideas about this land. Various landed states asserted their right to trans-Ohio tracts by dint of their English charters or other founding instruments, but landless states worried about the interstate imbalance of wealth and power that might result from the union's recognition of such claims, not to mention the further problems of sorting out individual states' competing assertions. Moreover, hadn't the 1763 Proclamation and 1774 Act abrogated individual colonial claims to the Northwest? Given that all the states were waging a common struggle against Britain, shouldn't the Western prize go to the union as a whole? The Articles of Confederation as drafted in 1777 said nothing about this contentious matter, but landless Maryland refused to ratify the Articles until New York and Virginia finally took steps to cede their Western claims.

With the Treaty of Peace of 1783, England abandoned its own claim to the Northwest and agreed to recede behind the Great Lakes. Over the next couple of years, the remaining landed states relinquished their jurisdiction over this area. Thereafter, despite its lack of formal authority, only Congress could act in this region. And if it did act, and act quickly, it could help solve America's two most pressing problems.

First, the union was broke, with enormous war debts to pay and empty coffers. If managed right—with good land surveys, good domestic government, and a good Indian policy—the West would become, in the words of The Federalist No. 38, "a mine of vast wealth." The first wave of income would flow—and indeed, by late 1787 had already begun to flow—from land sales themselves; thereafter, Western settlers could begin to pay their fair share of continental expenses—though under both the Articles and the Constitution, any extensive revenue plan for the West raised the awkward specter of taxation without (congressional) representation.[48]

Second, the nation was militarily vulnerable. Britain had promised in 1783 to abandon its Western forts but then made no effort to do so; and of course there were also the Indian tribes to consider. But if the West could be properly organized, settlers in search of cheap land would invade the region and by their very presence comprise an invincible American army—or more precisely, an American militia of nonprofessionals. The magic magnet of Western land would not only pull Americans from the coast over the mountains but would also draw countless thousands across the ocean. With each boatload of new settlers from the Old World, the United States would grow that much stronger against Europe itself and Europe's New World outposts.

As Wilson declared in Pennsylvania,

> the increase of numbers increases the dignity and security, and the respectability, of all governments. . . . This applies with peculiar force to this country, the smaller part of whose territory is yet inhabited. We are representatives, sir, not merely of the present age, but of future times; not merely of the territory along the sea-coast, but of regions immensely extended westward. We should fill, as fast as possible, this extensive country, with men who shall live happy, free, and secure. . . . By these means, we may draw members from the other side of the Atlantic, in addition to the natural sources of population.[49]

Thus Americans would reverse the policies of King George, whom the Declaration had scolded for trying to "prevent the population of these States; for that purpose obstructing the Laws for Naturalization of Foreigners; refusing to pass others to encourage their migrations hither, and raising the conditions of new Appropriations of Lands."

National defense, immigration, and revenue enhancement would all mutually reinforce. If enough seed money and organization could be scraped together to conduct land surveys and to defend settlers against Indian depredations—and in turn restrain these settlers from unprovoked assaults against Indians—Congress could expect to reap sizable financial returns that could then be plowed back into additional surveys and defense structures. With its vast agricultural lands and its plentiful timber, minerals, and furs, the West promised a self-financing perpetual-motion machine that required only enough energy to prime the pump. Eventually, improved inland roads through the Appalachians could combine with man-made canals to knit the East and West together in a tight and mutually advantageous economic system. Facing an ocean of water on one side and an ocean of land on the other, the original thirteen states would be shielded by two great buffer zones of freedom, with a mercantile armada of commercial ships defending the coastline and an advancing militia of pioneers securing the hinterlands.

Of course, Western territory would be more than a buffer zone; it would also be the nursery of new states. In 1774, the English Parliament's refusal to guarantee some system of provincial self-government to the people of Quebec had outraged Americans. This was not how the West should be won. The Northwest Ordinance sketched out a strikingly different vision, in which Westerners would initially elect a temporary general assembly and send a nonvoting delegate to Congress. Thereafter, the ordinance promised that the territory would be divided up into smaller states, each of which would be entitled to frame a permanent state constitution on "republican" principles and be admitted into the union "on an equal footing with the original States, in all respects whatever."[50]

Having themselves been mistreated as colonists, Americans in the Northwest Ordinance solemnly vowed not to mistreat their own new colonies. The older states would help their younger siblings grow up and would thereafter regard them as equals, rather than as permanent adolescents—the status to which Mother England had wrongly relegated her own New World wards.

Article IV wisely omitted all the messy details, timetables, and formulas of the Northwest Ordinance. A Constitution designed to cope with all future territories and states for all time called for considerable flexibility. The Articles of Confederation had likewise aimed for flexibility on the topic of new states but had in fact bungled the job by codifying a mathematical glitch, an eighteenth-century forerunner of the late-twentieth-century Y2K bug. According to the Confederation document, Canada could automatically join the union, while any "other colony" might do so if nine states agreed. The nine-state rule built into this admissions clause, and indeed into the Confederation's governing structure more generally, would have imploded had, say, five new states entered the union from the Northwest Territory, along with other new states south of the Ohio River, such as Kentucky and Tennessee. In an expanded union of twenty states, nine would have ceased to make any sense as the magic number for admitting further states or enacting major Confederation policies. Although this technical glitch might have been patched over with an amendment replacing the words "nine states" with "two-thirds of the states" everywhere in the Confederation document, any such amendment would have required unanimous state approval, enabling any one state to derail it. By contrast, the Constitution was sleekly designed to work in a union of nine states or ninety, via general rules pegged to percentages rather than fixed numbers. For example, Article IV authorized Congress to admit new states by way of ordinary statutes—statutes that under Article I would require either regular majorities of House and Senate quorums or two-thirds override votes in the event of presidential veto.

Nor was the fixed number nine the only flaw in the Confederation's framework for admitting new states. Did the Confederation's admissions clause require a simple vote of nine state delegations *in Congress,* or did it instead call for the votes of nine *state legislatures?* Both readings were plausible. And what did the Confederation document mean when it spoke of any "colony" that would be eligible for admission? Some Confederation congressmen construed this to refer only to British domains such as Nova Scotia and the Floridas. Others read "colony" generically to refer to any new candidate for union membership. The status of an entity that had once been part of a state was also unclear under the Articles. In the late 1780s, these ambiguities ensnared Kentucky's urgent pleas for admission in a web of legal confusion that only thickened when, in mid-1788, the Confederation Congress got definitive word that it would soon be going out of business. In the end, the old Congress failed to act decisively on Kentucky's bid. The Confederation's admissions clause thus flunked its first and only real test. Relief for Kentuckians and other Westerners would arrive only after the Constitution's Article IV framework went into effect.[51]

THE CONFEDERATION'S ADMISSIONS CLAUSE had explicitly promised that Canada could join the union with "all the advantages" and implicitly held out the same promise of equal treatment to any other colony that might be admitted. Likewise, the Northwest Ordinance guaranteed that new states would one day be welcomed on an equal footing. Against this backdrop, the Constitution never promised in so many words that all federal territory would at some point ripen into statehood. Nevertheless, the fact that Article IV addressed both federal territory and new states in a single integrated section both reflected and reinforced a general expectation that territories would indeed mature into new states that in due course would be admitted on equal terms.

True, the specific words "equal footing" did not appear. Yet this idea shone through in the document's general structure and in many of its specific rules. Apart from a reference in the 1808 clause to "the States now existing"—a clause that implicitly allowed Congress to ban transatlantic slave imports into new states even before 1808—the Constitution nowhere distinguished between the original states and later ones. All states, old and new alike, would get two Senate seats apiece and live under a universally applicable population formula for House seats. All would play by the same rules in the electoral college and in the Article V amendment process. All would be guaranteed republican forms of government, protected against involuntary dismemberment or invasion, and so on. Gouverneur Morris later bragged about how he had successfully blocked a specific textual guarantee of equal footing; but regardless of the outcome of this textual battle, Morris had lost the structural war. The original thirteen states would have no privileged place within America's New World order.[52]

Of course, American-style state equality and state republicanism meant that new states, just like old ones, would be free to make bad choices. Even if Congress could keep slavery out of a federal territory during its critical adolescent period, federal lawmakers had no general authority to prevent a new adult state, after its admission, from embracing slavery, just as they had no right to prevent an old state from backsliding. Only over a few un-usual venues—federal forts and the national capital city—was congres-sional power seen as more than transitional.

Yet even as new states in the nineteenth century eventually came to claim the same formal rights and owe the same formal duties as their elder siblings, the youngsters exhibited a distinct cultural character. The origi-nal thirteen colonies predated the birth of the United States; these thirteen could indeed be said to have created the union. By contrast, the new states (with rare exceptions like Texas) were undeniably created by the union it-self. In 1861, a Virginian like Robert E. Lee could look back at many gen-erations of Lees who had served in the Virginia House of Burgesses long before 1776. From Lee's point of view, *of course* Virginia came before America, chronologically and emotionally. But from where he stood, Abraham Lincoln had a different view of the country and its history. The union had itself given birth to his home state of Illinois and also to Indi-ana, where he had spent much of his boyhood, having arrived there at the very moment when it was moving from federal territorial status to state-hood. As Lincoln saw it, "the Union is older than any of the States; and, in fact, it created them as States."[53]

The West would also prove to be a land of newcomers and self-made men. Old money and famous fathers would count for less here. Thus, the new states would give antebellum America its two most dramatic stories of ascent from low birth to high office in the figures of Andy Jackson and

Abe Lincoln. Two of the three youngest elected presidents in this era—Lincoln and Polk—would come from the West,[54] as would Jackson, who had earlier served as one of America's youngest senators. From 1789 to 1850, new states would choose young men for the Senate at almost twice the rate set by the original thirteen states but would generally choose a very different breed of young man. Exactly half (thirteen of twenty-six) of the young Eastern senators were sons, sons-in-law, or nephews of prominent politicians, while none (zero of twenty-four) of the young Westerners fit this category. On the contrary, several of the West's most notable senators were famously self-made, such as Tennessee's Jackson, Kentucky's Henry Clay, and Illinois's Stephen Douglas. Nowhere were the New World ideals of opportunity and upward mobility—at least for white males—embodied more dramatically than in America's new states.[55]

"a Republican Form of Government"

Well-educated twenty-first-century Americans have been taught that the Constitution established a "republican" form of government in emphatic contradistinction to a "democratic" one; that the framing generation invariably associated a republic with the idea of filtered, representative government, as opposed to more direct modes of popular participation; and that the Founders loathed the label and reality of direct democracy.[56] All these well-learned lessons need to be unlearned if we are to understand the Constitution in general and the Article IV republican-form-of-government clause in particular. Under this clause, "the United States shall guarantee to every State in this Union a Republican Form of Government."

Modern-day misinterpretations typically take Madison's *Federalist* No. 10 as their point of departure: "A republic, by which I mean a government in which the scheme of representation takes place, opens a different prospect, and promises the cure for which we are seeking. Let us examine the points in which it varies from pure democracy. . . . [A] great point[] of difference between a democracy and a republic [is] the delegation of the government, in the latter, to a small number of citizens elected by the rest." Madison reiterated his distinction between "a republic and a democracy" in *The Federalist* No. 14 and also criticized the ancient Greek brand of direct democracy in No. 63.

Yet Madison himself, in these very passages, admitted that he was swimming against the tide of standard eighteenth-century usage.[57] Thus, in No. 10 he stipulated his own definition: "A republic, by which *I mean* . . ."

(as opposed to "a republic, by which is generally meant . . ."). In No. 14, he confessed that the "prevalen[t]" understanding "confound[s] a republic with a democracy." Sure enough, Madison's contemporaries often referred casually to England's House of Commons and state lower houses—all of which were based on principles of representation—as particularly "democratic" or "democratical" elements of their respective constitutions.[58] Conversely, late-eighteenth-century "republics" could indeed make use of certain forms of direct political participation—as had, for example, Massachusetts in ratifying its state constitution and in its general tradition of town meetings. Ancient Greek governments, which had practiced various forms of direct democracy, were also commonly described as "republics." In fact, such a description appears in no less than three of the four *Federalist* essays immediately preceding Madison's stipulated definition in No. 10.[59]

Of course, if Madison's definition did in fact sway large numbers of would-be ratifiers, then its new-minted linguistic distinction might deserve to carry some weight in sound constitutional interpretation. But *The Federalist* No. 10 went largely unnoticed at the Founding. And nowhere in that essay did Publius purport to explain the meaning of the specific Article IV clause featuring the word "Republican." When Publius did turn to Article IV, he offered a very different and less idiosyncratic account of republicanism.

At the same time that Madison was drawing his fine linguistic distinction, other leading Federalists were obliterating it, proclaiming that a "republican" government could be either directly or indirectly democratic. Explicitly equating a "republic" with a "democracy" in the Pennsylvania ratifying convention, Wilson repeatedly pronounced the Constitution "democratic" and "democratical." For Wilson, the crucial distinction was not between a "republic" and a "democracy," but rather between a democracy/republic on the one side and "monarchy" or "aristocracy" on the other. In a proper republic/democracy, "the people at large retain the supreme power, and act *either* collectively *or* by representation." The Constitution met this test, Wilson declared. "All authority, of every kind, is derived by REPRESENTATION from the PEOPLE, and the DEMOCRATIC principle is carried into every part of the government." Similarly, South Carolina's Charles Pinckney described a republican government as one in which "the people at large, *either* collectively *or* by representation, form the legislature."[60]

Repeatedly, Federalists explained the central meaning of republican government—especially in discussing the meaning of Article IV's use of the word "Republican"—by defining republics not in contradistinction to democracies but rather in opposition to monarchies and aristocracies. Thus, Iredell in North Carolina read Article IV to mean that "no state should have a right to establish an aristocracy or a monarchy." Similarly, an early Federalist essay, "Plain Truth," explained that the clause would guarantee against "monarchical or aristocratical encroachments," and Tench Coxe, in another essay, read the clause to mean that state constitutions "cannot be royal forms, cannot be aristocratical, but must be republican." When Madison/Publius himself turned to expound Article IV in *The Federalist* No. 43, he declared that "in a confederacy founded on republican principles, and composed of republican members, the superintending government ought clearly to possess authority to defend the system against aristocratic or monarchial innovations." Later, in No. 84, Publius pointed to the Constitution's ban on titles of nobility as "truly . . . the corner-stone of republican government"—a passage that called to mind Jefferson's celebrated 1784 plan for Western territories, which had provided that territorial governments "shall be in republican forms, and shall admit no person to be a citizen who holds any hereditary title."[61]

The *Federalist* essays, when read as a whole, painted a very different picture of the central meaning of republican government than the one that has been peddled to many modern Americans. Time and again, Publius linked "republican" government with various aspects of popular sovereignty. For instance, moments before its stilted definition, *The Federalist* No. 10 casually linked republicanism with majority rule ("the republican principle")—a linkage that recurred in Hamilton/Publius's Nos. 21 and 78. When discussing the most fundamental attributes of republican government, Publius associated the idea with "the capacity of mankind for self-government" and with "the right of the people to alter or abolish the established Constitution, whenever they find it inconsistent with their happiness." A true republican government "derives all its powers directly or indirectly from the great body of the people." The "genius of republican liberty . . . demand[s] . . . that all power should be derived from the people." Thus, as Publius took pains to remind his audience, the Constitution itself was being founded "on republican principles"—founded, that is, "on the assent and ratification of the people of America, given by deputies elected for the special purpose."[62]

This, indeed, was the general understanding of republicanism across America. Samuel Johnson's 1786 dictionary defined "Republican" as "Placing the government in the people." Ratification pamphlets and speeches described republican government as one in which "the people are sovereign"; in which "the people are consequently the fountain of all power"; in which "all authority should flow from the people"; in which "all laws are derived from the consent of the people"; in which power resides in "the hands of the people at large"; and in which "the majority govern."[63]

When the word "democracy" appeared in the Founding era, it was often associated with, rather than defined against, republicanism—even by Madison himself. Madison's preferred system of filtered representation over an extended geographic sphere, which *The Federalist* No. 10 proudly labeled "the *republican* remedy for the disease most incident to *republican* government," had earlier been described by Madison at Philadelphia as "the only defence agst. the inconveniences of *democracy* consistent with the *democratic* form of Govt."[64] In the 1790s, when various political groups sprang up in sympathy with the outlook of men such as Madison and Jefferson, some local groups called themselves "Republican Societies," others "Democratic Societies," and still others "Democratic-Republican Societies." The political party that Madison and Jefferson created in this decade was variously described as the "Republican" party and the "Democratic-Republican" party. (Today's Democratic Party claims the "Republican" Jefferson as one of its founders.)

Thus, the essence of the Article IV guarantee of each state's "Republican" form of government was not to prohibit town meetings or initiatives or referenda or juries or any other form of direct popular participation.* Rather, the big idea was to shore up popular sovereignty. The electorate of

---

*Many modern scholars quote various democracy-bashing statements made at Philadelphia as smoking-gun evidence of the Constitution's antidemocratic spirit. For instance, Randolph spoke of the dangers arising from "the democratic parts of our [state] constitutions" and of the need to check "the turbulence and follies of democracy." Gerry said that "the evils we experience flow from the excess of democracy" and that he had been "too republican heretofore." *Farrand's Records*, 1:26–27, 48, 51 (May 29 and 31). Alas, scholars who invoke these particular statements rarely remind readers that both Gerry and Randolph refused to sign the final version of the Constitution. (As noted in Chapter 1, Randolph later supported ratification for geostrategic reasons; see page 49.) True, Gerry and Randolph did not stand in isolation; other Philadelphians said antidemocratic and antirepublican things behind closed doors. An early compilation of such statements appears in Chapter VII of Charles Beard's hugely influential 1913 book, *An Economic Interpretation of the Constitution of the United States*. But what do such quotations prove? Many of the statements were made on behalf of proposals that the Convention ultimately *voted down*—a point rarely noted by Beardians. If the question is whether the framers themselves were all zealous democrats/republicans, Beard's evidence clearly suggests that the answer is no. But the real question is—or should be—whether the *Constitution itself* as finally enacted (and amended early on) was strongly democratic/republican when viewed in its legal and historical context. To answer that question, we must go beyond private grumblings to consider public words and deeds—namely, the text and the act of constitution. (Even today, politicians privately bellyache about democracy, but that fact alone does not make our current system undemocratic.) The statements showcased by Beard and others do give rise to a puzzle: Why would men with less than fully democratic instincts propose a strongly democratic (in context) document? There

a given state, acting by "a majority of the people in a legal and peaceable mode" would of course retain the right to "alter or abolish" their state constitutions (subject to the overriding dictate of federal supremacy), but the United States would protect against "changes to be effected by violence"—usurpations, military coups, and so on.[65]

Three complementary visions inspired this guarantee. First, the Constitution would offer a kind of democratic insurance policy. If any individual state system of self-government fell sick and needed help, sister republics would come to its aid.[66] In so doing—and here were the second and third ideas—sister republics would also be protecting themselves, both individually and collectively. A monarch or tyrant in any one state would pose a geostrategic threat to each and every neighboring state.[67] Thus Article IV not only guaranteed that each state would honor the basics of republican government, but also promised to protect each state from any "Invasion" or "domestic Violence," instigated by a neighbor state or otherwise.[68] In addition, an unrepublican state government might tend to undermine the republican character of the *federal* government, whose own institutions would rest largely on state-law pillars. For example, a warped state government might corrupt the integrity of that state's elections to the federal House, Senate, and electoral college.

In the North Carolina ratification debates, Iredell explained that "if a monarchy was established in any one state, it would endeavor to subvert the freedom of the others, and would, probably by degrees succeed in it. This must strike the mind of every person here, who recollects the history of Greece, when she had confederated governments. The king of Macedon, by his arts and intrigues, got himself admitted a member of the Amphictyonic council, which was the superintending government of the Grecian republics; and in a short time he became master of them all."[69] In *The Federalist* No. 43's discussion of the Article IV guarantee, Madison had said much the same thing, quoting Montesquieu as follows: "Greece was undone . . . as soon as the king of Macedon obtained a seat among the Amphictyons."

Of course, when Southerners like Madison and Iredell spoke of republican governments that derived from "the people," they did not mean

is, however, a simple solution to the puzzle: In order to get their proposal ratified and legitimated, the framers had to move toward the strong democratic/republican end of the continuum—much as grumbling politicians today often find themselves obliged to restrain their worst antidemocratic impulses.

to include slaves. (Nor had ancient Greek democracies/republics.) In legal contemplation, slaves were akin to aliens, who likewise had no rights to participate in republican governments.

What about free black men? In the antebellum era, such men constituted such a small percentage of each state's total population that their status under the republican-government clause aroused rather little interest. But at the end of the Civil War, this once-obscure issue leaped into prominence—as we shall see in more detail in a later chapter. Once four million slaves had won their freedom by dint of Lincoln's Emancipation Proclamation and the Thirteenth Amendment, which forever abolished slavery, free blacks came to comprise more than a quarter of the population of every ex-Confederate state. Yet under Southern state laws, none of these freedmen could vote or be voted for. Could any ex-Confederate government that excluded so wide a slice of its *free* people from the franchise be truly "Republican" in form, within the meaning of Article IV? If not, exactly how should the federal government enforce the republican guarantee in former slave states that had suddenly become unrepublican?

These questions urgently confronted the members of the Reconstruction Congress, who had to decide which state governmental regimes and electoral systems were sufficiently republican to warrant inclusion in the federal House and Senate. Eventually, the sleeping giant of the Article IV republican-guarantee clause would awaken and utterly transform the nature of the union as originally envisioned by the likes of Madison and Iredell.

Chapter 8

THE LAW OF
THE LAND

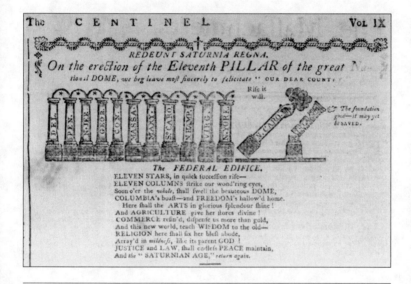

The CENTINEL   VOL IX

REDEUNT SATURNIA REGNA.

On the erection of the Eleventh PILLAR of the great National DOME, we beg leave most sincerely to felicitate " OUR DEAR COUNTRY."

Rise it will.

The foundation good—it may yet be SAVED.

The FEDERAL EDIFICE.

ELEVEN STARS, in quick succession rise—
ELEVEN COLUMNS strike our wond'ring eyes,
Soon o'er the *whole*, shall swell the beauteous DOME,
COLUMBIA's boast—and FREEDOM's hallow'd home.
Here shall the ARTS in glorious splendour shine !
And AGRICULTURE give her stores divine !
COMMERCE refin'd, dispense us more than gold,
And this new world, teach WISDOM to the old—
RELIGION here shall fix her blest abode,
Array'd in *mildness*, like its parent GOD !
JUSTICE and LAW, shall costless PEACE maintain,
And *the* " SATURNIAN AGE," *return again.*

THE ELEVENTH PILLAR (AUGUST 2, 1788).
Pursuant to Article VII, eleven of the original thirteen states formed a new, more perfect union in 1787–88. But what would become of North Carolina and Rhode Island?

$\mathscr{T}$HE PHILADELPHIA CONSTITUTION ended as it had begun, underscoring its own exalted political and juridical status. In a closing coda consisting of three short Articles featuring seven self-references to "this Constitution" (words that had first appeared at the end of the Preamble), the document proclaimed itself America's "supreme Law," superior to all other legal texts precisely because it was to be ordained, and could later be altered, by America's supreme lawgiver—the people of the United States.

"Amendments"

Mistakes happen—and the men drafting and ratifying the Constitution of 1787 had no illusions that they had gotten every issue exactly right. Even had they somehow believed that their blueprint would solve every problem in sight, they understood that new challenges and opportunities in the unforeseeable future might require new approaches. America's experience in its first decade of independence had sobered its solons. By 1787, many state constitutions that had won accolades in 1776 seemed badly in need of repair. The Articles of Confederation, framed by some of America's leading lights, had proved inadequate almost from the start. Could anyone absolutely guarantee that the Philadelphia Constitution itself would not suffer a similar fate? Hence the wisdom of leaving the door to future constitutional amendments wide-open.[1]

In one sense, the amendment issue defined the first and most fundamental item of business to be addressed at Philadelphia. State governments had sent their leading citizens to the city of brotherly love not to propose a new Constitution openly repudiating the Articles of Confederation, but rather to ponder possible amendments to the Confederation document rendering it adequate to its basic purpose. This charge presented a paradox, for it quickly became apparent to the delegates that the Confederation document's biggest—and indeed, fatal—flaw was its practical unamendability. According to the closing passage (Article XIII) of that document, any amendment to the Articles required the agreement of all thirteen state legislatures. Experience had shown that such unanimity was all but impossible to achieve. Repeatedly, the Confederation Congress in the early and mid-1780s had proposed amendments that would have enhanced the union's ability to perform its core functions; each time, one or more states had said no. Given that the tiny and refractory state of Rhode Island had refused even to send a delegation to Philadelphia, there seemed little hope that every legislature would eventually bow to the far more sweeping changes that the drafters agreed to consider as the Convention began.

This brute political reality prompted the delegates to unshackle themselves from their instructions. Instead of urging amendments to the Articles, they decided to float an entirely new Constitution that would not need to be ratified by each and every state legislature. Thus, the Confederation's closing passage led ironically but directly to the Constitution's diametrically opposed closing words, Article VII, which audaciously proposed that nine states could put the new document into effect amongst themselves.

We shall consider Article VII in more detail shortly. But before we reach that concluding Article, we should note how the old Confederation's amendment clause also influenced the new Constitution's amendment clause—Article V. Once the Constitution had won the approval of nine or more state conventions, this new amendment clause would allow future constitutional alterations to go into effect if ratified by three-quarters of the (remaining) states. To the men at Philadelphia, the moral of the Confederation's closing passage was that an overly stiff amendment mechanism in a governing document ultimately doomed the document to irrelevance by inviting outright repudiation. If the Constitution aimed to avoid the same fate, its own amendment procedures needed to be easier to activate. Thus, the Article V amendment clause decisively rejected the old requirement of state unanimity—a requirement that flowed logically from a pure confederacy of sovereign states but that would hardly befit the more perfect union envisioned by the new Constitution.

During the ratification period, the kinetic interplay between the old Article XIII and the new Article V helped propel the Constitution forward, as Federalists cleverly urged skeptics to ratify an admittedly imperfect Philadelphia document and then work to amend it. Consider for example the predicament of moderates who worried that the new Constitution went too far in strengthening the central government but who conceded that the old Articles had not gone far enough. If such moderates voted the Constitution down, they would be stuck with the Confederation, which was all but impossible to change. A yes vote, by contrast, could easily become a "yes, but" vote. Once the Constitution's new rules were in place, these new rules would include Article V, which would facilitate further alterations. Such alterations could adjust the basic structure of the new system, add a more comprehensive catalogue of explicit constitutional rights, and move in any other direction that seemed advisable.[2]

EVEN AS ARTICLE V openly repudiated the Confederation's amendment provision, it also impliedly rejected the amendment models furnished by the first state constitutions, none of which seemed to have gotten the matter quite right. In 1776, Connecticut and Rhode Island had simply continued operating under old Crown charters that made no mention of amendment procedures. Though this gaping silence in its foundational text ultimately created little difficulty in Connecticut, which adopted a new constitution in 1818, events would play out rather differently in Rhode Island. When Rhode Islanders finally turned to the task of constitutional revision in the 1840s, the absence of procedural guidance in the Crown charter helped plunge the state into a constitutional crisis and virtual civil war as two dueling governments each claimed to be the lawful successor of the Crown-chartered regime.

The first state constitutions of Virginia, North Carolina, and New York likewise made no explicit mention of amendment procedures. Yet unlike the two Crown charters, perhaps these three documents implicitly addressed the issue by analogy to the very process by which these constitutions had been ordained at the outset of the Revolution. None of these three constitutions had themselves been established by the people in some dramatically special vote. Rather, they had been promulgated by de facto legislatures elected in the ordinary way.[3] Thus, a strong argument could be made (though in Virginia the argument would ultimately be rejected by the judiciary in 1793) that these constitutions were little more than fancy statutes. If so, why couldn't a later legislature simply repeal what an earlier, ordinary legislature had enacted?[4] And if such legislative repeals were indeed permissible, what was to stop a future sitting legislature from, say, canceling the next set of elections and extending its own term of office for several extra years, as Parliament had notoriously done in 1716?

New Jersey's constitution of 1776 expressly gave the legislature general authority to amend its provisions by ordinary enactment, although it exempted a handful of items, one of which was the annual-election rule, from legislative amendment. How annual elections or other exempted items might ever be altered if the people of New Jersey truly desired a change, this document did not say. Apart from these exemptions, the document offered no external check against legislative overreaching. South Carolina's constitution of 1778 was not much better. It expressly provided for amendment by legislative enactment, though it did require would-be amenders to give ninety days' notice of their plan and obliged them to win a majority of the entire membership of each legislative house, as distinct from a majority of an ordinary quorum.[5]

In Delaware, a sitting legislature could generally amend the constitution by a supermajority vote. Here, too, unscrupulous lawmakers might one day agree among themselves to aggrandize their power or escape proper limits on their authority (including regular elections) with little external check. Maryland provided for amendment by way of two legislative votes sandwiching an intervening general election. This model provided an external check against outrageous legislative self-dealing—namely, the voters themselves in the intervening election. But Maryland failed to give the citizenry an equally effective external prod; the state specified no explicit mode of amending the constitution except via the legislature. If the people wanted not to block an outrageous amendment but rather to effect a rather modest one—say, an amendment limiting legislative power—how could they detour around whatever roadblocks to reform that the legislature might erect? The electorate could of course vote only for lawmakers pledged to support the favored constitutional reform, but unless that reform issue dominated all other concerns in two consecutive elections, the ballot box was a rather blunt instrument.[6]

Georgia's constitution of 1777 aimed to cure the problem by enabling citizens to petition for a special convention that would propose amendments. But the document failed to say exactly what would happen after the convention met. Would convention delegates have authority to promulgate amendments on their own say-so? Then what was to prevent a runaway convention from imposing all sorts of unwanted rules on the people? Alternatively, would the convention's proposed amendments need to be ratified by another body? In that case, who would ratify, and how? Some of these questions would find answers in 1789, when the state adopted a new constitution, but these events of course came after the federal ratification process and thus benefited from the lessons of that experience and from Article V itself.[7]

None of the ten states that we have canvassed (except, possibly, Delaware) could be said to have ordained its constitution by some extraordinarily inclusive act of popular participation. Thus, none of these states offered the delegates at Philadelphia direct guidance about how a constitution that had in fact been established in some exceptionally democratic way by *the people themselves* might later be amended. The remaining three states—Pennsylvania, Massachusetts, and New Hampshire—had each undergone a more populist ordainment process. Interestingly enough, all three amendment clauses followed the same pattern, identifying a specific date, or set of dates, in which an amendment process might be triggered by an institution outside the legislature. In Pennsylvania, a Council of Censors would convene every seven years, with authority to summon an amending convention. In Massachusetts, the voters themselves, via their townships, could initiate the amendment process in 1795. New Hampshire blended these two plans, combining Massachusetts's township model with Pennsylvania's septennial date for its first revision.[8]

Yet none of these three documents explained how the people *at any other time* might properly alter what they had originally ordained. If these amendment clauses were the exclusive means of constitutional revision, didn't they abridge the theoretically inalienable right of the people to alter or abolish? Theory aside, if these clauses were read as exclusive, were their seven- to fifteen-year waiting periods wise? What if an urgent set of issues arose before the fixed review period?

Such questions could never have been far from the minds of the Philadelphia delegates. After all, they were hoping that these three states, along with the other ten, would ratify the proposed federal Constitution sometime before mid-1788. Though these hoped-for ratifications would amend existing state constitutions, the amendments would need to occur seven years before the 1795 date specified in Massachusetts and several years ahead of the scheduled review dates in Pennsylvania and New Hampshire. Ratification in these three states would thus depend on reading the state constitutional-amendment clauses as nonexclusive even though these texts did not expressly say so.

GIVEN THE ABSENCE of any genuinely well-specified amendment provision in any antecedent document, the Philadelphia framers did a respectable job in Article V, avoiding many of the grossest errors of earlier Revolutionary efforts. Aside from a couple of special rules dealing with slave importation and equal state representation in the Senate, Article V proclaimed that constitutional amendments would become valid whenever proposed by a two-thirds vote of each house of Congress and ratified by three-quarters of the states, acting either through legislatures or special conventions. (The choice between the two ratification modes was Congress's.) Also, whenever two-thirds of the state legislatures so petitioned,

Congress would be obliged to call a special convention to propose amendments and to send that convention's proposals to the states for ratification under the same rule of three-quarters.

This system combined most of the virtues of the state amendment clauses while sidestepping most of their vices. First, in order to safeguard all the important restrictions imposed on Congress by the people in the rest of the Constitution, Article V wisely denied Congress the unilateral authority to lift those restrictions. In this way Article V buttressed the Constitution's status as a law far superior to an ordinary congressional statute subject to ordinary congressional repeal. A mere congressional supermajority requirement for amendment, à la Delaware, would not have done the trick. After all, sitting congressmen might at some point be virtually unanimous that the next election should be canceled or that all restrictions on their own powers should be lifted. Thus Article V sensibly required Congress to get outside approval, a requirement that would deter many self-aggrandizing amendments from even being proposed and would prevent other ill-advised schemes from being adopted.

Second, in order to prevent a self-dealing Congress from simply bottling up needed reforms that might limit its own powers, Article V offered an alternative amendment-proposal system that would not depend on congressional will. This alternative—a federal convention—might never need to be deployed in order to have its desired effect. Its mere potential availability might suffice to pry needed amendment proposals from a Congress desirous of maintaining control over the amendment agenda. (As shall become evident later in our story, this is precisely what happened with the Bill of Rights, which the First Congress drafted largely to silence cries for a new convention.)

Third, in order to guard against a despotic federal convention that might try to crown itself king, Article V made clear that if and when summoned into existence, its federal convention could merely propose amendments that would need to be independently ratified. This limit on Article V proposing conventions was important not only if and when such conventions in fact materialized, but at every other moment as well. By making its proposing convention less terrifying to would-be amenders, Article V rendered this instrument a more credible weapon to be brandished by those whose main goal was to prod Congress itself into action.

Fourth, in order to avoid the danger that self-dealing state legislatures might thwart needed reforms limiting their own powers or shifting additional authority to the central government, Article V allowed Congress to bypass these bodies in favor of special state ratifying conventions. Here, the Article V amendment process paralleled the Article VII ordainment process, in which the Philadelphia framers themselves outflanked potentially obstructionist and self-serving state legislatures.

Finally, in order to enable the nation to respond to a crisis whenever it arose, Article V imposed no date restrictions on the amendment process—except, of course, for its special concession to slavery interests in a proviso guaranteeing the transatlantic slave trade immunity from constitutional amendment until 1808. The only other item to receive special treatment in Article V was the rule of equal state representation in the Senate; this rule, said Article V, could not be changed to any state's detriment without that state's consent. Essentially, this meant that the Senate—the vestige of the old Confederation Congress—could be reapportioned only by a Confederation-like amendment process of state unanimity.

FOR ALL ITS IMPROVEMENTS upon its predecessors, Article V was neither an embodiment of pure republicanism nor an exemplar of perfect draftsmanship. After all, here were perhaps the most important rules in the entire document, specifying how and by whom everything else might be changed—a meta-Constitution operating on a higher conceptual plane than the rest of the document (except the ordainment rules of the Preamble and Article VII). Yet Article V left a great deal uncertain.

For example, could a proposing convention be limited by subject matter? Would any congressional action triggering a proposing convention need to come before the president for his signature or veto? Who would decide the delegate-selection rules for such a convention, states or Congress? Within the convention itself, what voting rules and apportionment ratios would apply, and who would decide these questions? How would ratifying conventions in the several states be structured? By whom?[9]

Just beneath these technical questions lurked deeper puzzles. Could an amendment modify the rules of amendment themselves? In other words, were the provisions of Article V themselves subject to amendment? (If not, where did Article V say that?) Were some things unamendable by dint of the Constitution's very essence?[10] For example, did the bedrock idea of republican self-government mean that strong protection for core political expression was an unrepealable feature of the entire constitutional project? Apart from this bedrock (if any existed), could a legitimate amendment purport to make itself (or any other random provision of the Constitution) immune from further amendment?

Also, to what extent did Article V set out the exclusive mechanism of constitutional amendment? While compliance with Article V would generally suffice to amend, was strict compliance also necessary? For instance, did Congress have any authority to call a proposing convention on its own? Article V said that Congress was *required* to call one when enough state petitions poured in, but could Congress summon it otherwise?[11] If a majority of all American voters petitioned for a proposing convention, would Congress be morally or legally obliged to respond? Could a convention or Congress submit a proposed amendment for ratification by the whole American people in some especially direct fashion outside Article V—say, a national ratifying convention or a national referendum?

Answers to some of these questions might be deduced from other parts of the constitutional text and from the popular-sovereignty logic implicit in the very act of constitution that took place in 1787-88. For example, one might plausibly infer from the Preamble's text about the rights of "our Posterity" and from the very act of ordainment that what We, the People originally established, We could later amend. Ongoing popular sovereignty formed the Constitution's bedrock principle, which could not be abrogated without undermining the very foundation of the document. On this view, if some putative amendment purported to eliminate the right of a later generation to adopt still further amendments, such an attempted abrogation of a genuinely *inalienable* right would not be a permissible amendment of the Constitution's general project. Rather, it would represent an impermissible repudiation of the basic legitimating concept. Thus, in general the Constitution had to remain subject to amendment.

But if so, that very openness to amendment would then itself become an unamendable aspect of the Constitution! That the Constitution at this precise point might seem to burst into open paradox should not surprise us, on reflection. For the very idea of popular sovereignty, like the mathematical idea of infinity and the theological idea of omnipotence, gave (and continues to give) rise to mind-bending questions: Is infinity, when raised exponentially to an infinite power, one infinity or something more? If God is omnipotent, can He create a rock so heavy that even He cannot lift it? Can the People truly bind themselves?

"Provided that . . ."

It might at first appear that Article V itself squarely repudiated the idea of universal amendability in its two special provisos relating to the transatlantic slave trade and Senate equality. But Article V's slave-trade clause merely "Provided that no Amendment which may be made prior to the

Year One thousand eight hundred and eight shall in any Manner affect the first and fourth [i.e., the slave-trade] Clauses in the *Ninth Section of the first Article.*" What about an amendment in, say, 1795 that did not purport to amend Article I's slave-trade rules in any manner whatsoever, but instead simply amended out the special proviso of Article V itself? Once that amendment had passed, why couldn't a second amendment then change the Article I slave-trade rules directly? (Indeed—though this might have risked the loss of a needed legal fig leaf—why couldn't Congress propose the two amendments simultaneously, with joint ratification of both proposals then occurring in the several states?)

Nothing like this sly scheme was ever seriously attempted in the early republic. Had it been, outraged slavocrats would doubtless have claimed that it violated the evident spirit of the slave-trade pact. But such a double amendment would have satisfied the literal text of Article V and would also have comported with the Constitution's general principle of ongoing popular sovereignty. Strictly read, the law entitled Deep South slavocrats to their pounds of flesh, but not one drop of blood. Or at least so a late-eighteenth-century Portia might have argued, extrapolating from the clear-statement principles of *Somerset's Case.* From this perspective, the odiousness of the slave trade and chattel slavery offered special reasons for construing the Article V 1808 clause (and, more broadly, all anti-freedom clauses) with special strictness.

Nor did Article V's other proviso—that "no State, without its Consent, shall be deprived of it's [sic] equal Suffrage in the Senate"—contradict the idea of general amendability. Even had these words been airtight, they did not purport to make anything formally unamendable. Rather, they merely provided for an alternative amendment procedure that in effect required unanimity among the states.

In fact, however, the proviso was far from airtight, perhaps reflecting the unconsidered manner in which it was adopted late in the Philadelphia deliberations.[12] (The fabled Connecticut Compromise concerning House and Senate apportionment had taken place much earlier and had overlooked the amendment issue.) As written, the proviso would be triggered only by amendments concerning the Senate's *apportionment,* as distinct from its *authority.* Thus, the ordinary Article V rules, and not the special state-unanimity regime, would apply to an amendment restricting Senate powers—even, it would seem, a clever amendment removing most of the Senate's powers and relocating them to a (proportionately representative) new-minted "Second Chamber."[13] Upon ratification of such an amendment, the Senate would, in keeping with the proviso, continue to follow the two-senators-per-state rule, but this vestigial chamber would sink into irrelevance as the new "Second Chamber" took over most of the old senatorial functions. As a practical matter, then, the structure of America's upper house has always been governed by the same basic Article V system applicable to all other amendments, despite the proviso.

If this analysis is correct, then the biggest concession to small states in Article V lay not in the proviso, but in its more general system, which trebly (perhaps quadruply) privileged the equality of all states, large and small. First, any amendment proposed by Congress had to win a two-thirds vote in the Senate as well as the House. Second, Article V required that a special proposing convention be held whenever two-thirds of equally weighted states so petitioned. (Also, Article V nowhere made clear that the proposing convention would follow rules of proportional representation, as opposed to the one-state, one-vote rule that had applied at Philadelphia's proposing convention.) Third, the Article V ratification process would also count all states equally, whether they acted by legislature or by convention.

This privileging of small states made it less likely that the Senate would ever be eclipsed by a new-minted and proportionately representative "Second Chamber." Why would small-state senators/legislatures/conventions ever agree to diminish their own state's power? Yet even here, it is possible to imagine ways in which such a transition might be made, if Americans in small states ever came to view the Senate and/or Article V as genuinely unfair. An amendment, after all, could propose a new "Second Chamber"—and even a new, more proportionately representative amendment procedure—and could further propose that such new constitutional rules would go into effect only, say, thirty years after ratification. Such a delay would drain away much of the small-state resistance based solely on naked self-interest. Many small-state citizens and leaders might easily imagine that three decades hence they or their children could well have moved to some larger state. In effect, the time delay would enable Americans to focus on the pure issue of apportionment *principle,* behind a veil of ignorance about how the rule might work to their individual advantage or detriment.

This was almost precisely the point that Gouverneur Morris made in Philadelphia as he urged small states in 1787 to repudiate the Confederation's equal-state voting rule, not just for the new federal House but also for its new Senate. In Morris's words, "Our ideas [should] be enlarged to the true interest of man, instead of being circumscribed within the narrow compass of a particular Spot. And after all how little can be the motive yielded by selfishness for such a policy. Who can say whether he himself, much less whether his children, will the next year be an inhabitant of this or that State."[14]

This final sentence made perfect—indeed, literal—sense to Morris, a wealthy bachelor who did in fact glide from state to state. (He had represented New York in the Confederation Congress, was representing Pennsylvania at the Philadelphia Convention, and would later represent New York again in the U.S. Senate.) By contrast, most other delegates could in fact "say" with considerable certainty that they would be staying put "the next year." Thus small-state leaders adamantly refused to abandon the idea of Senate equality at Philadelphia, for such an idea did indeed suit their "selfishness."

Had Morris and his allies proposed a proportionate Senate to be phased in after a thirty-year delay, might they have overcome selfish small-state resistance?[15] It was precisely Morris's failure to follow out the larger lessons of his own insight—the failure to move from "the next year" to "the next generation"—that limited his efficacy both on small-state apportionment and also, as has been seen, on slave apportionment. In both cases, delegates with the better argument from democratic principle missed the chance to overcome self-interest by shifting the debate from the immediate present to the intermediate future.

IT REMAINS TO TACKLE the intriguing issue of Article V exclusivity: Did that Article specify the exclusive means of constitutional change, or did We the People retain a right to alter the Constitution by returning to the same popular-sovereignty ground rules under which We ordained it? Though Article V never expressly said that it was the "only" mechanism of amendment, this textual omission hardly ended the matter. Elsewhere the Constitution often clearly implied other types of exclusivity without quite saying so expressly. For instance, the Article III roster of cases and controversies omitted the word "only," but surely it gave federal courts jurisdiction solely over the nine listed categories of lawsuits, and no others.

In Article V, as elsewhere, we need to read the constitutional text in the larger context of constitutional history and structure. Let's begin by asking how the federal Constitution should have been read had Article V not existed. Would the document simply have been unamendable? Plainly the better view, in light of the parallel issues raised by the three state constitutions that had no amendment clause, would have been that the federal Constitution could have been altered by recourse to the same popular-sovereignty rules under which it had been ordained.[16] The exclusivity issue thus boiled down to this: Did Article V *supplement* the background right of the People to alter, or did it *supplant* and *implement* that right?

Even on the supplemental view, Article V would remain a hugely important addition to the document. Thus, a nonexclusive reading would hardly render Article V superfluous. Without this Article, direct recourse to the people themselves, in a manner akin to the original ordainment, would have always been required for every amendment, howsoever minor. Even a unanimous Congress backed by every state legislature would have had no right to change a single word in the document. But thanks to Article V, ordinary public servants in Congress and state legislatures were indeed empowered to amend the basic charter that limited their own authority. In specifying precisely how such ordinary lawmaking bodies could amend, Article V presumably set forth the *only* way these legislators could do so without seeking direct approval from the people themselves in an ordainment-like process.

The vast majority of modern lawyers, judges, and scholars would go a step further and read Article V's explicit provisions to furnish the only way of effecting amendments, period.[17] Thus, the legal and political mainstream reads Article V to supplant the background reordainment right, or put differently, to fully implement the people's right to alter what We have ordained. There is much to be said for this view. However, there are also a few things to be said on the other side.

For starters, Article V's procedures, if exclusive, gave regular government servants a troubling monopoly. Only ordinary lawmakers elected in the ordinary way in state legislatures and Congress could get the amendment ball rolling. But what if the people wanted to impose new federal constitutional limits on both sets of government—say, term limits for all legislators? Ordinary elections might not effectively register the popular will and judgment in such a case. Ordinary property qualifications and eligibility rules would apply to these elections, in contrast to the exceptionally inclusive participation rules embodied in the ordainment process.[18] Also, Article V's rules were nonegalitarian, weighting each small-state citizen more than each large-state citizen in three (or four) distinct ways.

Beyond these theoretical concerns, the best argument for Article V nonexclusivity came not from what the Constitution *said,* but rather from what it *did.* In 1787, as has been seen, most states had Article V analogues in their state constitutions—that is, clauses or articles setting forth the rules for state constitutional amendment. Often, Article V analogues used explicit language seeming to affirm exclusivity: "no" amendments could occur except via the specified procedure. Nevertheless, a great many states ratified the federal Constitution in 1787–88—and thereby amended their state constitutions[19]—without complying with the procedures specified in their Article V analogues.

Thus, up and down the continent at the Founding, Article V analogues were, in political fact and not simply in abstract theory, treated as nonexclusive. Each analogue was read as supplementing rather than supplanting the popular-sovereignty process of direct appeal to the state people themselves, assembled in a ratifying convention. Throughout the nineteenth century, states would continue to treat their Article V analogues as nonexclusive for purposes of state constitutional amendment.

If the Founding act itself necessarily traveled through a nonexclusive reading of state Article V analogues, shouldn't Article V likewise be read as nonexclusive? In 1788 a *state* ratifying convention of the *state* people had sufficed to amend the *state* constitution outside the *state* Article V analogue. After 1788, why shouldn't a *national* ratifying convention of the *national* people likewise suffice to amend the *national* Constitution outside Article V itself? Prior to 1788, each state people had been sovereign, but in 1788, these state peoples had merged to form the sovereign people of the United States. Thus, if Congress, acting outside Article V, upon the urging of a mass popular movement, were on its own motion to call a national proposing convention which in turn put forth amendments to be ratified by a national ratifying convention, why wouldn't the new rules adopted by such a ratifying body deserve to be treated as America's supreme law, having derived from the people themselves? Both in public debates in 1787 and in a famous law lecture he gave a few years later, James Wilson appeared to endorse just such a possibility. "The people may change the constitution[] whenever and however they please. This is a right of which no positive institution can ever deprive them." "A majority of the society is sufficient for this purpose."[20] Post-Founding state constitutional practice lent additional plausibility to Wilson's musings: In the century after 1789, a large number of states amended their constitutions or promulgated new constitutions via popular sovereignty procedures outside the bounds of their state Article V analogues.[21]

The best Founding-era argument against Wilson's reasoning sounded in federalism. On this account, the canonical formulation of which appeared in Madison's *Federalist* No. 39, even though the Founding repudiated a strong notion of continued state sovereignty it fell short of creating an undifferentiated continental polity. According to Madison, America under the Constitution would become a complex compound of federal and national elements, as reflected in the intricate—and exclusive—balance struck by Article V. From this perspective, practice under and outside state constitutional analogues to Article V failed to provide any square precedent for construing Article V itself.

The slavery issue added a further complication. Southern leaders, as has been seen, strongly resisted a House apportioned by free population or by voting population, and likewise opposed direct popular election of the president. The Constitution also avoided any uniform national voter-eligibility rule for Article I elections of representatives and for Article VII elections of ratification-convention delegates. In all these contexts, strongly egalitarian national rules would have failed to give Southern states sufficient credit for their slave population and/or control over their franchise base. Any popular right of national constitutional amendment by a national referendum—especially if Congress could widen the ordinary voting rules for such a referendum—would likewise have risked strong slavocrat opposition had such a right been expressly asserted in the Constitution. Yet the possibility of a national ratifying *convention* did not quite raise the same concern; much would depend on how slaves would be counted in apportioning the ratifying convention itself. As shall soon become evident, a similar issue in fact arose in connection with the Article VII ratifying conventions held within each state in 1787–88.

To be sure, the prospect of a national ratifying convention outside Article V raised hard questions about precisely how the process would work. For example, who would be allowed to vote for and in such a convention? Slavery aside, how would convention delegates be apportioned—by analogy to the federal House, or the federal Senate, or some composite?

Hard as they were to answer, these questions did not raise unique embarrassments for nonexclusivists like James Wilson. In fact, similar questions existed within Article V itself. If, pursuant to Article V, two-thirds of the state legislatures petitioned for a national convention to *propose* amendments, what suffrage and delegate-eligibility rules would apply, and how would *that* convention be apportioned? In the summer of 1787, each state government (except Rhode Island's) had sent a delegation that cast an equal vote in the Philadelphia Convention. But of course that Convention took place under a pure confederacy (or alternatively, outside the confederacy in an informal meeting of equal states). Would similar election and apportionment rules make sense after Americans had repudiated a pure confederacy in favor of a more perfect—and, in particular, a more proportionately and directly representative—union? At Philadelphia, Madison reminded his colleagues that, even within Article V, the very notion of a proposing convention opened up a large can of worms. "Difficulties might arise as to the form, the quorum &c. which in Constitutional regulations ought to be as much as possible avoided."[22]

At the Founding, the intriguing issue of Article V exclusivity appeared to divide the two deepest Federalist thinkers, James Wilson and James Madison. The intervening years have treated Madison kindly. At a theoretical level, most citizens and scholars have never even heard of Wilson's ideas about constitutional amendment. At a practical level, Americans have participated in two centuries of formal amendments within the Article V tradition, while the nation has never explicitly pursued a non–Article V amendment path by express analogy to its ordainment process.[23]

Yet if the citizenry's national popular-sovereignty right is indeed inalienable, perhaps it remains possible for this right to be exhumed and exercised by some future generation, in a world where a majority of Americans actually finds the idea of amendment outside Article V plausible, principled, and necessary. That future world, it must be emphasized, remains very far from the general sentiment today—perhaps in part because many current Americans have lost touch with the populist foundations of the Constitution itself. But there is a mountain of American history still to be written. Forever is a long time; perhaps it is too soon to count Wilson out.

"This Constitution . . . shall be the supreme Law"

While Article V invited readers to imagine the Constitution as it might one day become, Article VI reminded readers of what the Constitution would be even in the absence of amendments. In tandem with the Preamble, this penultimate Article marked the Constitution's most sustained meditation upon itself. Whereas the Preamble first introduced the self-referential phrase "this Constitution," Article VI echoed that phrase four times in three short paragraphs, clarifying the precise status of the document vis-à-vis the old Confederation, the new federal government, and state governments.

Article VI began by smoothing over the juridical rupture between the old "Confederation" and the new "Constitution," reassuring America's creditors and treaty partners that the new United States would stand behind all the "Debts" and "Engagements" of its predecessor, even if the new union ultimately failed to encompass all thirteen of the original states. Had any of the thirteen persisted in refusing to join the new union, negotiations between the new United States and its former member state(s) might have been needed to settle old accounts. As events actually came to pass, all thirteen states ultimately reunited, and financial adjustments among them occurred wholly within the framework of the new federal government.

The middle paragraph of Article VI mapped out America's new legal hierarchy. At the apex stood "this Constitution," the "supreme Law of the Land." Then came federal statutes and treaties that conformed to the Constitution, and below them came state constitutions, and ordinary state laws.

This ranking of laws reflected a democratic gradient. The Constitution trumped all other laws because it derived more directly and emphatically from the highest lawmaker: the entire American people, whose ordainment would set the whole system in motion. Ordinary federal laws emerging from ordinary congressional votes could not claim the same extraordinary populist mandate.[24] Thus, federal statutes would be valid only insofar as they complied with the federal Constitution—including of course any future constitutional amendments, which would become valid only after having cleared much higher democratic hurdles than the ones set out for ordinary congressional lawmaking.

Alongside its explicit declaration that federal statutes would have legal vitality only insofar as they were "in Pursuance" of the Constitution, Article VI provided that only treaties made "under the Authority" of the United States were legally binding—and of course the new government would have no "Authority" to enter into a treaty that violated the Constitution itself.[25] Reinforcing the opening paragraph of Article VI, the treaty clause also made clear that the new union would continue to view all treaties entered into by the old Confederation as legally binding. Indeed, the remainder of Article VI provided that these old treaties would be enforceable as law in state and federal courts and thus more legally effective than ever before.

If the federal Constitution outranked federal laws and treaties because of its superior democratic pedigree, those laws and treaties in turn outranked state constitutions and state laws for similar reasons. Emerging from continental elections and enactments, federal laws and treaties would embody the judgment of America as a whole, as distinct from the more parochial view of any particular local part. Thus, valid federal statutes and treaties would become part of the "supreme Law of the Land," with priority over any inconsistent state-law norm, even one that appeared in a state constitution.

Under the Articles of Confederation, states had pledged to abide by the Articles themselves and congressional pronouncements and treaties thereunder. Yet nowhere had the Articles expressly proclaimed confederate rules to be "law," enforceable as such in ordinary courts. As a result, when states flouted their confederate duties, state courts had often shown little interest in stopping the violations. Part of the problem was that the Confederation document had never come before the people themselves for ratification. Having been created by ordinary state legislatures, the Confederation in effect remained the creature of these masters, several of whom derived their own mandates from state constitutions that had been more directly blessed by the people. Democratically, many of these state constitutions thus seemed to outrank the Articles themselves. Even a state statute, if adopted after the Articles, might be thought to supercede the Confederation document from a parochial perspective. Though state legislators who renounced what their predecessors had previously agreed to might be viewed as "unwise" or "perfidious"—to borrow Madison's words at Philadelphia[26]—judges within that state might well believe themselves obliged to follow the most recent pronouncement of the democratic will.

Ratification of the new Constitution by the American people themselves, explained the Federalists, would put an end to the old state-centered approach.[27] Lest any residual doubt linger in the mind of a state judge, Article VI issued a pointed directive to "the Judges in every State" that proper federal legal norms took precedence over state rules. If state courts disregarded or misapplied this directive in any case arising under the federal Constitution, laws, or treaties, Article III authorized federal courts sitting in appellate jurisdiction to review and reverse their state-court brethren.[28]

The final paragraph of Article VI obliged a host of state and federal policymakers to take personal oaths of allegiance "to support this Constitution." We have already seen, in the presidential-oath clause, the evident importance placed by the framers on personal oaths of allegiance. As with the president's special oath, Article VI allowed a man to "Affirm[]" his support rather than swear to it in an oath, thereby accommodating public servants who had religious or other conscientious objections to oath-taking. As a further gesture of religious inclusiveness and tolerance, Article VI forbade any "religious Test" for any federal office or post—a prohibition that swept far beyond anything in early state constitutions.

If we step back from the details and ponder the larger pattern of the Preamble and Articles VI and VII, we can only marvel at the ingenious ways in which "this Constitution" worked to pull itself up by its own boot-straps. The Preamble began, and Article VII ended, the document by propping it up with the weight of countless thousands of voters, whose support for ratification would give the text unrivaled *democratic political legitimacy*. Beyond this, the first paragraph of Article VI sought to boost the Constitution *economically* and *internationally* by assuring America's creditors and allies that their loans would be repaid and their treaties hon-ored. These assurances, combined with reinforcing rules and structures elsewhere in the document encouraging debt repayment and treaty com-pliance, would give powerful interest groups at home and well-wishers abroad reasons to root for the Constitution rather than against it.[29] Then came a paragraph infusing the document with *juridical* authority as "supreme Law" enforceable in ordinary courts, thereby throwing the weight of lawyers and judges behind it. There followed a series of oath-taking requirements enlisting the *conscience* and *honor* of America's leaders in the service of the Constitution. In a few short paragraphs at its beginning and end, "this Constitution" thus validated itself in a remarkably shrewd manner, imparting extraordinary strength to a mere piece of paper ini-tially composed by a few dozen men acting largely on their own authority.

"Treaties"

Perhaps the hardest questions raised by the Article VI legal hierarchy con-cerned the subtle interplay between federal statutes and federal treaties. Consider, for example, the dilemma of a judge confronted by two appar-ently conflicting federal legal commands and thus forced to decide which of the two he was oath-bound to obey. If one command derived from the Constitution itself and the other came from some other legal source, the supremacy clause and the Constitution's general structure of popular sov-ereignty dictated a clear answer: The Constitution would always trump. Thus, a duly ratified constitutional amendment—"valid to all Intents and Purposes, as Part of this Constitution"—would prevail over a contrary federal statute or treaty. True, if a treaty was already in place, a later con-stitutional amendment expressly repudiating it might place the United States in breach of international law, but American judges would never-theless be obliged to follow the Constitution as the "supreme Law of the Land" for domestic-law purposes.

But what if a federal *statute* and a federal *treaty* conflicted? If statutes ranked higher than treaties, the statute should prevail. Conversely, if treaties ranked higher, the treaty should trump.

Modern judges have embraced neither hierarchical solution, instead deeming statutes and treaties as legal equals for certain domestic-law purposes.[30] Generally speaking, the judicial rule when dealing with legally equal enactments is that the more recent enactment prevails over the earlier one.[31] Thus, if a legislature enacts a given rule on Monday and a contradictory rule on Tuesday, judges ordinarily treat the latter statute as having duly repealed the former. The same of course holds true for constitutional amendments; the more recent amendment effectively displaces the earlier amendment in the event of conflict between the two. (For example, we shall see in Chapter 11 how the Twenty-first Amendment, ratified in 1933, duly repealed the Prohibition edict of the Eighteenth Amendment, ratified in 1919.)

By allowing federal treaties to repeal federal statutes and, symmetrically, statutes to repeal treaties,[32] the modern judiciary has paid insufficient heed to the text of Article VI itself, ignoring the apparent legal hierarchy implicit in that text. In *Marbury v. Madison,* Chief Justice Marshall, in emphasizing the legal priority of the Constitution, deemed it "not entirely unworthy of observation" that the Article VI supremacy clause listed the Constitution *first.*[33] Isn't it likewise worthy of notice that this very same clause listed federal statutes *ahead of* federal treaties, thereby implying a rank order between the two? Everywhere else in the supremacy clause, textual priority signified legal superiority. First came the Constitution, then federal statutes, then treaties, then state constitutions, then state laws: "This Constitution, and the Laws of the United States which shall be made in Pursuance thereof; and all Treaties made, or which shall be made, under the Authority of the United States, shall be the supreme Law of the Land . . . any Thing in the Constitution or Laws of any State to the Contrary notwithstanding."

As has been seen, the Constitution deserved priority over lesser laws because of its superior democratic pedigree. A similar argument would seem to support the priority of federal statutes over federal treaties. After all, treaties cut the House of Representatives out of the loop. Both English and colonial tradition regarded the lower branch of a bicameral legislature as the people's house, the institution most closely in touch with the voters, thanks to direct election, wide membership, and short terms of service.

If federal statutes were seen as superior to federal treaties, a treaty would not suffice to undo a federal statute but would suffice to trump past and future state constitutions and state laws.[34] A simple example may help clarify the various vertical and horizontal effects of a treaty under this reading of Article VI. Imagine a late-eighteenth-century Anglo-

American friendship treaty giving English subjects a right to own real property in America and American citizens a corresponding right to own real property in England.[35] Upon ratification, such a federal treaty would automatically oust all state laws that barred aliens from owning land, insofar as those laws applied to Englishmen. The treaty would also impose an international-law duty on Congress to repeal any noncompliant federal land laws already on the books in the territories or the national capital (areas over which Congress had exclusive jurisdiction). But the treaty would not of its own force effect this federal statutory repeal. Instead the House of Representatives would need to agree to a repealing statute—as would of course the Senate and (absent override) the president.

The federal land statutes themselves, however, might explicitly or implicitly have contained sunset provisions, allowing these laws to lapse whenever a treaty so provided (or indeed, on the occurrence of any number of other contingencies). For instance, in the case of a congressional declaration of war, the declaration itself might ordinarily best be read, unless it specified otherwise, to sunset upon the ratification of a peace treaty. But in such scenarios, the treaty would not, strictly speaking, repeal the earlier statute. Rather, the earlier statute would merely lapse, thanks to triggers expressly or implicitly contained *in that very statute itself.*

Though this simple way of thinking about federal statutes and treaties may well startle some modern lawyers and judges, it shouldn't.[36] In fact, modern judges already do implicitly acknowledge the primacy of statutes over treaties, and the pivotal role of the House of Representatives, in one of the foundational doctrines of American treaty law, which deems certain treaties to be "non-self-executing." Such treaties are understood to require an implementing statute before they can operate fully as domestic law. For example, it is widely conceded that a duly enacted treaty cannot itself authorize a new expenditure, impose a new internal tax, create a new federal crime, raise a new army, or declare a war.[37] A treaty might commit the nation to do any or all of these things as a matter of international law, but for domestic-law purposes a statute is necessary to carry out—to execute—the commitment. The general intuition behind this doctrine is that some things cannot be done domestically unless the people's House concurs.[38] But if so, why shouldn't the repealing of an old federal statute be included on the list of those things that require House agreement in a new statute?

On various occasions in the 1790s and early 1800s, allies of Thomas Jefferson went even further, suggesting that no treaty could operate of its own self-executing force over any of the domains reserved by the Constitution to Congress (and thus, in part, to the House).[39] The Jeffersonian test went too far and has never won widespread approval. In today's world of sweeping congressional power, this test would make almost all treaties non-self-executing. Moreover, even in the early republic the Jeffersonian approach threatened to unduly restrict the vertical force of federal treaties over state laws in regulatory fields where Congress had the power to pre-empt state law but had opted to remain silent. The Jeffersonian test, had it ever been strictly followed, would have curiously made treaties under the Constitution harder to enforce against states than had been the case under the old Articles of Confederation. Under the Articles, whenever nine of the thirteen states (that is, two-thirds) agreed to a treaty in the Confederation Congress, all states would in theory be bound thereby. (Getting actual compliance was of course another matter.) But under the Jeffersonian test a great many treaties seeking to limit state laws in the interest of national security would need to be adopted *twice* by the Confederation Congress's successor entities—first by a two-thirds vote of the Senate and then by an ordinary federal statute. Why, we might well ask, should two continental votes always be needed? So far as states' rights were concerned—the ver-tical effect of the supremacy clause—why shouldn't treaty ratification by two-thirds of a Senate selected by state governments suffice, much as a similar treaty-ratification process had sufficed (or at least should have suf-ficed) under the Articles?*

The horizontal effect of a treaty—its capacity to oust previous federal laws or substitute for a federal statute in certain delicate areas, such as taxing, spending, criminalization, militarization, and war declaration—raised a different set of issues. In other words, a treaty displacing state laws was one thing; a treaty undoing preexisting federal laws or substituting for an act of Congress was something else entirely.

If modern courts have tended to muddle through horizontal-effect is-sues via a vaguely contoured doctrine of non-self-execution, perhaps they may be excused for their imprecision because the framers themselves were of several minds and failed to offer crystalline guidance. At Philadelphia, delegates John Francis Mercer and George Mason—the only two to ad-

---

*If anything, the federal treaty process was surely designed to be more nationalistic than the treaty regime under the Articles of Confederation, whose ninth Article had withheld from the union general authority to make "treat[ies] of commerce . . . whereby the legislative power of the respective states shall be restrained from imposing such imposts and duties on foreigners, as their own people are subjected to, or from prohibiting the exportation or importation of any species of goods or commodities whatsoever." Such fetters on treaty making under the Confed-eration had made it that much harder for the union to negotiate favorable trade deals with major economic powers and the Philadelphia plan pointedly granted the president and Senate treaty authority unconstrained by these earlier limits.

dress the repeal issue directly—agreed that treaties should not be "final so as to alter the laws of the land" or "repeal" a federal law unless such treaties had been "ratified by legislative authority. This was the case of Treaties in Great Britain."[40] Pennsylvania's Gouverneur Morris went much further, proposing that "no Treaty shall be binding on the U.S. which is not ratified by a law."[41] This proposal failed; evidently, the delegates did not intend that every treaty be wholly non-self-executing. (To put the historical point more structurally, if every single treaty were non-self-executing, the treaty process would begin to approximate an unnecessary fifth wheel in the machinery of federal lawmaking.) But neither did the framers endorse the opposite idea that every treaty could execute itself by repealing contrary federal laws and creating the precise domestic-law equivalent of a federal statute.

Much of the conceptual difficulty arose from the lack of any closely applicable historical model on either side of the Atlantic. In England, the king had unilateral authority to make treaties and thereby bind the nation as a matter of international law, but as James Wilson observed at Philadelphia, echoing Mercer, many of these treaties were non-self-executing, domestically. "In the most important Treaties, the King of G. Britain [was] obliged to resort to Parliament for the execution of them."[42] Yet the precise juridical status of treaties under English law was subject to varying interpretations,[43] and in any event the relevance of the English system for Americans was contestable. After all, in the New World regime taking shape at Philadelphia, treaties would themselves be formed not by the fiat of a hereditary monarch, but rather by a continentally elected president who had secured the approval of two-thirds of an elected Senate. Nor did the experience of American colonies and Revolutionary states—entities that had never made treaties or conducted general foreign affairs on their own—provide the framers with much direct guidance.

The Articles of Confederation also cast little light on the precise question at hand. Under that document, both proto-lawmaking on major issues and treaty making occurred in the same body and by the same vote: nine states out of thirteen in the Confederation Congress. The special complexities of the horizontal effect that confronted the Philadelphia framers emerged only when the legal tracks of lawmaking and treaty making were decisively separated by the Constitution itself, with authority over these two tracks vested in different (but overlapping) institutions and governed by different voting rules.

In an influential analysis of the horizontal-effect issue during the ratification process, Wilson depicted federal treaties as subordinate to federal statutes:

Though the treaties are to have the force of laws, they are in some important respects very different from other acts of legislation. . . . The House of Representatives possess no active part in making treaties, yet their legislative authority will be found to have strong restraining influences upon both President and Senate. In England, if the king and his ministers find themselves, during their [treaty] negotiation, to be embarrassed because an existing law is not repealed, or a new law is not enacted, they give notice to the legislature of their situation, and inform them that it will be necessary, before the treaty can operate, that some law be repealed, or some be made. And will not the same thing take place here?

In the Virginia debates, Federalist Francis Corbin reinforced Wilson's view, arguing that it was "as clear as that two and two make four" that treaties would be subordinate to "the Constitution itself, *and the laws of Congress*" but paramount over state law. Madison promptly allied himself with Corbin, reading Article VI to "restrain[] the supremacy of [treaties] to the laws of particular states, and not to Congress."[44]

Taking the matter one step further, North Carolina's ratifying convention endorsed a constitutional amendment designed to reduce ambiguity by codifying the Wilson/Madison approach as follows: "No treaties which shall be directly opposed to the existing laws of the United States in Congress assembled shall be valid until such laws shall be repealed, or made conformable to such treaty; nor shall any treaty be valid which is contradictory to the Constitution of the United States."[45]

Wilson's and Madison's remarks and North Carolina's proposed clarification hardly ended the treaty-statute debate, and over the next decade the horizontal effect of treaties bedeviled the republic's most eminent statesmen. In fierce debates triggered by the 1793 Neutrality Proclamation and the 1795 Jay Treaty, Madison famously squared off against his former allies Hamilton, Jay, and Washington. Several years later, similar issues swirled around the controversial treaty-based extradition of a sailor whose contested identity and citizenship—was he American or British?—only compounded the constitutional complexities.[46] Jeffersonians took one position, Adamsonians another. Much as the Founding Federalists could all agree upon the need for strong vertical federal judicial review over states while disagreeing about the optimal scope of horizontal judicial review against Congress, so, too, with the vertical dimension of treaty supremacy over states as distinct from the horizontal effect of treaties vis-à-vis Congress.

"Conventions"

Article VII, the Philadelphia Constitution's closing sentence, elaborated its opening words by specifying how "We the People of the United States" would in actual fact ordain and establish the Constitution—namely, via the ratifications of nine or more state "Conventions."

The evident link between the Preamble's "People" and Article VII's "Conventions" prompts several basic questions.* In what sense were conventions truly the people themselves? Indeed, how were ratifying conventions any different than ordinary legislatures? Wouldn't direct state referenda have been more truly populist devices for ratification?

We have already seen one dramatic way in which conventions more authentically embodied the people than did ordinary legislatures—namely, the ratifying conventions that met between 1787 and 1790 operated under special voting and eligibility rules, allowing a wider swath of Americans to vote and serve. Moreover, each convention emerged from a special election with only one question on the agenda: Should the Constitution be ratified? Voters in each state had the Constitution in hand long before the delegate election occurred. A vote for convention delegates thus approximated a direct referendum on the document, as opposed to a typical legislative election selecting lawmakers empowered to address any and all issues, howsoever unforeseeable, that might arise during the legislative term.

Above and beyond these arguments from popular-sovereignty theory and high principle, realpolitik considerations also encouraged the Philadelphia delegates to detour around existing state legislatures. The Philadelphia plan, after all, diminished the role of state legislatures in many ways—by adding to the formal list of laws that state legislatures could not enact, by expanding Congress's policy-making mandate, by weakening state legislative control over Congress, by creating a powerful set of new central governmental officials who might compete against state governments for popular affection, and by giving the central government a bulging kit bag of new tools to bring states into line. Though ordinary citi-

---

*Though Article VII did not say in so many words that its ratifying conventions were to be chosen directly by the people, the Philadelphia delegates did state the point explicitly in their brief September 17, 1787, cover letter to the Constitution, which called for the submission of the proposed Constitution to "a Convention of Delegates, chosen in each State by the People thereof." *Farrand's Records,* 2:665. The idea that the new Constitution should come before some special "assembly or assemblies . . . to be expressly chosen by the people" was an essential ingredient of the original Virginia Plan; see ibid., 1:22 (May 29).

zens might happily authorize the transfer of power from one set of their agents (state legislators) to another set (federal officials), self-interested state lawmakers themselves were apt to view this transfer as a demotion and resist it accordingly. Also, because most states had bicameral legislatures, legislative ratification would have nearly doubled the opportunities for opponents to ambush the Constitution or play inappropriate logrolling games.[47]

In one sense, high theory and realpolitik defined two sides of the same coin. The men at Philadelphia, America's consummate insiders, found themselves obliged to play a classic outsiders' game. These statesmen understood that American peace and prosperity required a dramatic restructuring of power away from state legislatures. Yet such legislatures were shrouded in decades, if not centuries, of legal tradition and republican ideology. To overcome such entrenched and putatively republican power centers, Philadelphians had to summon into existence an even greater authority—the American people themselves. And to prove their populist bona fides, George Washington and company needed to propose a democratic ratification process that would be universally perceived as fair— a wide-open process under which the Philadelphians might well lose, precisely so as to give their plan unprecedented political legitimacy and momentum if instead it somehow managed to win.*

But why, we might ask, didn't the framers simply call for direct referenda? Here, too, their decision reflected both high principles and low politics. The very idea of a direct popular vote on an issue, as distinct from an election of representatives, was not one that had been implemented on an extensive geographic scale anywhere on the planet prior to 1787; even the Swiss had yet to stage a national referendum. True, New Englanders had traditions of town meetings, but these traditions did not exist in most other parts of the American continent. Also, when the voters of Massachusetts and New Hampshire had ratified state constitutions in 1780 and 1784, respectively, these men had done so by assembling in person in their townships and had voted only after extended public discussions and deliberations had taken place in these township meetings. In short, modern no-talk-just-vote drive-through referenda, California style, did not exist as an obvious conceptual alternative for the Founders.

For all its efforts to be a publicly accessible document, the proposed

---

*It is at precisely this point that the standard Beardian accounts of the Constitution—with their tendency to dwell on the closed-door sessions at Philadelphia and their inclination to assume or imply that ratification was a rigged game—are at their weakest.

Constitution had many intricacies that deserved extended deliberation—
deliberation that the convention format could accommodate far better
than could the referendum model. Thus, when the Rhode Island legislature refused to call a ratifying convention in 1788 and instead staged a
direct-referendum, Federalists boycotted the scheme as procedurally irregular. Two years later, the state would finally assemble a convention,
which in the end would vote to ratify by the slim margin of thirty-four to
thirty-two.

Even had the Philadelphia framers themselves preferred direct referenda, they had no power to effect such elections on their own. They
needed to rely on state governments to set the ground rules—specifying
who could vote, when, how, and so on—and to administer the ratification
process. Yet state governments in many places might well have resisted the
direct-referendum model, had it been proposed. By this point in our story,
one obvious reason for such likely resistance should be familiar: slavery.
Direct popular election would have embodied the modern ideal of one-
man, one-vote, but in most states circa 1787 this principle had never fully
operated—indeed, no censuses had yet occurred. As has been seen, South
Carolina would end up resisting direct election of presidential electors and
state governors throughout the entire antebellum era. Doubtless this state
government would likewise have resisted any sort of direct referendum in
1787–88. Conventions enabled state governments to follow standard apportionment rules already in place for lower state houses—rules that in a
state like South Carolina gave plantation belts extra weight.

Some modern scholars have noted that had the document come directly before South Carolina's voters, it likely would have failed to win
a popular state majority, and that the same democratic embarrassment
probably applied to a few other states.[48] Less noted today is the likelihood
that in still other states—such as Massachusetts—apportionment rules
gave Anti-Federalists more than their fair share of convention delegates.[49]
Whether or not various apportionment imperfections tended to cancel
out, the crucial fact to keep in mind is that the Philadelphia framers had
no effective way to put their document directly to South Carolinian
voters—or the voters of any other state—even had the solons so desired.
Had direct voting been a realistic option, perhaps the Philadelphia delegates would have availed themselves of it and crafted their document
somewhat differently. But knowing that they needed to win in a *convention* in South Carolina and elsewhere, the drafters structured their document with the rules of *that* game in mind. Democratic bootstrapping had
its limits. At some point, the framers had to build their new edifice by

working with preexisting institutional building blocks and by working around immovable stumbling blocks.

PERHAPS THE BIGGEST stumbling block that the framers worked around was the Confederation's concluding passage, which required that all thirteen states approve any decisive legal change. We have already seen why the Philadelphia delegates abandoned the magic number thirteen; but why did Article VII embrace the number nine as opposed to, say, eight or ten or three? Why *any* nine, as opposed to nine contiguous states or nine states with a certain minimal total population?

Here, too, both principle and pragmatism came into play. As a matter of theory, the best formal legal justification for repudiating the Articles of Confederation stressed its status as a breached treaty. But if only one state thought the Confederation a gross failure that deserved to be repudiated, would such a state have been morally justified (or prudent, for that matter) in abandoning the Confederation if all twelve of its sisters forcefully denied that the treaty had indeed been materially breached? Article VII, while allowing each state to decide for itself, proposed that the Confederation should be buried only if an overwhelming majority of the states agreed that it deserved to die. The Confederation itself had given special weight to the decisions of nine states—the threshold for deciding most important issues of Confederation policy. Thus in proposing a nine-state trigger, the framers were in a sense working within the framework of the Articles even as they were also working to end that framework.[50] (In the 1860s, by contrast, secessionists won the endorsement of only a minority of states—eleven out of thirty-four—and did so in a more perfect union that was emphatically designed to be indissoluble by such unilateral actions.)

The number nine also made good practical sense, promising to create a sufficient critical mass—of land, population, and wealth—so as to give the new Constitution tolerable prospects for success. Given the powerful geostrategic considerations driving the new Constitution, its framers surely hoped that the nine or more ratifying states would be generally contiguous and would include certain states that, as a practical matter, were indispensable. But specifying all the possible permutations of nine out of thirteen would have been a drafting challenge (to put it mildly)[51] and would also have unwisely increased Anti-Federalist leverage in critical states such as Virginia and New York—states where the document in the end barely squeaked through.

Indeed, precisely by *not* conditioning ratification on New York's, Virginia's, or any other single state's approval, the framers ingeniously made it more likely that such indispensable states would join. New Yorkers eventually ratified the document in July 1788 only because it was clear that—thanks to ten prior state ratifications—the new ship *Constitution* was setting sail with or without them. Similarly, it was precisely Article VII's pointed refusal to wait for a yes from Rhode Islanders that in the end helped secure that yes. By promising to embark with any nine crew members, Article VII ultimately induced all thirteen to come aboard.*

But on April 30, 1789, as George Washington solemnly swore to "preserve, protect and defend the Constitution," only eleven states were with him. Article VII had done its main work but had not forever closed its doors to North Carolinians and Rhode Islanders, who might perhaps be persuaded to join if the new government proved itself willing to consider needed constitutional amendments. Indeed, thanks to the Article VII convention format, as distinct from a no-talk-just-vote referendum or an infinite array of simultaneous town meetings, leading Federalists had heard directly from many of their most prominent critics, had visibly engaged these critics in extensive high-profile discussions, and had offered face-to-face assurances that they would duly consider various additional constitutional reforms, many of which were crystallized in the Article VII conventions themselves.

Thus, Article VII's ratification conventions did not merely end the ordainment process but also began the amendment process. Though this Article in 1788 stood as the Constitution's dramatic rear portico, the textual culmination of ordainment, today it sits somewhere in the middle of the document—a perfectly placed internal passageway linking the original text of ordainment on one side with the subsequent texts of amendment on the other.

Let us now cross through this passageway and enter the world of constitutional amendments.

*New York's dramatic yes vote to the Constitution in 1788 stood in sharp contrast to that state's decisive no vote to a proposed federal impost amendment to the Articles of Confederation in 1786. Given the Articles' rule of unanimity, New York's no doomed the revenue plan and was for many Americans the last straw, confirming the imbecility of the Confederation and the practical impossibility of reforming the Articles from within. For evidence that New York's 1786 no vote was a major and proximate cause of the Philadelphia Convention, see Robert A. Feer, "Shays's Rebellion and the Constitution," *New Eng. Qtly.* 42 (1969): 388, 390, 397–98, 401–2, 409–10.

Chapter 9

MAKING AMENDS

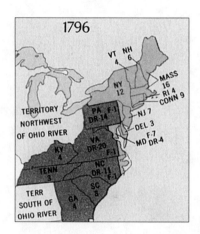

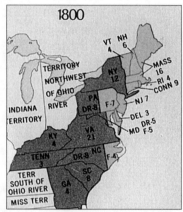

THE PRESIDENTIAL ELECTIONS OF 1796 AND 1800.

In two contests pitting Adams against Jefferson, the nation divided sharply along regional lines. In the first election, Adams won by an electoral vote of seventy-one to sixty-eight, and in the second Jefferson triumphed seventy-three to sixty-five—thanks to his New York running mate Aaron Burr, whose involvement would create its own set of issues. In the wake of these elections, the Twelfth Amendment changed the rules of the game in 1804.

...ation by a dependent...
...quence of the states in 1791... ...Chapter 2
83. The original second amendment... fell short in the 1790s... eventually rebound...
...become the Twenty-seventh Amendment, ratified in 1992... shall consider its curious...
Chapter 14. Readers seeking additional background on the original first amendment or a...
...ed analysis of the Founders' Bill of Rights more generally may wish to consult my earlier...
...and Reconstruction (1998).

$\mathscr{O}$F THE TWENTY-SEVEN AMENDMENTS that Americans have made to the Constitution over the course of two centuries, twelve occurred in the document's first decade and a half—an average rate of almost one amendment per year (compared to an average of less than one amendment per decade thereafter). The first ten amendments, today known as the Bill of Rights, secured a broad range of vital liberties, including freedom of expression and religion, the right to bear arms, immunity from unreasonable searches, and various jury-trial privileges. In both word and deed, the Bill dramatized the rights of "the people," a phrase that appeared no less than five times. Yet that phrase in effect excluded slaves, as did the substance of all the early amendments—especially the Twelfth, which brought the presidency closer to the voters but reinforced slavocrats' unfair advantage in the electoral college.

"Congress shall make no law . . ."

Self-denial is a wondrous thing to behold and an intriguing one to explain. In September 1789, the First Congress voted (by the requisite two-thirds of each house) to propose twelve constitutional amendments protecting a host of rights and freedoms against federal encroachment. By the end of 1791, ten of these twelve had won enough state ratifications (from eleven of the fourteen states then in the union) to become valid for all intents and purposes.* But why, we might ask, did federal lawmakers agree to a Bill of Rights that, after all, limited their own power?

In part, no doubt, because of a love of liberty and a belief in basic American freedoms. Many of these early amendments distilled familiar principles that had already found expression in several state constitutions and state bills of rights. Also, in proposing to restrain the federal government, members of the first federal legislature were tying not just their

---

*The original first amendment, regulating congressional size, fell one state shy of the needed three-quarters of the states in 1791. (For more discussion of this proposal, see Chapter 2, page 82.) The original second amendment also fell short in the 1790s but eventually rebounded to become the Twenty-seventh Amendment, ratified in 1992. We shall consider its curious tale in Chapter 12. Readers seeking additional background on the original first amendment or an extended analysis of the Founders' Bill of Rights more generally may wish to consult my earlier book *The Bill of Rights: Creation and Reconstruction* (1998).

own hands but also the hands of their successors. In a world of frequent congressional rotation, where extended tenure in the national seat often meant spending many nights far from home, most members of the First Congress probably did not expect to continue into, say, the Sixth. (If they did, they were wildly unrealistic. Less than 20 percent of the men who voted on the proposed amendments in 1789 remained in Congress a decade later.)[1] Thus, at least some 1789 congressmen voting to restrain post-1789 Congresses may have done so in order to protect their own expected noncongressional positions in the future, whether as officeholders in the federal executive or judicial branch, as state governmental leaders of some sort, or as private citizens.

We should also note that while the Bill of Rights plainly limited Congress, it applied against other branches of the federal government as well. Even the First Amendment, which began by proclaiming that *"Congress* shall make no *law"* of a certain sort, has properly come to be construed more broadly. In essence, the amendment declared certain preexisting principles of liberty and self-government—*"the* free exercise" of religion and *"the* freedom of speech, [and] of the press"—that implicitly applied against all federal branches (not just Congress) and all federal actions (not just laws). Thus a president today may not condition a pardon on a promise that the recipient will join a particular church or will refrain from speaking out against the administration; nor may federal judges impose a religious test on courtroom spectators or bar them from publishing criticisms of the judiciary. None of the other nine amendments in the Bill of Rights used the word "Congress," and hence there was never any doubt that they, too, applied against all federal branches, often in their core applications. For instance, the Fifth through Eighth Amendments, regulating civil and criminal litigation, imposed limits not just on congressional lawmaking but also on the nonstatutory practices of federal prosecutors and judges.

While the First Congress proposed to restrain itself, its successors, and other federal branches, it suggested no new limits on state governments. Nor did it propose any new federal powers. Tellingly, none of the amendments ratified prior to the Civil War aimed to rein in state governments or expand the regulatory domain of the federal government. (By contrast, the vast majority of the amendments ratified thereafter would indeed strengthen the center in one or both of these ways, as we shall see in later chapters.) To be sure, Congressman James Madison, who spearheaded the 1789 amendment project, prefigured postbellum developments when he advocated a sweeping amendment that would have prohibited *state* abridg-ments of free expression, freedom of religion, and the right to criminal jury trials. Though Madison steered this proposal through the House, which presciently numbered it amendment fourteen, a Senate structured to embody special sensitivity to states' rights refused to go along. In this rejection of what Madison himself deemed "the most valuable amendment in the whole list," we can see several interrelated factors at work in the process that led to the First Congress's epic act of self-denial.[2]

For starters, let's recall that the American people themselves, in several state ratifying conventions, had demanded various amendments that would clarify implicit limits on federal power and add new limits. No convention had called for additional constraints on state government. Though the assorted convention suggestions lacked formal legal status, many Federalist delegates had either voted for these informal proposals or otherwise signaled a willingness to consider them after ratification had been won. Beyond these implicit promises, several members of the First Congress—Madison most notably—had been obliged to offer additional pledges to their constituents in the first congressional elections, which occurred in late 1788 and early 1789.[3]

And if all this were not enough to tug on the First Congress's collective conscience, there was of course the next round of elections to keep in mind. Every House member who desired to retain his seat would in two short years need to explain to his constituents why he had either supported or opposed a federal bill of rights—and in some cases, why he had kept or betrayed a personal pledge to back such a bill. Most senators in the First Congress found their own political leashes unusually short. Whereas a senator elected after 1789 could generally look forward to a full six-year term before being judged again by his state legislature, two-thirds of the first senators were denied this luxury. In order to launch the Senate system of staggered elections, Article I, section 3 provided that one third of the Senate class of 1789 would need to face reelection after only two years of service, while another third would be given an initial term of four years.

The prospect of a second constitutional convention further helped to concentrate the congressional mind. During the Virginia ratification convention, presiding officer Edmund Pendleton had reassured skeptics by predicting that if congressmen motivated by "self-interest" ever balked at desirable amendments, the people would "assemble in Convention" to "reform" the system and "punish" the obstructionists.[4] In New York, Jay and Hamilton had even agreed to support an Article V amendment-proposing convention if moderate Anti-Federalists would first ratify the Philadelphia plan as written.[5] By mid-1789, only two state legislatures—Virginia's and New York's—had formally requested a new convention, but if the First Congress failed to act, political pressure for such a convention might begin to build, and a new political bandwagon might start to roll. If the bandwagon were to gain momentum, who could tell whether Congress could halt or detour it? If, instead, the First Congress itself took the lead in formulating amendments, it might be able to harness some of the outside reformers' political energy, steering the process toward amendments that Congress favored, or at least did not strongly disfavor. On the day that Madison introduced his proposed Bill of Rights, three of his colleagues pointed to the prospect of a second convention as a decisive reason to move quickly on his proposal.[6]

Co-opting the opposition agenda could also help achieve national cohesion and enhance national security. A thoughtfully drafted set of amendments could both cement the loyalty of Anti-Federalists across the continent and woo North Carolina and Rhode Island back into the union. In his First Inaugural Address, President Washington went out of his way to mention that suitably drafted amendments might answer various "objections which have been urged against" the Constitution and thereby reduce skeptics' "inquietude." Though as president he had no official part to play in the amendment process,[7] Washington devoted more than 10 percent of his brief address to the topic of amendments, advising Congress to consider whether the new Constitution might be revised so as to "impregnably fortif[y]" the "characteristic rights of freemen" without "endanger[ing] the benefits of an united and effective government." When Madison himself tried to explain the urgency of amendment to his colleagues, he stressed not just the intrinsic propriety of a bill of rights, but also its usefulness as an olive branch to those who had opposed—and in two states were still opposing—the Constitution:

> There is a great number of our constituents who are dissatisfied with it [the Constitution]; among whom are many respectable for their talents and patriotism [and who are] inclined to join their support to the cause . . . if they were satisfied on this one point. We ought not to disregard their inclination, but, on principles of amity and moderation, conform to their wishes, and expressly declare the great rights of mankind secured under this constitution. . . . But perhaps there is a stronger motive. . . . It is to provide those securities for liberty which are required by a part of the community; I allude in a particular manner to those two States that have not thought fit to throw themselves into the bosom of the Confederacy. . . . A re-union should take place as soon as possible.[8]

Representative Elbridge Gerry, a Philadelphia Convention alumnus who had opposed the Constitution, echoed Madison. "There are two States not in the Union; it would be a very desirable circumstance to gain them. I should therefore be in favor of such amendments as might tend to invite them and gain their confidence; good policy will dictate to us to expedite that event." Several weeks later, Gerry reiterated the point. "There are two States not in the Union; but which we hope to annex to it by the amendments now under deliberation. These are inducements for us to proceed and adopt this amendment, independent of the propriety of the amendment itself." Notably, the First Congress resolved to send copies of its proposed amendments not just to the eleven states in the union but also "to the Executives of the States of Rhode Island and North Carolina."[9]

YET EVEN AS MADISON aimed to placate Anti-Federalists, he also sought to place his own imprint on a federal bill of rights. In reviewing the scores of suggestions spawned by the ratification process, he screened out all proposals that would have radically weakened the new federal government or warped its basic structure. Instead, he generally endorsed clauses that either *clarified* or *codified*—that is, clauses that clarified limits that Federalists had claimed were implicit in their plan all along, or that codified principles that were common practice among the states (which Washington had described as the "*characteristic* rights of freemen").

Much of the First Amendment, for instance, simply textualized the Federalist party line in 1787–88 that Congress had no proper authority to censor opposition speech or meddle with religion in the several states. The First Amendment's particular phraseology—"*Congress shall make no law* . . . abridging the freedom of speech, or of the press"—sounded in federalism and enumerated power, invoking and inverting a prominent Article I clause under which "*Congress shall* have Power . . . To *make all Laws*" that were necessary and proper to federal ends. Anti-Federalists had worried that the sweeping "make all Laws" language might enable Congress to pass general censorship statutes. Federalists had repeatedly responded that such pretextual federal legislation, going far beyond the legitimate purposes underlying the various enumerated powers, would be constitutionally improper. By turning Article I's "Congress shall . . . make all Laws" language into "Congress shall make no law" phraseology, the First Amendment underscored that Congress lacked authority under the necessary-and-proper clause, or any other Article I enumeration, to censor expression in the states. The other main object of the "make no law" amendment—religion—also lay beyond Congress's Article I enumerated powers, according to leading Federalists in the ratification process. Thus it made sense to yoke religion and speech in a single federalism-related provision, even though no previous state bill of rights had linked the two topics.[10]

Likewise, the Tenth Amendment distilled into a single sentence a principle that supporters of the Constitution had insisted was already part of the document's general structure: The new federal government would enjoy only those powers explicitly enumerated or otherwise implicit in the Constitution's general framework. In crafting the language of this textual nod to states' rights, Madison nevertheless avoided anything that might revive the Articles of Confederation's stingy formula limiting the central government to powers *"expressly"* enumerated. When South Carolina's Thomas Tudor Tucker proposed adding the word "expressly," Madison rallied his allies to beat back the unwanted addition: "It was impossible to confine a Government to the exercise of express powers; there must necessarily be admitted powers by implication, unless the constitution descended to recount every minutia."[11]

Madison also tried to sneak a few of his own pet ideas into the first round of amendments, but with limited success. His biggest defeat came when the Senate killed his beloved "No state shall" proposal, which ill fit the general public mood. None of the state conventions or leading Anti-Federalist speakers had urged this or any other sweeping new prohibition on state government. Nor did the idea of restricting states resonate with the Anti-Federalist impulse that Madison himself was urging Congress to heed. To disaffected states' rightists and partisans of America's long tradition of local self-rule, Madison's suggested expansion of federal control over states doubtless looked more like a musket shot than an olive branch. True, Madison's proposal did follow the logic of his own *Federalist* No. 10, which had emphasized the need to rein in state legislatures prone to majority tyranny. But this particular *Federalist* essay had few adherents in the late 1780s, especially among moderates and states' rightists. Just as Madison in 1787 failed to persuade the Philadelphia framers to give Congress a veto over state laws that it deemed unconstitutional, so in 1789 he failed to persuade Congress to propose sweeping new limits on state government.*

---

*In the next chapter, we shall see how the Reconstruction generation succeeded precisely where the prescient Madison failed. The Fourteenth Amendment, ratified in 1868, would begin by proclaiming that "No state shall" violate fundamental civil rights—including rights of expression, religion, and jury trial—and would end by empowering Congress to overrule offending state laws.

Madison did a better job crafting another of his favorite ideas—property protection—into words that fit the spirit of the age and escaped the blue pencils of his colleagues. Though no state convention had demanded that the federal government pay just compensation whenever it took private property for public use, Madison's proposal to that effect (a proposal that left state practices unhindered) harmonized with a general Anti-Federalist desire to limit central officialdom. Also, by tacking his just-compensation clause onto an omnibus amendment guaranteeing various procedural rights previously endorsed by several ratification conventions, Madison drew attention away from his own original contribution. His "No state shall" amendment, by contrast, stood by itself and was thus easier to spot and to kill.

"the right of the people"

In both its enactment and its script, the Bill of Rights began and ended with the people. As we have seen, the initial political demand for the Bill bubbled up from the general citizenry during a uniquely democratic ratification process; and the prompt willingness of a supermajority of state legislatures to agree to ten of the amendments proposed by congressional supermajorities further attested to the general popularity of these proposals. The text of the Bill itself poetically recapitulated its own populist enactment saga. Just as the idea of a bill of rights had begun with the people assembling in conventions and petitioning for change in 1787–88, so the Bill's opening sentence insisted that future generations of "the people" would likewise retain the right to assemble and petition.[12] Though the First Amendment radiated beyond the core case of a constitutional convention, such a convention exemplified "the right of the people peaceably to assemble" and make their views known. And just as the amendment process would culminate in 1791 with ratifications by state governments under the citizenry's watchful eye, so the Bill's closing sentence affirmed the vast reservoir of authority reserved to "the States respectively, *or to the people*." Perhaps the most fundamental power reserved to "the people" was their power to participate in the process of constitutional amendment, as the people dramatized in the very enactment of the Bill.

Between its opening and closing appearances in the Bill of Rights, the phrase "the people" surfaced three more times, in three amendments whose full significance has eluded many modern-day interpreters, who miss the popular-sovereignty overtones of this phrase.

LET'S BEGIN WITH THE WORDS of the Second Amendment: "A well regulated Militia, being necessary to the security of a free State, the right of the people to keep and bear Arms, shall not be infringed." This simple sentence has perplexed most modern readers. How do the two main clauses with different subject-nouns fit together? Do these words guarantee a right of *militias,* as the first clause seems to suggest, or a right of *people,* as the second clause directly asserts? In one corner, gun controllers embrace a narrow, states'-rights reading, insisting that the amendment merely confers a right on state governments to establish professional state militias like the modern National Guard. On this view, no ordinary citizen is covered by the amendment. In the other corner, gun lovers read the amendment in a broad, individual-rights way, arguing that it protects a right of every person to have weapons for self-protection, for hunting, and even for sport. Virtually nothing having to do with personal weaponry is outside the scope of the amendment on this view. Neither modern reading does full justice to the eighteenth-century text.

The states'-rights reading slights the fact that the amendment's actual command language—"shall not be infringed"—appeared in its second clause, which enunciated a right of "the people" and not "the States." Surely the Tenth Amendment, which contradistinguished "the States" and "the people," made clear that these two phrases were not identical and that the Founders knew how to say "States" when they meant states. Also, the eighteenth-century "Militia" referred to by the first clause was miles away from the modern National Guard, which is nowadays composed of a relatively narrow band of paid, semiprofessional volunteers. For the Founders, the general militia encompassed a wide swath of the adult free male citizenry, much as does the modern Swiss militia.

But the individual-rights reading must contend with textual embarrassments of its own. The amendment announced a right of "the people" collectively rather than of "persons" individually. Also, it used a distinctly military phrase: "bear Arms." Though a deer hunter or target shooter carries a gun, he does not, in the strictest sense, *bear arms.*[13] The military connotation was even more obvious in an earlier draft of the amendment, which contained additional language stating that "no one religiously scrupulous of bearing arms shall be compelled to render military service in person." Even in the final version, the military phrase "bear Arms" was sandwiched between a clause discussing the "Militia" and a clause (the Third Amendment) regulating the quartering of "Soldier[s]" in times of "war" and "peace." State constitutions on the books in 1789 consistently used the phrase "bear arms" in military contexts and no other.[14]

By now it should be evident that we need to understand how all the words of the amendment fit together and also how they dovetailed with other words in the Constitution. The amendment's syntax has perplexed modern readers precisely because these readers persistently misconstrue the words "Militia" and "people" by imposing twentieth- and twenty-first-century definitions on an eighteenth-century text. In 1789, the key subject-nouns were simply slightly different ways of saying roughly the same thing. As a general matter, the Founders' militia were the people and the people were the militia. Indeed, an early draft of the amendment linked the two clauses with linchpin language speaking of "a well regulated militia, composed of the body of the people."[15] This unstylish linchpin was later pulled out, but the very grammatical structure of the final amendment as a whole equated the "Militia" of the first clause with "the people" of the second. As the amendment envisioned the republican ideal, those who voted should serve in the military; and those who served should vote.

Beneath these words lay a profound skepticism about a permanent, hierarchical standing army that might not truly look like America. Such an army might come to embody a dangerous culture within a culture, a proto-military-industrial complex threatening republican equality and civilian supremacy. The amendment's root idea was not so much guns per se, nor hunting, nor target shooting. Rather the core idea concerned the necessary link between democracy and the military: We, the People, must rule and must assure ourselves that our military will do our bidding rather than its own. According to the amendment, the best way to achieve this goal would be via a military that would represent and embody us—the people, the voters, the democratic rulers of a "free State." Rather than placing full confidence in a standing army filled with aliens, convicts, vagrants, and mercenaries—men who would not truly represent the electorate and who might well pursue their own agendas—a sound republic should rely on its own armed citizens, a "Militia" of "the people." Thus, no Congress should be allowed to use its Article I, section 8 authority over the militia as a pretextual means of dissolving America's general militia structure—this was the core meaning of the operative "shall not be infringed" command.

Let's call this the republican reading, as opposed to the states'-rights and individual-rights readings that dominate modern discourse. States' rightists anachronistically read the "Militia" to mean the government (the paid professional officialdom) rather than the people (the ordinary citizenry). Equally anachronistically, individual rightists read "the people" to mean atomized private persons, each hunting in his own private Idaho, rather than the citizenry acting collectively. But when the original Constitution spoke of "the people" rather than "persons," the collective connotation was primary. In the Preamble, "the People" ordained and established the Constitution as public citizens meeting together in conventions and acting in concert, not as private individuals pursuing their respective hobbies. The only other reference to "the people" in the Philadelphia Constitution of 1787 appeared a sentence away from the Preamble, and here, too, the core meaning was public and political, not private and individualistic. Every two years, "the People"—that is, the voters—would elect the House.

To see the key people/person distinction another way, let's recall that (nonslave) women in 1787 had various rights as "persons" (such as freedom of worship and the entitlement to due process) but did not directly participate in the acts of "the people." Thus, eighteenth-century women did not vote for constitutional conventions or for Congress, nor did they serve on juries, nor were they part of the people/militia at the heart of the Second Amendment. Elsewhere in the Bill of Rights, the phrase "the people" generally gestured toward voters as the core rights-holders, even as the phrase in certain contexts plainly radiated beyond the core group.

Founding history confirms a republican reading of the Second Amendment, whose framers generally envisioned Minutemen bearing guns, not Daniel Boone gunning bears. When we turn to state constitutions, we consistently find arms-bearing and militia clauses intertwined with rules governing standing armies, troop-quartering, martial law, and civilian supremacy. A similar pattern may be seen in the famous English Bill of Rights of 1689, where language concerning the right to arms immediately followed language condemning unauthorized standing armies in peacetime. Individual-rights advocates cannot explain this clear pattern that has everything to do with the military and nothing to do with hunting. Yet states' rightists also make a hash of these state constitutional provisions, many of which used language very similar to the Second Amendment to affirm rights *against* state governments.

Founding-era militias were closely akin to Founding-era constitutional conventions, electorates, and jurors. In each context, state law helped define the precise boundaries of "the people," specifying when and how the people could properly act. Yet these webs of state law did not thereby transform any of these entities into an ordinary government agency.

Rather, in each case, the law enabled "the people" to act outside ordinary governmental channels and thereby check the professional officialdom.

With the analogies between militias, juries, conventions, and electorates in mind, we can see the kernel of truth in each main modern account and also what's missing from each. States' rightists are correct to see the militia as a local body organized by law. So too with, say, the jury. Twelve private citizens who simply got together on their own to announce the guilt of a fellow citizen would not be a lawful jury, but a lynch mob. Similarly, self-selected clusters of private citizens who choose to own guns today are not a well-regulated militia of the people; they are gun clubs. But what the states'-rights reading misses is that when the law summons the citizenry together, these citizens nevertheless in some sense act *outside* of government, rather than as a professional and permanent government bureaucracy. Just as today's Environmental Protection Agency is obviously not a true jury, so the modern semiprofessional National Guard is not a general militia. Individual-rights advocates rightly recoil at their adversaries' authoritarianism but wrongly privatize what is an inherently collective and political right. It is as if some private citizen insisted that the First Amendment guaranteed him the right to conduct his own political opinion poll and on the basis of its results proclaim himself president.

Yet to see all this is to see what makes the Second Amendment so slippery today. The legal and social foundations on which the amendment was built have washed away over the years. The Founders' juries—grand, petit, and civil—are still around today, but the Founders' militia is not. America is not Switzerland. Voters no longer muster for militia practice in the town square.

How could this erosion of the Second Amendment's very foundation have occurred? Part of the answer can be found in a major drafting omission: The amendment effectively barred the *federal* government from using its authority under Article I to dissolve America's militia structure but imposed no direct ban on state and local governments. The amendment simply presupposed—yet failed to guarantee—the continued existence of general militia laws and practices at the state and local level. Over the years, these local structures and practices have crumbled into practical irrelevance.

Drafting loopholes aside, the Civil War and Reconstruction generated a powerful constitutional counternarrative to the (romanticized) Revolutionary War vision at the heart of the Founders' Second Amendment. The very birth-logic of the Reconstruction Amendments—the process by which they came to be proposed and ratified—depended on the good offices (and good officers) of the Union Army. As constitutional events of the highest import, these amendments necessarily valorized the central army and called into question the anti-army ideology driving the Founders' Second Amendment. But even as Reconstruction Republicans buried their fathers' Second Amendment, they helped unearth a new understanding of its intriguing language. Reading the amendment's words in the light of their own lived experience, they deemphasized militias and states' rights while accentuating an individual right of all citizens—women as well as men, nonvoters as well as voters, civilians as well as militiamen—to keep guns in private homes for personal self-protection.

We shall briefly consider a few of the fascinating details of this death and rebirth in the next chapter. For now, it suffices to observe that, much as other "rights of the people" may be read broadly, beyond their core textual and historical concerns, so, too, may the right of the people to keep and bear arms.

CONSIDER NEXT THE LANGUAGE of the Fourth Amendment, affirming that the "right of the people to be secure in their persons, houses, papers, and effects, against unreasonable searches and seizures, shall not be violated." Here, the collective phraseology of "the people" immediately gave way to more individualistic language of "persons." Clearly, this amendment seemed to center on the domain of domesticity—on "persons" in their private "houses" as distinct from the people in the public square. Why, then, did the Fourth even mention the more republican-sounding phrase "the people"?

Perhaps to highlight the part that civil jurors, acting collectively and representing the electorate, were expected to play in deciding which searches and seizures were reasonable and how much to punish government officials who searched or seized improperly. Private "persons" would remain the core rights-holders, but "the people" on civil juries would retain a vital role in shaping the boundaries of the right. In the first draft of Madison's proposed civil-jury amendment, we can, if we listen with care, detect distinct echoes of the Fourth Amendment and also of the Second: "In [civil] suits at common law . . . the trial by jury, as one of the best securities to the rights of the people, ought to remain inviolate."[16] The multiple textual harmonies at play here—"security" (Second Amendment), "secure" (Fourth Amendment), and "securities" (civil-jury draft amendment); "shall not be infringed," "shall not be violated," and "ought to remain inviolate"; and, of course, "the right[] of the people" in all three places—suggest that all three amendments aimed to protect popular rights via institutions (the militia and the jury) that would embody "the people" themselves.

THE POPULISM EVIDENT in the Second Amendment's people/militia and the Fourth Amendment's people/jury resurfaced again in the Ninth Amendment, which declared that "the enumeration in the Constitution, of certain rights, shall not be construed to deny or disparage others retained by the people." On one level, this amendment worked alongside cognate language in the Tenth (which affirmed "powers . . . reserved . . . to the people") to reaffirm that, qua popular sovereign, the American people would "retain[]" and "reserve[]" the right to alter or abolish what they had ordained and established.

But the Ninth also operated on several other levels. As a federalism provision, it buttressed the Tenth Amendment's reaffirmation that the central government would wield only limited powers. The Tenth made clear that Congress had no inherent power to legislate in all cases whatsoever but said not a word about how interpreters should decide whether Congress had express or implied power over a given topic. The Ninth worked alongside the Tenth to suggest that nothing in the Bill of Rights should be read as conferring additional government power. For instance, readers should not infer from the language of the Fifth Amendment just-compensation clause that Congress enjoyed a general power of eminent domain. Rather, eminent-domain power, like all other powers, had to be deduced from the Constitution's earlier enumerations of governmental authority. This federalism aspect of the Ninth Amendment helps explain why no state constitution circa 1789 contained language closely analogous to it (or to the Tenth Amendment, for that matter). After all, no state constitution had purported to confer only certain enumerated legislative powers.

Beyond its federalism dimension, the Ninth Amendment warned readers not to draw certain types of strong negative inferences about constitutional rights. Thus, the *textual* enumeration of various constitutional rights was not to be read to negate other constitutional rights derivable from the document's *general structure*. Similarly, a text that explicitly *expressed* certain rights was not to be read to negate closely related rights that were merely *implied*. For instance, the mere fact that the First Amendment enumerated free-speech and free-exercise rights against Congress did not mean that Americans lacked similar rights against the president and federal courts, if those rights could indeed be properly inferred from the Constitution as a whole or from the spirit of the First Amendment itself. Likewise, the Sixth Amendment's enumerated right of the accused to enjoy the assistance of counsel should not be read to negate his unenumerated right to represent himself, given that this latter right was implicit in the Sixth Amendment's general logic. Nor did the Sixth Amendment's express statement of the right of "the accused" to enjoy a public trial negate the idea that the public also had a right to attend the trial even if the accused proved willing to waive his own entitlement. The people's independent right to attend was strongly implicit in the Constitution's general structure of governmental transparency, and in the wording of Article III, which spoke of presumptively open "courts" as distinct from closed "chambers."

In 1787 and 1788, Federalists had repeatedly warned that a bill of rights, if incautiously drafted, might actually weaken certain protections in the original Constitution by unintentionally expanding federal powers and restricting implicit rights. In response, the Anti-Federalists had delighted in poking logical holes in the Federalists' defense and casting doubt on the Federalists' good faith. The Ninth Amendment offered a happy democratic synthesis of these clashing positions. One side would get its bill of rights, and the other side would save face via an amendment that solved the arguable drafting problem that it had identified. Though the Ninth Amendment was perhaps unnecessary as a matter of logic—making express what would otherwise have been the most sensible constitutional inference—the same thing might be said of several other provisions of the Bill of Rights, such as the Tenth Amendments and parts of the First Amendment.

It remains for us to ponder the possible existence of other Ninth Amendment "rights" of "the people," rights that might not be inferable from the Constitution's text and structure but that nevertheless might deserve constitutional status.* Although no major Supreme Court case has ever been decided solely on the basis of the Ninth Amendment, some modern judges and scholars have suggested that this amendment should be read to invite judges to mint an expansive set of new rights as the judiciary deems fit. However, the very language of the amendment itself would suggest that judges (and other constitutional interpreters, for that matter)

*The Ninth Amendment suggested that various rights of "the people" were not to be *denied* or *disparaged* by the existence of the Bill of Rights, but this command obviously presupposed a baseline, namely, what would the status of a given right have been in the absence of the Bill of Rights?

who range beyond the Constitution's text and structure must give "the people" their due: Any rights that are to be enforced in the name of the Ninth Amendment must genuinely be rights of *"the people."*

Rights of "the people" need not involve the collective people as direct rights-holders. The Fourth Amendment, after all, focused on individual persons as core rights' bearers, yet nevertheless involved the people (via civil juries) as implementers and interpreters of the rights at stake. More generally, all the provisions of the Bill of Rights might be said to be rights of "the people" insofar as these rights emerged from a populist process. Modern judges (and others) seeking to discover and declare unenumerated rights of "the people" should look for rights that the people themselves have truly embraced—in the great mass of state constitutions, perhaps, or in widely celebrated lived traditions, or in broadly inclusive political reform movements. In short, judges seeking guidance on the real rights of "the people" must give due weight to the very sources and sorts of legal populism that helped generate the Bill of Rights itself.[17]

"trial by jury"

Of the five amendments in the Bill of Rights that did not directly invoke "the people," three explicitly referred to the closely related idea of the "jury." The Fifth Amendment guaranteed a role for federal grand juries, the Sixth Amendment elaborated the parameters of federal criminal-trial juries, and the Seventh Amendment preserved certain entitlements to and of civil juries.

This pattern faithfully reflected the broader legal culture of post-Revolutionary America. During the 1760s and early 1770s, the British Empire had repeatedly sought to evade local jury trials via expanded uses of juryless admiralty, vice admiralty, and chancery courts and via laws authorizing trials in England for crimes committed in America. In response, the colonists had demanded an end to all such evasions. In 1765, delegates representing nine state assemblies met in an intercolonial Stamp Act Congress to declare, among other things, "that trial by jury is the inherent and invaluable right of every British subject in these colonies" and that imperial extensions of "the jurisdiction of the courts of Admiralty beyond its ancient limits, have a manifest tendency to subvert the rights and liberties of the colonists." A decade later, in response to a fresh set of British provocations, the First Continental Congress insisted on Americans' right "to the great and inestimable privilege of being tried by their peers of the vicinage, according to the course of [common] law"; and the Second Continental Congress reaffirmed Americans' entitlement to "the accustomed and inestimable privilege of trial by jury, in cases affecting both life and property." The Declaration of Independence featured three distinct paragraphs condemning the Empire's violations of the rights to and of local juries. Every state that penned a constitution between 1775 and 1789 featured at least one express affirmation of jury trial, typically celebrating the jury with one or more of the following words: "ancient," "sacred," "inviolate," "great[]," and "inestimable." The Northwest Ordinance also affirmed "trial by Jury" and, in a separate provision, a man's right not to be deprived of his liberty or property in the absence of "the judgment of his peers, or the law of the land."[18]

Small wonder, then, that even though the Philadelphia framers explicitly guaranteed in Article III that "the Trial of all Crimes, except in Cases of Impeachment, shall be by Jury; and such Trial shall be held in the State where the said Crimes shall have been committed," Anti-Federalists demanded much more—more guarantees of local criminal trials within a state, more explicit safeguards of the historic role of grand juries, and more security for civil juries. Amendments V–VII aimed to give the people what they wanted while accommodating certain practical considerations confronting the new continental government.

The Fifth Amendment required grand-jury indictments for all serious federal crimes but carved out an exception for matters of military justice within the army or navy or within the militia when called into actual federal service. (While expressly exempting the military only from the ordinary civilian system of pretrial indictments, the amendment also implicitly recognized that military justice more generally could be governed by a distinct set of procedures across the board; thus, military trials themselves have traditionally operated outside the ordinary Article III rules governing judges and juries.) Two other clauses of the Fifth Amendment further affirmed jury rights, though not in so many words. First, the amendment promised that all federal actions depriving persons of "life, liberty, or property" would comport with "due process of law"—an English-law term of art that had long been linked to the right to grand and petit juries. Second, the Fifth Amendment ban on double jeopardy empowered duly instructed trial jurors to irreversibly acquit a criminal defendant, even in the face of overwhelming evidence of guilt, if these twelve men, good and true, saw fit to do so.

The Sixth Amendment supplemented Article III by specifying that criminal juries would be "impartial" and that they would represent not merely the "State" but also the intrastate "district" wherein the crime had occurred. This was rather less than the Anti-Federalists had demanded, however, for the amendment pointedly avoided any entitlement to a jury from the common-law "vicinage" and indeed allowed Congress to treat an entire state as a single district. Similarly, the Seventh Amendment promised that the right of civil juries would be "preserved" but failed to identify with precision the proper preservation baseline. Would a federal civil jury need to preserve the jury-trial right as it existed in each state at the time of the Founding or as it existed in the forum state at the time of the trial? Or should federal courts instead look to English practice circa 1790?

The complexities surrounding the vicinage/district debate and the preservation-baseline issue arose in part because federal jury trials needed to apply in a wide variety of current and future states featuring different state court jury practices, practices that were also subject to change within any given state. By allowing Congress to define districts, the Sixth Amendment freed the federal criminal system from the intricacies of state-vicinage rules, much as Article I, section 4 allowed Congress to trump state-defined district lines for congressional seats. Similarly, the Supreme Court eventually opted to use the uniform metric of Founding-era English practice as a Seventh Amendment baseline and thereby avoid the welter of conflicting state practices.[19] As a result, Article III civil litigation could more easily be consolidated and transferred across state lines within a unitary system of federal court justice.

The remaining provisions of the Sixth Amendment paralleled the celebrated English Treason Trials Act of 1696 but extended its safeguards to all federal criminal defendants, whether or not accused of treason. Thanks to this amendment, every man facing federal charges would be guaranteed the rights to receive proper notice of those charges, to subpoena his own witnesses, and to have legal counsel. Even before the states had ratified this proposal, Congress adopted an omnibus crime bill in 1790 recognizing these rights in language lifted directly from the English Act of 1696.[20] The Sixth Amendment also declared rights to speedy trials and to confrontation of prosecution witnesses—entitlements that, although absent from the landmark English statute, had appeared repeatedly in state constitutions.[21] Supplementing this Sixth Amendment package, the Fifth Amendment declared that a federal criminal defendant (who had no common-law right to testify on his own behalf) would retain the right to resist any demand that he testify against himself. Rooted in English and American practice,[22] this right prevented the government from tricking or tormenting an innocent soul into a false confession.

Completing the complement of judicial-procedure rules based on English law, the Eighth Amendment copied the English Bill of Rights verbatim—save for a substitution of "shall not be" for "ought not to be"—in forbidding excessive bail, excessive fines, and cruel and unusual punishments. Though the jury went unmentioned here, its very absence helps explain the special appeal of this amendment to pro-jury eighteenth-century Americans. Precisely because judges, in setting bail and imposing criminal sentences, would often be acting on their own, without jury oversight, special safeguards were necessary to prevent them from running amok.

"Judicial power . . . shall not . . . extend"

An amendment enacted shortly after the Bill of Rights also aimed to rein in federal judges who seemed at risk of going too far—indeed, who had already gone too far.

To appreciate the impulse animating this (the Eleventh) amendment, we need to understand the first constitutionally significant case ever decided by the Supreme Court, *Chisholm v. Georgia*.[23] In 1792 the executor of a South Carolina merchant brought suit in the original jurisdiction of the Supreme Court against the state of Georgia. The plaintiff sought damages against the state, which he claimed had breached a war-supplies contract. Georgia declined to argue the case orally and instead filed a written objection asserting its sovereign immunity from suit.

Five justices heard the case and delivered five individual opinions. Perhaps because Georgia's tactics created an awkward procedural posture requiring the state to present sovereign immunity as a jurisdictional bar rather than as a substantive defense, all five justices tended to collapse the two distinct questions posed by the lawsuit. First, the jurisdictional issue proper: Did the Court have judicial power to entertain a lawsuit brought by a private citizen against a state government? Second, the substantive issue: Could a state government be held liable in damages for a mere breach of contract? Four justices appeared to answer yes to both questions. Justice Iredell dissented.

The plaintiff argued that the straightforward language of Article III allowed the Supreme Court to hear any lawsuit—whether or not based on federal law—that arose between a "State and Citizens of another State." The Judiciary Act of 1789 seemed to confirm the breadth of this part of the Article III roster, authorizing the Court to hear all civil suits "where a state is a party, except between a state and its [own] citizens."[24] The majority of the Court agreed with the plaintiff's jurisdictional analysis, rejecting Georgia's argument that the Judiciary Article and the Judiciary Act tacitly applied only to suits brought *by* states *against* private parties and not the reverse. The majority justices then proceeded to imply that Georgia was not only suable by a private citizen in a jurisdictional sense, but also suable in a substantive sense—that is, liable to a private citizen in damages for its breach of contract.

This was a bold leap. Under the common law of Georgia and South Carolina—and indeed, of every other state in 1792, it would appear—no damages lay for a breach of contract by the state itself. At common law, such a contract, though morally binding upon a state, was not legally enforceable against it in a damage suit unless the state itself consented to the suit. Anyone who did not like this rule was free to avoid making contracts with the state, or to demand some other up-front compensation or collateral to offset the risk of subsequent nonpayment.

What justified the Court majority's disregard of Georgia's valid state-law defense? After all, the Tenth Amendment seemed to promise that state laws would continue to govern unless such laws were properly displaced by some valid federal legal norm. Indeed, the Judiciary Act of 1789 expressly directed federal courts to follow substantive state law as "rules of decision" in the absence of some preempting federal law.[25] Given that the very purpose of federal court jurisdiction in a case pitting Georgian interests against South Carolinian interests was to ensure the impartial application of state law, lest state courts discriminate against out-of-staters, by what right did federal judges simply disregard the substantive law of *both* states?

We must be clear on what the majority justices did *not* say. Nowhere did they claim that Georgia, in breaching its contract, had violated any federal statute or federal constitutional provision. In particular, the justices never claimed that Georgia's breach violated the Article I, section 10 ban on state laws impairing the obligation of contract.* Yet the justices

---

*The contract clause was designed to prevent the impairment of a preexisting legal obligation, not to create a new legal obligation where none had existed before. Thus, there is reason to doubt the soundness of the Court's later approach in *Fletcher v. Peck,* 10 U.S. (6 Cranch) 87 (1810), which applied the contract clause to a contract in which the state itself was a party. In light of the basic purpose of the contract clause—the avoidance of retroactive impairments—any invocation of this clause by *Chisholm* would have been ironic, giving the creditor a legally enforceable claim ex post facto when at the time of the contract he had bargained only for a morally enforceable claim (and had presumably been compensated in other ways for the risk of nonpayment). Such a dramatic retroactive change in the legal rules, leading to unjust enrichment of one contracting party, would seem antithetical to the basic spirit of the clause.

nevertheless seemed prepared to hold Georgia liable, despite its substantive state-law defense.

The *Chisholm* decision provoked widespread resentment, culminating in an amendment designed to overrule the Court. (Here again, in the emphatic reversal of the justices' first decision of any significance, we see the weakness of the early Court. Only three more times in all the rest of American history would the public successfully mobilize against a specific Court case and overrule it via amendment.)[26] Some arch states' rightists objected in principle to the notion that a state could ever be dragged into federal court and forced to pay money, even in cases where the state *had* violated a valid federal law or the federal Constitution itself. But this extreme faction did not command enough support to ram through an amendment banning all federal lawsuits against states. Instead, just as moderate Federalists had compromised with moderate Anti-Federalists to find common ground in a bill of rights, so once again common ground was found, repudiating *Chisholm,* but on a much narrower basis that even nationalists could live with.

Had states'-rights extremists prevailed, the Eleventh Amendment would have read something like this: "No State shall ever be sued in any Article III court by any private party." Language similar to this was indeed floated by *Chisholm*'s critics immediately after the Court announced its decision, but this language was never seriously considered.[27] The amendment that did pass—proposed by Congress in 1794 and ratified the following year—featured much narrower wording: "The Judicial power of the United States shall not be construed to extend to any suit *in law or equity,* commenced or prosecuted against one of the United States *by Citizens of another State, or by Citizens or Subjects of any Foreign State.*"

This amendment simply rewrote the particular state-party language in Article III that had authorized federal jurisdiction in *Chisholm.* Because the federal judiciary had shown itself to be overly activist in adjudicating state-law disputes brought by out-of-state litigants against state governments, these diversity lawsuits would henceforth be relegated to state courts. But all other Article III clauses would remain intact, even though such clauses might well authorize federal court suits against states if federal laws were at issue.

In other words, moderate Federalists were willing to lop off some of the bottom tier of Article III, which covered various *state-law* controversies, but carefully crafted the amendment so as to preserve intact the top tier of *federal* law cases. This explains why the Eleventh Amendment's text spoke only of ousting jurisdiction over certain cases in "law or

equity"—phraseology that artfully preserved mandatory Article III jurisdiction over federal admiralty law. Likewise, the amendment's last fourteen words left intact top-tier federal jurisdiction whenever a citizen sued
his *own* state on the basis of a federal-law claim in law or equity. The Federalists who in the late 1780s had painstakingly structured Article III so as
to give federal courts the last judicial word over all federal questions thus
managed to maintain this basic structural principle in the mid-1790s.

On this reading, the Eleventh Amendment's text cohered nicely with
the Constitution's general structure. The goal of both the Article IV
privileges-and-immunities clause and Article III's companion diversity
clauses was to end state discrimination against citizens of sister states.
Chisholm had gone too far, giving out-of-staters an outright (and unfair)
advantage: Inexplicably, the Court had said that a South Carolinian creditor could recover damages against Georgia even though an identically
situated Georgian creditor would have received nothing from a Georgia
court.[28] In repudiating *Chisholm,* the Eleventh Amendment restored interstate equality. Since a Georgian could constitutionally sue Georgia in
federal court if the state violated federal rights, a South Carolinian could
likewise sue Georgia under federal law but would henceforth have no special *Chisholm*-like diversity-clause access in state-law suits.[29]

Although the Eleventh Amendment itself (properly construed) did
not bar private damage actions against states, it could be and was argued
in the Founding era that general structural considerations nevertheless
immunized states from such lawsuits. In eighteenth-century England, for
example, the Crown could not be sued absent its consent. Why, then,
asked some Americans, shouldn't state governments (and the federal government, for that matter) likewise enjoy structural immunity?

The short answer was that, in America, neither federal institutions
nor state governments were truly sovereign. Only the people were. In England, the king-in-Parliament was the source of all law, and so no law
could be wielded against the king or Parliament without their consent.
But in America, We the People, via the Constitution itself, had laid down
certain laws that did indeed bind all government officials and entities.
Whenever a government violated the Constitution, that government was
not truly sovereign and thus could not, properly speaking, claim a sovereign's immunity. Similar logic applied whenever a state government violated valid federal laws, for such laws had themselves been authorized in
the Constitution by the true sovereign, the American people.

A government might nevertheless properly insulate itself from liability
for constitutional violations so long as it assured meritorious plaintiffs that

some other legal remedy would make them whole. At the Founding, plaintiffs could typically sue government officials directly whenever such officials had acted unconstitutionally. In such cases, courts generally awarded plaintiffs damages even when the unconstitutional conduct had occurred in good faith; in turn, the government typically indemnified the officials involved and thus indirectly footed the bill.

But in the twentieth century, the Supreme Court began to widen immunities for errant officials while also slamming the courthouse door on injured citizens seeking redress directly against the state or federal government itself. The door has often remained shut even in cases where the government itself has clearly violated constitutional rights. To make matters worse, the modern Court has tried to defend some of its stinginess by hiding behind the words of the Eleventh Amendment, stretching these words beyond all recognition. According to the current Court, the amendment itself and its animating principles prohibit a multitude of federal-law claims against states, even in admiralty cases and in lawsuits brought by citizens against their own states—fact patterns far beyond the amendment's text. Instead of respecting the Constitution's general theme of popular sovereignty, today's Court has exalted *governmental* sovereignty and in fact made it harder for twenty-first-century Americans to achieve redress than it ever was in eighteenth-century England. Instead of honoring the celebrated common-law maxim that "for every right, there should be a remedy,"[30] the modern Court seems intent on insisting that for many a right there must be no remedy. Sovereignty means never having to say you're sorry.[31]

Thus an amendment born in judicial error has bred more judicial error. *Chisholm* was only the first of a long line of embarrassing judicial pronouncements on the topic of state (and federal) suability.

"Electors shall . . . vote . . . for President and Vice-President"

When Americans in 1804 enacted the Twelfth Amendment close on the heels of eleven predecessor amendments, no one could have known that more than sixty years would elapse before a thirteenth would follow. What the Twelfth's drafters and ratifiers could and did know was that the Philadelphia delegates' device for electing presidents and vice presidents had badly misfired and needed to be repaired as soon as possible, preferably before the next presidential contest.

In retrospect, we can detect cracks in the framers' electoral-college system even in the first presidential election, which occurred in early 1789.

Under the rules cobbled together at Philadelphia, each elector would ballot for his top two presidential choices, at least one of whom had to be an out-of-stater. If the highest vote-getter had the support of a majority of electors, that candidate would become president and the next highest vote-getter, regardless of his vote total, would automatically become vice president. But this double-ballot system created a problem in 1789. If virtually all electors wanted Washington as president and Adams as vice president, yet viewed Adams as a distant second choice to Washington, how could they effectively communicate this ensemble of preferences? If each elector voted sincerely for his top two choices, there would be no way of formally signaling the huge difference between the two. Washington and Adams might emerge with nearly identical numbers, thereby creating the illusion that the two were close substitutes in the collective mind of the college.

Working quietly behind the scenes to forestall this result, Hamilton urged various electors to divert their second votes away from Adams (their true second choice) toward lesser candidates. In the end, the scheme worked rather well (from Hamilton's, if not Adams's, perspective). Each of the 69 participating electors cast one vote for Washington, 34 cast their second votes for Adams, 9 gave their second ballots to Jay, and 26 scattered their second votes across an assortment of regional favorites and lesser figures. The cumulative results gave Washington an emphatic mandate reflecting his status as head and shoulders above Adams. In the next presidential election, held in 1792, a similar pattern emerged. Washington won the support of all 132 electors, Adams got 77 votes, and George Clinton came in third with 50.

Yet the 1789 results had come about in part through a coordinated scheme of strategic voting that operated in tension with the spirit of the system created at Philadelphia. Article II had required electors to cast secret ballots on the same day in separate states so as to make it difficult for large blocs of electors to form cabals. And precisely because Article II aimed to discourage enforceable agreements among electors, the situation was rife with the possibility of double cross, if one or more electors pledged to do one thing and then turned around and did something else. Where the margins between the top three candidates were wide, as they were in both 1789 and 1792, a handful of breached promises would do little damage. In a tight race, however, even a small number of strategic defections might make all the difference, as evidenced by the elections of both 1796 and 1800–01.

In 1796, the first post-Washington election, the emerging Federalist faction offered the nation a geographically balanced ticket of Northerner John Adams and Southerner Thomas Pinckney. The opposing Republican faction rallied around Southerner Thomas Jefferson as their leader, with Northerner Aaron Burr a distant second choice. In this new, more openly partisan landscape, the double-ballot system gave rise to several interrelated risks. First, the risk of in-party inversion: Though most Federalists agreed that Adams, the incumbent vice president, deserved the top spot on the ticket, not all Federalists shared this ranking. If a small handful of Northern Federalist delegates diverted their second ballots from Pinckney—so as to assure that Adams would end up with more votes than his running mate—there was always a danger that Southern Federalist delegates might double-cross them by diverting a greater number of ballots away from Adams, thereby giving Pinckney the top spot. In effect, a handful of Federalist schemers could invert the party ticket from Adams-Pinckney to Pinckney-Adams.

The double-ballot system also risked cross-party inversion. If Republicans knew they were going to lose, they might at the last minute strategically cast a few votes for Pinckney and thus reverse the Federalist ticket. To minimize both in-party and cross-party inversion risks, Northern Federalists would need to throw a substantial number of their second ballots away from Pinckney. But this broad diversion would create yet a third risk by opening an electoral window through which Jefferson might slip ahead of Pinckney into second place overall and thereby capture the vice presidency for himself. As the 1796 contest played out, Jefferson did indeed enter through the open window. Adams won with seventy-one votes, and strategic Northern diversions left Pinckney with only fifty-nine, enabling Jefferson, with sixty-eight votes, to claim second prize.

Between 1797 and 1801, Americans witnessed a curious spectacle plainly envisioned by Article II, but previously hidden from view by Washington's preeminence: Two closely matched rivals who had run against each other now stood as president and vice president. During these years, political factions continued to harden, thanks largely to the polarizing events of the French Revolution and the Federalists' overreaction in the notorious Alien and Sedition Acts. The election of 1800 featured a rematch between Adams and Jefferson, but this time with much greater interparty hostility and much tighter intraparty discipline. Once again, each party offered up a geographically balanced ticket—Adams and Charles Cotesworth Pinckney (Thomas's older brother) for the Federalists, and Jefferson and Burr for the Republicans. With enmity between the parties so intense and the race so tight, virtually no wasting of votes occurred; any extra diversion by one party would open a window for the other. Thus, only one Federalist elector threw a vote away from Pinckney so as to signal the Federalists' preference for Adams at the top of the ticket. More important, no Republican electors diverted, with the result that Jefferson and Burr ended up tied, with seventy-three votes apiece as compared to sixty-five for Adams and sixty-four for Pinckney.

This tie at the top highlighted yet a fourth electoral-college imperfection, which Hamilton had foreseen in 1789 but which had subsequently receded from view. Even though almost all Republicans had in their minds voted for Jefferson first and Burr second, on the formal paper ballots these two candidates emerged as equals. (Indeed, a single sly Republican elector could have double-crossed his party by diverting his vote from Jefferson and thus inverting the ticket; likewise, had Federalists known for certain that they were going to lose, their electors could have crowned whichever Republican candidate they honestly preferred.)

Compounding the problem, the Constitution gave the decisive choice in tie-vote situations to the House of Representatives, operating under a quirky set of balloting rules reminiscent of the old Confederation. Each state delegation in the House would act as a unit—one state, one vote—with an absolute majority of state delegations required for victory. But what if, thanks to absenteeism and divided state delegations (whose votes would count as zero rather than one-half for each candidate), neither Jefferson nor Burr could command such an absolute majority? To make matters worse, the House entrusted with this all-important decision in 1801 would be filled with lame ducks whose party had just been trounced at the polls. Although Federalists had entered the 1800 contest with a substantial House majority, Republicans running under the Jefferson/Burr banner had won more than 60 percent of the seats. Yet it would be the old—electorally repudiated—body that would choose the new president. The new House was not due to convene until nine months *after* Inauguration Day.

True, nothing in the Philadelphia Constitution had explicitly mandated that the presidential election be resolved by the outgoing representatives as distinct from the incoming ones. In 1789, for obvious reasons, the electoral ballots for George Washington were unsealed and counted by the newly chosen (eleven-state) First Congress rather than the old Confederation Congress. The new Congress had been summoned into existence on March 4, 1789, and its term therefore ended on March 3, 1791. But what about Washington's term? The First Congress certified Washington's election on April 6, 1789, and he took the oath on April 30. Had either of these two dates been used to mark the beginning of the president's four-year term, the way would have been clear for future *incoming* Congresses to count presidential ballots in early March, as had the first incoming Congress. But without giving the matter much thought, Congress decided in a 1792 law—the same sorry statute that put legislative leaders atop the presidential succession list—that Washington's first term had truly begun, *nunc pro tunc,* at the precise moment that Congress's had, on March 4, 1789.[32] Thus in 1793 Washington took his second oath of office on March 4. The unforeseen consequence of this date choice, however, was to mandate that future electoral-college disputes be decided by congressional lame ducks rather than spring chickens.

When the Federalist-dominated lame ducks met in early February 1801, they initially deadlocked. In a sixteen-state union, the winner needed the votes of nine state delegations, yet after thirty-five consecutive ballots over the course of a week, Jefferson remained stuck at eight votes, with six state delegations backing Burr and two evenly divided (and thus not counted). Though Federalist Burrites in Congress have been depicted by some modern writers as political saboteurs and dirty tricksters defying Jefferson's popular mandate, the Constitution plainly gave the House the right to pick either Burr or Jefferson. (As previously noted, had any prescient Federalist elector been so inclined earlier in the process, he could have single-handedly inverted the Republican ticket by switching his second ballot from Pinckney to Burr.) And as we shall see, Jefferson's popular mandate was not quite so popular as many today might think.

The real legitimacy crisis in February 1801 sprang not from the possibility that the House might pick Burr over Jefferson, but rather from the danger that it might choose *neither.* What if congressional Federalists simply kept the deadlock going until the end of the congressional term on March 3? Would Adams continue to hold office by dint of inertia—beyond his allotted four years? For how long? Even if Adams were to summon the new Congress into emergency session, by what authority could that body purport to untie the Burr-Jefferson knot, given that it was not the Congress that had opened the ballots? If Adams refused to budge, could Jefferson and Burr jointly summon Congress on March 4 on the theory that surely one of them was the new president and thus had authority to convene Congress, which once in session could then choose between them *nunc pro tunc,* à la 1789? (This was Madison's proposal, a clever if concededly extra-constitutional improvisation in a devilish situation.)[33]

Alternatively, might the dawn of March 4 trigger the 1792 succession law designed to deal with situations where both president and vice president were dead or disabled? Was a lapsed president the same in law as a disabled one? If the act did apply, the first in line would be the president pro tempore of the Senate, but no person occupied this position in early February 1801, as Vice President Jefferson took care to hold the Senate chair continuously while the House drama was playing itself out. Could the Senate nevertheless proceed to name a president pro tempore while Jefferson presided? And what about Madison's earlier argument that the act was itself unconstitutional, and that only a true officer—such as the secretary of state—could be named? (An anonymous newspaper essay in 1801 made the case for the secretary of state as the most apt successor. The essay's author may well have been John Marshall, who himself was—you guessed it—secretary of state.)[34] Could the lame ducks properly enact a new succession act naming Marshall, or anyone else they preferred, as interim president? For what interim?

In short, America in February 1801 neared the brink of a constitutional crisis as March 4 irresistibly drew closer while the House refused to make way. The air swirled with far more constitutional questions than answers, and rumblings arose from several state militias ready to march—or so it was widely rumored—if Adams overstayed his term or the Republicans were otherwise deprived of what they believed was rightfully theirs.

And then, on the thirty-sixth ballot ending a week of stalemate, the House anointed Jefferson over Burr by a vote of ten states to four, with two states divided. The succession crisis was over.

OR AT LEAST, over for the moment. For the Constitution mandated a presidential election every four years, and what had happened once could happen again unless Americans repaired Article II's defective machinery. Enter the Twelfth Amendment, proposed in December 1803 and ratified half a year later, just in time for the presidential election of 1804. Under the amendment's provisions, each elector would cast *one* ballot for president and a *wholly separate* (non-presidential) ballot for vice president. Political parties could henceforth openly designate tickets that could not easily be inverted or subverted. A party that commanded an electoral-vote majority would automatically win both presidency and vice presidency, and it would be clear from the start which party candidate was running for the top spot and which was instead slated solely for the vice presidency.

The amendment also provided a revised backup system: If no presidential candidate received an absolute majority of electoral votes, the House (acting under the old one state, one vote rule) would decide among the top three candidates (as opposed to the top five under the original Philadelphia plan). Though this new backup system might conceivably jam up much as the old one had threatened to do in February 1801, the new one would itself be less likely to be triggered in the first instance, thanks to the introduction of separate ballots for presidents and vice presidents. Also, in the event of a House deadlock in the presidential contest, the amendment provided that the incoming vice president could act as president—an option that had not been available under the Philadelphia plan whereby any House deadlock over the presidency also left the nation without an incoming vice president.

The amendment failed to make clear what would happen if both the presidential and vice-presidential selection machinery simultaneously seized up. Under the amendment's new rules, unless one of the vice-presidential candidates won an absolute majority of electoral votes for the number two job, the Senate would proceed to choose between the top two electoral-vote recipients, with the winner needing the support of a majority of the entire Senate. If, thanks to absenteeism, neither candidate could command an absolute Senate majority, and if the House simultaneously found itself deadlocked over the presidential contest, the ghost of February 1801 might return to haunt the nation.

THROUGH ITS SEEMINGLY small modifications of the original electoral college, the Twelfth Amendment in fact worked rather large changes in the basic structure of the American presidency and its relation to other parts of the American constitutional order. First, by knowingly facilitating the efforts of political parties to run presidential–vice presidential tickets—tickets likely to be linked to slates of local and congressional candidates—the amendment paved the way for increased involvement of ordinary citizens in the presidential-selection process. Even if an ordinary voter did not know the presidential candidates directly, he could with relative ease learn about party ideologies and traditions. He could also make plausible inferences about each party's presidential candidate by directly assessing that party's local candidates, whom he *was* well positioned to know personally or with one degree of separation. In 1800, the last presidential election held under the Philadelphia plan, only one-third of the states allowed voters to pick electors directly. In 1804, the first election under the amendment, this number doubled. By 1828, voters were directly choosing electors in twenty-one of the twenty-four states.[35]

Alongside the increased informal role for ordinary voters would come a decreased formal role for Congress in the presidential-selection process. By eliminating double-ballot rules apt to create electoral-college deadlocks and misfires, the Twelfth Amendment lessened the likelihood that any given presidential election would be decided by Congress. The new system would thus work to enhance the executive's formal independence from the legislature. After its dramatic selection of Jefferson over Burr, Congress would be called upon to act in only two of the ensuing fifty presidential contests—directly in 1824–25 and indirectly in 1876–77.

The Twelfth Amendment also helped shape a new kind of vice president, a rather diminished figure compared to his Philadelphia-plan predecessor. Under Article II, the vice president was supposed to be a genuinely presidential personage, a statesman who had in fact received the second-highest vote total for the presidency itself. Under the amendment, the vice presidency would instead go to a man who no elector had picked—and that perhaps no elector would pick—for the top job. The Philadelphia plan had undeniably generated vice presidents of stature in the persons of Adams and Jefferson, twin giants of the American Revolution who would each go on to become president in his own right. (Whether Burr himself, the last man elected vice president under the Philadelphia plan, was of remotely comparable gravitas is a harder question that continues to divide historians.) By contrast, the first two vice presidents elected under the Twelfth Amendment, George Clinton and Elbridge Gerry, were political warhorses well past their prime. Both died in office—Clinton in his second vice-presidential term, Gerry in his first—and Clinton was said to have viewed his final post as a "respectable retirement."[36] According to one leading scholar of the vice presidency, only one "statesman of the first or second rank" held the office between Burr and Theodore Roosevelt a full century later; and that one, John C. Calhoun, would in fact resign (thereby leaving the country bereft of a vice president) in order to serve as a United States senator.[37]

Most important of all, the Twelfth Amendment sired a new kind of president, apt to be far more openly populist and partisan than his predecessors. Modeling himself as an American version of Bolingbroke's fabled Patriot King, Washington had tried to stand as a man above party, with Hamilton as his right hand and Jefferson as his left. (Republican critics complained that in practice, he had often favored his right hand.) In the Age of Jackson, however, Washington's initial effort to embody a president above party would decisively give way to a more modern model of the president as an avowed party leader. Though the Twelfth Amendment did not compel this shift, it plainly enabled it.

In the words of one early expert on the Twelfth Amendment, Lolabel House, "The enormous consequence of [the amendment] has been to make party government constitutional." A more recent book by Tadahisa Kuroda, *The Origins of the Twelfth Amendment,* seconds this assessment: "The amendment modifying the electoral college had a partisan motive and in effect recognized the existence of national political parties." Modern commentators who stress that the Constitution presupposed the absence of organized national parties and aimed to discourage the development of such parties may well be right about the text that emerged from Philadelphia with Washington's signature but are wrong about the document as it came to be revised in the shadow of Jefferson's ascension.[38]

THE TWELFTH AMENDMENT also gave the nation a more visibly and undeniably slavocratic presidential-selection system than the one that America had ratified in the late 1780s. In 1803, it could not be persuasively argued that Article II's rules had in fact worked to boost small states. In the four presidential elections that had taken place thus far, the rules had thrice crowned a man from the largest state (in electoral votes) and once anointed a man from the second-largest state. The runner-up slot had also gone to a big-state man every time. Six of the seven largest states (in free population, circa 1800) had sent men to the executive cabinet, while only one of the ten smallest states had done so.[39]

The Twelfth Amendment itself, by both omission and commission, would only compound the big-state advantage, as was repeatedly emphasized during congressional debate over the measure. After 1800 it was evident both that any state seeking to maximize its clout had to select a statewide slate of electors, winner-take-all, and also that under a general regime of state-winner-take-all, big states would enjoy an advantage. Though prominent proposals had surfaced after 1801 to require states to renounce winner-take-all systems, the framers of the Twelfth Amendment spurned all such proposals and instead increased the big-state advantage in two distinct ways. First, the Amendment's separate ballots for presidents and vice presidents reduced the likelihood of an electoral-vote tie between running mates and thus increased the odds that elections would be decided by the electors themselves (in a system favoring big states) rather than in the House (operating on a one-state, one-vote rule).

Second, in the event no presidential candidate had an electoral-vote majority, the House could choose only among the top three vote-getters, rather than among the top five. This, too, shrank the domain over which the state-equality principle would operate.[40]

Several congressmen attacked the amendment for its obvious weakening of the influence of small states, and tiny Delaware in fact refused to ratify the amendment on these grounds.[41] However, by 1803 politically savvy Americans had come to see that the nation's deepest fissures ran not between big states and small states, but rather between free states and slave states.[42] Every actual combination of president and vice president (and indeed every losing ticket as well) had balanced a Northerner and a Southerner. Many of the major debates in Congress—over the assumption of state debt, the location of a national capital, the establishment of a federal bank, the apportionment of representatives after the first census, the ratification and enforcement of the Jay Treaty, and much more—had either highlighted or thinly papered over obvious sectional differences. In both 1796 and 1800, electors had divided along sectional lines,* and even the final vote in the House on February 17, 1801, had called attention to the geographic gradient. The four states that held out to the bitter end for (Northerner) Burr over (Southerner) Jefferson were all located in New England: Connecticut, Rhode Island, Massachusetts, and New Hampshire.

The election of 1800–01 had also drawn the nation's attention, in the most dramatic fashion possible, to the Philadelphia plan's proslavery bias. In 1787–89, many Northern ratifiers had failed to understand the full significance of the words "three fifths." Refighting the last war, they had focused more on apportioning taxes than on allocating House members and presidential electors. But by 1803, everyone understood that virtually no revenue would come from direct taxes subject to the three-fifths clause. (Only once, in 1798, had a small direct tax been levied.)[43] By contrast, the hard-fought and razor-close election of 1800–01 had made the three-fifths clause's electoral significance obvious to anyone with eyes and a brain.

For without the added electoral votes created by the existence of Southern slaves, John Adams would have won the election of 1800—as everyone at the time plainly understood. Jefferson's (and Burr's) electors came from states that had a smaller total free population than the states whose electors backed Adams. Had the electoral college been apportioned on the basis of

*See the election maps on the first page of this chapter.

free population—with no three-fifths bonus—Jefferson would have ended up with about four electoral votes less than Adams rather than eight votes more. As one New England paper sharply put the point, Jefferson was riding "into the TEMPLE OF LIBERTY, upon the *shoulders of slaves*."[44]

Congressional critics of Mr. Jefferson, and of the electoral-college amendment that his political party was pushing, repeatedly called attention to the unpleasant facts underlying his claimed mandate. In 1802, Connecticut Congressman Samuel Dana declared that if Republican reformers were in earnest about changing the electoral rules, they should ponder a wider range of issues, including whether the apportionment of representatives (and thus presidential electors) "should be in proportion to the whites, or in proportion to the whites compounded with slaves." The following year, Representative Seth Hastings of Massachusetts argued that if any amendment should be made in the wake of the preceding presidential election, it should be one establishing "an equal representation of free citizens, and free citizens only," thereby undoing the Philadelphians' "compromise . . . by which one part of the Union has obtained a great, and in my opinion, unjust advantage over other parts of the Union. A compromise, sir, by which the Southern States have gained a very considerable increase of Representatives and Electors, founded solely upon their numerous black population." Echoing his colleague, fellow Bay Stater Samuel Thatcher chafed at the "peculiar inequality" between regions created by "the representation of slaves," who would add "eighteen Electors of President and Vice President at the next election."[45]

In the upper house, New Hampshire Senator William Plumer likewise called attention to the "eighteen additional Electors and Representatives" created by chattel slavery. "Will you, by this amendment, lessen the weight and influence of the Eastern states, in the elections of your first officers, and still retain this unequal article in your Constitution? Shall property in one part of the Union give an increase of Electors, and be wholly excluded in other States? Can this be right?"[46] Yet the Twelfth Amendment's Republican backers were plainly not interested in fixing *this* aspect of the presidential-selection system, even as they freely altered other parts of the Article II machinery. Ultimately, the New England states accounted for six of the ten votes against the amendment in the Senate, while in the House, states north of New Jersey generated thirty-one of the forty-two no votes.[47]

In short, whereas Article II originally created the presidency in the image of George Washington, Amendment XII refashioned the office in the likeness of Thomas Jefferson and in a manner that prefigured Andrew Jackson.* After the adoption of this amendment, America's presidential-election rules—and thus America's presidents—would generally be more democratic, more partisan, and more openly slavocratic. Prior to the amendment, America's first president had taken steps to free his slaves, and America's second president had none who needed freeing. America's third president—a transitional figure elected under Article II and re-elected under Amendment XII—had passionately condemned slavery in his early years but did rather little to back up his youthful rhetoric after his slavery-supported triumph in 1801. The next dozen presidents—mostly Southern slaveholders or Northern doughfaces—likewise did little to challenge slavery.

AND THEN, IN ONE of those delicious ironies that abound in history, the Twelfth Amendment eventually came to advantage an emphatically anti-slavery candidate. In 1804, this future president had yet to be born, and the state from which he sought the presidency did not even exist. Surely no one at the turn of the nineteenth century could have foreseen the long and twisting path that would lead from a proslavery Twelfth Amendment to an abolitionist Thirteenth. Yet lead it did. Thanks to the Twelfth Amendment, the presidency in 1860–61 went to a partisan dark horse who commanded less than 40 percent of the popular vote and who probably could not have won an outright national majority in a one-on-one matchup against his leading rival. Though this 1860 winner managed a virtual clean sweep of the North, he was reviled in the (white) South; he received not a single popular vote—none!—in the ten states south of Virginia. His name, of course, was Abraham Lincoln, and the next great wave of amendments would reflect the new political coalition that he helped bring into power.

---

*In his First Annual Message to Congress, on December 8, 1829, Jackson himself advocated a constitutional amendment that would eliminate both the office of presidential elector and the backup system of congressional selection. In their place, Jackson proposed a system of direct election. The devil of course was in the details—direct election would occur only within each state, with the final continental results tallied up using the three-fifths formula. "I would there-fore recommend such an amendment of the Constitution as may remove all intermediate agency in the election of the President and Vice President. *The mode may be so regulated as to preserve to each State its present relative weight in the election.*" *Senate Journal,* 19:9–10 (emphasis added).

A New Birth of
Freedom

"Shall I Trust These Men (*left*), And Not This Man (*right*)?"
(August 5, 1865)

At the end of the Civil War, America—depicted here as Lady Columbia—confronted momentous questions. Under what conditions should white rebels who had taken up arms against her be restored to their civil and political rights? What new rights should be extended to loyal blacks who had devoted their lives and limbs to her defense?

$\mathcal{F}$OUR SCORE YEARS after the Founding, a new generation arose to transform what their fathers had brought forth on the continent. In what can only be described as a constitutional revolution, the nation ended slavery, made every person born under the flag an equal citizen, guaranteed a host of civil rights to all Americans, and extended equal political rights to black men. Hard as it was to get America to make these promises, getting her to keep them would prove harder still. Full compliance would not occur until a Second Reconstruction in the late twentieth century. For women, too, the First Reconstruction would taste bittersweet, as daughters of the republic won promises of civil rights but not the key political right to vote.

"Neither slavery nor involuntary servitude"

From 1864 through 1870, Americans of all sorts—women and men, blacks and whites, civilians and soldiers, Easterners and Westerners, exblues and ex-grays—engaged in a massive democratic struggle over the meaning of democracy itself. The result, breaking more than a half-century of constitutional silence, was a trilogy of constitutional amendments. First, in 1865, the Thirteenth Amendment ended slavery forever. Then came the Fourteenth Amendment, proposed in 1866 and ratified in 1868, making all persons born in America—blacks no less than whites, women no less than men—full and equal citizens, and pledging to protect all fundamental civil rights against state and federal encroachment. But this package of "civil" rights purposefully omitted the "political" right to vote and kindred "political" rights to hold office and serve on juries. Hence the need for yet another amendment—the Fifteenth, proposed in 1869 and ratified the next year—guaranteeing black men precisely these "political" rights.

From a modern perspective, this trilogy might seem to form an indivisible and inevitable postwar ensemble, but to Americans living through this tumultuous time, each amendment arose in its own unique historical moment; each raised its own set of issues; and in each amendment battle neither side could know whether additional battles would follow. Let us, then, begin by pondering the first of this grand trilogy, the Abolition Amendment.

Though the Constitution of 1787–88 did not abolish slavery, it would be nice to think that the Founding Fathers designed a document whose arc would inexorably bend toward freedom and equality. Alas, the facts do not bear out this comforting thought.

True, many framers piously hoped that one day slavery would disappear. Yet they did little to hasten or guarantee that day, even when doing so might have been relatively painless—say, by constitutionally excluding slavery from all future Western territories. In fact, the Constitution's basic structure tilted the long-run game against the forces of freedom. To recap: For every slave bought or bred (both before and after 1808) the slavocracy's clout in Congress and the electoral college would increase, thanks to the three-fifths clause. In a process akin to compound interest, the effects of this one little number would grow exponentially as time passed, giving the Slave Power far more than its fair share of federal House seats, state legislative (and therefore federal Senate) seats, and electoral-college seats (and therefore far more chances to dominate the presidency, the cabinet, and the Court). If the long-term tendencies of this constitutional system were not evident to all in 1787, they surely were by 1804, when the document was amended in a manner that blessed its proslavery bias.

What, then, happened to derail this train and to place the nation on a different track heading in the opposite direction? In brief: Lincoln, secession, war, black arms-bearing, and victory.

ABRAHAM LINCOLN IN 1858 knew two great truths. First, slavery was wrong. As he later put it, "If slavery is not wrong, nothing is wrong."[1] Second, it would be well-nigh impossible to right this wrong overnight, to abolish slavery immediately and everywhere. Sparring with Stephen Douglas in a series of celebrated debates across the length and breadth of Illinois, Lincoln at one point declared that if and when the nation ventured onto his own preferred path of long-term reform, "I do not suppose that in the most peaceful way ultimate extinction would occur in less than a hundred years at the least."[2]

The sluggish pace at which abolition had taken place even in the North justified Lincoln's cautious assessment. Although New York had passed a gradual emancipation statute in 1799, as of 1820 the state still had over ten thousand bondsmen, ranking it alongside Missouri. In Connecticut, slavery had never been a particularly widespread practice. Nevertheless it took more than a half-century to uproot it; the state enacted its first gradual-emancipation law in 1784 and did not end all slavery until 1848.

Similarly, New Jersey, which had begun the abolition process in 1804, did not put a decisive end to slavery until 1847, and a few blacks remained unfree until the Civil War. In some places, it seemed as if abolition meant *ending slavery* as a system more than *freeing actual slaves* then in bondage.[3]

Although Lincoln lost his 1858 bid to oust Douglas from the U.S. Senate, in 1860 the two men again squared off, this time with two other men in the ring and the presidency at stake. As before, Lincoln stood for long-term reform: Slavery's spread into virgin territory must stop, immediately and absolutely, but in states where slavery had already insinuated itself, a different strategy was in order. Thus the 1860 Republican Party platform seemed to forswear federal abolition in the states, pledging allegiance to the "inviolate . . . right of each State to order and control its own domestic institutions according to its own judgment exclusively."

How, then, would Lincoln's proposed bar on new slave territory achieve his ultimate goal of general emancipation? In a word: gradually. Free territories would one day ripen into free states. Southeastern slavery would eventually be surrounded. Aided perhaps by federal financial sweeteners, upper-South states such as Delaware, Maryland, Kentucky, and Missouri would eventually begin to adopt long-run systems of compensated emancipation, possibly accompanied by voluntary emigration of freedmen to Africa or Central America. Once slavery stopped growing and instead began to shrink, the state-led emancipation process might spread southward and accelerate—a compound-interest story in reverse—as local leaders began to devise smooth exit strategies. Perhaps (though candidate Lincoln never quite said so), once antislavery leaders held sway over the vast majority of the nation, they might amend the federal Constitution to provide for universal emancipation on a gradual and compensated basis.

Winning just under 40 percent of the national vote in a four-man race, Lincoln prevailed in 1860 by sweeping every free state save New Jersey and thereby capturing 180 electoral votes, compared to 123 electoral votes for the rest of the field. Even had all the popular votes cast against Lincoln gone to a single anyone-but-Abe candidate, Lincoln would still have emerged victorious thanks to his outright majorities in Northern states totaling 169 electoral votes. Still, for every two Lincoln men at the polls, three other men had voted against Lincoln. America's first openly antislavery president could hardly claim a ringing mandate. Nor would Lincoln's new party be likely to overwhelm all others in Congress, having won only about 108 out of 237 House seats and controlling roughly 30 of the 66 Senate seats.[4]

All these facts and figures point to a sobering conclusion: *Had the Slave Power simply acquiesced in the election of 1860, nothing like immediate emancipation could ever have occurred in the 1860s.* Had slavocrats continued to play the game—as they had been playing (and generally winning) it prior to 1860—they could have won or tied many more rounds in the short and intermediate run. Slavery would probably have continued for at least another half-century even had Lincoln and his new party managed to accomplish all they realistically hoped for and more in his constitutionally guaranteed four years.

But the Slave Power did not acquiesce. Before Lincoln raised his right hand on March 4, 1861, seven states had already purported to secede and to form their own Confederacy. (Several of the state-secession votes occurred in assemblies skewed by state-law variants of the federal three-fifths clause—laws that gave plantation belts undue weight in the ultimate outcome.)

To woo the Deep South back into the Union and to deter the upper South from joining the Confederacy, the lame-duck Congress on March 2, 1861, voted by the requisite two-thirds of each house to propose a new amendment to the Constitution.[5] Despite its clumsy grammar and customary euphemism,[6] the proposal's thrust was plain enough: If, thanks to a strategy of containment and encirclement, antislavery forces were ever to command overwhelming national majorities, these forces would be barred from amending the Constitution to give Congress abolition power over slave states. Several notable Republican congressmen voted for this measure, and Lincoln himself, in his Inaugural Address, pointedly mentioned it and expressed "no objection."

To be sure, the proposal squared with Lincoln's and the Republicans' chief campaign theme, read narrowly. Republicans had focused on slavery in the territories (and implicitly in the national seat), not in the states. Also, the very clumsiness of the written proposal made its proslavery rules potentially vulnerable to future Portias. (What if a future amendment did not *empower Congress* to abolish slavery, but *itself* abolished slavery directly?) Nevertheless, the Slave Power's muscular grip on American politics was nowhere more evident than on March 4, 1861. In what was then rightly seen as the most antislavery moment in American history, with the first inauguration ever of an openly antislavery president, that president—following the lead of his own antislavery party in Congress—blessed an amendment to make slavery in the states *forever* immune from congressional abolition.

And then came a bombshell—quite literally. When Confederate

forces began their military assault on Fort Sumter in early April, they sparked a process that brought about precisely what they sought to prevent: immediate, uncompensated, and universal abolition, something that could never have happened had they just held their fire. Rarely in history have cannons backfired so explosively.

In response to Sumter's fall, Lincoln took immediate steps to suppress the insurrection. Four upper-South states (Virginia, North Carolina, Tennessee, and Arkansas) thereupon entered the Confederacy, which now formed an eleven-state bloc boycotting the federal Congress. A handful of loyal congressmen from Confederate states nevertheless continued to serve in the Capitol, as did congressmen from the four slave states (Delaware, Maryland, Kentucky, and Missouri) that remained in the Union. Alongside them were congressmen from the nineteen free states. Ironically enough, it was secession itself that for the first time in history created a Congress dominated by antislavery statesmen.

At first, Lincoln and the Republicans proceeded cautiously on the antislavery front. The president's primary goal was to bring the South back into the Union with as little bloodshed as possible. Radical abolitionist measures early on would ruin any prospects for rapprochement. At its July special session, Congress endorsed a resolution, cosponsored by then-Senator Andrew Johnson, defining Union war aims narrowly. "This war is not waged . . . for any purpose . . . of overthrowing or interfering with the rights or established institutions of those States [in revolt], but to defend and maintain the supremacy of the Constitution."[7]

Lincoln also had to guard his rear flank. Any quick move against slavery in 1861 might weaken his hold over the four loyal slave states, at least two of which were geostrategically indispensable. Were Maryland to heed its secessionist elements and follow Virginia into the Confederacy—in 1860, Lincoln had won less than 3 percent of Maryland's popular vote—the District of Columbia would be surrounded and all but impossible to defend. Kentucky's position along the banks of the Ohio River also made it essential. (Lincoln had won less than 1 percent of the vote in this, his birth state.) Legend has it that Lincoln once quipped that "I hope to have God on my side, but I must have Kentucky."

As time passed, hopes of a quick victory and early re-Union faded while Lincoln's hold over the middle states improved. In mid-April 1862, the first anniversary of the Sumter affair, Republicans in Congress began to implement their modest antislavery agenda. First, the two houses enacted a suggestive but vague joint resolution, which in its entirety declared "that the United States ought to cooperate with any State which may adopt gradual abolishment of slavery, giving to such State pecuniary aid, to be used by such State in its discretion, to compensate for the inconveniences, public and private, produced by such change of system." That same week, Congress passed a detailed statute that freed all existing slaves in the District of Columbia, barred future slavery there, and authorized government compensation—up to $300 per slave—for loyal masters.[8]

Two months later, Congress banned slavery in all federal territory, without any provision for compensation and in direct defiance of the Taney Court's pronouncements in *Dred Scott*. Yet perhaps this move was more modest than it looked. The 1862 Act borrowed language verbatim from the Northwest Ordinance of 1787, which had been construed by the Washington Administration only to bar the bringing of new slaves into the Northwest, not to free the slaves already there. If the new act were similarly construed, or if the relatively few masters with slaves in extant territories were to remove them posthaste into a (Union) slave state, then no issue of emancipation or compensation would arise. Also, a pair of federal Confiscation Acts in 1861 and 1862 allowed federal officers to free certain slaves of individual rebels. In practice, however, these laws had rather limited emancipatory effect.[9]

In September 1862 Lincoln proclaimed his own, more expansive, emancipation plan. In all places that continued to be under rebel control on New Year's Day 1863, the Union government would cease to recognize the claims of masters, even loyalists. Slaves in these places would (if and when the Union Army arrived) be liberated. On January 1, Lincoln finalized the Emancipation Proclamation, declaring all slaves in rebel lands—some three million souls—to be "forever free."

With a stroke of the executive pen, Lincoln changed the meaning of the war and the course of American history. No longer was the struggle merely one to restore the Union as it was. Henceforth, it would be a war for Freedom alongside Union. Lacking specific statutory warrant for his Proclamation—one of the most sweeping measures ever undertaken in America—Lincoln pointed to his Article II power as America's commander in chief in a time of actual war. The war itself had destroyed or imperiled a vast amount of liberty and property, of innocent civilians as well as soldiers. Why should slave masters' property claims be regarded with extreme tenderness, if such claims interfered with the Union's ability to win the war? And emancipation would, in Lincoln's eyes, surely help win the war by encouraging Southern slaves to come to the aid of the Union Army and also by preventing the English government from entering into any diplomatic alliance with the Confederacy. If the war were only about American union, the English might well pursue their own imperial ambitions to divide (and perhaps one day reconquer?) their former colonies. But once Lincoln's Proclamation redefined the meaning of the war, linking Union with Freedom, antislavery British public opinion would prevent any unholy alliance between Great Britain and the Confederacy.

Ironies and harmonies intermingled. Unilateral executive power, widely feared at the Founding, was now being used to secure freedom on an epic scale. True, the Proclamation itself emancipated none of the slaves in Union states and exempted certain designated Confederate lands already under Union control. Yet the very fact that the Proclamation was *not* universal reinforced Lincoln's legal authority to make it. The holes and exceptions were themselves proof that Lincoln's was indeed a *military* (and thus executive) decision as distinct from a *moral* one (which would have required express legislative backing). In the 1780s, George Washington had worked to create a union for geostrategic reasons—to push England out of the American heartland. Now, four score years later, Abraham Lincoln was redefining the meaning of that union for analogous geostrategic reasons—to *keep* England out of the heartland.

Having taken the plunge toward abolition in various states—albeit states in rebellion—Lincoln strengthened his moral standing with a plan to extend abolition to the four loyal slave states (and presumably to any future ex-Confederate state rejoining the Union). Lincoln's plan, unveiled in his December 1862 Annual Message, envisioned three new constitutional amendments. The first would guarantee federal compensation to any slave state that abolished slavery prior to 1900. Lincoln's earlier one-hundred-year notion had now shrunk to thirty-seven years, but even this was a far cry from the eventual reality of immediate universal emancipation in 1865. Lincoln's proposal should remind us that the ultimate Thirteenth Amendment solution—freedom now, forever, and everywhere—was hardly foreordained even after the Emancipation Proclamation. Lincoln's additional constitutional proposals would have provided federal compensation for all loyal masters whose slaves had been liberated by "the chances of the war" and federal subsidies for any "free colored persons" willing to emigrate to Africa, Central America, or elsewhere.

To explain why the Thirteenth through Fifteenth Amendments that America in fact enacted from 1865 to 1870 differed so sharply from the Thirteenth through Fifteenth Amendments that Lincoln was dreaming of in late 1862 (and also from the Thirteenth Amendment that Lincoln had tentatively blessed in March 1861), we must turn away from the words of whites and attend to the deeds of blacks. We must also venture beyond the elected leaders in Washington, D.C., to ponder the voters in the (loyal) states.

Black Americans reacted to the Proclamation by making it their own and taking freedom into their own hands. Emancipation would not merely be given by one white, but also earned by countless blacks. In the South, slaves fled plantations and flocked toward Union Army lines in droves, crippling the Confederate economy while pledging their allegiance to Lincoln. The Proclamation had promised that slaves fleeing rebel soil would "be received into the armed service of the United States," and thousands of such men poured into the Union ranks. Thrilled by the promise of freedom for their Southern kinsmen, Northern free blacks likewise rushed to volunteer in Lincoln's army. In Kentucky, more than half of the male slaves of fighting age signed up, spurred by federal promises of freedom for all such enlistees, and later, promises of freedom for their families as well. All told, roughly 180,000 blacks served in blue—more than 20 percent of all African American males of military age.[10]

After blacks voted for Lincoln with their feet and arms, whites did so with their ballots. Without some good news from the battlefield (thanks in no small measure to blacks), Lincoln might well have lost his 1864 bid for reelection, and emancipation might have been stopped in its tracks or even rolled back. Had Democratic nominee George McClellan prevailed at the polls, might he have ended the emancipation process by allowing the Confederacy to take its remaining slaves and leave the Union? Might he have gone even further? What if, as America's new commander in chief, he tried to repeal his predecessor's Proclamation as applied to any slave whose Confederate master sought to reclaim him? Lincoln's thumping victory, with 212 electoral votes to McClellan's 21, made all such questions moot. Lincoln's allies also gained ground in congressional elections, with Republicans looking forward to controlling more than two-thirds of the seats in each house of the Thirty-ninth Congress.

In its 1864 platform, Lincoln's party had pledged to amend the Constitution so as to effect the "utter and complete extirpation" of slavery from "the soil of the Republic," and in the afterglow of their November triumph, Republicans moved quickly to redeem this promise. On January 31, 1865, the lame-duck Thirty-eighth Congress voted for a resoundingly abolitionist Thirteenth Amendment, which received the support of two-thirds of the non-seceding true-blue states in July and two-thirds of all states, including the former Confederacy, in December. The speedy ratification process in true-blue states highlighted the link between Lincoln and this amendment: First to say yes was Lincoln's home state of Illinois, and the three states that had gone against Lincoln in 1864—New Jersey, Delaware, and Kentucky—all declined to ratify.[11] By mid-1865, the latter two were the Union's only remaining slave states. Maryland and Missouri had freed their slaves in late 1864 and early 1865 respectively, and West Virginia had been required to adopt an abolition plan as part of its 1863 admission to the Union.

The Thirteenth Amendment blended traditional language with transformative substance. The specific wording banning "slavery [and] involuntary servitude" derived from the Confederation Congress's Northwest Ordinance of 1787 and had also appeared in subsequent congressional statutes, including the Territorial Act of 1862. But the 1787 law had been applied only to bar carrying new slaves into the West, not to emancipate those already there. The 1862 law may have swept further, but not much, and emancipation in the District of Columbia had operated only over a minuscule area. In sharp contrast, the Thirteenth Amendment freed everyone—immediately and without compensation—unlike all prior federal laws and most antebellum state emancipation statutes. And of course, the amendment promised a *permanent* end to America's slavery system: Neither states nor the federal government would be allowed to revive slave codes, import new slaves, or otherwise permit bondage to creep back onto American soil (save as a criminal punishment, subject to due process).

The old words of the Northwest Ordinance had also expanded along another dimension in the intervening decades. If a man agreed to sell himself into servitude for a number of years and then later changed his mind and tried to walk away, could courts compel him to perform what he had promised, or should judges merely require him to pay damages for his contractual breach? In the early nineteenth century, courts tended to look at the moment of initial consent and deem various indentures to be *voluntary*—at least if these service agreements did not extend beyond seven years. By the 1860s, courts looked instead to the hour of breach. Under the new liberationist view, to hold a man to service who wanted *at that moment* to leave was indeed to impose an impermissible *involuntary* servitude.

While the Thirteenth Amendment clearly condemned traditional forms of unfree labor—chattel slavery itself, debt peonage, and so on—the antebellum experience had also dramatized a variety of other, less obviously economic forms of degradation, dehumanization, and unfreedom. While slave men had been worked against their will in the fields, paradigmatic slavery for women and children had taken other forms above and beyond field work—sexual exploitation and child abuse, for example. By banning *all* forms of "slavery [and] involuntary servitude," the Thirteenth Amendment cast a wide net not merely over the nation's economy but also over its social structure and its domestic institutions.[12]

Government-sanctioned slavery was forever prohibited, but the amendment went even further, condemning various types of private domination perpetrated in the absence of formal legal authority or in the teeth of formal legal prohibition. Whenever one person improperly held another in bondage, the amendment applied: "slavery [and] involuntary servitude . . . shall [not] exist." Hence, as soon as a state became aware of the existence of de facto slavery within its borders, the state had an obligation to end it.

Despite its seemingly traditional language, the Thirteenth Amendment thus marked a radical break with the antebellum federal Constitution. That prewar document had imposed few limits on what a state could do to its own inhabitants, whereas the Thirteenth pulverized bedrock legal principles and practices in more than one-third of the states and imposed new affirmative federal obligations on every state. The old Constitution had insulated property-holders from uncompensated takings, but the new one ratified and extended the largest redistribution of property in American history.[13] Slaves were worth more than any other capital asset in the nation except land. In 1860, human chattel represented about three times as much wealth as the entire nation's manufacturing and railroad stock, yet the Thirteenth made no provision for compensation, even of loyal masters in true-blue states. (Section 4 of the Fourteenth would go even further, prohibiting any federal or state compensation of slave masters.) A structurally proslavery Constitution became, in a flash, stunningly antislavery.[14]

The naked constitutional text misleads: A casual reader encounters a Thirteenth Amendment whose words seem to follow smoothly after the first seven Articles and the first twelve amendments, in one continuous constitutional tradition linking the Founders to their twenty-first-century posterity. What the bare text does not show is the jagged gash between Amendments Twelve and Thirteen—a gash reflecting the fact that the Founders' Constitution *failed* in 1861–65. The system almost died, and more than half a million people did die. Without these deaths, the Thirteenth Amendment's new birth of freedom could never have occurred as it did.

"Congress shall have power"

America's first eleven amendments had all aimed to limit the federal government, and the Twelfth had neither added to nor detracted from federal authority. By contrast, the Thirteenth expanded the federal government's role in broad language, borrowed from some of the most sweeping passages of the Philadelphia document and antebellum case law.

Here, too, it is worth juxtaposing the Thirteenth Amendment as enacted in 1865 with the would-be Thirteenth Amendments that Congress proposed in 1861 and that Lincoln floated in 1862. The 1861 proposal would have forever forsworn congressional power over slavery in the states, and the 1862 plan likewise left the abolition issue to the several states (this time, with a federal financial sweetener). But the Thirteenth Amendment that prevailed at the end of the war reflected the spirit of nationalism that had been summoned up by the war itself. Not only did the amendment's opening words impose large duties on states, obliging them to prohibit slavery now and forever, but the amendment's closing words explicitly conferred new powers upon Congress: "Congress shall have power to enforce this [amendment] by appropriate legislation."*

Whereas the Founders' first successful amendment told Congress that it could "make no law" over a certain domain (religion), the Reconstructors' first successful amendment told Congress that it could indeed make many laws over a different domain (emancipation). While the Founders' opening amendment had cleverly inverted the final paragraph of Article I, section 8 ("Congress shall have Power . . . To make all Laws which shall be necessary and proper . . ."), the Reconstructors' opening amendment essentially echoed this sweeping Article I language. Article I said that Congress would have all "proper" power; the Thirteenth Amendment said that Congress would have all "appropriate" power.

But why, we might wonder, did the amendment use a synonym (and etymological cousin) rather than track Article I's sweeping clause verbatim? Most likely because Congress preferred to use the language that the Supreme Court had itself used in construing congressional power broadly. In John Marshall's classic opinion in *McCulloch v. Maryland* (whose lan-

---

*Building on the foundations laid by the Thirteenth Amendment, seven of the fourteen subsequent amendments have featured similarly worded congressional enforcement clauses. See U.S. Const. amends. XIV, XV, XVIII, XIX, XXIII, XXIV, XXVI. Three other post-Reconstruction amendments have conferred new powers on Congress, but in rather different language. See U.S. Const. amends. XVI, XX, XXV.

guage about a "government of the people, . . . by them, . . . and for their benefit" would find its way into Lincoln's Gettysburg Address), the great chief justice had, in a famous passage, construed the necessary-and-proper clause to permit all congressional laws "which are appropriate."[15] *McCulloch* was read in the nineteenth century as providing a generous understanding of congressional power. In the antebellum period, no Court opinion—with the arguable exception of the malodorous Taney opinion in *Dred Scott*—had ever held that a congressional statute flunked *McCulloch*'s deferential test of congressional power. Reconstructors pointed in particular to one case, *Prigg v. Pennsylvania,* where the justices had shown notable deference to Congress in upholding federal power to legislate under the *McCulloch* test of "appropriateness." Republicans relished the irony that this language, which had long been used to support proslavery congressional laws (like the law at issue in *Prigg*) would henceforth authorize a wide assortment of antislavery congressional laws.

In particular, Reconstructors insisted that the Abolition Amendment's "appropriate" clause allowed Congress to legislate not merely against slavery itself, but against all the "badges" and relics of a slave system.[16] In 1866, Congress passed an expansive Civil Rights Act protecting the civil rights of blacks in every state, North and South. The act prohibited race discrimination even in states that had never known slavery, on the theory that such forms of discrimination were vestiges of slavery. Critics objected that Congress lacked authority to intrude so deeply into traditionally state-law issues, and Andrew Johnson vetoed the bill.

On April 9, 1866, Congress overrode, in a dramatic vote that made headlines and indeed made history: Never before had any Congress ever surmounted a president's veto of a major bill. The two-thirds vote in each house on this bill foreshadowed the eventual two-thirds votes on the Fourteenth Amendment later that spring. In fact, as all at the time understood, the linkage between the enacted Civil Rights Act and the proposed Civil Rights Amendment was even tighter than this: One of the main purposes of the amendment was to provide an incontrovertible constitutional foundation for the act, which Johnson and his allies persisted in labeling unconstitutional even after its passage in April.

As most Reconstruction Republicans viewed the matter, since antebellum Congresses had been allowed to promote a slave system, postwar Congresses should have equal latitude to destroy all remnants of that system. Illinois Senator Lyman Trumbull argued that if a narrow view of the Abolition Amendment's "appropriate" clause were to prevail, the trumpet of freedom that we have been blowing throughout the land has given an "uncertain sound," and the promised freedom is a delusion. . . . I have no doubt that under this provision . . . we may destroy all these discriminations in civil rights against the black man. . . . It was for that purpose that the second clause of that amendment was adopted, which says that Congress shall have authority, by appropriate legislation, to carry into effect the article prohibiting slavery. Who is to decide what that appropriate legislation is to be? The Congress . . . [which may] adopt such appropriate legislation as it may think proper.[17]

Whatever we might think of Trumbull's words and Congress's votes in isolation, we must understand that they did not stand alone. In emphatic response to critics who resisted broad congressional legislation under the "appropriate" clause of the Thirteenth Amendment, Congress, as noted, promptly proposed a *Fourteenth* Amendment with its own "appropriate" clause calling for sweeping congressional enforcement. In debates over this proposed Civil Rights Amendment, congressmen repeatedly quoted the language and the deferential approach of *McCulloch* and *Prigg* as exemplifying the spacious view of congressional power they were espousing. An early draft of the Fourteenth in fact copied Article I verbatim: "The *Congress shall have power to make all laws which shall be necessary and proper* to secure to the citizens of each State all privileges and immunities . . . and to all persons in the several States equal protection in the rights of life, liberty, and property."[18] Later, this draft language gave way to revised language of "appropriate" congressional enforcement legislation, plainly patterned on the phraseology used at the end of the sibling Thirteenth Amendment.

And—here is the key point—the American people ratified the Fourteenth Amendment, with evident understanding of the breadth of its, and also the Thirteenth's, language authorizing "appropriate" federal legislation. Knowing full well that Congress believed that this language authorized transformative new federal statutes to uproot all vestiges of unfreedom and inequality—and having seen with their own eyes that Congress had already acted on a similar belief in connection with the Thirteenth Amendment—Americans said yes. We do.

"Amendment"

But exactly who was the "We" who did this deed? And how did We "do" it? Who counted, and who did not—and why—in the very enactment of the Thirteenth and Fourteenth Amendments? Who opposed this transformation, and why?

These are questions close to the heart of Professor Bruce Ackerman's epic work-in-progress, *We the People: Foundations, Transformations, Interpretations*. No serious student of America's Constitution can disregard Ackerman's provocative agenda. To understand the full meaning of Reconstruction, twenty-first-century Americans must come to grips with the acts of amendment alongside the texts of amendment. We must ask not simply *what* the words of the key constitutional clauses meant in the 1860s and mean today, but also *how* these words came to become part of America's supreme law. Nevertheless, we should resist some of the specific answers that Ackerman gives to the important questions that he poses. As he tells the story, the Reconstruction Amendments emerged from a process akin to civil disobedience, with amenders thrusting aside the letter and spirit of Article V. Though Ackerman ultimately proclaims America's Reconstruction to be legitimate, he does so on the basis of his own ingenious theory of permissible constitutional change. This theory, which he mints more than a century after the events in question, repudiates much of what the Reconstruction Republicans claimed to be doing during the amendment process itself—namely, *complying* with Article V as best they could in the uniquely tumultuous and utterly unprecedented circumstances created by the Civil War.

Here are Ackerman's main objections to, quarrels with, and questions concerning the orthodox view that the Reconstruction Amendments in fact emerged from a process generally faithful to Article V's letter and spirit:

1. In December 1865, the very month in which the Thirteenth Amendment came to be ratified, the Reconstruction Congress refused to seat House members and senators purporting to represent the defeated Southern states. Yet these states were, in legal contemplation, part of an indivisible union. After all, such was Lincoln's theory justifying the federal government's forceful resistance to the South's attempted secession. Indeed, the ex-Confederate states were explicitly counted in tallying the various ratifications of the Thirteenth Amendment, which, under the rules of Article V, needed the approval of three-fourths of

the state legislatures. How could ex-Confederate states be both in the union for Article V purposes and out of it for Article I purposes?

2. Congress continued to operate without widespread Southern representation until mid-1868. (Some defeated Southern states did not regain their seats until 1870.) In 1866 a rump Congress proposed the Fourteenth Amendment by a two-thirds vote of each house, but that Article V hurdle would never have been cleared had the eighty excluded Southern members been present. The Senate's exclusions marked a particularly large break with traditional constitutional principles, which had placed each state's right to equal Senate representation in a privileged position, immune even from ordinary Article V amendment.

3. In 1867, the rump Congress enacted legislation purporting to outline the terms under which the defeated states would be readmitted into Congress and allowed to resume internal self-government. In effect, Congress conditioned each state's readmission upon that state's prior ratification of the Fourteenth Amendment. As with the Thirteenth Amendment, this process counted various states for Article V while excluding them from Article I. In fact, the process featured a double standard within Article V itself. If the Southern state assemblies ratifying the Thirteenth and Fourteenth Amendments were valid "legislatures" for Article V purposes, how could the federal assembly excluding these states count as a proper "Congress" for Article V purposes?

4. The combination of congressional carrots and sticks obviously coerced the affected states, tainting the Southern yes votes that emerged from the ratification process. Congress's actions amounted to a "naked violation[] of Article V," which presumed that states would have a truly free choice to say yea or nay to any proposed amendments.

5. The above-noted points are not merely the product of modern constitutional sensibilities. Rather, these and related arguments were voiced loudly by Old Guard critics in the 1860s, especially President Andrew Johnson. Yet the Reconstruction Congress reacted to critics by threatening them with the same aggressive tactics it was using against the defeated states. In particular, the Congress impeached and almost convicted Johnson for his defense of a traditional understanding of the constitutional ground rules, and the legislature took steps to restrict Supreme Court review of Reconstruction laws.[19]

So saith Ackerman. Yet at the end of the day, he deems the irregular process of Reconstruction to be constitutionally legitimate. On his view, although the Reconstruction Republicans "played fast and loose" with the

Founding document and acted in ways that "simply cannot be squared" with the Constitution's text, the amenders nonetheless won the support of the American electorate, albeit in ways wholly outside Article V.[20]

There is, however, another, more orthodox account of the amendment process that better fits the understandings of the amenders themselves, who denied that their actions were "naked violations" of the Constitution, and who never claimed that they were in fact pursuing some non–Article V mode of amendment. On this orthodox view, Reconstruction Republicans plausibly acted within the general Article V framework, even as they repeatedly found themselves obliged to improvise, interpolate, and make commonsensical judgment calls to resolve many difficult legal issues that were arising for the first time in the mid-1860s (and that have never recurred).

LET'S BEGIN WITH the fact that when the Thirty-ninth Congress met for the first time, on December 4, 1865, both the House and Senate refused to seat members from the former rebel states. Even if these refusals plainly violated the Constitution—in fact, they did not, but let's bracket that issue for now—none of this would undermine the legality of the Thirteenth Amendment. Assuming that, as of December 1865, all ex-Confederate states should be counted in the amendment calculus, the United States consisted of thirty-six states, twenty-seven of which would be needed to ratify any amendment under Article V's rule of three-quarters. Even before Congress convened, twenty-five states had ratified the amendment. On December 4 and December 6—the first and third days of the new congressional session—North Carolina and Georgia added their respective assents, thus giving the abolition amendment the needed twenty-seven state ratifications. In what sense were the various state ratification decisions—almost all of which had occurred long before the Thirty-ninth Congress had said a single word or done a single thing—tainted by the seating decisions?

Perhaps it might be said that North Carolina and Georgia ratified only because of the illegal coercion/exclusion that began on December 4. But this is hard to swallow. Congress had said nothing at this point to suggest that a state, merely by ratifying the amendment, would thereby gain admission. In fact, the House and Senate had refused to seat *any* of the ex-rebel states, even the ones (Virginia, Louisiana, Tennessee, Arkansas, South Carolina, and Alabama) that *had* already ratified the Thirteenth. In any event, Oregon and California, both of which were eligible to sit in

Congress from the outset, said yes to the amendment, on December 8 and 19, thus putting it over the top regardless of North Carolina and Georgia.

Nor is there any constitutional embarrassment in the fact that the Confederate states were not generally represented in the Thirty-*eighth* Congress, which proposed the Thirteenth Amendment in a lame-duck session in January 1865, shortly after Lincoln's triumphant reelection. Article I, section 5 provided that a simple majority of each house "shall constitute a Quorum to do Business," including the business of proposing constitutional amendments, even if one or more states chose to boycott or otherwise failed to send properly elected congressmen. Longstanding practice dating back to the Washington Administration confirmed that this section meant what it said. In the First Congress, New York's senators had failed to show up until late July 1789, yet in their absence Congress enacted several statutes, all duly signed into law by Washington. When Congress proposed the Bill of Rights later that year, the union consisted of a different group of states than the ones that later ratified the Bill. (The proposing group excluded, while the ratifying group eventually included, North Carolina, Rhode Island, and Vermont.)

Granted, the Thirteenth Amendment had won only the support of two-thirds of the voting members in each house, as distinct from two-thirds of the total membership, including absent and excluded members. But the same thing was true of the Twelfth Amendment. In proposing and ratifying the Twelfth, each house and several states had explicitly considered and rejected critics' contention that two-thirds of a quorum did not suffice. In fact, in 1789 the Bill of Rights was itself certified only to have received the support of two-thirds of the House members who voted on it, and House records failed to indicate whether it had cleared any higher bar.[21]

Thus far, we have been assuming that after Appomattox, all defeated states should be counted in both the (ratifying-states) numerator and the (total-states) denominator of Article V. But the Thirteenth Amendment would also be valid if we instead treated all eleven state governments in the former Confederacy as having lapsed, and thus not properly included in either numerator or denominator. On this view, only twenty-five true-blue state governments were in fact constitutionally operative in 1865, with nineteen needed to ratify under Article V. Long before December 4, nineteen true-blue states had indeed ratified the abolition amendment. So whichever way we count, the Thirteenth Amendment plainly cleared the Article V bar. As for the Fourteenth Amendment, the necessary nineteen true-blue states said yes as of mid-February 1867.[22]

Although several leading Republicans, including Senator Charles Sumner and Representative John Bingham, endorsed a true-blue-only approach to Article V, this approach was never the official policy of the Reconstruction Congress.[23] But neither did Congress (or individual Republican leaders, for that matter) claim to be nakedly violating Article V or amending the Constitution outside Article V, à la Ackerman.[24] So if forced to choose which aspects of these Amenders' approach to toss overboard in order to save the rest, modern readers could simply adopt a true-blue-only interpretation of Article V. Ackerman claims that anyone who accepts such an account necessarily repudiates Lincoln and the Unionists' general theory of indivisible nationhood, but in fact this claim blurs important legal distinctions.

BEFORE TURNING TO these distinctions, let's try to understand more precisely why the House and Senate refused to seat representatives and senators purporting to speak for the defeated states. One problem was plain to see: *The ex-Confederate elections had excluded all, or virtually all, blacks.*[25] Under the explicit language of Article I, section 5, each congressional house was made "the Judge of the Elections [and] Returns . . . of its own Members." If the state elections from the former Confederacy were constitutionally defective, then Congress had every right to refuse to seat the alleged victors. And if, under the best—or even a plausible—reading of the Article IV republican-government clause, no truly "republican" state circa 1865 had the right to disenfranchise a quarter or more of its adult free male population, then the House and Senate could indeed properly find that the Southern elections were defective.

Old Guard critics charged that Congress was acting in an unprincipled manner when it chose to count ex-Confederate-state yes votes on the Thirteenth Amendment while simultaneously denying that these states had genuine republican governments. But if all-white Southern elections were not truly republican, then of course the victors should not be rewarded with congressional seats. At the same time, it would seem perverse—an affront to common sense and basic fairness—to throw out these all-white governments' yes votes on a pro-black amendment.[26] Had free blacks been allowed to vote in the Southern congressional elections, the results might have been vastly *different:* A diametrically opposed set of candidates might have prevailed. But had free blacks been allowed to vote on the Thirteenth Amendment, they would surely have voted yes. Thus in any state where the whites-only government had already voted yes, the results would have been the *same*. (More precisely, in a fair election counting freedmen, there would have been an even wider margin of support for abolition.)[27] Hence Congress could indeed with a straight face "count these white governments when they said Yes on the Thirteenth Amendment but . . . destroy these governments in 1867 when they said No [to the Fourteenth]."[28]

As an analogy, consider a simple hypothetical in which congressional candidate A has received ten thousand more votes than B, but thirty thousand votes were destroyed before being counted. If the lost votes came from B's hometown and were destroyed by A's political cronies, then Congress might properly refuse to seat A. But if, instead, B's allies had destroyed ballots in A's stronghold, Congress should surely be permitted to let the election stand and to let A sit, since A managed to win even without counting all the additional votes he presumably racked up in his home base. For B's party to insist that the election that they in fact lost must be set aside thanks to their own misconduct would be sheer chutzpah.[29]

Whether or not a court of law or equity in the 1860s could properly have made these sorts of mixed legal-political calculations in deciding a contested election, the Constitution allowed each house to consider commonsense practicalities in judging congressional elections and returns. (A similar blend of law and politics applied when Congress sat judicially in the impeachment process.) Even the nineteenth-century judiciary, in applying the "de facto government" doctrine in various situations, generally rejected an all-or-nothing approach. Rather, courts declared themselves willing to uphold certain actions of a legally imperfect regime—issuances of marriage licenses, recordings of property deeds, and so on—while denying effect to other actions more strongly tainted by the regime's underlying legitimacy deficit.[30]

In fact, the judicial decisions on the books in 1865 lent considerable support to the Reconstruction Congress's approach. The pivotal precedent, ironically enough, was an 1849 Supreme Court opinion authored by slavocrat Roger Taney. The case, *Luther v. Borden,* arose out of a brief civil war in Rhode Island known as Dorr's Rebellion, whose underlying origins lay deep in Rhode Island history. During the American Revolution, when every other state except Connecticut adopted a new constitution, Rhode Islanders continued to operate under a charter of government initially granted by King Charles II in the 1660s. Lacking any explicit provisions for constitutional amendment, the charter failed to channel the passions of later reformers and traditionalists into a constitutional-revision process that both sides could accept. When the issue of constitutional change came to a boil in the early 1840s, each side sought to exploit procedural ambiguities to its own advantage. A political and military struggle ensued as two rival regimes each claimed to be the lawful government of Rhode Island.

In *Luther,* the Court declined to decide for itself which of the two camps deserved federal recognition as the state's proper republican government. That issue, opined Taney, was a political question that Congress should decide by determining which camp's leaders to seat in the House and Senate.

> For as the United States guarantee to each State a republican government, Congress must necessarily decide what government is established in the State before it can determine whether it is republican or not. And when the senators and representatives of a State are admitted into the councils of the Union, the authority of the government under which they are appointed, as well as its republican character, is recognized by the proper constitutional authority. And its decision is binding on every other department of the government.[31]

Quoting *Luther* chapter and verse in the 1860s, Sumner and his congressional allies stood on solid ground in insisting that Congress was entitled under Articles I and IV to "judge" congressional elections in a manner that enforced the Constitution's promise of a "Republican Form of Government." Going one step further, many leading congressmen also argued that Congress could properly choose to count only true-blue governments in Article V's numerator and denominator. Representative John Bingham—a highly respected lawyer from Ohio and the main author of the Fourteenth Amendment's opening section—explicitly invoked *Luther* in support of this view.[32]

Old Guard critics attacked Sumner and Bingham's sweeping conception of Article IV as a violation of the Founders' vision. But much had happened in the nation's first eighty years to give rise to a more robustly egalitarian and nationalistic conception of republican government than had prevailed in the 1780s. For starters, the intervening decades had witnessed a dramatic expansion of suffrage rights, at least among white men. State-law property qualifications, ubiquitous at the Founding, later sank into oblivion as universal free (white) male suffrage swept the land. By 1865, any state that automatically disenfranchised a quarter or more of its freemen—as did each ex-rebel state—was out of the American mainstream in a way that it would not have been in 1787. The question thus became, was the Article IV guarantee of republican government static or dynamic? Did the clause promise only that each American state would not retreat from the baseline set by its own 1787 practices, or should the clause also be read as promising that American states would keep pace with post-Founding reforms so as to remain in democracy's vanguard if the nation surged forward? The simple words of Article IV could be read either way, and certain passages from *The Federalist* seemed to lean toward a static test. Yet the fact that elected congressmen would be vital decision makers under this clause injected an inherently dynamic element into the republican-guarantee process.

Long before 1865, Congress had accustomed itself to judging local republicanism by applying dynamic democratic standards in the course of admitting new Western states. In the 1780s, a group of preexisting states had combined to give birth to the federal government. Over the next eighty years, the federal government itself became a prolific parent, siring new states at a rapid rate. By the outset of the Civil War, nearly two-thirds of the states in the Union were there only because Congress had chosen to admit them after assuring itself that these states met contemporary standards of republicanism. The process of admitting states had also sharpened congressional sensibilities concerning local electoral improprieties and had heightened congressional interest in local suffrage rules. These were the pulsating issues at the heart of the Bleeding Kansas controversy in the late 1850s, a controversy in which local electoral misconduct had touched the national conscience and aroused the Republican Party. Thus both Rhode Island's civil war in the 1840s and Kansas's civil war in the 1850s helped frame Congress's understanding of its own broad powers to judge local republicanism in the aftermath of a far wider civil war in the 1860s.

A long history of slavocratic contempt for core republican freedoms formed yet another factor inclining Sumner, Bingham, and company to a strongly nationalistic and democratic understanding of Article IV. In the decades ramping up to the Civil War, the Deep South's paranoid obsession with protecting its peculiar institution—an institution coming under increasingly sharp criticism in the outside world—spurred countless acts of tyranny and intolerance. The result was an arc of Southern unfreedom spiraling outward. At the spiral's center, slaves of course suffered brutal deprivations of life, liberty, and property. Then came serious repression of free blacks (whose very presence was feared to be a potential incitement to those in bondage); and then, increasingly, repression of whites themselves, both in the South and beyond. Several Southern states made it a crime—in some places, a capital offense—for a free white person to advocate abolition or to condemn slavery in strong language. Pulpits were silenced, presses confiscated, pamphlets burned, and abolitionist mail suppressed.

In the grip of a mind-set and political structure known by its critics as the Slave Power, Southern politicians even tried to silence Northerners. In the 1840s, slavocrats succeeded for a while in imposing gag rules that muzzled congressional free speech and debate over slavery. The Slave Power's assault on congressional free speech took more graphic shape in 1856, when a South Carolina representative, Preston Brooks, bludgeoned Charles Sumner into bloody unconsciousness on the floor of the Senate in reprisal for Sumner's fiercely antislavery speech "The Crime Against Kansas." Brooks was hailed in the South for his savage caning of an unarmed man. Though an overwhelming majority of Northern congressmen voted to expel Brooks, every Southerner save one voted to retain him, thereby causing the expulsion motion to fall short of the necessary two-thirds. Brooks received a second Southern vote of confidence when he resigned mid-session and his constituents returned him to Congress by a roaring margin that left no doubt about where they stood. On the eve of the Civil War, North Carolina went so far as to demand that various Northern congressmen and other Northern leaders be extradited to the Tar Heel State to face felony charges for having endorsed Hinton Helper's provocative antislavery tract *The Impending Crisis*.[33]

By 1860, the Slave Power exemplified all the evils that the original Article IV guarantee of republican government had aimed to avert. Aggressive slavocrats had flouted basic democratic freedoms within their own states, menaced freedom-lovers in neighboring states, and begun to corrupt the character of federal institutions that rested on state-law foundations. A society that criminalized core political expression and that in effect outlawed the Republican Party—recall that Lincoln got zero popular votes south of Virginia in 1860—was not merely un-Republican in a partisan sense but un-republican in a generic sense.

And then came the most un-republican act of all: secession itself. Howsoever distasteful Lincoln's triumph in 1860 may have been to some, his election was wholly lawful. If the Twelfth Amendment's rules had, just this once, advantaged an antislavery candidate, these rules had usually, and by design, done just the opposite; in a sound republic, turnabout was fair play. As Lincoln himself explained on July 4, 1861, republicanism's foundational premise required the losers of a fair election to abide by its results. The root question was "whether a constitutional republic, or a democracy—a government of the people, by the same people—can, or cannot, maintain its territorial integrity, . . . whether discontented individuals, too few in numbers to control administration, according to organic law, . . . [can] break up their Government, and thus practically put an end to free government upon the earth. . . . When ballots have fairly, and constitutionally, decided, there can be no successful appeal, back to bullets; . . . there can be no successful appeal, except to ballots themselves, at succeeding elections."[34]

This, then, was the backdrop against which the 1865 House and Senate declined to readmit Southerners until Congress could confidently assure itself that the new South would abide by the basic ground rules of republican government—as the old South had not. A central plank of Reconstruction policy as it eventually came to be hammered out in the Thirty-ninth Congress was that Southern governments would need to be based on a broad popular foundation that included free black voters alongside free whites. By voting in large numbers, Southern blacks would both embody the republican ideal of broad-based popular government and also prevent the revival of various unrepublican practices and tyrannical policies.[35]

Old Guard Democrats cried foul. The Southern elections in 1865 had generally followed the state election laws on the books in 1860. Since all Southern states in 1860 had been republics in good standing, eligible to be seated in Congress, Democrats argued that the new Southern states likewise deserved seats. Republicans countered that the act of secession itself and the unlawful war that the rebel states had waged against a duly elected Union government justified the Union's demands for new safeguards in rebel regions.[36] Also, Republicans argued that excluding *slaves* from the franchise in 1860 was one thing, but disenfranchising *free men* in 1865—many of whom had in fact fought for the Union Army—was something altogether different.[37]

Ackerman finds it "odd to suggest that the South had rendered itself un-republican by freeing the slaves."[38] Contrary to the tilt of this sentence, "the South . . . itself" did not of its own accord "free[] the slaves." Freedom came to the South thanks largely to Northern and national voices, arms, and votes[39]—Lincoln's Emancipation Proclamation, the Union Army's triumphs, the (Union) elections of 1862 and 1864, black self-help (in both North and South), and the Thirteenth Amendment itself, proposed in a true-blue Congress and ratified by an overwhelming majority of Northern states long before most Southern governments finally agreed to say yes (sometimes under pressure). Given that *the nation* had been instrumental in freeing the slaves, it was hardly odd to think that the nation also had to follow through by guaranteeing freedmen their proper place in a genuinely republican government.

But let's assume that each ex-Confederate all-white state government had freed its slaves by itself and solely out of the goodness of its heart. Once having done so, no state could properly stop there and deny freedmen the franchise. By analogy, consider the issue of immigration. A genuine republic need not allow the entire planet, filled with aliens living oceans away, to vote in its own domestic elections. Nor does a true republic need to allow massive immigration and naturalization. But if a republic does choose to admit and naturalize vast numbers of foreigners, it cannot allow them to remain permanently disenfranchised after they have become equal citizens. Or at least it cannot do so and continue to call itself a republic.

The Old Guard also accused congressional Republicans of hypocrisy. In 1865, only a handful of Northern states allowed blacks to vote. If the South had to enfranchise its blacks, why didn't the North? The most persuasive response from leading Republican congressmen was that in the South, but not the North, blacks amounted to a large slice of the free population. While accounting for 2 percent or less of the total population of most Northern states, free blacks constituted an outright majority in two Southern states (South Carolina and Mississippi), almost half in four others (Louisiana, Alabama, Georgia, and Florida), and more than a quarter in the remaining five ex-Confederate states (Virginia, North Carolina, Texas, Arkansas, and Tennessee). Northern voting restrictions, though illiberal and deeply regrettable to leading Reconstructionists, were not actionably unrepublican because the vast majority of Northern free males could in fact vote. Southern whites-only rules, by contrast, offended the basic republican ideal of a government that derived its power from the great mass of its citizens.[40]

As Sumner explained in an elaborate Senate speech in February 1866, the "denial of justice to the colored citizens in Connecticut and New York is wrong and mean; but it is on so small a scale that it is not perilous to the Republic." By contrast, Southern rules disenfranchised a "mighty mass," as Sumner proved by detailed recitation of the black and white population figures in Southern states. "Begin with Tennessee, which disenfranchises 283,079 citizens, being more than a quarter of its whole 'people'—Thus violating a distinctive principle of republican government. . . . But Tennessee is the least offensive on the list." At the other end of the Southern spectrum lay "South Carolina, which disfranchises 412,408 citizens, being nearly two-thirds of its whole 'people.' A Republic is a pyramid standing on the broad mass of the people as a base; but here is a pyramid balanced on its point. To call such a government 'republican' is a mockery of sense and decency. . . . It is not difficult to classify these States. They are aristocracies or oligarchies." Sumner added that had blacks been able to vote in 1860–61, "the acts of secession must have failed. Treason would have been voted down."[41]

Sumner had floated similar ideas on the very first day of the Thirty-ninth Congress, and analogous views would resound through the Capitol chambers over the ensuing months and years. For instance, Oregon Senator George H. Williams argued that American "history does not produce a case where one half, or a majority, or even one third of the free male citizens of a State have been excluded from all political power under a republican form of government."[42] In the House debates, Thomas Eliot denied that a republican government could ever disenfranchise "large classes of men" and "large masses of citizens," and Ralph Buckland declared that a state regime propped up by "a mere fraction of the people" was "contrary to the fundamental principles of republican government." Pennsylvania's John Broomall wondered how a government like South Carolina's could "be considered republican in form when four out of every seven adult males are denied the right of suffrage." Noting "with some sense of humiliation" the racial exclusions in his own state's laws, Broomall went on to point out that "but one in sixty is there excluded from participation" and that "easy consciences" might find solace in the "de minimus" nature of this Northern disenfranchisement.[43]

Though modern critics might be tempted to dismiss this self-serving Republican defense,[44] it drew strength from both Founding-era definitions of republicanism and contemporary realities. Southern black disenfranchisements in 1865 threatened to skew political power dramatically, both within Congress and within individual state legislatures. Reconstruction Republicans understood that the small numbers of free blacks in the North exerted little effect on either the overall apportionment of most Northern state legislatures or the apportionment of these states' congressional delegations. The situation was vastly different in the South, where several antebellum state constitutions had counted slaves at three-fifths or more for purposes of state legislative apportionment. Once the "mighty mass" of Southern blacks became free, unless they were also enfranchised, the white voters in black plantation belts might have even *more* voting power than before. In some ex-Confederate state legislatures, the old three-fifths bonus for disenfranchised slaves threatened to become a five-fifths bonus for disenfranchised freemen. In other Southern state legislatures, the system might warp even more dramatically, from zero-fifths to five-fifths. Not only would this massive and unevenly distributed body of non-voting freemen tilt future congressional elections even further toward the South, but *within* each Southern state the uneven distribution might well give revanchist districts far more federal and state seats than ever before, even though the white voters in such districts could hardly be trusted to virtually represent the interests of disenfranchised blacks.[45]

In response to Reconstruction Republicans' quantitative arguments, some Northern Democrats played a quantitative card of their own: If a republic required enfranchisement of the great mass of citizens, what about women?[46] Most of these critics did not sincerely advocate woman suffrage, but used the issue to prick the pretensions of their adversaries. If the republican-government principle required black suffrage in the South, taunted Pennsylvania Representative Benjamin Boyer, "then women should vote, for the same reason; and the New England States themselves are only *pretended* republics, because their women, who are in a considerable majority, are denied the right of suffrage."[47]

Republicans had an army of counterarguments at their disposal. Women as a rule had not voted at the Founding; nor did they vote in any state, North or South, East or West, in 1865.[48] Thus under either a static or a dynamic approach to Article IV, the actual practice of American government lent little support to any notion that the clause required woman suffrage. Instead, the basic principles of republican government would be met by broadly enfranchising men, who could in turn be relied on to virtually represent the interests of the women in their lives—their mothers, sisters, wives, and daughters. By contrast, Southern whites could not be trusted to represent the interests of those whom they had so recently and ruthlessly enslaved.[49] Within each state, the relatively even distribution of women across different districts also meant that male-only suffrage introduced no systemic skew into the process of state apportionment. Here, too, sex differed from race.[50] Moreover, certain political responsibilities properly accompanied the possession of political rights. Free men, black and white, had in the past been, and could in the future be, obliged to bear arms for the common defense. Women, by contrast, did not bear arms in the military and thus had a lesser claim on the franchise.[51]

IT REMAINS TO CONSIDER the Old Guard's objections to congressional demands that Southern states ratify the Fourteenth Amendment as a condition of reentry, and to examine whether Congress's treatment of the former Confederacy squared with Lincoln's theory of an indivisible union. Had Congress tried to extort Southern ratification of a proposed amendment wholly unrelated to Southern unrepublicanism, then we might indeed properly wonder whether Congress had abused its powers. (Imagine, say, a Congress that demanded Southern states agree to a tariff amendment aimed at benefiting Northern mercantile interests.) But in fact, the ratification conditions that Congress imposed were highly germane to the problem at hand—namely, Southern unrepublicanism—precisely because the amendment itself revolved in tight orbit around core principles of republican government.

For example, the Fourteenth's opening section served to protect fundamental "privileges" and "immunities"—especially freedom of speech, press, petition, and assembly—against future state abridgment. This section served to codify some of the specifics of republican government, offering a more detailed recipe for future state compliance with American-style republicanism.[52] State compliance with these safeguards would help prevent future acts of unrepublicanism ranging from censorship to armed insurrection. Also, the amendment's section 2 restructured congressional apportionment so as to induce states to practice a maximally inclusive republicanism (at least among men): Each and every state disenfranchisement of a free male citizen would reduce a state's clout in Congress.[53]

Finally, the very willingness of a given ex-Confederate state to ratify the amendment would itself credibly signal that the state had rejoined the republican ranks and sincerely renounced its earlier offenses against the republican ideal (including secession itself). Such a credible commitment was necessary to prove Southern good faith to a justifiably skeptical nation.[54] A mere promise in a state constitution—even a promise that blacks would henceforth be allowed to vote—could be repealed in a subsequent state amendment (whereas no state could unilaterally amend a *federal* constitutional provision).[55] Suspicion of the South's good faith ran especially high in the mid-1860s because a large percentage of Southern leaders had in fact treasonably betrayed their antebellum Article VI oaths to uphold the federal Constitution. In the first round of postbellum congressional elections, the supposedly "new" South had tried to send to the Capitol many of its old oath-breaking leaders and other prominent (former?) secessionists—four Confederate generals, four colonels, several Confederate congressmen and members of Confederate state legislatures, and even the vice president of the Confederacy, Alexander H. Stephens.[56] Troubling reports also began to pour into Congress concerning a host of abusive Southern actions all too reminiscent of prewar Slave Power misconduct: terrorism against blacks, violence targeted at white Unionists, voting fraud, and new laws ("Black Codes") aimed at reducing freedmen to virtual peonage.

True, the Fourteenth Amendment contained some provisions that ranged beyond a mere elaboration and implementation of Article IV republicanism. But more than three-quarters of true-blue states—states that had played by republican rules and had not taken up arms against a duly elected Union government—had freely ratified this amendment, which imposed equally stringent limits on all states, whether Northern or Southern. Congress was thus not trying to leverage its control over Southern states to validate an amendment that had failed to win overwhelming support among the states that were in fact republican.[57]

Which brings us at last to the question, why didn't Congress simply adopt a true-blue-only view of Article V? In February 1865, Congress resolved to count electoral votes only from the twenty-five true-blue states, expressly excluding the eleven rebel states from both the numerator (electoral votes cast for each candidate) and denominator (total electors lawfully appointed) of the Twelfth Amendment as applied to the presidential election of November 1864. Several of these eleven states—especially Louisiana, Arkansas, and Tennessee—were already well into the process of Reconstruction, and the new Louisiana and Tennessee governments had in fact purported to appoint presidential electors. Yet Congress refused to count any such returns.[58] If a true-blue-only approach properly applied in late 1864 and early 1865, why not later in 1865? Why not in 1866 and 1867? Indeed, why not as long as the ex-Confederate states failed to bring themselves into compliance with the standards of republican government, as judged by Congress in its seating decisions? If a true-blue-only approach properly applied to a presidential election—the very election whose ringing endorsement of Lincoln prompted Congress to propose the Thirteenth Amendment—why shouldn't the same approach apply to Article V ratification of that amendment?

Lincoln himself, shortly before his fateful evening at Ford's Theater, cautioned that "such a ratification would be questionable, and sure to be persistently questioned; while a ratification by three fourths of all the States would be unquestioned and unquestionable." Yet Lincoln also said in the same speech—his last public address—that "I do not commit myself against" a true-blue-only view of Article V.[59]

Why not? Ackerman claims that to rely on a true-blue-only tally would be to concede that the South was legally out of the Union—to embrace "secessionist" logic and thus repudiate Lincoln's theory of indivisible

Union.[60] If Ackerman is right, it would appear that Lincoln, by hedging in his final speech, misunderstood the meaning of his own theory of indivisibility. This seems unlikely. Perhaps there is a better way of understanding Lincoln's vision and that of his fellow Unionists?

Let's recall Lincoln's repeated emphasis on the *geographic* contours of the Union, and on its *"territorial"* integrity."[61] On a geostrategic view of the matter, neither a state government nor a state electorate could unilaterally remove the state's lands and waters from the Union; but a state government might nevertheless lapse into an unrepublican condition as a result of a coup d'état, an inadequate electoral base, a string of stolen elections, or any number of other problems. In such a case, Article IV would empower—indeed, oblige—the central government to restore republican government to the lapsed state, but until that restoration was complete, the Union might properly opt to administer the state as a de facto federal territory—fully *within* an indivisible Union but *without* a proper republican state government.[62] In effect, the postwar Congress could treat the South much as the prewar Congress had treated the West.

Ackerman describes the true-blue-only approach as if it proposed to deal with the South by brute force—as a "conquered province."[63] But this description blurs critical legal distinctions. In endorsing a true-blue-only approach, men such as Sumner and Bingham never denied the citizenship of all Americans, Southern as well as Northern, whether in operational states, lapsed states, de jure territories, or the national seat. Nor did these men advocate redrawing state boundaries at will or keeping Southern states out of Congress any longer than was necessary to guarantee republicanism. Rather, these true-blue congressmen proposed to nurse the South back into republican health, much as predecessor Congresses had weaned young territories into proper states to be thereafter admitted on equal footing. Such an approach was less a repudiation of Lincoln's vision of Union than an embodiment and sensitive adaptation of that vision—an exemplification of Lincoln's view, doubtless shaped by his own boyhood in the territory-turned-state of Indiana, that the Union had "in fact . . . created" the states.[64]

For all his questionable assertions, Ackerman nevertheless performs a mighty service in drawing our attention to three striking and interrelated aspects of the amendment process in the 1860s. First, the version of Article V on display in the 1860s was dramatically more nationalist than had been foreseen in the 1780s. Second, the ordinary rules of amendment were applied in an extraordinary way as a result of the constitutional crisis brought about by secession and emancipation. Third, Reconstruction pivoted on a remarkable reinterpretation of the Article IV republican-guarantee clause. The Constitution's sleeping giant had awakened.[65]

ANOTHER SLUMBERING GIANT that arose during the Civil War amendment process was the Union Army itself. For without that army's battlefield victories, Lincoln's Emancipation Proclamation would never have issued, nor would it have had any practical bite. Without the strong electoral support that Lincoln received from the troops, he might never have won reelection in 1864. Without federal soldiers in place to maintain order in the defeated Confederacy and to administer and monitor new Southern elections in compliance with congressional Reconstruction legislation, the Fourteenth Amendment could not have been ratified as it was. And without blacks' massive participation in the Union Army, it is doubtful whether the Fifteenth Amendment—extending the vote to a class of men who had nobly borne arms for their country—would ever have come to pass in this era.

Though nothing in the text of the Reconstruction Amendments explicitly purported to modify the Founders' intricate rules concerning armies and militias—rules that plainly disfavored central armies and glorified local militias—the very process of amendment gave birth to a new constitutional narrative.[66] If local Minutemen had played starring roles in the Founding story, the national army's boys in blue were the heroes of the new con-Founding story. Liberty would no longer be automatically associated with localism, as it had been for the generation of Americans who lived through the Revolutionary War. The antebellum, Civil War, and early Reconstruction experiences had proved that various states could be just as tyrannical as many Americans at the Founding had feared the federal government might be. These recent events had also shown that the central government—aided by a national army of both volunteers and draftees—could at times be freedom's best friend.

"born . . . citizens"

The Fourteenth Amendment's text began by repudiating the racialist vision of American identity that had animated Chief Justice Taney's infamous *Dred Scott* decision. Taney's 1857 opinion had proclaimed that a black man—even if born free in a state that treated him as a full and equal citizen—could never claim rights of citizenship under the *federal* Constitution. In 1862, Lincoln's attorney general opined that free blacks as a rule were federal citizens, despite Taney's words.[67] The Civil Rights Act of 1866 took aim at *Dred Scott* even more directly by legislating the principle of birthright citizenship: "All persons born in the United States and not subject to any foreign power, excluding Indians not taxed, are hereby declared to be citizens of the United States."[68] Two months later, Congress opened its proposed Fourteenth Amendment with similar anti-Taney language: "All persons born or naturalized in the United States and subject to the jurisdiction thereof, are citizens of the United States and of the State wherein they reside."

The amendment aimed to provide an unimpeachable legal foundation for the earlier statute, making clear that everyone born under the American flag—black or white, rich or poor, male or female, Jew or Gentile—was a free and equal citizen. As with the statute, the amendment did not encompass persons born on American soil who owed allegiance to some other jurisdiction—for instance, children of foreign diplomats or of tribal Indians. The amendment also made clear that non-native, naturalized Americans were entitled to claim the privileges of citizenship. This point could be teased out of other federal statutes and had thus been unnecessary to state in the 1866 Act, but it was worth reiterating in the amendment, lest any negative implication arise in this, the first explicit *constitutional* definition of American citizenship. Perhaps most important, the amendment clarified that to be an American citizen meant having rights not just against the federal government but also against one's home state.

These words codified a profound nationalization of American identity. Lacking any explicit definition of American citizenship, the Founders' Constitution was widely read in the antebellum era as making national citizenship derivative of state citizenship, except in cases involving the naturalization of immigrants and the regulation of federal territories. The Fourteenth Amendment made clear that all Americans were in fact citizens of the nation first and foremost, with a status and set of birthrights explicitly affirmed in a national Constitution. Henceforth the nation would not only define national citizenship, but state citizenship as well. Even for persons born on its own soil, a state would no longer enjoy carte blanche to designate some (that is, whites) as "citizens" and to treat others (free blacks) as lesser "inhabitants." Likewise, no state could henceforth bar any American citizen from choosing to become a state citizen—a point only implicit (at best) in the Founders' text. Article IV had obliged South Carolina to treat a Massachusetts *visitor* with a certain respect but had not stated explicitly that a Massachusetts man had an absolute right to *become* a South Carolinian, whatever other South Carolinians might think.

Many first-year law students are told, and today's Supreme Court is fond of reiterating, that the Fourteenth Amendment's key words targeted only the actions of state government. Though this claim may be true of the amendment's second sentence ("No State shall . . ."), it is plainly false as an account of the amendment's first sentence, which entitled citizens to rights against both state and federal officials. In tandem with the amendment's final sentence, these opening words also empowered Congress to dismantle various nongovernmental structures of inequality that threatened the amendment's vision of equal citizenship.

Though the word "equal" did not explicitly appear in the Fourteenth Amendment's first sentence, the concept was strongly implicit. All persons born under the flag were citizens, and thus *equal* citizens. The companion Civil Rights Act had spoken of the right of all citizens to enjoy "full and equal" civil rights, and a later Supreme Court case glossed the citizenship clause as follows: "All citizens are equal before the law."[69] Read alongside Article I's prohibitions on both state and federal titles of nobility, the citizenship clause thus proclaimed an ideal of republican equality binding on state and federal governments alike. Congress, if it chose, could go even further by enforcing the vision of equal citizenship against a host of unequal social structures and institutions. Taney's backdrop *Dred Scott* opinion had located citizenship in a broad context of social meaning and practice above and beyond state action. Blacks, said Taney in notorious language, could not be citizens because they were regarded by the white race—and not merely by white governments—as "beings of an inferior order, and altogether unfit to associate with the white race," with "no rights which the white man is bound to respect."[70]

Thus, when the Fourteenth Amendment overturned Taney, it did so with words suggesting that Congress could use its sweeping *McCulloch*-like enforcement power to enact statutes affirming that blacks were in fact and in law equal citizens worthy of respect and dignity. Such statutes could not compel whites to invite blacks to their dinner parties; such truly private consensual relations lay outside the ambit of equal citizenship. Suffrage rights also lay outside the domain of mere citizenship. For example, white women and children had long been viewed as equal citizens, but this fact did not thereby entitle them to vote. Black citizenship, as conceptualized by the Civil Rights Act and the Civil Rights Amendment, meant full and equal "civil" rights as distinct from "political" rights. But in enforcing the letter and spirit of the citizenship clause, Congress could indeed properly end widespread nongovernmental systems of exclusion in places such as hotels, theaters, trains, and steamships. Congress could also seek to protect blacks from racially motivated violence and thereby make plain that blacks did have rights that white men were bound to respect.

During the Reconstruction era, Congress enacted several statutes to this effect, some of which were struck down by a Supreme Court ill disposed to construe expansively the constitutional sentence that had been introduced to chastise the Court itself. The first Justice John Marshall Harlan (not to be confused with his Eisenhower-era grandson) dissented in the most important set of these stingy Reconstruction decisions, the 1883 *Civil Rights Cases,* as he would later dissent in *Plessy v. Ferguson.* In 1883, Harlan stressed the "distinctly affirmative character" of the citizenship clause and argued that postwar Congresses should have at least as much authority to protect blacks as prewar Congresses had enjoyed to harm them.[71]

Thirteen years later, Harlan explained in *Plessy* that the Constitution forbade government from creating a pervasive racial caste system. As Harlan saw it, any law whose preamble explicitly proclaimed blacks to be second-class citizens would plainly violate the Fourteenth Amendment, and the emerging system of racial apartheid known as Jim Crow broadcast precisely this unconstitutional message by its very operation. In purpose, in effect, and in social meaning, Jim Crow stretched its tentacles out to keep blacks down. Its whole point was to privilege whites and degrade blacks, in direct defiance of the Fourteenth Amendment's promise of equal citizenship. Though Jim Crow slyly claimed to provide formal, symmetric equality ("separate but equal"), in reality it delivered substantive inequality that made its regime practically indistinguishable from the postwar Southern Black Codes—the very set of laws that the amendment had undeniably aimed to abolish. Though Justice Harlan saw all this in 1896, his brethren did not. Not until the middle of the twentieth century would Court majorities embrace Harlan's vision, quietly at first and then with increasing confidence and emphasis.

EVEN AS THE CITIZENSHIP CLAUSE and the rest of the Fourteenth Amendment plainly took aim at the Black Codes, these words also targeted other—nonracial—forms of discrimination. Whereas the Fifteenth Amendment would later use the language "race, color, or previous condition of servitude" to extend suffrage to black men, the Fourteenth spoke more abstractly of all "citizens" entitled to various "privileges [and] immunities" and of all "persons" with a right to "due process" and "equal protection." At this level of abstraction, the amendment seemed to repudiate a multitude of inequalities beyond Black Codes and race laws.

But how to define this range? From one perspective it might be said that virtually all laws discriminate, treating some persons differently from others. Thus, most criminal codes treat arsonists differently from burglars and both differently from non-felons; tax codes often draw lines between homeowners and renters, between wage earners and dividend recipients, and so on. What makes ordinary tax codes qualitatively different from the Black Codes? Conversely, what sorts of nonracial laws might be more like the Black Codes than the tax codes?

Modern judges have wrestled with these issues by fixing their gaze on the phrase "equal protection" in the Fourteenth Amendment's over-worked second sentence. Yet perhaps additional guidance may be found in the overlooked first sentence, and in particular in its key word: "born." The amendment's text summoned up a provocative vision of birthright citizenship: Government could properly regulate its citizens' behavior—their conduct and choices—but should never degrade or penalize a citizen or treat that citizen as globally inferior to others simply because of his or her low birth status. The Black Codes, which subordinated certain people simply because they were born with dark skin, defined the paradigm case of impermissible legislation, but the grand idea that humans were born free and equal opened itself to broader interpretations—some plainly invited by Reconstruction Republicans, others less clearly foreseen yet nonetheless textually permissible. Laws that stigmatized those born out of wedlock, or that discriminated against American-born children of immigrants, or that doled out extra inheritance rights to firstborn children, or that heaped disabilities on anyone born a Jew or born female, or that gave special privileges to scions of the wealthy—all such legislation could plausibly be seen as violative of the equal-birth principle.[72]

The notion that all persons are born/created equal was hardly a new idea in 1866. Lincoln had insisted that this was *the* core idea of the Declaration of Independence, whose main draftsman himself had worked to overturn Virginia's primogeniture laws during the Revolution. In a farewell message penned fifty years after the Declaration, Jefferson had also famously reminded his countrymen that "the mass of mankind has not been born with saddles on their backs, nor a favored few booted and spurred, ready to ride them legitimately, by the grace of God."[73] Though the slaveholding Jefferson had not in life practiced what he preached on his deathbed, other Founding-era texts offered sturdier, less ironic foundations upon which Reconstruction Republicans could build. As of 1792, six states had outlawed or moved toward outlawing slavery, and in turn four of these six had enacted a Revolutionary-era state constitution. Every one of these four—and interestingly enough, only these four—featured a clause affirming that "all men" were "born" "equal."[74]

Whereas the Founding text used the word "men" in describing the principle of birthright equality, its Reconstruction descendant did not—and for good reason. Far more than is generally recognized today, the framers of the Reconstruction Amendments focused not merely on the race issue but also on intersecting issues of gender. Urgent questions of status and inequality topped the political agenda in the 1860s in a way that they had not in the 1780s. Once these issues had risen to the surface, conversations about race and sex intertwined in complex and fascinating ways. The justices debating the question of black citizenship in *Dred Scott* had found themselves obliged to ponder female citizenship; the framers of the Thirteenth Amendment had plainly understood that females were half the population seeking emancipation; and, as we have already begun to glimpse and shall soon see in more detail, women were central political actors in, and subjects of, the great drama surrounding the enactment of the Fourteenth and Fifteenth Amendments.

"No State shall"

Nowadays, the Fourteenth Amendment's second sentence ("No State shall . . .") is the handiest constitutional tool in the judicial kit bag, a constitutional provision deployed in court more often than any other—more often, perhaps, than all others combined. As a formal matter, this single sentence has come into play in most of the major constitutional cases decided by the modern Supreme Court. In its entirety, the sentence reads as follows: "No State shall make or enforce any law which shall abridge the privileges or immunities of citizens of the United States; nor shall any State deprive any person of life, liberty, or property, without due process of law; nor deny to any person within its jurisdiction the equal protection of the laws."

Today's Court construes these words to safeguard a vast array of rights against states—both substantive rights (like freedom of religion and expression) and procedural rights (such as a criminal defendant's entitlements to appointed counsel and trial by jury); both rights enumerated elsewhere in the Constitution (especially in the Bill of Rights) and unenumerated rights (most important, rights of privacy and sexual freedom); both political rights (paradigmatically the rights to vote, hold office, and serve on juries) and nonpolitical civil rights (including rights of minors, aliens, and other nonvoters). All of which should lead us to ask whether this sentence's text and enactment history in fact support this extraordinary judicial outpouring.*

Let's begin with what lawyers call the "incorporation" doctrine: the firmly settled judicial principle that the Fourteenth Amendment should be construed to "incorporate"—to apply—almost all of the provisions of the Bill of Rights against states. As we have seen, the First Congress designed the Bill of Rights in 1789 to rein in the *federal* government. This Bill safeguarded freedom of religion and expression, the right to keep and bear arms, entitlements to grand and petit juries, and so on, against violation by federal officials, but did not expressly guarantee any of these rights and freedoms against state officials. The First Amendment explicitly spoke of limiting "Congress," while the rest of the Bill was understood in the 1790s as a constraint on federal officials. For instance, when the Fifth Amendment said that "no person shall be . . . deprived of life, liberty, or property, without due process of law," the clear meaning to contemporaries was that no person could be so deprived *by the federal government*.

Of course, James Madison had sought to add to this catalogue a list of rights that "no state shall" abridge, but his pet amendment to this effect, which passed the House as its proposed "Art. XIV," did not clear the Senate. The incorporation doctrine reads Congressman Bingham's Fourteenth Amendment to do almost precisely what Congressman Madison tried and failed to do with his proto–Fourteenth Amendment. Indeed, Bingham went beyond Madison in a way that Madison himself would have envied. Madison's unsuccessful plan had said only that "no state shall infringe the right of trial by jury in criminal cases, nor the rights of conscience, nor the freedom of speech, or of the press." Bingham's successful plan said that "no State shall . . . abridge" a wide range of "privileges" and "immunities"—encompassing not merely the privileges mentioned by Madison's prototype but all fundamental civil rights and freedoms declared in the Bill of Rights and in other canonical legal sources.[75]

In ordinary nineteenth-century language, the various civil rights and freedoms mentioned in the Bill of Rights were indeed quintessential "privileges" and "immunities" of Americans. In fact, Bingham borrowed directly from the Bill itself with his language "No . . . shall . . . make . . . law . . . abridg[ing]"—all words lifted directly from the First Amendment.

---

*For much more discussion and documentation of the ideas summarized over the next several pages, the interested reader may wish to consult my earlier book *The Bill of Rights: Creation and Reconstruction,* especially Chapters 7–12.

Here the very text of the Fourteenth Amendment pointed the careful reader to its tight interlinkage with the Bill of Rights. Bingham's specific phraseology made special sense to his 1860s audience, because the most widely read (if also reviled) judicial opinion of the era was Taney's *Dred Scott,* which had explicitly described the Bill of Rights as "rights and privileges of the citizen." Elsewhere in the opinion, Taney referred to "liberty of speech," the right "to hold public meetings upon political affairs," and the freedom to "keep and carry arms" as core "privileges and immunities of citizens."[76] Though Bingham and his fellow Republicans emphatically rejected Taney's definition of *who* was a citizen, they largely agreed with Taney about *what* citizenship meant: American citizenship entitled a person to a broad set of "privileges and immunities" exemplified by the Bill of Rights. Henceforth, Bingham and others explained, no state would be allowed to abridge these fundamental freedoms.

Antebellum judicial case law had (properly) held that the Founders' Bill did not apply against states. Bingham was thus proposing an important change, as he explained in a series of prominent speeches in the House. Bingham repeatedly pointed his audience to the leading Supreme Court opinion, *Barron v. Baltimore,* authored by Chief Justice Marshall in 1833.[77] *Barron* said that if the First Congress had meant to apply the Bill of Rights to states, Congress would have used explicit words to that effect, just as the Philadelphia framers had used explicit words in Article I, section 10 when they imposed various limits on state governments. Taking his cue from *Barron,* Bingham decided to use the very Simon-Says language the *Barron* Court had called for; thus, his proposal borrowed the words "No State shall" verbatim from Article I, section 10.

Bingham's public explanations of his proposed amendment repeatedly linked the phrase "privileges or immunities of citizens" to "the bill of rights." The latter phrase appeared more than a dozen times in one key 1866 speech and six times in a later speech.[78] *The New York Times* summarized Bingham's amendment as "a proposition to arm the Congress . . . with the power to enforce the Bill of Rights," and Bingham himself published his key speech in a popular pamphlet whose title said it all: "One Country, One Constitution, and One People: Speech of the Hon. John A. Bingham of Ohio, in the House of Representatives, February 28, 1866, *In support of the proposed amendment to enforce the Bill of Rights.*"[79]

Other Reconstruction leaders echoed Bingham. For example, Senator Jacob Howard, speaking on behalf of the amendment's sponsors in a speech delivered before a packed gallery, reported that "privileges or immunities of citizens" encompassed "the personal rights guaranteed and secured by the first eight amendments of the Constitution." Howard then listed these rights one by one—"freedom of speech and of the press," "the right to keep and to bear arms," "the right to be tried by an impartial jury," and so on—and explained that "the course of decision of our courts and the present settled doctrine is, that all these immunities, privileges, rights . . . do not operate in the slightest degree as a restraint or prohibition upon State legislation. . . . The great object of the first section of this amendment is, therefore, to restrain the power of the States and compel them at all times to respect these great fundamental guarantees."[80] Both *The New York Times* and the *New York Herald* (the nation's bestselling newspaper in 1866) gave Howard's explanation front-page coverage and reprinted in full his Bill of Rights discussion.

Other leading Reconstruction Republicans sang from the same hymnal, and several elaborated the particular need to hold states to the specific guarantees in the federal Bill. The Slave Power had been able to prevail in antebellum America precisely because it had been allowed to trample basic rights such as free expression, freedom of worship, and due process. In their first national campaign, in 1856, Republicans had highlighted these outrages in a memorable slogan that told voters just what Republicans stood for: "Free Speech, Free Press, Free Men, Free Labor, Free Territory, and Fremont."

But why, we might wonder, did the Fourteenth Amendment's second sentence append a due-process clause to its earlier language requiring states to honor "the privileges or immunities of citizens"? If the privileges-or-immunities clause encompassed the various rights enumerated in the first eight amendments, those rights surely included the right to due process, which appeared explicitly in the Fifth Amendment. Wasn't the Fourteenth Amendment's inclusion of its own due-process clause weirdly redundant? In a word, no. As Bingham and Howard both explained,[81] the privileges-or-immunities clause would protect only *citizens* from oppressive state action. A separate due-process clause was thus needed to make clear that all "persons"—even aliens—were entitled to basic rights of procedural fairness. The citizen/person distinction took on particular significance because Taney's *Dred Scott* opinion had insisted that the federal Bill of Rights protected only "citizens" and that free blacks, as noncitizens, had no rights under the Bill. (This insistence explained why Taney could so quickly brush aside the due-process claims of free blacks threatened by the rigged procedures of the Fugitive Slave Act of 1850.) In making clear that even noncitizens had certain procedural rights that states (and by implication, the federal government) had to respect, the Fourteenth Amendment's second sentence continued the anti-Taney theme that plainly animated its first sentence.

Despite the wealth of textual, structural, and historical evidence supporting the incorporation doctrine, skeptics have raised important questions about the peculiar manner in which the Court eventually came to apply the Bill of Rights to the states—a judicial process that did not begin in earnest until the mid-twentieth century. What took the justices so long to see the light? And instead of emphasizing the clean textual argument that "privileges or immunities of citizens" encompassed the federal Bill in both ordinary language and case law circa 1866, the modern Court has used the Fourteenth Amendment's due-process clause as the vehicle for incorporation. Where various procedural rights are at issue—confrontation, compulsory process, counsel, and so on—the "due process" language is surely spacious enough to do the work. But how does a clause about *procedural* rights incorporate *substantive* freedoms such as freedom of expression and religion? The Court's odd answer—its doctrine of "substantive due process"—not only verges on oxymoron, but also perversely builds on *Dred Scott* itself, the Court's first effort to inject strong substantive content (there, the right to hold slaves) into the words "due process." To make matters worse, the Court has never satisfactorily explained why it has (thus far) declined to incorporate three provisions of the federal Bill—the right to keep arms, the right to be indicted by a grand jury, and the right to demand a civil jury in common-law cases.

But none of the skeptics' objections is a good argument against incorporation per se, as distinct from the particular manner in which the Court has effected and explained its doctrine. The best objection to the very idea of incorporation is thus this: If the Fourteenth Amendment meant to incorporate the first eight (or ten) amendments against the states, surely it could have expressed this purpose in more direct language.[82]

What this objection misses is that the Fourteenth Amendment aimed to incorporate various rights and freedoms in the Bill of Rights in a subtle way that meant both *more* and *less* than the first set of amendments as originally understood. Although "privileges or immunities" of citizens paradigmatically included the rights and freedoms in the federal Bill, these were not the *only* fundamental rights that henceforth no state could abridge. Other rights declared elsewhere in the Constitution—for example the "privilege" of habeas corpus protected against the federal government in Article I, section 9—defined additional core privileges that should be applied against states. Still other eligible candidates for inclusion in the civil-rights pantheon included fundamental freedoms affirmed by canonical legal texts, such as the American Declaration of Independence or the English Bill of Rights, or declared in various state constitutions, or promulgated by Congress in landmark civil-rights legislation (like the Civil Rights Act of 1866).

Though the modern Court has failed to appreciate Congress's general authority to enact "appropriate" enforcement laws defining new substantive "privileges or immunities of citizens," the Reconstruction Congress chose these broad words at the beginning and end of the amendment precisely to give itself and its successors a sweeping mandate to invalidate future state misconduct. In effect, the Fourteenth Amendment was designed to revive an idea that Madison had repeatedly put forth, unsuccessfully, at Philadelphia: Both Congress and the Court should have authority to keep states in line, with states generally held to standards set by whichever enforcer had the more generous understanding of the individual right in question.

Even as the precise language of the Fourteenth Amendment thus meant more than the first eight (or ten) amendments, it also meant less. Not every facet of the early amendments was truly a "privilege" of individual "citizens" as distinct from a right of states. For instance, part of the First Amendment had protected a state's authority to define its own policies regarding church establishments, yet this states'-rights aspect of the First Amendment made little sense if applied *against* states.

The Second Amendment gave rise to a particularly nice illustration of how the precise language of "privileges or immunities" incorporated core elements of the Bill of Rights while at the same time refining and redefining the Founders' text. At the Founding, the Second Amendment's affirmation of the people's right to bear arms intertwined with a strong commitment to local militias, a pronounced uneasiness about a federal army, and a tight focus on the political rights and responsibilities of voters/jurors/militiamen. Four score years later, this original vision had dissolved, thanks largely to the Civil War and to the very process by which the Fourteenth Amendment was to be ratified with the aid of the Union Army. Yet when filtered through the well-chosen language of "privileges or immunities of citizens," the Founders' Second Amendment could be refined into a rather different kind of right: a right/privilege to keep a gun at home for self-protection—a right of all citizens, female as well as male, acting individually rather than in a collective militia, wielding weapons in a private space rather than mustering on the public square.

In 1866, the prevalence in the South of marauding bands of white thugs, terrorizing black families whom state governments were failing to safeguard via genuinely "equal protection" of criminal laws, made an individual right to keep a gun in his—or her—home a core civil right deserving federal affirmation. This transformation of a Founding-era political right into a Reconstruction-era civil right was exemplified by a key congressional enactment in 1866, which declared that "laws . . . concerning *personal* liberty [and] *personal* security, . . . *including the constitutional right to bear arms,* shall be secured to and enjoyed by all the citizens."[83]

The words "privileges or immunities of citizens" not only enabled Reconstructionists to refine the Bill of Rights while generally applying these rights against states, but also made clear to the American public that the opening section of the Fourteenth Amendment applied only to civil rights and not to political rights such as voting, jury service, militia service, and officeholding. By conferring birthright citizenship on females as well as males—"*all* persons born" under the flag—the amendment's first sentence had strongly implied a focus only on civil rights. Citizenship itself did not imply voting or other political rights—a point that Justice Benjamin R. Curtis had famously stressed in his emphatic dissent in *Dred Scott.* Two years before that case, Congress itself had made clear in a naturalization statute that a foreign-born white woman who married an American husband would herself become a (nonvoting) "citizen" of the United States.[84]

The amendment's civil-rights focus sharpened in its second sentence, whose language borrowed from Article IV, which had likewise spoken of "Privileges" and "Immunities" of "Citizens." Article IV, it will be recalled, had affirmed an idea of *interstate equality of citizenship:* A Massachusetts citizen traveling in South Carolina would as a rule be entitled to be treated as a South Carolinian. The Fourteenth Amendment promised much more, namely, *full and equal in-state citizenship:* Every Massachusetts and South Carolina citizen would be entitled to claim a host of fundamental rights and freedoms (including the right to equality) against his or her own *home* state. But under both Article IV and the Fourteenth Amendment, the basic "privileges" and "immunities" of "citizens" would extend only to civil rights, not political rights. Under Article IV, a Massachusetts visitor would have no right to vote in a South Carolina election, serve on a South Carolina jury, et cetera. So, too, the Fourteenth Amendment guaranteed civil rights but not political rights against each citizen's home state.[85] In explaining the amendment's first two sentences to the American public and state legislatures being asked to support and ratify the amendment, Republican leaders repeatedly stressed these sentences' utter inapplicability to suffrage issues.[86] Northerners were not yet ready for a federal amendment mandating black (or woman) suffrage in every state.*

"Representatives shall be apportioned"

Yet the suffrage question demanded urgent attention in 1866. The Founders' Constitution had allowed the South to count nonvoting slaves at three-fifths, but after emancipation ex-slave states would be entitled to count all inhabitants at five-fifths, whether or not freedmen could vote. Emancipation thus ironically threatened to increase the South's clout in future Congresses (and electoral colleges).[87] Congress's 1867 resolve that ex-rebel states must extend the franchise to black men as a condition of reentry promised to solve part of the problem: If blacks could vote in the new South, then this Reconstructed region would *deserve* more seats. But what if a readmitted state later backslid by amending its state constitution to disenfranchise blacks? Suppose several states did this en masse and had enough pull in a future Congress to prevent exclusion or expulsion on republican-government grounds? And what about loyal states such as Kentucky, Maryland, and Delaware, where blacks made up a double-digit percentage of the population yet were not allowed to vote? Why should such states be allowed to count these nonvoters at a full five-fifths when white representatives could hardly be trusted to represent black interests?

Republicans grappling with these questions in 1866 faced several alternatives. First, Congress could propose a Fourteenth Amendment that would directly regulate state suffrage. Such an amendment could either constitutionalize universal adult male suffrage or, more modestly, forbid all race-based suffrage rules while allowing states to impose other sorts of voting restrictions (involving age, sex, residence, literacy, nativity, payment of poll taxes, absence of criminality, and so on). In 1869, Congress would ultimately propose the more modest version in its Fifteenth Amendment, but in 1866 even this was thought to go too far. Moderate Republicans

---

*The modern Supreme Court has read the language of the equal-protection clause to apply to voting rights; see, e.g., *Baker v. Carr,* 369 U.S. 186 (1962); *Reynolds v. Sims,* 377 U.S. 533 (1964). But the Thirty-ninth Congress designed this clause with nonvoting aliens—"persons" as distinct from "citizens"—quintessentially in mind and sold this clause to the American public as a guarantee of civil rights, as opposed to political rights. From the perspective of constitutional text, history, and structure, the voting-rights issues in cases such as *Baker* and *Reynolds* are better seen through the lens of the Article IV clause guaranteeing republican government. For a discussion of why courts may properly enforce this Article IV clause, notwithstanding certain overbroad readings of *Luther v. Borden,* see my essay "The Central Meaning of Republican Government," *U. Colorado LR* 65 (1994): 749, 753–54, 776–77, 780.

feared they could not sell the equal-suffrage idea in the North, where white bigotry remained a stubborn fact of life. Only five Northern states in 1864 let blacks vote on equal terms, while a sixth (New York) allowed blacks to vote if they met special property qualifications. Everywhere else, blacks were barred from the ballot. In 1865–67, equal-suffrage proposals went down to defeat in all six of the states that put the issue to a popular vote (twice in the case of Minnesota). While the vast majority of Republican voters supported these proposals, this sizable vanguard had yet to win control of the political center.[88]

A second possible approach would have linked House apportionment directly to each state's voting base rather than its overall population: The more persons a state let vote, the more seats it would get. Disenfranchising blacks would not be prohibited but rather penalized, via a loss of seats. Conversely, each state would have a strong republican incentive to expand its suffrage. But perhaps too strong? For example, a given state might double its federal clout by enfranchising women; other states might thereafter feel pressure to follow suit.[89] The question of woman suffrage—which had been a nonissue in the late 1780s—was far from hypothetical in the mid-1860s: Less than two years after the Fourteenth Amendment's ratification, the Wyoming Territory would embrace complete political equality for women (in voting, jury service, and officeholding). In 1865, a couple of states already allowed some women to vote in local school elections, and beginning in the mid-1870s, many more states would follow suit. A proposal for general woman suffrage appeared alongside a separate proposal for black suffrage on the Kansas ballot in 1867, though both measures were ultimately voted down by (white male) voters.[90]

Indeed, it was in no small measure the woman issue that ultimately dictated the precise shape of the Fourteenth Amendment's eventual solution to the urgent question of black suffrage. Had Congress opted to peg apportionment to each state's voting base, this would have solved the North-South imbalance only by creating a perceived East-West imbalance—an imbalance that itself reflected the uneven gender distribution among true-blue states. According to the 1860 census, females accounted for over 51 percent of the white population in Massachusetts but less than 30 percent in California. To switch from a population base to a voting base would (in the absence of woman suffrage) give the Massachusetts delegation roughly the same number of seats as she currently enjoyed but would dramatically increase California's share, since the Golden State boasted a much higher ratio of voters (or, put differently, had a much lower ratio of nonvoting women and children).[91] In debating the apportionment question, congressional Republicans openly discussed the gender issue[92] and in the end found themselves obliged to insert the word "male" into the Constitution—a word that the Founders had managed to omit.

The solution that ultimately became section 2 of the Fourteenth Amendment pegged apportionment to each state's overall population— including women, children, aliens, and other nonvoters—but with a twist. Whenever a state disenfranchised any part of its presumptive voting base, its federal apportionment would correspondingly drop. Thus if, say, Missouri disenfranchised the 7 percent of its population that was black, then it would receive 7 percent fewer seats. The penalty would bite regardless of whether the state formally used race as the basis for disenfranchisement or instead crafted some sly proxy (such as literacy) or indeed did anything that in fact disenfranchised any part of its presumptive voting base, black or white. The key to this strategy was to define a state's presumptive voting base in a manner that avoided penalizing the state for disenfranchising women or aliens. Hence section 2's gendered focus on each state's "male inhabitants" who were "twenty one years of age, and citizens of the United States."*

Women's-rights advocates, led by prominent women themselves, voiced their strong disapproval of section 2. Some of these early feminists, such as Lucy Stone, nevertheless eventually came to support the Fourteenth Amendment. For these crusaders, section 1's strong affirmation of basic civil rights for all citizens—black and white, male and female— outweighed section 2's implicit affirmation of political-rights inequality between black males and white females. For other champions of women's rights, including Susan B. Anthony and Elizabeth Cady Stanton, the insertion of the word "male" sent an unacceptably retrograde message, namely, that the federal Constitution cared not a whit whether women voted: presumptively, only men were voters. On New Year's Day, 1866, Stanton wrote to a (male) colleague that "if that word 'male' be inserted [into the Constitution], it will take us a century at least to get it out."[93]

The divisions within the women's-rights movement—divisions that would soon widen with the proposal and enactment of the Fifteenth Amendment—were particularly poignant because women reformers had

---

*One final wrinkle in this gendered formula allowed a state to disenfranchise without penalty all Confederate rebels and other criminals, lest the new South be deterred from meting out justice to those whose gross misconduct had unfit them for the ballot. In a similar spirit, section 3 of the Fourteenth Amendment rendered certain Confederate officials who had betrayed antebellum loyalty oaths ineligible to serve in Congress, federal office, or state government unless two-thirds of each congressional house voted to lift the ineligibility.

played leading roles in abolitionism and the crusade for racial justice. Sisters Sarah and Angelina Grimké had won acclaim for their antislavery lectures, while novelist Harriet Beecher Stowe was, in Lincoln's words, "the little woman who wrote the book that made this great war." In early 1864, the Women's National Loyal League presented Congress with an emancipation petition bearing one hundred thousand signatures, most of them women's; eventually the League gathered some four hundred thousand names. At the Eleventh National Woman's Rights Convention, held only a month before the Fourteenth Amendment cleared Congress, delegates unanimously applauded "Emancipation and the Civil Rights bill" by which "the negro and woman now hold the same civil and political status, alike needing only the ballot; and . . . the same arguments apply equally to both classes, proving all partial legislation fatal to republican institutions."[94] In a related campaign, thousands of women flooded Congress with petitions for woman suffrage.[95] Section 2 spurned these petitions even as it embraced the presumptive political rights of black men.

In later decades, this section's rules were never enforced as intended to penalize any actual disenfranchisement. Part of the problem arose during the 1870 census, when Congress began to confront some of the difficulties involved in determining the exact proportions of each state's actual disenfranchisements.[96] Thanks to Reconstruction legislation and the newly ratified Fifteenth Amendment, widespread black suffrage circa 1870 was a genuine reality in both the former Confederacy and the middle states, leaving section 2 with rather less work to do than had been feared in 1866. In later decades, when massive Southern disenfranchisement began to take root, the lapses in 1870 meant that there was no early institutional practice on which to build a sturdy section 2 enforcement apparatus. Ironically enough, perhaps section 2's largest legacy was its splintering effect upon the woman-suffrage movement. A clause aimed at including black men had its largest impact by dividing white women.

But all this is hindsight. Republicans in 1866 could hardly know that the very goal that they thought was politically unreachable—a national ban on race discrimination in suffrage—would soon become the law of the land and thereby shift future federal policy away from a regime of indirect apportionment incentives and toward a direct mandate on states.

"The right . . . to vote"

In the congressional election of 1860, race-blind suffrage rules prevailed in only five states, comprising less than one-half of 1 percent of the nation's blacks. In the congressional election of 1870, thanks to the newly ratified Fifteenth Amendment, equal suffrage was the supreme law of the land, binding in every state and in all elections, local, state, and federal. How could such a sea change occur? How could a rule that Republican leaders themselves saw as politically suicidal in mid-1866 win the assent of three-quarters of the states in early 1870?

The story of black ballots begins with black bullets. At war's end, it started to sink in that blacks in blue had helped save the Union. In March 1864, Lincoln was confidentially moving toward the notion that recon-structed Southern governments should enfranchise some blacks—in par-ticular, "the very intelligent, and especially those who have fought gallantly in our ranks." In another private letter, Lincoln declared himself "clear and decided" that blacks, "who have so heroically vindicated their man-hood on the battle-field, . . . have demonstrated in blood their right to the ballot, which is but the humane protection of the flag they have so fear-lessly defended." In a speech delivered four days before his death—formal remarks that grieving Americans soon came to realize were his last words to them—Lincoln went public with his new vision: "It is . . . unsatisfactory to some that the elective franchise is not given to the colored man. I would myself prefer that it were now conferred on the very intelligent, and on those who serve our cause as soldiers."[97]

On the first day of the Thirty-ninth Congress, Sumner took the posi-tion that no ex-Confederate state "can be accepted as republican, where large masses of citizens who have been always loyal to the United States are excluded from the elective franchise, *and especially where the wounded soldier of the Union, with all his kindred and race, and also the kindred of oth-ers whose bones whiten the battle-fields where they died for their country, are thrust away from the polls.*"[98] Sumner here both played the soldier card and upped the ante, openly urging not just ballot access for the black soldier himself, but for all black men.* While focusing particular attention on

---

*Sumner also played a property card, stressing the need to keep "faith with national soldiers *and national creditors.*" *CG*, 39-1:4 (Dec. 4, 1865) (emphasis added). Section 4 of the Fourteenth Amendment ultimately constitutionalized this theme. Just as the Founders in Article VI had pledged faith to creditors who had backed the United States in the Revolutionary War, so sec-tion 4 provided that "the validity of the public debt of the United States, authorized by law, in-cluding debts incurred for payments of pensions and bounties for services in suppressing insurrection or rebellion, shall not be questioned." Section 4 went on to prohibit any govern-mental payment of Confederate debt and also any compensation for slave masters, even loyal ones—a dramatic reversal of the compensation plan at the heart of Lincoln's proposed Four-teenth Amendment in late 1862.

Southern disenfranchisements, he also let it be known that he favored black suffrage in the North as well.[99]

Sumner's colleagues, however, were not yet prepared to follow his lead. The path from Sumter's fall to Sumner's rise was rather roundabout. In the end, black bullets won black ballots only indirectly, via a political ricochet. First, in 1866–68, Northern white Republicans imposed black suffrage on the former Confederacy while exempting their own states. Then, in 1869–70, Northern white Republicans eventually linked arms with new Southern black voters and black lawmakers to reform the North and also cement voting rights in the South.

DECEMBER 7, 1868, is a date that should live in glory. For the first time ever, a session of Congress (in this case, the third session of the Fortieth Congress) began with a membership that had been obliged to come before various electorates and state legislatures encompassing large numbers of blacks alongside whites. Although many Northern states continued to exclude black voters, the great majority of ex-Confederate states had finally rejoined Congress, thanks to their enactments of new state constitutions based on equal suffrage and their ratifications of the Fourteenth Amendment (which was proclaimed valid in late July). These readmissions left only three unreconstructed holdouts—Virginia, Texas, and Mississippi— outside the congressional fold.[100]

Much as they had cause to celebrate in December 1868, Republicans also had grounds for concern. True, the party had just won substantial victories in the November congressional races and could also look forward to the departure of Andrew Johnson in favor of General Ulysses Grant. Yet the general had won only 300,000 more popular votes than his Democratic rival, Horatio Seymour. Since roughly half a million blacks had voted, it appeared that most whites had actually backed the Democratic presidential ticket. If, however, another constitutional amendment could require Northern and middle states to extend the franchise to blacks, this infusion of new voters might give Republicans extra electoral security in the coming years. Also, by federalizing an equal-suffrage right that was then only a feature of state constitutions arguably subject to unilateral repeal, a new amendment could guarantee against the risk of future Southern backsliding.[101]

But why, we might ask, was the political climate in 1868–69 any more conducive to an equal-suffrage amendment than in 1866, when Republicans had carefully considered and rejected this option? For starters, Northern Republican crusaders in Congress could now join forces with new Southern Republicans who themselves had to answer to multiracial constituencies. Also, the Fifteenth Amendment would be conceived at a different stage of the electoral cycle than had the Fourteenth. In the spring of 1866, Republicans in the *first* session of the Thirty-ninth Congress knew that they had to come before the voters very soon and thus crafted their Fourteenth Amendment as the party's unofficial campaign platform. Since Northern (white) voters were not ready for a national mandate of political rights for blacks, Republicans promised only civil rights. But in the winter of 1869, members of the *third* (lame-duck) session of the Fortieth Congress had less to fear from potentially hostile voters, whom they would not need to face immediately. With any luck, by the time new elections rolled around, the Fifteenth Amendment itself would be the law of the land. If so, any lost white votes might be offset by grateful black votes; Republican congressmen in 1869 were thus freer than they had been in 1866 to vote their conscience with impunity.

Reformers had also won back the presidency between 1866 and 1869. Though Article V gave no formal role to the president, Andrew Johnson had wielded all his powers of patronage and persuasion to assail the reformist platform in 1866. Even after congressional reformers won a resounding vote of confidence from their Northern constituents in the midterm election of that year, Johnson himself (who was of course not on the 1866 ballot) remained in office as a stubborn reality to be reckoned with. In 1869, however, Republicans were united under Grant, and reformers could make their case with no fear that the president would use his pulpit to foment white bigotry against them. In fact, the new president used his Inaugural Address to "entertain the hope and express the desire" that the Fifteenth Amendment would be promptly ratified. Meanwhile, some white voters seemed to be warming to the idea of black suffrage. Though this idea had lost in all six states that put the issue to a vote between 1865 and 1867, it won in two states in 1868, one of which (Minnesota) had twice rejected the reform in prior votes. In any event, the Fifteenth Amendment would not come directly before the voters, but rather before Republican-dominated state legislatures whose members were more apt to toe the party line and who were themselves likely to benefit from the grateful votes of newly enfranchised blacks in future elections.[102]

Horizontal and vertical federalism issues also interacted in different ways in the mid- and late 1860s. Early on, the issue was whether a given

Northern state should *unilaterally* enfranchise its blacks. Some who believed in the abstract idea of equality might nevertheless have voted no, lest the new rule induce a massive influx of new blacks into the state.[103] But in 1869–70, the issue was whether *all* states should collectively enfranchise blacks. In this context, no state had reason to fear becoming a magnet. A state that ratified the Fifteenth Amendment did not thereby commit itself to equal suffrage unless and until all its neighbors would likewise be bound. In the end, every Northern state that said no to equal suffrage in 1865–67 said yes to the Fifteenth Amendment in 1869–70.

By its terms, the amendment did not mandate universal manhood suffrage. It merely prohibited race-based disenfranchisements. In later decades, this narrow draftsmanship would prompt countless shams and subterfuges whereby various states—especially ex-Confederate states—would use formally neutral voting rules, such as literacy tests and poll taxes, to exclude blacks from the ballot. In theory, such disenfranchisements should have triggered apportionment penalties under section 2 of the Fourteenth Amendment, but as already noted, this section was never enforced. Robust and sustained enforcement of black voting rights came only in the Second Reconstruction of the 1960s, when Congress used its sweeping enforcement powers under the Fifteenth Amendment's second section to enact "appropriate" legislation targeting state abuses. Here was yet another ricochet: An amendment that had been propelled forward by black votes in the South ultimately succeeded in revolutionizing black voting in the North, which in turn eventually brought the South back into line. (Much of the congressional support for 1960s enforcement laws occurred thanks to Northern black voters.)

America's Second Reconstruction also witnessed the end of American apartheid, the gross sham of "separate but equal" that the Court had blessed in the 1896 case of *Plessy v. Ferguson,* over the dissent of Justice Harlan. Harlan's dissent has come to be seen as based on the Fourteenth Amendment's guarantees of equal citizenship and equal protection, but Harlan himself took pains to stress the Fifteenth Amendment as well, which he read to guarantee that "no citizen should be denied, on account of his race, the privilege of participating in the political control of his country."[104] Of course, the amendment's text spoke only of "the right to vote," but Harlan evidently understood that this right in both letter and spirit encompassed not merely the equal right to *vote for legislators* and other elected officials, but also the equal right to vote *in legislatures,* the equal right to be *voted for* and *serve in* any elective post, and the equal right to vote *in juries* of all sorts.

Harlan further understood that the Fifteenth Amendment, so read, was by its very nature inherently integrationist. Standing alone, the Fourteenth promised equality, but as a conceptual matter, perhaps some forms of physical separation might well be equal. (Today, for example, physical separation of the sexes in public bathrooms and gym classes is thought to be equal and has met with the general approval of both sexes.) Though Jim Crow was in fact never equal—and thus violated the core idea of the Fourteenth—that amendment did not go so far as did the Fifteenth, which *necessarily* envisioned blacks and whites working side by side in jury rooms, legislative halls, and voting precincts.[105] As Harlan's dissent put the point in language interweaving the classic political rights, blacks had "risked their lives for the preservation of the Union" and were "entitled, by law, to participate in the political control of the State and nation" in "public stations of any kind." Whites and blacks needed to work alongside one another "in the jury box," "in a political assembly," and "when they approach the ballot-box."[106]

With this integrationist vision, the nation thus committed itself—at least on paper—to a role for blacks strikingly different than the one that had held sway in the minds of many antebellum antislavery reformers. Whereas Lincoln's proposed Fifteenth Amendment in late 1862 had envisioned blacks being invited to emigrate to Africa or Latin America, America's eventual Fifteenth Amendment in 1870 envisioned black men being invited to work alongside white men in governing the American Republic as full political equals.*

*True, the amendment did not in so many words affirm a right of blacks to be voted for or to serve on juries. But legislators and jurors surely *vote,* and thus the amendment's text was easily read to apply to these domains. As a matter of near-universal antebellum custom and state law, "all the citizens who exercise the elective franchise have the right of serving on a jury." Alexis de Tocqueville, *Democracy in America* (Phillips Bradley, ed., 1945), 2:378 (Appendix I–R to chap. 16, vol. 1). In *Neal v. Delaware,* 103 U.S. 370, 389 (1881), the Supreme Court, in an opinion by Justice Harlan, held that the Fifteenth Amendment automatically made blacks eligible jurors wherever preexisting state law had tied jury service to suffrage rules.

The Reconstruction Congress's views are also instructive. In the late 1860s, Georgia, after promising to respect the right of blacks to vote, expelled all duly elected blacks from the state legislature. Congress responded in 1869–70 first by refusing to seat Georgia's senators and then by reimposing military reconstruction on the state. Thus, at the very moment when the nation was pondering whether to adopt the Fifteenth Amendment, Congress was dramatizing that the right of blacks to vote might indeed entail their rights to vote for fellow blacks and to serve in government. Meanwhile, in Georgia itself, the lead opinion in the state Supreme Court declared that "the right of the people, if they please to choose a colored man for an office, is a necessary incident to the right to vote. The right to vote is worth but little to the colored man if he is restricted in the exercise of that right, so that he can only vote for men of a white color." *White v. Clements,* 39 Ga. 232, 268 (1869). In 1875, Congress evidently relied on the letter and spirit of the

Left out of this masculine picture, of course, were women, many of whom objected to the enfranchisement of black men while they themselves remained disenfranchised. But their very votelessness in 1869–70 made it that much easier for congressmen and state legislators to disregard their voices. Which raises the obvious question: How did America's women *ever* manage to lever their way out of votelessness and into suffrage? The answer lies in the next chapter of America's constitutional saga.

Black Suffrage Amendment to support enforcement legislation affirming the right of blacks to serve equally on juries. Compare U.S. Const. amend. XV ("The right of *citizens of the United States* to vote shall not be denied or abridged by *the United States or by any State on account of race, color, or previous condition of servitude*") (emphasis added) with the Act of March 1, 1875, ch. 114, sec. 4, 18 Stat. 335, 336 ("No *citizen* . . . shall be disqualified for service as grand or petit juror in any court *of the United States or of any State, on account of race, color, or previous condition of servitude*") (emphasis added). In three earlier Reconstruction statutes, Congress had likewise linked the language of the Fifteenth Amendment to the right to hold office. See Virginia Readmission Act of Jan. 26, 1870, 16 Stat. 62, 63 ("It shall never be lawful for the said State to deprive any *citizen of the United States, on account of race, color, or previous condition of servitude,* of the right to hold office") (emphasis added); Mississippi Readmission Act of Feb. 23, 1870, 16 Stat. 67, 68 (same); Texas Readmission Act of March 30, 1870, 16 Stat. 80, 81 (same). For more on the interlinkages among voting, officeholding, and jury service, see note 106 to this chapter, and see also Chapter 11, pages 426–28.

Chapter 11

PROGRESSIVE
REFORMS

WOMAN SUFFRAGE PARADE, MAY 6, 1912.

In 1912, the women of New York did not yet enjoy the right to vote, but they surely did have the right to speak, print, petition, assemble, and parade. Over the next five years, they translated these rights into a state constitutional right to vote; and then, in 1920, the Nineteenth Amendment became the supreme law of the land, guaranteeing women the vote in every state and federal election.

$\mathscr{P}$ROGRESSIVE-ERA CRUSADERS succeeded in broadening and deepening several major themes of the Reconstruction-era reformers who preceded them. Carrying forward the nationalism of the Reconstruction Amendment trilogy, early-twentieth-century amendments dramatically expanded congressional power. Much as zealous reformers in the mid-1860s had enacted large wealth transfers from slavocrats to freedmen, so a new generation of idealists in the mid-1910s aimed to reduce antirepublican extremes of wealth and want. Reenacting a good bit of the letter and spirit of the Fifteenth Amendment, the Nineteenth Amendment did for women what the older reform had done for black men.

"taxes on incomes"

The Sixteenth Amendment marked the third time that the American people rose up to say no to a Supreme Court decision that had favored propertied interests at the expense of other constitutional values. In the 1790s, the Eleventh Amendment overruled *Chisholm v. Georgia,* which had threatened to give some creditors more than they were legally entitled to under contracts they had made with state governments. In the 1860s, the Fourteenth Amendment likewise repudiated *Dred Scott,* which had glorified slaveholders' property rights as the Constitution's summum bonum. (Section 4 of the Fourteenth, it will be recalled, barred compensation for slave owners who had been stripped of their valuable chattels by emancipation—a bar that would have outraged Chief Justice Taney had he been alive.) As in the eighteenth and nineteenth centuries, so in the twentieth: In 1913, Americans once again declared that the Court had blundered.[1]

This time, the issue concerned the meaning of the Constitution's taxation provisions. In an unpersuasive and indeed unprecedented ruling in 1895, a bare majority of a sharply divided Court struck down the progressive federal income-tax law then in place.[2] In the Sixteenth Amendment, reformers undid the 1895 decision of *Pollock v. Farmers' Loan & Trust Co.* and made clear that Congress could indeed levy a progressive tax on income.

The specific issue in *Pollock* revolved around one of the Constitution's murkiest clauses, which provided (in Article I, section 9) that "no Capitation, or other *direct, Tax* shall be laid, unless in Proportion to the Census." A companion constitutional clause (in Article I, section 2) likewise provided that "Representatives *and direct Taxes* shall be apportioned among the several States . . . according to their respective Numbers." *Pollock* held that a tax on rental income was in effect a tax on the underlying land itself, and that such a land tax was a "direct" tax. A tax on dividend income was also a "direct" tax, said the Court. The Court went on to opine that under the Constitution these "direct" taxes had to be calibrated so that the amount collected from each state corresponded to that state's population as measured by the census.[3]

For instance, if state A and state B had identical populations, then tax rates would have to be set so that the total rental-dividend intake from each state was identical. If A's population was wealthier than B's, the tax rates in A would need to be lowered, or the rates in B raised, until the revenue from the two states evened up. As a practical matter, the state-adjustment approach demanded by the Court would be impossible to implement in any workable income-tax system operating in a union of some four dozen states. In effect, *Pollock* ruled out all federal income-tax systems that included rental or dividend income—as opposed to, say, taxes on the wage income of day laborers (which were not "direct" taxes under the Court's approach, and therefore did not require any special adjustments).

Even if the federal tax code could somehow be overhauled to meet the *Pollock* Court's demands, basic principles of progressivity would have to be sacrificed: Inhabitants of rich states would be entitled to pay lower rates than comparable inhabitants of poorer states. Though framed as a federalism constraint, *Pollock*'s state-adjustment rule doomed any politically feasible progressive tax system, given the notorious facts that most of the superrich at the turn of the century lived in a handful of states and that previous federal income taxes had fetched far more revenue per capita from these states.

As an interpretation of the Constitution, *Pollock* left much to be desired, as the four dissenters in the case made clear. Justice Harlan's dissent went so far as to describe the *Pollock* ruling as "a disaster to the country." Harlan, who would go on to write another famously prophetic dissent in the *Plessy v. Ferguson* case the following year, took special pains to condemn the *Pollock* Court's obvious over-reading of the words "direct tax"—words that, Harlan reminded his colleagues, had originally been designed largely to shield the Southern master class from heavy capitations—head taxes—on slaves.[4]

True, the Founding generation had been opaque about the exact location of the boundary line separating direct and indirect taxes. According to Madison's notes, at one point Philadelphia delegate Rufus King "asked what was the precise meaning of *direct* taxation? No one answd."[5] But under any one of several plausible tests, a tax on income was an *indirect,* transactional tax akin to "duties," "excises," and "imposts"—all of which were understood at the Founding to be classic "indirect" taxes not subject to the state-by-state accounting rule.[6]

Pollock also broke sharply with prior Supreme Court precedent. In the Court's first foray into the intricacies of direct taxation, the Justices in the 1796 case of *Hylton v. United States* had offered a narrow reading of "direct" taxes—the precise opposite of *Pollock*'s approach. *Hylton* had unanimously upheld the government tax in question—again, the opposite of *Pollock*. The *Hylton* justices had understood that the general requirement of state-by-state accounting would be unworkable for many types of taxes, and that this pragmatic fact was itself reason to think that the Founders held a highly restricted view of the kind of "direct" tax that would require such accounting. Key passages in *Hylton*'s seriatim opinions thus suggested that "direct taxes" should sensibly be defined as those levies that as a practical matter lent themselves to state-by-state accounting, census style.[7] This piece of early wisdom, too, *Pollock* disregarded. Finally, the levy that *Hylton* upheld was a luxury tax on the wealthy—specifically, a tax on the use of carriages. By contrast, it was the very fact that the federal income tax at issue in *Pollock* had targeted those most able to pay that rankled many of the *Pollock* Court's conservative defenders.

Although *Hylton* was the Court's first word on the topic of direct taxation, it was not the only precedent on the books in 1895 or even the closest one to the precise issue before the *Pollock* Court. During the Civil War, Congress had enacted an income tax, which a unanimous Court had upheld in the 1881 case of *Springer v. United States.*[8] *Pollock* in effect overruled *Springer.*

In 1913, however, the People in effect overruled *Pollock:* "The Congress shall have power to lay and collect taxes on incomes, from whatever source derived, without apportionment among the several States, and without regard to any census or enumeration."

With this amendment, and with several of the Progressive-era amendments that would soon follow, early-twentieth-century Americans reaffirmed two of the main themes of the Reconstruction Amendments— nationalism and equality—and extended these principles to new contexts. All three Reconstruction Amendments had ended with *McCulloch*-like clauses proclaiming that "Congress shall have power" to enforce the new constitutional order. The Sixteenth Amendment began with the same phrase. So, too, the Nineteenth (Woman Suffrage) Amendment would echo the Reconstruction-enforcement sections verbatim. Though devoid of similarly explicit congressional-empowerment language, the Seventeenth Amendment, which freed senators from their old dependence on state governments, was surely yet another nationalizing provision.

The Sixteenth, Seventeenth, and Nineteenth Amendments also all aimed to make America more equal—the Nineteenth by protecting women's equal voting rights; the Seventeenth by introducing one-person, one-vote rules within individual state elections for U.S. senators; and the Sixteenth by affirming the legitimacy of a progressive income-tax system that would take more from rich persons and rich states, a tax system that would target not merely wage income of laborers but also rental and dividend income of investors. Nationalism and egalitarianism intertwined in the income-tax context: Any individual state that imposed high taxes on the wealthy risked being underbid by lower rates in neighboring states, but the national government could avoid this sort of bidding war with a uniform federal policy. While the amendment's text formally addressed only *national income* taxes, its spirit smiled upon a range of other state and federal taxes—wealth taxes, for example—aimed at the affluent.

Make no mistake, both sides in the national income-tax debate understood that such taxes had always been, and were likely to be, *progressive* income taxes—in particular, taxes that targeted the rich. Such taxes openly sought to democratize the economy. This, indeed, was the very reason that *Pollock*'s defenders so disliked these taxes.

Prior to the Civil War, at least seven states had adopted income taxes. High exemptions and graduated rates—the basic features of a progressive tax structure—were commonplace in these states.[9] Congress followed this pattern when introducing a federal income tax in the 1860s. For instance, the 1865 federal tax code exempted all persons who made less than $600, taxed income between $600 and $5,000 at 5 percent, and subjected all income above $5,000 to a steeper 10 percent rate. Later federal laws tweaked the specifics but preserved the basic structure, under which more than three-quarters of federal revenue came from the seven wealthiest states: New York (which itself generated more than 30 percent of the total national intake), Massachusetts, Pennsylvania, Ohio, Illinois, New Jersey, and Connecticut. Under the law struck down in *Pollock*, incomes over $4,000 were taxed at 2 percent; all others were exempt. According to Treasury Department estimates, less than 1 percent of the population had been subject to this levy.[10]

The 1908 Democratic Party Platform minced no words when it urged "the submission of a constitutional amendment specifically authorizing Congress to levy and collect a tax upon individual and corporate incomes, *to the end that wealth may bear its proportionate share of the burdens of the Federal Government.*"[11] Republican President Theodore Roosevelt had previously endorsed the idea of an income tax, and in 1909, America's new president, William Howard Taft, likewise gave his blessing.

Though presidents play no formal part in the Article V process, Taft, as the leader of his party, carried great weight (literally and otherwise). Taft also urged Congress to adopt a constitutional amendment rather than a mere statute reinstating an income tax and daring the Court to say no. Though the Court might well uphold such a statute and overrule *Pollock*, Taft felt that such an act of judicial abasement would weaken a vital branch of government whose independence needed to be nurtured. (A dozen years later, ex-president Taft would be named chief justice, allowing him to preside over the Court that he so admired and that he had sought to shelter, even at some risk to his own political fortunes.) With the backing of both party establishments, the Income Tax Amendment eventually sailed through both houses of Congress early in the Taft Administration and was ratified almost four years later, as Taft was preparing to leave the White House to make way for Democrat Woodrow Wilson, whose party convention in 1912 had ringingly endorsed the then-pending Income Tax Amendment.

In the first income-tax statute enacted after the new amendment was in place, Congress once again opted for a progressive tax structure that exempted a large swath of low- and middle-income persons and taxed the rest at a sloping rate, beginning at 1 percent for an individual making $3,000 and topping out at 7 percent for income over $500,000. The $3,000 minimum threshold effectively limited the tax to the top 1 percent of the economic order.[12] In 1916 the Supreme Court unanimously upheld the new tax law, expressly rejecting the notion that the "progressive feature" of the tax somehow rendered it unconstitutional.[13] The American People had spoken and—this time, at least—the Court listened.

"Senators . . . elected by the people"

Proposed in 1912 and ratified the following year, the Seventeenth Amendment provided that United States senators would henceforth be chosen directly by voters rather than by state legislatures. Along with a supermajority of the House, two-thirds of the Senate—a Senate whose members had been chosen under the old constitutional regime—agreed to this change, as did three-quarters of the state legislatures, who thereby reduced their own power. How and why did this happen?

Largely for a reason that by now should begin to look familiar: The electorate demanded change and had the power to make politicians pay attention. In 1789, Congress proposed a bill of rights limiting its own legislative authority largely because Americans had voiced their desire for such a bill in the previous year's ratification process. Members of the First Congress understood that if they refused to heed the people's message, they would have to answer for that refusal at the next election. So, too, as national presidential parties began to emerge before and after the election of 1800, state legislatures generally found themselves obliged to yield up to their constituents the right to choose presidential electors. Once popular election of electors became relatively common in the states, holdout legislatures found it increasingly difficult to deny their constituents the power that voters in sister states were already wielding. Thus, although nothing in the original Constitution or the 1804 Presidential Selection Amendment formally required direct popular election of each state's presidential electors, a strong tradition to that effect had emerged by 1830.

Democratization of the Senate selection process took longer but followed a roughly parallel path. In brief, individual states began experimenting with a variety of methods that gave voters a more direct say in senatorial elections; and once these practices began to take root and spread from state to state, voters in holdout states began to insist that they, too, deserved the right to pick United States senators directly.

One of the first major innovations in Senate-selection practice occurred in the late 1850s in Illinois. According to Don E. Fehrenbacher, the 1858 Senate race between Lincoln and Douglas "had no precedent in American politics." Lincoln's earlier bid for the Senate, in 1854, had exemplified the old way of proceeding. In that year, Lincoln "had waited until *after* the general election in November to announce his candidacy, and then he had conducted a quiet letter-writing campaign among the *legislators,* with whom the choice rested." But in 1858, the fledgling Republican Party held a state convention in June, nearly five months *before* the election. At this convention, Republicans unanimously named Lincoln as the party's "first and only choice . . . for the United States Senate." Meanwhile, the Democrats were signaling that they would back incumbent Douglas for reelection. Both men proceeded to make their case directly before the voters, in a campaign that quickly became legendary thanks to its famous debates. The novel, if implicit, message of this way of proceeding was that Illinois's voters themselves could in effect pick their United States senator. If they wanted Lincoln, they should vote the Republican ticket for state legislature; if Douglas, the Democratic state ticket.[14]

Yet this makeshift could only effect a crude approximation of direct popular election. For one thing, the Lincoln-Douglas framework made sense only when the U.S. Senate race was the single real issue at stake in a state legislative election. This system required both voters and state legislators to be loyal party men; it left no room for a voter to register a preference for a state legislator of one party and a U.S. senator of the other party. Also, it was vulnerable to all the ordinary quirks of legislative apportionment. In 1858 itself, for instance, Lincoln's Republicans outpolled Douglas's Democrats by a popular vote of approximately 50 percent to 48 percent, but Douglas managed to eke out a state legislative majority, thanks to a variety of factors. Not all state districts were equally populous or fairly drawn; turnout rates varied across districts, as did margins of victory; not all state seats were up for reelection in 1858; and so on.[15]

Three decades later, states began to experiment with direct primary elections for Senate candidates within each party. This model made it likely that each party candidate would be the people's choice within his own party but failed to guarantee that the legislature would in fact crown the man whom most voters would have preferred in a head-to-head race between the top Democrat and the top Republican—a race that could not easily be accommodated within the primary-election framework. Nevertheless, the Senate-primary system, operational in twenty-eight of the forty-six states in 1910,[16] did enhance the democratic character of the federal upper chamber and proved especially significant in the South and other places where one party was dominant and the primary election was thus the main event.

At the turn of the century, Oregon began to experiment with a different approach, which went through several iterations and refinements both in Oregon itself and in copycat states such as Nebraska, Oklahoma, Montana, and Nevada. Under the Oregon Plan, the state at its general election allowed voters to directly express their preferences among the candidates for the United States Senate. In an early version of the plan, individual state lawmakers could, if they chose, officially pledge to support the winner of the voters' preference-poll. Once this pledge was taken, even a Republican state legislator would be honor-bound to vote for a Democratic senator if the Democrat were to win the preference-poll, and vice versa. In a later version, Oregon voters in 1908 enacted a state initiative "instruct[ing]" the state legislature to ratify the people's choice.[17]

By early 1913, more than half of the states had already committed themselves to a form of direct election—either the direct-primary approach in one-party states or some version of the Oregon Plan. Thus, when senators and state legislatures from these states supported the Direct Senate Election Amendment, they were voting to constitutionalize rules that were already largely in place or about to be in place.*

Several major reform impulses drove the movement for direct election. As a result of intense partisanship, state-law quorum rules, and clever parliamentary maneuvering, state legislatures had often deadlocked when balloting for the Senate. These deadlocks—nearly fifty between 1891 and 1905—had routinely meant that for months a state had only one senator (and in the case of Delaware during one especially contentious two-year period, no senator) in the federal upper chamber. Meanwhile, the Senate tussles had often distracted state governments from attending to other pressing business. Direct election promised to solve these problems.[18]

Supporters of direct election also argued that their system would result in cleaner, less corrupt government and would counter the undue effects of large corporations, monopolies, trusts, and other special-interest groups in the Senate election process. The Senate was at risk of becoming—indeed, to critics had already become—a bastion of privilege, a millionaires' club mocking the republican ideal. Nor was the corruption limited to the senators themselves. It also infected state governments, as big-city bosses and other insiders paid off state lawmakers for their votes in Senate contests.

The Seventeenth Amendment solution was to provide that each senator be elected by "the people" of his state—more precisely, the same voters who chose state legislators and therefore the House of Representatives. Senate vacancies would be filled by special election, as with the House, with the proviso that a state's governor might make an interim appointment until a special election could be held.

How DID THE NEW SYSTEM later unfold? To what extent did it redeem the hopes of its backers? If the reformers' goal was to slash the number of wealthy senators, the amendment might be thought less than a complete

---

*Nevertheless, Southern legislatures were notably slower to jump aboard the constitutional bandwagon, given that the amendment envisioned a large federal role over the time, place, and manner of Senate elections. Only four of the thirty-six necessary ratifications came from the ex-Confederacy. (Louisiana added her superfluous yes a year later.) For more background on the states'-rights and race issues lurking beneath the amendment's surface, see Alan P. Grimes, *Democracy and the Amendments to the Constitution* (1978; reprint, 1987), 79–82.

success. The Senate largely remained a millionaires' club.[19] Nor can it be said that the amendment reduced the amount of money required to mount a successful Senate bid. Direct elections cost money—lots of it. Indeed, more money was probably required to prevail among the voters than to wage a successful campaign among a smallish number of state legislators.

Yet perhaps this greater amount of money was later being spent in less corrupt ways—on campaigns aiming to reach ordinary voters, inform them about the issues, and draw them into the political process, in contrast to old-style bribes slipped into the waiting pockets of state-capital bigwigs. As the Founders themselves understood, it is harder to bribe a large group of ad hoc decision-makers—such as ordinary voters—than a small group of standing officials. (Recall that this anticorruption idea inclined many at the Founding to trust jurors more than judges and to structure the electoral college so as to minimize the risk of bribery.) Thus, one of the bigger effects of the Seventeenth Amendment's reform of the *federal* legislature was a modest reduction in *state* governmental corruption. Also, by creating a one-person, one-vote regime within each state, direct election lessened the impact of state malapportionment and gerrymandering long before the Supreme Court began to condemn these practices in the 1960s.

The other major federalism dimension of the Direct Senate Election Amendment was more pronounced. Liberated from all dependence on state governments, modern senators were freer to pursue policies that state officials might not like. In the domain of constitutional rights, directly elected senators were in general more wont to expose and rectify the wrongdoing of state public servants. In other regulatory contexts, the federal government proved more inclined to displace state laws and even impose mandates on state government. Thus, the Seventeenth Amendment fit snugly into a long line of post–Civil War provisions enhancing the authority of the federal government. Over the centuries, We the People of the "United States" have placed increased emphasis on the word "United" and have correspondingly diminished the status of "States."

The transformation of the Senate also affected bicameralism and the separation of powers, subtly reconfiguring the Senate's relations with the House, with the presidency, and with the judiciary. As to the latter, the Seventeenth Amendment's democratization of the Senate, alongside the Twelfth's democratization of the presidency, perhaps gave the judiciary a greater sense of constitutional uniqueness than it had at the Founding. Under the Philadelphia plan, the indirect election of the Senate and president made it somewhat more likely that these entities would check a directly elected House—or put differently, made the Senate and the president somewhat more like the Supreme Court. But as the Senate and the president moved toward House-style direct election—albeit with distinct electoral cycles and voting bases—only the judiciary continued to stand outside the direct-election system. Yet if an enhanced sense of judicial separateness did in fact result from the Direct Senate Election Amendment, this dynamic manifested itself only gradually. Sitting senators or ex-senators were appointed to the Supreme Court at roughly the same rate in the three decades before and the three decades after the Seventeenth Amendment—one per decade, on average. But in the last fifty years, not a single sitting senator or former senator has been named to America's highest court.[20]

Within Congress itself, the direct election of senators enhanced the status of the Senate vis-à-vis the House. In addition to their more select membership and more secure tenure, senators could now claim to be the people's choice in a way that they could not before 1913. Prior to the amendment, six men who had served in the House but not the Senate—Madison, Polk, Lincoln, Hayes, Garfield, and McKinley—went on to become president. Since then, no (mere) representative has gained the White House.[21]

Meanwhile, the Seventeenth Amendment probably did enhance the presidential prospects of senators by sharpening their populist electoral skills, public visibility, and perceived electabilty. In the early republic, the Senate was a notable nursery for future presidents. After Washington (who of course as the first president had no opportunity for a prior job under the new Constitution), eleven of the next fourteen presidents had served in the Senate, either as a senator or as the Senate's presiding officer (i.e., the vice president of the United States) or both. But the Civil War marked the start of a new, middle-republic pattern, in which popularly elected governors tended to outshine legislatively chosen senators as successful presidential candidates. After Grant's departure, five of the next nine presidents were big-state governors—two Ohioans, two New Yorkers, and a New Jerseyan.[22]

Then came the Direct Senate Election Amendment. By strengthening the populist credentials of senators, the amendment helped restore members of the upper chamber to their early preeminence (alongside generals and diplomats) as presidential prospects. This change was nicely visible in the two presidential elections that immediately followed the Seventeenth's enactment. The first, exemplifying the middle-republic model, featured two big-state ex-governors, Woodrow Wilson and Charles Evans Hughes. In the second, in 1920, Ohio's sitting governor, James Cox, ran against one of that state's sitting senators, Warren G. Harding. As a member of the Senate class of 1915, Harding was in the very first set of men to reach the Senate the "clean" way—under the new, Seventeenth Amendment regime. Six years later, the presidency was his.

This was a sign of things to come. While before enactment of the amendment only three of the ten most recent presidents had previously served in the Senate (as either a senator or a vice president), after enactment seven of the next ten presidents would be Senate veterans. An even more dramatic shift appears if we focus only on actual *senators* who were later *elected* president—a category that describes only one of the ten men most recently elected to the White House before the ratification of the Seventeenth Amendment, but that encompasses five of the next ten elected presidents.[23] Similarly, while ex-senators accounted for only two of the ten most immediate pre-amendment vice presidents, they would account for six of the next ten. Interestingly enough, since 1944 every Democratic Party Convention save one has named a current or former senator as its vice-presidential nominee.*[24]

"intoxicating liquors . . . prohibited"

While the Sixteenth, Seventeenth, and Nineteenth Amendments aimed to change the face of America's economy and its polity, the Eighteenth, which ushered in the Prohibition era, aimed to transform America's social fabric. It failed, and less than fifteen years after its enactment it was explicitly repealed by yet another amendment, the Twenty-first.

The crusade to ban liquor in America won its first major victory in 1851, when Maine enacted a statewide prohibition law.[25] Several states fol-

*Direct Senate election also indirectly affected the relationship between the upper legislative chamber and the executive cabinet. Prior to direct election, it was not uncommon for a sitting senator to resign his post, serve in the cabinet, and then return to the Senate when his cabinet stint had ended. State legislatures often encouraged this career path; while serving in the cabinet, a once-and-future senator could continue to advance the interests of his home state. To induce a sitting senator to resign from the upper chamber (as required by the Article I, section 6 incompatibility clause), state legislatures implicitly promised to hold the retiree's seat and reelect him to the Senate once his cabinet service was over. Direct election has made this sort of implicit deal all but impossible to strike: Voters en masse are too large, diffuse, and ad hoc to offer the sort of assurance of reelection that state legislatures had been able to provide. Before the enactment of the Seventeenth Amendment, thirteen cabinet officers were once-and-future senators; since then, not a single senator has joined the cabinet and then returned to the Senate at the end of his or her cabinet service. For more analysis, see Vikram David Amar, "Indirect Effects of Direct Election: A Structural Examination of the Seventeenth Amendment," *Vanderbilt LR* 49 (1996): 1347, 1355–60.

lowed, but most of these laws, including Maine's, were quickly repealed. Renewed state campaigns ensued in later decades, and by 1917 prohibition was in place in roughly half the states, although many of these places were not "bone dry." Some states, for example, allowed the sale of beer and wine and/or the private use (as distinct from the commercial sale) of other spirits.[26]

The temperance/prohibition movement held special appeal in Western states, where it went hand-in-hand with the emerging woman-suffrage movement.[27] Women and children had often been victimized by drunken men; and the saloons where men had gathered were seen as vicious, corrupt dens. Much as Progressives sought to purify Senate elections from the corrupting influences of bosses and corporate insiders; much as they aimed to purify the economy by busting trusts and reducing the power of wealthy special interests; much as they hoped to purify politics by enfranchising the fairer sex; so many reformers aspired to purify American society more generally by destroying saloons and the "wet" big-city political machines that operated with and through them.

World War I gave reformers additional momentum. Since grain and sugar were in short supply, Prohibition could be packaged as a patriotic act as well as a moral policy. Prominent brewers were of German descent, and the war made it easy to stigmatize all things German. (As a rule, Prohibition ran strongest among rural, native-born Americans who looked askance at recent immigrants and urban culture.) Proposed by Congress in late 1917, the Prohibition Amendment was ratified in early 1919, and by its own terms went into effect "one year [after] ratification." By mid-1919, forty-five of the forty-eight states had said yes to this amendment; and in 1922, New Jersey belatedly did the same, making Rhode Island and Connecticut the sole holdouts.[28]

But in early 1933, the House and Senate—which had voted for the Eighteenth Amendment by overwhelming margins only a decade and a half earlier—voted by equally overwhelming margins to repeal it via the Twenty-first Amendment. By the end of the year, thirty-seven states had agreed.[29] How and why did this constitutional about-face occur?

In part, because Prohibition's repeal involved a different cast of characters. State and congressional apportionment rules in the 1910s had tended to favor rural and heavily native-born regions, but by the early 1930s, new electoral maps began to reflect America's increasingly urban and immigrant population. Yet malapportionment lived on in many states, prompting Anti-Prohibitionists to sidestep state legislatures altogether in the ratification process. Instead, state conventions were assembled to vote on the new amendment—a ratification option permitted by Article V but never before invoked by Congress. In most states, convention delegates were selected in statewide at-large elections—a process that detoured around the apportionment thicket.[30]

More significantly, many Americans who had initially supported Prohibition later came to believe that it was a mistake—a failed experiment in an era that celebrated scientific experimentation. Drinking remained common but had simply been driven underground. The old saloon had given way to the new speakeasy (where women as well as men were now welcome). Organized crime had moved into the liquor business. Big-city corruption had actually seemed to increase, as had murder rates, gangsterism, and related evils associated with criminalization itself. Data suggested that rates of illegal drinking were also rising, not falling, as time went on. Rich and powerful groups managed to get around the law, as did clever entrepreneurs. One type of grape juice, for instance, was sold with a "warning" label stating that U.S. Department of Agriculture tests indicated that if the juice were allowed to age for sixty days, it would ripen into wine with an alcoholic content of 12 percent.[31] With the onset of the Depression in 1929, critics increasingly argued that Prohibition placed a drag on the economy, costing thousands of legitimate jobs and closing off an important source of tax revenue. In 1932, the Democratic Party Platform openly called for repeal of the Prohibition Amendment, while the Republican Party Platform proclaimed more equivocally that the American people should revisit the issue. When the proposed repeal amendment reached the floor of Congress, more than a dozen senators who had voted for the Prohibition Amendment now voted to kill it.[32]

ALTHOUGH ITS ATTEMPT to transform American society fell short, the Prohibition Amendment did usher in a notable procedural innovation. Section 3 of the amendment provided that the amendment itself would be "inoperative" unless ratified within seven years. No previous amendment had so provided in its text, although three of the next four amendments (all but the Woman Suffrage Amendment) would follow this lead.

But how, it might be asked, could such an extra requirement be squared with Article V, which imposed no explicit time limit on the ratification process? If the Prohibition Amendment had been ratified in *eight* years, wouldn't such ratification have satisfied Article V? If so, wouldn't the amendment have been "valid to all Intents and Purposes" under Article V, notwithstanding section 3?

Actually, nothing in section 3 said otherwise. Had the amendment been ratified in its eighth year, a good case could indeed be made that it then would have become "valid." Section 3 merely provided that in such an event, the "valid" amendment would be substantively meaningless—moot, inert, self-negating, of no "operative" significance. Upon ratification, section 3 itself would be as valid as sections 1 and 2; and section 3 told all interpreters simply to disregard the earlier sections if ratification occurred late. In this sense, section 3 was akin to section 1 itself, which had introduced— again for the first time in an amendment—a time-delay rule, under which Prohibition would not go into effect until "one year" after ratification. Section 3 in effect simply changed "one year" to "never" in the event of late ratification.

The broader significance of this seemingly technical point comes into focus when we realize that what section 3 of the Eighteenth did for time, another section of a future amendment could do along other dimensions. For instance, section 3 of a hypothetical Twenty-eighth Amendment proposed in the year 2020 could provide that the amendment would be "inoperative" unless ratified by four-fifths of the states, rather than a mere three-quarters. Or it could provide that the amendment would be "inoperative" unless endorsed by the president; or agreed to by supermajorities within individual state legislatures; or unless approved by a national referendum; or unless ratified by states totaling more than 50 percent of the national population.

Of course, none of these requirements could formally lower the Article V bar or displace it—that would be pure bootstrap. But by raising the formal bar through a provision specifying when an amendment truly becomes "operative," future section 3 analogues could, as a practical matter, move America toward a more directly democratic system of amendment. If a future section 3 required a national referendum vote of approval before the Twenty-eighth Amendment were to become "operative," that fact alone might put pressure on some fence-sitting state legislators to say yes. A yes vote by such a legislator would become less a vote on the proposed Twenty-eighth's substance, and more a vote to "let the people decide."

Doubtless, the framers of the Prohibition Amendment did not appreciate that they were opening a procedural Pandora's box with the seemingly innocuous provision of section 3—any more than they foresaw all the unintended substantive consequences of Prohibition itself. But despite their intent, section 3 raises intriguing questions and possibilities for twenty-first-century Americans pondering the permutations of permissible constitutional change. Perhaps the Prohibition Amendment still has something to say after all—even after its formal repeal.

"The right . . . to vote"

In August 1920, some ten million women who had never been allowed to vote in a general election became the full political equals of men thanks to the ratification of the Nineteenth Amendment. In sheer numbers, this Woman Suffrage Amendment marked the single biggest democratizing event in American history. (Even the most extraordinary feats of the Founding and Reconstruction eras had involved the electoral empowerment and/or enfranchisement of hundreds of thousands, not millions.) Much as the unprecedented power wielded by American voters under the original Constitution broke sharply with traditional English practice—and just as the widespread enfranchisement of blacks during Reconstruction went far beyond what anyone could have forecast before the Civil War—so also woman suffrage in 1920 came as a thunderclap. As late as 1909, women voted equally with men only in four Western states comprising less than 2 percent of the nation's population. How, then, did women get from the wilderness to the Promised Land in so short a span?

To answer that question, it is useful to begin by pondering how women got from bondage into the wilderness—that is, how they managed to get equal voting rights in four Rocky Mountain states in the late nineteenth century. The rules of territorial expansion and the dynamics of interstate federalism are surely part of the story.

In 1869–70, Wyoming Territory broke new ground by according women equal rights with men to vote and hold office.[33] Twenty years later, Wyoming entered the Union as the first woman-suffrage state. Colorado, Utah, and Idaho soon followed suit. An overly simple yet relatively robust explanation for these developments is that women were an especially rare and precious resource in the West. Under the laws of supply and demand, where women were exceptionally scarce, men had to work that much harder to attract and keep them. By letting women vote with their hands, perhaps Western men hoped that women would vote with their feet—and head West. Much as the Founding Fathers had structured a Constitution whose promises of freedom and democracy sought to pull skilled European immigrants across the ocean, so their pioneer grandsons in the West evidently aimed to draw American women through the plains and over the mountains.[34]

Data from the 1890 census provide some support for this admittedly crude theory. For every hundred native-born Wyoming males, there were only fifty-eight native-born females. No other state had so pronounced a gender imbalance. Colorado and Idaho were the fifth and sixth most imbalanced states overall in 1890. The other early woman-suffrage state, Utah, had a somewhat higher percentage of women (thanks to its early experience with polygamy), but even Utah had only eighty-eight native-born females for every hundred native-born males, ranking it eleventh among the forty-five states in the mid-1890s. Also, the second, third, fourth, and seventh most imbalanced states—Montana, Washington, Nevada, and Oregon—would all embrace woman suffrage in the early 1910s, several years ahead of most sister states. In all these places, men voting to extend the suffrage to women had little reason to fear that males might anytime soon be outvoted en masse by females.[35]

Contemporaneous comparative data from across the oceans are also suggestive. In 1893, New Zealand became the first nation in the world to give women the vote—though until 1919 it withheld from them the right to serve in Parliament. From one perspective, New Zealand's niche within the British Empire was not altogether different from Wyoming's within the American continent: a remote outpost eager to attract new settlers, especially women. At the turn of the century, New Zealand males outnumbered females by a ratio of nine to eight. Among certain communities of New Zealand immigrants from the European continent, the gender imbalance exceeded two to one. Neighboring Australia gave women the vote in national elections in 1902, when there were fewer than ninety nonindigenous females for every hundred nonindigenous males. Before and after Australia's continental enfranchisement, each of the six states that united to form the nation in 1901 followed its own suffrage rules for elections to local parliaments. The least densely populated and most gender-imbalanced region—Western Australia, where men outnumbered women more than three to two—was the second-fastest to give women the vote, doing so in 1899, nearly a full decade before the most populous and balanced area, Victoria, finally became the last state to embrace woman suffrage.[36]

Above and beyond any individualistic desire to woo women that may have motivated the men of Wyoming and other Western regions, federal territorial policy provided a modest if unintended spur to woman suffrage. In general, Congress in the nineteenth century waited for each territory to achieve a certain critical population mass before admitting that territory to statehood. Although Congress followed no single formula applicable to all places and all times, each Western territory understood that rapid population growth would enhance its prospects for early statehood. Every new woman in the West would not only bring to a territory her own person but might also help produce future growth through childbearing. And if Congress ever decided to focus not on a given territory's total number of inhabitants but rather on the size of its voting base, then woman suffrage would almost double the key number.

In its early years, the story of woman suffrage was in effect the opposite of the initial black-suffrage experience. In 1866–68, Northern states had imposed black suffrage on the South while largely declining to embrace it for themselves, partly because these states wanted to discourage Southern blacks from coming north. But at almost the very moment that Northern whites were seeking to discourage a large influx of Southern blacks, Western men were seeking to encourage a large influx of Eastern women.[37]

Although the stories of black and woman suffrage thus diverged in their early chapters, they later converged—much as the very language of the Nineteenth Amendment obviously echoed the Fifteenth, simply substituting "sex" for "race" as an impermissible basis for future state or federal disenfranchisement. In the Fifteenth Amendment saga, once large numbers of blacks could vote in a large number of states, the stage was set for universalization of the equal-suffrage principle. So, too, the Nineteenth Amendment finally became a reality only after a substantial number of states had embraced woman suffrage. In the case of both blacks and women, white male lawmakers for whom they had never voted ultimately proved somewhat more eager to enfranchise them than did their fellow voters.

As early as 1878, Elizabeth Cady Stanton and other leading women began appearing before the United States Senate to speak in support of a proposed constitutional amendment that would do for sex what the Fifteenth Amendment had done for race. Introduced by a male senator, California's A. A. Sargent, the proposed amendment's words had in fact been drafted by a woman, the crusading suffragist Susan B. Anthony, in collaboration with Stanton.[38] In 1920, this amendment would eventually prevail in the exact form in which Anthony had initially drafted it, but only after Anthony's acolytes had transformed the landscape of state practice.

Between 1896 (when Utah and Idaho became the third and fourth woman-suffrage states) and 1909, no new states gave women the vote in general elections. Yet even in this period of seeming quiescence, powerful subterranean forces were at work. A few additional states joined an already substantial list of others willing to let women vote in school board elections and/or other municipal matters. More important, merely by voting on a routine basis in the Rocky Mountain West, women pioneers were proving by their daily example that equal suffrage was an eminently sensible and thoroughly American way of life suitable for adoption in sister states.[39]

Eventually, suffragists—inspired by early crusaders like Anthony, Stanton, and Lucy Stone, and by the more quiet examples of thousands of ordinary Rocky Mountain women—succeeded in spreading woman suffrage to neighboring Western states. From this broad and expanding base the movement began to successfully colonize the East. In effect, Western egalitarians aimed to even up the continental balance of trade: The East had sent bodies out West, but the idea of woman suffrage would migrate in the other direction—reprising the American Revolution itself, in which colonial children had sought to teach Mother England the true meaning of liberty. Seen from a different angle, suffragists hoped to do for horizontal federalism what the Founders had done for vertical federalism: Just as the Philadelphia Constitution had provided a model for state emulation, so Western states might lead the way for the rest.

The special challenge confronting suffragists in this colonizing phase was that in each and every non-suffrage state, voteless females somehow had to persuade male voters and/or male lawmakers to do the right thing and share the vote. The ultimate success of the indefatigable suffragists ironically proved that the old saw—that men would virtually represent the interests of women—contained at least a grain of truth. For had all men been implacably indifferent to the voices of women, suffrage would never have happened. Of course, if virtual representation was a half-truth, it was also a half-lie. The very fact that so many women were so urgently and ceaselessly demanding the vote—waging, in the years prior to 1920, a total of fifty-six full-blown state-referendum campaigns, not to mention countless lobbying efforts before state legislatures, Congress, and national party conventions[40]—was itself evidence to men of good faith that these women did *not* believe that virtual representation was an adequate substitute for actual representation.

From 1910 through 1914, the pace of reform quickened dramatically, as seven additional states—six in the West, and Kansas in the Midwest—gave women full suffrage rights. Meanwhile, other democratic reforms were bubbling to the top of the political agenda and capturing the national imagination. At the state level, provisions empowering voters to participate in initiatives, referenda, recalls, and direct primaries were sweeping the country.[41] At the federal level, the Direct Senate Election Amendment became law in 1913, less than a year after being proposed by Congress. Corruption was out, and good government was in—and women were widely associated with the latter. Also, the Progressive era placed strong emphasis on education and literacy, and in many places women had higher literacy rates than men.

The pace of change further accelerated when various Midwestern and Eastern state legislatures began allowing women to vote for president even where women could not vote for congressmen or state legislators. By the end of 1919, a dozen states fell into the presidential-suffrage-only category, and two more allowed women to vote generally in primary elections, including presidential primaries.[42] These legal changes typically did not require amendments of state constitutions or direct appeals to the voters. Presidential suffrage thus offered a handy hedge for many a state lawmaker who hesitated to get too far ahead of his (currently all-male) voting base but who also was beginning to see that one day—soon—women would be voting even in state races.

Meanwhile, more states—including, for the first time, Eastern and Midwestern heavyweights such as New York (in 1917) and Michigan (in 1918)—were clambering aboard the full-suffrage bandwagon. By the end of 1918, women had won full suffrage rights in a grand total of fifteen states. Because federal lawmakers in all these places would now need to woo female as well as male voters, suffragists could look forward to strong support in Congress from this bloc. Eventually, congressmen from full-suffrage states would favor the Nineteenth Amendment by a combined vote of 116 to 6, adding extra heft to the House support and providing the decisive margin of victory in the Senate.[43]

True, in some places in the mid-1910s, woman suffrage went down to defeat at the hands of all-male electorates. For example, in 1912, male voters in Ohio, Wisconsin, and Michigan all said no, and in 1915, suffragists lost in Massachusetts, Pennsylvania, New Jersey, and New York. But by this point, savvy politicians were beginning to appreciate the mathematical logic of what historian Alexander Keyssar has aptly labeled the suffrage "endgame."[44] Once women got the vote in a given state, there would be no going back, for women themselves would never consent to their own political suicide. Unlike, say, Southern blacks, women would likely always have enough votes to keep the ballot after they first got it. Conversely, whenever suffragists failed to win the vote in a given state, they would be free to raise the issue again and again and again: Tomorrow would always be another day, and democracy's ratchet would inexorably do its work. Thus, in 1917, New York women won what they had failed to win in 1915; and in 1918 suffragists prevailed in Michigan after recent defeats in 1912 and 1913.

Another aspect of the endgame: If and when women did get the vote, woe unto the diehard anti-suffrage politician who had held out until the bitter end! Each state legislator or congressman from a non-suffrage state had to heed not just the men who had elected him, but also the men *and women* who could refuse to reelect him once the franchise was extended. (After ratification of the Direct Senate Election Amendment, every U.S. senator had to focus on the statewide voters rather than a tiny clump of political chums in the state capital.) The experience in Ohio, where male voters had refused to enfranchise women in 1912 and again in 1914, nicely illustrated the underlying electoral math. Senator Warren Harding voted for the Woman Suffrage Amendment and went on to capture the White House in 1920. Conversely, Senator Atlee Pomerene opposed the amendment and was voted out of office in 1922.[45]

By the end of 1919, no serious presidential candidate could afford to be strongly anti-suffrage, since such a stance might well doom his prospects in the twenty-nine states that already embraced either full suffrage or some version of presidential suffrage. To win the White House without several of these states would be the political equivalent of filling an inside straight. Thus even a senator from a non-suffrage state had to think twice about opposing woman suffrage if he harbored any long-term presidential aspirations.

America's decision to enter World War I added still further momentum to the movement. In a military crusade being publicly justified to Americans as a war to "make the world safe for democracy," the claims of those Americans excluded from full democratic rights took on special urgency. Because America claimed to be fighting for certain ideals, it became especially important to live up to them. All across Europe, women were winning the vote in countries such as Norway, Denmark, Holland, Sweden, and even Austria and Germany. Surely, suffragists argued, the United States should not lag behind any of these places. Also, women on the home front were making vital contributions to the general war effort, economically and socially, even if they did not bear arms on the battlefield itself. In a word, America's women were *loyal*—as America's blacks had been in the 1860s—and wars generally serve to remind nations of the value of loyalty. Widespread nativist anxiety about German aliens in America, and even about naturalized citizens from Central Europe, also fueled the suffrage crusade, given that a disproportionate percentage of women across the country were American-born.

Wars generally increase executive power, and World War I was no exception. In September 1918, President Woodrow Wilson dramatized his support for a national woman-suffrage amendment by appearing in person before the Senate to plead for constitutional reform. Reminding his audience that women were "partners . . . in this war," Wilson proclaimed the amendment a "vitally necessary war measure" that would capture the imagination of "the women of the world" and enhance America's claim to global moral leadership in the postwar era. Several months after this flamboyant presidential intervention, Congress formally proposed the Woman Suffrage Amendment. The endgame had entered its final stage.[46]

The scene then shifted back to the several states. In Congress, suffrage opponents had understandably but unsuccessfully urged that the amendment proposal should be sent for ratification not to the forty-eight regular state legislatures, but rather to ad hoc state conventions, as permitted by Article V. State ratifying conventions would have been apt to approximate state referenda. Single-shot convention delegates would have had less reason than regular legislators to worry about the future political rewards or punishments that women could mete out once suffrage was won. Supporters of the amendment thus resisted the bait offered up by opponents; women's odds were better with state legislatures, even though this traditional ratification track would generally require the amendment to win bicamerally in every state.

In the final stage of the struggle for woman suffrage, the only substantial opposition to the Susan B. Anthony Amendment (as it was generally called) came from the South. This was the sole region that had yet to jump aboard the accelerating full-suffrage bandwagon. Also, Southerners who by the turn of the century had effectively nullified the Black Suffrage Amendment in their region had little sympathy for a Woman Suffrage Amendment written in parallel language and reaffirming the root principles of national voting rights and national enforcement power. As South Carolina's Senator Ellison D. Smith put the point in 1919, "Here is exactly the identical same amendment applied to the other half of the Negro race. The southern man who votes for the Susan B. Anthony Amendment votes to ratify the Fifteenth Amendment."[47] In late August 1920, Tennessee became the key thirty-sixth state needed for ratification, but only the third of eleven ex-Confederate states to say yes to the Anthony Amendment.

READ NARROWLY, THE NINETEENTH AMENDMENT guaranteed women's equal right to vote in ordinary local, state, and federal elections, both for candidates (mayors, governors, senators, et cetera) and on ballot issues (in initiatives, referenda, bond measures, and so on). Yet fairly read, the Anthony Amendment swept even further, promising that women would bear equal rights and responsibilities in all political domains, including, for example, an equal right to stand for election and to sit on juries. Though the Supreme Court has never quite articulated the principle of the Anthony Amendment in this way, much of the Court's current case law does indeed approximate this principle in its results.[48]

Consider, for example, the right of women to serve on juries equally with men—a right that today's Court squarely recognizes even though its relevant opinions typically fail to highlight the Anthony Amendment. This failure is puzzling. After all, the words of the amendment—words that Progressive-era Americans understood to have been drafted by Susan B. Anthony herself in the 1870s—guaranteed women's right "to vote" in all venues. If these words applied when citizens voted for mayors or in referenda, why didn't they apply when citizens voted in jury boxes? Also, the Woman Suffrage Amendment was plainly pegged to the Black Suffrage Amendment. A landmark congressional statute enacted in 1875— a statute that was on the books both in 1878 when the Anthony Amendment first reached Congress and in 1920 when the Amendment finally prevailed—seemed to say that the principles of the Black Suffrage Amendment applied to jury service as well.[49] If this was (and indeed remains) true of the Black Suffrage Amendment, why not of the Woman Suffrage Amendment? Just as Susan B. Anthony herself had condemned all-male electorates, so she had famously rejected all-male juries—in a notorious early-1870s episode that *The New York Times* briefly recalled for its readers on the very day that it reported Congress's enactment of what the *Times* referred to as "the Susan Anthony amendment."[50]

Beyond these basic points from the Anthony Amendment's text and history, we should note that most states in the early twentieth century provided that jurors should be drawn from the pool of eligible voters. Even if the Anthony Amendment did not by itself make women equal jurors, didn't it do so in tandem with state laws and practices linking jury service to suffrage rules? Many state supreme courts and state legislatures in the Progressive era construed the Nineteenth Amendment and/or its state constitutional counterparts to have precisely this effect, though other states failed to see the light.[51] More broadly, the amendment's implicit logic undercut many of the old justifications for keeping women out of the halls of power. For example, any argument that women could be kept off juries because they lacked sufficient capacity to make important decisions would seem to be refuted by the Anthony Amendment itself: Since the amendment empowered women to vote as equals for constitutional conventions and for presidents, it plainly presupposed that women did indeed have the right stuff to be equal partners in all serious matters of governance.[52]

To see the sweep of the Anthony Amendment from one final angle, let's consider a simple question: Did women have an equal right to run for president? Suppose, for example, that a state legislature in 1922 passed a law disqualifying all female candidates for president and specifying that any vote for a woman in that state would be legally invalid. Would such a law have been constitutional? Surely most American citizens and judges today would think not.

But where, exactly, did the Constitution say that a woman had a right to run? In what clause, precisely, did the document limit gendered state laws regulating presidential elections? If we look to the original Constitution of 1788, it is hard to see where such a right or a limit existed in word or deed. After all, the text consistently referred to the president with the words "he" and "his"—never "she" or "her." Anti-Federalists and Federalists debated at length whether American presidents would come to resemble English kings but said nary a word about queens. The original Constitution also seemed to provide state legislatures virtual carte blanche in regulating how presidential electors would be chosen. And of course, "the People" doing the ordaining in the Founding era were men.

Nor would the Reconstruction Amendments as written and originally understood provide much help to our hypothetical female candidate. The Fourteenth Amendment's text guaranteed only civil rights in emphatic contradistinction to political rights like the right to vote or the right to run. As for the Thirteenth Amendment, ineligibility to be president would hardly seem the equivalent of slavery. And the Fifteenth Amendment forbade only racial discriminations.

But just as it *would* be a violation of the spirit of the Fifteenth Amendment to prevent blacks from seeking office, so, too, with the Nineteenth Amendment and women. As the Reconstruction Congress itself had illustrated in highly visible decisions made prior to the ratification of the Fifteenth Amendment,[53] the right *of* blacks to vote included their right to vote *for* blacks. The right of blacks *to vote* also implied their right *to be voted for*. Similar logic applied to the companion Woman Suffrage Amendment.[54]

To read the Constitution any more narrowly than this would fail to do justice to an amendment that in the public mind bore the name of Susan B. Anthony and that was enacted thanks not only to ordinary voters, but also to elected officials working alongside (and at times beyond) them.

"the 20th day of January, and . . . the 3d day of January"

Much as the Seventeenth and Nineteenth Amendments had aimed to democratize Senate elections and the general voting base, so the Twentieth Amendment aimed to democratize the political calendar. Though this rather technical amendment clipping the wings of electoral lame ducks can hardly be placed on the same plane as the enfranchisement of ten million women, the amendment did succeed in improving American-style popular sovereignty.

Proposed in March 1932 and ratified in early 1933, the Twentieth aimed to reduce the power of lame-duck politicians—public servants who had been repudiated by the voters at the polls but who had yet to be replaced by their spring-chicken successors. Tackling the problem of a lame-duck president, section 1 moved up Inauguration Day from the old March 4 to a new date, January 20. Current events gave the issue special poignancy. When Congress proposed the amendment, everyone knew that President Herbert Hoover was unlikely to be reelected in November. Yet everyone also understood that the soon-to-be-lame-duck president would remain in power for four months after being repudiated, with no mandate (and perhaps little inclination) to do anything, despite the widespread view that immediate action was needed to pull the country out of its Depression.

The ratification track record of the Lame Duck Amendment reflected the country's mounting frustration once the voters did indeed say no to Hoover and yes to Roosevelt. In January 1933 alone, twenty-eight states ratified the reform amendment, and before long every single one of America's forty-eight states had said yes to the new calendar. Although none of this hastened FDR's inauguration—under a time-delay rule, à la Prohibition, the new political calendar would not become operative until the following electoral cycle—the amendment's prompt ratification did mean that future generations would not have to wait as Depression-era Americans had been made to.*

---

*The Twentieth Amendment's time-delay rule for its own implementation presents a puzzle: Why would an amendment designed to reduce time delays between popular elections and government policy-making itself introduce a special time-delay rule for its own operation? At least two interrelated answers would seem to be at work. First, constitutional rules often operate on

By comparison to established English parliamentary practice, in which new governments typically took power very shortly after elections, even the new presidential starting date of January 20 involved an awkwardly long period of political limbo. But under the original Constitution as revised by the 1804 Presidential Selection Amendment, the November election would not formally decide the presidency. Rather, the Constitution provided for several postelection proceedings—the meeting of the electors, the counting of their votes in Congress, and congressional balloting in the event that no candidate had a clear electoral-vote majority. To accommodate all this, section 1 preserved a considerable window between Election Day and Inauguration Day.*

Sections 1 and 2 of the amendment also tackled the problem of the congressional calendar. Henceforth biannual congressional terms would begin on January 3, not March 4. And instead of presumptively meeting every December, as the Philadelphia Constitution had provided, Congress would presumptively convene in January. In practice, this meant that members elected in November would come into power only two months later—a marked contrast to the older practice under which the first meeting of Congress was presumptively held in December of the year *following* the election, a full *thirteen* months after the voters had spoken. The new January 3 start date also meant that future lame-duck congressional sessions would be nonexistent or very short indeed—for the new Congress would take power right after New Year's Day.

By providing a start date for Congress three weeks *before* Presidential Inauguration Day, the Twentieth Amendment would also enable any electoral-college misfires to be handled by the *incoming* Congress—as had not happened, for example, in the elections of 1800–01, 1824–25, and 1876–77, when lame-duck Congresses had decided the identity of the

---

a different, more extended temporal plane than ordinary governmental policy-making. In some situations, a time-delay rule in a proposed constitutional amendment may create a desirable veil of ignorance, forcing amenders to focus on long-run principle rather than short-run advantage. (For an example, see Chapter 8, page 294.) Second and related, without a time delay certain changes in the constitutional order might be thought to violate vested rights or strong expectations worthy of respect.

*In 1916, Woodrow Wilson had toyed with another possible way to shorten this window. Were Wilson, the incumbent, to lose to Republican challenger Charles Evans Hughes, Wilson could choose to appoint Hughes secretary of state—a post that under the presidential-succession law then in effect would place Hughes next in line after the vice president. If Wilson and his vice president, Thomas Marshall, were then to resign, Hughes could take over long before March 4. As things turned out, Wilson won and nothing became of this musing. In 1920–21, Wilson took no steps to hasten Harding's ascension. See generally Edward S. Corwin, *The President: Office and Powers, 1787–1957* (4th rev. ed. 1957), 358–59.

president. In these previous elections, had congressional lame ducks not acted, no one could have, for the new Congress had no right to convene before Inauguration Day (and, indeed, was not ordinarily due to assemble until many months after Inauguration). By staggering the starting dates for the legislature and the executive, the Lame Duck Amendment aimed to ensure (though it oddly failed to state explicitly) that all future presidential-election decisions would be made by congressmen—and congresswomen!—with fresh electoral mandates.[55]

Other sections of the amendment tidied up a variety of technical issues of presidential selection and succession—for example, by clarifying that in the event of the death of a president elect, the incoming vice president elect would become president on Inauguration Day.[56] Details aside, the basic thrust of the Twentieth Amendment as a whole was to render the constitutional calendar more republican by bringing the legislative and executive branches into closer temporal alignment with the most recent expression of the people's wisdom on Election Day.

YET EVEN AFTER THESE REFORMS—and after the more sweeping changes introduced by other Progressive Amendments—American democracy remained visibly imperfect. If the Sixteenth Amendment had authorized federal progressive income taxes on the rich, it had done nothing to stop regressive and suffrage-limiting state poll taxes on the poor. Even as the Seventeenth Amendment had democratized Senate elections within individual states, it had left the District of Columbia—a non-state—wholly unrepresented in America's basic republican system. Although the Nineteenth Amendment had extended the vote to millions of loyal women, it had overlooked millions of loyal young adults who were also important partners in America's wars. And while Congress in the early twentieth century conferred citizenship on all Indians in reservations, thereby filling a gap left open by the Fourteenth Amendment,[57] the promises of the Reconstruction Amendments generally remained unfulfilled for most black Americans.*

In short, the American People still had much to do.

---

*For example, by 1910, "only 15 percent of adult black men in Virginia were registered to vote; in Mississippi and Alabama the figure stood at less than 2 percent." Mary J. Farmer and Donald Nieman, "Race, Class, Gender, and the Unintended Consequences of the Fifteenth Amendment," in David E. Kyvig, ed., *Unintended Consequences of Constitutional Amendment* (2000), 141, 148.

Chapter 12

≈

MODERN MOVES

MARCH ON WASHINGTON, AUGUST 28, 1963.
During the Second Reconstruction, Americans took to the streets to demand equality and justice for all. Three of the four amendments ratified between 1960 and 1972 broadened rights of political participation.

*I*N THE SHADOW of extended military struggles against an assortment of Old World tyrants, late-twentieth-century Americans continued to debate and refine their own New World alternative. New constitutional rules hedged against domineering presidents and self-dealing congressmen and improved the presidential-succession process. Young adults and poor people won additional rights of democratic participation, as did residents of the nation's capital city. A Second Reconstruction aimed to redeem the promises of the First. Perhaps most important of all, the most recent generation of Americans has kept the door open for future generations to introduce their own reforms. Two centuries after the Founding, America's more perfect union thus remains what it has always been—an imperfect work in progress.

"No person . . . more than twice"

With only two exceptions, America's amendments have come in generational spurts in times of high political energy. After a Founding-era flurry, the next burst of amendments did not occur until Reconstruction, followed by decades of constitutional quietude. Then came a cluster of constitutional reforms in the Progressive era and another pair of amendments in the Great Depression. Four of the remaining six amendments became law during the Kennedy-Johnson-Vietnam years. The Twenty-second Amendment, which prohibited any person from being elected to the presidency more than twice, stands as a counterexample to the general rule of generational clusters: Ratified in 1951, this lonely amendment was separated by almost two decades from its immediate predecessor and by another decade from its immediate successor.* Yet if we pull the camera back, even this amendment can be seen to fit into a larger modern pattern: Of the seven amendments adopted between 1932 and 1972, all but one focused wholly or in part on issues of presidential election and succession.

The Two Term Amendment codified an unwritten tradition dating back to George Washington. Whether America's first president had in fact set out to establish a strict resignation norm may be debated, for he of-

---

*The other generational outlier is the Twenty-seventh Amendment, whose strange two-century odyssey from proposal to enactment we shall ponder later in this chapter.

fered his countrymen no extended explanation as he stepped down at the end of eight years. When Jefferson declined a third term, he began to elaborate the emerging precedent by publicly invoking the ideal of republican rotation.[1] After Madison and Monroe followed suit, any successor who might dare aspire to a third term knew that he would be inviting nearly impossible political comparisons: Did he really think he was greater than every one of these Founders?

Nevertheless, the two-term tradition did not stop all post-Founding presidents from dreaming to go where none had gone before. Not only was the norm a purely informal one, but in at least three ways, its message was ambiguous. First, did it bar all third terms or merely three *consecutive* terms? Ulysses S. Grant, whose military credentials as the Republic's savior naturally invited comparisons to George Washington, construed the resignation norm narrowly. In 1876, he mounted no campaign for a third term, but four years later he did reach for the Republican nomination, which barely eluded his grasp.[2] In 1896, Grover Cleveland also declined to rule out a third term, which would have been only his second straight one. (Four years of President Benjamin Harrison had separated Cleveland's first two terms.) But Cleveland, a Democrat, had alienated his party, which turned its back on the incumbent in favor of William Jennings Bryan. The official Democratic platform that year "declare[d] it to be the unwritten law of this Republic, established by custom and usage of 100 years, and sanctioned by the examples of the greatest and wisest of those who founded and have maintained our Government, that no man should be eligible for a third term of the Presidential office."

The next decade highlighted a second ambiguity: How should the "custom and usage of 100 years" be applied to partial terms? When Theodore Roosevelt succeeded the slain William McKinley six months into McKinley's second term and then won election in his own right three years later, was he free to run for a second full term, or did tradition argue against any bid for eleven and a half straight years? In the event, Roosevelt announced that he would step aside after seven-plus years in power: "The wise custom which limits the President to two terms regards the substance and not the form." "Under no circumstances will I be a candidate for or accept another nomination." Three years after leaving office, however, Roosevelt was back in the ring contending for another stint and noting that, strictly speaking, he was seeking only his second *full* term. When confronted with his earlier pledge, Roosevelt resorted to the distinction between consecutive and nonconsecutive terms. As he saw it, if at some moment he were to decline "a third cup of coffee," no one should think he was forever forswearing the beverage. "I meant, of course, a third consecutive term."[3]

A final ambiguity concerned the absolutism of the norm. Might exceptional circumstances arise that warranted an extra term? *The Federalist* No. 72 had warned that in a crisis, the nation might urgently require the leadership of a particular man, whose prior service to the republic should never render him ineligible at the hour of greatest need. Washington said much the same thing in private correspondence with Lafayette, and even Jefferson would later muse about the propriety of a third term in rare circumstances.[4] In 1920 Woodrow Wilson apparently dreamed of a third consecutive term to complete the work of world pacification that he had begun and that the Senate had undone when it sank his plan for an American role in the League of Nations.[5] Wilson's failing health, however, made his musings wildly unrealistic. Less than two decades after his defeat at the hands of the Senate, his worst fears had come to pass: The European armistice failed and the old world war resumed. In response, Franklin Roosevelt sought and won an unprecedented third term in 1940 and then a fourth in 1944. With America first on the edge and then at the center of the largest military struggle in world history, the incumbent and the voters placed a premium on executive continuity.

Roosevelt died early in his fourth term. Less than two years later, in March 1947, Congress proposed an amendment to limit presidential re-eligibility and codify the pre-FDR practice. Ratification occurred in early 1951.

By reducing fluid traditions to a fixed text, the amendment resolved several earlier ambiguities. The new rules capped all terms, not merely consecutive ones. A rounding rule allowed a vice president who had taken over in the event of presidential death or disability to be twice elected to the presidency if his earlier service was for less than two years, and to be elected only once otherwise. In effect this codified Theodore Roosevelt's initial decision to count his sizable partial term as a full one.[6] A similar two-year rounding rule would apply to any other officer who had acted as president under congressional succession statues. Finally, the amendment made clear that its new commands were absolute, softened only by a special set of transition rules applicable to current and past incumbents.[7]

Yet some ambiguities have remained to the present day. The Two Term Amendment's opening words barred a person from being *"elected"* president more than twice. But what about a two-term incumbent who thereafter sought and won the vice presidency and then moved back into the Oval Office as a result of the new president's death, disability, removal, or resignation? Would it matter if the resignation had been prearranged?[8] What if our two-termer had subsequently become vice president not by being elected to that office but by appointment thereto under the later Presidential Succession Amendment?[9] Even if all such vice-president-turned-president gambits were deemed to violate the Constitution's letter and spirit, should the same broad reading apply if a two-termer later became, say, secretary of state and was then called upon to act as president in a double-vacancy scenario, pursuant to a valid congressional succession statute?[10]

WE HAVE SEEN REPEATED constitutional illustrations of the deep truth that the presidency was from the beginning, and remains, the nation's most personal office. Thus, in 1787–89 the Federalists sculpted the original Executive Article in Washington's image; in 1803–04 Republicans reshaped the office via an amendment to accommodate Jefferson; and in 1932–33 Americans amended the constitutional rules yet again with the lame-duck Herbert Hoover's failures in mind. The Two Term Amendment provides yet another example of America's personalized presidency. The amendment emerged as a posthumous rebuke to the memory of Franklin Roosevelt. Never again, the text made clear, should one man presume to be elected to the nation's—*the world's*—most powerful office more than twice. The specters of Hitler, Mussolini, and Stalin only added to America's mid-century anxiety about any political system that revolved around the same man for an extended period.* What was needed, instead, was a new kind of presidency transcending the idea that any one person could ever be indispensable in a way that FDR had seemed to be.

True, the text of the Two Term Amendment nowhere mentioned "that man" by name, any more than it referred to Harry Truman or Herbert Hoover. But when its transition-rules section spoke of "any person holding the office of President, when this Article was proposed by the Congress," this clause did indeed apply to a class of one. The text might as well have referred to "all persons named Harry Truman and born in

---

*A similar anxiety manifested itself in state constitutions. In 1950, nearly two-thirds of the states allowed governors to seek unlimited reelection. Today, only a quarter of the states do so. Compare *The Book of the States* (1950–51), 8:625 with ibid. (2002), 34:161–62. Much as states in the post-Founding era began to remodel their state governors in the image of the Philadelphia Constitution's Executive Article, so it would appear that states have generally revised their gubernatorial models to mirror the Two Term Amendment. Note however that state constitutions commonly cap only the number of *consecutive* terms that one person may serve as governor.

Lamar, Missouri, on May 8, 1884." So, too, Hoover was the only living ex-president to whom other transition rules applied. Most important of all, the amendment's chief rule—no third elected terms—had FDR written all over it, tracking as it did a prominent plank of the Republican plat-forms of 1940 and 1944.

In one of history's little ironies, an amendment whose most ardent supporters were FDR's Republican critics has had its greatest bite in re-stricting the Republican Party itself, by preventing the GOP from tapping Dwight Eisenhower and Ronald Reagan for third terms in the elections of 1960 and 1988, respectively. In both years, these popular incumbents might well have been preferred by both the party faithful and the general elec-torate, had they remained eligible. Thus far, the only other men formally barred from seeking third terms by the amendment have been Richard Nixon, Bill Clinton, and George W. Bush. It seems wildly unlikely that post-Watergate Republicans would ever have preferred Nixon as their leader in 1976, regardless of the amendment. Whether Clinton would have been the Democrats' top choice in 2000 but for the Two Term Amend-ment is harder to say. The constitutional cap itself profoundly affected Clinton's years in office; without that cap, politics would have played out rather differently.

Nor is this last point unique to Clinton. For every second-term presi-dent since FDR, the amendment has removed an important arrow in the old presidential quiver. Prior to 1951, a two-term president was unlikely to seek and win a third term, but the mere possibility that he might do so strengthened his control over his allies and helped keep his foes in check. Overly aggressive tactics against him by opposition leaders might prod him into action, provoking him to transform the next presidential contest into a personal referendum between himself and his detractors. Deprived of this option by the amendment, successful presidents in the modern era have been easier targets—sitting ducks from Day One of Term Two. Of the four constitutional lame ducks from 1951 to 2001—Eisenhower, Nixon, Reagan, and Clinton—the last three met with fierce congressional opposition in their second terms, thanks to high-visibility investigations in the Watergate and Iran-Contra scandals and the Lewinsky affair. The up-shot: the nation's first presidential resignation under threat of impeach-ment and its first actual impeachment of an *elected* president.[11] If the aim of the Two Term Amendment was to take the presidency down a notch, it has thus far succeeded beyond all expectations.

A related result of the amendment has been to oblige second-term presidents to pin their hopes for political protection and vindication on their vice presidents. Americans seeking to reward Ronald Reagan in his second term could give him an indirect vote of confidence—a third term of sorts—by electing his handpicked vice president, George H. W. Bush, to replace him. So, too, with Bill Clinton and his anointed successor, Al Gore.[12] Indeed, since the adoption of the Two Term Amendment, America has witnessed a remarkable rise in the status of her vice presidents. Of the vice presidents chosen between the 1804 adoption of the Presidential Selection Amendment (which effectively downgraded the vice presidency) and the 1951 ratification of the Two Term Amendment (which indirectly upgraded it), less than one in six ever went on to win a major-party nomination to the presidency itself. After 1952—the first election under the new rules—more than half of the VPs would later head the party ticket. Starting with Eisenhower, every one of the five retiring presidents in the late twentieth century watched his party tap his handpicked vice president as its next presidential candidate—a result that occurred only twice in all the years from Jefferson through Truman. Along this dimension, it would seem that the amendment has been a remarkable success, prompting presidents to pick stronger VPs and encouraging the republic to avoid thinking of any one man as utterly indispensable.[13]

"The District"

The capital city of a nation that began as the world's leading democracy and that continues to see itself in that light has never been an equal participant in that democracy. But in 1961, Americans ratified an amendment— the Twenty-third, to be precise—that integrated the District of Columbia into the electoral-college system.

The constitutionally awkward status of the District may be teased out of the nation's very name: United *States*. How should Americans conceptualize parts of the nation that lack the status of states? Answers to this question have varied over time. When the phrase "united states" was first emblazoned across the Declaration of Independence, Americans were not yet thinking of anything other than states. No union territory existed. Rather, individual states laid (conflicting) claims to the ultramontane West. The text of the Articles of Confederation said nothing about a collective Western territory, but as we have seen, landless Maryland refused to ratify that text until landed states such as Virginia agreed to cede their Western claims to the union. Members of the Confederation Congress then proceeded to improvise a framework for the West that culminated in the Northwest Ordinance of 1787.

The Philadelphia framers made special provision in Article IV for direct federal governance of union territory and also provided in Article I for a federally run national seat. Early in the Washington Administration, Congress famously decided to locate the capital on the banks of the Potomac, not far from Mount Vernon. Because this new capital city was emphatically not a state, it would of course have no seats in the House, Senate, or electoral college. Nor would it have any constitutional right of home rule. Rather, Congress would have plenary legislative power over the District, as over the Western territories.

Throughout the antebellum era, the status of the District hardly seemed peculiar. After all, countless thousands of Americans in the West were receiving roughly similar constitutional treatment. Also, until the 1860 census, the District had fewer residents than even the tiniest state. But as the continental territories inexorably graduated into states, the sense of anomaly grew, as did the District's population. By 1900, the District could claim more residents than could any one of the six least populous states. Four of these had been admitted to statehood in the preceding dozen years. Only the District, it seemed, was doomed to *permanent* nonstatehood.

To be more precise, the District's status increasingly began to resemble not the ordinary continental territories, but rather a few extraordinary entities of distinctly diminished constitutional status: Indian reservations* and America's overseas possessions, such as Hawaii, the Philippines, and Puerto Rico. And the District had one other obvious thing in common with these other subordinated units: a sizable percentage of nonwhite residents. Blacks accounted for a third of the District's population in 1900 and more than half in 1960.

In fact, the District's black inhabitants had been a huge part of its history from the earliest days of the Republic. The First Congress chose a site along the banks of the Potomac to accommodate the South, in exchange for Southern concessions on other issues. The specific decision to encapsulate the city of Alexandria within the District assured that a large number

---

*On the constitutional status of Indian reservations, it should be noted that both the original Constitution (in Article I, section 2) and the later Fourteenth Amendment (in its own section 2) pointedly excluded "Indians not taxed"—that is, tribal Indians living on reservations—from congressional apportionment. In addition, the first section of the Fourteenth Amendment, granting birthright citizenship to all persons born under the American flag, excluded those not "subject" to U.S. "jurisdiction"—paradigmatically, Indians on reservations. This Indian exclusion appeared in plainer language in the text of the companion Civil Rights Act of 1866, 14 Stat. 27. In 1924, Congress conferred citizenship by statute on American Indians. Act of June 2, 1924, ch. 233, 43 Stat. 253.

of slaves would be part of the national capital from the outset. (This part of the District was eventually ceded back to Virginia in the 1840s.) In the aftermath of the Civil War, Reconstruction Republicans debated long and hard over the status of blacks in the national capital. In 1865, white voters in the District overwhelmingly rejected the idea of black suffrage, with nearly seven thousand opposed and only thirty-five in favor. But precisely because the District was not wholly self-governing, this vote hardly ended the matter. Congress enfranchised the District's blacks in early 1867, two months before it imposed black suffrage on the South and two years before it proposed universalizing black suffrage in the Fifteenth Amendment. In 1868, the capital city elected two black aldermen. Nevertheless, District self-government existed only within the limits laid down by Congress, which in 1874 reasserted its own control over the area.[14]

For much of the early twentieth century, District residents sought increased powers of home rule and a larger role in national governance. Why, we might wonder, did such pleas go unheeded until the 1960s? Conversely, why did this amendment finally succeed when it did?

THE STORY OF RACE, war, and suffrage in the mid-nineteenth century repeated itself somewhat in the mid-twentieth. As America's blacks had once proved themselves on the battlefields of the Civil War, so in World War II more than a million African Americans served in uniform. Much as an all-out struggle against the Slave Power had helped mobilize many whites against grotesque forms of racial subordination, so a war against Nazism helped delegitimate all American ideas that resembled Hitler's creed of Aryan Supremacy. And just as America's leaders in the Civil War had worried about the need to secure support overseas—by wooing British public opinion, for example—so America's leaders in the Cold War came to understand the importance of winning the hearts and minds of black- and brown-skinned peoples in Africa and Asia.[15]

Abolishing American apartheid would obviously improve the nation's image in these emerging military and ideological battlegrounds, and so would ending the seeming imperialism within the American federal system, whereby brown-skinned folk in Hawaii and black-skinned citizens in the District of Columbia found themselves at a distinct disadvantage in the basic governing structure. It is not entirely a coincidence that Hawaiian statehood and the D.C. Amendment came to pass less than two years apart, or that this last state to join the union was the first to ratify the D.C. plan, only a week after the amendment cleared Congress. (Alaska, featuring its own sizable proportion of nonwhite natives—and exquisite proximity to the Soviet Union, a major plus for Cold War surveillance and other military purposes—had become the forty-ninth state just before Hawaii's admission.[16]) To see the connection between race and the D.C. Amendment from another angle, we need only note that of the eleven states that failed to ratify the amendment, ten came from the old Confederacy. The only ex-gray state that said yes was Tennessee, and the only ex-blue state that said no was Kentucky.

We should also note the specific timing of Congress's proposal, for it gently reminds us that America's presidency, though no formal part of the amendment process, nevertheless influences that process. Congress proposed the amendment in June 1960—only months before what was expected (and what in fact turned out) to be a presidential horse race down to the wire between Nixon and Kennedy. Black voters were being wooed by both sides. Republicans reminded blacks that theirs was the party of Lincoln, while Democrats (outside the South) proclaimed themselves the heirs of FDR and Truman. In 1948, with the Democratic Platform officially endorsing "extension of the right of suffrage to the people of the District of Columbia," the national black vote had given Truman his margin of victory.[17] More recently, Eisenhower had made inroads among blacks in 1956. In 1960, neither party could afford to take the Negro vote for granted. It is thus fitting that an amendment giving black voters more power—the first such amendment since Reconstruction—was proposed under a Republican president and ratified under a Democrat.

Yet the amendment's domain was limited. First, it folded the District into the electoral-college system but not into the House or Senate. (Even in presidential elections, if no candidate won an electoral-vote majority, the matter would continue to be decided in the House, where D.C. would have no vote.) In 1978, Congress would eventually propose a broader amendment integrating D.C. into the federal legislature,[18] but over the next seven years, less than half the needed states would agree. By this time, black voters had decisively migrated to the Democratic camp and Republican politicians were loath to give their rivals two new Senate seats and at least one new House seat. Since 1970, Congress has allowed D.C. to send a nonvoting representative to the House and has extended speech and debate privileges to this official.[19]

Second, the D.C. Amendment failed to offer District of Columbia voters any home-rule powers over the capital city itself. In 1973, when the chairmanship of the House Committee on the District of Columbia passed from a white South Carolinian to a black Michigander, Congress enacted a new statute vesting various powers in a locally elected mayor and city council.[20]

Third, the D.C. Amendment capped the District's electoral votes. As with every state, the District was guaranteed a three-elector minimum, but the amendment went on to provide that in no case would the District, regardless of its population, receive more electoral votes than the smallest state. For example, in 1964, the District cast only three electoral votes, even though several less populous states—New Hampshire, North Dakota, Hawaii, Idaho, Montana, and South Dakota—got four votes apiece. On the other hand, thanks to the three-elector minimum, all these states and the District as well could be said to enjoy a leg up on the next tier of slightly larger states. For instance, Colorado, Oregon, and Arkansas each had well over twice the District's population in 1964, but each only cast six electoral votes.

Finally, the amendment provided no ironclad guarantee that the District's voters would in fact choose electors directly. Technically, the electors would be chosen "as the Congress may direct." In theory, Congress itself might try to appoint electors on behalf of the District. True, any state legislature might likewise resolve to appoint that state's electors. But the obvious difference was that disgruntled state voters could throw grabby state legislators out of office, whereas District residents would have no comparable power over Congress. Thus, the democratic anomaly of the District has been reduced but not eliminated.

"The right . . . to vote"

Much as the Twenty-third Amendment promised more democracy for the residents of the District, so the Twenty-fourth and Twenty-sixth Amendments extended the constitutional right to vote to two other segments of American society who had yet to receive their democratic due: the poor, and young adults. In the midst of these new voting-rights amendments, America also adopted a landmark voting statute redeeming the promise of her earliest voting-rights amendment.

Proposed in 1962 and ratified two years later, the Twenty-fourth Amendment guaranteed that "the right of citizens of the United States to vote" in federal elections "shall not be denied or abridged by the United States or any State by reason of failure to pay any poll tax or other tax." This language echoed and extended the phraseology of the Fifteenth and Nineteenth Amendments. What the Black Suffrage Amendment had done for race and the Woman Suffrage Amendment had done for sex, the Anti–Poll Tax Amendment did for class. Henceforth, neither state law nor federal law could disenfranchise a person merely because he or she was too poor to pay a poll tax.

Or at least that would be the explicit rule for *federal* elections—of representatives, senators, and presidents. (Reflecting the increasing importance of primary elections—John Kennedy's path to power in 1960—the amendment explicitly applied to all congressional and presidential primary contests.)[21] The amendment did not reach state and local elections. Yet nothing in the amendment blessed poll taxes in these nonfederal proceedings. The issue was simply left to be resolved by state and federal statutes and by earlier federal constitutional provisions, including the republican-government clause and the Reconstruction Amendments.

In 1965, only a year after the Anti–Poll Tax Amendment became part of the Constitution, Congress enacted a landmark Voting Rights Act targeting a host of electoral tests and devices designed to disenfranchise blacks. Though this act was hardly limited to poll-tax suffrage laws, it surely encompassed them, for such laws did indeed disfavor blacks in both purpose and effect. In the early 1960s, poll-tax suffrage laws were in place in only five states—all in the former Confederacy.[22] In one section of the act specifically aimed at poll-tax suffrage laws, Congress declared that such laws "in some areas ha[ve] the purpose or effect of denying persons the right to vote because of race or color" and further declared that "the constitutional right of citizens to vote is denied or abridged in some areas by the requirement of the payment of a poll tax as a precondition to voting." Explicitly invoking its own authority to enforce the Reconstruction Amendments, Congress directed the attorney general to seek judicial invalidation of such state laws.[23]

In 1964, in its first case construing the Anti–Poll Tax Amendment, the Supreme Court took pains to note that Virginia's poll tax "was born of a desire to disenfranchise the Negro." Speaking for the Court, Chief Justice Earl Warren pointedly quoted one of the original sponsors of Virginia's poll-tax suffrage rule, which dated back to 1902: "Discrimination! Why, that is precisely what we propose[:] . . . to discriminate to the very extremity of permissible action under the limitations of the Federal Constitution, with a view to the elimination of every negro voter who can be gotten rid of, legally, without materially impairing the numerical strength of the white electorate."[24] In 1966, the Virginia poll-tax regime was back before the justices, who proceeded to invalidate it and the laws of three other states (all Southern) that still conditioned voting rights on poll-tax payments. Thus the Court extended and deepened the constitutional norm that Congress and the ratifying states had so recently championed.

As with the newborn District of Columbia Amendment and the gestating Voting Rights Act, the Anti–Poll Tax Amendment embodied a renewed commitment to voting equality for the dispossessed. The issue of race visibly hovered over all three measures. Indeed, in its very text, the Anti–Poll Tax Amendment reaffirmed the grand phrases of the Black Suffrage Amendment—a bow by the Second Reconstruction generation to their First Reconstruction forefathers and foremothers. Once again, the North was bringing the South back into line.

This time, however, electoral reform took hold in the South as had not happened a century earlier. Thanks to the 1964 amendment and the 1965 statute, blacks soon came to vote and win elections in record numbers in both North and South. For instance, in Mississippi—which had a long history of discriminatory poll-tax laws and policies—black voter registration zoomed from less than 10 percent in 1964 to nearly 60 percent within a few years. Overall, roughly a million new Southern black voters entered the rolls in the late 1960s, and the region never reverted to its pre-LBJ status.[25] Another suggestive sign that North and South were finally reuniting: Whereas none of the seventeen men elected president in the first hundred years after the shelling of Fort Sumter had listed an ex-Confederate state as his home, no less than five of the seven men elected president immediately following the Anti–Poll Tax Amendment ran as proud sons of the South. Three of these five won overwhelming support from Southern black voters, and the other two notably named black leaders to high governmental office.[26]

Indeed, evidence of modern racial and geographic reunification may also be discerned in the ratification pattern of the major voting amendments themselves. As we have seen, the First Reconstruction ultimately failed to create a durable Southern culture committed to broad democratic participation. In the Progressive era, only three of the eleven ex-Confederate states ratified the Woman Suffrage Amendment, whose letter and spirit so obviously recalled the Black Suffrage Amendment. And in the early days of America's Second Reconstruction, only one ex-gray state (Tennessee) said yes to the D.C. Amendment, and only two (Tennessee and Florida) ratified the Anti–Poll Tax Amendment.[27] But only a few years later, the South would finally abandon its historic hostility to federal voting-rights amendments. As we shall now see, in the enactment of America's most recent "right to vote" amendment, in 1971, the South at long last embraced a more expansive understanding of voting rights: All told, nine Southern states ratified this Youth Suffrage Amendment.

THE AMENDMENT THAT PROVIDED the occasion for this belated reunification of North and South once again echoed the language of the Black Suffrage and Woman Suffrage Amendments but this time extended the "right . . . to vote" along the *youth* axis. According to the text of this—the Twenty-sixth—amendment, "The right of citizens of the United States, who are eighteen years of age or older, to vote shall not be denied or abridged by the United States or by any State on account of age." Proposed in late March 1971, the amendment became part of the Constitution less than four months later.

The astonishing speed with which this amendment rocketed through the ratification process, combined with its fast and nearly unanimous passage through Congress—no senators opposed it, and only nineteen House members voted no—might at first seem hard to explain. Consider, for example, earlier amendments extending the right to vote. By the time Congress floated the Fifteenth in 1869, almost half the states, comprising three-fourths of the nation's blacks, already had race-neutral voting laws in place. So, too, woman suffrage became universal only after most states had jumped aboard an accelerating bandwagon, using state constitutions and state statutes to guarantee women either full or presidential suffrage. Long before the enactment of the Twenty-fourth Amendment, all but five states had repudiated poll-tax suffrage. And although it did not feature the same explicit "right . . . to vote" formula, the Seventeenth Amendment likewise codified a direct-Senate-election practice that prevailed in most states. By contrast, as of 1969, only two states (Georgia and Kentucky) let eighteen-year-olds vote. Alaska and Hawaii set the bar at nineteen and twenty years, respectively. All other states drew the line at age twenty-one. How, we might wonder, did this settled practice unravel so quickly?

The late 1960s and early 1970s were years of extraordinary dynamism, and the Twenty-sixth Amendment was propelled forward by three of the era's most powerful currents—the civil-rights/voting-rights movement,* a youth culture, and the great debate over Vietnam. As to the first, anyone with eyes could see that a genuine voting-rights revolution was underway,

---

*Whereas reformers in the First Reconstruction sharply distinguished between "civil rights" and "voting rights," these two concepts tightly intertwined in the reform discourse of the Second Reconstruction.

featuring the enfranchisement of Southern blacks on a massive scale; the abolition of state malapportionment under the judicial banner of "one man, one vote"; the complete elimination of entrenched Southern poll-tax suffrage laws; the repudiation of literacy tests and other exclusionary devices nationwide; the end of long residency requirements; the partial political empowerment of the District of Columbia; and more. To many at the time, it seemed that all these good turns deserved another for young adults. Thus the first congressional move toward youth suffrage came by way of a statutory amendment to the Voting Rights Act, which was up for renewal in 1970. When the Supreme Court, in a case captioned *Oregon v. Mitchell*,[28] struck down parts of this statutory fix as an impermissible exercise of federal authority, Congress promptly moved to constitutionalize its commitment to youth suffrage.

At about the same time, individual states began to reevaluate their suffrage-age laws. In 1970 alone, sixteen states held referenda on the issue, with six lowering their age rules and ten standing pat.[29] Even where voters had declined to press forward, state and federal lawmakers from these regions had good political reason to do so wherever the (older) electorate had been remotely close to evenly divided. After all, pro-suffrage lawmakers might expect to personally benefit from the grateful votes of the newly enfranchised in a way that old voters would not. Also, the Voting Rights Act of 1970, as modified by the Supreme Court in *Mitchell,* had opened all *federal* elections to eighteen-year-olds. State lawmakers understood that there would be major administrative and cost advantages in harmonizing state ballot rules with the new federal framework.

As to the second current, we should note that the percentage of Americans under twenty, which had been falling steadily for more than a century, surged between 1950 and 1960 and remained high throughout the 1960s. The baby-boom generation that came of age in this era embodied a fierce willingness to question authority and to consider innovative modes of thought and new ways of life. In response to the fact that the number twenty-one was a longstanding tradition, many were inclined to shout, "So what?" After all, segregation was a tradition, malapportionment was a tradition, public school prayer was a tradition—and yet all these traditions and many others were being visibly swept away by waves of change.

As to the third current, leading antiwar protesters denied the basic legitimacy of a Vietnam policy that directly affected an age cohort that had no vote in the matter. As of 1968, Americans under twenty-one made up roughly one quarter of the troops and an even higher percentage of casualties in the war.[30] In the minds of antiwar activists back home, mass disenfranchisement justified mass disobedience. (Activists also proffered other justifications for civil disobedience.) Arrayed against these critics, prominent supporters of the war from Richard Nixon on down agreed that the generation doing much of the fighting deserved a seat at the table. As conservatives came to see the matter, once young adults were enfranchised, there would be one less pretext for defiance of law and order. Since the number twenty-one was admittedly arbitrary (as, indeed, any number would be), both pro- and antiwar leaders came to agree that the same number should be used for both political rights like the vote and political responsibilities like the draft.[31] As had previously occurred after the Revolutionary and Civil Wars and during World War I, an extraordinary military mobilization thus led America to expand the suffrage.[32]

The three great currents of the late 1960s swirled together in complex ways. For instance, no one in the civil-rights debate or the war debate could ignore the fact that America's blacks were once again fighting in large numbers. True, Vietnam was known as "LBJ's War," and LBJ was the president who had made the Voting Rights Act a reality for America's blacks; but it was also true that America's leading civil-rights spokesman, Martin Luther King, Jr., had spoken forcefully against the war before his death. Nor were the antiwar and civil-rights movements wholly separate from the wider youth culture. Young Americans thronged the streets to demand peace and justice, infusing both political movements with their unique energy and charisma. More broadly, census data indicated that nonwhites made up a disproportionate percentage of America's teenagers. Thus the new South's speedy ratification of the Youth Suffrage Amendment signaled real racial progress. For once, the South was embracing rules that might disproportionately *enfranchise* and *advantage* nonwhites.

"removal . . . or . . . death or resignation"

Sandwiched between the two modern voting-rights amendments, the Twenty-fifth Amendment revised the rules of presidential disability and succession. As with earlier provisions regulating the presidency, the Presidential Succession Amendment promulgated its commands in impersonal language but with a particular person in mind.

Numbed by the shocking events of November 22, 1963, a grieving nation replayed the assassination of John F. Kennedy over and over, both in its news media and in its collective memory. As tragic as this dark day had been, sober analysts quickly began to appreciate that it could have been much worse: Although Kennedy himself had been killed, the nation had dodged a fatal bullet. What if, instead of dying within minutes of being shot in the head, JFK had in fact survived, drifting in and out of consciousness, with uncertain prospects for a full mental recovery? What if the bullet had badly impaired his cognitive functions but in a way that he himself did not understand and refused to acknowledge? In these situations, it was far from clear whether the vice president could lawfully assume the powers and duties of the presidency. Nor was it clear how and by whom any question of arguable presidential disability had to be decided. In a nuclear world where each side in the Cold War had the capability of striking the other in a matter of minutes, could America afford to be effectively leaderless for even a short interval? Could the nation risk the mere possibility of a shaky finger on the button? In the shadow of the Cuban Missile Crisis of 1962, these were hardly idle questions.

As statesmen pondered possible statutory and constitutional responses, they discovered that American history was littered with relevant lessons. One issue related to the formal legal status of the vice president in the event of presidential death or disability: Did the VP actually *become* president, or would he merely serve as *acting* president? This nice question had first arisen in 1841, when President William Henry Harrison died after only a month in office. Although the Executive Article's text and history suggested that in cases of presidential death or disability the vice president would merely assume the "Powers and Duties" of president,[33] Harrison's running mate, John Tyler, had other ideas. As he eventually came to see the matter, he was not merely the vice president acting as president. Rather, he was in law and in fact the president of the United States. While this difference in label itself mattered in a title-conscious world, more than nomenclature was at stake. As president, Tyler could demand a presidential salary—five times his old vice-presidential salary and constitutionally immune from congressional tinkering in a way that his old salary was not. (Arguably, no salary change should have been permitted for a vice president *acting as president,* but this interpolation would have locked Tyler into a low base pay. Also, the mere existence of ambiguity surrounding an *acting* president's salary guarantee might have weakened Tyler's ability to resist congressional encroachments or blandishments.)

When "Presidents" Millard Fillmore and Andrew Johnson followed the Tyler precedent, ambiguity shifted to a different aspect of the problem. If a vice president in fact became president when he took over for his dead running mate, would the same be true if he acted to fill a power vacuum in a *disability* situation? This unresolved question weighed heavily on Vice President Chester A. Arthur in the summer of 1881. President James A.

Garfield had been shot in June and lay in bed for months, unable to function. If Arthur put himself forward in this period, would he thereby become "president" under the Tyler-Fillmore-Johnson precedent? If so, what would happen if Garfield recovered (as at first seemed likely)? If an assertive Arthur had legally become president, would a healthy Garfield be out of luck (and out of a job)? In that case, Arthur in effect would have staged a palace coup. To make matters worse, the Constitution failed to say who should decide whether a president was disabled, and statutes offered little guidance.

Yet another complication: Garfield and Arthur represented different wings of the Republican Party. In the political lingo of the day, Garfield was a "Half-breed," Arthur a "Stalwart." Charles Guiteau, the madman who shot Garfield, had told the police, "I am a Stalwart and Arthur will be president!" On Guiteau's person, authorities found a letter addressed to Arthur making specific recommendations for cabinet reshuffling. Although there was no evidence that Arthur or his fellow Stalwarts had conspired with the deranged assassin, the facts surrounding the shooting received considerable publicity. In this situation, any quick move by Arthur to displace Garfield would have been a public-relations fiasco. Indeed, in the 1860s, some of Andrew Johnson's detractors had made much of the fact that John Wilkes Booth had tried to visit the vice president only hours before shooting Lincoln. A century later, it hardly helped another Vice President Johnson—Lyndon—that JFK had been assassinated in LBJ's home state.

In pondering the lessons of the past, constitutional reformers in the mid-1960s also paid heed to the events at the end of Wilson's presidency. Although the president had been incapacitated by a series of strokes, Vice President Thomas Marshall had failed to step forward. Here was evidence that, even without the special complications created by assassinations and loose conspiracy-talk, vice presidents were unlikely to act unilaterally to fill the executive breach. Too much ambiguity surrounded both their status if they did act and the proper procedures they should follow in establishing presidential disability.

PROPOSED IN JULY 1965 and ratified in February 1967, the Twenty-fifth Amendment aimed to solve several of the problems that JFK's assassination had made shockingly visible. The amendment began by codifying and cabining the Tyler precedent: When a president died or resigned or was removed by the impeachment process, the vice president would himself "*become* President,"[34] but in situations of disability, the vice president would simply serve as "Acting President," assuming the "powers and duties of [his] office" without prejudice to the disabled president's right to resume office if and when the disability ended.

Other provisions of the amendment clarified two different mechanisms by which executive authority could flow from a president to his VP and back in disability situations. Under section 3 of the amendment, a president could voluntarily relinquish his authority and then unilaterally reclaim it at any later time. This mechanism—which built upon an informal arrangement that was first worked out between President Eisenhower and Vice President Nixon, and was later embraced by Presidents Kennedy and Johnson—could be used whenever a president was to undergo planned surgery, or in any other situation where it made sense for him to hand off power smoothly with an expectation of having it smoothly handed back.[35]

Section 4 addressed situations when a president might be disabled but was not in a position to acknowledge that fact, whether because he was unconscious, unreachable, or deranged by the disability itself. In such circumstances, the vice president would be authorized to step into the breach, so long as he had the support of a majority of the cabinet or whatever "other body [that] Congress may by law provide," such as a team of medical experts. Precisely because the vice president would not be *unilaterally* stepping forward, he might be more likely to act when needed. After all, the cabinet or "other body" would be standing with him and vouching for him, thus reducing any public perception of overeagerness on his part—the Chester Arthur problem. Conversely, precisely because the vice president would need to win the immediate approval of others—either cabinet officers whom the disabled president had himself picked or some "other body" specially named by Congress—genuine acts of vice-presidential usurpation would be deterred. If the president later chose to challenge the vice president's actions, and if the VP declined to back down, Congress itself would make the final disability decision, with the scales tilted in the president's favor: The president would regain power unless two-thirds of each house ruled that he was in fact "unable to discharge" the office.

These provisions both clarified and enhanced the constitutional status of the vice president as America's executive heir apparent. Section 3 made plain that the vice president's core job description involved not merely presiding over the Senate but also filling in for the president on a temporary basis in a multitude of short-term disability situations. Section 4 gave the vice president an even more central role, as the one indispensable actor in that section's elaborate script.[36] Executive power would flow only if the president himself relinquished it under section 3 or if the vice president chose to invoke section 4. All other actors in the system had lesser roles—the courts were out of the picture, the cabinet could be displaced by Congress, and Congress itself would act only after the vice president had stepped forward.

These enhancements of vice-presidential authority reinforced trends initiated by the Two Term Amendment. Unsurprisingly, the Two Term Amendment and the Presidential Succession Amendment were both proposed and enacted during the presidencies of former vice presidents—Truman and Johnson, to be specific. Although Article V gave presidents no formal part in the amendment process, most of America's amendments have in fact been affected, for better or worse, by the superintending presence of America's chief executive. Thus, we should not be surprised to see two pro-vice-presidential amendments emerging in the Truman-through-Ford era, a span in which former vice presidents occupied the Oval Office for an unprecedented twenty-one out of thirty-two years.

ONE OTHER PROVISION of the Presidential Succession Amendment further enhanced the vice president's constitutional status, by providing for the filling of any vice-presidential vacancy that might arise—whether because the vice president had died or resigned or been removed, or because he had himself become president following another man's death, resignation, or removal. The framers had not provided for replacing vacant VPs—an omission that tended to suggest that these number twos were not especially important in their own right. Prior to the Presidential Succession Amendment, the nation over the course of its history had operated without a vice president for more than thirty-seven years. Had anything happened to the president in these years, congressional succession laws would have come into play.

Section 2 of the amendment created a new system, in which a president would nominate, and the entire Congress—both House and Senate—would confirm a new vice president whenever the second spot fell vacant. In this new constitutional system—envisioning as it did close cooperation between America's top two executive officers, as exemplified by section 3 handoffs of power back and forth—a president would be allowed to handpick his constitutional lieutenant and heir apparent, subject to congressional oversight, which would both deter any improper nomination and also give the incoming vice president a national vote of confidence.

Section 2 also promoted executive-party continuity. For example, in 1972, when Americans voted for Republican Richard Nixon, section 2 dramatically increased the likelihood that the country would indeed get four years of Republican executive policies, regardless of what might happen to Nixon himself or his running mate, Spiro Agnew. As subsequent events played out, Vice President Agnew resigned in 1973 and was replaced by Gerald Ford, whom Nixon handpicked and Congress confirmed under section 2. When Nixon himself resigned in 1974, Ford thereupon became president and named Nelson Rockefeller to be *his* vice president (again, under section 2). Americans in 1972 had voted for four years of Republicans, and the Presidential Succession Amendment helped give them just that.

Yet problems still remain. Most are caused by a 1947 presidential-succession statute that allows congressional leaders to assume presidential power in double-vacancy scenarios, contrary to constitutional text and history, and in disregard of compelling arguments put forth early in our history by Congressman James Madison.[37] However bad the 1947 statute was when enacted, it has become even worse in the intervening decades: Its underlying vision and specific procedures run precisely counter to the letter and spirit of the later Presidential Succession Amendment. Under the amendment, if a president and vice president vacate their offices sequentially, party continuity is generally assured; but under the statute, if both officers were to die or resign or be ousted via impeachment simultaneously, presidential power might well flow to a congressional leader of the opposite party—the very party that Americans voted *against* in the previous presidential election. The 1967 amendment was based on a vision of close cooperation between a president and his handpicked vice president, with power flowing back and forth smoothly in temporary-disability situations. The 1947 statute, by contrast, makes back-and-forth handoffs to legislative leaders nearly impossible in cases of short-term disability.[38] The amendment constitutionalized a model of proxy succession in which each president would name the person to complete his term: Nixon to Ford to Rockefeller. The statute, instead, has codified a very different model, denying presidents the right to name their own proxies. The amendment was obviously designed to fill vice-presidential vacancies promptly; but the statute has created perverse incentives for delays in the congressional confirmation process. It took a Democrat-controlled Congress 121 days to confirm Republican Vice President Nelson Rockefeller. Had anything untoward happened to President Ford in the interim, a Democrat would have moved into the Oval Office under the 1947 law.

The bad news, in short, is that the 1967 amendment did not solve all of the problems of presidential succession. In particular, America's succession system remains vulnerable to mishap in situations where both the president and vice president die or become disabled at the same time—an unlikely event to be sure, but one more imaginable than ever in a twenty-first-century world of global terrorism. The good news, however, is that most of the problems could be fixed rather easily by repealing the unconstitutional and unworkable Presidential Succession Act of 1947 and replacing it with a proper Madisonian system of cabinet succession. Much as Americans responded to the tragedy of November 22, 1963, by revising the Constitution's succession system, so Americans in the wake of September 11, 2001, have good reason to rethink our statutory succession system before tragedy strikes again.[39]

"the compensation . . . of the Senators and Representatives"

America's last and youngest amendment is also one of her first and oldest. Proposed by the First Congress in 1789, the Twenty-seventh Amendment was finally ratified by the last necessary state in 1992. In other words, an amendment that was legally conceived on the same day as the federal Bill of Rights did not emerge from the constitutional birth canal until more than two centuries later. Some scholars have contended that this proposal died long ago in utero, and that its words in 1992 were thus stillborn—invalid for all constitutional intents and purposes.[40] Yet the federal executive branch has certified the Twenty-seventh as a validly ratified amendment, and Congress has overwhelmingly concurred. (The vote, held in May 1992, was 414 to 3 in the House and 99 to 0 in the Senate.)[41] The judiciary has never gainsaid this orthodoxy, and every day countless thousands of official and unofficial copies of the Constitution roll off printing presses or appear in cyberspace with the words of the Twenty-seventh included. How did all this happen? And what if anything does this amendment's strange journey tell us about the amendment process in general?

The second of twelve amendments proposed by Congress in September 1789 aimed to regulate congressional compensation.* Lest lame-duck federal lawmakers try to line their pockets on the way out the door— voting themselves pay increases after they had been booted out by the electorate—the proposal provided that no change in congressional salary could go into effect until after an intervening general election.[42] In late 1789 and the early 1790s, only six states ratified this Salary Amendment, far short of the three-quarters required by Article V.

Yet the proposal's root norm remained a powerful one in America. When Congress in 1816 enacted the first congressional pay increase since 1789 and refused to delay its effect until after the next election, angry voters across the country responded by ousting congressional incumbents in record numbers. In the wake of this tidal wave, a duly chastened Congress prospectively repealed the salary increase. History repeated itself, more or less, in the 1870s. In 1873, Congress voted itself a retroactive 40-percent pay increase. Critics promptly dubbed the bill the Salary Grab Act, and in early 1874 Congress repealed the increase in the face of intense public opposition. Unmollified, angry voters turned against the congressional party in power by using the next election to effect what historian Eric Foner has described as "the greatest reversal of partisan alignments in the entire nineteenth century."[43]

Something else happened in 1873 that merits our attention: The state of Ohio gave its kiss of approval to the 1789 Salary Amendment, which had been slumbering for decades, undisturbed since Virginia's ratification as the sixth approving state in 1791. With the 1874 repeal of Congress's salary grab, no other state in the 1870s emulated Ohio's example. There the matter stood for an entire century. Then, in 1978, Wyoming added its blessing to the sleeping provision. At this point, our story took a most unlikely turn. A Texas college student, Gregory Watson, stumbled across the issue and began writing to state legislatures urging them to ratify what Watson believed to be a still-live amendment proposal. Amazingly, states began to follow this advice, ratifying at a steady clip over the next decade— two states in 1983–84, eight more in 1985–86, another seven in the next two years, then nine more in 1989–90, and yet another seven in 1991–92. All told, thirty-four states said yes in the modern era. These thirty-four yesses, when added to the six ayes in the Founding era and Ohio's lonely

---

*As we saw in Chapter 8, the first proposed amendment, addressing the issue of congressional size, was never ratified. The remaining ten amendments were ratified in 1791 and have generally become known as the "Bill of Rights," though this phrase does not appear in the document itself.

approval in 1873, meant that the Salary Amendment had indeed won the assent of more than the thirty-eight states required by Article V.

But even if this process strictly complied with the letter of Article V—proposal by two-thirds of Congress and ratification by three-fourths of the states—did it satisfy the larger spirit of that Article and of America's Constitution more generally? Bolstered by dicta from a 1921 Supreme Court case,[44] some distinguished scholars have argued that proposal and ratification must be sufficiently contemporaneous so as to guarantee that at some specific moment in time a genuine national consensus does indeed exist on each and every amendment. By analogy, for any given proposal—call it P—to become a valid federal statute, it is not enough for P to win the support of the House, Senate, and president at wildly different times. If the House votes for P in Year One and the Senate finally says yes in Year Ten, and then a president endorses P in Year Fifteen, this does not a valid law make. Rather, all three lawmaking organs (or the first two by extraordinary votes in the case of a veto by the third) must agree at roughly the same time—within the same congressional term. Why shouldn't a similar contemporaneousness rule apply if P is a proposed constitutional amendment rather than a mere proposed statute?

Partly because Article I is organized around bright-line rules for contemporaneousness that have no Article V counterpart. An ordinary statute must pass within a single term of Congress, and a bright legal line separates the last day of one term from the first day of the next, regardless of how close together these two days lie on an ordinary calendar. But no such bright lines punctuate the Article V amendment process, which is sensibly governed by its own set of principles. The most important of these principles, for the issue at hand, is the last-in-time rule. Just as, within a single house, a lawmaker is generally free to change his vote until the moment at which the final tally is announced, so each state is free to change its ratification vote at any time prior to the magic moment when the last requisite state has said yes, at which point the amendment automatically becomes part of the Constitution. A state that initially says no to a proposed amendment is later free to say yes—and vice versa. Each state's most recent action is the one that counts, and this rule helps assure that a certain sort of ratification contemporaneousness will indeed exist. A state that said yes long ago is legally deemed to continue to say yes until it changes its mind. On this view, a state such as Virginia that said yes in the 1790s legally continued to say yes in the 1990s, and thus its yes *was* contemporaneous with yes votes that were first voiced much later. If Virginia did not want to be counted as a continuing yes, it had only to say no at any time. (Alternatively, perhaps it could have placed a sunset provision in its initial yes vote.)

Without this last-in-time idea, Article V would not make good sense, regardless of the time span between proposal and ratification. Let's imagine some ratification period—whether 150 days or 150 years—during which states one by one initially say yes to a proposed amendment and then immediately repent and repeal their ratifications. If one were to count only yes votes and ignore the last-in-time no votes, then this amendment might be deemed to be ratified even though it never won the considered approval of anything close to a supermajority of states.

Though the text of America's Constitution did not explicitly specify the last-in-time rule, the act of constitution in the Founding period did allow North Carolina and Rhode Island to say yes to the Philadelphia plan after they had initially said no. True, in the 1860s, when Ohio and New Jersey voted to rescind their prior ratifications of the Fourteenth Amendment, Congress and the executive branch disregarded these valid rescissions and purported to treat both states as having ratified. This was a grave mistake—and unnecessary: Even without these two states, the Fourteenth had enough other yes votes to clear the Article V bar.[45] Several later amendments—the Fifteenth, Sixteenth, and Twenty-second, for example—have been ratified by states that had previously rejected them, and these last-in-time ratifications have been duly counted.[46]

But if a later yes properly displaces an earlier no, shouldn't the reverse also hold true? Otherwise, the system would feature a perverse ratchet: Heads we win, tails let's play again. Within each state, one yes would always trump one hundred nos, whether before or after or both. How could this be a sensible system of popular sovereignty?

Logically, the last-in-time rule should also apply to Congress itself. If Congress, after having proposed an amendment, would like to cancel its proposal, it should be allowed to do so by joint resolution.[47] Perhaps the hardest question is whether the repealing resolution would need to win the support of two-thirds of each house (by analogy to the original proposal) or whether, instead, a simple majority of each should suffice (by analogy to other joint resolutions, and to maximize a current Congress's power to retract outdated proposals).[48] Thus far, this nice question has not arisen in practice, and—like most of the Article V questions that we have been pondering in the last few paragraphs—has never been definitively addressed by the Supreme Court or the other federal branches.[49]

In the case of the Salary Amendment, for example, no repeal issue ever arose: Congress never purported to repudiate its original proposal.

On the contrary, Congress in fact overwhelmingly reaffirmed its 1789 proposal in 1992. So the simple answer to scholarly skeptics of the Salary Amendment is that this proposal did indeed enjoy at a single moment—in 1992, to be precise—the legal support of Congress itself and of more than three-quarters of the states, all of whom had, in their last words on the subject, said yes. We do.*

---

*This is as good a place as any to mention the handful of congressionally proposed amendments to which states have refused to say "We do." In the nation's history, the great majority of would-be amendments that have made their way through Congress have eventually been ratified. In fact, only six amendment proposals have cleared the congressional bar and then failed during the ratification process. First, an amendment proposed by Congress in 1789, which aimed to regulate congressional size, fell one state shy in the 1790s, and thereafter became moot thanks to congressional expansions that occurred even in the absence of formal ratification. See Chapter 2, page 82. Second, in 1810 Congress proposed an amendment stripping American citizenship from any person who, without the consent of Congress, accepted any "title of nobility" from "any emperor, king, prince or foreign power." 2 Stat. 613. The proposal further disqualified all such persons from holding any state or federal office. Evidencing early Americans' revulsion to European-style aristocracies, this proposal received widespread support but fell short of the requisite three-fourths; twelve out of eighteen states said yes. Third, in 1861, Congress proposed the Corwin Amendment, shielding slavery in the states. Two states (Ohio and Maryland) ratified early in the Civil War, and a third (Lincoln's own Illinois) purported to ratify but did so in an irregular way. Congress in all but name rescinded this proposal when it sent a new proposed Thirteenth Amendment—abolishing slavery everywhere—to the states in early 1865. In any event, ratification of that amendment wholly mooted the earlier Corwin proposal; see generally Chapter 10. Fourth, Congress in 1924 proposed an amendment that would have empowered the federal government to "limit, regulate, and prohibit the labor of persons under eighteen years of age." 43 Stat. 670. In pointed contrast to most other amendments proposed just before and after this one, this proposal contained no sunset clause. Over the ensuing decade and a half, twenty-eight states ratified, well short of the needed thirty-six. When, in the late 1930s and early 1940s, the New Deal Court itself began to recognize congressional power to regulate child labor and analogous aspects of the national economy, the proposal was in effect overtaken by events. The chief pre–New Deal Supreme Court case that the proposal was designed to repudiate, *Hammer v. Dagenhart,* 247 U.S. 251 (1918), was overruled by the New Deal Court in 1941. In 1939, the Court pointedly declined to rule that the proposal had lapsed due to the passage of time; see *Coleman v. Miller,* 307 U.S. 433. Fifth, in 1972, Congress proposed an Equal Rights Amendment prohibiting both state and federal policies that "denied or abridged" the "equality of rights under the law . . . on account of sex." 86 Stat. 1523. The enacting resolution provided for a seven-year ratification window. At the end of this period, only thirty-five of the needed thirty-eight states had at some point said yes, and several of these yes states had already recanted. During the pendency of this proposal, Supreme Court case law came rather close to reading an ERA-like idea into the general equality language of the Fourteenth Amendment. Here, too, the proposal might be said to have been overtaken by events; as with the congressional-size amendment and the child-labor amendment, the ERA was in effect codified even without formal ratification. Finally, in 1978, Congress proposed an amendment treating the District of Columbia as a state for purposes of congressional representation and electoral-college participation. 92 Stat. 3795. The proposed amendment text contained a seven-year sunset clause, and within those seven years, the proposal received yes votes from only sixteen states.

"   "

It might seem that with the Twenty-seventh Amendment we have reached the end of the document, and of our story. Not quite. Perhaps the most important aspect of the document's tail end is that at any given moment it is merely provisional, awaiting a future amendment that will for a time become the new end, and another after that, and still another and another ad infinitum. The document has no final resting place—it started with a bang and keeps going. Viewed this way, the document's real end is the vast creative white space looming just beyond the latest amendment, inviting today's people to consider what words they might deem suitable to insert in that space—leaving room, of course, for tomorrow's people to do the same. So read, the document's textual end poetically draws attention to its teleological end—to secure to every generation of Americans the blessings of liberty, including our public liberty to govern ourselves and make amends.

This final textual flourish reminding each generation of its collective rights and responsibilities came about without much Founding forethought. Although the Preamble's poetry and Article V's prose proclaimed an openness to future amendment, nowhere did the Philadelphia document make clear exactly where in the text future amendments would fit or how they should be styled. Nor had earlier state constitutions established any clear pattern for the proper textual form of constitutional revisions. Only a handful of Revolutionary state constitutions had emerged from special constitutional conventions, and no alterations of these prototype documents had taken place prior to 1789, when the First Congress met to consider possible changes to the federal Constitution.

In that Congress, Madison initially proposed to directly rewrite the Philadelphia document so as to generate a new "uniform and entire" text—much as twenty-first-century Americans word process a modern document by blending old and new phrases, excising here and inserting there to create a seamless new version displacing its predecessor. During the ratification debates of 1787–88, state conventions had at times appeared to suggest such a direct-rewrite format for amendments. Thus, South Carolina ratifiers resolved "that the third section of the sixth article ought to be amended, by inserting the word 'other' between the words 'no' and religious." At one point in a long list of desired amendments, the New York ratification delegates suggested that "the words *without the Consent of the Congress,* in the seventh clause of the ninth section of the first article of the Constitution, be expunged." Likewise, the North Carolina convention of 1788 endorsed an amendment "that the latter part of the 5th paragraph of the 9th section of the 1st article be altered to read" in a particular way. Yet even these suggestions were ultimately ambiguous on the style point. When read carefully, they did not rule out the possibility of adding new provisions at the end of the document declaring that earlier specified sections or clauses "are hereby amended to read as follows" or "are hereby repealed."[50]

When critics in the First Congress raised questions about his proposed direct-rewrite format, Madison ultimately yielded. The Philadelphia text would be left untouched, and amendments would be added to the end of the document. The First Congress endorsed twelve such amendments in 1789, and when ten of the original twelve won ratification in 1791, they were accordingly renumbered and appended as a postscript to the Philadelphia plan. With the model for amendment format and placement thus established, it seemed only natural for Americans to append their next amendment, ratified in 1795, as a post-postscript, and thereafter to tack each subsequent amendment onto the end of the one before.

Though the full implications of this style of amendment escaped detailed analysis in the 1780s and 1790s, America's ultimate decision to array amendments in chronological order has happily encouraged the Constitution's readers to attend to the document's history and trend line. Each discrete amendment bears a precise date that locates its message within the broader saga of American history. Readers can tell at a glance which changes were made when and can easily trace the direction of documentary change both issue by issue and more comprehensively.

For example, we need only see the date 1868 alongside the Fourteenth Amendment to understand its underlying impulse. This is a *Reconstruction* Amendment, and its words about birthright citizenship, privileges and immunities, equal protection, congressional apportionment, and congressional power should be read in light of the obvious evils that the 1860s reformers were aiming to abolish. An alternative word-processing regime whereby later generations rewrote the Philadelphia Constitution directly, interweaving old and new language, would have obscured the link between particular words and specific historical events.

More generally, the document's chronological format highlights the grand arc of constitutional history. Readers can see at a glance, for example, how democracy has swept forward across the centuries, through an eighteenth-century Bill of Rights repeatedly affirming "the rights of the people"; a trio of nineteenth-century amendments ending slavery, proclaiming liberty and equality, and enfranchising black men; and a cluster of twentieth-century amendments extending the vote to women, the poor, and the young, and further democratizing the Senate (via direct election), the House (via shortened lame-duck terms), and the presidency (via term limits and reforms of selection and succession rules). Had Americans opted to directly rewrite the Founding text rather than adding amendments to the end in chronological order, this strong vector would have been less visible. For example, it would have been harder to see that although the Founding-era texts contained several special safeguards for creditors and property holders, later generations of American constitutionalists have scaled back protections for the rich while embracing increasingly strong claims of civil and political equality. Reformers freed slaves without compensating slave masters in the 1860s, embraced a predictably progressive income tax in the 1910s, and banned various disenfranchisements of the poor in the 1960s. This increasing inclusion has been evident in deed as well as word: "We the people," who have done all this amending, have included groups that our forebears excluded from their acts of Founding and early amendment.[51]

And the American people are not yet done. History is still happening. That is the plain meaning of the blank space. Had amendments been blended into the original text, the document at every given moment might have seemed perfect and complete as is—"uniform and entire," in Madison's formulation.[52] By contrast, the manner of hanging amendments onto the end serves to highlight the document's obvious incompleteness and open-endedness. Why only twenty-seven amendments, as opposed to twenty-eight, or twenty-nine, or ninety-six? Hence the vast creative white space at the bottom.

Or perhaps I should say the top; it all depends on one's angle of view. The very word "Founding" suggests that the beginning text goes on the bottom, as a foundation upon which later layers proceed to build upward toward the boundless creative space above. This is the image that the Founding generation itself conjured up in the Great Seal of the United States, a grand yet perpetually unfinished pyramid gesturing upward, with a blank space near the apex as a constant reminder that America is always a work in progress.

By adding new texts rather than directly editing old ones, We the People have made amends without hiding our past mistakes. The open space thus tops a pyramid that is not only unfinished but visibly imperfect. Indeed, America's mode of add-on amendment draws special attention to those provisions—such as the three-fifths clause and the fugitive-slave clause—that we have later abandoned yet nonetheless kept in view as a lesson to careful readers.

If modern Americans were to spend more time examining our repudiated constitutional past, perhaps we might more fully understand our constitutional present and better imagine our constitutional future. Take the electoral college. The very presence of a Presidential Selection Amendment separate and detached from the original Executive Article calls attention to the Philadelphia framers' now-superseded presidential system. The original system failed to anticipate the rise of national presidential parties and therefore quickly needed to be replaced. This fact alone might prompt us to ask, "What other important developments related to presidential elections—or anything else—did the Philadelphia Founders fail to anticipate? Are there perhaps other repair jobs that need to be done by the American people today?" Indeed, the textual layout of sequential amendments helps us see an intriguing pattern at a glance: Of the seventeen amendments ratified after 1791, three (the Twelfth, Twentieth, and Twenty-third) have directly and specifically modified the electoral college; five more (the Fourteenth, Fifteenth, Nineteenth, Twenty-fourth, and Twenty-sixth) have indirectly modified the college by counteracting its facilitation of widespread disenfranchisement; and two others (the Twenty-second and Twenty-fifth) have reformed closely related rules governing who shall sit in the Oval Office. All told, ten of the seventeen post-1791 amendments have tried to push the system of presidential selection and succession toward increased democracy. Might all these amendments point the way to still further democratic reforms of the presidential-election process?

Of course, today's and tomorrow's people are also free to decide that the amendments moving away from the Founders' plan were the real mistakes that should be repealed, just as the Anti-Prohibition Amendment of 1933 repealed the mistaken Prohibition Amendment of 1919. The people may change direction. In deciding where to go—how to fill the creative white space—We the People confront an expanding constitutional text that has a built-in Socratic dialogue, preserving and highlighting conflicting approaches to certain vexing issues in American history. Thus, today's American people have before us in the very text itself an original electoral-college model in Article II, a Twelfth Amendment variant facilitating partisan tickets, and a Twenty-third Amendment version wedging the District of Columbia into a state-based system. In pondering, say, the war on drugs, we have both the Prohibition Amendment and its opposite before our eyes, representing two contrasting approaches to the legal regulation of intoxicating substances.

Indeed, the document even showcases two contrasting styles of constitution-writing. The first stylistic Constitution, from Preamble to Article VII, offers a model of a "uniform and entire" text. The second stylistic Constitution, beginning with the First Amendment and continuing up to the blank space beyond the Twenty-seventh, offers a model of generational layers, a constitutional Grand Canyon of accreting rules and principles. In the First Congress, Madison argued that the second model would entail "very considerable embarrassment" because it would often "be difficult to ascertain to what parts of the instrument the amendments particularly refer."[53] Congressman John Vining agreed, arguing that a layered approach to amendments would eventually make the document resemble "a careless written letter" with "more attached to it in a postscript than was contained in the original composition."[54] Had Madison and Vining prevailed on the point of style, subsequent generations of Americans might never have had a clear picture of how a layered approach might look and work. Ironically, precisely because the layered approach preserved the Philadelphia text in its totality, Americans do have at least a picture of what an "entire and complete" composed copy might look like. And if Americans today or tomorrow prefer that "entire and complete" style of expressing our deepest constitutional aspirations, nothing prevents us from adopting a Twenty-eighth Amendment that would substitute an entirely new constitutional text for the "careless written letter" that we now use. The amendment might, for instance, begin by proclaiming that "upon adoption of this amendment, the Constitution of the United States, in its entirety, shall read as follows."

Beyond the niceties of stylistic format lurk large substantive issues. In general, may amendments prospectively modify the rules of amendment themselves? If We the People truly are sovereign, what limits on our amending power properly exist precisely in order to preserve that sovereignty for ourselves and our successors? What other limits on amendment properly exist in the name of Justice? How and by whom are such limits to be enforced? These are among the Constitution's most challenging questions, and the very vastness of the space at the end beckons each generation to look deep within itself, and deep within the document, for answers.

These hard questions, of course, would need to be confronted regardless of how amendments were stylistically woven into or tacked onto the pre-amendment text. However, a direct-rewrite format would not necessarily have ended the document in a manner that dramatically called attention to the Constitution's broad openness to amendment and to arguable limitations on that openness. The (perhaps unintended) genius of amendments at the end is that this format forces modern Americans to confront these deep issues not just once, in Article V, but repeatedly, as we encounter amendment after amendment by generation after generation—and then come to the vast white space bidding our generation to say and do something worthy of inclusion.

What words, if any, will the current generation of Americans inscribe into our supreme law? How might we leave our posterity an even richer constitutional legacy than the one we have inherited from our Founding (and Amending) Fathers (and Mothers)? Time will tell. America's constitutional saga continues.

Postscript

Any reader hardy enough to have made it thus far deserves both my thanks and an explanation. What have I been trying to prove in the preceding pages? Which interpretive methods have informed my tale, and why? Substantively, how does the foregoing account fit with, or run against, other writings on the Constitution? Where might critics justly take issue with the conclusions I have presented? What is missing from this constitutional biography? Where should lay readers and scholars go from here?

Method

This book has tried to offer a comprehensive account of America's Constitution, introducing the reader both to the legal text (and its consequences) and to the political deeds that gave rise to that text.

Surprisingly enough, virtually nothing else in print aims to do this. There is of course a vast outpouring of superb work on the Constitution. But within the legal literature, most books and articles focus on some specific aspect of constitutional law—executive power, judicial review, free speech, or what have you—and make no effort to encompass the constitutional system as a whole. Many law-trained authors concentrate on Supreme Court decisions, thereby privileging the *United States Reports* over the United States Constitution. Other law books are dense treatises aimed only at legal professionals. While political scientists routinely analyze Congress, the presidency, and the judiciary, they, too, rarely ponder the Constitution as a whole. True, historians have offered rich accounts of the Founding era and its colorful personalities. Yet these chroniclers have devoted less attention to the Constitution as a legal text, and what work they have done on the document often focuses only on the original version framed at Philadelphia. Rarely do they carry the story forward to include all the amendments over the next two centuries.* Finally, there are a few general classroom textbooks about the Constitution, most of which are distillations of conventional wisdom pitched at an average ninth grader. In the preceding pages I have aimed higher, targeting undergraduates, law students, graduate students, history buffs, civil libertarians, opinion leaders, politicians, judges, lawyers, teachers, professors, and general-interest readers.

In my effort to synthesize law, history, and political science (about which I shall say more in a moment), I owe large debts to distinguished scholars in all three fields. For instance, although my general constitutional narrative and Bruce Ackerman's diverge at critical junctures, I have followed his lead in analyzing the Constitution not merely as a text but as a deed; like him, I pay special attention to the fascinating manner in which our Constitution was made and amended. Ackerman (a law professor) has also inspired me, as have Robert Dahl (a political scientist) and Edmund Morgan (a historian), to measure America's democracy against the experience of other nations, especially England.[1] Issues of race, class, and gender inclusion and exclusion figure prominently in my analysis. Here, I follow the flow of a great many extraordinary scholars; some of my favorites are William Wiecek, David Brion Davis, Eric Foner, Paul Finkelman, Ray Diamond, Mary Dudziak, Garry Wills, Michael Klarman, Sidney Aronson, Pauline Maier, Rogers Smith, Alexander Keyssar, Linda Kerber, Joanne Freeman, and Reva Siegel. I have also brought Congress and the president onstage as leading constitutional actors; in this, I have been especially edified by the work of historians David Potter, Eric McKitrick, Stanley Elkins, Don E. Fehrenbacher, William Freehling, Clinton Rossiter, Jack Rakove, Les Benedict, Ralph Ketcham, Forrest McDonald, and Shlomo Slonim; political scientists Edward Corwin, Leonard D. White, William Riker, Nelson Polsby, Norman Ornstein, Morris Fiorina, David Mayhew, Donald Robinson, James Ceaser, Jeffrey Tulis, David Nichols, Barry Weingast, and Stephen Skowronek; and legal scholars Charles Black, David Currie, Larry Kramer, Michael Gerhardt, Jeff Powell, Dan Farber, and Steve Calabresi. As these scholars have deepened my understanding of separation of powers, so other writers have helped me rethink

*For notable treatments of the amendments as distinct from the Founding document, see Alan P. Grimes, *Democracy and the Amendments to the Constitution* (1978); Richard Bernstein with Jerome Agel, *Amending America* (1993); and David E. Kyvig, *Explicit and Authentic Acts: Amending the Constitution, 1776–1995* (1996).

federalism. In the tradition of Gordon Wood, Willi Paul Adams, Rosemary Zagarri, Marc Kruman, Donald Lutz, G. Alan Tarr, and Rakove, I seek to locate the federal Constitution against the backdrop of its state constitutional counterparts. And I am especially indebted to Frederick Marks III, for his brilliant work establishing the primacy of national-security and foreign-policy concerns in the making of the Constitution.

Law, history, and political science—these three disciplines form the legs of the stool on which this book rests. Yet each discipline in isolation may be faulted. For instance, constitutional lawyers, trained to read cases and paid to argue in court, have generally overemphasized the judges' doctrine and overlooked the People's document. The standard legal narrative has missed many of the ways in which the American people have historically outpaced the American judiciary in affirming and embodying liberty and democracy. For their part, many political scientists have also tended to rush past the document, paying more attention to abstract mathematical models than to the treasure trove of real-life questions that constitutional historians and lawyers have stumbled across—involving, for instance, the interplay between state and federal constitutions, the antebellum apportionment of each branch, and the processes by which the Constitution was first created and later amended. As one who teaches in both a law school and a political-science department, I have written this book to help show my colleagues what they are missing.

I have also written this book as a gentle prod to my friends in history departments across the country. For understandable reasons, historians have fallen in love with James Madison, a brilliant and prescient thinker as well as a spectacularly effective doer who kept great records. But even if he was indeed the most interesting person in the room at Philadelphia—at least for a modern intellectual historian*—the basic point about the Constitution is that it became law only after it left that (closed) room. Constitutional historians should resist the temptation to organize their narrative around Philadelphia, even if there is a great tale to be told there, filled with dramatic moments and a fabulous cast of characters whom many lay readers will al-

---

*At certain junctures, I have tried to introduce the lay reader to James Wilson as a foil to James Madison. Though Wilson failed to leave copious records and did not die in glory, he surely lived well and deserves more credit as another brilliant Founding thinker and doer who presaged the future. Compared to Madison, Wilson was far more fluent in law, embraced popular sovereignty more enthusiastically and systematically, and was far less personally complicit in the evil of slavery as an institution. As an immigrant of modest origins who rose to meteoric heights, becoming America's foremost legal scholar and one of Washington's first picks for the Supreme Court, James Wilson exemplified the promise of the New World.

ready know by name (and want to learn more about).[2] The real constitutional drama, as I see it, began when the Philadelphia Convention ended, when—for the first time in world history—a continental people came onstage to say yes or no. And that drama has continued ever since, as a widening circle of Americans has struggled with our imperfect legacy. But in most standard Philadelphia stories, the historian-authors and the readers are exhausted (as were some of the Philadelphia delegates themselves) by the end of the summer of 1787. There is little room left in these narratives for the ensuing process of popular conversation, contestation, and amendment.

Even if an adventurous historian takes the constitutional story up through the Bill of Rights or the entire Washington Administration, the curtain then typically comes down. What happened later is "not my period," the historian tells himself. But what happened later is the reason many people today look to the Founding with reverence rather than revulsion. What happened later is that We the People eventually abolished slavery and promised equal rights to blacks and, later, women. This puts the "not-my-period" historian in a bind. To emphasize just how central slavery was in the 1789 document is to tell a dark tale about the Founding—to leave the ultimate story of redemption to some other historian of a later period. The path of least resistance is thus to mute slavery's significance in the Founding text,[3] and to imply that slavery's ultimate repudiation was the natural if delayed culmination of the Founders' system. This is a pretty picture, but is it true?

I have argued that it is not. The Founding regime was proslavery, although many in the 1780s may not have foreseen the full extent of this bias. The Reconstruction broke sharply with the antebellum system and did so only because of the cataclysm of the Civil War. Before that, slavocrats had come to dominate antebellum America, thanks to the compound-interest effect of the three-fifths clause. Narratively, this thesis has unfolded rather easily in the foregoing chapters precisely because my tale did not end in 1787 or 1789 or 1791 or 1797 or 1801. My *constitutional* story has been redemptive even if my *Founding* story was less so.*

---

*Doubtless, some sophisticated readers may be tempted to dismiss my general account as "Whig history"—a tale of inexorable progress: Onward and upward! However, I do not think history always works this way; nor do I think that American history has always played out in this manner. I do believe that the *Constitution* itself has, *thus far* and *in general,* followed a progressive course. But not because of any supernatural telos or historical inevitability. For instance, my Reconstruction story is one of boomerang—of postwar progress made possible by prewar regression. (Even here, much of this initial progress was erased until the Second Reconstruction.) Similarly, the story of Prohibition and its repeal is hardly unilinear. Nor is there any guarantee that future amendments will in fact continue in the same direction as have past amendments.

A FEW FINAL STRAY THOUGHTS about the methodological moves I have been making in this book. The careful reader will have noted my aspiration to holism—my desire to unite law, history, and political science; to view the document over its entire life span; to see how various textual provisions and institutional patterns fit together; to ponder both rights and structure, and to examine their interrelation; to analyze both constitutional politics (how did the text come to be enacted?) and constitutional law (what did the enacted text mean?); to attend to all the branches of government, and not just the judiciary; to weigh state constitutionalism alongside the federal document; to consider both domestic- and foreign-policy dimensions of America's Constitution; and to show the reader both the core situations in which a given text was meant to apply and salient instances where a text was plainly *not* meant to apply.

Modern Americans are fond of debating whether the Constitution was conservative or liberal. The answer to this question will often depend on the baseline: liberal or conservative compared to what? To avoid anachronism, and to keep myself honest, I have repeatedly resorted to four historical baselines in analyzing the original Constitution: English practice in the Georgian era, American colonial customs, Revolutionary state constitutional norms, and the rules of the Articles of Confederation. In assessing later amendments, I have continued to treat state-constitutional practice as a useful baseline, with brief attention to international norms, especially when the overseas experience itself entered into the American constitutional conversation (as occurred most obviously in the crusade for woman suffrage).

Wherever possible, I have tried to give the reader facts and figures— lots of them—as a modest constraint on my own potential biases. Even if numbers cannot keep any author completely honest (for each author inevitably must choose to use some sets of numbers and not others), well-chosen numbers can perhaps exert a certain democratic pull because they aggregate the experience of many persons and thus counterbalance a potential narrative temptation to overrely on a few particularly notable and quotable big names—the "great men" (sic) of history. Even if I am wrong about the democratizing effect of numbers, the Constitution itself is filled with numbers, and I have not shied away from them. In my view, a well-chosen number can be every bit as interesting as a well-chosen quote. I thus hope that some of the numbers I have compiled will inspire lay readers and scholars to assemble additional data sets to supplement or challenge the ones that I have featured.

Though I reckon myself a constitutional textualist, I have in two ways gone beyond textual analysis as conventionally practiced by lawyers. First, I have tried to understand the meaning inherent in the basic *acts* of constitution and amendment. In my view, the late-1780s process of ordainment incarnated the animating principle of popular sovereignty, and the illegality of future unilateral secession was an essential part of the very enactment—the "We do" moment—in all-important New York and elsewhere. Likewise, the manner in which the Fourteenth Amendment occurred necessarily committed the nation to a robust reading of national republicanism and a new vision of the national army. Though no part of the text of the Fourteenth Amendment, these understandings were part of the amendment's very essence.

Second, I have paid special heed to the practices of President Washington. This seemed particularly appropriate because the American people in 1787–89 understood that the Constitution was designed for Washington, whose precedent-setting actions would surely help concretize its meaning—especially the meaning of its open-textured Executive Article. Likewise I have stressed early implementing legislation by the Reconstruction Congress out of respect for its explicit enforcement role in the Reconstruction Amendment texts.

So much, then, for what this book has tried to do. What has it left undone? At least two major omissions are worth noting. First, in countless places, where I have in essence said, "The Constitution as written meant X," I might just as well have said that "although the issue is not black-and-white, and thoughtful analysts have disagreed and continue to disagree, on balance, I personally believe (unless and until I see good new evidence to the contrary, or otherwise come to be persuaded that I have erred) that the best reading of the Constitution as written—putting case law to the side for present purposes—is probably . . . X." For reasons of readability, I have not added all the quibbling qualifiers on every page. But no reader should think that all the views in this book are constitutional gospel accepted by all denominations. Instead, as promised in the Preface, I have tried to offer my own current best judgment on constitutional issues that have been contested for centuries and will probably continue to be contested for centuries more, if the Republic endures.

The largest omission is that mine has been a tale of the *written* and *enacted* Constitution—of the ordained and amended document, as distinct from judicial doctrine and the infinity of American experiences that have left no clear textual trace in the written Constitution itself. I shall briefly return to this large omission, and its important implications, in the concluding paragraphs of this Postscript.

Substance

A reader seeking a single hard-edged thesis in this book may come away disappointed. I offer not a polemic but a portrait, which seeks to illuminate a landmark text much as a standard biographer might shed light on the life of some prominent person. Just as a conventional biographer might explore his subject's inner "constitution" (that is, her deep convictions and contradictions) alongside her outward actions, so I have tried to examine both the document's external impact and its internal structure—its "personality," so to speak. While my narrative has notable themes—for example, I claim that the Founders' Constitution was more democratic, more slavocratic, and more geostrategically inspired than is generally recognized, and that subsequent amendments deepened the document's democratic and geostrategic dimensions while eventually reversing its slavocratic tilt—my largest claim is simply this: America's Constitution deserves careful study and still has much to teach us, if we would but listen.*

Within each chapter, I have tried to offer pointed perspectives and concrete conclusions in the hope that some of my analysis may resolve old debates and even start new ones. A brief recap of some of the more distinctive claims implicit and explicit in the preceding chapters may help readers locate this biography within the wider constitutional literature.

By LAVISHING SOME FIFTY PAGES on a single constitutional sentence, this book's opening chapter aims to restore the Preamble to its proper place as the Founders' foundation. The modern Supreme Court has had almost nothing to say about the Preamble, and modern law students likewise skate past this text with Olympic speed. Earlier generations paid far more attention to the document's grand opening. In each of its three most significant opinions—*Marbury v. Madison, Martin v. Hunter's Lessee,* and *McCulloch v. Maryland*—the Marshall Court expounded on the Preamble, as did

---

*Though this thesis may seem banal, it runs counter to strong trends in recent legal scholarship. See, e.g., Richard A. Posner, *Overcoming Law* (1995); Michael Klarman, "Antifidelity," *Southern California LR* 70 (1997): 381; David Strauss, "Common Law Constitutional Interpretation," *U. of Chicago LR* 63 (1996): 877; David Strauss, "The Irrelevance of Constitutional Amendments," *Harvard LR* 114 (2001): 1457.

Lincoln in his First Inaugural Address and his brief remarks at Gettys-burg.[4]

Contra Charles Beard and his disciples, I argue that the Preamble's words and deeds made clear that the Constitution was essentially demo-cratic. Previous scholarship has failed to emphasize—indeed failed to notice—that in the "We do" moment of the 1780s, most states waived vari-ous property qualifications, following a pattern set by earlier acts of popu-lar constitutionalism in Pennsylvania, Massachusetts, and New Hampshire. Most modern authors have also missed the plain meaning of the New York ratification experience, in which Federalists decisively repudiated the idea of unilateral secession.* Further, scholars have failed to notice how the Preamble's "more perfect Union" was modeled on the indivisible union of England and Scotland in 1707. As I see it, Lincoln thus stood on rock-solid ground in the 1860s, as becomes even clearer once we appre-ciate the centrality of national-defense and geostrategic concerns at the Founding—concerns that neo-Beardians have tended to play down in their efforts to play up the class/property issue.

Chapter 2 measures Congress along several different democratic dimensions—size, salary, eligibility, apportionment, frequency of election, and so on. Here, too, it would seem that modern observers have over-looked or distorted many of the document's strikingly democratic features and have slighted the significance of geographic/geostrategic considera-

---

*Here, too, historians' penchant for period specialization may be partly to blame. Civil War his-torians are not always fluent in the facts of the Founding; and those who have ranged beyond their niche have sometimes stumbled. For instance, Kenneth M. Stampp's important essay "The Concept of a Perpetual Union," *J. of Am. Hist.* 65 (1978): 5, makes no mention of the New York convention vote on the secession issue, misses the basic argument of Publius's early essays, gives insufficient weight to the Federalists' roaring silence—their notable failure to affirm any right of unilateral secession—and slights many keys and cues in the Founding act and text. Con-versely, historians of the Founding have often failed to show much interest in the intense seces-sion debate that occurred many decades later. For example, in *Original Meanings,* his sweeping book on "Politics and Ideas in the Making of the Constitution," Jack Rakove devotes only a sin-gle passing sentence to the vote against a proposed secession right in the New York convention and offers no analysis of the possible significance of this 1788 vote for the great legal debate of the 1860s. Nor does Rakove ponder secession anywhere else in his grand narrative. See Jack N. Rakove, *Original Meanings* (1996), 127; cf. ibid., 435 (index entry). For an extended analysis of se-cession by a constitutional lawyer with a strong interest in history, see Daniel Farber, *Lincoln's Constitution* (2003), 70–91. Yet even this fine account overlooks some important data from the New York ratifying convention—as did my own earlier work on secession; see, e.g., "Of Sover-eignty and Federalism," *Yale LJ* 96 (1987): 1425, 1451–66; "Abraham Lincoln and the American Union," *Illinois LR* 2001: 1109. For a classic early work placing more emphasis on the New York vote, see Andrew C. McLaughlin, *A Constitutional History of the United States* (1935), 209–11, 218 n. 46.

tions that loomed large in the Federalist vision. My pages also seek to measure the slavocratic dimension of the three-fifths clause. Debate over this question recently erupted in the pages of *The New York Times,* when Gordon Wood reviewed Garry Wills's book *"Negro President."*[5] In my view, the underlying issues are clarified by noting that no state constitution circa 1787 gave special apportionment credit to slave property as such; nor had any colony prior to 1776, nor did England, nor did the Articles of Confederation. All these baseline facts support Wills's bottom line that the three-fifths clause was strikingly proslavery. In fairness to Wood, however, Wills did not emphasize any of these baseline facts; nor have most other modern slavery scholars paid close attention to these baselines. For better or worse, my suggestion that a sliding-scale alternative to the three-fifths clause might have been an acceptable compromise in the late 1780s (had it been clearly presented) is, so far as I know, original—as is my emphasis on the antidynastic aspects of the Constitution's age qualifications.

Chapter 3 features a noneconomic reading of the commerce clause that runs somewhat counter to what today's Supreme Court says, but that fits rather well with what the Court has in fact done and what it should do in future cases. This reading also makes good sense of the basic purpose of the Philadelphia plan and of early congressional legislation dealing with Indian tribes. In canvassing Article I restrictions on Congress and on the states, I place less emphasis than have others on the contracts clause and more emphasis on those antiaristocracy aspects of Article I that foreshadowed the Reconstruction Amendments.

The next two chapters focus on America's presidency, highlighting the unity, energy, and dispatch inherent in this republican office—in short, dynamism without dynasty. Following Hamilton, these pages put forth a moderately strong reading of the Article II vesting clause and stress the president's central role in foreign affairs. In defending the president's unilateral power to abrogate treaties in certain situations, I take a relatively strong position on an issue where no scholarly consensus has yet emerged; but my views square with actual practice and dovetail with general arguments from constitutional structure. In detailing various ways in which the Executive Article was designed against the backdrop of European monarchies and early American dynasties, I have tried to extend the republican story that Wood began in his brilliant book *The Radicalism of the American Revolution.* Some parts of my congressional and presidential saga—focusing on salary and property rules, age limits, oath clauses, immigrant eligibility, and so on—might well have been entitled *The Radicalism of the American Constitution.* But other parts of my narrative—exploring the corrupting impact of the three-fifths clause on all the branches of government—could just as well have been captioned *The Anti-Radicalism of the American Constitution.*

My general account of the judiciary in Chapter 6 may come as a surprise to modern lawyers and judges, who tend to exaggerate the role of judges at the Founding. Many historians and political scientists, however, have already begun to cut the early bench down to size by reminding us that Founding-era juries were far more active, and Founding-era judges far less so, than their modern counterparts. To explain the modern judiciary's privileged position within the current constitutional system, we must thus focus on *post*-Founding developments; I try to offer a few new suggestions about how, when, and why this judicial rise came about. I also try to bring to light some underappreciated facts and figures about early judicial appointment and apportionment. Doctrinally, I follow the First Congress and the Marshall Court in construing Article III as comprising two sharply distinct tiers of jurisdiction, the first mandatory and the second not. While this reading has much to commend it, readers should be warned that modern scholars and judges have yet to achieve consensus on this question.

The next two chapters, summarizing Articles IV through VII, contain several distinctive claims. The trans-Appalachian West features prominently in my tale, as does the idea of popular self-rule. While many modern pundits sharply distinguish between democracies and republics and then read that distinction into the Article IV republican-government clause, I argue that this approach is utterly unwarranted. I am more tentative on the topic of Article V exclusivity; but my mere willingness to seriously consider James Wilson's apparent view that the people might perhaps amend the Constitution outside this Article separates me from most orthodox legal scholars. Also, my account of treaties' special status within a three-level hierarchy of federal law is a novel conceptualization, albeit one that generally coheres with modern practice.

My account of the antebellum amendments in Chapter 9 continues several themes at work in my earlier book *The Bill of Rights: Creation and Reconstruction.* In my current retelling of the story, I have emphasized the significance of the 1788 ratification debates more than I did previously, and also emphasized how the first congressional elections served as a second referendum of sorts on the new Constitution. On the Eleventh Amendment and state sovereign immunity, I follow the mainstream of modern legal scholarship, which has little praise for current case law; four of the nine current justices have also attacked the root premises of doctrine in this area. In stressing the role of slavery in the presidential election of 1800–01 and the subsequent Twelfth Amendment, I build upon Garry Wills's recent book and present additional evidence generally supportive of Wills's insights.

The next chapter, "A New Birth of Freedom," also unfolds themes previously sketched in *The Bill of Rights: Creation and Reconstruction*—the Fourteenth Amendment's incorporation of the Bill of Rights; the amendment's basic distinction between civil and political rights; the interconnections among voting, jury service, officeholding, and military service; and the salience of women's-rights issues in the Reconstruction conversation. Compared to current case law, I place less emphasis on the equal-protection and due-process clauses, and I argue for a more robust reading of the birthright-citizenship clause and the privileges-or-immunities clause. Also, my insistence on a broad congressional enforcement role places me much closer to the Warren Court approach than to the more recent Rehnquist Court vision. Further, I offer some new thoughts about how and why the Fifteenth Amendment came about when it did.

While my Reconstruction chapter features an explicit critique of Bruce Ackerman's account of the 1860's, my final two chapters can be read as an implicit critique of Ackerman's more Court-centered and less textualist view of twentieth-century constitutional law. Ackerman organizes his grand narrative around *Lochner v. New York,*[6] a case that, to him, rests on a highly plausible defense of freedom of contract. I read this 1905 case differently. *Lochner* allowed various government restrictions on freedom of contract; what it forbade was legislation seeking to redistribute economic power from haves to have-nots.[7] If *Lochner* is indeed a case about redistribution rather than freedom of contract per se, then the Court was wrong to follow *Lochner* after 1913, the year when the American people, via the Income Tax Amendment, emphatically embraced the propriety of redistribution. Ackerman apparently believes that the Court was correct to *Lochner*ize until the Constitution was (on his view) implicitly amended in the New Deal. I offer a different account, in which modern America's enhanced nationalism and commitment to economic equality are properly derived from the explicit Progressive Amendments. As I see it, while Ackerman claims to champion twentieth-century popular sovereignty, he in fact slights the actual and extraordinary outburst of constitutional creativity in the 1910s. As for the New Deal, this alleged "constitutional moment" left virtually no textual trace in the Constitution itself.[8] Hence, my most direct engagement with the New Deal is via the Two Term Amendment—an *anti*-FDR text.

Likewise my story of the late twentieth century highlights the mobilized citizenry and the Congress, with less focus on the Supreme Court as the sole engine or index of change. As I tell the tale, the status of blacks changed not merely thanks to *Brown v. Board of Education,* but largely as a result of Second Reconstruction enforcement statutes, such as the Voting Rights Act of 1965. Once we focus on Congress as an enforcement agent, we are reminded that over the course of American history, the Court has not always played the hero in the saga of civil and political rights for the dispossessed. *Brown* was of course preceded by *Plessy;* and *Plessy* in turn blessed state segregation laws that Congress had in fact preempted in its first wave of Reconstruction statutes—statutes that the Court struck down in the 1880s.

More generally, my concluding chapters contain several notable theories and lots of new evidence about how the truly epic constitutional changes of the last century—woman suffrage, direct Senate election, progressive federal taxation, the democratization of the constitutional calendar, the transformation of the vice presidency, and the Second Reconstruction—actually came to pass and then rippled through the political system. New, too, is my suggestion that the Prohibition Amendment contains deep within it heretofore unnoticed yet potentially transformative implications for the process of future constitutional amendment.

Posterity

A parting thought. Much as America's Constitution is a democratic and intergenerational project—the product of many minds over many years—so, too, is constitutional scholarship. The document has no fixed end point, and scholarship on the Constitution must likewise go on indefinitely. I would hope that future scholars might proceed on at least two fronts. First, we need more empirical and institution-oriented work. For example, I can imagine literally dozens of detailed microstudies that could profitably carry forward the intellectual agenda sketched out in my opening chapters on Congress and the presidency. There are still so many unanswered questions: Precisely how much, or how little, did slavery skew apportionment maps in each state and in each decade of antebellum America? What other factors shaped apportionment in state and congressional races, and in the judiciary? What was the state-by-state experience with political dynasties? How prominent were dynastic concerns after Jackson? How did woman suffrage influence state dynastic practice, as daughters, wives, and widows became eligible political heirs? How and why have state executive branches evolved over the centuries? And so on.

Second, we need new scholarship that breaks free of the methodological constraints that I have imposed on myself in this project. While this book has focused on the written and enacted Constitution, I myself do not believe that all of American constitutionalism can be deduced simply from the document. At key points the text itself seems to gesture outward, reminding readers of the importance of unenumerated rights above and beyond textually enumerated ones.

Thus we need at least one more book to start where this one ends, giving readers a detailed account of America's *unwritten* Constitution. Such a book could canvass Supreme Court case law; could assess quasi-constitutional framework statutes that have emerged and endured in America; could ponder other foundational American legal texts such as the Declaration of Independence and the Northwest Ordinance; could examine unwritten customs of Americans worthy of constitutional protection; could systematically consider other modern constitutions across the globe for the wisdom doubtless embedded in many of these documents/traditions; could reflect on the teachings of past and present political philosophers; and could assess particularly plausible proposals for new constitutional amendments. In other words, such a future book could profitably take the interested reader in any number of directions that today's narrative has not.

But before we turn to judicial doctrine and to other potential sources of constitutional wisdom beyond the written Constitution, it is useful—indeed, indispensable—to understand precisely what the document did and did not mean to those who enacted and amended it. While this book should not be the last word for serious constitutionalists, I hope that, for some readers at least, it will be a first step.

THE CONSTITUTION
OF THE
UNITED STATES*

We the People of the United States,

in Order to form a more perfect Union, establish Justice,

insure domestic Tranquility, provide for the common defence,

promote the general Welfare, and secure the Blessings of Liberty

to ourselves and our Posterity, do ordain and establish this

Constitution for the United States of America.**

*The version of the Founding text reprinted here derives from the hand-signed parchment as distinct from the printed version of the document simultaneously approved at Philadelphia. The print and the parchment differed in minor details of punctuation and capitalization, and a strong case could be made for treating the printed version as the legally official one. (It was the version sent to the states for ratification.) However, it has become conventional to use the parchment copy for most purposes. For more background on the printed version, and the story of how it came to fade from public view over the centuries, interested readers may wish to consult my brief bicentennial essay, "Our Forgotten Constitution," *Yale LJ* 97 (1987): 281. The amendment texts reprinted here derive from S. Doc. 103–6 (1992, reprint, 1996).
**The numbers that appear in the margins of the following pages refer to the pages of the preceding chapters that discuss each particular passage in the Constitution. The Preamble above is covered on pages 3–53, 106, 247, 292, 299, 308, 324, and 471–72.

ARTICLE. I.

57–64 *Section. 1.* All legislative Powers herein granted shall be vested in a Congress of the United States, which shall consist of a Senate and House of Representatives.

15, 58, 64–66, 69, 74–76, 145, 156 *Section. 2.* The House of Representatives shall be composed of Members chosen every second Year by the People of the several States, and the Electors in each State shall have the Qualifications requisite for Electors of the most numerous Branch of the State Legislature.

66–72, 163, 473 No Person shall be a Representative who shall not have attained to the Age of twenty five Years, and been seven Years a Citizen of the United States, and who shall not, when elected, be an Inhabitant of that State in which he shall be chosen.

20–21, 55, 76–93, 150–51, 156–59, 345–46, 406–7, 439n., 473 Representatives and direct Taxes shall be apportioned among the several States which may be included within this Union, according to their respective Numbers, which shall be determined by adding to the whole Number of free Persons, including those bound to Service for a Term of Years, and excluding Indians not taxed, three fifths of all other Persons. The actual Enumeration shall be made within three Years after the first Meeting of the Congress of the United States, and within every subsequent Term of ten Years, in such Manner as they shall by Law direct. The Number of Representatives shall not exceed one for every thirty Thousand, but each State shall have at Least one Representative; and until such enumeration shall be made, the State of New Hampshire shall be entitled to chuse three, Massachusetts eight, Rhode-Island and Providence Plantations one, Connecticut five, New-York six, New Jersey four, Pennsylvania eight, Delaware one, Maryland six, Virginia ten, North Carolina five, South Carolina five, and Georgia three.

133 When vacancies happen in the Representation from any State, the Executive Authority thereof shall issue Writs of Election to fill such Vacancies.

132, 171–72, 198–99 The House of Representatives shall chuse their Speaker and other Officers; and shall have the sole Power of Impeachment.

36, 58, 74–76, 85–86, 144–45, 293–95 *Section. 3.* The Senate of the United States shall be composed of two Senators from each State, chosen by the Legislature thereof, for six Years; and each Senator shall have one Vote.

132–33, 144, 317 Immediately after they shall be assembled in Consequence of the first Election, they shall be divided as equally as may be into three Classes. The Seats of the Senators of the first Class shall be vacated at the Expiration of the second Year, of the second Class at the Expiration of the fourth Year, and of the third Class at the Expiration of the sixth Year, so that one third may be chosen every second Year; and if Vacancies happen by Resignation, or otherwise, during the Recess of the Legislature of any State, the Executive thereof may make temporary Appointments until the next Meeting of the Legislature, which shall then fill such Vacancies.

No Person shall be a Senator who shall not have attained to the Age of thirty Years, and been nine Years a Citizen of the United States, and who shall not, when elected, be an inhabitant of that State for which he shall be chosen.

The Vice President of the United States shall be President of the Senate, but shall have no Vote, unless they be equally divided.

The Senate shall chuse their other Officers, and also a President pro tempore, in the Absence of the Vice President, or when he shall exercise the Office of President of the United States.

The Senate shall have the sole Power to try all Impeachments. When sitting for that Purpose, they shall be on Oath or Affirmation. When the President of the United States is tried, the Chief Justice shall preside: And no Person shall be convicted without the Concurrence of two thirds of the Members present.

Judgment in Cases of Impeachment shall not extend further than to removal from Office, and disqualification to hold and enjoy any Office of honor, Trust or Profit under the United States: but the Party convicted shall nevertheless be liable and subject to Indictment, Trial, Judgment and Punishment, according to Law.

Section. 4. The Times, Places and Manner of holding Elections for Senators and Representatives, shall be prescribed in each State by the Legislature thereof; but the Congress may at any time by Law make or alter such Regulations, except as to the Places of chusing Senators.

The Congress shall assemble at least once in every Year, and such Meeting shall be on the first Monday in December, unless they shall by Law appoint a different Day.

Section. 5. Each House shall be the Judge of the Elections, Returns and Qualifications of its own Members, and a Majority of each shall constitute a Quorum to do Business; but a smaller Number may adjourn from day to day, and may be authorized to compel the Attendance of absent Members, in such Manner, and under such Penalties as each House may provide.

Each House may determine the Rules of its Proceedings, punish its Members for disorderly Behaviour, and, with the Concurrence of two thirds, expel a Member.

Each House shall keep a Journal of its Proceedings, and from time to time publish the same, excepting such Parts as may in their Judgment require Secrecy; and the Yeas and Nays of the Members of either House on any question shall, at the Desire of one fifth of those Present, be entered on the Journal.

112   Neither House, during the Session of Congress, shall, without the Consent of the other, adjourn for more than three days, nor to any other Place than that in which the two Houses shall be sitting.

15–16, 58, 72–74, *Section. 6.* The Senators and Representatives shall receive a Compensation
99, 101–4, 200–01 for their Services, to be ascertained by Law, and paid out of the Treasury of the United States. They shall in all Cases, except Treason, Felony and Breach of the Peace, be privileged from Arrest during their Attendance at the Session of their respective Houses, and in going to and returning from the same; and for any Speech or Debate in either House, they shall not be questioned in any other Place.

63, 78, 131, 171–73, No Senator or Representative shall, during the Time for which he was
182, 415*n.* elected, be appointed to any civil Office under the Authority of the United States, which shall have been created, or the Emoluments whereof shall have been encreased during such time; and no Person holding any Office under the United States, shall be a Member of either House during his Continuance in Office.

107 *Section. 7.* All Bills for raising Revenue shall originate in the House of Representatives; but the Senate may propose or concur with Amendments as on other Bills.

60–64, 137, 143, Every Bill which shall have passed the House of Representatives and
175, 181–85, 203, the Senate, shall, before it become a Law, be presented to the President of
362 the United States; If he approve he shall sign it, but if not he shall return it, with his Objections to that House in which it shall have originated, who shall enter the Objections at large on their Journal, and proceed to reconsider it. If after such Reconsideration two thirds of that House shall agree to pass the Bill, it shall be sent, together with the Objections, to the other House, by which it shall likewise be reconsidered, and if approved by two thirds of that House, it shall become a Law. But in all such Cases the Votes of both Houses shall be determined by yeas and Nays, and the Names of the Persons voting for and against the Bill shall be entered on the Journal of each House respectively. If any Bill shall not be returned by the President within ten Days (Sundays excepted) after it shall have been presented to him, the Same shall be a Law, in like Manner as if he had signed it, unless the Congress by their Adjournment prevent its Return, in which Case it shall not be a Law.

Every Order, Resolution, or Vote to which the Concurrence of the Senate and House of Representatives may be necessary (except on a question of Adjournment) shall be presented to the President of the United States; and before the Same shall take Effect, shall be approved by him, or being disapproved by him, shall be repassed by two thirds of the Senate and House of Representatives, according to the Rules and Limitations prescribed in the Case of a Bill.

Section. 8. The Congress shall have Power To lay and collect Taxes, Duties, Imposts and Excises, to pay the Debts and Provide for the common Defence and general Welfare of the United States; but all Duties, Imposts and Excises shall be uniform throughout the United States;

To borrow Money on the credit of the United States;

To regulate Commerce with foreign Nations, and among the several States, and with the Indian Tribes;

To establish an uniform Rule of Naturalization, and uniform Laws on the subject of Bankruptcies throughout the United States;

To coin Money, regulate the Value thereof, and of foreign Coin, and fix the Standard of Weights and Measures;

To provide for the Punishment of counterfeiting the Securities and current Coin of the United States;

To establish Post Offices and post Roads;

To promote the Progress of Science and useful Arts, by securing for limited Time to Authors and Inventors the exclusive Right to their respective Writings and Discoveries;

To constitute Tribunals inferior to the supreme Court;

To define and punish Piracies and Felonies committed on the high Seas, and Offences against the Law of Nations;

To declare War, grant Letters of Marque and Reprisal, and make Rules concerning Captures on Land and Water;

To raise and support Armies, but no Appropriation of Money to that Use shall be for a longer Term than two Years;

To provide and maintain a Navy;

To make Rules for the Government and Regulation of the land and naval Forces;

To provide for calling forth the Militia to execute the Laws of the Union, suppress Insurrections and repel Invasions;

To provide for organizing, arming, and disciplining, the Militia, and for governing such Part of them as may be employed in the Service of the United States, reserving to the States respectively, the Appointment of the Officers, and the Authority of training the Militia according to the discipline prescribed by Congress;

To exercise exclusive Legislation in all Cases whatsoever, over such District (not exceeding ten Miles square) as may, by Cession of Particular States, and the Acceptance of Congress, become the Seat of the Government of the United States, and to exercise like Authority over all Places purchased by the Consent of the Legislature of the State in which the Same shall be, for the Erection of Forts, Magazines, Arsenals, dock-Yards, and other needful Buildings;— And

To make all Laws which shall be necessary and proper for carrying into Execution the foregoing Powers, and all other Powers vested by this Constitution in the Government of the United States, or in any Department or Officer thereof.

Section. 9. The Migration or Importation of such Persons as any of the States now existing shall think proper to admit, shall not be prohibited by the Congress prior to the Year one thousand eight hundred and eight, but a Tax or duty may be imposed on such Importation, not exceeding ten dollars for each Person.

The Privilege of the Writ of Habeas Corpus shall not be suspended, unless when in Cases of Rebellion or Invasion the public Safety may require it.

No Bill of Attainder or ex post facto Law shall be passed.

No Capitation, or other direct, Tax shall be laid, unless in Proportion to the Census or Enumeration herein before directed to be taken.

No Tax or Duty shall be laid on Articles exported from any State.

No Preference shall be given by any Regulation of Commerce or Revenue to the Ports of one State over those of another: nor shall Vessels bound to, or from, one State, be obliged to enter, clear, or pay Duties in another.

No Money shall be drawn from the Treasury, but in Consequence of Appropriations made by Law; and a regular Statement and Account of the Receipts and Expenditures of all public Money shall be published from time to time.

No Title of Nobility shall be granted by the United States: And no Person holding any Office of Profit or Trust under them, shall, without the Consent of the Congress, accept of any present, Emolument, Office, or Title, of any kind whatever, from any King, Prince, or foreign State.

Section. 10. No State shall enter into any Treaty, Alliance, or Confederation; grant Letters of Marque and Reprisal; coin Money; emit Bills of Credit; make any Thing but gold and silver Coin a Tender in Payment of Debts; pass any Bill of Attainder, ex post facto Law, or Law impairing the Obligation of Contracts, or grant any Title of Nobility.

No State shall, without the Consent of the Congress, lay any Imposts or Duties on Imports or Exports, except what may be absolutely necessary for executing it's inspection Laws: and the net Produce of all Duties and Imposts, laid by any State on Imports or Exports, shall be for the Use of the Treasury of the United States; and all such Laws shall be subject to the Revision and Controul of the Congress.

51, 115–17, 120, No State shall, without the Consent of Congress, lay any Duty of Ton-
187–88, 254 nage, keep Troops, or Ships of War in time of Peace, enter into any Agreement or Compact with another State, or with a foreign Power, or engage in
War, unless actually invaded, or in such imminent Danger as will not admit
of delay.

ARTICLE. II.

151, 131–48, *Section. 1.* The executive Power shall be vested in a President of the
163–64, 185–86 United States of America. He shall hold his Office during the Term of four
Years, and, together with the Vice President, chosen for the same Term, be
elected, as follows.

20–21, 143, Each State shall appoint, in such Manner as the Legislature thereof
148–59, 313 may direct, a Number of Electors, equal to the whole Number of Senators
and Representatives to which the State may be entitled in the Congress: but
no Senator or Representative, or Person holding an Office of Trust or Profit
under the United States, shall be appointed an Elector.

148–50, 166–68, The Electors shall meet in their respective States, and vote by Ballot
336–41, 429 for two Persons, of whom one at least shall not be an Inhabitant of the same
State with themselves. And they shall make a List of all the Persons voted
for, and of the Number of Votes for each; which List they shall sign and certify, and transmit sealed to the Seat of the Government of the United States,
directed to the President of the Senate. The President of the Senate shall, in
the Presence of the Senate and House of Representatives, open all the Certificates, and the Votes shall then be counted. The Person having the greatest Number of Votes shall be the President, if such Number be a Majority
of the whole Number of Electors appointed; and if there be more than one
who have such Majority, and have an equal Number of Votes, then the
House of Representatives shall immediately chuse by Ballot one of them for
President; and if no Person have a Majority, then from the five highest on
the List the said House shall in like Manner chuse the President. But in
chusing the President, the Votes shall be taken by States, the Representation from each State having one Vote; A quorum for this Purpose shall consist of a Member or Members from two thirds of the States, and a Majority
of all the States shall be necessary to a Choice. In every Case, after the
Choice of the President, the Person having the greatest Number of Votes of
the Electors shall be the Vice President. But if there should remain two or
more who have equal Votes, the Senate shall chuse from them by Ballot the
Vice President.

154 The Congress may determine the Time of chusing the Electors, and
the Day on which they shall give their Votes; which Day shall be the same
throughout the United States.

129, 159–66, 473 No Person except a natural born Citizen, or a Citizen of the United States, at the time of the Adoption of this Constitution, shall be eligible to the Office of President; neither shall any Person be eligible to that Office who shall not have attained to the Age of thirty five Years, and been fourteen Years a Resident within the United States.

132, 166–73, 447–49 In Case of the Removal of the President from Office, or of his Death, Resignation, or Inability to discharge the Powers and Duties of the said Office, the Same shall devolve on the Vice President, and the Congress may by Law provide for the Case of Removal, Death, Resignation or Inability, both of the President and Vice President, declaring what Officer shall then act as President, and such Officer shall act accordingly, until the Disability be removed, or a President shall be elected.

15–16, 131, 181–83, 473 The President shall, at stated Times, receive for his Services, a Compensation, which shall neither be encreased nor diminished during the Period for which he shall have been elected, and he shall not receive within that Period any other Emolument from the United States, or any of them.

62–63, 178–83, 473 Before he enter on the Execution of his Office, he shall take the following Oath or Affirmation:— "I do solemnly swear (or affirm) that I will faithfully execute the Office of President of the United States, and will to the best of my Ability, preserve, protect and defend the Constitution of the United States."

51, 131, 137, 185–89, 192–93, 197, 356 *Section. 2.* The President shall be Commander in Chief of the Army and Navy of the United States, and of the Militia of the several States, when called into the actual Service of the United States; he may require the Opinion, in writing, of the principal Officer in each of the executive Departments, upon any Subject relating to the Duties of their respective Offices, and he shall have Power to grant Reprieves and Pardons for Offences against the United States, except in Cases of Impeachment.

21, 111, 131, 137, 142, 189–95, 197, 218–20 He shall have Power, by and with the Advice and Consent of the Senate, to make Treaties, provided two thirds of the Senators present concur; and he shall nominate, and by and with the Advice and Consent of the Senate, shall appoint Ambassadors, other public Ministers and Consuls, Judges of the supreme Court, and all other Officers of the United States, whose Appointments are not herein otherwise provided for, and which shall be established by Law: but the Congress may by Law vest the Appointment of such inferior Officers, as they think proper, in the President alone, in the Courts of Law, or in the Heads of Departments.

132, 195 The President shall have Power to fill up all Vacancies that may happen during the Recess of the Senate, by granting Commissions which shall expire at the End of their next Session.

Section. 3. He shall from time to time give to the Congress Information of the State of the Union, and recommend to their Consideration such Measures as he shall judge necessary and expedient; he may, on extraordinary Occasions, convene both Houses, or either of them, and in Case of Disagreement between them, with Respect to the Time of Adjournment, he may adjourn them to such Time as he shall think proper; he shall receive Ambassadors and other public Ministers; he shall take Care that the Laws be faithfully executed, and shall Commission all the Officers of the United States.

76, 132, 178, 195–98

Section. 4. The President, Vice President and all civil Officers of the United States, shall be removed from Office on Impeachment for, and conviction of, Treason, Bribery, or other high Crimes and Misdemeanors.

145, 198–203, 222

ARTICLE. III.

Section. 1. The judicial Power of the United States, shall be vested in one supreme Court, and in such inferior Courts as the Congress may from time to time ordain and establish. The Judges, both of the supreme and inferior Courts, shall hold their Offices during good Behaviour, and shall, at stated Times, receive for their Services, a Compensation, which shall not be diminished during their Continuance in Office.

15–16, 181, 194, 205–26

Section. 2. The judicial Power shall extend to all Cases, in Law and Equity, arising under this Constitution, the Laws of the United States, and Treaties made, or which shall be made, under their Authority;— to all Cases affecting Ambassadors, other public Ministers and Consuls;— to all Cases of admiralty and maritime Jurisdiction;— to Controversies to which the United States shall be a Party;— to Controversies between two or more States;— between a State and Citizens of another State;— between Citizens of different States,— between Citizens of the same State claiming Lands under Grants of different States, and between a State, or the Citizens thereof, and foreign States, Citizens or Subjects.

211, 225–29, 252, 295, 334–35, 474

In all Cases affecting Ambassadors, other public Ministers and Consuls, and those in which a State shall be Party, the supreme Court shall have original Jurisdiction. In all the other Cases before mentioned, the supreme Court shall have appellate Jurisdiction, both as to Law and Fact, with such Exceptions, and under such Regulations as the Congress shall make.

121, 211, 229–33

The Trial of all Crimes, except in Cases of Impeachment, shall be by Jury; and such Trial shall be held in the State where the said Crimes shall have been committed; but when not committed within any State, the

15, 233–42, 330

Trial shall be at such Place or Places as the Congress may by Law have directed.

35, 242–45   *Section. 3.* Treason against the United States, shall consist only in levying War against them, or in adhering to their Enemies, giving them Aid and Comfort. No Person shall be convicted of Treason unless on the Testimony of two Witnesses to the same overt Act, or on Confession in open Court.

242–43   The Congress shall have Power to declare the Punishment of Treason, but no Attainder of Treason shall work Corruption of Blood, or Forfeiture except during the Life of the Person attainted.

Article. IV.

249, 255–56   *Section. 1.* Full Faith and Credit shall be given in each State to the public Acts, Records, and judicial Proceedings of every other State. And the Congress may by general Laws prescribe the Manner in which such Acts, Records and Proceedings shall be proved, and the Effect thereof.

249–56, 335, 381, 391   *Section. 2.* The Citizens of each State shall be entitled to all Privileges and Immunities of Citizens in the several States.

201, 255–56, 258–59   A Person charged in any State with Treason, Felony, or other Crime, who shall flee from Justice, and be found in another State, shall on Demand of the executive Authority of the State from which he fled, be delivered up, to be removed to the State having Jurisdiction of the Crime.

21, 256–64   No Person held to Service or Labour in one State, under the Laws thereof, escaping into another, shall, in Consequence of any Law or Regulation therein, be discharged from such Service or Labour, but shall be delivered up on Claim of the Party to whom such Service or Labour may be due.

51, 270–76   *Section. 3.* New States may be admitted by the Congress into this Union; but no new State shall be formed or erected within the Jurisdiction of any other State; nor any State be formed by the Junction of two or more States, or Parts of States, without the Consent of the Legislatures of the States concerned as well as of the Congress.

17, 51, 58, 264–70, 439   The Congress shall have Power to dispose of and make all needful Rules and Regulations respecting the Territory or other Property belonging to the United States; and nothing in this Constitution shall be so construed as to Prejudice any Claims of the United States, or of any particular State.

16, 51, 58, 264–70, 439   *Section. 4.* The United States shall guarantee to every State in this Union a Republican Form of Government, and shall protect each of them against Invasion; and on Application of the Legislature, or of the Executive (when the Legislature cannot be convened) against domestic Violence.

Article. V.

12–13, 16, 21,
34–35, 91, 285–99,
300, 364–80,
416–17, 454–58,
463, 474

The Congress, whenever two thirds of both Houses shall deem it necessary, shall propose Amendments to this Constitution, or, on the Application of the Legislatures of two thirds of the several States, shall call a Convention for proposing Amendments, which, in either Case, shall be valid to all Intents and Purposes, as Part of this Constitution, when ratified by the Legislatures of three fourths of the several States, or by Conventions in three fourths thereof, as the one or the other Mode of Ratification may be proposed by the Congress; Provided that no Amendment which may be made prior to the Year One thousand eight hundred and eight shall in any Manner affect the first and fourth Clauses in the Ninth Section of the first Article; and that no State, without its Consent, shall be deprived of it's equal Suffrage in the Senate.

Article. VI.

299–300, 302,
396n.

All Debts contracted and Engagements entered into, before the Adoption of this Constitution, shall be as valid against the United States under this Constitution, as under the Confederation.

33–34, 37, 51, 121,
178–79, 190–92,
299–307

This Constitution, and the Laws of the United States which shall be made in Pursuance thereof; and all Treaties made, or which shall be made, under the Authority of the United States, shall be the supreme Law of the Land; and the Judges in every State shall be bound thereby, any Thing in the Constitution or Laws of any State to the Contrary notwithstanding.

16, 62–63, 166, 180,
301–2

The Senators and Representatives before mentioned, and the Members of the several State Legislatures, and all executive and judicial Officers, both of the United States and of the several States, shall be bound by Oath or Affirmation, to support this Constitution; but no religious Test shall ever be required as a Qualification to any Office or public Trust under the United States.

Article. VII.

6–7, 14–16, 29–30,
33–34, 283, 286,
301, 308–12

The Ratification of the Conventions of nine States, shall be sufficient for the Establishment of this Constitution between the States so ratifying the Same.

5–6, 80, 134–35

Done in Convention by the Unanimous Consent of the States present the Seventeenth Day of September in the Year of our Lord one thousand seven hundred and Eighty seven and of the Independence of the United States of America the Twelfth In witness whereof We have hereunto subscribed our Names,

Attest William Jackson Secretary

Go. Washington — Presidt. and Deputy from Virginia.

New Hampshire	John Langdon
	Nicholas Gilman
Massachusetts	Nathaniel Gorham
	Rufus King
Connecticut	Wm: Saml. Johnson
	Roger Sherman
New York	Alexander Hamilton
New Jersey	Wil: Livingston
	David Brearley.
	Wm. Paterson.
	Jona: Dayton
Pennsylvania	B Franklin
	Thomas Mifflin
	Robt Morris
	Geo. Clymer
	Thos. Fitzsimons
	Jared Ingersoll
	James Wilson
	Gouv Morris
Delaware	Geo: Read
	Gunning Bedford jun
	John Dickinson
	Richard Bassett
	Jaco: Broom
Maryland	James McHenry
	Dan of St Thos. Jenifer
	Danl. Carroll.
Virginia	John Blair—
	James Madison Jr.
North Carolina	Wm. Blount
	Richd. Dobbs Spaight.
	Hu Williamson
South Carolina	J. Rutledge
	Charles Cotesworth Pinckney
	Charles Pinckney
	Pierce Butler.
Georgia	William Few
	Abr Baldwin

AMENDMENT I [1791]

Congress shall make no law respecting an establishment of religion, or prohibiting the free exercise thereof; or abridging the freedom of speech, or of the press; or the right of the people peaceably to assemble, and to petition the Government for a redress of grievances.

AMENDMENT II [1791]

A well regulated Militia, being necessary to the security of a free State, the right of the people to keep and bear Arms, shall not be infringed.

AMENDMENT III [1791]

No Soldier shall, in time of peace be quartered in any house, without the consent of the Owner, nor in time of war, but in a manner to be prescribed by law.

AMENDMENT IV [1791]

The right of the people to be secure in their persons, houses, papers, and effects, against unreasonable searches and seizures, shall not be violated, and no Warrants shall issue, but upon probable cause, supported by Oath or affirmation, and particularly describing the place to be searched, and the persons or things to be seized.

AMENDMENT V [1791]

No person shall be held to answer for a capital, or otherwise infamous crime, unless on a presentment or indictment of a Grand Jury, except in cases arising in the land or naval forces, or in the Militia, when in actual service in time of War or public danger; nor shall any person be subject for the same offence to be twice put in jeopardy of life or limb; nor shall be compelled in any criminal case to be a witness against himself, nor be deprived of life, liberty, or property, without due process of law; nor shall private property be taken for public use, without just compensation.

AMENDMENT VI [1791]

In all criminal prosecutions, the accused shall enjoy the right to a speedy and public trial, by an impartial jury of the State and district wherein the crime shall have been committed, which district shall have been previously ascertained by law, and to be informed of the nature and cause of the accusation; to be confronted with the witnesses against him; to have compulsory process for obtaining witnesses in his favor, and to have the Assistance of Counsel for his defense.

AMENDMENT VII [1791]

In Suits at common law, where the value in controversy shall exceed twenty dollars, the right of trial by jury shall be preserved, and no fact tried by a jury, shall be otherwise re-examined in any Court of the United States, than according to the rules of the common law.

AMENDMENT VIII [1791]

Excessive bail shall not be required, nor excessive fines imposed, nor cruel and unusual punishments inflicted.

AMENDMENT IX [1791]

The enumeration in the Constitution, of certain rights, shall not be construed to deny or disparage others retained by the people.

AMENDMENT X [1791]

The powers not delegated to the United States by the Constitution, nor prohibited by it to the States, are reserved to the States respectively, or to the people.

AMENDMENT XI [1795]

The Judicial power of the United States shall not be construed to extend to any suit in law or equity, commenced or prosecuted against one of the United States by Citizens of another State, or by Citizens or Subjects of any Foreign State.

AMENDMENT XII [1804]

The Electors shall meet in their respective states and vote by ballot for President and Vice-President, one of whom, at least, shall not be an inhabitant of the same state with themselves; they shall name in their ballots the person voted for as President, and in distinct ballots the person voted for as Vice-President, and they shall make distinct lists of all persons voted for as President, and of all persons voted for as Vice-President, and of the number of votes for each, which lists they shall sign and certify, and transmit sealed to the seat of the government of the United States, directed to the

President of the Senate;—The President of the Senate shall, in the presence of the Senate and House of Representatives, open all the certificates and the votes shall then be counted;—The person having the greatest Number of votes for President, shall be the President, if such number be a majority of the whole number of Electors appointed; and if no person have such majority, then from the persons having the highest numbers not exceeding three on the list of those voted for as President, the House of Representatives shall choose immediately, by ballot, the President. But in choosing the President, the votes shall be taken by states, the representation from each state having one vote; a quorum for this purpose shall consist of a member or members from two-thirds of the states, and a majority of all the States shall be necessary to a choice. And if the House of Representatives shall not choose a President whenever the right of choice shall devolve upon them, before the fourth day of March next following, then the Vice-President shall act as President, as in the case of the death or other constitutional disability of the President.—The person having the greatest number of votes as Vice-President, shall be the Vice-President, if such number be a majority of the whole number of Electors appointed, and if no person have a majority, then from the two highest numbers on the list, the Senate shall choose the Vice-President; a quorum for the purpose shall consist of two thirds of the whole number of Senators, and a majority of the whole number shall be necessary to a choice. But no person constitutionally ineligible to the office of President shall be eligible to that of Vice-President of the United States.

AMENDMENT XIII [1865]

18, 114, 126–27, 351–60, 363–76, 427, 457 n., 459–60 *Section 1.* Neither slavery nor involuntary servitude, except as a punishment for crime whereof the party shall have been duly convicted, shall exist within the United States, or any place subject to their jurisdiction.

361–63, 407–8 *Section 2.* Congress shall have power to enforce this article by appropriate legislation.

AMENDMENT XIV [1868]

18, 126–27, 349, 351, 362–92, 405, 427, 439 n., 459, 475 *Section 1.* All persons born or naturalized in the United States and subject to the jurisdiction thereof, are citizens of the United States and of the State wherein they reside. No State shall make or enforce any law which shall abridge the privileges or immunities of citizens of the United States; nor shall any State deprive any person of life, liberty, or property, without due process of law; nor deny to any person within its jurisdiction the equal protection of the laws.

377, 392–95, 399, *Section 2.* Representatives shall be apportioned among the several States
439n., 461 according to their respective numbers, counting the whole number of persons in each State, excluding Indians not taxed. But when the right to vote
at any election for the choice of electors for President and Vice President of
the United States, Representatives in Congress, the Executive and Judicial
officers of a State, or the members of the Legislature thereof, is denied to
any of the male inhabitants of such State, being twenty one years of age, and
citizens of the United States, or in any way abridged, except for participation in rebellion, or other crime, the basis of representation therein shall be
reduced in the proportion which the number of such male citizens shall
bear to the whole number of male citizens twenty one years of age in such
State.

377, 394n. *Section 3.* No person shall be a Senator or Representative in Congress, or
elector of President and Vice President, or hold any office, civil or military,
under the United States, or under any State, who, having previously taken
an oath, as a member of Congress, or as an officer of the United States, or as
a member of any State legislature, or as an executive or judicial officer of
any State, to support the Constitution of the United States, shall have engaged in insurrection or rebellion against the same, or given aid or comfort
to the enemies thereof. But Congress may by a vote of two thirds of each
House, remove such disability.

360, 396n., 405 *Section 4.* The validity of the public debt of the United States, authorized
by law, including debts incurred for payment of pensions and bounties for
services in suppressing insurrection or rebellion, shall not be questioned.
But neither the United States nor any State shall assume or pay any debt or
obligation incurred in aid of insurrection or rebellion against the United
States, or any claim for the loss or emancipation of any slave; but all such
debts, obligations and claims shall be held illegal and void.

361n., 363, 407–8 *Section 5.* The Congress shall have power to enforce, by appropriate legislation, the provisions of this article.

AMENDMENT XV [1870]

18–19, 349, 351, *Section 1.* The right of citizens of the United States to vote shall not be
383, 395–401, 421, denied or abridged by the United States or by any State on account of
425–28, 445, 459,
461 race, color, or previous condition of servitude.

361n., 399, 407–8, *Section 2.* The Congress shall have power to enforce this article by appro-
443 priate legislation.

AMENDMENT XVI [1913]

361n., 405–9, The Congress shall have power to lay and collect taxes on incomes, from
475–76 whatever source derived, without apportionment among the several States, and without regard to any census or enumeration.

AMENDMENT XVII [1913]

408–15, 422–24, The Senate of the United States shall be composed of two Senators from
445, 476 each State, elected by the people thereof, for six years; and each Senator shall have one vote. The electors in each State shall have the qualifications requisite for electors of the most numerous branch of the State legislatures.

When vacancies happen in the representation of any State in the Senate, the executive authority of such State shall issue writs of election to fill such vacancies: Provided, That the legislature of any State may empower the executive thereof to make temporary appointments until the people fill the vacancies by election as the legislature may direct.

This amendment shall not be so construed as to affect the election or term of any Senator chosen before it becomes valid as part of the Constitution.

AMENDMENT XVIII [1919]

323, 415–19, 461 *Section 1.* After one year from the ratification of this article the manufacture, sale, or transportation of intoxicating liquors within, the importation thereof into, or the exportation thereof from the United States and all territory subject to the jurisdiction thereof for beverage purposes is hereby prohibited.

361n. *Section 2.* The Congress and the several States shall have concurrent power to enforce this article by appropriate legislation.

417–19, 476 *Section 3.* This article shall be inoperative unless it shall have been ratified as an amendment to the Constitution by the legislatures of the several States, as provided in the Constitution, within seven years from the date of the submission hereof to the States by the Congress.

AMENDMENT XIX [1920]

18–19, 361n., 403, The right of citizens of the United States to vote shall not be denied or
408, 419–28, 445, abridged by the United States or by any State on account of sex.
459–61, 476

Congress shall have power to enforce this article by appropriate legislation.

AMENDMENT XX [1933]

429–30, 461, 476 *Section 1.* The terms of the President and Vice President shall end at noon on the 20th day of January, and the terms of Senators and Representatives at noon on the 3d day of January, of the years in which such terms would have ended if this article had not been ratified; and the terms of their successors shall then begin.

429 *Section 2.* The Congress shall assemble at least once in every year, and such meeting shall begin at noon on the 3d day of January, unless they shall by law appoint a different day.

361n., 430 *Section 3.* If, at the time fixed for the beginning of the term of the President, the President elect shall have died, the Vice President elect shall become President. If a President shall not have been chosen before the time fixed for the beginning of his term, or if the President elect shall have failed to qualify, then the Vice President elect shall act as President until a President shall have qualified; and the Congress may by law provide for the case wherein neither a President elect nor a Vice President elect shall have qualified, declaring who shall then act as President, or the manner in which one who is to act shall be selected, and such person shall act accordingly until a President or Vice President shall have qualified.

361n., 430 *Section 4.* The Congress may by law provide for the case of the death of any of the persons from whom the House of Representatives may choose a President whenever the right of choice shall have devolved upon them, and for the case of the death of any of the persons from whom the Senate may choose a Vice President whenever the right of choice shall have devolved upon them.

428 *Section 5.* Sections 1 and 2 shall take effect on the 15th day of October following the ratification of this article.

417 *Section 6.* This article shall be inoperative unless it shall have been ratified as an amendment to the Constitution by the legislatures of three-fourths of the several States within seven years from the date of its submission.

AMENDMENT XXI [1933]

303, 416–17, 461 *Section 1.* The eighteenth article of amendment to the Constitution of the United States is hereby repealed.

Section 2. The transportation or importation into any State, Territory, or possession of the United States for delivery or use therein of intoxicating liquors, in violation of the laws thereof, is hereby prohibited.

416–17 *Section 3.* This article shall be inoperative unless it shall have been ratified as an amendment to the Constitution by conventions in the several States, as provided in the Constitution, within seven years from the date of the submission hereof to the States by the Congress.

AMENDMENT XXII [1951]

433–38, 451, 461, 475 *Section 1.* No person shall be elected to the office of the President more than twice, and no person who has held the office of President, or acted as President, for more than two years of a term to which some other person was elected President shall be elected to the office of the President more than once. But this Article shall not apply to any person holding the office of President, when this Article was proposed by the Congress, and shall not prevent any person who may be holding the office of President, or acting as President, during the term within which this Article becomes operative from holding the office of President or acting as President during the remainder of such term.

417 *Section 2.* This Article shall be inoperative unless it shall have been ratified as an amendment to the Constitution by the legislatures of three-fourths of the several States within seven years from the date of its submission to the States by the Congress.

AMENDMENT XXIII [1961]

438–42, 444, 446, 461 *Section 1.* The District constituting the seat of Government of the United States shall appoint in such manner as the Congress may direct:

A number of electors of President and Vice President equal to the whole number of Senators and Representatives in Congress to which the District would be entitled if it were a State, but in no event more than the least populous State; they shall be in addition to those appointed by the States, but they shall be considered, for the purposes of the election of President and Vice President, to be electors appointed by a State; and they shall meet in the District and perform such duties as provided by the twelfth article of amendment.

361n. *Section 2.* The Congress shall have power to enforce this article by appropriate legislation.

AMENDMENT XXIV [1964]

18, 431, 442–46, *Section 1.* The right of citizens of the United States to vote in any primary
459–61 or other election for President or Vice President, for electors for President
or Vice President, or for Senator or Representative in Congress, shall not be
denied or abridged by the United States or any State by reason of failure to
pay any poll tax or other tax.

361n. *Section 2.* The Congress shall have power to enforce this article by appropriate legislation.

AMENDMENT XXV [1967]

169, 172–73, *Section 1.* In case of the removal of the President from office or of his death
447–50, 461 or resignation, the Vice President shall become President.

451–52 *Section 2.* Whenever there is a vacancy in the office of the Vice President,
the President shall nominate a Vice President who shall take office upon
confirmation by a majority vote of both Houses of Congress.

449–51 *Section 3.* Whenever the President transmits to the President pro tempore of
the Senate and the Speaker of the House of Representatives his written declaration that he is unable to discharge the powers and duties of his office, and
until he transmits to them a written declaration to the contrary, such powers
and duties shall be discharged by the Vice President as Acting President.

361n., 449–51 *Section 4.* Whenever the Vice President and a majority of either the principal officers of the executive departments or of such other body as Congress
may by law provide, transmit to the President pro tempore of the Senate
and the Speaker of the House of Representatives their written declaration
that the President is unable to discharge the powers and duties of his office,
the Vice President shall immediately assume the powers and duties of the
office as Acting President.

Thereafter, when the President transmits to the President pro tempore
of the Senate and the Speaker of the House of Representatives his written
declaration that no inability exists, he shall resume the powers and duties of
his office unless the Vice President and a majority of either the principal officers of the executive department or of such other body as Congress may by
law provide, transmit within four days to the President pro tempore of the
Senate and the Speaker of the House of Representatives their written declaration that the President is unable to discharge the powers and duties of
his office. Thereupon Congress shall decide the issue, assembling within
forty-eight hours for that purpose if not in session. If the Congress, within

twenty-one days after receipt of the latter written declaration, or, if Congress is not in session, within twenty-one days after Congress is required to assemble, determines by two-thirds vote of both Houses that the President is unable to discharge the powers and duties of his office, the Vice President shall continue to discharge the same as Acting President; otherwise, the President shall resume the powers and duties of his office.

AMENDMENT XXVI [1971]

Section 1. The right of citizens of the United States, who are eighteen years of age or older, to vote shall not be denied or abridged by the United States or by any State on account of age.

Section 2. The Congress shall have the power to enforce this article by appropriate legislation.

AMENDMENT XXVII [1992]

No law varying the compensation for the services of the Senators and Representatives shall take effect, until an election of Representatives shall have intervened.

Notes

WORKS FREQUENTLY CITED

Adams, *FAC* Willi Paul Adams, *The First American Constitutions: Republican Ideology and the Making of the State Constitutions in the Revolutionary Era* (Rita Kimber and Robert Kimber, trans., expanded ed. 2001)

AHR *The American Historical Review*

Annals† Joseph Gales, Sr., *The Debates and Proceedings in the Congress of the United States . . .* (1834–), 24 vols. (*"Annals of the Congress of the United States"*)

APSR *American Political Science Review*

Blackstone's Comm. William Blackstone, *Commentaries on the Laws of England,* 4 vols. Note: the star (*) pagination refers not to Blackstone's 1765 first edition, but to a revised (and differently paginated) edition from the 1780s that soon became the standard for later printings.

CG† *Congressional Globe*

Cong. Rec.† *Congressional Record*

DHRC Merrill Jensen, John P. Kaminski, and Gaspare J. Saladino, eds., *The Documentary History of the Ratification of the Constitution* (1976–), 20 vols.

†Available online on the Library of Congress website "A Century of Lawmaking." Many of these LOC databases are word-searchable. Detailed citations are generally omitted for other easily web-searchable materials such as the Collected Works of Abraham Lincoln, electoral-college results, the *Federalist* essays, historical census data, Inaugural Addresses, and national political-party platforms.

Elliot's Debates†	Jonathan Elliot, ed., *The Debates in the Several State Conventions on the Adoption of the Federal Constitution....* (1888), 5 vols.
Farrand's Records†	Max Farrand, ed., *The Records of the Federal Convention of 1787* (rev. ed. 1966), 4 vols.
Ford, *Essays*	Paul Leicester Ford, ed., *Essays on the Constitution of the United States* (1892)
Ford, *Pamphlets*	Paul Leicester Ford, ed., *Pamphlets on the Constitution of the United States* (1888)
Hamilton, *Papers*	Harold C. Syrett, ed., *The Papers of Alexander Hamilton* (1961–), 27 vols.
HWS	Elizabeth Cady Stanton, Susan B. Anthony, et al., eds., *History of Woman Suffrage* (1881– ; reprint, 1985), 6 vols.
JCC†	*Journals of the Continental Congress*
Jefferson, *Papers*	Julian P. Boyd, ed., *The Papers of Thomas Jefferson* (1950), 30 vols.
Jefferson, *Writings* (Ford)	Paul Leicester Ford, ed., *The Writings of Thomas Jefferson* (1895), 10 vols.
LJ	*Law Journal*
LR	*Law Review*
Maclay's Journal†	Edgar S. Maclay, ed., *Journal of William Maclay* (1890)
Madison, *Papers*	William T. Hutchinson, William M. E. Rachal, et al., eds., *The Papers of James Madison* (1962), 17 vols.
Madison, *Writings* (Hunt)	Gaillard Hunt, ed., *The Writings of James Madison* (1910), 9 vols.
OED	*Oxford English Dictionary*
Stat.†	*Statutes at Large*
Storing's Anti-Fed.	Herbert J. Storing, ed., *The Complete Anti-Federalist* (1981), 7 vols.
Story, *Commentaries*	Joseph Story, ed., *Commentaries on the Constitution of the United States* (1833; rev. ed. 1991), 3 vols.
Washington, *Writings*	John C. Fitzpatrick, ed., *The Writings of George Washington, from the Original Manuscript Sources, 1745–1799* (1939), 39 vols.
Wilson, *Works*	Robert Green McCloskey, ed., *The Works of James Wilson* (1967), 2 vols.
WMQ	*The William and Mary Quarterly,* 3d series (1944–)

1: IN THE BEGINNING

1. In Connecticut, all town inhabitants were eligible to vote for ratification-convention delegates, whereas only town freemen—a narrower category de jure, and a much narrower category de facto—voted for ordinary state legislators. Charles J. Hoadly et al., eds., *Public Records of the State of Connecticut* (1894–   ), 6:355. Connecticut's state historian, Christopher Collier, estimates that there were almost twice as many inhabitants as freemen in the late 1780s. Conversation with ARA, August 2002; see also Christopher Collier, "A Constitutional History of the Connecticut General Assembly: A Preliminary Sketch" (paper prepared for the Connecticut Humanities Council Institute, Hartford, Conn., June 1988), 10–12. In North Carolina, all taxpayers could vote for the state house of commons, but only those with fifty-acre freeholds could vote for the state senate. Adams, *FAC,* 324. The ratification-convention elections tracked the more inclusive house rules. Walter Clark, ed., *The State Records of North Carolina* (1902), 20:196–97, 370–72, 514–16, 526–27; Charles Beard, *An Economic Interpretation of the Constitution* (1913; reprint, 1986), 240–41. New York also had different suffrage qualifications for its two state houses. Adams, *FAC,* 318. All these rules were waived in the 1788 election for ratification-convention delegates. *The New-York Journal and Daily Patriotic Register,* April 30, 1788, 3; John P. Kaminski, "New York: The Reluctant Pillar," in Stephen L. Schechter, ed., *The Reluctant Pillar: New York and the Adoption of the Federal Constitution* (1985), 75.

2. New Hampshire, Massachusetts, New York, New Jersey, Maryland, North Carolina, and South Carolina each had higher property qualifications for membership in the upper house than the lower house. Adams, *FAC,* 315–27. All seven declined to impose upper-house requirements on ratification-convention delegates; four—Massachusetts, Maryland, North Carolina, and South Carolina—did not impose even the lower-house property requirements on convention delegates; a fifth (New York) had no property qualifications for lower-house members and imposed none on convention delegates; while a sixth state (New Hampshire) widened delegate eligibility in a different way. Only New Jersey appeared to hold convention delegates to all the same eligibility rules applicable to its lower-house members.

In particular: New Hampshire provided that certain former loyalists ineligible to serve as representatives in the state's general court could nevertheless serve as convention delegates. Albert Stillman Batchellor, ed., *Early State Papers of New Hampshire* (1892), 21:165; cf. Beard, *Economic Interpretation,* 240. Although Massachusetts generally required each member of the state house of representatives to have a freehold of £100 or a ratable estate of £200, Adams, *FAC,* 316, the state imposed no property qualifications on convention delegates. It provided that the convention election should track lower-house rules of *voter eligibility* and *apportionment,* but said nothing about property qualifications for delegates. *Debates and Proceedings in the Convention of the Commonwealth of Massachusetts, Held in the Year 1788* (1856), 22–24. In New York, all freemen were eligible to serve as convention delegates, regardless of whether they met the freehold requirement for state senate membership. *The New-York Journal and Daily Patriotic Register,* April 30, 1788, 3; Adams, *FAC,* 318. New Jersey apparently applied its lower-house membership qualifications (a personal estate worth £50 proclamation money clear of debts, Adams, *FAC,* 319) to convention delegates in catchall language that delegate elections should "be conducted agreeably to the mode, and conformably with the Rules and Regulations prescribed for conducting . . . Elections" of "Representatives in General Assembly." United States Department of State Bureau of Rolls and Library, *Documentary History of the Constitution of the United States of America, 1786–1870* (1894–1905; reprint, 1998–99), 2:61–62. Maryland explicitly provided that all resident citizens could serve as convention delegates, squarely rejecting a proposal from the state senate that delegates must meet the £500 property qualification for the state house of delegates. *Votes and Proceedings of the Senate of Maryland, November Session, 1787,* 5–7; Forrest McDonald, *We the People* (1958; reprint, 1992), 149; Adams, *FAC,* 322. For both its 1788 and 1789 conventions, North Carolina explicitly allowed all freeholders to serve as convention delegates, even though the state required members of its lower house of commons to meet a property qualification of one hundred acres freehold. Clarke, *Records of North Carolina,* 20:196–97, 370–72, 514–16, 526–27; Adams, *FAC,* 324. In South Carolina, the senate proposed to require delegates to meet the eligibility rules for the state house of representatives, but the house rejected this proposal. The final result was a law that explicitly limited the convention election to those "intitl'd to Vote for Representatives to the General Assembly" while leaving convention delegates unmentioned and—presumably—unlimited by any property qualification whatsoever. Michael E. Stevens, ed., *The State Records of South Carolina: Journals of the House of Representatives, 1787–1788* (1981), 330–33; Adams, *FAC,* 325.

It also bears notice that in Massachusetts ordinary laws could be vetoed, subject to a two-thirds vote to override in each house, by a governor obliged to meet even higher property thresholds than those applicable to state house and senate members. Adams, *FAC,* 316. In New York, the state governor and a council collectively wielded a defeasible veto; only freeholders were eligible to serve as governor. Ibid., 318. Ratification by conventions bypassed these pro-property rules as well.

Although Connecticut did not impose higher property qualifications for membership in the legislature than for voting, it did require that both voters and lawmakers be freemen worth 40s. per year or with personal estates valued at £40. Ibid., 317. The state did not impose these restrictions on convention delegates in 1787. Hoadly, *Public Records of Connecticut,* 6:355. Pennsylvania allowed all taxpayers to vote for and all freemen to serve in the one-house state assembly. Georgia's rules for voting were almost as generous, but that state did impose property qualifications on members of the single-branch legislature. Adams, *FAC,* 320, 327.

    Summing the various data from this and the preceding note, we find that ten of the thirteen states used broader suffrage rules for the convention and/or used broader delegate-qualification rules or simply had an especially expansive franchise to begin with. The three states outside this general pattern were Rhode Island, Delaware, and Virginia.

    The data presented here contrast sharply with the picture painted by Charles Beard in his controversial 1913 book, *An Economic Interpretation of the Constitution.* Oddly, though Beard elsewhere lavished attention on the issue of property qualifications for representatives, he omitted all mention of the topic in analyzing the ratification process, focusing instead only on property qualifications for voters. Compare his fourth chapter, on "Property Safeguards in the Election of [Philadelphia] Delegates," with his eighth chapter, on "The Process of Ratification." Perhaps this striking inconsistency is explained by the simple fact that the convention-delegate qualification data undercut his general thesis. (For a reading of Beard's general method that might support this explanation, see Forrest McDonald's provocative introduction to the 1986 reprint edition of Beard's book.) Harder to explain, however, is the failure of later scholars, including Beard's many critics, to highlight the issue of convention-delegate qualifications.

3. "We the People of the States of New Hampshire, Massachusetts, Rhode Island and Providence Plantations, Connecticut, New York, New Jersey, Pennsylvania, Delaware, Maryland, Virginia, North Carolina, South Carolina and Georgia do ordain declare and establish the following Constitution for the Government of ourselves and of our Posterity." *Farrand's Records,* 2:152. For an earlier snippet in Wilson's hand, see ibid., 150. Although Wilson penned these documents, they were composed as part of a five-man drafting committee. Possibly, the initial impetus behind the words "We the People" came from some other committee member(s) and Wilson was merely the scribe, but this seems unlikely. The distinctive emphasis on popular sovereignty in these opening words reverberated with themes that Wilson had sounded early and often at Philadelphia—see, e.g., ibid., 1:49, 52, 68, 69, 127, 132–33, 151, 153–54, 179, 252–53, 259, 279, 359, 361, 365, 379, 405–6—and would continue to sound in the ratification debates and thereafter. Wilson's draft language also echoed the preamble of his 1776 state constitution: "We, the representatives of the freemen of Pennsylvania . . . [to] promote the general happiness of the people of this state, and their posterity, . . . do . . . ordain, declare and establish the following . . . CONSTITUTION of this com-

monwealth." Cf. Mass. Const. (1780), Preamble ("We, therefore, the people of Massachusetts, . . . do agree upon, ordain, and establish . . . the CONSTI-TUTION OF THE COMMONWEALTH OF MASSACHUSETTS").

4. *Elliot's Debates,* 2:470.

5. See, e.g., ibid., 4:23 (William R. Davie) ("The act of the Convention is but a mere proposal, similar to the production of a private pen"); 24 (William Maclaine) ("The Constitution is only a mere proposal"); 206 (Richard Dobbs Spaight) (similar); 282 (Charles Cotesworth Pinckney) (similar); 3:37–38 (Edmund Pendleton) (similar). Proposing a new Constitution did go beyond the Philadelphia delegates' commissions, as Madison explicitly admitted in *Federalist* No. 40, but that fact alone hardly made the proposal "illegal." Unless and until ratified by the people and thereby made supreme law, the proposal was no more than—but also no less than—a lawful exercise of free expression, akin to a political pamphlet proposing future legislation or future withdrawal from a treaty. For a different interpretation—one which in my view erroneously collapses the distinction between a document lacking the force of law behind it and a document that is itself "illegal"—see Bruce Ackerman, *We the People: Foundations* (1991), 328–29 n. 4. For more discussion of various issues of legality, see n. 72 below.

6. According to the *OED,* the word *fiat* has long been used "with reference to *'fiat lux'* (let there be light) Gen. i. 3 in the Vulgate: A command having for its object the creation, formation, or construction of something." In a 1791 lecture, Wilson returned to the Genesis motif via a soft allusion to the God who made Adam from clay: "As to the people . . . [f]rom their authority the constitution originates: . . . in their hands it is as clay in the hands of the potter." Wilson, *Works,* 1:304. Compare James Madison's public remarks in 1796, describing the Philadelphia proposal as "nothing but a dead letter, until life and validity were breathed into it by the voice of the People," *Farrand's Records,* 3:374, with Genesis 2:7: "And the LORD God formed man of the dust of the ground, and breathed into his nostrils the breath of life; and man became a living soul."

7. For a powerful discussion, see Jed Rubenfeld, *Freedom and Time* (2001), 13, 163–68.

8. See generally Pauline Maier, *American Scripture* (1997), 47–96.

9. Among America's future leaders, those who had opposed independence or hesitated in 1776 generally atoned for these lapses by joining the patriot cause while the fate of the Revolution still hung in the balance. For example, although moderate John Dickinson declined to vote for independence in July 1776, neither did he vote against it; and he quickly showed his true colors by fighting the British on the battlefield. Connecticut's William Samuel Johnson refused to take an oath of allegiance to an independent Connecticut in 1777, but he did so two years later. Similar stories can be told concerning several other early loyalists who went on to leadership positions in independent

America, such as Pennsylvania's Tench Coxe and New Hampshire's Woodbury Langdon. Maryland's Philip Barton Key was slower to renounce his
youthful loyalism, and slower, too, to achieve eventual political rehabilita-
tion. On the post-ratification political survival of Anti-Federalists, see Richard E. Ellis, "The Persistence of Antifederalism after 1789," in Richard Beeman
et al., eds., *Beyond Confederation: Origins of the Constitution and American National Identity* (1987), 295–314.

10. See generally Adams, *FAC,* 61–95; Allan Nevins, *The American States During
and After the Revolution, 1775–1789* (1924), 129; Gordon S. Wood, *The Creation of the American Republic, 1776–1787* (1969), 307, 332; Marc W. Kruman,
*Between Authority and Liberty: State Constitution Making in Revolutionary
America* (1997), 15–33, 55–56.

11. On the Massachusetts and New Hampshire Constitutions, see n. 31. Professor Lutz has identified important American colonial documents—church
covenants and more localized secular compacts and agreements—that have
the same basic "We . . . do" structure as the Preamble and that helped prepare
the ground for the dramatic acts of popular ratification in the 1780s. Donald
S. Lutz, *The Origins of American Constitutionalism* (1988), 13–34. See also Andrew C. McLaughlin, *The Foundations of American Constitutionalism* (1932),
13–37.

12. Wilson, *Works,* 2:773–74. A similar, if more rhetorically restrained, meditation appears in the opening paragraphs of *Federalist* No. 38. For a still earlier
speech of Wilson in the same genre, see *Elliot's Debates,* 2:422.

13. See Del. Const. (1776), Declaration of Rights, sec. 6 ("the right in the people
to participate in the Legislature, is the foundation of liberty and of all free
government"); Md. Const. (1776), Declaration of Rights, art. V (similar);
Wood, *Creation,* 24–25, 60–61, 362; Gordon S. Wood, *The Radicalism of the
American Revolution* (1991), 104.

14. For Wilson, see *Elliot's Debates,* 2:434–35, 437. Wilson reiterated the point in
his later lectures. Wilson, *Works,* 1:304. For Iredell, see *Elliot's Debates,* 4:230.
For the Virginia convention, see ibid., 1:327.

15. *Elliot's Debates,* 1:327.

16. In Virginia, Edmund Pendleton had specifically linked the right of popular
amendment to the people's right to "assemble." Ibid., 3:37. For more discussion of the interlinkages between the Preamble, the First Amendment right
of "the people" to assemble, and the rights and powers of "the people" guaranteed by the Ninth and Tenth Amendments, see Akhil Reed Amar, *The Bill
of Rights: Creation and Reconstruction* (1998), 26–32, 119–22.

During the ratification debates, Wilson declared that "this single sentence in the Preamble is tantamount to a volume and contains the essence of
all the bills of rights that have been or can be devised." *DHRC,* 2:383–84. Parroting this line, *Federalist* No. 84 claimed that the Preamble was "a better
recognition of popular rights, than volumes of those aphorisms which make

the principal figure in several of our State bills of rights." Congressman John Vining of Delaware expressed a similar view in the First Congress. "A bill of rights was unnecessary" given the Preamble's "practical declaration" of popular sovereignty. *Annals,* 1:467 (June 8, 1789).

17. In response to a proposal to add language to the Preamble expressly declaring, à la Virginia and New York, that "the people have an indubitable, unalienable and indefeasible right to reform or change their Government," Representative James Jackson of Georgia argued that the Preamble's "words, as they now stand, speak as much as it is possible to speak; it is a practical recognition of the right of the people to ordain and establish Governments, and is more expressive than any other mere paper declaration." *Annals,* 1:451 (June 8, 1789), 741 (Aug. 13). Connecticut's Roger Sherman agreed: "If this right is indefeasible, and the people have recognised it in practice, the truth is better asserted than it can be by any words whatever. The words 'We the people' in the original constitution, are as copious and expressive as possible; any addition will only drag out the sentence without illuminating it." Ibid., 746 (Aug. 14). For earlier language from Wilson stressing the Preamble's "practical" import, see p. 13; *Elliot's Debates,* 2:434.

18. Both the Massachusetts and New Hampshire Constitutions, which had been ordained by the voters themselves, contained specific clauses contemplating bills of credit. See Mass. Const. (1780), pt. II, ch. II, sec. I, art. XI; N.H. Const. (1784), pt. II (unnumbered para. beginning "No monies shall be issued . . .").

19. See, e.g., U.S. Const., art. I, sec. 10, para. 1 ("No state shall . . . coin Money; emit Bills of Credit; make any Thing but gold and silver Coin a Tender in Payment of Debts"). For a candid acknowledgment of the fact that the federal Constitution would effect amendments of existing state constitutions, see *Federalist* No. 44. For more discussion, see James Madison to George Washington, April 16, 1787, in Madison, *Papers,* 9:385; *Farrand's Records,* 1:317 (Madison), 2:88, 92–93 (Mason, Rufus King, and Madison), 3:229 (Luther Martin's "Genuine Information"); Kaminski, "New York," 74.

20. Mass. Const. (1780), pt. II, ch. VI, art. X; *DHRC,* 14:220 (diary of John Quincy Adams) ("I think it my duty to submit. . . . In our Government, opposition to the acts of a majority of the people is rebellion to all intents and purposes"). Cf. *Elliot's Debates,* 2:157 (Ames: "such a [constitution] as the majority of the people approve *must* be submitted to by this state; for what right have an eighth or tenth part of the people to dictate a government for the whole?"). For discussion of the possible implications of this principle for federal constitutional amendment under (or outside) Article V, see Chapter 8.

21. See John Locke, *The Second Treatise of Government* (1690), secs. 221, 243.

22. *Elliot's Debates,* 2:432; *DHRC,* 2:348–49. For later statements from Wilson to the same effect, see Wilson, *Works,* 1:77–79, 317.

23. *Elliot's Debates,* 2:458. See also ibid., 432–33.

24. For Iredell, see ibid., 4:229–30. For Publius, see *Federalist* No. 78. See also No. 40 (invoking "the transcendent and precious right of the people to 'abolish or alter their governments as to them shall seem most likely to effect their safety and happiness' ").

25. On England, see generally Lois G. Schwoerer, *The Declaration of Rights, 1689* (1981); Edmund S. Morgan, Inventing the People: *The Rise of Popular Sovereignty in England and America* (1988), 110–21. On the Greeks, see Plutarch, *The Rise and Fall of Athens: Nine Greek Lives* (Ian Scott-Kilvert, trans., 1960), 67; *Federalist* No. 38.

26. Federalist Governor Samuel Huntington offered similar remarks in his state ratifying convention. *Elliot's Debates,* 2:200.

27. For a detailed refutation of this canard, see Adams, *FAC,* 96–114. Adams demonstrates that "democracy" and "republic" were broadly synonymous from 1776 to 1787, and that although some Federalists, such as Madison, tried to contradistinguish the two words, other leading Federalists continued to use them synonymously. Adams dismisses as "pseudo-learned" the notion "that the founding fathers intended the United States to be a republic but not a democracy." We shall return to these issues in Chapter 7's analysis of the Article IV guarantee of a republican form of government.

28. See, e.g., *Federalist* No. 14 ("the structure of the Union . . . has been new modelled by the act of your [Philadelphia] convention, and it is that act on which you are now to deliberate and to decide"); No. 22 ("The fabric of American empire ought to rest on the solid basis of THE CONSENT OF THE PEOPLE. The streams of national power ought to flow immediately from that pure, original fountain of all legitimate authority"); No. 39 ("the Constitution is to be founded on the assent and ratification of the people of America, given by deputies elected for the special purpose"); No. 40 (proposed Constitution is "submitted TO THE PEOPLE THEMSELVES"—the "supreme authority"); No. 43 ("The express authority of the people alone could give due validity to the Constitution"); No. 46 ("ultimate authority, wherever the derivative may be found, resides in the people alone"); No. 49 ("the people are the only legitimate fountain of power, and it is from them that the constitutional charter, under which the several branches of government hold their power, is derived"); No. 53 ("The important distinction so well understood in America, between a Constitution established by the people and unalterable by the government, and a law established by the government and alterable by the government, seems to have been little understood and less observed in any other country"); No. 78 (Constitution declares will of "the people" and a "fundamental principle of republican government . . . admits the right of the people to alter or abolish their established Constitution"); No. 84 ("Here, in strictness, the people surrender nothing; and as they retain every thing, they have no need of particular reservations. 'WE, THE PEOPLE of the United

States, to secure the blessings of liberty to ourselves and our posterity, do ORDAIN and ESTABLISH this Constitution for the United States of America.' Here is a [clear] recognition of popular rights").

29. In *Federalist* No. 10, Madison/Publius elaborated on how congressional representation in a large and diverse country would afford "a republican remedy for the diseases most incident to republican government"—an argument that Madison at Philadelphia had labeled "the only defence agst. the inconveniences of democracy consistent with the democratic form of Govt." *Farrand's Records,* 1:134–35. See also *Federalist* No. 36 ("door [of eligibility for Congress] ought to be equally open to all"); No. 39 ("Could any further proof be required of the republican complexion of this system, the most decisive one might be found in its absolute prohibition of titles of nobility, both under the federal and the State governments; and in its express guaranty of the republican form to each of the latter"); No. 52 ("the door [to Congress] is open to merit of every description, . . . without regard to poverty or wealth, or to any particular profession of religious faith"); No. 57 (voters will encompass "the great body of the people"—"not the rich, more than the poor" or the "haughty heirs of distinguished names, more than the humble sons of obscurity and unpropitious fortune"; voters may choose officeholders regardless of "wealth" or "birth"); No. 69 (noting "total dissimilitude" between president as "an officer elected by the people" and "re-eligible as often as the people of the United States shall think him worthy of their confidence" and "king of Great Britain, who is an HEREDITARY monarch, possessing the crown as a patrimony descendible to his heirs forever"); No. 70 (defending the compatibility of "a vigorous Executive" with "the genius of republican government" based on "a due dependence on the people [and] a due responsibility"); No. 76 (Senate confirmation will discourage unfit presidential appointments based on "family connection"); No. 78 (judicial review will ensure that legislatures abide by limits imposed by "the people themselves"); No. 84 ("prohibition of titles of nobility . . . may truly be denominated the corner-stone of republican government; for so long as they are excluded, there can never be serious danger that the government will be any other than that of the people"); No. 85 (cataloguing "the additional securities to republican government, to liberty and to property" contained in the Constitution: the suppression of local insurrections, factions, and despots; the diminution of the risk of foreign intrigue that would be triggered by dissolution of the union; the prevention of extensive military establishments that would result from disunion and wars between the states; the express guaranty of republican government; the bans on state and federal titles of nobility; and the ban on state practices undermining property and credit).

30. *Elliot's Debates,* 2:434, 482, 523 (emphasis deleted).

31. On Pennsylvania, see Samuel B. Harding, "Party Struggles Over the First Pennsylvania Constitution," in *Annual Report of the American Historical Asso-*

ciation for the Year 1894 (1895), 371–79; Chilton Williamson, *American Suffrage* (1960), 92–96; Adams, *FAC,* 75–76; Alexander Keyssar, *The Right to Vote: The Contested History of Democracy in the United States* (2000), 16; Maier, *American Scripture,* 66; see also Kruman, *Between Authority,* 26. On Massachusetts, see "The Call for a Convention, June, 15, 1779," in Oscar Handlin and Mary Handlin, eds., *The Popular Sources of Political Authority* (1966), 402–3; see also Samuel Eliot Morison, "The Struggle Over the Adoption of the Constitution of Massachusetts, 1780," *Proceedings of the Massachusetts Historical Society* 50 (1917): 355. In 1778, an earlier proposed constitution had also come before Massachusetts town meetings that had waived standard provincial property requirements in favor of universal adult male suffrage. "Resolve of May 5, 1777," in Handlin, 174–75. See also Adams, *FAC,* 3, 87–88; Kruman, *Between Authority,* 30–32. However, the Bay State principle that a constitutional election required the broadest popular suffrage was clouded by an apparent property qualification for early participation in the 1795 amendment process—a process that was ultimately deemed nonexclusive; see Chapter 8. New Hampshire gave the ratification power to "the Inhabitants of this State in their respective Town meetings," with no mention of any property qualifications. No property qualifications limited membership in the conventions elected to frame the proposed document: "every Town, Parish & District" could choose delegates "as they shall judge . . . expedient." Nathaniel Bouton, ed., *State Papers: Documents and Records Relating to the State of New Hampshire* (1874) 8:774–76, 897–98. See also Williamson, *American Suffrage,*105–6; Richard Francis Upton, *Revolutionary New Hampshire* (1936), 175–87; Wood, *Creation,* 289.

32. The Delaware experience, tracking that of Pennsylvania, also deserves mention. For brief accounts, see Wood, *Creation,* 332–33; Adams, *FAC,* 72–74 & n. 46; Kruman, *Between Authority,* 28–30.

33. *Farrand's Records,* 2:90 (Gorham), 92 (King). Cf. ibid., 2:215 (Gorham: "He had never seen any inconveniency from allowing such as were not freeholders to vote"); *Elliot's Debates,* 2:35 (King: "He never knew that *property* was an index to abilities. We often see men, who, though destitute of property, are superior in knowledge and rectitude"). For state constitutions formally excluding clergy from legislative membership, see Va. Const. (1776) (unnumbered para. beginning "The two Houses of Assembly . . ."); Del. Const. (1776), art. 29; Md. Const. (1776), art. XXXVII; N.C. Const. (1776), art. XXXI; Ga. Const. (1777), art. LXII; N.Y. Const. (1777), art. XXXIX; S.C. Const. (1778), art. XXI.

34. Recall the successful claims of propertyless Pennsylvania militiamen in 1776 that their arms-bearing entitled them to the franchise; see p. 17. Benjamin Franklin, who had supported the militiamen's claims in 1776, returned to the linkage between suffrage and military service in his closed-door remarks to the Philadelphia drafters strongly opposing any constitutionally mandated

property qualifications for voting in federal elections: "In time of war a country owed much to the lower class of citizens. Our late war was an instance of what they could suffer and perform. If denied the right of suffrage it would debase their spirit and detatch [sic] them from the interest of the country." *Farrand's Records,* 2:210. For more discussion, see Chapter 2, pp. 67.

35. Anxiety about slave revolts appeared prominently in the Declaration of Independence, which condemned George III for "excit[ing] domestic insurrections amongst us." See Maier, *American Scripture,* 147.

36. See Keyssar, *Right to Vote,* 20, 54. Note that voting by widows did not raise some of the concerns that might have arisen from voting by wives subject to common-law coverture servitude to their husbands.

37. On the Philadelphia society, see Wood, *Radicalism,* 186. On the more general movement against slavery, see Act for the Gradual Abolition of Slavery, 1780, in Alexander James Dallas, ed., *Laws of the Commonwealth of Pennsylvania* (1795–1801), 1:838–43; William Wiecek, *The Sources of Antislavery Constitutionalism in America, 1760–1848* (1977), 40–51, 60–61, 89–90; Edmund Cody Burnett, *The Continental Congress* (1941), 598–600. On the slave trade, see Nevins, *American States,* 445–48.

38. For more details, see Chapter 7. For general background, see Jack P. Greene, *Peripheries and Center: Constitutional Development in the Extended Polities of the British Empire and the United States, 1607–1788* (1986). And for a quick yet nuanced sketch of various similarities and differences among the colonies, see John M. Murrin, "A Roof without Walls: The Dilemma of American National Identity," in Beeman et al., eds., *Beyond Confederation,* 333–48.

39. *JCC,* 1:101–13 (Oct. 21–26, 1774).

40. Granted, there were important differences of capitalization and even caption between the famous hand-signed document and an earlier printed version of the Declaration, the so-called Dunlap broadside. For now, I seek merely to identify possible readings of the Declaration's intriguing text. Ultimately, I shall place far more weight on the act of declaration itself, on the general structure of the Continental Congress, and on the more definitive legal acts and texts of Confederation and Constitution. For discussion of the two Declaration texts, see Maier, *American Scripture,* 150–53; Carlton F. W. Larson, "The Declaration of Independence: A 225th Anniversary Re-interpretation," *Washington LR* 76 (2001): 701, 724–27.

41. Thus, when the Declaration discussed how the king had "dissolved Representative Houses" and attempted to suspend the "Legislative powers," thereby causing such powers to revert to the hands of "the People at large for their exercise," this meant the people *within each colony.* In various colonies, local patriots, with the encouragement of the Continental Congress, created new de facto provincial legislatures to replace the old de jure colonial assemblies dissolved by the Crown. The king had never dissolved the Continental

Congress (which was not typically described as a "Representative House" vested with formal "Legislative powers").

42. For a similar reading, see Wood, *Creation*, 356–57.

43. Hoadly, *Public Records of Connecticut*, 1:3 (emphasis added). See generally Claude H. Van Tyne, "Sovereignty in the American Revolution: An Historical Study," *AHR* 12 (1906): 538.

44. See Nevins, *American States*, 62; Adams, *FAC*, 48–49, 62, 78, 275–78, 286; Curtis Putnam Nettels, "The Origins of the Union and of the States," *Proceedings of the Massachusetts Historical Society* 72 (1963): 74; Jack Rakove, *The Beginnings of National Politics* (1979), 95, 97–98, 100. The situation in Pennsylvania was somewhat unusual as the old colonial assembly and patriot critics outside the assembly vied for control during the late spring and early summer of 1776. Eventually, patriots muscled their way forward as the old assembly crumbled.

45. *JCC*, 4:342, 357–58 (the "recommend[ations]" of May 10 and May 15, 1776); 6:1087–92 (Jefferson's notes paraphrasing June 8 arguments of James Wilson, Robert R. Livingston, Edward Rutledge, and John Dickinson, and the responses of John Adams, Richard Henry Lee, George Wythe, and others); *Elliot's Debates*, 1:56–60 (same). To repeat, these remarks occurred long after the mid-May votes on state constitution making, votes that some nationalist scholars have adduced as proof of the supremacy of the union over individual states in 1776. On the legal significance of the word "recommend[]," see n. 61 below.

46. This anxiety also helps explain the first Continental Congress's "Letter to the Inhabitants of Quebec," in *JCC*, 1:105–13 (Oct. 26, 1774).

47. Actually, New York lagged slightly behind the others, abstaining on the votes in early July and then explicitly endorsing independence in its Revolutionary provincial congress a few days later. For details, see Maier, *American Scripture*, 45.

48. Whereas the Continental Congresses of 1774 and 1775 had operated on a one-state, one-vote rule, Franklin's 1754 Albany Plan had proposed giving larger colonies, like Franklin's own Pennsylvania, more seats, an idea Franklin repeated in a plan he brought before the Continental Congress on July 21, 1775. *JCC*, 2:195, 199. Pennsylvanian Joseph Galloway's 1774 plan for an intercolonial assembly had also been heading in the direction of proportionality before it was derailed in the First Continental Congress. Ibid., 1:49–51, 102 n. 1 (Sept. 28 and Oct. 21, 1774).

49. *JCC*, 5:425, 431.

50. The leading English law dictionary of the day presented "Treaties, Leagues, and Alliances" as a single entry, and Blackstone's *Commentaries* treated the three categories en masse. Giles Jacob, *A New Law Dictionary*, Owen Ruffhead and J. Morgan, eds., (9th ed., enl. 1772); *Blackstone's Comm.*, 1:*257.

51. At the Philadelphia Convention, Wilson challenged Luther Martin's extreme claim that "the separation from [Great Britain] placed the 13 states in a state of nature towards each other"—a claim that seemed to deny even an implicit military and diplomatic alliance in the fight against Britain. According to Wilson, the United States on July 4, 1776, "were independent, not *Individually* but *Unitedly*" and the states "were confederated as they were independent." *Farrand's Records,* 1:324. This correction did not contest that the states were merely *confederated;* and thus Wilson supported the Article VII rule that each state was ultimately free to go its own way in ratifying the Constitution or not—a rule that logically implied that each state was ultimately sovereign prior to joining the more perfect union. See ibid., 1:123, 127, 482, 469. Wilson had himself made secessionist threats on behalf of Pennsylvania in late July, 1776. Rakove, *Beginnings,* 161. Many nationalist interpreters of the Declaration have stressed Wilson's "Unitedly" language while omitting his key word "confederated" and ignoring other statements and actions of Wilson that undercut a strong notion of national indivisibility prior to 1788. See, e.g., Samuel H. Beer, *To Make a Nation: The Rediscovery of American Federalism* (1993), 236, 325.

    In 1796 Supreme Court Justice Samuel Chase, who like Wilson had signed the Declaration, wrote that he considered it "as a declaration, not that the United Colonies *jointly,* in a *collective* capacity, were independent states, &c. but that *each* of them was a sovereign and independent state, that is, that *each* of them had a right to govern itself by its own authority, and its own laws, without any controul from any other power upon earth." *Ware v. Hylton,* 3 U.S. (3 Dall.) 199, 224–25 (1796). Chase went on to admit that "Congress properly possessed the great *rights of external sovereignty*" and further presumed that acts of Congress prior to the ratification of the Articles were authorized by general acquiescence. Ibid., 231–32. See also *Penhallow v. Doane's Administrators,* 3 U.S. (3 Dall.) 54, 91–96 (1795) (Iredell, J.) (suggesting that authority of the Continental Congress prior to the ratification of the Articles rested on the acquiescence of the people of each state individually, rather than the people of America en masse; and that Congress enjoyed "high powers of . . . *external sovereignty*" that a state could avoid only by "withdrawing from the confederation").

52. Mass. Const. (1780), pt. I, art. IV (emphasis added).

53. N.H. Const. (1784), pt. I., art. VII.

54. Because the Articles did not take effect until ratified by every state, their provision prescribing term limits for congressmen began to operate only in 1781, resulting in mandatory departures beginning in 1784. On this point, see Rakove, *Beginnings,* 218. See also ibid., 287–88 ("Congress fixed March 1, [1781], as the day the confederation would finally take effect"). For Rakove on "threats of disunion," see ibid., 161. For Lynch, see *JCC,* 6:1080.

55. The issue was far from hypothetical. In the early 1780s, little Rhode Island

scuttled a proposed amendment that eleven larger states had endorsed. One other low-population state—Georgia—had yet to act. For corrections to Madison's claim in *Federalist* No. 40—a claim often repeated by standard histories—that twelve states had endorsed the 1781 impost amendment, see Jackson Turner Main, *The Antifederalists: Critics of the Constitution, 1781–1788* (1961), 72–74 & n. 2; Forrest McDonald, *E Pluribus Unum: The Formation of the American Republic, 1776–1790* (2d ed. 1979), 54; Rakove, *Beginnings,* 316, 338.

56. *Farrand's Records,* 1:250.

57. Cf. ibid., 256 (Randolph labeling Confederation Congress "a mere diplomatic body").

58. For details, see Chapter 2.

59. Emmerich de Vattel, *The Law of Nations* (1760), bk. I, ch. I, sec. 10 (emphasis added). For a similar analysis of Vattel and the Articles of Confederation, see Wood, *Creation,* 355. See also Gordon S. Wood, *The Making of the Constitution* (1987), 5–6. On Vattel's influence in America, see generally Peter S. Onuf and Nicholas Onuf, *Federal Union, Modern World* (1993), 1–26; Locke, *Second Treatise,* sec. 14. *Blackstone's Comm.,* 1:*97 n. e (added in 1766 ed.); see also ibid., 4:*i* (supplement to 1st ed.).

60. But see *Farrand's Records,* 1:323 (Rufus King, denying that states were " 'sovereign[]' in the sense contended for by some"—note the qualification—because individually they did not "make war, nor peace, nor alliances, nor treaties").

61. For a similar suggestion, see Larson, "Declaration of Independence," 721–63. Generally, the evidence adduced by modern scholars on behalf of a "nationalist" interpretation of the confederation period proves little about the status of secession rights. See Richard B. Morris, *The Forging of the Union* (1987), 55–79; Rakove, *Beginnings,* 173–74 n.; Beer, *To Make a Nation,* 195–206. The military, diplomatic, and state-constitutional coordination among the states, via instructed congressmen, did not negate the ultimate authority of each state (by which I mean of course the people within each state, rather than the state government as such) on the secession issue. Morris draws overbroad nationalist lessons from the First Continental Congress, which coordinated petitions and boycotts within a framework of avowed loyalty to the king rather than of military resistance or independence. It is hard to see this Congress as claiming the general powers of a de facto government. See generally Van Tyne, "Sovereignty." As for the Second Continental Congress, Morris and Beer downplay several decisive points: (1) Emerging de facto governments within each colony generally picked the delegates, and retained the right to instruct or recall them. (2) Never, prior to independence, did the view or practice prevail that Congress had any right to legislate for dissenting colonies or to prevent their unilateral exit. (3) By contrast, the emerging de facto governments within each state—as the successors of long-established colonial

governments operating with the same traditional geographic boundaries and featuring similar lawmaking bodies—did claim and exercise precisely this right to bind local dissenters. Thus, when the American people acted in 1775–76, they acted within each colony in coordination with patriots in other colonies rather than as an undifferentiated continental "collectivity," as Morris would have it. *Forging,* 76. Ultimately, Morris and like-minded scholars conflate the people/government distinction with the national/state distinction. The Revolution was effected by the people, to be sure, but not by a single collective and indivisible national people. These commentators also at times conflate issues of external sovereignty vis-à-vis the rest of the world with the unilateral secession issue that would later vex the Union. Troubling, too, is the treatment these commentators give to the key law words both present in and absent from several of the most important legal texts. In a passage that Beer pointedly reiterates, Rakove claims that "the idea that the confederation was essentially only a league of sovereign states was ultimately a fiction. Congress was in fact a national government, burdened with legislative and administrative responsibilities." Rakove, *Beginnings,* 184–85; Beer, *To Make a Nation,* 196. Yet the Articles used the law words "confederation," "league," and "sovereign" states while studiously not using the law words "national," "government," or "legislative" to describe Congress. (Nor did Congress's basic structure resemble any legislature that existed in America or elsewhere. Rather, the Confederation Congress resembled a traditional international assemblage of ambassadors, akin to today's United Nations.) Similarly, Beer says that words like "recommendation" in the documents on which he relies do not mean what they say, and that the legal language of the Articles was mere "rhetoric" because "all disdained the compact federalism of leagues and of confederations." Ibid., 195–96, 199–200, 419 n. 13. For a rather different view, which explains the important differences between recommendations and laws, see Richard P. McCormick, "Ambiguous Authority: The Ordinances of the Confederation Congress, 1781–1789," *Am. J. of Legal Hist.* 41 (1997): 411.

However one might construe the complicated events and legal texts of 1775–76 standing alone, the later Articles of Confederation explicitly codified a system of state sovereignty. Most important of all, the very act of constitution itself, in Article VII, proceeded on the basis of preexisting state sovereignty, at least on the secession issue. Thus, state sovereignty as of September 1787 is the theory *of the Constitution itself.* How can a strong nationalist interpretation of the pre-constitutional period explain the fact that the act of constitution itself was, as Madison stressed in *Federalist* No. 39, emphatically "not . . . *national,* but . . . *federal"*?

62. See, e.g. *Farrand's Records,* 1:34 (Gouverneur Morris); see also *OED* entry on "federal" (defining "federal" as "Of or pertaining to a covenant, compact, or treaty," with examples dating from 1660). For more primary source refer-

ences, see Main, *Antifederalists,* 120 n. 5. See generally Martin Diamond, "The Federalist's View of Federalism," in *Essays in Federalism* (1961), 21–64; Martin Diamond, "*The Federalist* on Federalism: 'Neither a National nor a Federal Constitution, but a Composition of Both,' " *Yale LJ* 86 (1977): 1273; Beer, *To Make a Nation,* 222–24.

63. Story, *Commentaries,* 1:227, sec. 246 (quoting unidentified wag) (emphasis deleted); James Madison, "Vices of the Political System of the U. States," in Madison, *Papers,* 9:348–57.

64. For Wilson on "partial union," see *Farrand's Records,* 1:123. According to Yates's notes, Wilson argued that whichever states "do ratify it [the proposed Constitution] will be immediately bound by it, and others as they may from time to time accede to it." Ibid., 127. Charles Pinckney endorsed Wilson's idea and presciently proposed nine states as the minimum threshold. Ibid., 123. Madison wrote that Wilson's "hint was probably meant in terrorem to the smaller States of N. Jersey & Delaware." Ibid., 123 n. For later suggestions along similar lines, see ibid., 320–21, 327 (Madison), 462 (Nathaniel Gorham), 482 (Wilson), 541 (Elbridge Gerry). Cf. ibid., 2:90 (Gorham suggesting that nonconcurrence of Rhode Island and a few other states, perhaps including New York, should not prevent other states from forming a new union amongst themselves). For Paterson on Wilson's "hint," see ibid., 1:179. See also ibid., 445 (Martin) (if "the three great States should league themselves together, the other ten could do so too"). For Wilson's conclusion that "the States only which ratify can be bound," see ibid., 2:469. The following day, the language of Article VII was amended to make this point explicit. Ibid., 475.

65. It might be suggested that the proposed Constitution would merely amount to a new side alliance among nine or more of the thirteen states, and that such alliances were permissible so long as (1) the allying states lived up to all the rules of the Articles of Confederation when dealing with the remaining states, and (2) the allying states secured the blessing of the Congress under the Articles (which, presumably, they would have been able to do by so instructing their confederate delegates). See Articles of Confederation (1781), art. VI, para. 2 (outlining procedures for side deals among two or more confederate states.) I have not encountered evidence that friends of the Constitution ever advanced this argument. Generally, they seemed to concede that governance under the Constitution would be incompatible with continuation of the Articles of Confederation, and maintained a prudent silence on the precise nature of the relationship the new union would work out with any nonratifying states. See, e.g., *Federalist* No. 43.

66. This was emphatically George Washington's general view of treaties and other international agreements. Edmund S. Morgan, *The Meaning of Independence* (1976), 49–50.

67. *Blackstone's Comm.* 1:*97 n. e (added in 1766 ed.); see also ibid., 4:*i* (supplement to 1st ed.).

68. Vattel, *Law of Nations,* bk. II, ch. XIII, sec. 200. See also ibid., sec. 202 ("That the violation of one article in a treaty may occasion the breaking the whole"). See also Hugo Grotius, *Of the Rights of War and Peace* (1715; reprint, 2001), bk. II, ch. XV, sec. XV ("If either Party break the League, the other is freed, because each Article of the League has the force of a Condition") (emphasis deleted).

69. See Madison, "Vices," in Madison, *Papers,* 352–53. General Jedidiah Huntington appealed to the breached treaty argument in May 1787, urging the Connecticut legislature to send a delegation to Philadelphia: "The compact between the several states has not any penalty annexed to it for the breach of its conditions . . . whenever therefore any state refuses a compliance with a requisition made agreeably to the confederation, all obligation on the part of the other states is dissolved." *DHRC,* 13:106.

70. *Farrand's Records,* 1:122–23, 315. Lest anyone miss the point, Madison reminded his colleagues that "the violations of the federal articles had been numerous & notorious." See also ibid., 485. In one speech, Madison may well have had a copy of Blackstone in hand as he sharply distinguished, as had Blackstone, "between a *league* or *treaty,* and a *Constitution.* . . . The doctrine laid down by the law of Nations, in the case of treaties is that a breach of any one article by any of the parties, frees the other parties from their engagements. In the case of a union of people under one Constitution, the nature of the pact has always been understood to exclude such an interpretation." Ibid., 2:93.

71. Pinckney's comments appeared a week before the publication of *Federalist* No. 43 in New York: "The Confederation was a compact . . . that had been repeatedly broken by every state in the Union; and all the writers on the laws of nations agree that, when the parties to a treaty violate it, it is no longer binding." *Elliot's Debates,* 4:308. According to Iredell, "Perhaps every state has committed repeated violations of the demands of Congress. . . . The consequence is that, upon the principle I have mentioned, (and in which I believe all writers agree,) the Articles of Confederation are no longer binding." Ibid., 230. Note, however, that Iredell did not refer to the Articles as a "treaty" and thus his comments are more ambiguous than Madison's and Pinckney's. Pinckney's legal analysis was disputed by Rawlins Lowndes. Ibid., 310. The breached-treaty defense also appeared in private correspondence. See, e.g., John Brown Cutting to William Short, circa Jan. 9, 1788, in *DHRC,* 14:497; Samuel Holden Parsons to William Cushing, Jan. 11, 1788, in Bernard Bailyn, ed., *The Debate on the Constitution* (1993), 1:753.

72. For the argument that the Federalists' restraint also reflected the legal weakness of the breached-treaty defense of secession, see Bruce Ackerman and Neal Katyal, "Our Unconventional Founding," *U. of Chicago LR* 62 (1995): 475. Though I share Ackerman and Katyal's view that arguments from realpolitik and general principle often dominated narrow legal analysis in de-

bates about Article VII, I remain skeptical of some of their strong claims and characterizations concerning what they refer to as "the Federalists' flagrant illegalities." Ibid., 476.

In particular: The fact that some Philadelphia delegates went beyond the terms of their commissions (as commissioners, envoys, diplomats, and ambassadors sometimes do when distinctly advantageous negotiating opportunities present themselves) does not itself constitute "illegality." Also, various descriptions of events as "extra-constitutional" should not be read as "unconstitutional." For instance, a private opinion poll or a nonbinding popular vote for U.S. senator in 1900 might be outside the constitution, yet not in violation of it. On the issue of Article VII ratification, Ackerman and Katyal claim that if A, B, and C mutually league together and B breaches, A and C remain bound to each other. Ibid., 554. Not always. If all the states between New Hampshire and Georgia breached, the very essence of the confederacy—its main purposes and presuppositions—might well have failed so completely so as to free the remaining parties, separated as they were by a thousand miles and unable to enjoy the military and other benefits that had underlain their initial agreement to join. Beyond issues of breach lay questions concerning what contract lawyers call "fundamental failures of conditions precedent" and "impossibility" and what international lawyers refer to as the (changed-circumstances) doctrine of *rebus sic stantibus.* Ackerman and Katyal argue that a party with unclean hands (that is, a party itself guilty of some breach) might not have a perfect legal right to rescind. Ibid., 555. By the same token, however, neither would a complaining party with unclean hands have a perfect legal right to object and receive specific performance. Ackerman and Katyal also note that formal rescission requires official acts. Ibid. True enough, but these acts *followed* rather than preceded the ninth state's ratification. Until then, no rescission had occurred, and even after that, the announced rescission was not to be immediate. The very lack of immediacy made the rescission more justifiable, by giving the old confederacy time to wind up affairs in an equitable manner. Thus, the continuing actions of the Confederation Congress after the ninth ratification and before the convening of the First Constitutional Congress are not inconsistent with a breached-treaty approach, contra Ackerman and Katyal at 556–58. Finally, it is critical to note that the proposed rescission was not unilateral but multilateral. Nine states would have to agree. If they did, these states were enough to constitute a definitive majority of the old Confederation Congress—the only juridical entity that would be in a position to resolve whatever dispute might arise should one or more of the nonratifying states claim legal injury. In other words, the only real "international court" that existed in 1787 was the Confederation Congress itself, and the new Constitution would take effect if and only if nine states—a controlling majority of that Congress— agreed that dissolution of the old Confederation was justified.

73. Jay made a similar observation in an October 13, 1786, report to the Confederate Congress on state breaches of America's 1783 Peace Treaty with Britain. *JCC,* 31:870 (noting desirability of union response to state breaches that "points at no particular State" and thus "cannot wound the feelings of any").

74. See n. 3 above.

75. At the outset of Article VI, the Constitution did use the word "Confederation," but only to distinguish the old regime of the Articles from the new order being proposed by the Constitution itself. Also, Article I, section 10 forbade states from entering into any "Treaty, Alliance, or Confederation." The phrase "this Constitution" appeared in the necessary-and-proper clause of Article I, section 8; in the Article II, section 1 clause requiring that a president generally be a natural-born citizen; in the Article III, section 2 clause extending the judicial power to all federal question cases; in the Article IV, section 3 clause governing federal property; and in a cluster of provisions in Articles V through VII.

76. When this supremacy clause was first introduced at Philadelphia by Luther Martin, it failed to specify the supremacy of the federal Constitution over state constitutions. *Farrand's Records,* 2:28–29. Martin fumed at the delegates' subsequent modification of the clause, and with good reason, for the modification decisively repudiated his view that the new Constitution should remain a classic confederacy among thirteen sovereign peoples. Ibid., 3:287.

77. *Federalist* No. 15 (describing the Constitution as repudiating the idea of "a league or alliance between independent nations" in "a treaty . . . depending for its execution on the good faith of the parties" in favor of "a government" with the "power of making laws"); No. 33 (distinguishing between "a mere treaty, dependent on the good faith of the parties" and a "government" whose "laws . . . pursuant to the powers intrusted to it by its constitution, must necessarily be supreme over those societies, and the individuals of whom they are composed"); Madison, "Vices," in Madison, *Papers,* 352 (defining a "Constitution" as an instrument by which separate states "are become one sovereign power"). See generally Locke, *Second Treatise,* sec. 14 (distinguishing between "league" and pact "to enter into one community, and make one body politic"); *Blackstone's Comm.,* 1:*97 n. e (similar).

78. For Nasson, see *Elliot's Debates,* 2:134. "Letters of a Federal Farmer (IV)," in Ford, ed., *Pamphlets,* 311 (emphasis added). Robert Yates, "Essays of Brutus (XII)," in *Storing's Anti-Fed.,* 2:424–25. A similar view was expressed by another New York Anti-Federalist in "Letters of Cato (II)," in ibid., 108. For the Pennsylvania Anti-Federalists, see *DHRC,* 2:630 ("The Address and Reasons of Dissent of the Minority of the Convention of the State of Pennsylvania to Their Constituents"); ibid., 393, 407–8, 447–48 (Whitehill, Smilie, Findley). For Martin, see *Farrand's Records,* 3:158–59, 223.

79. *Elliot's Debates,* 3:44, 22, 55. For similar Anti-Federalist readings of the Preamble, see Main, *Antifederalists,* 122 n. 10.

80. *Farrand's Records,* 2:93 (quoted). See also Madison, "Vices," in Madison, *Papers,* 352 (distinguishing "a league of sovereign powers" and a "political Constitution by virtue of which they are become one sovereign power").

81. An act for rendring the union of the two kingdoms more intire and compleat (1707), 6 Anne, c. 6 (emphasis added).

82. *Elliot's Debates,* 2:463 (Wilson), 4:187 (Johnston), 3:586–87 (Wythe). See also ibid., 2:540 (Thomas McKean) (the proposed Constitution "unites the several states, and makes them like one, in particular instances and for particular purposes—which is what is ardently desired by most of the sensible men in this country").

83. On Virginia, see p. 11 above. Several conventions did however endorse specific suggested amendments, and also tried to make explicit their understandings of various constitutional provisions for whatever weight this contemporaneous legislative history might merit in subsequent interpretations. See *Elliot's Debates,* 1:319–37, 3:656–63.

84. For Hamilton on "slender" chances, see his letter to Madison, June 25, 1788, in Hamilton, *Papers,* 5:80. On the proposed compromise, *Elliot's Debates,* 2:411. For Federalist insistence on "full confidence" rather than "condition[s]," see Hamilton, *Papers,* 5:193–95. See also *Elliot's Debates,* 2:412. On the defeat of Lansing's proposal, see ibid. This vote goes unmentioned by the great historian Kenneth M. Stampp, and surely qualifies his claim that "no state convention made the right of secession the subject of extended inquiry." "The Concept of a Perpetual Union," *J. of Am. Hist.* 65 (1978): 5, 20. Stampp also claims that *The Federalist* and the Federalists generally had little to say on the topic of secession. Ibid. For a very different reading of the dominant Federalist argument for union, and its overwhelming (if implicit) repudiation of a subsequent right of unilateral secession, see pp. 40–53 below.

85. Madison's letter to Hamilton, July 20, 1788, is in Madison, *Papers,* 11:189. For Hamilton on the "perpetual compact," see "New York Ratifying Convention. First Speech of July 24," in Hamilton, *Papers,* 5:193–95. See also Kaminski, "New York," 112; Stampp, "Concept," 18 n. 51. For Hamilton's earlier wavering, see Hamilton to Madison, July 19, 1788, in Hamilton, *Papers,* 5:177–78. For Hamilton and Jay's repudiation of "a right to withdraw," see excerpt from *The Daily Advertiser,* July 28, 1788, in ibid., 5:194–95.

86. For Lincoln's claim that "none of our states, except Texas, ever was a sovereignty," see his Special Session Address to Congress, July 4, 1861, in which Lincoln also made clear that "Texas gave up [her sovereign] character on coming into the Union." For Jefferson Davis's state-sovereignty reading of the Declaration and Articles of Confederation, see his *The Rise and Fall of the Confederate Government* (n.d.; reprint, 1958), 1:86–94.

87. *Gibbons v. Ogden,* 22 U.S. (9 Wheat.) 1, 187 (1824).

88. Adams, *FAC,* 228.

89. In the words of the 1766 Declaratory Act that grated on colonial ears, Parlia-

ment "hath, and of right ought to have, full power and authority to make laws and statutes of sufficient force and validity to bind the colonies and people of *America* . . . in all cases whatsoever." An act for the better securing the dependency of his Majesty's dominions in *America* upon the crown and parliament of *Great Britain* (1766), 6 Geo. 3, c. 12. The Declaration of Independence famously rejected Parliament's acts of "pretended Legislation" and claims to "a jurisdiction foreign to our Constitution, and unacknowledged by our laws."

90. See Declarations of the Stamp Act Congress, Oct. 19, 1765 ("IV. That the people of these colonies are not, and from their local circumstances cannot be, represented in the House of Commons in Great-Britain"). See generally Adams, *FAC,* 131, 231; Greene, *Peripheries and Center,* 37, 123; Morgan, *Inventing the People,* 242; cf. Beer, *To Make a Nation,* 168–77.

91. On assemblies' control of congressmen, see Van Tyne, "Sovereignty," 529–31; Morgan, *Inventing the People,* 263; Morris, *Forging,* 56–58, 77–79. To the pattern of annual elections, there were only three exceptions: In Rhode Island and Connecticut, elections occurred twice a year; in South Carolina, once every two years. *Federalist* No. 53. For an example of an assembly changing its name, the Virginia House of Burgesses became the House of Delegates. For continuity (and some differences) between colonial and state legislatures, see Nevins, *American States,* 1–2, 88–97, 118–19; Adams, *FAC,* 27, 34–35, 52, 61–95; Greene, *Peripheries and Center,* 164–65; Morgan, *Inventing the People,* 245, 247, 257. On increased legislative size, see generally Jackson Turner Main, "Government by the People: The American Revolution and the Democratization of the Legislatures," *WMQ* 23 (1966): 391.

92. Recall Patrick Henry's words calling the Philadelphia plan a step "as radical as that which separated us from Great Britain."

93. See Adams, *FAC,* 2, 267, 289, 290–300, 310; Lutz, *Origins,* 138.

94. For Lansing, see *Farrand's Records,* 1:250. See also ibid., 338 (Lansing) ("The system was too novel & complex"). For Martin, see ibid., 439. See also ibid., 3:292 ("Martin's Reply to the Landholder") (describing Philadelphia plan as a "motley mixture" and "strange hotch-potch"—an "innovation in government of the most extraordinary kind"); "Letters of Centinel (XV)," in *Storing's Anti-Fed.,* 2:196. For similar traditionalist objections to the Constitution's novelty, see, e.g., "Essays of John DeWitt (I)," in ibid., 4:18; "Letters of Agrippa (IV)," in ibid., 4:76; "A Republican Federalist (V)," in ibid., 4:178.

To put my point in Professor Ackerman's framework: Even if some leaders in 1776 took steps toward indissoluble nationhood, their proposals failed to be codified by the decisive legal text of the Articles of Confederation, and the Constitution itself properly presupposed that no indivisible continental nation existed in 1787. Professor Beer therefore gets matters backward when he suggests that Americans repudiated a century of local governance in favor of continental nationhood in 1775–76 (when little focused discussion of indivisibility occurred, and the legal data are mixed at best) even as he downplays the focused federalism debate that did occur in 1787–89. See Beer, *To Make a Nation,* 321. Beer also errs in suggesting that the federal origins of the act of constitution somehow support later "nullifiers and secessionists." Ibid. On the contrary, it was in this very debate that America squarely focused on nullification and secession—indeed practiced them by nullifying the Articles and seceding from the Confederation—and forswore the future permissibility of unilateral nullification or secession under the Constitution's decisively different, more perfect union.

95. On the minimal impact of No. 10 in the Founding era, see Douglass Adair, *Fame and the Founding Fathers: Essays by Douglass Adair,* Trevor Colbourn, ed. (1974), 75–76; Larry D. Kramer, "Madison's Audience," *Harvard LR* 112 (1999): 611. For an important exposition of the themes of the early *Federalist* essays apart from No. 10, see Frederick W. Marks III, *Independence on Trial: Foreign Affairs and the Making of the Constitution* (1973), 167–75. For two other useful correctives, featuring incisive overviews of the great federalism debate of the late 1780s, see David F. Epstein, "The Case for Ratification: Federalist Constitutional Thought," in Leonard W. Levy and Dennis J. Mahoney, eds., *The Framing and Ratification of the Constitution* (1987), 292–304; Peter S. Onuf, "State Sovereignty and the Making of the Constitution," in Terence Ball and J.G.A. Pocock, eds., *Conceptual Change and the Constitution* (1988), 78–98. For an extended quantitative analysis of the ratification conversation, see William H. Riker, *The Strategy of Rhetoric: Campaigning for the American Constitution* (1996).

96. *Annals,* 1:454–55, 784 (June 8 and Aug. 17, 1789).

97. *DHRC,* 13:595, 14:531–33, 15:575–78, 16:597–600.

98. *Federalist* No. 8; *Blackstone's Comm.,* 1:*418. See also *Federalist* No. 41 (principal reliance on "maritime strength" would enable America to emulate "the insular advantage of Great Britain"; navies are "most capable of repelling foreign enterprises" but "can never be turned by a perfidious government against our liberties"). In an August 11, 1786, letter to James Monroe, Thomas Jefferson observed that a "naval force can never endanger our liberties, nor occasion bloodshed; a land force would do both." Jefferson, *Papers,* 10:225.

99. For "BORDERING nations," see *Federalist* No. 5. On the elevation of the military, see No. 8. Elsewhere in this essay, Publius links standing armies with a loss of "liberty."

100. Ibid., Nos. 4–5.

101. Ibid., No. 11. See also No. 5 (explicitly invoking union of England and Scotland as model for American union). In a pamphlet published in mid-April 1788, Jay reiterated the point:

The old Confederation [is falling apart]. Then every State would be a little nation, jealous of its neighbors, and anxious to strengthen itself by foreign alliances, against its former friends. Then farewell to fraternal affection, unsuspecting intercourse; and mutual participation in commerce, navigation and citizenship. Then would arise mutual restrictions and fears, mutual garrisons,— and standing armies, and all those dreadful evils which for so many ages plagued England, Scotland, Wales, and Ireland, while they continued disunited, and were played off against each other. . . . You know the geography of your State, and the consequences of your local position. Jersey and Connecticut, to whom your impost laws have been unkind . . . cannot, they will not love you— they border upon you, and are your neighbors; but you will soon cease to regard their neighborhood as a blessing.

John Jay, "An Address to the People of the State of New-York," in Ford, *Pamphlets,* 84.

102. *Federalist* No. 15.

103. On "dismemberment," see ibid., No. 1. The first paragraph of this essay sounds the alarm, by suggesting that the very "existence of the UNION" is at stake. For further emphasis on the theme of imminent dissolution of the confederacy, see Nos. 5, 8, 15. On the danger of thirteen separate states, see Nos. 2–8, 25. On regional confederacies and "territorial disputes," see No. 7. For Wilson on a land dispute between Connecticut and Pennsylvania over Wyoming district, see *Elliot's Debates,* 2:528.

104. On the Atlantic as a defense, see *Federalist* Nos. 5, 8. On financing the navy, see No. 12. On taxes' superiority to requisition, see Nos. 4, 15, 25. On the army, see No. 4.

105. On the need to deter Europeans, see ibid., Nos. 4, 5, 7. See also Nos. 16, 18, 19, 41, 85. On state violations of the treaty and British retention of forts, see Nos. 3, 15.

106. On relations with Europe, see ibid., No. 11. On interstate relations, see No. 12.

107. On trade wars, see ibid., Nos. 4, 6. William Shakespeare, *Henry V,* 4.3.60–67 ("We few, we happy few, we band of brothers; / For he to-day that sheds his blood with me / Shall be my brother; be he ne'er so vile, / This day shall gentle his condition; / And gentlemen in England, now a-bed / Shall think themselves accurs'd they were not here; / And hold their manhoods cheap whiles any speaks / That fought with us upon Saint Crispin's day"). For similar brotherly language from Jay in a 1788 pamphlet, see "Address," in Ford, *Pamphlets,* 86 ("people of America [should] remain . . . as a *band of brothers*"). For Wilson's paraphrase of Jay's *Federalist* No. 2 in the Pennsylvania debates, see *DHRC,* 2:346 ("while we consider the extent of the country, so intersected and almost surrounded with navigable rivers, so separated and detached from the rest of the world, it is natural to presume that Providence has designed us for an united people, under one great political compact").

108. *Ibid.,* No. 11, whose "nursery" image in turn built on *Federalist* No. 4.
109. On the economies of union, see *Federalist* Nos. 4, 13, 25.
110. *Farrand's Records,* 1:463–65.
111. In Wilson's words:

> A number of separate states, contiguous in situation, unconnected and disunited in government, would be, at one time, the prey of foreign force, foreign influence, and foreign intrigue; at another, the victims of mutual rage, rancor, and revenge. . . . Would it be proper to divide the United States into two or more confederacies? . . . Animosities, and perhaps wars, would arise from assigning the extent, the limits, and the rights, of the different confederacies. . . . The danger resulting from foreign influence and mutual dissensions, would . . . be . . . great. . . .
>
> [Under the Constitution, states] would not be exposed to the danger of competition on questions of territory, or any other that have heretofore disturbed them. . . . The several states cannot war with each other. . . . What a happy exchange for the disjointed, contentious state sovereignties! The adoption of this system will also secure us from danger, and procure us advantages from foreign nations.

> *Elliot's Debates,* 2:427–28, 527–28.

> In Ellsworth's words:

> A union is necessary for the purposes of a national defence. . . . Witness England, which, when divided into separate states, was twice conquered by an inferior force. . . . A *union,* sir, is likewise necessary, considered with relation to economy. . . . We must unite, in order to preserve peace among ourselves. If we be divided, what is to prevent wars from breaking out among the states? . . . Union is necessary to preserve commutative justice between the states. . . . [Otherwise, the] European powers will . . . play the states off one against another.

> Ibid., 185–86, 190.

> In Randolph's words:

> Call to mind the history of every part of the world, where nations bordered on one another, and consider the consequences of our separation from the Union. . . . A numerous standing army, that dangerous expedient, would be necessary. . . . If you wish to know the extent of such a scene, look at the history of Scotland and England before the union; you will see their borderers continually committing depredations and cruelties of the most calamitous and deplorable nature, on one another. . . .
>
> . . . I allude to the Scotch union. If gentlemen cast their eyes to that period, they will find there an instructive similitude between our circumstances and the situation of those people. The advocates for a union with England declared that

NOTES FOR PAGE 49

it would be a foundation of lasting peace, remove all jealousies between them, increase their strength and riches, and enable them to resist more effectually the efforts of the Pretender. These were irresistible arguments. . . . and the predictions of the advocates for that union have been fully verified. The arguments used on that occasion apply with more cogency to our situation. . . .

We are next informed [by Patrick Henry] that there is no danger from the borders of Maryland and Pennsylvania, and that my observations upon the frontiers of England and Scotland are inapplicable. He distinguishes republican from monarchial borderers, and ascribes pacific meekness to the former, and barbarous ferocity to the latter. There is as much danger, sir, from republican borderers as from any other. History will show that as much barbarity and cruelty have been committed upon one another by republican borderers as by any other. We are borderers upon three states, two of which are ratifying states. . . .

Ibid., 3:75, 123, 197. See also ibid., 603 ("If, in this situation, we reject the Constitution, the Union will be dissolved, the dogs of war will break loose, and anarchy and discord will complete the ruin of this country").

112. Also indispensable, in the eyes of many, was Virginia's leading resident, George Washington, for whom the new constitutional presidency had been designed. If Virginia did not ratify, would Washington serve? Without Washington to set the right precedents and give the office proper ballast, could the new union be successfully launched? On Washington's centrality, see Chapter 4, pp. 134–35.

113. See, e.g., *Elliot's Debates,* 3:242 (George Nicholas) ("England, before it was united to Scotland, was almost constantly at war with that part of the island. The inhabitants of the north and south parts of the same island were more bitter enemies to one another than to the nations on the Continent. England and Scotland were more bitter enemies, before the union, than England and France have ever been, before or since. Their hatred and animosities were stimulated by the interference of other nations. Since the union, both countries have enjoyed domestic tranquillity, the greatest part of the time, and both countries have been greatly benefited by it. This is a convincing proof that union is necessary for America, and that partial confederacies would be productive of endless dissensions, and unceasing hostilities between the different parts").

114. "Farewell Address," in Richard B. Morris, ed., *Great Presidential Decisions: State Papers that Changed the Course of History* (rev. ed. 1967), 37–38 ("Every part of our country . . . must derive from union an exemption from those broils and wars between themselves which so frequently afflict neighboring countries not tied together by the same governments. . . . Likewise, they will avoid the necessity of those overgrown military establishments which, under any form of government, are inauspicious to liberty, and which are to be regarded as particularly hostile to republican liberty"). On Washington as a surveyor and strategist, see generally Edmund S. Morgan, *The Genius of*

George Washington (1980), 7–8, 14–16, 18–19, 22–25, 60–63, 67–87; Morgan, *Meaning of Independence,* 41–52.

115. *JCC,* 1:105, 111 (Oct. 26, 1774) (emphasis deleted).

116. *JCC,* 1:112.

117. Patrick Henry put the point crisply: "The history of Switzerland clearly proves that we might be in amicable alliance with [other] states without adopting this Constitution. Switzerland is a confederacy." *Elliot's Debates,* 3:62. See also ibid., 142–43, 211 (Patrick Henry and James Monroe) (further elaborating the Swiss analogy). For a smattering of the many approving references to Switzerland in the Anti-Federalist literature, see, e.g., "Letters of Centinel (IV)," in *Storing's Anti-Fed.,* 2:163; "Essay of A Democratic Federalist," in ibid., 3:62; "Essays by a [Maryland] Farmer (III, V)," in ibid., 5:30–31, 46–48.

118. For Ellsworth, see Elliot's Debates, 2:188. For other discussions of Swiss geography and/or disharmony, see ibid., 3:69–70, 130–31, 235 (Randolph, Madison, and John Marshall).

119. *JCC,* 1:106.

120. For details, see Akhil Reed Amar, "Abraham Lincoln and the American Union," *U. of Illinois LR* (2001): 1109, 1110–18.

2: NEW RULES FOR A NEW WORLD

1. On the word "Congress," see Edward Dumbauld, *The Constitution of the United States* (1964), 52, 62; Jack N. Rakove, *Original Meanings: Politics and Ideas in the Making of the Constitution* (1996), 206.

2. See Chapter 5, n. 30. See also Rakove, *Original Meanings,* 206, 253; John C. Yoo, "Globalism and the Constitution: Treaties, Non-self-execution, and the Original Understanding," *Columbia LR* 99 (1999): 1955, 2009–11.

3. Informally, various state legislatures would continue to claim authority to "instruct" their federal senators in the antebellum era. In turn, some senators at times felt honor-bound to resign if they refused to follow these supposed "instructions." See generally William Riker, "The Senate and American Federalism," *APSR* 49 (1955): 452.

4. In fact, however, few congressmen did seek extended reelection in the first century. See generally Jack N. Rakove, "The Structure of Politics at the Accession of George Washington," in Richard Beeman et al., eds., *Beyond Confederation: Origins of the Constitution and American National Identity* (1987), 261–94; Nelson W. Polsby, "The Institutionalization of the U.S. House of Representatives," *APSR* 62 (1968): 144–68; Morris P. Fiorina et al., "Historical Change in House Turnover," in Norman Ornstein, ed., *Congress in Change: Evolution and Reform* (1975), 24–57; Douglas Price, "Careers and Committees in the American Congress: The Problem of Structural Change," in William O. Aydelotte, ed., *The History of Parliamentary Behavior* (1977), 28–62.

5. *Farrand's Records,* 2:666.

6. See generally Jackson Turner Main, "Government by the People: The American Revolution and the Democratization of the Legislatures," *WMQ* 23 (1966): 391–407.

7. *Federalist* Nos. 48 (Madison) and 71 (Hamilton).

8. Ibid., Nos. 48 (Madison quoting Jefferson) and 51 (Madison).

9. Ibid., Nos. 48, 51.

10. For elaboration and qualification of this general presidential authority, see Chapter 5, pp. 183–85.

11. *Farrand's Records,* 1:99 (Franklin), 486 (Madison). Mason echoed Franklin's point. Ibid., 101. For more discussion of executive bargaining in the colonial era, see Forrest McDonald, *The American Presidency: An Intellectual History* (1994), 109–110.

12. We shall consider this special army rule in Chapter 3, p. 116. For now, it suffices to say the army exception proves the rule by establishing that the Constitution purposely avoided a global mandatory-expiration-date device.

13. The clever system faced a severe challenge whenever one branch deemed a given policy constitutionally impermissible while another branch viewed the policy as constitutionally mandatory.

14. For discussions of the importance of political honor at the Founding, see generally Douglass Adair, *Fame and the Founding Fathers: Essays by Douglass Adair,* Trevor Colbourn, ed. (1974); Joanne B. Freeman, *Affairs of Honor: National Politics in the New Republic* (2001).

15. See generally Bruce Ackerman, *We the People: Foundations* (1991), 230–322; Bruce Ackerman, "The New Separation of Powers," *Harvard LR* 113 (2000): 633; Laura S. Fitzgerald, "Cadenced Power: The Kinetic Constitution," *Duke LJ* 46 (1997): 679.

16. While Professor Morgan has parenthetically noted that "in Rhode Island and Connecticut [Confederation congressmen] were chosen at large by the voters," Professor Rakove has written that "both Connecticut and Rhode Island permitted congressional delegates to be nominated by popular vote, but the state assemblies retained the right of election." Edmund S. Morgan, *Inventing the People: The Rise of Popular Sovereignty in England and America* (1988), 264; Rakove, *Original Meanings,* 208. It would appear that the truth is somewhere in between: Rhode Island allowed voters to select congressmen (with the legislature authorized to fill vacancies), whereas Connecticut law allowed voters to nominate seven delegates from whom the legislature would then choose two to four to represent the state. *Rhode Island General Assembly Laws* (March 1777, 2d Session), 18; Charles J. Hoadly et al., eds., *Public Records of the State of Connecticut* (1894–   ), 2:264 (session of May 13, 1779); Richard Buel, Jr., *Dear Liberty: Connecticut's Mobilization for the Revolutionary War* (1980), 213–15.

17. Morgan, *Inventing the People,* 264 (quoting Patrick Henry).

18. New Hampshire, Massachusetts, New Jersey, Maryland, North Carolina,

South Carolina, and Georgia all fell into this category. In New York, state senators did not themselves face extra-high property qualifications, but those who elected them did. Adams, *FAC*, 315–27.

19. New York, North Carolina, and Maryland all had bicameral voter-qualification rules, and New York also limited its gubernatorial elections to a propertied subset of assembly voters. In most states, of course, governors were not directly elected by the citizenry, but were instead picked by (propertied) legislators. For details, see ibid., 318 (N.Y.), 322 (Md.), 324 (N.C.).

20. Other provisions of Article I seemed to envision federal bureaucracies to collect customs duties, deliver mail, and conduct censuses. Customs officials would likely confine themselves to port cities, and neither they nor postal officials would directly monitor state political functions. Census officials conducting decennial counts would likely be less intrusive than federal election officials overseeing biennial elections.

21. See generally Chilton Williamson, *American Suffrage: From Property to Democracy, 1760–1860* (1960); Bernard Bailyn, *The Origins of American Politics* (1965), 30–31, 86–88; Adams, *FAC*, 315–27; Morgan, *Inventing the People*, 137, 146, 175; Alexander Keyssar, *The Right to Vote: The Contested History of Democracy in the United States* (2000), 7.

22. "No Person shall be a Representative who shall not have attained to the Age of twenty five Years, and been seven Years a Citizen of the United States, and who shall not, when elected, be an Inhabitant of that State in which he shall be chosen." U.S. Const., art. I, sec. 2, para. 2. "No Person shall be a Senator who shall not have attained to the Age of thirty Years, and been nine Years a Citizen of the United States, and who shall not, when elected, be an inhabitant of that State for which he shall be chosen." Ibid., sec. 3, para. 3. On the exclusivity of these provisions, see generally *Powell v. McCormack*, 395 U.S. 496 (1969); *U.S. Term Limits v. Thornton*, 512 U.S. 1286 (1994). See also *Federalist* Nos. 52 and 60; *Elliot's Debates*, 2:257 (Hamilton); *Farrand's Records*, 2:249–50 (Madison).

23. In practice, some members of Commons found clever ways around its steep property qualifications. Even these techniques typically required the cooperation or patronage of some wealthy figures behind the scenes.

24. Md. Const. (1776), art. XXVII; N.H. Const. (1784), pt. II (unnumbered para. concerning "the delegates of this state to the Congress").

25. New York and Pennsylvania were the only exceptions. See Adams, *FAC*, 315–27.

26. Unicameral Georgia also restricted membership in its assembly to propertied men. Ibid.

27. Mass. Const. (1780), pt. II, ch. I, sec. II, art. I; N.H. Const. (1784), pt. II (unnumbered para. beginning "There shall be annually elected . . ."); S.C. Const. (1778), art. XV.

28. See *Farrand's Records*, 1:512–13, 533, 567, 581–82 (Morris); 428, 2:121 (Mason);

1:144, 529, 542, 562, 580–81 (Butler); 196, 534, 582 (Rutledge); 541, 562, 582, 595 (King); 596 (C. C. Pinckney); 542 (Davie); 560 (Williamson); 469–70 (Baldwin); 486, 562, 2:204 n. 17 (Madison). Gerry, who ultimately declined to sign the Constitution, favored legislative apportionment based on a "combined ratio of numbers of Inhabitants and of wealth, and not of either singly." Ibid., 1:540–41. For more on Madison, see Rakove, *Original Meanings,* 41.

29. *Farrand's Records,* 2:201–210.
30. Professor Rakove has argued that "the fact that the Convention could not simply promulgate a constitution on its own authority . . . had an immensely liberating effect on its deliberations." Rakove, *Original Meanings,* 102. My account aims to stress the complementary chastening effect, drawing the eventual proposals toward the populist pole of the spectrum of opinion at Philadelphia.
31. *Farrand's Records,* 2:248–51.
32. Ibid., 249. (On a more humorous note, Franklin added that "some of the greatest rogues he was ever acquainted with, were the richest rogues.") Whereas Franklin made the republican point by looking to the future, several weeks earlier John Dickinson had reached a somewhat similar conclusion by reference to the classic republican traditions of antiquity. Arguing against "any recital of qualifications in the Constitution," Dickinson "doubted the policy of interweaving into a Republican constitution a veneration for wealth. He had always understood that a veneration for poverty & virtue, were the objects of republican encouragement. It seemed improper that any man of merit should be subjected to disabilities in a Republic where merit was understood to form the great title to public trust, honors & rewards." Ibid., 123. But see ibid., 1:150 (Dickinson "wished the Senate to consist of [men] distinguished for their rank in life and their weight of property, and bearing as strong a likeness to the British House of Lords as possible").
33. For the Federalists, see *Elliot's Debates,* 2:482 (Wilson) (emphasis deleted); *Farrand's Records,* 2:210 (McHenry's notes on Franklin), 3:146–47 (McHenry summarizing Franklin); *Elliot's Debates,* 2:35–36, 51 (Sedgwick and King), 3:8–9, 395 (Nicholas and Madison); *Federalist* No. 57. See also Tench Coxe, "An Examination of the Constitution of the United States (IV)," in Ford, *Pamphlets,* 145 ("No qualification in monied or landed property is required by the proposed plan; nor does it admit any preference from the preposterous distinctions of birth and rank"). For Anti-Federalists criticizing the absence of property qualifications for congressmen, see *Elliot's Debates,* 2:22 (Pierce); "Letters from the Federal Farmer (XII)," in *Storing's Anti-Fed.,* 2:294–95.
34. *Farrand's Records,* 2:237, 268–69. For similar remarks by Ellsworth, Madison, and Franklin., see ibid., 235–38. In the First Congress, the nine immigrant Americans were Representatives Aedanus Burke, Thomas Fitzsimons, James Jackson, John Laurance, and Thomas Tudor Tucker, and Senators Pierce

Butler, Samuel Johnston, Robert Morris, and William Paterson. The four signers in this group were Fitzsimons, Butler, Morris, and Paterson.

35. Ibid., 218. Modern historians have confirmed Mason's critique of Parliament. According to Morgan, by the beginning of the seventeenth century, most members of Commons "were country gentlemen not actually resident in the boroughs that elected them." Morgan, *Inventing the People,* 42.

36. See Coxe, "An Examination (II)," in Ford, *Pamphlets,* 141 ("No ambitious, undeserving or inexperienced youth can acquire a seat in this house [the Senate] by means of the most enormous wealth, or most powerful connections, till thirty years have ripened his abilities, and fully discovered [i.e., revealed] his merits to his country—a more rational ground of preference surely than mere property"). In his next essay (III), Coxe linked the twenty-five-year age limit in the House to a republican desire to limit undue advantages of those with "wealth" and "powerful connections." Ibid., 143–44. For more background on the egalitarian dimension of age rules, see Holly Brewer, *By Birth or Consent: Children, Law, and the Anglo-American Revolution in Authority* (2005).

37. On Congress as a possible springboard for future offices and honors, see generally David R. Mayhew, *America's Congress: Actions in the Public Sphere, James Madison Through Newt Gingrich* (2000), 129–67. The eight early senatorial youngsters who did *not* go on to be presidents or runners-up were Thomas Worthington, John Rutherfurd, William Hill Wells, Samuel White, James Ross, David Stone, Richard Stockton, and Ray Greene. Zachary Taylor was the sole antebellum president never to have served in Congress. (For this tally, I have included membership in the Continental and/or Confederation Congress; Mayhew does the same, ibid., 159 & n. 40.) Among the favorite sons who went on to become president in antebellum America, Harrison and Tyler were both sons of Virginia governors; Pierce was the son of New Hampshire's governor, and of course John Quincy Adams was the son of President John Adams.

As for state constitutions, while no state lower house had age requirements beyond those for voters, four states did require their *upper*-house members to be elder statesmen of sorts—Delaware, Maryland, and Virginia set the age bar at 25, and South Carolina did so at 30. Also, North Carolina required its governor to be at least 30.

38. Of the dozen youngest men to reach the Senate in this decade, Rhode Island's Ray Greene was the son of the state's ex-governor William Greene, Jr. (who was in turn the son of colonial Governor William Greene); Virginia's Stevens Thomson Mason was the son of Thomson Mason, one of the state's handful of top judges, who was in turn the younger brother of George Mason, author of the state bill of rights and also a Philadelphia framer; New Jersey's Richard Stockton was the son and namesake of one of the signers of the Declaration of Independence, the younger brother-in-law of another signer,

Benjamin Rush, and the nephew (on both sides) of Elias Boudinot, a member of the Continental Congress and, later, the federal House; Virginia's James Monroe was the nephew of Joseph Jones, a member of the Continental Congress who had also served in high state judicial office; and New York's Rufus King was the son-in-law of Continental Congressman John Alsop.

Of the seventy older senators, Virginia's John Taylor (age 38 when he came to the Senate) was orphaned in boyhood and thereafter raised by his uncle Edmund Pendleton, a Continental congressman, speaker of the state house of delegates, president of the state supreme court of appeals, and president of the Virginia ratifying convention; Connecticut's James Hillhouse (42) was the son of Confederation Congressman William Hillhouse and the nephew of Governor Matthew Griswold; New Jersey's Franklin Davenport (43) was Benjamin Franklin's nephew; Rhode Island's Theodore Foster (48) was the son-in-law of Governor Arthur Fenner, Jr.; South Carolina's Ralph Izard (48 or 49) was the grandson of the first Crown-appointed governor, Robert Johnson; Delaware's Philemon Dickinson (51) was the younger brother (by seven years) of John Dickinson, a Continental congressman, state president, and Philadelphia framer; Georgia's George Walton (53 or 54) was the younger brother (by about twelve years) of Continental Congressmen John Walton; Connecticut's Jonathan Trumbull, Jr. (55) was the son and namesake of the state's first and long-serving governor, and the younger brother (by three years) of Joseph Trumbull, who had been elected to the Continental Congress but did not serve; North Carolina's Samuel Johnston (55) was the nephew of a colonial governor, Gabriel Johnston; and Virginia's Richard Henry Lee (57) was the son of Thomas Lee, longstanding president of the colonial council and briefly its royal governor. (Also, Richard Henry's younger brother, Francis Lightfoot Lee, was a signer of the Declaration of Independence, as of course was Richard Henry himself. Yet another younger brother, Arthur Corbin Lee, had served in the Confederation Congress.)

My tally omits several relations that ill fit the "favorite son" metaphor. For example, William Blount (47) was the older brother (by ten years) of Representative Thomas Blount; New Hampshire's John Langdon (47) was, as a state president and signer of the Constitution, more prominent than his brother, Woodbury, who was two years older but had followed John as a Continental congressman (and also served briefly on the state supreme court); and Delaware's Joshua Clayton (53) was married to the adopted daughter of ex-senator and future governor Richard Bassett, but Clayton was in fact a year older than Bassett, and had already served as the state's last president and first governor. Other early senators were the scions of famous families, but not of famous *political officeholders.* Most notably, Aaron Burr (35) comes to mind— the son and namesake of Princeton University's president, and the grandson of the great theologian Jonathan Edwards.

Of the thirty-seven men who reached the House before the age of 32, thirteen were sons, sons-in-law, nephews (by blood or marriage), and/or younger brothers of leading statesmen: Tennessee's William Charles Cole Claiborne (21 or 22), Maryland's Richard Sprigg, Jr. (26 or 27), Virginia's Francis Preston (28), Richard Bland Lee (28), and Francis Walker (29), Delaware's James Asheton Bayard, Sr. (29), South Carolina's John Rutledge, Jr. (30 or 31) and William Loughton Smith (30 or 31), Massachusetts's Harrison Gray Otis (31), New Jersey's Jonathan Dayton (31), New York's Edward Livingston (31) and Hezekiah Lord Hosmer (31), and Kentucky's Alexander Dalrymple Orr (31).

Of the remaining 218 House members, I have found only 22 with comparable family ties to elder statesmen: John Francis Mercer (32), Roger Griswold (33), Nicholas Gilman (33), Thomas Blount (34), Dwight Foster (35), Chauncy Goodrich (36), Lewis Richard Morris (36), Carter Bassett Harrison (36 or 37), James Hillhouse (37), Richard Brent (37 or 38), John Laurance (38 or 39), Frederick Augustus Conrad Muhlenberg (39), Richard Dobbs Spaight (40), John Baptista Ashe (41 or 42), Michael Jenifer Stone (41 or 42), James Armstrong (45), Joseph Bradley Varnum (44 or 45), Matthew Lyon (46), Thomas Pinckney (47), Elias Boudinot (48—brother-in-law), Jonathan Trumbull, Jr. (48), and Samuel Maclay (54). Remarkably, only one of the fifty-plus men who reached the House at age 50 or above was a favorite son/nephew/younger brother, so far as I have been able to determine.

The biographical information presented in this note is based solely on the *Dictionary of American Biography,* the *Biographical Directory of the American Congress,* and the "Political Graveyard" website. These sources are doubtless incomplete, but there is no reason to think that omissions are biased along the age axis.

39. The Pennsylvania and Maryland Constitutions adopted a different approach in the shadow of Wilkes, allowing expulsion upon a simple majority vote, but prohibiting a second expulsion on the same grounds in the event voters decided to return the expelled man to the house. See Pa. Const. (1776), sec. 9; Md. Const. (1776), art. X. On Wilkes and what he meant to American patriots, see generally Pauline Maier, *From Resistance to Revolution: Colonial Radicals and the Development of American Opposition to Britain, 1765–1776* (1972), 162–69; *Powell v. McCormack,* 395 U.S. 527–31. See also Raymond William Postgate, *That Devil Wilkes* (1929); George F. E. Rudé, *Wilkes and Liberty: A Social Study of 1763 to 1774* (1962).

40. Morgan, *Inventing the People,* 176.

41. See Jack N. Rakove, *The Beginnings of National Politics* (1979), 216–39.

42. Gordon S. Wood, *The Radicalism of the American Revolution* (1991), 292. For further discussion of the egalitarian significance of legislative salary, see Rakove, "The Structure of Politics," 262, 270; Rakove, *Original Meanings,* 226.

43. *Farrand's Records,* 1:372 (Gorham), 2:291 (Broom); *Elliot's Debates,* 2:52–53

(Taylor and Sedgwick); Story, *Commentaries,* 2:318–19, sec. 849; J. R. Pole, *Political Representation in England and the Origins of the American Republic* (1966), 285–86.

44. Pa. Const. (1776), sec. 17; Mass. Const. (1780), pt. II, ch. I, sec. III, art. II, para. 4; N.H. Const. (1784), pt. II (unnumbered para. beginning "The travel of each representative . . ."). In Revolutionary Maryland, the highly propertied senate on several occasions resisted efforts by lower-house delegates to increase the delegates' per diem allowance. See Jackson Turner Main, *The Upper House in Revolutionary America, 1763–1788* (1967), 112–13.

45. Pole, *Political Representation,* 51, 286. See also Morgan, *Inventing the People,* 160. In 1811, Massachusetts began to pay house members state salaries; see Allan Nevins, *The American States During and After the Revolution, 1775–1789* (1924), 182. Cf. Story, *Commentaries,* 2:318–19, sec. 849.

46. Cf. *Farrand's Records,* 1:374 n. *.

47. Ibid., 215–16 (Mason), 377 (Randolph), 372 (Williamson), 373 (Madison), 426–27 (C. C. Pinckney), 513 (Morris). See also ibid., 219 (Butler and Rutledge arguing against the payment of senators). Note that even Hamilton—hardly a doctrinaire democrat behind closed doors (or anywhere else)—played the equality card, noting that "payment by the States would be unequal as the distant States would have to pay for the same term of attendance and more days in travelling to & from the seat of the Govt." Ibid., 373. For a similar view, see ibid., 2:290 (Morris).

48. Ibid., 2:291 (Sherman); *Elliot's Debates,* 3:368–74, 372 (Madison).

49. *Farrand's Records,* 1:216, 374.

50. Bailyn, *Origins,* 67–68.

51. Gordon S. Wood, *The Creation of the American Republic, 1776–1787* (1969), 166; Nevins, *American States,* 18.

52. Ibid., 166; Marc W. Kruman, *Between Authority and Liberty: State Constitution Making in Revolutionary America* (1997), 81–86.

53. On the two-year House term, see *Federalist* No. 53; *Elliot's Debates,* 2:10 (Ames), 533 (McKean), 4:29 (Maclaine). According to Madison, "One year will be almost consumed in preparing for and traveling to & from the seat of national business." *Farrand's Records,* 1:214. For related Madisonian musings, see ibid., 361, 422. For discussion of the Senate's six-year term, see *Federalist* Nos. 53, 62–64; *Elliot's Debates,* 2:25 (Cabot), 45–48 (Ames and King), 291 (R. R. Livingston), 302, 306–7 (Hamilton), 533 (McKean), 4:41 (Iredell); "Letters of Fabius by John Dickinson (II)," in Ford, *Pamphlets,* 170–71. See also Chapter 4, pp. 144–45.

54. *Farrand's Records,* 1:361 (Madison).

55. See also *Elliot's Debates,* 2:227 (Smith), 3:33 (Mason).

56. Ibid., 2:38 (Dana); cf. *Federalist* No. 84 (noting that the new Congress would "consist of . . . the same number of which Congress, under the existing Confederation, may be composed" but mistakenly referring to this number as

sixty-five rather than ninety-one). See generally Morgan, *Inventing the People*, 275.

57. See Frederick W. Marks III, *Independence on Trial: Foreign Affairs and the Making of the Constitution* (1973), 128–29; Richard B. Morris, *The Forging of the Union, 1781–1789* (1987), 1, 91–93, 97–98; McDonald, *American Presidency*, 143–45, 194. In the canonical book on the Confederation Congress, the index entry for "decrease in attendance, thin, no quorum" under the heading of the "Continental Congress" features references to more than forty pages. Edmund Cody Burnett, *The Continental Congress* (1941), 732.

58. *JCC*, 34:vii. From the end of October 1785 through April 1786—a six-month span—there were only three days when nine proper state delegations showed up on the floor. Burnett, *Continental Congress*, 647.

59. *Elliot's Debates*, 4:280 (C. C. Pinckney).

60. See generally Main, "Government by the People," 391–407; Jackson Turner Main, *The Sovereign States, 1775–1783* (1973), 202; Wood, *Creation*, 167.

61. *Federalist* No. 55; *Elliot's Debates*, 3:97 (Nicholas). The Carolinas' assemblies were even larger than Virginia's.

62. Morgan, *Inventing the People*, 275.

63. *Elliot's Debates*, 3:281 (Grayson); "Essays of Brutus (III)," in *Storing's Anti-Fed.*, 2:381–82.

64. See Akhil Reed Amar, *The Bill of Rights: Creation and Reconstruction* (1998), 10–14 and sources cited in accompanying endnotes. See also *Elliot's Debates*, 2:36 (Taylor). Referring to the clause concerning House size, Madison/Publius began *Federalist* No. 55 by acknowledging that "scarce any article, indeed, in the whole Constitution seems to be rendered more worthy of attention, by the weight of character and the apparent force of argument with which it has been assailed."

65. *Farrand's Records*, 1:569 (Gerry); *Elliot's Debates*, 2:228–29, 248–49 (M. Smith), 3:262–63 (Mason), 281 (Grayson).

66. Ibid., 2:246–47 (M. Smith); "Letters from the Federal Farmer (III)," in *Storing's Anti-Fed.*, 2:235; "Essays of Brutus (IV)," in ibid., 2:386; "Essay by Cornelius," in ibid., 4:143. See generally Rakove, *Original Meanings*, 232.

67. See *Elliot's Debates*, 2:243–51 (M. Smith), 473–74 (Wilson), 3:32–33, 262, 266–67 (Mason), 322 (Henry), 426 (Mason); "Essays of Brutus (III)," in *Storing's Anti-Fed.*, 2:377–82. For additional sources, see Amar, *Bill of Rights*, 316 n. 29.

68. Del. Const. (1776), Declaration of Rights, sec. 6; Md. Const. (1776), Declaration of Rights, art. V; John Adams, "Thoughts on Government: Applicable to the Present State of the American Colonies (1776)," in Michael Kammen, ed., *Deputyes & Libertyes: The Origins of Representative Government in Colonial America* (1969), 199, 200. See also *Farrand's Records*, 1:48–49 (Mason, describing the lower house as "the grand depository of the democratic principle of the Govt."); "Essays of Brutus (III)," in *Storing's Anti-Fed.*, 2:379–82 (refer-

ring to "that branch of the legislature, which is called the democratic" and to the "democratic branch of the legislatures of the several states" and arguing that representatives "should resemble those who appoint them").

69. Edmund S. Morgan, *The Meaning of Independence* (1976), 40; Morris, *Forging,* 91, 93; Rakove, "The Structure of Politics," 261–63.

70. Baldwin, Carroll, Clymer, Fitzsimons, Gerry, Gilman, Madison, Sherman, and Williamson served in the first House; Bassett, Butler, Ellsworth, Few, Johnson, King, Langdon, Robert Morris, Paterson, Read, and Strong served in the Senate.

71. *Farrand's Records,* 1:568–69 (Madison), 2:553–54 (Hamilton).

72. Ibid., 554. New York cast no vote. For additional evidence linking the issue of size to travel distance, see ibid., 1:569 (Sherman); *Elliot's Debates,* 2:273–74 (Hamilton).

73. *Farrand's Records,* 2:644.

74. One of the thirty-nine acted by proxy. Absent on the Convention's last day, John Dickinson authorized fellow delegate George Read to sign in his place. Ibid., 3:587. If Dickinson thus pledged without penning, William Blount did just the reverse, signing to "attest" the Convention's actions while telling fellow delegates that he did not thereby pledge to support the plan back home. Ibid., 2:646. In fact, Blount did end up backing the plan publicly.

75. Ibid., 2:638 (Mason). For other objectors to the number sixty-five, see "Essays of Brutus (III)," in *Storing's Anti-Fed.,* 2:377–82; and the sources cited in Amar, *Bill of Rights,* 10–14 and accompanying endnotes.

76. *Federalist* Nos. 55–58; *Elliot's Debates,* 2:534 (McKean); *Farrand's Records,* 3:260 (Strong); *Elliot's Debates* 3:11–12 (Nicholas), 2:238–39, 251–53 (Hamilton). Strong's fellow Philadelphian Nathaniel Gorham projected farther into the future, predicting 360 members "in fifty years," while Judge Dana predicted a more modest increase "soon." Ibid., 2:37–38. Note that the "take it for granted" language is a dead giveaway that Nicholas was cribbing from *Federalist* No. 55. See also *Elliot's Debates,* 2:270–71 (Harrison) (Article I "contemplates and secures a regular increase of the representation"); Coxe, "An Examination of the Constitution (III)," in Ford, *Pamphlets,* 143 ("When the increasing population of the country shall render the body too large at the rate of one member for every thirty thousand persons, they will be returned at the greater rate of one for every forty or fifty thousand").

77. *Elliot's Debates,* 2:243 (M. Smith).

78. Ibid., 251–52.

79. Ibid., 1:322 (Mass.), 326 (N.H.), 329 (N.Y.), 3:659 (Va.), 4:244 (N.C.). For more discussion, see Amar, *Bill of Rights,* 14.

80. 1 Stat. 97.

81. For the precise figures, see Story, *Commentaries,* 2:136, sec. 669.

82. Pa. Const. (1776), sec. 13; N.Y. Const. (1777), art. XV. On publicity more generally, see Adams, *FAC,* 247–49; Kruman, *Between Authority,* 81; Daniel N.

Hoffman, *Governmental Secrecy and the Founding Fathers: A Study in Constitutional Controls* (1981), 12–20.

83. For praise of this clause, see Coxe, "An Examination (III)," in Ford, *Pamphlets,* 144. Several state constitutions—Virginia's, for example—lacked comparable guarantees. See *Elliot's Debates,* 3:202 (Randolph).

84. Coxe, "An Examination (II)," in Ford, *Pamphlets,* 140, 142.

85. See generally Hoffman, *Governmental Secrecy,* 47–88.

86. *Farrand's Records,* 1:569 (Ellsworth), 260 (Strong); *Elliot's Debates,* 2:10, 45–46 (Ames), 265–66 (Hamilton), 283 (Jay), 3:229–230 (Marshall); *Federalist* No. 56; "Letters of Fabius," in Ford, *Pamphlets,* 170; "Letters of a Landholder (IV)," in Ford, *Essays,* 152.

87. *Federalist* No. 56; Wood, *Creation,* 170; Rosemarie Zagarri, *The Politics of Size: Representation in the United States, 1776–1850* (1987), 37.

88. Bailyn, *Origins,* 81; Morgan, *Inventing the People,* 146.

89. Bailyn, *Origins,* 83; Pauline Maier, *American Scripture: Making the Declaration of Independence* (1997), 113; Zagarri, *Politics of Size,* 43; Kruman, *Between Authority,* 65, 73; Nevins, *American States,* 19–20.

90. On the imperfect shift toward proportionality, see generally Pole, *Political Representation,* 172–89, 198–204, 260–77, 314–38, 526–39 (esp. 262–65, 274–76, 315–21, 535–36); Zagarri, *Politics of Size,* 36–60; Adams, *FAC,* 228–43; Kruman, *Beyond Authority,* 65–76. On South Carolina's notorious malapportionment, see Nevins, *American States,* 1, 96, 133, 174, 192, 200–1; Jackson Turner Main, *The Antifederalists: Critics of the Constitution, 1781–1788* (1961), 22–23.

91. Pa. Const. (1776), sec. 17; N.Y. Const. (1777), arts. V, XVI.

92. My assessment of Senate apportionment thus differs from Professor Rakove's, as I elaborate in n. 110 below.

93. *Farrand's Records,* 1:534, 578–79 (Mason), 533, 583 (Morris), 584 (Madison), 605 (Wilson).

94. See *Elliot's Debates,* 2:27 (Parsons), 49 (Dana), 51 (King), 3:367 (Madison), 4:71–72 (Steele); *Farrand's Records,* 2:241. Note that Tench Coxe did assume the existence of equipopulous districts and assured his readers that "no decayed or venal borough" such as "old Sarum" would exist. Coxe, "An Examination (III, IV)," in Ford, *Pamphlets,* 143, 153 n. *. In 1964, the Warren Court, per Justice Black, held that the Constitution required equipopulous congressional districts within a state, and that federal courts could properly enforce this constitutional mandate. See *Wesberry v. Sanders,* 376 U.S. 1 (1964). Though the Court based this decision solely on the language of Article I—House members must be chosen by "the People of the several States"—such a reading is hard to defend on the basis of Founding-era sources and understandings, as the second Justice Harlan's dissenting opinion made clear. As we shall see in Chapter 10, a more defensible basis for the modern Court's result in *Wesberry* involves the reconstruction of Founding-era apportionment rules and understandings in the Fourteenth Amendment.

95. *Farrand's Records,* 1:132–33 (Wilson, who also said that representation was necessary "only because it is impossible for the people to act collectively"), 561 (Paterson), 562 (Madison, who said that representatives "ought to vote in the same proportion in which their citizens would do, if the people of all the States were collectively met").

96. On euphemism regarding the proslavery clauses, see ibid., 588 n. * (Carroll), 595 (Wilson), 2:415–16 (Mason and Morris), 3:210 (Martin); *Elliot's Debates,* 4:102, 176 (Iredell).

97. *Farrand's Records,* 1:201 (Gerry), 561 (Paterson), 2:220 (King), 221–23 (Morris and Dayton).

98. See, e.g., Joel Tiffany, *A Treatise on the Unconstitutionality of American Slavery* (1849, reprint, 1969), 62–63; Frederick Douglass, "Glasgow Speech, Mar. 26, 1860," in Philip S. Foner, ed., *The Life and Writings of Frederick Douglass* (1950), 2:467–80. See generally William M. Wiecek, *The Sources of Antislavery Constitutionalism in America, 1760–1848* (1977), 273; Don E. Fehrenbacher, *The Slaveholding Republic: An Account of the United States Government's Relations to Slavery* (2001), 299.

99. Raymond T. Diamond, "No Call to Glory: Thurgood Marshall's Thesis on the Intent of a Pro-Slavery Constitution," *Vanderbilt LR* 42 (1989): 93, 112–13.

100. *Farrand's Records,* 2:222 (Morris). See also ibid., 1:561 (Paterson), 588 (Morris), 2:220 (King), 364, 3:211 (Luther Martin); "Essays of Brutus (III)," in *Storing's Anti-Fed.,* 2:379; *Elliot's Debates,* 2:226–27 (Melancton Smith).

101. Virginia's numbers do not include Kentucky, which was admitted as a separate state in mid-1792—before the general House expansion pursuant to the first census.

102. Fehrenbacher, *Slaveholding Republic,* 40. For earlier scholarship emphasizing the proslavery aspects of the three-fifths clause, see generally Donald L. Robinson, *Slavery in the Structure of American Politics, 1765–1820* (1971); Wiecek, *Sources of Antislavery,* 62–83; William M. Wiecek, "The Witch at the Christening: Slavery and the Constitution's Origins," in Levy and Mahoney, eds., *Framing,* 167–84; Paul Finkelman, "Slavery and the Constitutional Convention: Making a Covenant with Death," in Beeman et al., eds., *Beyond Confederation,* 188–225; Diamond, "No Call to Glory," 93. For an effort to play down the significance of slavery in this clause, see Howard A. Ohline, "Republicanism and Slavery: Origins of the Three-Fifths Clause in the United States Constitution," *WMQ* 28 (1971): 563.

103. *Farrand's Records,* 2:222 (Morris); *Elliot's Debates,* 4:283 (C. C. Pinckney). Cf. ibid., 31 (Davie).

104. To be specific, Georgia and Kentucky would each have lost one of their two seats; Maryland two of its eight, North Carolina two of its ten; South Carolina, two of its six; and Virginia six of its nineteen. On the other side of the

Mason-Dixon Line, New York's inability to count her twenty thousand slaves (at three-fifths) would have dropped her from ten to nine seats.

105. See, e.g., *Farrand's Records,* 1:500 (Bedford), 561 (Morris), 578 (Mason), 584–86 (Madison), 595 (King), 604–5 (Morris), 2:9–10 (Madison), 3:187 (Martin); *Elliot's Debates,* 3:102, 347, 359 (Nicholas), 4:276–77 (Rutledge), 283 (C. C. Pinckney), 5:108 (Madison's letter to Randolph, April 8, 1787); David Ramsay, "An Address to the Freemen of South Carolina on the Subject of the Federal Constitution," in Ford, *Pamphlets,* 375; *Annals,* 1:899 (Madison, Sept. 4, 1789). Cf. *Farrand's Records,* 3:501 (Grayson). See generally Staughton Lynd, "The Compromise of 1787," *Political Science Qtly.* 81 (1966): 225–50; Drew R. McCoy, "James Madison and Visions of American Nationality in the Confederation Period: A Regional Perspective," in Beeman et al., eds., *Beyond Confederation,* 226–58.

106. See Wiecek, *Sources of Antislavery,* 144–48.

107. The data here are all drawn from Stanley B. Parsons, William W. Beach, and Dan Hermann, comps., *United States Congressional Districts, 1788–1841* (1978). For a powerful analysis of regional variation within the antebellum South, see William W. Freehling, *The Road to Disunion: Secessionists at Bay, 1776–1854* (1990). See also Virginia Const. (1830), art. III, sec. 6 (apportioning state congressional districts via three-fifths formula).

108. Merrill D. Peterson, ed., *Democracy, Liberty, and Property: The State Constitutional Conventions of the 1820's* (1966), 277, 324–25 (discussing arguments of Benjamin Watkins Leigh and quoting arguments of Abel P. Upshur at the Virginia convention of 1829–30); *Proceedings and Debates of the Virginia State Convention of 1829–1830* (1830; reprint 1971), 1:75, 115, 126–27, 163–64 (Upshur, Morris, Scott, and Leigh).

109. For states counting slaves at three-fifths, see N.C. Const. (1776), amend. art. 1, sec. 1, para. 2 (1835) (house of commons proportioned by "Federal population"—that is, the three-fifths formula); Md. Const. (1776), amend. sec. 10 (1837) (house of delegates based on "federal numbers"); Fla. Const. (1838/45), art. IX, secs. 1–2 (both houses). For states counting slaves at five-fifths, see La. Const. (1845), title II, art. 15 (Senate); La. Const. (1852), title II, arts. 8, 15 (both house and senate); Md. Const. (1851), art. III, sec. 3 (house of delegates).

110. Professor Rakove thus oversimplifies when he argues that it "was not, after all, the three-fifths clause that gave southern states the leverage they needed to keep the Union safe for slavery, but rather the Senate." *Original Meanings,* 93. This false dichotomy overlooks various ways in which the three-fifths clause itself fed back into the antebellum Senate's composition, via the clause's indirect effects on slave-state legislative apportionment and slave-state abolition policy. (Remember, any slave state that pursued a policy of abolition plus emigration would end up losing House seats. Slave states thus faced actual

disincentives to become free states.) And, as Garry Wills has shown, the three-fifths clause powerfully influenced presidential elections and presidential territorial policies—policies that in turn surely helped shape the long-run composition of the Senate. Additionally, Wills points to certain proslavery congressional policies—including the 1840 gag rule and the 1854 Kansas-Nebraska Act—where the three-fifths skew in the House proved decisive. Garry Wills, *"Negro President": Jefferson and the Slave Power* (2003), 219–20, 225.

It also bears emphasis that when the Constitution was adopted, Senate equality was generally thought to favor New England, given the strong expectation that population would flow southward in the years ahead—an expectation that Rakove himself stresses. *Original Meanings,* 54, 72, 77, 91. Thus, Rakove's point about the Senate as it came to operate in the early-to-mid-1800s is best understood as one of history's many ironies, rather than as a serious argument that *in the 1780s,* Senate equality was somehow more predictably vicious than the three-fifths clause. On the Senate as a proslavery institution in the late antebellum era, see Barry R. Weingast, "Political Stability and Civil War: Institutions, Commitment, and American Democracy," in Robert H. Bates et al., *Analytic Narratives* (1998), 148–93.

111. Fehrenbacher, *Slaveholding Republic,* 47. For Fehrenbacher's magisterial account of slavocracy in the Taney era, see Don E. Fehrenbacher, *The Dred Scott Case: Its Significance in American Law and Politics* (1978).

3: CONGRESSIONAL POWERS

1. *Blackstone's Comm.,* 1: *166–67. For subsequent judicial discussion, see *Williamson v. United States,* 207 U.S. 425, 436–46 (1908); *Gravel v. United States,* 408 U.S. 606, 614 (1972). For analysis of *Williamson*'s reliance on Blackstone's treatise, whose language changed as new editions came out in the late 1760s through the early 1780s, see Akhil Reed Amar and Neal Kumar Katyal, "Executive Privileges and Immunities: The Nixon and Clinton Cases," *Harvard LR* 108 (1995): 701, 710 & n. 43.

2. Thomas Jefferson, *A Manual of Parliamentary Practice* (2d ed. 1812), sec. III, reprinted in Wilbur Samuel Howell, ed., *Jefferson's Parliamentary Writings: "Parliamentary Pocket-Book" and A Manual of Parliamentary Practice* (1988), 360. See also Story, *Commentaries,* 2:325–28, secs. 856–62.

3. 1 W. & M., ch. 2, sec. 9 (1689); Articles of Confederation, art. V, cl. 5. Mass. Const. (1780), pt. I, art. XXI; N.H. Const. (1784), pt. I, art. XXX; Vt. Const. (1786), ch. 1, art. XVI. For an engaging general discussion, see Zachariah Chafee, *Three Human Rights in the Constitution* (1956), 4–89.

4. Wilson, *Works,* 1:421.

5. See Leonard W. Levy, *Emergence of a Free Press* (1985), 14–15.

6. See, for example, statements from Noah Webster, Ellsworth, Hamilton, Wilson, Randolph, Hugh Williamson, Richard Dobbs Spaight, Iredell, and the

two Pinckneys, cited in Akhil Reed Amar, *The Bill of Rights: Creation and Reconstruction* (1998), 326 n. 78.

7. *Annals,* 1:453–54 (June 8, 1789), 4:934 (Nov. 26, 1794).

8. *Elliot's Debates,* 4:569, 575–76.

9. See *New York Times v. Sullivan,* 376 U.S. 254, 273–76, 282–83 (1965). For scholarly commentary on the *Sullivan* case, and/or on the conceptual inter-linkage between the Constitution's two speech clauses, see Alexander Meiklejohn, *Political Freedom: The Constitutional Powers of the People* (1960), 34–36; Alexander Meiklejohn, "The First Amendment is an Absolute," *Supreme Court Rev.* (1961): 245, 256; Harry Kalvin, Jr., "The New York Times Case: A Note on 'The Central Meaning of the First Amendment,' " *Supreme Court Rev.* (1964): 91.

10. *Blackstone's Comm.,* 1:*164–66.

11. Resolutions of the Continental Congress, October 14, 1774, *JCC,* 1:69; Allan Nevins, *The American States During and After the Revolution, 1775–1789* (1924), 62–63, 85; Edmund S. Morgan, *The Challenge of the American Revolution* (1976), 3–42, esp. 23–25; Jack P. Greene, "Origins of the American Revolution," in Leonard W. Levy and Dennis J. Mahoney, eds., *The Framing and Ratification of the Constitution* (1987), 36–53.

12. 6 Geo. 3, ch. 12 (emphasis added).

13. For the financial details of 1781, I have relied on Leonard W. Levy, "Introduction: American Constitutional History, 1776–1789," in Levy and Mahoney, eds., *Framing,* 7. A rather less dire view of Confederation finances is presented in Merrill Jensen, *The New Nation* (1950). In 1786, New York sank a proposed amendment to the Articles of Confederation that would have allowed the union to levy an impost on certain items. For evidence and analysis suggesting that this rejection operated as a major factor precipitating the Philadelphia Convention, see Robert A. Feer, "Shays's Rebellion and the Constitution," *New England Qtly.* 42 (1969): 388, 390, 397, 398, 401, 402, 409, 410. See also E. James Ferguson, "What Were the Sources of the Constitutional Convention?" in Gordon S. Wood, ed., *The Confederation and the Constitution* (1979), 12; Jack N. Rakove, "The Road to Philadelphia, 1781–1787," in Levy and Mahoney, eds., *Framing,* 107.

14. Cf. Frederick W. Marks III, *Independence on Trial: Foreign Affairs and the Making of the Constitution* (1973), 45 ("the international law of this time regarded consistent failure to pay debts as a just cause for armed intervention by the creditor nation").

15. See, e.g., *United States v. Lopez,* 514 U.S. 549 (1995); *United States v. Morrison,* 529 U.S. 598 (2000). For a particularly narrow view of congressional power under this clause, see *Lopez,* 514 U.S. 584–602 (Thomas, J., concurring). For prior scholarship generally supportive of the Thomas approach, see Richard A. Epstein, "The Proper Scope of the Commerce Power," *Virginia LR* 73 (1987): 1387; Raoul Berger, "Judicial Manipulation of the Commerce

Clause," *Texas LR* 74 (1996): 695. For a somewhat broader view that nevertheless insists that the clause applies only to interstate *economic* matters, see
Grant S. Nelson and Robert J. Pushaw, "Rethinking the Commerce Clause:
Applying First Principles to Uphold Federal Commercial Regulation but
Preserve State Control Over Social Issues," *Iowa LR* 85 (1999): 1. None of
these interpretations comes to grips with the basic inadequacy of a purely
economic reading of "commerce" in relation to Indian tribes.

16. *OED* entry on "commerce." Note that my textual argument here is not that
"Commerce" *must* be read to apply beyond economic matters, but only that it
may properly be read this way, if constitutional context and structure so warrant.

17. *Farrand's Records,* 2:321, 493.

18. Imagine, for example, a situation in which one state's regulation of upstream
land created adverse effects for residents of downstream states. Federal
power over admiralty jurisdiction would not necessarily cover such a case if
the stream were non-navigable. On the international front, imagine a
transnational incident that called for a domestic federal-law solution as distinct from an international agreement, compact, or treaty.

19. If a broad interpretation of "Commerce" were rejected, a similar result could
be reached, albeit more roundaboutly, by reading Article I's necessary-and-
proper clause in tandem with Article III's diversity clauses. Under Article III,
section 2, federal judicial power permissibly extended to any controversy,
whether or not economic, between the governments and/or citizens of diverse states, and between Americans and foreigners. Just as the necessary-
and-proper clause has been read to allow Congress to enact substantive
federal laws to govern all Article III admiralty proceedings, so, too, this clause
could be read to allow Congress to legislate whenever an altercation spilled
across state or national lines—whenever, in Article III's phrasing, a "Contro-
vers[y]" arose "between" interstate or international parties. For analysis of
the Article III admiralty clause as a font of congressional power, see Note,
"From Judicial Grant to Legislative Power: The Admiralty Clause in the
Nineteenth Century," *Harvard LR* 67 (1954): 1214. Although Article III's diversity clauses differed from its admiralty provisions in some respects—see,
e.g., Henry J. Friendly, "In Praise of *Erie,* and of the New Federal Common
Law," *N.Y.U. LR* 39 (1964): 383—these clauses could likewise be read to permit Congress to step in whenever states cannot agree amongst themselves
and/or foreigners are involved.

20. *Farrand's Records,* 1:164 (C. C. Pinckney and Madison), 172 (Wilson).

21. Ibid., 165.

22. See *Federalists* Nos. 33, 44; *Elliot's Debates,* 2:537–38 (McKean).

23. *McCulloch v. Maryland,* 17 U.S. (4 Wheat.) 316, 408, 407 (1819). As Washington's biographer, Marshall was acutely aware that the lack of funds during
the Revolution had imperiled the war effort both by increasing the risk of

outright British success on the battlefield and also by making the continental army more vulnerable to desertion and mutiny.

24. For a thoughtful analysis, see William W. Van Alstyne, "The Role of Congress in Determining Incidental Powers of the President and of the Federal Courts: A Comment on the Horizontal Effect of the Sweeping Clause," *Law & Contemporary Problems* 40 (Spring 1976): 102.

25. *Blackstone's Comm.,* 1:*267; compare Bernard Bailyn, *The Origins of American Politics* (1968), 25, 69; Forrest McDonald, *The American Presidency: An Intellectual History* (1994), 106–7.

26. See *Blackstone's Comm.,* 1:*273, *275–76, *277–79, 2:*405–7, 4:*159.

27. Nevins, *American States,* 19. On the traditional right of English monarchs to fix the legislative meeting place, see Edward Dumbauld, *The Constitution of the United States* (1964), 96.

28. *McCulloch,* 17 U.S. 316, 421. For an intriguing, if occasionally overexuberant, effort to revive a focus on propriety and pretext, see Gary Lawson and Patricia B. Granger, "The 'Proper' Scope of Federal Power: A Jurisdictional Interpretation of the Sweeping Clause," *Duke LJ* 43 (1993): 267.

29. *Elliot's Debates,* 3:453, 598–99.

30. Ibid., 4:286 (Pinckney), 102 (Iredell); *Annals,* 1:1523–24 (March 23, 1790) (report).

31. Joint Resolution of March 2, 1861, 12 Stat. 251.

32. *Farrand's Records,* 2:509 (Sherman).

33. By English tradition dating back to the Mutiny Act of 1689, Parliamentary authorization of military-discipline law and military funding lapsed annually, obliging the monarch to summon Parliament every year if he wanted to keep up an army. But nothing would have prohibited a particularly pliant Parliament (which had to come before the electorate only on a septennial basis) from creating a standing authorization of a standing army. See *Blackstone's Comm.,* 1:*414–15; Story, *Commentaries,* 3:73–74, sec. 1185.

34. *Federalist* Nos. 28 (Hamilton), 46 (Madison).

35. Ibid., No. 28.

36. At one point in the drafting debates, Gouverneur Morris moved to name these three states in the importation clause, but he withdrew his motion after George Mason suggested it might "give offence to the people of those States." *Farrand's Records,* 2:415–16.

37. Ibid., 1:592 (C. C. Pinckney) ("S. Carola. has in one year exported the amount of £600,000 Sterling all of which was the fruit of the labor of her blacks. . . . He hoped a clause would be inserted in the system restraining the Legislature from . . . taxing Exports").

38. *Elliot's Debates,* 3:453–54 (Madison); *Farrand's Records,* 2:375 (Ellsworth). For other references to the omission of this clause as a possible deal-breaker, see ibid., 364–65, 371–74, 559 (remarks of both Pinckneys, John Rutledge, and Roger Sherman).

39. Scholars have disagreed about the precise significance, or lack thereof, of Shays's Rebellion on the events leading up to and beyond the Philadelphia Constitution. For a smattering of views, see Feer, "Shays's Rebellion"; David Szatmary, *Shays' Rebellion: The Making of an Agrarian Insurrection* (1980), 120–34; Richard D. Brown, "Shays's Rebellion and the Ratification of the Federal Constitution in Massachusetts," in Richard Beeman et al., eds., *Beyond Confederation: Origins of the Constitution and American National Identity* (1987), 113–27; Bruce Ackerman, *We the People: Transformations* (1998), 44–46. In this book, I have not featured this rebellion as a major causal force driving the Constitution of 1787–88. As Robert Feer notes, many of the leading Federalists of the late 1780s, concerned as they were about the union's general imbecility in financial matters and foreign affairs, had voiced the need for a major overhaul of the Articles of Confederation long before the Massachusetts insurrection broke out. Conversely, the Philadelphia delegate who spoke out most about the Rebellion, Elbridge Gerry, ended up opposing the Constitution; several other leaders who had helped put down the rebellion, such as New York's George Clinton and Samuel Adams, also ultimately opposed the Constitution or joined the Federalist cause rather late. Rhetorically, it was awkward for leading Federalists to invoke the insurrection as conclusively evidencing the need for a continental reform that would use the Massachusetts Constitution as a major template for the new federal Constitution. After all, leading Anti-Federalists could and did counter that the rebellion confirmed the orthodox view that geographically extended governments, such as the Appalachian-straddling regime in Massachusetts, were particularly vulnerable to breakdown of the sort evidenced by the Rebellion. Also, as Brown has demonstrated, the officialdom's strong response to the Rebellion ultimately generated a backcountry backlash that tended to work against ratification of the Philadelphia plan in Massachusetts, and perhaps elsewhere. For an illuminating geostrategic perspective on the Rebellion, see Marks, *Independence on Trial,* xi–xiv, 102–5.

40. *Federalist* No. 28.

41. Abraham Lincoln, Special Session Address, July 4, 1861; *Ex parte Merryman,* 17 F. Cas. 144 (C.C. Md. 1861) (Case No. 9487). For more discussion of Lincoln's actions, with special emphasis on the legal propriety of disobeying a lower court ruling alleged to have been made without jurisdiction, see Daniel Farber, *Lincoln's Constitution* (2003), 115–43, 157–63, 188–92. A somewhat more skeptical view of Lincoln's activities may be found in J. G. Randall, *Constitutional Problems Under Lincoln* (1926), 118–39. See also Chapter 4.

42. *Federalist* No. 44; "Vices of the Political System of the U. States," in Madison, *Papers,* 9:349; *Farrand's Records,* 2:26 (Morris).

43. *Federalist* Nos. 10, 44; Madison to Jefferson, March 19, 1787, in Madison, *Papers,* 9:318.

44. Madison to Jefferson, October 17, 1788, in Madison, *Papers,* 11:297.

45. See, e.g., *Fletcher v. Peck,* 10 U.S. (6 Cranch) 87, 138 (1810). A long line of Supreme Court case law has applied the Bill of Attainder clauses to prohibit what English law referred to as "bills of pains and penalties"—that is, legislative enactments singling out a person or persons by name for some form of disfavored treatment short of capital punishment, such as banishment, deprivation of the right to vote, loss of liberty or property, or extreme humiliation. See generally *Cummings v. Missouri,* 71 U.S. (4 Wall.) 277, 323 (1866); *United States v. Lovett,* 328 U.S. 303, 315–18 (1946); *United States v. Brown,* 381 U.S. 437, 441–42 (1965). The great weight of scholarly commentary has endorsed this approach; see, e.g., Story, *Commentaries,* 3:209–11, sec. 1338; Laurence H. Tribe, *American Constitutional Law* (2d ed. 1988), 641–56; Chafee, *Three Human Rights,* 149–55; Note, "The Bounds of Legislative Specification: A Suggested Approach to the Bill of Attainder Clause," *Yale LJ* 72 (1965): 330 (authored by John Hart Ely). For a (somewhat cranky) dissenting view, which fails to give due weight to structural considerations alongside textual and historical evidence, see Raoul Berger, "Bills of Attainder: A Study of Amendment by the Court," *Cornell LR* 63 (1978): 355, 356. For additional elaboration of my own views on the deep structure of the attainder clauses, see Akhil Reed Amar, "Attainder and Amendment 2: *Romer's* Rightness," *Michigan LR* 95 (1996): 203.

46. For bans on ex post facto laws, see Del. Const. (1776), Declaration of Rights, sec. 11; Md. Const. (1776), Declaration of Rights, art. XV; N.C. Const. (1776), Declaration of Rights, art. XXIV; Mass. Const. (1780), pt. I, art. XXIV; N.H. Const. (1784), pt. I, art. XXIII. For various prohibitions of bills of attainder, see Md. Const. (1776), art. XVI; N.Y. Const. (1777), art. XLI; Mass. Const. (1780), pt. I, art. XXV; see also Vt. Const. (1786), ch. II, art. XVII.

47. For an engaging exploration of honor and dishonor in the Founding era, see Joanne B. Freeman, *Affairs of Honor: National Politics in the New Republic* (2001).

48. Adams to Gerry, April 23, 1784, in Henry A. Cushing, ed., *Writings of Samuel Adams* (1968), 4:301; Gordon S. Wood, *The Radicalism of the American Revolution* (1991), 241.

49. *Federalist* Nos. 39 (Madison), 84 (Hamilton). Note also that Jefferson's famous 1784 plan for Western lands had provided that Western governments "shall be in republican forms, and shall admit no person to be a citizen who holds any hereditary title." *JCC,* 26:119, 227 (March 1 and April 23, 1784). For more discussion, see Chapter 7.

4: America's First Officer

1. *Farrand's Records,* 2:135, 152, 167, 171.

2. See generally the sources cited in Chapter 2, nn. 57–58. See also Forrest McDonald, *E Pluribus Unum: The Formation of the American Republic, 1776–1790* (2d ed. 1979), 38, 62, 69, 228, 237.

3. For a gripping account of a moment when the machinery of continuity almost broke down, threatening to leave America leaderless, see Bruce Ackerman's forthcoming book, *America on the Brink*.

4. As was common at the outset of an incoming presidential administration, the Senate was in session in early and mid-March to advise and consent to the new president's cabinet nominations and to transact other Senate business. The full Congress, including the newly elected House of Representatives, was not scheduled to meet until the end of the year.

Some modern critics have faulted Lincoln for not summoning Congress into session immediately upon his inauguration. However, until secessionists actually began bombarding Sumter on April 12, Lincoln could hardly be certain that the crisis would ripen into armed conflict. (To avoid provocation, Lincoln had refrained from sending any fresh troops or additional ammunition to the besieged garrison and in early April gave notice to Southern officials of his intent merely to resupply the fort with foodstuffs.) See generally David M. Potter, *Lincoln and His Party in the Secession Crisis* (rev. ed. 1962), 358–74. Also, few leaders in early 1861 anticipated that the military conflict begun at Sumter would last as long or cost as much in blood and treasure as it ultimately did. The two-and-a-half-month lag between Lincoln's April 15 call and the July 4 meeting conformed to the general pattern established by the only previous occasions when presidents had called the full Congress into special session. In late March 1797 President John Adams had summoned Congress to meet in mid-May; in May 1837 President Van Buren had triggered a special session to begin in September; and in mid-March 1841 President Harrison had ushered Congress to an emergency session to begin on May 31. (In August 1856, as a sitting Congress rose to adjourn, President Pierce told lawmakers to remain for a special session to commence three days later—a very different situation than gathering representatives from across the continent for their first meeting.)

5. Lincoln to Matthew Birchard and others, June 29, 1863; Forrest McDonald, *The American Presidency: An Intellectual History* (1994), 401.

6. In 1861 Congress enacted a blanket law retrospectively blessing Lincoln's previous actions, and in 1863 Congress enacted a forward-looking statute authorizing presidential suspensions of habeas corpus under certain conditions. Act of Aug. 6, 1861, ch. 63, sec. 3, 12 Stat. 326; Act of March 3, 1863, ch. 81, 12 Stat. 755. An argument can also be made that Lincoln's suspension of habeas was warranted by militia laws on the books in early 1861; see Dan Farber, *Lincoln's Constitution* (2003), 164; but cf. Edward S. Corwin, *The President: Office and Powers, 1787–1957* (4th rev. ed. 1957), 139.

7. For instance, the recess-appointments clause defined the precise expiration dates for such appointments and specified the scope of the Senate's shared role. For more discussion, see Chapter 5.

8. See Henry P. Monaghan, "The Protective Power of the Presidency," *Columbia LR* 93 (1993): 1.

9. Among the broader provisions, see, e.g., N.Y. Const. (1777), art. XVII; N.J. Const. (1776), art. VIII; Md. Const. (1776), art. XXXIII; S.C. Const. (1778), art. XI.

10. With its Hydra-headed executive council, Revolutionary Pennsylvania presented a unique case. What if an executive quorum could not be mustered in an emergency? In early 1777 the Continental Congress had felt obliged to help plug an apparent vacuum in the state's executive authority in order to secure public safety in a crisis. See Richard B. Morris, *The Forging of the Union, 1781–1789* (1987), 64. Morris quotes the reaction of Continental Congressman James Duane, upon being informed that the state executive council had adjourned for a month: "Executive adjourned, say you, how is this possible?" Ibid., 123.

11. The linguistic variation among the early states tracked variations in colonial usage; see *OED* entry on "president."

12. *Maclay's Journal*, 24.

13. See Allan Nevins, *The American States During and After the Revolution, 1775–1789* (1924), 173–74; Adams, *FAC*, 68–70.

14. For a related suggestion, crediting Rutledge's fellow South Carolinian Charles Pinckney with the initial impetus behind the word "President," see Charles C. Thach, Jr., *The Creation of the Presidency, 1775–1789* (rev. ed. 1969), 108–17. Although Pinckney did not sit on the drafting Committee of Detail, he did submit a plan to the committee featuring the word "President"; see *Farrand's Records*, 2:135, 3:606.

15. *Annals,* 1:36 (May 14, 1789), 331–32 (May 11, 1789); *Maclay's Journal,* 1–43, esp. pp. 24, 27, 28.

16. We might also wonder why the debate over the executive title was so much less extensive at the Philadelphia Convention than in the First Congress. One possible answer: Washington himself was in the room at Philadelphia, making extended debate in that venue more awkward. Also, John Adams—who smiled upon grander titles—presided over the congressional debate but had been absent from the Philadelphia deliberations.

17. *Maclay's Journal,* 10, 28.

18. Ibid., 10–11; *Annals,* 1:332 (May 11, 1789).

19. Ibid., 333–34 (May 11, 1789).

20. *Maclay's Journal,* 4, 9, 25; *Annals,* 1:332 (May 11, 1789) (Tucker).

21. The first major override, of the Reconstruction Congress's landmark Civil Rights Act, occurred in April 1866. For discussion of this notable event, see Chapter 10, p. 362. Prior to that, Congress had overridden six relatively inconsequential bills—the first dealing with revenue cutters and steamers (on the last full day of Tyler's presidency, in March 1845) and the other five deal-

ing with a cluster of internal improvements in 1856 (during the Pierce Administration). For a relatively comprehensive list of early vetoes, see Edward Campbell Mason, *The Veto Power: Its Origin, Development and Function in the Government of the United States (1789–1889)* (rev. ed. 1967), 141–207.

22. The other two states with longer executive terms were Delaware (three years) and South Carolina (two years). See Adams, *FAC,* 328–31.

23. Two states, New Hampshire and Vermont, currently elect governors biannually. In a handful of other states, a gubernatorial veto may be overridden by special legislative majorities less than two-thirds. *The Book of the States* (2002), 34:104–5, 161–62.

24. See, e.g., *Federalist* No. 15 ("Regard to reputation has a less active influence when the infamy of a bad action is to be divided among a number than when it is to fall singly upon one"); No. 63 ("A sense of national character . . . can never be sufficiently possessed by a numerous and changeable body. It can only be found in a number so small that a sensible degree of praise and blame of public measures may be the portion of each individual; or in an assembly so durably invested with public trust that the pride and consequence of its members may be sensibly incorporated with the reputation and prosperity of the community"); No. 74 ("the sense of responsibility is always strongest in proportion as it is undivided").

25. For more information on the other two nonannual states (Maryland and Virginia), see p. 144. For details on all the states, see Adams, *FAC,* 328–31.

26. *Book of the States,* 73, 161–62.

27. Ga. Const. (1789), art. II, sec. 10; Ky. Const. (1792), art I, sec. 28; N.H. Const. (1792), pt. II, sec. XLIV. All three provided that a veto could be overridden by a two-thirds vote of each house. In 1799, a new Kentucky constitution provided for override by a majority of the entire number of elected legislators (as opposed to a majority of those voting) in each house. Ky. Const. (1799), art. II, sec. 25.

28. The six embracing independent election were Vermont, New Hampshire, Pennsylvania, Delaware, Kentucky, and Tennessee. Georgia and South Carolina—the two most southern—were the outliers here. As for longer executive terms, the two outliers were the two most northern states, New Hampshire and Vermont. In 1799, Kentucky eliminated gubernatorial reeligibility. Ky. Const. (1799), art. III, sec. 3. Between 1810 and 1862, every one of the seventeen new states entering the union gave its governor a veto pen and an independent electoral base. In Illinois, this pen was at first shared with a council of revision; override procedures varied across the states, as did gubernatorial election rules. For details, see John A. Fairlie, "The Veto Power of the State Governor," *APSR* 11 (1917): 473.

29. Military language laced Madison's brief notes of this first day, with various references to "General" Washington, "Col. Hamilton," and "Major Jack-

son." *Farrand's Records,* 1:3–4. For an early reference to "Mr. President," see, e.g., ibid., 1:29 (May 30, 1787, Journal entry).

30. See generally Frederick W. Marks III, *Independence on Trial: Foreign Affairs and the Making of the Constitution* (1973).

31. In a nutshell, this paragraph distills my answer to Professor Wood, who has provocatively argued that "the new national government framed in 1787 went way beyond what the weaknesses of the Articles demanded. . . . The new Constitution of 1787 therefore cannot be explained by the obvious and generally acknowledged defects of the Articles of Confederation." Gordon S. Wood, *The Making of the Constitution* (1987), 14. See also Gordon S. Wood, *The Creation of the American Republic, 1776–1787* (1969), 474–75 ("the new national government . . . was not . . . meant merely to save the Union, for strengthening the Confederation along the lines of the New Jersey plan could have done that"). I suggest that while Wood is right to emphasize the importance of the state experience alongside the federal in the 1780s, the big story may be somewhat simpler than the one he has told. In Wood's epic narrative, the federal Constitution aimed centrally at fixing broken state constitutions. Madison's ideas and certain provisions of Article I, section 10 loom large in this telling. In my narrative, whether or not the federal Constitution aimed to *cure* the problems that existed locally, it had to *avoid repeating* the flaws of imbalance that state constitutions had exemplified. That is, widespread Federalist dissatisfaction with state constitutions helps explain why the federal Constitution created a more balanced central-government structure, and why the Philadelphia Convention could not accept the imbalanced New Jersey plan. Madison—who was indeed obsessed by the failures of state government—pushed for a stronger version of Article I, section 10 and a congressional veto of all state laws, but he did not succeed in getting all that he wanted at Philadelphia. Apart from certain admittedly important provisions of Article I, section 10, much of the Constitution that was adopted (as distinct from the one Madison dreamed about) can indeed be explained as a response to the "weaknesses of the Articles" in a manner that avoided replicating the evident weaknesses of the state governments. For a critique of Wood on somewhat similar grounds, and Wood's spirited reply, see his exchange with Shlomo Slonim in "Forum: The Founders and the States," *Law and Hist. Rev.* 16 (1998): 527.

32. *Farrand's Records,* 1:97.

33. See Steven G. Calabresi and Christopher S. Yoo, "The Unitary Executive During the First Half-Century," *Case Western Reserve LR* 47 (1997): 1474–75.

34. See also *Elliot's Debates,* 4:103–4 (Davie), 315 (C. C. Pinckney).

35. Ibid., 2:448 (Wilson) ("Being elected by the different parts of the United States, he . . . will watch over the whole" and in considering whether to sign or veto laws "will have before him the fullest information" including "official

communications, foreign and domestic"); 3:499 (Nicholas) (president would have "no local views, being elected by no particular state, but [by] the people at large"); 4:120 (Davie) ("the President, . . . being elected by the people of the United States at large, will have their general interest at heart"); *Federalist* No. 68 (successful candidate for presidency would need to have "the esteem and confidence of the whole Union"); No. 75 (describing the president as "the constitutional representative[ ] of the nation"). At Philadelphia, Gouverneur Morris had spoken of the president as "the general Guardian of the National interests." *Farrand's Records,* 2:541.

36. Another longtime secretary of state, Henry Clay, perennially contended for the presidency. Also, Daniel Webster had sought the presidency before his two stints as secretary of state. For a recent meditation on the political significance of yet another longstanding secretary of state, Timothy Pickering, see Garry Wills, *"Negro President": Jefferson and the Slave Power* (2003).

37. The military accomplishments of some of the post-Polk generals placed them well below the heroic heights attained by the pre-Polk generals. For example, General Pierce was no General Jackson on the battlefield. Nevertheless, Pierce's "most notable national service had been as a brigadier in the Mexican War." Stephen Skowronek, *The Politics Presidents Make: Leadership from John Adams to Bill Clinton* (rev. ed. 2002), 180.

38. See Chapter 2, n. 53.

39. *Farrand's Records,* 1:426. For Gerry's counterargument that such a long Senate term "would never be adopted by the people," see ibid., 425.

40. Cf. ibid., 2:283 (Charles Pinckney "hoped to see that body [the Senate] become a School of Public Ministers, a nursery of Statesmen").

41. Cf. Corwin, *President,* 14; Arend Lijphart, *Parliamentary Versus Presidential Government* (1992), 11–12.

42. *Federalist* No. 69; see also *Elliot's Debates,* 4:74 (Iredell).

43. See, e.g., *Farrand's Records,* 3:216 (Luther Martin); *DHRC,* 3:426 (Benjamin Gale, Nov. 12, 1787, Connecticut town meeting).

44. Retirements within the four-year terms, by contrast, have come to be viewed very differently—appropriate only in cases of disability or disgrace.

45. Jefferson to Vermont legislature, Dec. 10, 1807, quoted in Corwin, *President,* 332. In 1787, Jefferson had complained to both Adams and Madison that the Article II four-year clause would in practice degenerate into a system of de facto life tenure. See Jefferson to Adams, Nov. 13, 1787, in Jefferson, *Papers,* 12:351 ("He may be reelected from 4. years to 4. years for life. Reason and experience prove to us that a chief magistrate, so continuable, is an officer for life"); Jefferson to Madison, Dec. 20, 1787, in ibid., 12:441 ("The power of removing him every fourth year by the vote of the people is a power which will not be exercised").

46. Winston S. Churchill, *Triumph and Tragedy* (1953), 586–87.

47. In 1798, when war with France loomed on the horizon, President Adams

asked the retired Washington to lead America's army. Washington agreed, but then insisted that Hamilton be made second in command. When Adams balked, Washington threatened to resign. Though perhaps intemperate, Washington acted within his rights. He had not asked to lead the army, and was willing to withdraw; but he was not willing to accept military responsibilities without having the staff members of his own choice to help him. For various accounts, see Leonard D. White, *The Federalists: A Study in Administrative History* (rev. ed. 1964), 243–47; James Thomas Flexner, *George Washington: Anguish and Farewell (1793–1799)* (1972), 4:391–412; David McCullough, *John Adams* (2001), 507, 510–13; Stanley Elkins and Eric McKitrick, *The Age of Federalism* (1993), 599–606.

48. One note on terminology: The Constitution itself nowhere uses the phrase "electoral college," nor did the men of the late 1780s. As this phrase is now customary usage, I freely use it in this book.

49. *Farrand's Records,* 2:500. But see ibid., 512, 523 (Gouverneur Morris challenging this assumption).

50. This tally counts as "small" those states with less than the average (mean) state population. (The result turns out to be the same whether we use free population or total population as the relevant baseline in the antebellum era.) To see the point from a different angle, note that if the presidential electoral system were genuinely well structured to avoid disfavoring small-state candidates, we should expect that in any given presidential election, the winner should be as likely to hail from one of the many smaller states comprising half of the nation's total (free) population as from one of the few largest states comprising the other half. Using this (different) measure of state size, over the course of many elections, half the winners should be small-state men, half big-state men. Yet of the fifty-three presidential elections held since 1787, small-state men have won only ten times, while big-state men have won a whopping thirty-four times. (On nine occasions, the winner's home state straddled the 50 percent dividing line.)

51. In 1876–77, Congress once again played an important role in deciding a presidential election, but not by balloting for president, as occurred in 1801 and 1825. Rather, the 1877 Congress resolved the status of certain disputed state electoral votes and declared that Rutherford Hayes had won a first-heat electoral-college majority.

52. For general explanations of this effect—an example of what political scientists refer to as "Duverger's Law"—see Maurice Duverger, *Political Parties* (1951), Barbara North and Robert North, trans. (2d ed. 1962), 216–28; V. O. Key, *Politics, Parties, and Pressure Groups* (1952), 224–31; Anthony Downs, *An Economic Theory of Democracy* (1957), 114–25; Doug Rae, *The Political Consequences of Electoral Laws* (1967), 95–96.

53. The idea of a North-South balance within the federal executive branch surfaced both early and late at Philadelphia. See, e.g., *Farrand's Records,* 1:113–14

(George Mason's endorsement of an executive triumvirate composed of representatives of "Northern," "Middle," and "Southern" states); 66 n. 9, 92 (similar views by Randolph); 2:537 (Mason's proposal for six-man subpresidential executive council, with two representatives apiece from "Eastern," "middle," and "Southern" states); 639 (Mason's reiteration of a regionally balanced executive council).

54. Ibid., 1:486.

55. Ibid., 2:31.

56. In 1788–89, four out of ten states chose electors by popular vote, either at large or by districts; four others gave legislatures free rein, and two states used mixed systems. The biggest shift to popular election occurred in 1804, precisely at the time of the adoption of the Twelfth Amendment. In 1800, five of sixteen states allowed voters to choose electors directly; in 1804, eleven of seventeen did so. See Neal R. Peirce and Lawrence D. Longley, *The People's President: The Electoral College in American History and the Direct Vote Alternative* (1981), 247.

57. *Farrand's Records,* 2:31 (Mason), 501 (Baldwin and Wilson).

58. For the specifics, see Peirce and Longley, *People's President,* 247–49.

59. Adams, *FAC,* 316, 322, 325–26.

60. *Farrand's Records,* 2:122, 248–49 (C. C. Pinckney), 249 (Rutledge).

61. For other Federalist discussion of this issue, see ibid., 1:290–91, 300 (Hamilton), 2:109–11 (Madison), 500 (Morris), 3:390 (C. Pinckney in Senate), 394 (Morris in 1802); *Elliot's Debates,* 2:512 (Wilson), 3:486 (Randolph), 4:104–5, 304–5, 315 (Davie, Spaight, and C. C. Pinckney); Noah Webster, "An Examination into the Leading Principles of the Federal Constitution," in Ford, *Pamphlets,* 25, 35, 37; "Letters of Fabius by John Dickinson (II)," in ibid., 171–72. For Anti-Federalist anxiety about the threat of foreign influence over American presidential elections, see *Elliot's Debates,* 3:220 (Monroe), 484 (Mason), 490 (Grayson).

62. Ibid., 2:512 (Wilson).

63. As did similar language in *Federalist* Nos. 60, 64, and 69.

64. *Elliot's Debates,* 3:494. See also ibid., 502 (Nicholas, similar).

65. Ibid., 2:511 (Wilson), 3:494 (Madison).

66. *Federalist* No. 68.

67. For useful correctives, see, e.g., Paul Finkelman, *Slavery and the Founders: Race and Liberty in the Age of Jefferson* (2d ed., rev. ed. 2001), 6–22; Donald L. Robinson, *"To the Best of My Ability": The Presidency and the Constitution* (1987), 82–83; Wills, *"Negro President,"* 1–13, 50–61. See also Shlomo Slonim, "The Electoral College at Philadelphia: The Evolution of an Ad Hoc Congress for the Selection of a President," *J. of Am. Hist.* 73 (1986): 35.

68. *Farrand's Records,* 1:68–69 (Wilson), 2:29, 52–54 (Morris), 2:55–56 (King and Wilson).

69. Ibid., 56–57 (Madison).

70. Ibid., 111. On Madison's assumptions about future population growth, see Chapter 2, nn. 105, 110.

71. *Farrandi Records* 2:32. In the vote following Williamson's remarks, only Pennsylvania supported direct popular election of the continental executive; see ibid.

72. Don E. Fehrenbacher, *Constitutions and Constitutionalism in the Slaveholding South* (1989), 54.

73. To be sure, electors could have been chosen in (malapportioned) districts rather than via statewide elections, but a district system would have weakened the state's overall clout compared to sister states following winner-take-all rules. For comprehensive data on state methods of elector selection, see Peirce and Longley, *The People's President,* 247–49.

74. "Letters from the Federal Farmer (XIV)," in *Storing's Anti-Fed,* 2:307, 312.

75. Tench Coxe, "An Examination of the Constitution (I)," in Ford, *Pamphlets,* 133, 137–38.

76. "Observations Upon the Proposed Plan of Federal Government, April 2, 1788," (attributed to "A Native of Virginia"), reprinted in *DHRC,* 9:655, 679.

77. I omit from this tally sons who died before their fathers became president.

78. Dorothy Twohig, ed., *The Papers of George Washington: Presidential Series* (1987), 2:162–63. This passage was later deleted, perhaps on the advice of James Madison. Special thanks to Gordon S. Wood for kindly bringing this passage to my attention.

79. For Boston, see "To the Citizens of the United States," in *Independent Chronicle,* Oct. 31, 1796, 2; McCullough, *John Adams,* 462. For Pennsylvania, see Noble E. Cunningham, Jr., ed., *The Making of the American Party System, 1789–1809* (1965), 150 (reprinting broadside of Oct. 3, 1796) (emphasis altered). In a forceful letter of July 29, 1791, to Jefferson, Adams himself denied that he had ever advocated hereditary government for independent America. McCullough, *John Adams,* 431.

80. Gordon S. Wood, *The Radicalism of the American Revolution* (1991), 84, 48.

81. Ibid., 48.

82. Peter E. Russell, *His Majesty's Judges: Provincial Society and the Superior Court in Massachusetts, 1692–1774* (1990), 52. In 1771, the province's highest court included John Cushing III—whose father John Cushing II had sat on the court and whose son William Cushing would follow suit; Chief Justice Benjamin Lynde, Jr., whose father, Benjamin Lynde, Sr., had also been chief; and Foster Hutchinson, whose older brother Thomas Hutchinson was the former chief justice and acting governor. Ibid., 141–42, 146–47, 164, 167–68, 176.

83. Va. Const. (1776), Declaration of Rights, sec. 4.

84. Md. Const. (1776), Declaration of Rights, art. XL ("no title of nobility, or

hereditary honours, ought to be granted in this State"); N.C. Const. (1776), Declaration of Rights, art. XXII ("no hereditary emoluments, privileges or honors ought to be granted or conferred in this State").

85. N.H. Const. (1784), pt. I, art. IX.

86. Mass. Const. (1780), pt. I, art. VI. Adams here evidently borrowed from the language of George Mason's first draft of the Virginia Bill of Rights of 1776, whose final version omitted Mason's concluding language condemning hereditary officeholding as "unnatural and absurd." See Wood, *Radicalism,* 181.

87. On "corruption of blood," see *Blackstone's Comm.,* 2:*254–56.

88. See Chapter 2, n. 36–38.

89. For a somewhat similar musing, see Corwin, *President,* 35. Cf. *Farrand's Records,* 2:101 (Williamson: President "will spare no pains to keep himself in for life, and will then lay a train for the succession of his children").

90. This tally counts only biological children born in wedlock and still alive at the time of the end of the president's term. Thus, the childless presidents were Washington, Madison, Jackson, Polk, Pierce, and Buchanan; the daughters-only presidents were Jefferson and Monroe; and the presidents with at least one son were John Adams, John Quincy Adams, Van Buren, Harrison, Tyler, Taylor, Fillmore, Lincoln, Johnson, and Grant. Of the childless presidents, only Pierce ended his tenure with an unsuccessful bid for another term. Note that although Grant stepped down in the 1876 election, he sought a third (nonconsecutive) term in 1880; see Chapter 12.

   The tally may be somewhat misleading in the case of Jackson, who adopted his wife's nephew shortly after birth and gave him the name Andrew Jackson, Jr. However, the improvident young Jackson was very far from being a potential political successor. It is also worth noting that many presidents who lost their bids for a second term might well have declined to seek a third; the composite data presented here reflect not only the resignation decisions made by presidents, but also the choices made by the American people, who would appear to have been rather more reluctant to give second terms to presidents with sons.

91. For example, a child born abroad of American parentage would be eligible, so long as the citizenship rules in place at the time of his birth so provided. See generally Jill A. Pryor, Note, "The Natural-Born Citizen Clause and Presidential Eligibility: An Approach for Resolving Two Hundred Years of Uncertainty," *Yale LJ* 97 (1988): 881.

92. For the First Congress, see Chapter 2, p. 70. The first Court's six members included the Scottish-born James Wilson and the English-born James Iredell. In the early cabinet, Alexander Hamilton had emigrated from the West Indies, Albert Gallatin from Switzerland, George Washington Campbell from Scotland, Alexander Dallas from Jamaica, and James McHenry from Ireland.

93. Robert Morris was born in England; Pierce Butler, Thomas Fitzsimons, James McHenry, and William Paterson were Irish-born; Wilson came from Scotland; and Hamilton from the West Indies. Also, William Davie, a Philadelphia delegate who was not present at the signing, was born in England.

94. See Richard Krauel, "Prince Henry of Prussia and the Regency of the United States, 1786," *AHR* 17 (1911): 44–51. See also Louise Burnham Dunbar, *A Study of "Monarchial" Tendencies in the United States, from 1776 to 1801* (1922), 54–75; William M. Wiecek, *The Guarantee Clause of the U.S. Constitution* (1972), 42–50.

95. Max Farrand, *The Framing of the Constitution of the United States* (1913), 173–75; Max Farrand, *The Fathers of the Constitution: A Chronicle of the Establishment of the Union* (1921), 134. See also *Farrand's Records,* 3:72–73 (Martin), 73–74 (extract from the Pennsylvania Journal), 80–81 (Sydney).

96. Ibid., 73–74 (extract from the Pennsylvania Journal). See also Farrand, *Framing,* 173. For details on the newspapers that ran this item in mid-August, see Richard B. Bernstein with Jerome Agel, *Amending America* (1993), 345 n. 1.

97. On the apparent link between this clause and American fears of monarchy and aristocracy, see Charles Gordon, "Who Can Be President of the United States: The Unresolved Enigma," *Maryland LR* 28 (1968): 1, 5. See also Wiecek, *Guarantee Clause,* 43 ("The subject of an American monarchy . . . aroused a latent xenophobia in many otherwise levelheaded Americans because it seemed that aliens had been most forward in proposing quasi-monarchial schemes"). Cf. Act of Jan. 29, 1795, 4 Stat. 414, which required an alien seeking to become a naturalized citizen to expressly renounce any "hereditary title" or "order of nobility." For background discussion, see *Annals,* 4:1033–40 (Jan. 1, 1795).

98. Only New York and Virginia lacked religious tests in 1787. (In 1788, the New York legislature added a test.) Connecticut and Rhode Island did impose political exclusions on religious grounds, but their Crown charters did not mandate these exclusions. In the state constitutions, see Mass. Const. (1780), pt. II, ch. VI, art. 1; N.H. Const. (1784), pt. II (unnumbered paras. beginning "Provided, nevertheless, That no person . . . ," "All persons qualified to vote . . . ," and "The President shall be chosen . . ."); Pa. Const. (1776), sec. 10; N.J. Const. (1776), art. XIX; Del. Const. (1776), art. 22; Md. Const. (1776), Declaration of Rights, arts. XXXV–XXXVI; N.C. Const. (1776), art. XXXII; S.C. Const. (1778), arts. III, XII, XIII; Ga. Const. (1777), arts. VI, XIV–XV, XXIV.

99. Delaware, Georgia, and South Carolina eliminated their religious qualifications; Pennsylvania softened its requirements; and New Hampshire did not change. A dramatic change also occurred in Vermont, whose 1786 constitution required lawmakers to affirm their belief in "one God, . . . the Old and New Testament[s] . . . and . . . the Protestant religion" but whose 1793/6 constitution omitted all this. See Vt. Const. (1786), ch. II, sec. XII.

100. Corwin, *President,* 61.

101. Mass. Const. (1780), pt. II, ch. II, art. III; N.Y. Const. (1777), art. XX. The constitutions of Delaware, Virginia, and North Carolina all mentioned inability, and Georgia mentioned sickness. See Del. Const. (1776), art. 7; Va. Const. (1776) (unnumbered para. beginning "A Privy Council . . ."); N.C. Const. (1776), art. XIX. None of these three states gave chief executives particularly broad powers or an independent electoral base.

102. Va. Const. (1776), Declaration of Rights, art. IV; N.C. Const. (1776), Declaration of Rights, art. III. See also Mass. Const. (1780), pt. 1, art. VI ("consideration of services rendered to the public"); N.H. Const. (1784), pt. I, art. X ("not for the private interest or emolument of any one man, family or class of men").

103. *Farrand's Records,* 2:535. For the subsequent history of this clause at Philadelphia, see ibid., 599 n. 23, 626.

104. *Elliot's Debates,* 3:487–88.

105. Act of Mar. 1, 1792, 1 Stat. 239, 240. Madison's criticisms were nicely summarized in a February 21, 1792, letter to Edmund Pendleton:

> 1. It may be questioned whether these are *officers,* in the constitutional sense. . . . 3. As they are created by the Constitution, they would probably have been there designated if contemplated for such a service, instead of being left to Legislative selection. 4. Either they will retain their *legislative* stations, and their incompatible functions will be blended; or the incompatibility will supersede those stations, & then those being the substratum of the adventitious functions, these must fail also. The Constitution says, Congs. may declare *what officers* &c. which seems to make it not an appointment or a translation; but an annexation of one office or trust to another office. The House of Reps. proposed to substitute the Secretary of State, but the Senate disagreed, & there being much delicacy in the matter it was not pressed by the former.

See Madison, *Papers,* 14:235–36.

106. *Farrand's Records,* 2:573 (emphasis added), 599.

107. Other clauses confirm the distinction between federal legislators on the one hand and officers of the United States on the other. Article II provided in the alternative that "no Senator or Representative, or Person holding an Office . . . under the United States" could be a presidential elector. Likewise, the Article VI oath clause contradistinguished "Senators and Representatives" from "all executive and judicial Officers . . . of the United States."

108. An even earlier precedent was set in the Washington Administration, where for a time Treasury Secretary Hamilton actually ran the War Department as well while Secretary Henry Knox was away for an extended period. See McDonald, *American Presidency,* 227.

109. Thus Madison's letter italicized the words *"what officers,"* and explained that

the Constitution envisioned "not an appointment" of a person to the position of acting president but rather "an annexation of one office or trust to another office." See Madison to Edmund Pendleton, Feb. 21, 1792, in Madison, *Papers,* 14:236.

110. For additional arguments that Madison was constitutionally right and the 1792 Act was constitutionally wrong, see Akhil Reed Amar and Vikram David Amar, "Is the Presidential Succession Law Constitutional?" *Stanford LR* 48 (1995): 113. Several other recent scholars have also tended to side with Madison; see, e.g., Steven G. Calabresi, "The Political Question of Presidential Succession," *Stanford LR* 48 (1995): 155. For a more agnostic view, see John F. Manning, "Not Proved: Some Lingering Questions About Legislative Succession to the Presidency," *Stanford LR* 48 (1995): 141. For earlier scholarly commentary, see Ruth C. Silva, "The Presidential Succession Act of 1947," *Michigan LR* 47 (1949): 451; Ruth C. Silva, *Presidential Succession* (1951); John D. Feerick, *From Failing Hands: The Story of Presidential Succession* (1965).

111. Madison to Edmund Pendleton, Feb. 21, 1792, in Madison, *Papers,* 14:236.

112. Act of Jan. 19, 1886, 24 Stat. 1; 3 U.S.C. 19.

5: Presidential Powers

1. Coronation Oath Act (1689), 2 W. & M. ch. 6. See also *Blackstone's Comm.,* 1:*234–36.

2. See Pa. Const. (1776), sec. 10 ("I do believe in one God. . . ."); Del. Const. (1776), art. 22 ("I . . . do profess faith in God the Father. . . ."); Ga. Const. (1777), art. XXIV ("so help me God"); Mass. Const. (1780), pt. II, ch. VI, art. I ("I believe the Christian religion," and "So help me, God"); N.H. Const. (1784), pt. II (unnumbered paras. beginning "I, A. B. do truly . . ." and "I, A. B. do solemnly . . .")("So help me God"). Note that the textual applicability of Pennsylvania's oath to state executive officials was somewhat unclear.

3. Coronation Oath Act (1689), 2 W. & M. ch. 6.

4. Ibid.

5. Act of June 25, 1798, 1 Stat. 570. For Jefferson's objections, see Kentucky Resolves of Nov. 10, 1798, para. 9, in *Elliot's Debates,* 4:542–43.

6. On expectations for the president at the Founding, see generally James W. Ceaser, *Presidential Selection: Theory and Development* (1979), 41–87; Ralph Ketcham, *Presidents Above Party: The First American Presidency, 1789–1829* (1984); Jeffrey K. Tulis, *The Rhetorical Presidency* (1987), 29–55. On inaugural addresses, see ibid., 51, 180.

7. In its very first statute, the First Congress codified rules for administering the Article VI oath, thereby confirming the importance of oaths in the Founding era. See Act of June 1, 1789, 1 Stat. 23.

8. *Elliot's Debates,* 2:446 (Wilson) (emphasis deleted).

9. For Franklin's suggestion, see *Farrand's Records,* 1:81–85. For Washington's

declared willingness to forego a salary, see *Senate Journal,* 1:20 (April 30, 1789). Though Ames's specific remark was directed at compensation for the vice president, the republican point obviously applied to the president as well; see *Annals,* 1:674 (July 16, 1789). For more discussion, see David P. Currie, *The Constitution in Congress: The Federalist Period, 1789–1801* (1997), 32–34; Forrest McDonald, *The American Presidency: An Intellectual History* (1994), 215. In his final Annual Message to Congress, Dec. 7, 1796, Washington himself declared that sufficient salaries for federal officers were necessary because "it would be repugnant to the vital principles of our government, virtually to exclude from public trusts, talents and virtue, unless accompanied by wealth." *Senate Journal,* 2:299 (Dec. 7, 1796). For the statute setting the president's salary, see Act of Sept. 24, 1789, 1 Stat. 72.

10. *Farrand's Records,* 1:21. Note the use of the juristic word "Magistracy" to describe the executive, a common mode of expression and thought in 1787.

11. As Dr. Franklin tartly observed early in the Philadelphia proceedings, "It was true the King of G.B. had not . . . exerted his negative since the [Glorious] Revolution: but that matter was easily explained. The bribes and emoluments now given to the members of parliament rendered it unnecessary, everything being done according to the will of the Ministers." Ibid., 1:99. Other monarchical tools obviating resort to the veto included dissolutions of Parliament and threatened expansions of the House of Lords.

12. McDonald, *American Presidency,* 115–16; Bernard Bailyn, *The Origins of American Politics* (1968), 71, 72 n. 19, 114–16, 155.

13. Recall, in this context, Franklin's discussion of how the game was played in colonial Pennsylvania; see Chapter 2, p. 62.

14. Mass. Const. (1780), pt. II, ch. II, sec. I, art. XIII. Unlike Article II, Massachusetts failed to insulate sitting governors from the tantalizing temptation of immediate pay increases. The legislature might "enlarge[]" (though not diminish) gubernatorial salaries with no clear rule that the increase could only go into effect in subsequent gubernatorial terms.

15. Allan Nevins, *The American States During and After the Revolution, 1775–1789* (1924), 219; J. H. Benton, Jr., *The Veto Power in the United States: What is it?* (1888), 42–43 n*.

16. *Annals,* 3:539 (April 5, 1792).

17. Under Article I, section 7, a president would ordinarily have ten days (excepting Sundays) to decide whether to sign a bill into law, to allow it to become a law without his signature, or to veto it by returning it to Congress for reconsideration and possible override. If, however, he received a bill at the end of a legislative session at a time when he could not return it to Congress, he might prevent its enactment simply by withholding his signature— putting the bill in his "pocket," so to speak.

18. See generally Edward Campbell Mason, *The Veto Power: Its Origin, Development and Function in the Government of the United States (1789–1889)* (1890),

142–50. For various views of the early veto power, see Carlton Jackson, *Presidential Vetoes: 1792–1945* (1967); Robert J. Spitzer, *The Presidential Veto: Touchstone of the American Presidency* (1988); Charles L. Black, Jr., "Some Thoughts on the Veto," *Law & Contemporary Problems* 40 (1976): 87; Nolan McCarty, "Presidential Vetoes in the Early Republic" (unpublished manuscript).

19. Similarly, certain instances of post-enactment executive review might prevent hard-to-reverse effects of a statute from ever occurring. Some distinguished scholars have suggested that the very existence of the constitutional veto option negates a president's authority of executive review—the power to decline to enforce a duly enacted statute he deems unconstitutional. See, e.g., Edward S. Corwin, *The President: Office and Powers, 1787–1957* (4th rev. ed. 1957), 66. This suggestion ignores basic differences between the veto and executive review. A president's veto is in key respects far broader. For example, it can be used purely on policy grounds, while executive review can only be used to resist an *unconstitutional* law. Moreover, a veto, if successful, prevents a bill from ever becoming a law; executive review does not. Because of its breadth, the veto is subject to important counterbalances—primarily the possibility of override. Executive review is subject to its own counterbalances. Because executive review does not erase a law from the statute books (nor does judicial review, for that matter), in some situations the law itself might be effectively revived if a successor president (or a successor Court in the case of judicial review) does not share its predecessor's constitutional doubts. To put the general point another way: No one should think that if a president vetoes a criminal law and the veto is overridden, he somehow may not properly pardon those who violate the law. The pardon power, the executive review power, and the veto power are overlapping yet distinct. Each has its own unique logic and set of counterbalances.

20. *McCulloch v. Maryland,* 17 U.S. (4 Wheat.) 316, 401–02 (1819). For a less idealistic account of Washington's signing of the bank bill, see McDonald, *American Presidency,* 231–32.

21. *Register of Debate,* 22–1:76 App. (July 10, 1832).

22. The views I present today are well within the mainstream of this debate. In the case law, a relatively robust reading of the Executive Article vesting clause may be found in Chief Justice Taft's classic opinion for the Court in *Myers v. United States,* 272 U.S. 52 (1926). On the other side stands the canonical concurrence of Justice Jackson in the famous steel-seizure case, which came close to denying that the vesting clause added any residuum beyond the later executive powers listed; *Youngstown Sheet & Tube Co. v. Sawyer,* 343 U.S. 579, 640–41 (1952). Several fine scholars have been inclined to side with Jackson. See, e.g., Corwin, *President,* 4; Lawrence Lessig and Cass R. Sunstein, "The President and the Administration," *Columbia LR* 94 (1994): 1, 47–48 & n. 195. But these scholars are unable to explain, textually, where the president

gets various powers that he has always exercised and that even these scholars generally concede he should exercise. To read out the vesting clause is thus to do one of three things: (1) Reject much of actual executive practice going back to George Washington, practice that made good constitutional sense when done and continues to make good sense. (2) Uphold various actions of Washington and Lincoln—and most other well-respected presidents—by stretching the enumerated list of executive powers beyond recognition. But what is gained by this? (3) Uphold actual practice by creating wholly non-textual doctrines. Again, what is gained thereby? For thoughtful moderate positions in this debate, which side with Hamilton in treating the vesting clause as a source of residual power but resist overly exuberant definitions of that residuum, see Henry P. Monaghan, "The Protective Power of Presidency," *Columbia LR* 93 (1993): 1; H. Jefferson Powell, *The President's Authority Over Foreign Affairs: An Essay in Constitutional Interpretation* (2002).

23. See generally *Federalist* Nos. 70–77.
24. *Blackstone's Comm.,* 1:*231.
25. The justices themselves made this clear in a notable 1793 exchange with the executive branch in which they declined to give the Washington Administration the informal legal advice it sought. See "Correspondence of the Justices (1793)," reprinted in Richard H. Fallon, Jr., et al., eds., *Hart and Wechsler's The Federal Courts and the Federal System* (5th ed. 2003), 78–79.
26. See Chapter 3, n. 41; Chapter 4, n. 4–6.
27. I offer more background and analysis of this provision in Akhil Reed Amar, "Some Opinions on the Opinions Clause," *Virginia LR* 82 (1996): 647.
28. Among the weak-executive states, see, e.g., Del. Const. (1776), art. 7 (legislative override); Md. Const. (1776), art. XXXIII (similar); N.C. Const. (1776), art. XIX (similar); Va. Const. (1776) (unnumbered para. beginning "A Governor, or chief magistrate, shall be chosen . . .") (similar); Ga. Const. (1777), art. XIX (suspensive power only); cf. N.J. Const. (1776), art. IX (postconviction pardon only, by decision of collective council); Pa. Const. (1776), sec. 20 (collective council, no executive pardon in cases of treason or murder). South Carolina made no mention of pardons. For the strong-executive states, see Mass. Const. (1780), pt. II, ch. II, art. VIII; N.Y. Const. (1777), art. XVIII. New Hampshire later copied the Massachusetts model; see N.H. Const. (1784), pt. II (unnumbered para. beginning "The power of pardoning offences . . .").
29. Article II did not give presidents general power to pardon crimes before they had occurred—a power of "dispensing with" and "suspending" laws that the English Parliament had pointedly denied the English Crown in the 1689 Bill of Rights. In the bloodless Whiskey Rebellion, Washington, via General Henry Lee, promised a general amnesty to insurrectionists willing to abandon their revolt. See Washington's Proclamation of July 10, 1795, reprinted in Phillip Kurland and Ralph Lerner, eds., *The Founders' Constitution* (1987),

4:20. Washington later pardoned the two men who were convicted of treason in the affair.

30. For evidence that the Confederation Congress's "executive" powers were part of the baseline for the executive powers vested in the presidency, see *Farrand's Records,* 1:21 ("besides a general authority to execute the National laws, it [the national executive] ought to enjoy the Executive rights vested in Congress by the Confederation"). See also "Letters from the Federal Farmer (X)," in *Storing's Anti-Fed.,* 2:284 ("the present Congress is principally an executive body"). For additional evidence that Article II "executive Power" was understood early on to vest the president with a residuum of authority to conduct foreign affairs, see Saikrishna B. Prakash and Michael D. Ramsey, "The Executive Power over Foreign Affairs," *Yale LJ* 111 (2001): 231; Powell, *President's Authority.* For a somewhat more restrained reading of that residuum, see Harold Hongju Koh, *The National Security Constitution: Sharing Power After the Iran-Contra Affair* (1990), 76.

31. For general background, see Charles Warren, "The Mississippi River and the Treaty Clause of the Constitution," *George Washington LR* 2 (1934): 271. For a nice elaboration of Madison's decisive geostrategic argument that the Mississippi crisis had been caused by the Confederation's weakness and that the solution was thus to bolster the central government so that it could deal with Spain from a position of strength, see Lance Banning, "Virginia: Sectionalism and the Common Good," in Michael Allen Gillespie and Michael Lienesch, eds., *Ratifying the Constitution* (1989), 261–99, esp. 266, 275–76, 282–83, 288.

32. See, e.g., *Elliot's Debates,* 3:347, 499–500 (Madison and George Nicholas); cf. *Farrand's Records,* 2:541 (Gerry), 543 (Williamson, Spaight, King); see also ibid., 4:58. In practice, the Senate would seem the most apt interpreter and enforcer of this boundary. If a majority of the Senate deems a simple statute sufficient, then a statute suffices. If, instead, a majority of the Senate deems a treaty necessary above and beyond a statute, it can decline to support a statute in the absence of a supplementary treaty. Cf. Bruce Ackerman and David Golove, "Is NAFTA Unconstititutional?" *Harvard LR* 108 (1995): 799, 920.

33. As Hamilton explained in his influential *Pacificus* No. 1 essay:

> The President is the constitutional EXECUTOR of the laws. Our Treaties, and the laws of Nations form a part of the law of the land. He, who is to execute the laws must first judge for himself of their meaning. In order to the observance of that conduct, which the laws of nations combined with our treaties prescribed to this country, in reference to the present War in Europe, it was necessary for the President to judge for himself whether there was any thing in our treaties incompatible with an adherence to neutrality.

> Hamilton, *Papers,* 15:43. For more discussion, see generally Prakash and Ramsey, "The Executive Power over Foreign Affairs"; Powell, *President's Authority.*

The president's unilateral authority (for domestic-law purposes) to declare a treaty inoperative in the case of a foreign breach or the demise of a foreign government should not be confused with the power to simply disregard a treaty that the president no longer likes—to abrogate in any and all cases. Abrogation power in a case of breach or demise (or some closely analogous situation) is best construed as *executing* a treaty under the explicit and implicit conditions of the treaty itself.

To understand why, consider the basic rules governing statutes. A statute that explicitly provides that its provisions may or must lapse whenever condition X arises is not violated—rather, it is honored—when X occurs and its provisions thereupon lapse. In general, the decision whether statutory condition X has in fact occurred is to be made not by the House or Senate but rather by the executive branch, subject to the possibility of judicial review. Cf. *INS v. Chadha,* 462 U.S. 919 (1983). See also pp. 63–64. A similar analysis applies to treaties, with the important difference that judicial review of the president's treaty-based determinations is apt to be especially deferential or even nonexistent in the case of certain types of treaties implicating various national-security issues or other matters beyond the judiciary's traditional areas of competence. If a treaty explicitly provides for its own termination upon the occurrence of event X, the president, and not the House or Senate, is the branch that determines whether X has in fact occurred. At least in the absence of some clear treaty language to the contrary, every treaty implicitly incorporates background rules of international law that permit the treaty to lapse in the event of substantial breach or the demise of one of the parties to it. Thus, when the French monarchy fell and Louis XVI was beheaded, President Washington properly determined for himself whether these events permitted the U.S. to declare its 1778 treaties with France as lapsed, and whether the U.S. should exercise this (implicit) treaty option if it in fact existed. A president might choose to involve the Senate (or the House or the cabinet or informal advisors) in making these and related sorts of determinations—as, for example, Franklin Pierce apparently chose to do in 1856—but is not obliged to do so. On Pierce, see David Gray Adler, *The Constitution and the Termination of Treaties* (1986), 172–73.

Adler and other scholars (including Arthur Bestor, whose work is discussed below) have argued that treaty termination must generally be symmetric to treaty formation, and that the Senate must thus play a role. There are many reasons to doubt the soundness of this argument in its strong form. First, true symmetry would involve not just the Senate and president, but also America's initial treaty partner. The result of such truly symmetric action would simply be a new, superseding treaty. (Just as a statute may generally repeal and supersede a previous statute, so may a later treaty supersede an earlier one.) But the fact that a new treaty can often supersede an old one does not mean that similar legal effect should follow from the actions of the president and Senate acting without a treaty partner. Outside the appointments-making context, joint formal action by the president and Senate alone is simply not contemplated by the Constitution: It is of zero legal effect; cf. *Chadha*. In other words, the Constitution simply does not recognize a special category of joint executive-Senate action in treaty abrogations; rather, the document provides for new treaties, new statutes, and unilateral executive actions, each of which has its own distinct logic and boundaries. (It also bears note that even in a new-treaty situation, the Senate's role is not quite equal to the president's. Prior to Senate ratification of the second treaty, the mere willingness of the foreign government to agree to new rules might well constitute a temporary waiver of its rights under the earlier treaty. So might various other forms of presidential agreements with foreign governments.)

Second, even after the Senate has given its advice and consent to a treaty, the final decision whether to ratify the treaty internationally is made by the president alone. Given this baseline fact, there is indeed a kind of symmetry (albeit not of the sort that Adler advocates) when a president acting alone deems a treaty no longer valid in cases of material breach or the juridical demise of America's treaty partner.

Third, the Adler approach, while (unsuccessfully) aiming to achieve symmetry between treaty making and treaty breaking, ends up creating large asymmetries between the Senate's two Article II advice-and-consent roles, involving treaties and appointments. A more satisfying interpretation of Article II would minimize this latter set of asymmetries: The president's unilateral abrogation power in cases of breach and demise would roughly parallel his unilateral power to remove top executive officers at will and lower-level executive officers for cause. In both situations, Senate advice and consent would properly apply to the initial creation of certain juridical facts (appointments and treaties) but not to their later undoing. In both situations, the president's unilateral authority to undo is best understood as encompassed by his general grant of executive power as informed and supplemented by other enumerated presidential powers.

Finally, it should be remembered that as American history has in fact unfolded, treaties have often been displaced by means other than joint presidential-Senate action; see Adler, *Termination,* 190. Thus, the Adler approach finds little support in Supreme Court case law—see *Goldwater v. Carter,* 444 U.S. 996 (1979)—and runs counter to the presidentialist view espoused by the *Restatement (Third) of the Foreign Relations of the United States* (1987), section 339.

34. See Corwin, *President,* 195–96, 435–46 n. 75. For one attempt to tally the data (informed by a general hostility to presidential unilateralism) see Adler, *Termination,* 149–90.

35. Act of July 7, 1798, 1 Stat. 578. For interpretations of this enactment, see *Bas v. Tingy,* 4 U.S. (4 Dall.) 37, 40–41 (1800); Corwin, *President,* 435 n. 75; Adler, *Termination,* 157.

36. Corwin, *President,* 436 n. 75.

37. See n. 33 above.

38. On Washington's independent post-advice-and-consent deliberation, see James Thomas Flexner, *George Washington: Anguish and Farewell (1793–1799)* (1972), 4:210 ("Washington had hoped to pass the buck. He would hold forth on the glories of legislative leadership, and then do what the Senate advised. But now that the treaty lay on his desk with the recommendation that he ratify, he could not bring himself to shirk what he felt was his responsibility. On July 21, Randolph wrote to Monroe, 'The President has not yet decided upon the final measure to be adopted by himself' "); Powell, *President's Authority,* 66 ("Washington hesitated over ratifying the treaty and then delayed promulgating it, even after word of Britain's acquiescence in the Senate's condition"). See also Story, *Commentaries,* 3:371–72, sec. 1517, ("although the president may ask the advice and consent of the senate to a treaty, he is not absolutely bound by it; for he may, after it is given, still constitutionally refuse to ratify it"). For the need for broad presidential discretion over negotiations in cases calling for "perfect SECRECY and immediate DESPATCH," see *Federalist* No. 64. For the analogous recognition that "the Senate can make no treaties; they can approve of none unless the President . . . lays it before them" and the recognition that in this sense the senators were "only auxiliaries to the President," see *Elliot's Debates,* 2:466, 477 (Wilson). Note also that Washington negotiated treaties without prior legislative consultation; see Koh, *National Security,* 78; Stanley Elkins and Eric McKitrick, *The Age of Federalism* (1993), 396–97. For a narrow view of presidential authority that would seem to call much of this Washingtonian practice into question, see Arthur Bestor, "Respective Roles of Senate and President in the Making and Abrogation of Treaties—The Original Intent of the Framers of the Constitution Historically Examined," *Washington LR* 55 (1979): 1. Putting aside questions of text, structure, function, and practice—where Bestor's wooden legal arguments leave much to be desired—even his history may be questioned. For example, he omits the role of the vesting clause in the great removal debate of 1789 and fails to appreciate that the Confederation Congress was itself a collective *executive* body. His reading of the tea leaves from the secret Philadelphia Convention is also questionable. For a more nuanced account, see Jack N. Rakove, "Solving a Constitutional Puzzle: The Treaty-making Clause as a Case Study," in *Perspectives in American History,* n.s. 1 (1984): 233.

39. For a balanced and informative general account of the appointments process as it has taken shape and evolved, see Michael J. Gerhardt, *The Federal Appointments Process: A Constitutional and Historical Analysis* (2000).

40. On Washington's views, see his letter to Eleanor Francois Elie, May 25, 1789, in Washington, *Writings,* 30:334 (emphasis added). For early statutes structuring executive offices, see Act of July 27, 1789, 1 Stat. 28, 29 (secretary of foreign affairs—later renamed secretary of state); Act of Aug. 7, 1789, 1 Stat. 49, 50 (secretary of war); Act of Sept. 2, 1789, 1 Stat. 65, 67 (secretary of treasury). Cf. Act of Sept. 24, 1789, 1 Stat. 73, 93 (attorney general). Although the attorney general was not made the head of a department, and nothing in the authorizing statute addressed the removal issue explicitly, he was brought within the sweep of the Article II opinions clause and thus made wholly subordinate to the president. See also Act of Aug. 7, 1789, 1 Stat. 50, 53 (recognizing presidential removal power over territorial officers); Act of Sept. 22, 1789, 1 Stat. 70 (creating postmaster general "to be subject to the direction of the President"). For Madison's remarks, see *Annals,* 1:480–81 (June 16, 1789). For evidence that Madison's invocation of the Article II vesting clause as a font of power was part of a much larger pattern of understanding in the first years of the Washington Administration, see generally Powell, *President's Authority.* For the early track record of presidential removal of non-cabinet officers, see Steven G. Calabresi and Christopher S. Yoo, "The Removal Power: The Unitary Executive During the First Half-Century," *Case Western Reserve LR* 47 (1997): 1451.

On the other side of the ledger, it should be noted that in *Federalist* No. 77, Hamilton/Publius had suggested in passing that the Senate would play a symmetric advice-and-consent role in both appointments and removals. This suggestion has not prevailed in the court of history, or the Supreme Court for that matter. During Reconstruction, Congress enacted the Tenure of Office Act, which purported to require senatorial consent to certain cabinet firings. When President Andrew Johnson nevertheless unilaterally removed Secretary of War Edwin Stanton, Congress proceeded to impeach Johnson. The president was ultimately acquitted, and in *Myers v. United States,* 272 U.S. 52 (1926), Chief Justice Taft, speaking for the Court, pronounced the Tenure of Office Act unconstitutional, a ruling that the Court has repeatedly reiterated in subsequent case law.

41. Thus, early presidents, beginning with Washington, claimed broad supervisory authority over a geographically dispersed corps of federal prosecutors, and at times issued binding instructions to these subordinate executive officers. For example, on March 13, 1793, Washington wrote William Rawle, the U.S. attorney for the district of Pennsylvania, "instruct[ing]" Rawle to "enter a Nolle prose qui on the indictment aforesaid." Washington, *Writings,* 32:386. See generally Leonard D. White, *The Federalists: A Study in Administrative History* (1961), 31 n. 15, 408 & n. 10. Calabresi and Yoo, "Removal Power," 1483–84.

42. More precisely, the Senate thwarted more than 10 percent (three of twenty-eight) of the pre-1830 nominations to the Supreme Court, while rejecting none of the sixty-plus cabinet nominations in this period.

43. On Washington's appointments, see White, *Federalists,* 262, 278. On the appointment of John Quincy Adams, see *Senate Executive Journal,* 1:242 (May 31, 1797). On the nomination of Smith, see ibid., 357, 384 (Dec. 8, 1800, and Feb. 21, 1801); David McCullough, *John Adams* (2001), 520, 563; White, *Federalists,* 251, 278–80. For brief accounts of the Senate's role in reviewing Adams's nomination of another in-law, Joshua Johnson, see *Senate Executive Journal,* 1:350–51 (Apr. 28–May 5, 1800); White, *Federalists,* 280. Adams also appointed his nephew by marriage, William Cranch, to the federal bench; see Sydney H. Aronson, *Status and Kinship in the Higher Civil Service: Standards of Selection in the Administrations of John Adams, Thomas Jefferson, and Andrew Jackson* (1964), 148–49; McCullough, *John Adams,* 563.

44. Thus, in August 1789, the Senate declined to confirm President Washington's nomination of Benjamin Fishbourn to a naval post in Georgia; apparently, the appointment did not meet with the approval of the Georgia senators; see Corwin, *President,* 73; White, *Federalists,* 87 n. 44, 259. Two weeks later, the Senate declined to approve another Georgia candidate for a different post (as a commissioner to negotiate with the Indians of Georgia); once again the Senate as a whole in effect delegated its collective veto to the Georgia delegation. McDonald, *American Presidency,* 221.

45. Under the "inferior Officers" track, Congress could, for example, allow courts to pick subordinate clerks and magistrates, a cabinet officer to select his deputy, and the president to name his immediate staffers—all without Senate confirmation. In each case, the appointing entity was expected to supervise and take responsibility for the actions of its "inferior" officer. For more discussion, see Akhil Reed Amar, "Intratextualism," *Harvard LR* 112 (1999): 747, 804–12.

46. See George Washington to James Madison, May 5, 1789, in Washington, *Writings,* 30:310–11 ("As the first of every thing, *in our situation* will serve to establish a Precedent, it is devoutly wished on my part, that these precedents may be fixed on true principles").

47. See *Elliot's Debates,* 2:534, 538 (Thomas McKean) (The president who nominates is "the responsible person," in contrast to Pennsylvania's collective nomination system); Ibid., 480 (Wilson) (similar).

48. See *Farrand's Records,* 2:539 (Wilson) (favoring executive council "provided its advice should not be made obligatory on the President"). For additional sources and discussion, see generally Amar, "Opinions Clause." While some scholars have tried to point to the opinions clause as evidence of the weakness of the presidency as envisioned by the Founders, see, e.g., Lessig and Sunstein, "President," 32–38, this gets the matter precisely backward. Read in context, the opinions clause resoundingly affirmed that a president would not be saddled with a state-style executive council whom he would have to cajole. Cabinet officers would answer to the president, not vice versa.

49. *Elliot's Debates,* 4:110. See also James Iredell, "Answers to Mr. Mason's Objections to the new Constitution," in Ford, *Pamphlets,* 348.

50. Wilson, *Works,* 1:318–19.

51. For general analysis of the presidential-impeachment process, see Charles L. Black, Jr., *Impeachment: A Handbook* (1974); Michael J. Gerhardt, *The Federal Impeachment Process: A Constitutional and Historical Analysis* (2d ed. 2000). My own views on the topic may be found in Akhil Reed Amar, "On Impeaching Presidents," *Hofstra LR* 28 (1999): 291.

52. The Constitution did not explicitly specify whether disqualification would require a two-thirds vote or a simple majority. Twice in American history, the Senate has imposed disqualification—each time by simple a majority vote after a two-thirds vote to convict. Thoughtful commentators have raised serious questions about this practice; see Gerhardt, *Impeachment,* 77–79.

53. For the contrarian argument that the Constitution, rightly read, provided for Article III appellate review of the Senate's impeachment decisions, see Raoul Berger, *Impeachment: The Constitutional Problems* (1973), 108–26. In this Watergate-era book, Berger conceded that the Founders made "no express mention of judicial review . . . with respect to impeachment" and in fact pointedly shifted impeachment trials away from Article III courts. Ibid., 118–19, 121. Berger also seemed to admit that Article III appellate review of impeachments would run counter to what leading Federalists said about impeachment during the ratification process; see, e.g., *Federalist* No. 65. Nevertheless, Berger claimed that impeachments were covered by the general Article III language vesting federal courts with jurisdiction over "all Cases" arising under the Constitution. Berger, *Impeachment,* 116–18. Berger simply overlooked the limiting Article III words, "Law and Equity." Impeachment cases were neither strictly legal nor strictly equitable, but were rather a unique category—quasi-political/quasi-judicial proceedings purposefully removed from the general domain of Article III courts, just as the veto was a unique kind of quasi-executive/quasi-legislative power wielded by the president notwithstanding the general vesting clause of Article I. Nothing in the Constitution's text, history, or structure suggested any intent to allow direct appeals of impeachment to the Supreme Court (or any other court). Jurisdictional statutes have never so provided; nor has the Supreme Court (or any other court) ever purported to enjoy such an appellate jurisdiction over the High Court of the Senate.

Of course, an impeachment conviction might be challenged *collaterally* in a common-law or equitable proceeding—say, a mandamus case for reinstatement or a suit for salary due. In such a proceeding, an Article III court (or a state court, for that matter) might well have jurisdiction, but would generally be obliged to give res judicata effect to the impeachment court's judgment, so long as it could be said that the impeachment court truly had jurisdiction, regardless of the correctness of its substantive rulings (from a collateral court's viewpoint). Collateral review should be limited to cases in which the impeachment court plainly exceeded its limited jurisdiction, as might be the case, for example, if it purported to try a conceded non-officer, or impose a sentence other than removal and disqualification. When a house of Congress in good faith adjudicates the legal and factual issues concerning a would-be member's age, residence, or citizenship, these judgments should indeed be treated as res judicata because the Constitution explicitly makes each house the "judge" of such issues. So, too, the Senate is generally the judge of fact and law in impeachments. Cf. *Powell v. McCormack,* 395 U.S. 486, 521 n. 42 (1969); see generally *Nixon v. United States,* 506 U.S. 224, 237 (1993).

Elsewhere, Berger oddly argued that congressmen could be impeached because members of Parliament were impeachable in England; Berger, *Impeachment,* 224–33. But of course, in England even private persons were impeachable; and the Constitution plainly broke with this aspect of English law. Berger's argument on this point made a hash of constitutional text, structure, and precedent. Textually, only "Officers of the United States" are impeachable. Perhaps impeachment could properly extend to *former* officers who should be disqualified from future officeholding, but not to Congress members generally, who are not and cannot be "Officers of the United States," thanks to the Article I, section 6 incompatibility clause. Structurally, the Constitution provided for expulsion, not impeachment, of rotten federal lawmakers. And in the impeachment of Senator William Blount in the late 1790s, a majority of the Senate sitting as a high court of impeachment read the Constitution in just this way, rejecting contrary English practice. See generally Gerhardt, *Impeachment,* 48, 75–77.

54. *Farrand's Records,* 1:88, 230; 2:132, 186; *Elliot's Debates,* 3:500 (Madison); 4:126–27 (Iredell); *Annals,* 1:517 (Madison, June 17, 1789).

55. Although it has been suggested that Judge Pickering was charged with the technical crime of blasphemy, see Berger, *Impeachment,* 60 n. (summarizing the position taken by attorney Simon Rifkind), the word "blasphemy" nowhere appeared in the articles of impeachment. *Annals,* 13:318–22 (Jan. 4, 1804).

56. *Maclay's Diary* 166–67. For more discussion of a sitting president's implicit structural immunity from criminal prosecution, see generally Akhil Reed Amar, "On Prosecuting Presidents," *Hofstra LR 27* (1999): 671.

57. *Blackstone's Comm.,* 1:*244.

58. The veto numbers may be found in Mason, *Veto Power,* 141–55.

59. N.Y. Const. (1777), arts. XX, XXXIII; Mass. Const. (1780), pt. II, ch. I, sec. II, art. VIII.

60. The Philadelphia Convention explicitly considered and defeated a proposal

that would have obliged an impeached officer to step aside during his trial; see *Farrand's Records,* 2:612–13. In the Virginia ratifying debates, Madison appeared to suggest that Congress would have power to suspend an impeached president prior to conviction, but pointed to nothing in the Constitution's text to support this claim; see *Elliot's Debates,* 3:498.

6: Judges and Juries

1. Jay to John Adams, Jan. 2, 1801, in Henry P. Johnston, ed., *The Correspondence and Public Papers of John Jay* (1890), 4:285.
2. Chief justices who followed the Crown included New Hampshire's Theodore Atkinson, Massachusetts's Peter Oliver, New York's William Smith II, New Jersey's Frederick Smyth, Pennsylvania's William Allen, North Carolina's Martin Howard, South Carolina's Thomas Knox Gordon, and Georgia's Anthony Stokes. Although Virginia had no formal position of chief justice, the governor who presided over the colony's highest court, Lord Dunmore (John Murray), remained loyal to George III, as did Maryland's governor, Sir Robert Eden, who acted as the presiding chancellor in that colony's chancery court. (In Maryland, a separate common-law provincial court existed, but information about this court is rather sparse; it would appear that William Hayward, a patriot, headed the court at the outbreak of the Revolution.) In the three other colonies with chancery courts presided over by governors, these Crown men—New York's William Tyron, New Jersey's William Franklin, and South Carolina's Lord Charles Greville Montagu and his brief successor, Lord William Campbell—all sided with their king. See generally L. Edward Purcell, *Who Was Who in the American Revolution* (1993); Lorenzo Sabine, *Biographical Sketches of Loyalists of the American Revolution* (1864).

    On the other side of the ledger, Rhode Island's chief justice, Stephen Hopkins, openly joined the patriot cause and in fact signed the Declaration of Independence. (Former Chief Justice James Helme, who continued to serve in the 1770s as an associate justice, joined the ranks of loyalists.) In Connecticut, where officers of doubtful sympathies were ousted in the Stamp Act crisis a decade before the Revolution, openly loyalist judges were almost nowhere to be seen in the mid-1770s. Chief Justice Matthew Griswold was a patriot, and Associate Justice Samuel Huntington signed the Declaration of Independence. See generally Oscar Zeichner, *Connecticut's Years of Controversy, 1750–1776* (1949). In Delaware, it would appear that the colonial chief justice, Richard McWilliams, did not become an active loyalist; in fact, one of its associate justices, Caesar Rodney, signed the Declaration.
3. The three were New Jersey's Richard Stockton, Pennsylvania's John Morton, and Delaware's Caesar Rodney, each of whom served as an associate justice on his colonial supreme court. This tally omits service as a local justice of the peace or comparable low-level judicial office. Also omitted, as noted in the

text, are the six signers from Connecticut and Rhode Island, three of whom—Connecticut's Roger Sherman and Samuel Huntington and Rhode Island's Stephen Hopkins—had served on their respective supreme courts.

4. The six Philadelphians who had already served in high judicial positions were Blair, Brearly, Johnson, Read, Rutledge, and Sherman. The three whom Washington named to the Supreme Court in 1789 were Blair, Rutledge, and Wilson; the two whom he later put on the Court were Paterson and Ellsworth (who was not present for the Philadelphia signing ceremony); and the two whom he named to district courts were Bedford and Brearly. Washington also named Rutledge as a recess appointment to the chief justiceship in 1795; Rutledge was sworn in, but the Senate later rejected his permanent appointment.

5. The eleven Philadelphians in the first Senate were Bassett, Butler, Ellsworth, Few, Johnson, King, Langdon, Robert Morris, Paterson, Read, and Strong. The eight Philadelphians in the 1789 House were Baldwin, Daniel Carroll, Clymer, Fitzsimons, Gerry, Gilman, Madison, and Sherman. (In 1790, North Carolina's Williamson would make nine out of a total of sixty-five.) Gerry, it will be remembered, had opposed the Constitution. Ellsworth, King, and Strong were not present at the Philadelphia signing ceremony but did back the Constitution during the ratification process. Among the members of the first cabinet, Hamilton and Randolph had served at Philadelphia, where the latter had declined to sign the document, only to become a key proponent thereafter.

6. Raoul Berger has argued that a misbehaving federal judge may be removed by other judges via a common law writ of scire facias, as was the case in England. Raoul Berger, *Impeachment: The Constitutional Problems* (1974), 127–34. Others have challenged this general account of English law and/or its proper application to America's Article III. See, e.g., Martha Andes Ziskind, "Judicial Tenure in the American Constitution: English and American Precedents," *Supreme Court Rev.* (1969): 135, 137–38; Peter M. Shane, "Who May Discipline or Remove Federal Judges? A Constitutional Analysis," *U. of Pennsylvania LR* 142 (1993): 209, 234–35. However this debate is resolved, several points are worth emphasizing. First, Berger does not claim that Congress must provide for such removal writs, only that it may do so. Second, early Congresses in fact did not do so. Third, in English common law, it appears that the writ was to be initiated in the name of the appointing authority—that is, the executive, not the judiciary itself. Berger, *Impeachment,* 182. Thus such a writ, even if permissible, hardly evidences a truly inherent judicial power of self-police.

7. Here, too, I focus on the Court's inherent powers (or lack thereof) as opposed to the power Congress might choose to give the Court.

8. *Farrand's Records,* 1:21 (emphasis added).

9. See generally Edwin C. Surrency, "The Courts in the American Colonies,"

Am. J. of Legal Hist. 11 (1967): 253, 347; David E. Engdahl, "What's in a Name? The Constitutionality of Multiple 'Supreme' Courts," *Indiana LJ* 66 (1991): 457, 468–72.

10. *Blackstone's Comm.,* 3:*56.

11. Elmer Beecher Russell, *The Review of American Colonial Legislation by the King in Council* (1915), 221; Forrest McDonald, *The American Presidency: An Intellectual History* (1994), 103.

12. A list of pre-1888 Supreme Court cases invalidating state laws may be found in 131 U.S. ccxxvii–cclvii (1888).

13. Indeed, fierce debate over the precise number and meaning of cases continues to rage among legal historians even today. According to one recent tally:

> There are seven cases from the Revolutionary era in which courts arguably invalidated statutes. (Given the scholarly record, there is dispute as to which of these cases involved exercises of judicial review and which involved statutory construction.) All of these cases involved statutes that either limited the right to a jury trial or that in some way affected judicial authority, such as by resolving a dispute between parties or by altering the evidentiary or pleading rules. . . . [These cases are as follows:] *Symsbury Case,* 1 Kirby 444 (Conn. Super. Ct. 1785) (statute resolving a land dispute); "Ten-Pound Act" Cases (N.H. 1786), described in 2 William Winslow Crosskey, *Politics and the Constitution in the History of the United States* 969–71 (1953) (statute limiting jury trial invalidated by two courts); *Holmes v. Walton* (N.J. 1780), described in Austin Scott, "Holmes v. Walton: The New Jersey Precedent," 4 *Am. Hist. Rev.* 456 (1899) (statute limiting jury trial); *Rutgers v. Waddington* (N.Y. City Mayor's Ct. 1784), reprinted in 1 Julius Goebel, Jr., *The Law Practice of Alexander Hamilton: Documents and Commentary* 393 (1964) (statute affecting pleading and admissibility of evidence); *Bayard v. Singleton,* 1 N.C. 5 (1 Mart. 48) (1787) (statute limiting jury trial); *Trevett v. Weeden* (R.I. 1786), described in James M. Varnum, *The Case, Trevett v. Weeden: On Information and Complaint, for Refusing Paper Bills in Payment for Butcher's Meat, in Market, at Par with Specie* (Providence, John Carter 1787), reprinted in 1 Bernard Schwartz, *The Bill of Rights: A Documentary History* 417, 425 (1971) (statute limiting jury trial).

Paul M. Schwartz and William Michael Treanor, "*Eldred* and *Lochner:* Copyright Term Extension and Intellectual Property as Constitutional Property," *Yale LJ* 112 (2003): 2331, 2371–72 & n. 242. For other recent discussions, compare Larry D. Kramer, *The People Themselves: Popular Constitutionalism and Judicial Review* (2004) with Saikrishna B. Prakash and John C. Yoo, "The Origins of Judicial Review," *U. of Chicago LR* 70 (2003): 887, 929–40, and Saikrishna B. Prakash and John C. Yoo, "The Constitutional Origins of Judicial Review: Questions for Critics of Judicial Review," *George Washington LR* 72 (2003): 354, 369–71.

14. See generally *Wayman v. Southard,* 23 U.S. (10 Wheat.) 1, 21–22 (1825); William W. Van Alstyne, "The Role of Congress in Determining Incidental

Powers of the President and of the Federal Courts: A Comment on the Horizontal Effect of the Sweeping Clause," *Law & Contemporary Problems* 40 (Spring 1976): 102.

15. David M. Potter, *The Impending Crisis: 1848–1861* (1976), 292 n. 45; Charles Warren, *The Supreme Court in United States History* (rev. ed. 1926), 2:289 n. 2.

16. This phrase first appeared in an opinion of the Court in *Baker v. Carr,* 369 U.S. 186, 211 (1962). Cf. *Cooper v. Aaron,* 358 U.S. 1, 18 (1957) (proclaiming, in a context involving state defiance of the Court's mandate rather than congressional or presidential disagreement with the Court's judgment, that "the federal judiciary is supreme in the exposition of the law of the Constitution"); *Youngstown Sheet & Tube Co. v. Sawyer,* 343 U.S. 579, 595 (1952) (Frankfurter, J., concurring) (describing "judicial process as the ultimate authority in interpreting the Constitution").

17. For more discussion of the carriage-tax case, *Hylton v. United States,* and its implications for the later federal Income Tax Amendment, see Chapter 11, pp. 407–9. Congress granted the Court general power to review federal criminal cases by the Act of Mar. 3, 1891, ch. 517, sec. 5, 26 Stat. 826, 827–28. Until two years before that enactment, the Court's criminal appellate jurisdiction over lower federal courts was generally limited to habeas proceedings and decisions in which the federal circuit court below was divided on a question of law.

18. Act of Sept. 24, 1789, 1 Stat. 73; Act of June 23, 1790, 1 Stat. 128.

19. On the other hand, congressional staffs have also mushroomed since the Founding.

20. For the key statutes giving the Supreme Court more power and leeway over lower courts, see Act of Mar. 3, 1891, 26 Stat. 826, 827–28; Act of Dec. 3, 1914, 38 Stat. 790; Act of Sept. 6, 1916, 39 Stat. 726; Act of Feb. 13, 1925, 43 Stat. 936.

21. Note that the Constitution itself generally gave all federal judicial officers, whether on the Supreme Court or some other federal court, the same simple republican title: "Judge." In an eighteenth-century world sensitive to fine gradations of formal title, the Judicial Article referred without generic distinction to "the Judges, both of the supreme and inferior Courts," and the Executive Article likewise spoke simply of the "Judges of the supreme Court." Elsewhere, however, the Constitution did single out one federal judicial officer for a special title and a unique honorific role: America's "Chief Justice" would preside at any presidential impeachment, though he would have no vote in the matter. Modern legal nomenclature, which sharply distinguishes between "associate justices" on the Supreme Court, and "judges" on other federal courts, derives not from the Constitution but rather from the Judiciary Act of 1789 and subsequent practice.

22. See especially the Judiciary Act of 1925, 43 Stat. 936.

23. Jeffrey K. Tulis, *The Rhetorical Presidency* (1987), 51, 180; Edward S. Corwin,

The President: Office and Powers, 1787–1957 (4th rev. ed. 1957), 279. On the Court's discretionary docket, see the statutes cited in n. 20 above.

24. The Article II appointments clause allowed Congress by law to dispense with presidential nomination and senatorial confirmation of "inferior Officers." Although some scholars have argued that lower court Article III judges are "inferior Officers," Congress has never treated them as such. True, the Constitution generally obliges lower federal court judges to follow the rulings of a legal superior, the Supreme Court, but this fact alone does not suffice to make them inferior officers. (Ambassadors and cabinet heads are generally obliged to follow the orders of their legal superior, the president, but have never been thought to be inferior officers.) The better view would seem to be that life-tenured judges, whose decisions need not always be appealable to the Supreme Court (or any other court), require full-blown presidential nomination and Senate confirmation. Where truly "inferior" judicial officers are involved (say, federal magistrates or masters), the appointments clause allows Congress to hand appointment decisions not merely to the Supreme Court, but to any other Article III "Court[] of Law." This language tends to confirm that Article III judges are indeed akin to cabinet heads, who are likewise authorized to appoint truly "inferior Officers" within their own respective departments.

25. Wilson came to America from Scotland, Iredell from England, and Paterson from Ireland. Jay was well-born and linked by marriage to the prominent Livingston family—his father-in-law, William, was a Philadelphia framer and longstanding New Jersey governor; Blair's father, John, had served as president of colonial Virginia's council and acting governor of the province; Cushing's father, John III, and grandfather John II had sat on colonial Massachusetts's highest court; Iredell's brother-in-law was Samuel Johnston, North Carolina's governor from 1787 to 1789; Ellsworth was, by marriage, the grandnephew of one Connecticut governor, Roger Wolcott, and the first cousin once removed of two other governors, Matthew Griswold and Oliver Wolcott, Sr. (who had signed the Declaration of Independence); and Bushrod Washington was George Washington's nephew. On the lower federal bench, North Carolina's John Sitgreaves and Georgia's Joseph Clay were both English-born. Well-born and/or well-connected federal district judges included Gunning Bedford, Jr., James Duane, Francis Hopkinson, Nathaniel Pendleton, William Drayton, Cyrus Griffin, and William Paca. Edmund Pendleton and Thomas Pinckney also enjoyed high social status; both men were confirmed as district judges but declined.

26. In addition to those who served on the early Court, Washington named and the Senate confirmed an old friend and former aide of Washington's, Robert Hanson Harrison of Maryland, who declined the appointment. My tally omits potential nominees who Washington sounded out informally but never offically nominated—most notably Patrick Henry, Edward Rutledge,

and Charles Cotesworth Pinckney, all approached in the mid-1790s (by which time Henry, a strong Anti-Federalist in 1788, had begun to drift toward Federalism; the other two men had been Federalists from the start).

27. Gunning Bedford, David Brearly, James Duane, Richard Law, John Sullivan, William Paca, Edmund Pendleton, Thomas Johnson, and Thomas Pinckney had all backed the Constitution in their respective ratifying conventions. The three last-mentioned men declined Washington's commission in 1789. Paca had come late to the Federalist cause but voted yes when it counted. For Washington's appraisal of Paca, see his Nov. 30, 1789, letter to James McHenry in Washington, *Writings,* 30:471.

On Harry Innes's Anti-Federalism, see *DHRC,* 8:385–86 (letter from Harry Innes to John Brown, Feb. 20, 1788), 433–35 (Feb. 29 circular letter cosigned by Innes). On Brown's Federalism, see ibid., 10:1579–80 (letter from John Brown to unnamed Kentucky-district convention delegates, June 5, 1788). See generally Mary K. Tachau, *Federal Courts in the Early Republic: Kentucky, 1789–1816* (1978), 34–37; Richard S. Arnold, "Judicial Politics Under President Washington," *Arizona LR* 38 (1996): 473, 486. On James Innes, see *Dictionary of American Biography;* Washington letter to Lafayette, Apr. 28, 1788. On Washington's general approach to appointments, see McDonald, *American Presidency,* 225 (Washington "refused to appoint known enemies of the Constitution. No one was appointed unless Washington knew him personally or someone Washington trusted attested to his character").

28. Jefferson to Madison, Oct. 15, 1810, in Jefferson, *Writings,* 9:283; Joseph Story, *Life and Letters of Joseph Story,* William W. Story, ed. (1851), 1:128. See generally Morgan D. Dowd, "Justice Joseph Story and the Politics of Appointment," *Am. J. of Legal Hist.* 9 (1965): 265–85.

29. President Tyler nominated candidates of both political parties in 1844–45, but did so at a time when he himself was a man without a clear party affiliation.

30. On the promise/prediction distinction and the Senate's general role in judicial appointments, see Vikram D. Amar, Note, "The Senate and the Constitution," *Yale LJ* 97 (1988): 1111.

31. Prices had indeed fluctuated wildly in many states during and immediately after the Revolution, and the Philadelphia framers were acutely aware of the inflation issue as they crafted the salary rules of Articles I, II, and III. On several occasions, Madison suggested a kind of automatic cost-of-living adjustment pegged to the price of wheat or some other constitutionally designated benchmark. *Farrand's Records,* 1:216, 373, 2:45, 291–92. See also ibid., 2:142 (Committee of Detail draft).

32. McDonald, *American Presidency,* 118–19.

33. Del. Const. (1776), art. 12; Md. Const. (1776), art. XLVIII; Mass. Const. (1780), pt. II, ch. III, art. I; N.H. Const. (1784), in Thorpe, 4:2466 (unnumbered para. beginning "The tenure, that all commission officers shall have by law in their offices . . ."); N.Y. Const. (1777), art. XXIV (until the age of sixty); N.C. Const.

(1776), art. XXXIII; S.C. Const. (1778), XXVII; Va. Const. (1776), in Thorpe, 7:3817 (unnumbered para. beginning "The two Houses of Assembly shall, by joint ballot . . .").

34. In Massachusetts and New Hampshire, the process of address involved the governor and council as well as the legislature; in South Carolina and Maryland, it involved both legislative houses; while in Delaware the general assembly had the unilateral power to remove by address. Maryland required a two-thirds vote in each house.

35. Of the six states with fixed judicial salaries—Virginia, Pennsylvania, Delaware, South Carolina, Massachusetts, and New Hampshire—all except Virginia and Pennsylvania had address; Virginia and South Carolina gave their governors no power of judicial nomination or appointment, while Delaware submerged its president in a collective-appointments process; and Pennsylvania lacked life tenure.

36. Among the states, New York and South Carolina were the two major exceptions, requiring a two-thirds vote to convict an impeachment defendant. See N.Y. Const. (1777), art. XXXIII; S.C. Const. (1778), art. XXIII. On Chase and Pickering, see Chapter 5, n. 55.

37. For state antecedents of this federal law, see, e.g., Del. Const. (1776), art. 23; Md. Const. (1776), art. XL. The federal statute itself, Act of Apr. 30, 1790, ch. 9, sec. 21, 1 Stat. 112, 117, has raised the eyebrows of some modern constitutional scholars; see, e.g., Shane, "Discipline," 228. For a compelling defense of the constitutionality (and common sense) of this act, see Maria Simon, Note, "Bribery and Other Not So 'Good Behavior': Criminal Prosecution as a Supplement to Impeachment of Federal Judges," *Columbia LR* 94 (1994): 1617. Far more doubtful, of course, would be any claim of a *state* court applying *state* criminal law to automatically oust a *federal* officer from his office.

38. For discussion of the writ of scire facias as a possible device for ousting a misbehaving federal judge, see n. 6 above.

39. *Stuart v. Laird,* 5 U.S. (1 Cranch) 299 (1803); *Marbury v. Madison,* 5 U.S. (1 Cranch) 137 (1803).

40. Even had Marshall's Court insisted that that the "midnight" judges were constitutionally entitled to keep their vested commissions and to draw their promised salaries, Jefferson's Republican Congress would still have had no obligation to let these Federalist judges hear important cases. Congressional power to shape lower court jurisdiction was virtually plenary—yet another facet of its early primacy.

41. Among the fifty states, only tiny Rhode Island follows the federal model of life tenure. See *The Book of the States* (2002), 34:203–6, table 5–1. Similarly, no other leading democracy in the world has followed Article III. Vicki C. Jackson and Mark Tushnet, *Comparative Constitutional Law* (1999), 489–91.

42. For example, Charles Evans Hughes resigned in June 1916 to become the Republican Party presidential nominee; James Byrnes resigned in 1942 to join

the Roosevelt Administration and later became governor of South Carolina; and William Douglas was a leading contender for the vice-presidential nomination in 1944 and later considered running for president.

43. In Article I, the vesting clause and the roster of specific powers textually interlocked via the word "herein"—the roster was the primary place where the "legislative Powers herein granted" were indeed granted. So, too, Article III's opening words and later roster textually interlocked: The roster explicitly defined the scope of "the judicial Power" vested in federal courts by the opening words. No similar interlock appeared in Article II. Nothing in its opening words spoke of specific executive powers "herein" granted (à la Article I) and nothing in its roster said that "the executive power shall comprise" a finite list of specified items (à la Article III).

44. Although state judges could point to state-constitutional safeguards of office, none of the state systems on the books in 1787 fully matched the federal package. Also, future state-constitutional amenders might unilaterally alter or abolish whatever state-constitutional safeguards existed in 1787.

45. Some scholars have contended that the 1789 Act and later laws in fact made minor exceptions to Article III jurisdiction in a handful of federal question cases. Other scholars have disagreed. For present purposes, I put aside this trivia. Readers interested in pursuing the issue should consult the sources cited in the following note.

46. In earlier works, I have tried to elaborate and defend this two-tiered reading in great detail. See Akhil Reed Amar, "A Neo-Federalist View of Article III: Separating the Two Tiers of Federal Jurisdiction," *Boston U. LR* 65 (1985): 205; Akhil Reed Amar, "*Marbury,* Section 13, and the Original Jurisdiction of the Supreme Court," *U. of Chicago LR* 56 (1989): 443; Akhil Reed Amar, "The Two-Tiered Structure of the Judiciary Act of 1789," *U. of Pennsylvania LR* 138 (1990): 1499. Some scholars have embraced this reading, while others have challenged it. For leading academic criticisms, see, e.g., Daniel J. Meltzer, "The History and Structure of Article III," *U. of Pennsylvania LR* 138 (1990): 1569; John Harrison, "The Power of Congress to Limit the Jurisdiction of Federal Courts and the Text of Article III," *U. of Chicago LR* 64 (1997): 203. For direct responses to the critics, see Akhil Reed Amar, "Reports of My Death Are Greatly Exaggerated: A Reply," *U. of Pennsylvania LR* 138 (1990) 1651; Robert J. Pushaw, Jr., "Congressional Power Over Federal Court Jurisdiction: A Defense of the Neo-Federalist Interpretation of Article III," *B.Y.U. LR* (1997): 847.

47. Though the Founding generation did not expect that federal judges would frequently void duly enacted federal statutes, the Founding document did plainly vest federal courts with the power of judicial review. As Article VI made clear, the Constitution was America's highest law, superior to any federal statute that might conflict with it; and as Article III made clear, federal judges could apply this supreme law in cases brought before them. Though

separated by many intervening paragraphs, the relevant clauses of these two Articles tightly intermeshed, like perfectly calibrated gears of an eighteenth-century clockwork. Thus, Article III vested federal courts with jurisdiction over all cases arising under "this Constitution, the Laws of the United States, and Treaties made, or which shall be made, under their Authority," and Article VI used matching language to affirm the legal supremacy of "this Constitution, and the Laws of the United States . . . and all Treaties made, or which shall be made, under [their] Authority." Records from the drafting sessions at Philadelphia confirm that this intermeshing language was no accident, but rather was indeed part of a conscious design in contemplation of judicial review.

Today's lawyers and layman understandably but erroneously tend to conflate the "supreme Law" in Article VI with the "supreme Court" in Article III, and to assume that America's highest court is uniquely responsible for interpreting America's highest law. Articles III and VI do indeed fit together, but not because both happened to use the word "supreme." The Article III power of judicial review was vested in all federal courts, not just the Supreme Court. Nor did anything in Article III or Article VI vault the judiciary above the legislature and executive. The Constitution was America's highest *law* and the Supreme Court was America's highest *court,* but neither Article III nor Article VI nor the two put together said that the Supreme Court (or the federal judiciary as a whole) was America's highest *branch* or the document's unique interpreter. With no change in meaning, Article III might just as easily have described America's highest court as a federal "Court of Appeals," Article I might instead have spoken of Congress as the country's "supreme" standing legislature, and Article II might well have referred to the president as the nation's "supreme" executive/defender. In fact, early drafts from Philadelphia did explicitly speak of a central government "consist[ing] of a Supreme Legislative, Judiciary and Executive." *Farrand's Records,* 2:129.

48. Admiralty cases would generally involve interstate or international shipping and navigation matters that needed to be governed by a uniform body of federal-law principles preempting what would otherwise be a crazy quilt of potentially contradictory state rules. Because earlier language in the Article III roster covered only federal-law cases that were brought "in Law and Equity," a special admiralty clause was necessary to ensure federal judicial control over this distinct branch of federal law.

In colonial America, ordinary common-law courts had generally steered clear of admiralty cases, which fell within the compass of special imperial courts whose jurisdiction sometimes combined several colonies into a single admiralty district. Although states began to hear various admiralty issues after independence, the Articles of Confederation empowered Congress to create a new continental court to review all lawsuits involving captures of enemy ships—a power that Congress started exercising even before the Articles won final approval. The Articles also authorized Congress to designate trial courts for serious crimes on the high seas. Thus, the large federal judicial presence in admiralty proposed by Article III ran no risk of encroaching upon traditional state jurisdiction or intruding into a domain where state regulation made sense. In Hamilton/Publius's words in *Federalist* No. 80, "The most bigoted idolizers of State authority have not thus far shown a disposition to deny the national judiciary the cognizances of maritime causes."

49. Shifting the last judicial word on federal law to state judges would have been as odd as shifting the federal appointments or commander-in-chief power to state governors. Beneath this simple argument from organizational-chart symmetry lay deeper principles of judicial independence and the rule of law. To prevent retroactive modifications of statutory commands and ensure evenhanded interpretation, the framers committed adjudication to federal judges independent of the enacting legislature. State judges lacked this independence. In some states, the very legislators who elected federal senators had assumed judicial powers; see *The Federalist* No. 48; Edward S. Corwin, "The Progress of Constitutional Theory Between the Declaration of Independence and the Meeting of the Philadelphia Convention," in Gordon S. Wood, ed., *The Confederation and the Constitution* (1979), 18. Allowing such legislator-judges to speak the last judicial word on the meaning of congressional enactments would have been uncomfortably close to allowing congressmen to adjudicate their own laws.

50. After considerable discussion, delegates endorsed James Madison's proposal that the jurisdiction of the national judiciary "shall extend to all cases arising under the Natl. laws: And to such other questions as may involve the Natl. peace & harmony." *Farrand's Records,* 2:46 (Madison's notes—for a slightly differently worded version in the official Journal, see ibid., 39). This language hinted at a two-tiered approach, singling out federal-law cases over which federal jurisdiction would be mandatory ("*shall* extend . . ."), while suggesting a non-mandatory approach for other types of lawsuits ("*such* questions as *may* . . .").

When Madison's proposal reached a five-man Committee of Detail, the Committee's initial draft revised it as follows:

The jurisdiction of the supreme tribunal shall extend
    1. to all cases arising under the laws passed by the general [Legislature] . . . and
    3. to *such* other cases, as the national legislature may assign, as involving the national peace and harmony,

    . . .

    in disputes between citizens of different states
    in disputes between different states; and
    in disputes, in which the subjects or citizens of other countries are concerned.

Ibid., 146–47 (Committee of Detail IV). This draft obviously distinguished between a mandatory tier of cases in which federal jurisdiction "shall"—that is, must—"extend" to "all" federal-law matters, and a permissive tier of cases involving nonresidents, where the "national legislature" would have discretion to grant or withhold federal jurisdiction. As is often true of first drafts, there were some important omissions, and when Committeeman John Rutledge remembered admiralty cases (which might arise under traditional admiralty precedents in the absence of a specific federal statute), he scribbled in a reference to them. The next major Committee draft, penned by James Wilson, folded admiralty into the first tier while preserving the basic two-tiered structure of earlier drafts via the selective use of the word "all":

The Jurisdiction of the Supreme (National) Court shall extend to all Cases arising under Laws passed by the Legislature of the United States; to all Cases affecting Ambassadors (and other) public Ministers, . . . to all Cases of Admiralty and Maritime Jurisdiction; to Controversies between a State and a Citizen or Citizens of another State, between Citizens of different States and between Citizens (of any of the States) and foreign States, Citizens, or Subjects.

Ibid., 172–73 (Committee of Detail IX). All subsequent Committee drafts retained this basic two-tiered structure, which the full Philadelphia Convention ultimately endorsed.

51. *Martin v. Hunter's Lessee,* 14 U.S. (1 Wheat.) 304, 327–36 (1816). For Story's later scholarly insistence on his two-tiered approach, see Story, *Commentaries,* 3:572–73 & n. 2, sec. 1696. For post-*Martin* Supreme Court opinions authored by Marshall himself seconding Story's two-tiered approach, see *Cohens v. Virginia,* 19 U.S. (6 Wheat.) 264, 378 (1821); *Osborn v. Bank of the United States,* 22 U.S. (9 Wheat.) 738, 819–22 (1824); *American Insurance Company v. Canter,* 26 U.S. (1 Pet.) 511, 545 (1828). In the post-Marshall Court, see, e.g., *Rhode Island v. Massachusetts,* 37 U.S. 657, 672–74 (oral argument), 721 (Baldwin) (1838); *The Moses Taylor,* 71 U.S. (4 Wall.) 411, 428–29 (1867); *Stevenson v. Fain,* 195 U.S. 165, 166–67 (1904).

52. For example, precisely which cases fell within the Court's original jurisdiction, and why? If read hastily and without attention to the roster, the paragraph might be thought to say that the Court could preside at trial in each and every lawsuit in which a "State" was a "Party"—even when a state sued one of its own citizens in a wholly state-law dispute. Yet this hasty reading would defy common sense. A state-party case with no federal-law ingredient and no diversity configuration lay outside the Article III roster's comprehensive list of lawsuits suitable for federal courts. Surely, the Supreme Court had no right to try a case that was not even on the roster.

Plainly, the original/appellate paragraph was written to be read in conjunction with the roster itself. This paragraph echoed the roster's ambassadors/ministers/consuls language verbatim, and also explicitly referred readers to the "Cases before mentioned" in the roster. Thus, "those [cases] in which a State shall be Party" did not mean *"all"* such cases—a key word pointedly absent here, as it was in the roster itself when listing various state-party lawsuits. As John Marshall would make clear in the 1821 case of *Cohens v. Virginia,* 19 U.S. at the Supreme Court had original jurisdiction only when the roster gave federal courts authority *because* a state was a party—that is, only in second-tier suits where the word "state" itself appeared in the roster, in various diversity controversies pitting states against nonresidents. For a later case that muddied the waters, slightly, see *U.S. v. Texas,* 143 U.S. 621 (1892). The result of this case can best be reconciled with Marshall's approach by viewing the lawsuit in question as a de facto controversy between one state (Texas) and its sister states (represented by the federal government itself). For more discussion of this and other technical questions concerning the Court's original jurisdiction, see Amar, *"Marbury,"* 488–98.

53. The record is held by Walter Jones, who argued more than three hundred cases. For details of the three Confederation-era cases, see Amar, "Two-Tiered Structure," 1561 n. 222. For brief mention of the general role of congressmen as Supreme Court advocates, see David R. Mayhew, *America's Congress: Actions in the Public Sphere, James Madison Through Newt Gingrich* (2000), 76.

54. *Marbury v. Madison,* 5 U.S. (1 Cranch) 137, 174 (1803). For a classic example of modern scholarly criticism of this passage and a presentation of alternative readings of Article III, see William W. Van Alstyne, "A Critical Guide to *Marbury v. Madison," Duke LJ* 1969:1, 30–33. See also David P. Currie, *The Constitution in the Supreme Court* (1985), 1:68–69.

55. *Federalist* No. 81 (Hamilton); *Elliot's Debates,* 3:518 (Pendleton); Jay to Washington, circa Sept. 13, 1790, in Maeva Marcus et al., ed., *The Documentary History of the Supreme Court of the United States, 1789–1800* (1985), 2:89–91, and in Story, *Commentaries,* 3:440 n. 1, sec. 1573; Chase to Marshall, Apr. 24, 1802, in George Lee Haskins and Herbert A. Johnson, *History of the Supreme Court* (1981), 2:172–76 n. 182.

56. See Act of Sept. 24, 1789, 1 Stat. 73, 81, "The Supreme Court . . . shall have power to issue writs of prohibitions (c) to the district courts, when proceeding as courts of admiralty and maritime jurisdiction, and writs of *mandamus,* (d) in cases warranted by principles and usages of law. . . ." Note that this passage nowhere purported to give the Court "jurisdiction" over all mandamus cases. Instead, it spoke of "power"—a word that appeared elsewhere in the Judiciary Act but never to confer jurisdiction. In every other part of this long statute, whenever Congress sought to confer jurisdiction it always used the word "jurisdiction" or the word "cognizance."

57. For more discussion of what this statute in fact said, and why Marshall may have indulged a misreading of it, see Amar, *"Marbury,"* 453–63.

58. See, e.g., *Elliot's Debates,* 3:446–47 (Henry), 4:290 (Lowndes).

59. Ibid., 1:504 (letter from R. H. Lee to Edmund Randolph, Oct. 16, 1787), 381 (Martin), 4:154 (Spencer); *Storing's Anti-Fed.,* 2:319 ("Letters from the Federal Farmer (XV)," Jan. 18, 1788), 3:159 ("Minority of the Convention of Pennsylvania," Dec. 18, 1787).

60. *Elliot's Debates,* 1:504 (letter from R. H. Lee to Edmund Randolph, Oct. 16, 1787); 3:447, 545, 578 (Henry), 569 (Grayson); 4:150, 211 (M'Dowall), 154 (Spencer). For statements by the ratifying conventions themselves, see ibid., 3:658 (Va.), 4:243 (N.C.), 1:334 (R.I.).

61. Ibid., 1:323 (Mass.), 325 (N.H.), 328 (N.Y.); see also ibid., 2:110 (Holmes).

62. Tench Coxe, "An Examination of the Constitution (IV)," in Ford, *Pamphlets,* 149; *Federalist* No. 81; *Elliot's Debates,* 2:488, 518–19 (Wilson), 3:546 (Pendleton), 573 (Randolph), 4:145, 171 (Iredell), 307 (C. C. Pinckney).

63. *Elliot's Debates,* 2:488 (Wilson), 4:166, 171 (Iredell), 306–08 (Pinckney); Coxe, "An Examination (IV)," 149–50; Oliver Ellsworth, "Letters of a Landholder (VI)," in Ford, *Essays,* 165.

64. *Federalist* No. 81; *Elliot's Debates,* 2:112 (Gore), 488 (Wilson), 539–40 (McKean), 4:144 (Spaight), 145, 165–66, 170–71 (Iredell), 260, 307–8 (C. C. Pinckney).

65. State practice varied on the availability of jury trial for petty offenses. Article III's emphatic language "all" in effect treated every *federal* offense as inherently non-petty.

66. *Elliot's Debates,* 2:450, 477 (Wilson), 113 (Gore).

67. Ibid., 493–94 (Wilson), 540 (McKean), 3:534 (Madison), 572–73 (Randolph).

68. *Farrand's Records,* 2:433 (Mason, Blair plan); *Elliot's Debates,* 2:493–94, 516–19 (Wilson), 3:660 (Va. proposal 14); *Storing's Anti-Fed.,* 3:63 n. 6.

69. Act of Sept. 24, 1789, 1 Stat. 73, 77, 80, 81, 88; for an earlier federal statute requiring indictment, see, e.g., Act of July 31, 1789, sec. 35, 1 Stat. 29, 47.

70. *Elliot's Debates,* 1:323 (Mass.), 326 (N.H.), 328 (N.Y.), 3:658–61 (Va.), 4:243–44, 246 (N.C.).

71. See, e.g., *Patton v. United States,* 281 U.S. 276 (1930). For more discussion, see Akhil Reed Amar, *The Bill of Rights: Creation and Reconstruction* (1998), 104–8.

72. See *Federalist* No. 83.

73. The list included Jefferson, Adams, Wilson, Iredell, and Kent, to name just a few. See Amar, *Bill of Rights,* 101 & sources cited therein.

74. *Georgia v. Brailsford,* 3 U.S. (3 Dall.) 1, 4 (1794).

75. Wilson, *Works,* 1:186; *Elliot's Debates,* 2:94 (Parsons); *DHRC,* 15:531 ("Aristides").

76. Imagine, for instance, a dispute between two farmers over the sale of a cow, in which the plaintiff farmer alleged that the defendant farmer failed to pay the agreed-upon sales price of $10, and the defendant replied that he did indeed offer $10 of federal paper money, which the plaintiff wrongly refused to accept as legal tender. Any court seeking to decide this private-party suit

might need to decide whether Congress indeed had the constitutional authority to issue paper money. Thus, American-style judicial review could arise in virtually any state or federal court and under a wide range of possible party configurations.

77. See generally Note, "The Changing Role of the Jury in the Nineteenth Century," *Yale LJ* 74 (1964): 170.

78. Act of Sept. 24, 1789, 1 Stat. 73.

79. *Elliot's Debates,* 3:158–59, 223. Madison's notes from the Philadelphia Convention confirm that the treason clause was drafted with awareness of a possible military "contest between the U—S— and a particular State," a contest in which "the laws of the U. States are to be paramount." *Farrand's Records,* 2:345–47 (Morris and Ellsworth).

80. *Blackstone's Comm.,* 2:*254–56.

81. Cf. Md. Const. (1776), Declaration of Rights, art. XXIV ("There ought to be no forfeiture of any part of the estate of any person, for any crime except in murder, or treason against the State, and then only on conviction and attainder").

82. *Elliot's Debates,* 2:487.

83. For the various press and criminal-procedure proposals, see ibid., 1:328 (N.Y.), 3:685–59 (Va.), 4:243–44 (N.C.); for the North Carolina ultimatum, see ibid., 1:331–22.

7: States and Territories

1. For an illuminating general discussion, see John M. Murrin, "A Roof Without Walls: The Dilemma of American National Identity," in Richard Beeman et al., eds., *Beyond Confederation: Origins of the Constitution and American National Identity* (1987), 333–48. Murrin's reminder that "until [the 1774 Continental] Congress met, more of its members had visited London than Philadelphia" is particularly arresting. Ibid., 340. On governor-sharing in the colonies, see Forrest McDonald, *The American Presidency: An Intellectual History* (1994), 107.

2. *JCC,* 2:195–99 (July 21, 1775).

3. In dicta, the Taney Court repeatedly affirmed that each state had a general right to exclude paupers and vagabonds from sister states. See, e.g., *New York v. Miln,* 36 U.S. (11 Pet.) 102 (1837); *The Passenger Cases,* 48 U.S. (7 How.) 283 (1849). Not until the middle of the twentieth century would the justices side with latter-day Franklins—see *Edwards v. California,* 314 U.S. 160 (1941)—and the Court has never squarely supported its modern approach by noting the evident contrast between Article IV and its Confederation precursor.

4. *Minor v. Happersett,* 88 U.S. (21 Wall.) 162, 169 (1875).

5. In at least one context, however, the Supreme Court has driven a wedge between these two clauses, treating corporations as state citizens for Article III

but not for Article IV. Compare *Marshall v. Baltimore & O.R.R.,* 57 U.S. (16 How.) 314 (1853), with *Paul v. Virginia,* 75 U.S. (8 Wall.) 168 (1869).

6. *JCC,* 4:60 (Jan. 16, 1776); Don E. Fehrenbacher, *The Slaveholding Republic: An Account of the United States Government's Relations to Slavery* (2001), 18–19.

7. *Elliot's Debates,* 1:90. We should not read too much into this single vote in isolation—Congress rejected every rewrite urged in 1778.

8. Ibid., 95 (emphasis added).

9. John Codman Hurd, *The Law of Freedom and Bondage in the United States* (1862), 2:4; Don E. Fehrenbacher, *The Dred Scott Case: Its Significance in American Law and Politics* (1978), 65.

10. Oscar Handlin and Mary Handlin, eds., *The Popular Sources of Political Authority: Documents on the Massachusetts Constitution of 1780* (1966), 192, 202, 217, 231–32, 248–49, 263, 282, 302, 312. For a particularly tart statement, see ibid., 277 (returns from Georgetown, May 25, 1778, "Rejected . . . Because [among other reasons] a Man being born in Afraca [sic], India or ancient American or even being much Sun burnt deprived him of having a Vote for Representative"). See generally Adams, *FAC,* 88.

11. See Story, *Commentaries,* 3:674–75, sec. 1800.

12. *Dred Scott v. Sanford,* 60 U.S. (19 How.) 393, 417 (1857).

13. In defense of Taney, it might be argued that the interstate-equality approach would break down altogether in a state that simply did not recognize any of its own in-state free blacks as "citizens." But for purposes of Article IV, "citizens" and "inhabitants" could be seen as functionally synonymous. (The Confederation precursor to Article IV used the two words synonymously.) Under this approach, a free black citizen of state A when sojourning in state B would be entitled to be treated as a free black inhabitant of B.

14. *Farrand's Records,* 2:443.

15. See Act of May 26, 1790, 1 Stat. 122. For discussion, see David P. Currie, *The Constitution in Congress: The Federalist Period, 1789–1801* (1997), 102–3.

16. For one especially thoughtful meditation, see Douglas Laycock, "Equal Citizens of Equal and Territorial States: The Constitutional Foundations of Choice of Law," *Columbia LR* 92 (1992): 249.

17. One unreported case from 1569 was said to have held that "England was too pure an Air for Slaves to breath [sic] in," and in 1784 the poet William Cowper wrote: "Slaves cannot breathe in England, if their lungs / Receive our air, that moment they are free / They touch our country, and their shackles fall." For discussion and citations, see William M. Wiecek, *The Sources of Antislavery Constitutionalism in America: 1760–1848* (1777), 34 n. 37.

18. *Smith v. Brown and Cooper,* 2 Ld. Raym. 1274, 91 Eng. Rep. 566 (K.B. 1701) (The case is also reported sub. nom. *Smith v. Browne and Cooper,* 2 Salk 666, 90 Eng. Rep. 1172); *Shanley v. Harvery,* 2 Eden 126, 28 Eng. Rep. 844 (Ch. 1762); *Blackstone's Comm.,* 1:*126–27.

19. For discussion, see Wiecek, *Sources of Antislavery,* 24; David Brion Davis, *The Problem of Slavery in the Age of Revolution: 1770–1823* (rev. ed. 1999), 471–80.
20. *Blackstone's Comm.,* 1:*424–25.
21. *Somerset v. Stewart,* Lofft 1, 19–20, 98 Eng. Rep. 499, 510 (K.B. 1772), reprinted in *Howell's State Trials* 20:2, 82.
22. *Elliot's Debates,* 3:453 (Madison), 4:176, 286 (Iredell and C. C. Pinckney); *Farrand's Records,* 3:84 (Blount, Williamson, and Spaight to Governor Caswell, Sept. 18, 1787).
23. Fehrenbacher, *Slaveholding Republic,* 103–4.
24. *JCC,* 32:343 (July 13, 1787) (Article the Sixth: "That any person escaping into the [said territory], from whom labor or service is lawfully claimed in any of the original States, such fugitive may be lawfully reclaimed and conveyed to the person claiming his or her labor or service as aforesaid"); Fehrenbacher, *Slaveholding Republic,* 207.
25. Act of Feb. 12, 1793, 1 Stat. 302. The law also allowed the slave-catcher, if he preferred, to seek the certificate from various state magistrates.
26. See p. 253 above. For a scathing attack on the 1808 clause from a passionate anti-slavery New Hampshireman, see *Elliot's Debates,* 2:203–4 (Atherton).
27. *Prigg v. Pennsylvania,* 41 U.S. (16 Pet.) 539 (1842).
28. *Jones v. Van Zandt,* 46 U.S. (5 How.) 215 (1847); Salmon P. Chase, *Reclamation of Fugitives from Service: An Argument for the Defendant, Submitted to the Supreme Court of the United States, at the December Term, 1846, in the case of Wharton Jones vs. John Vanzandt* (1847), 87–93.
29. Act of Sept. 18, 1850, 9 Stat. 462, 463–64. The 90 percent figure comes from William W. Freehling, *The Road to Disunion: Secessionists at Bay, 1776–1854* (1990), 536, who in turn relies on Stanley W. Campbell, *The Slave Catchers: Enforcement of the Fugitive Slave Law, 1850–1860* (1968).
30. *Ableman v. Booth,* 62 U.S. (21 How.) 506 (1859). My allusion here to Taney's infamous language in *Dred Scott* is not purely rhetorical. If one believed, as did Taney, that only citizens enjoyed Fifth Amendment due-process rights, and that blacks (even if free) could never be citizens, then it did indeed become rather easy to disregard the Fugitive Slave Act's evident failures of due process: Such failures injured only blacks with no Fifth Amendment standing. On the long tradition of judicial insistence on unbiased decision-makers, see, e.g., *Dr. Bonham's Case,* 8 Co. Rep. 107a, 77 Eng. Rep. 638 (C.P. 1610); *Federalist* No. 10 ("No man is allowed to be a judge in his own cause, because his interest would certainly bias his judgment, and, not improbably, corrupt his integrity").
31. *Dred Scott,* 60 U.S. (19 How.) 393, 407, 450 (1857).
32. *Elliot's Debates,* 2:452 (emphasis deleted).
33. Act of Aug. 7, 1789, 1 Stat. 50.
34. Act of Mar. 6, 1820, ch. 22, sec. 8, 3 Stat. 545, 548. Wiecek, *Sources of Anti-*

slavery, 115; Fehrenbacher, *Dred Scott,* 109. In private correspondence in 1819–20, Madison questioned Congress's plenary authority to bar slavery in federal territory, but offered no satisfying argument why the "ductile" language of the territory clause should be read at anything less than face value. See, e.g., Madison to Robert Walsh, Nov. 27, 1819, in Madison, *Writings* (Hunt), 9:4–6; Madison to Monroe, Feb. 23, 1820, in ibid., 24–25. Madison's judgment here is further called into question by his additional claim that extending slavery into new territory would ultimately benefit slaves, and the larger goal of gradual emancipation (and colonization). It would seem that Madison was more in the grip of slavocrat ideology than he realized, or than his admiring biographers have acknowledged. In general they have tended to avert their eyes from Madison in his most naked moments.

35. *Dred Scott,* 60 U.S. 450.
36. Act of May 26, 1790, 1 Stat. 123; Act of Apr. 2, 1790, 1 Stat. 106, 108.
37. Act of Apr. 7, 1798, 1 Stat. 549, 550.
38. See Staughton Lynd, "The Compromise of 1787," *Political Science Qtly.* 81 (1966): 231; Davis, *Problem of Slavery,* 155; Fehrenbacher, *Dred Scott,* 77–79.
39. Act of Mar. 2, 1805, sec. 1, 2 Stat. 322 (Orleans Territory); Fehrenbacher, *Dred Scott,* 89 (discussing 1802 federal acceptance of Yazoo strip cession from Georgia).
40. For more on slavocrats' foreign policy triumphs in the early republic as it actually unfolded, see Garry Wills, *"Negro President": Jefferson and the Slave Power* (2003), 33–46, 114–26, 147–58; Fehrenbacher, *Slaveholding Republic,* 89–133.
41. M. W. McKlusky, ed., *Speeches, Messages, and Other Writings of the Hon. Albert G. Brown* (1859), 594–95.
42. Davis, *Problem of Slavery,* 154.
43. *JCC,* 34:540–41 (Sept. 25, 1788); Wiecek, *Sources of Antislavery,* 109; Fehrenbacher, *Dred Scott,* 84–85; Paul Finkelman, *Slavery and the Founders: Race and Liberty in the Age of Jefferson* (2d ed. 2001), 52–55.
44. Fehrenbacher, *Dred Scott,* 76–77; Davis, *Problem of Slavery,* 154; Edmund Cody Burnett, *The Continental Congress* (1941), 598–600.
45. *Farrand's Records,* 2:370 (emphasis added); see also *Elliot's Debates,* 3:269–70, 452–53, 458. In linking the transatlantic-slave-trade issue with concerns about the spread of slavery into the West, Mason was not alone. For similar linkages, see ibid., 2:452 (Wilson); Madison to Monroe, Feb. 10, 1820, in Madison, *Writings* (Hunt), 9:22–23.
46. *Farrand's Records,* 3:430.
47. *Annals,* 1:1246–47 (Feb. 12, 1790); *Register of Debates,* 18–2:623 (Feb. 18, 1825); Madison to Robert J. Evans, June 15, 1819, in Madison, *Writings* (Hunt), 8:442–45. For Lincoln's plan, see Chapter 10.
48. On the first wave of revenues from the sale of a large chunk of Western land

to the Ohio Company of Associates, represented by Manasseh Cutler, see Max Farrand, *The Fathers of the Constitution: A Chronicle of the Establishment of the Union* (1921), 59–74.

49. *Elliot's Debates,* 2:462–63.

50. *JCC,* 32:342 (July 13, 1787). For an early articulation of the principles of territorial republicanism and equal footing, see ibid., 18:915 (Oct. 10, 1780) (proposal that the West be "formed into distinct republican states, which shall become members of the federal union, and have the same rights of sovereignty, freedom and independence, as the other states").

51. On the critical ambiguities of Article XI, see ibid., 26:251–52 (Apr. 20, 1784); Jefferson, *Papers,* 10:27–28 (answers to M. de Meusnier, circa Jan. or Feb. 1786). See generally Richard F. McCormack, "The 'Ordinance' of 1784," *WMQ* 50 (1993): 112, 117, 120. On Kentucky's travails, see *JCC,* 34:194, 198, 287–94 (June 2–3 and July 2–3, 1788); *DHRC,* 10:1579–80, 1661–63, 1667–68, 1677–78 (letters of June 5, 21, 22, and 25, 1788, from Congressman John Brown to unnamed delegates, and to James Breckinridge, John Steele, and Archibald Stuart).

52. For Morris, see *Farrand's Records,* 2:454, 3:404.

53. Special Session Address, July 4, 1861.

54. New Hampshire's Franklin Pierce became president at age 48; Tennessee's Polk at 49; Illinois's Lincoln at 52. For present purposes I am not counting unelected presidents—namely, Virginia's John Tyler and New York's Millard Fillmore, who assumed presidential powers at age 51 and 50, respectively.

55. "Young" senators are defined here as those who began serving before their thirty-fifth birthday. In addition to Virginia's Stevens Thomson Mason and James Monroe, Rhode Island's Ray Greene, New Jersey's Richard Stockton, New Hampshire's Franklin Pierce, and New York's Rufus King (all discussed in Chapter 2, nn. 37–38), Virginia's Armistead Thomson Mason was the son of the above-mentioned Stevens Thomson Mason; Maryland's Alexander Contee Hanson was the nephew of Continental Congressman Benjamin Hanson; South Carolina's Robert Young Hayne was the son-in-law of Governor (and framer) Charles Pinckney; New York's De Witt Clinton was the nephew of Governor and Confederate Congressman George Clinton; Rhode Island's Christopher Ellery was the nephew of William Ellery, who signed the Declaration of Independence; Delaware's John Middleton Clayton was the nephew of Governor and Senator Joshua Clayton; and Rhode Island's James Fenner was the son of Governor Arthur Fenner. As with the data presented in Chapter 2, n. 38, my tally in this note is based exclusively on information culled from three biographical databases. To repeat my caveat: These sources are incomplete, but any omissions should tend to cancel out across old and young legislators. For a study that confirms the anti-dynastic distinctiveness of the antebellum West, using different dynastic

criteria and addressing a different time period, see Alfred B. Clubok and Norman M. Wilensky, "Family Relationships, Congressional Recruitment, and Political Modernization," *J. of Politics* 31 (1969): 1035.

56. For paradigmatic examples of legal and historical scholarship in this vein, see, e.g., Charles A. Beard and Birl E. Shultz, *Documents on the State-Wide Initiative, Referendum, and Recall* (1912), 28–29; Charles A. Beard, *An Economic Interpretation of the Constitution of the United States* (1913); Hans A. Linde, "When Initiative Lawmaking is Not 'Republican Government': The Campaign Against Homosexuality," *Oregon LR* 72 (1993): 19; Hans A. Linde, "Who is Responsible for Republican Government?" *U. of Colorado LR* 65 (1994): 709.

57. For scholarship stressing that Madison was indeed attempting a linguistic innovation on this point, see, e.g., Adams, *FAC,* 110–13; James Farr, "Conceptual Change and Constitutional Innovation," in Terence Ball and J. G. A. Pocock, eds., *Conceptual Change and the Constitution* (1988), 23; J. G. A. Pocock, "States, Republics, and Empires: The American Founding in Early Modern Perspective," in ibid., 66; Terence Ball, " 'A Republic—If You Can Keep It,' " in ibid., 143–44, 159; Russell L. Hanson, " 'Commons' and 'Commonwealth' at the American Founding: Democratic Republicanism as the New American Hybrid," in ibid., 171–72, 180.

58. See Chapter 2, n. 68.

59. See, e.g., *Federalist* Nos. 6, 8, 9 (Hamilton). See also No. 18 (Hamilton and Madison). For yet another example, note Iredell's remarks quoted later in this chapter; see p. 280.

60. *Elliot's Debates,* 2:422, 433–34 (emphasis altered), 482 (emphasis altered) (Wilson), 4:328 (Pinckney, emphasis added). For more Wilson, see also ibid., 2:478, 523.

61. Ibid., 4:195 (Iredell); *DHRC,* 2:218 (Plain Truth, "Reply to an Officer of the Late Continental Army, Independent Gazatteer, 10 November"); Tench Coxe, "An Examination of the Constitution (IV)," in Ford, *Pamphlets,* 145, 147; *JCC,* 26:119, 277 (Mar. 1 and Apr. 23, 1784).

62. *Federalist* Nos. 37, 39, 43, 78.

63. "Letters of Centinel (I)," in *Storing's Anti-Fed.,* 2:139; *Elliot's Debates,* 3:298 (Pendleton), 4:326 (C. Pinckney); "Essays of Brutus (I)," in *Storing's Anti-Fed.,* 2:369; Tench Coxe, "An American Citizen (IV)," in Ford, *Pamphlets,* 145; *Elliot's Debates,* 2:196–97 (Ellsworth). See also R.I. Governor Collins to the Continental Congress, Apr. 5, 1789, quoted in Bruce Ackerman, *We the People: Transformations* (1998), 59. Early judicial opinions offered similar definitions. See, e.g., *Chisholm v. Georgia,* 2 U.S. (2 Dall.) 419, 457 (1793) (Wilson, J.) ("short definition" of "republican" government is "one constructed on this principle, that the Supreme Power resides in the body of the people"); *Penhallow v. Doane's Administrators,* 3 U.S. (3 Dall.) 54, 93 (1795) (Iredell, J.) (in "a Republic" the "sovereignty resides in the great body of the people").

64. *Federalist* No. 10 (emphasis added); *Farrand's Records,* 1:134–35 (emphasis added). Similarly, in 1789, Madison casually used the language of "[]democra[cy]" to discuss aspects of *representative* government in the states and the new federal system. Madison to Jefferson, Mar. 29, 1789, in Madison, *Papers,* 12:38. For a thoughtful discussion of what Madison evidently had in mind here, see Jack N. Rakove, "The Structure of Politics at the Accession of George Washington," in Beeman et al., eds., *Beyond Confederation,* 286–94.

65. *Federalist* Nos. 21, 78.

66. See ibid., Nos. 9, 10, 43.

67. See Baron de Montesquieu, *De L'Esprit Des Loix,* tome II, bk. 9, ch. 2 (1748) ("The spirit of monarchy is war and aggrandizement; the spirit of a republic is peace and moderation. These two kinds of government cannot easily subsist in a confederate republic") (my translation); William M. Wiecek, *The Guarantee Clause of the U.S. Constitution* (1972), 26, 66.

68. The possibility that the instigator of the violence in, or the invasion of, a given state might be unrepublican forces in a neighboring state helps explain the location of this guarantee in Article IV, which brought together a cluster of clauses addressing various horizontal relations between sister states. For a brief discussion of Shays's Rebellion, and its impact on the framers and ratifiers, see Chapter 3, n. 39.

69. *Elliot's Debates,* 4:195. See also *Farrand's Records,* 2:48 (Gorham) (without Article IV, "an enterprising Citizen might erect the standard of Monarchy in a particular State, might gather together partizans from all quarters, might extend his views from State to State, and threaten to establish a tyranny over the whole & the Genl. Govt. be compelled to remain an inactive witness of its own destruction").

8: THE LAW OF THE LAND

1. See, e.g., *Farrand's Records,* 1:202–3 (Mason) ("The plan now to be formed will certainly be defective, as the Confederation has been found on trial to be. Amendments therefore will be necessary, and it will be better to provide for them, in an easy, regular and Constitutional way than to trust to chance and violence"). For similar remarks by Hamilton, see ibid., 2:558.

2. See, e.g., *Federalist* No. 85; *Elliot's Debates,* 2:117, 157–58 (Jarvis, Ames), 3:636–37 (James Innes); *DHRC,* 15:50 (Joseph Barrell to Nathaniel Barell, Dec. 20, 1787). See generally Richard B. Bernstein with Jerome Agel, *Amending America* (1993), 22–25.

3. For a somewhat different view of constitution making in New York and North Carolina, see Marc W. Kruman, *Between Authority and Liberty: State Constitution Making in Revolutionary America* (1997), 21.

4. See Jefferson, "Notes on The State of Virginia," reprinted in Merrill D. Peterson, ed., *The Portable Thomas Jefferson* (1975), 166–67 ("the ordinary legislature may alter the constitution itself"). For the eventual judicial rejection of

this view, see *Kamper v. Hawkins,* 3 Va. (1 Va. Cas.) 20 (1793). For meditations on closely related issues, see *Farrand's Records,* 1:122–23 (Madison), 2:88–89 (Mason), 93 (Madison). On the last-in-time rule, see the later discussion in this chapter, p. 303.

5. N.J. Const. (1776), art. XXIII; S.C. Const. (1778), art. XLIV.
6. Del. Const. (1776), art. 30; Md. Const. (1776), art. LIX.
7. Ga. Const. (1777), art. LXIII.
8. Pa. Const. (1776), sec. 47; Mass. Const. (1780), pt. II, ch. VI, art. X; N.H. Const. (1784), pt. II (unnumbered para. beginning "To preserve an effectual adherence . . .").
9. For general discussions of some of these questions, see Walter E. Dellinger, "The Recurring Question of the 'Limited' Constitutional Convention," *Yale LJ* 88 (1979): 1623; Walter Dellinger, "The Legitimacy of Constitutional Change: Rethinking the Amendment Process," *Harvard LR* 97 (1983): 386; Charles L. Black, Jr., "Amending the Constitution: A Letter to a Congressman," *Yale LJ* 82 (1972): 189; Michael S. Paulsen, "A General Theory of Article V: The Constitutional Lessons of the Twenty-seventh Amendment," *Yale LJ* 103 (1993): 677.
10. For an interesting meditation, see Jeff Rosen, Note, "Was the Flag Burning Amendment Unconstitutional?" *Yale LJ* 100 (1991): 1073.
11. For an early skirmish over this issue in the First Congress, see *Annals,* 1:260–61 (May 5, 1789). In this debate, Madison argued that no proposing convention could be called in the absence of petitions from two-thirds of the states, while Tucker countered that Congress had discretion in such a case.
12. *Farrand's Records,* 2:630–31.
13. It might be objected that any amendment shifting power away from the Senate would properly fall within the proviso's spirit and thus require state unanimity. But this test would doom most of the amendments that have in fact been adopted, beginning with the Bill of Rights, which limited the Senate along with the rest of the federal government. Alternatively, it might be objected that the Senate proviso should apply to any amendment that reduces Senate power and that in some special way *targets* the Senate—for example, an amendment that drains more power from it than from the House. But this bridge, too, has already been crossed. The Twenty-fifth Amendment shifted considerable power from the Senate to the House. Without the amendment, in the event of the death of a president and the later death of his vice president (or vice versa), executive power would properly have flowed to a principal "officer" who had been confirmed solely by the Senate. But the Twenty-fifth Amendment shifted the power to confirm the replacement president in a sequential death scenario to the House and Senate acting jointly, thereby giving the House an equal role in what had previously been a Senate monopoly.
14. Ibid., 1:531. Morris's point here contrasted with his desire to permanently

privilege the original thirteen states over new ones—a contradiction that did not escape notice and comment by the eagle-eyed Madison; ibid., 584.

15. Though any given delegate was unlikely to move within any given year, the men at Philadelphia were surely more geographically mobile and cosmopolitan than most other Americans at that time. For some interesting facts and figures, see Richard D. Brown, "The Founding Fathers of 1776 and 1787: A Collective View," *WMQ* 33 (1976): 465.

16. Perhaps such recourse would result in a "new Constitution" rather than an "amendment," but little of substance turns on the label: A "new Constitution" could read virtually the same as the old, but for a few changes, while an "amendment" could supplant a great deal of the old document.

17. See, e.g., Laurence H. Tribe, "Taking Text and Structure Seriously: Reflections on Free-Form Method in Constitutional Interpretation," *Harvard LR* 108 (1995): 1221; Henry Paul Monaghan, "We the Peoples, Original Understanding, and Constitutional Amendment," *Columbia LR* 96 (1996): 121.

18. In addition, citizens favoring constitutional term limits would face special collective-action problems coordinating their efforts across legislative districts. Any individual district that voted against an incumbent who refused to endorse term limits might lose competitive clout in the ensuing legislature.

19. As supreme law, the new federal Constitution would displace various old state-constitutional rules—for example, rules allowing state legislatures to pass currency laws; see Chapter 1, n. 18. For more details on the state Article V analogues and their seeming exclusivity, see Akhil Reed Amar, "The Consent of the Governed: Constitutional Amendment Outside Article V," *Columbia LR* 94 (1994): 457, 469–81.

20. *Elliot's Debates,* 2:432; Wilson, *Works,* 1:304.

21. For a list of thirty-four conventions held prior to 1917 in eighteen states whose constitutions did not expressly authorize such conventions, see Roger Sherman Hoar, *Constitutional Conventions: Their Nature, Powers, and Limitations* (1917), 39–40. See also Bruce Ackerman, *We the People: Transformations* (1998), 80 ("On sixteen occasions before the Civil War, state legislatures refused to read [state constitutional] silence to imply exclusivity").

22. *Farrand's Records,* 2:630; see also ibid., 558 (Madison) ("How was a Convention to be formed? by what rule decide?"). Similar complexities plagued Article V's ratification rules allowing Congress to submit amendment proposals to state ratifying conventions. What would such conventions look like? How would they operate? What roles would Congress and state governments play in structuring these conventions?

23. For analysis of how the Reconstruction Amendments did in fact fit within the Article V framework—contrary to the interesting arguments of Professor Bruce Ackerman—see Chapter 10. Professor Ackerman also points to the New Deal as evidence of constitutional amendment outside of Article V,

but of course the only textual amendment adopted during FDR's tenure involved the narrow issue of Prohibition repeal.

24. Some federal statutes would require a two-thirds vote, but only to offset a presidential veto. Likewise, the two-thirds vote required for federal treaties would offset the absence of the House of Representatives in the treaty-making process.

25. *Elliot's Debates,* 3:507 (Nicholas).

26. *Farrand's Records,* 2:93.

27. Ibid. See also *Federalist* No. 22.

28. On the intentionally intermeshing language of Articles III and VI, see Chapter 6, n. 47.

29. For a nice quick discussion, see E. James Ferguson, "What Were the Sources of the Constitutional Convention?" in Gordon S. Wood, ed., *The Confederation and the Constitution* (1979), 7–8.

30. See, e.g., *The Head Money Cases,* 112 U.S. 580, 598 (1884) (treaties are in "the same category as other laws of Congress"); *Whitney v. Robertson,* 124 U.S. 190, 194 (1888); (treaties have same "force and effect" as "legislative enactment").

31. See generally *Federalist* No. 78.

32. The Supreme Court has regularly given effect (for domestic-law purposes) to federal statutes repudiating earlier treaties. See, e.g., *Whitney v. Robertson,* 124 U.S. at 194; *Chae Chan Ping v. United States,* 130 U.S. 581, 600 (1889); *Fong Yue Ting v. United States,* 149 U.S. 698 (1893); *Breard v. Greene,* 523 U.S. 371, 373 (1998). On the other side of the ledger, the Court has—but only once—allowed a treaty to displace a prior federal statute; see *Cook v. United States,* 288 U.S. 102 (1933). For commentary, see Edward S. Corwin, *The President: Office and Powers, 1787–1957* (4th rev. ed. 1957), 424; John C. Yoo, "Rejoinder: Treaties and Public Lawmaking: A Textual and Structural Defense of Non-Selfexecution," *Columbia LR* 99 (1999): 2218, 2244 n. 93.

33. *Marbury v. Madison,* 5 U.S. (1 Cranch) 137, 180 (1803).

34. For discussion of situations where a given federal action might require a treaty above and beyond a unilateral federal statute, see Chapter 5, p. 191.

35. My hypothetical treaty is in fact not wholly imaginary, but rather resembles certain provisions of the real-life Jay Treaty.

36. The precise legal status of treaties has been the subject of vigorous debate in law reviews of late. For one particularly notable exchange, see John C. Yoo, "Globalism and the Constitution: Treaties, Non-Selfexecution, and the Original Understanding," *Columbia LR* 99 (1999): 1955; Martins S. Flaherty, "History Right? Historical Scholarship, Original Understanding, and Treaties as 'Supreme Law of the Land,' " ibid., 2095; Carlos Vázquez, "Laughing at Treaties," ibid., 2154; Yoo, "Rejoinder," ibid., 2218. See also Julian G. Ku, "Treaties as Laws: A Defense of the Last in Time Rule for

Treaties and Federal Statutes," *Indiana LJ* 80 (2005): 1. While these essays are filled with important historical research and legal analysis, none of them highlights the critical distinction—as I see it—between the horizontal effect of a treaty on federal statutes and the vertical effect of a treaty on state law. My proposed synthesis places me somewhere in the middle of the contending positions mapped out by Professors Yoo, Flaherty, Vázquez, and Ku.

37. See, e.g., *Restatement (Third) of Foreign Relations Law of the United States* (1987), sec. 111 comment I & reporter's note 6.

38. It might be thought that no self-executing treaty could operate over any subject matter that the Constitution gave the Congress (and thus, in part, the House). Jeffersonians in effect so argued, but this proposed test of non-self-execution, if seriously applied, would have the curious effect of limiting the president and the Senate more than states (which in some domains are allowed to legislate concurrently with Congress and thus enact laws in the teeth of some congressional silences).

   Once the Jeffersonian test is rejected, are there attractive middle solutions that can help us make sensible distinctions among different congressional powers, identifying particular things that can be done only by federal statutes and not by self-executing treaties? Although Madison in 1796 publicly questioned the likely workability of any such middle position—*Annals,* 5:490–91 (Mar. 10, 1796)—perhaps he was too hasty. Consider, for example, a moderate solution that begins with the premise that certain treaties cannot be self-executing because the House must not be cut out of the loop in certain areas of special sensitivity—areas sometimes defined by the logic of particular patches of constitutional text, and other times marked out by more general considerations of constitutional history and/or constitutional structure. Such a test might indeed help explain why the Senate and president should not be allowed, via a self-executing treaty, to, for example, raise new internal taxes, authorize new spending, declare a war, raise a new army, or create a new federal crime. On the special House role in taxing and spending, we might note the special constitutional rules requiring House origination of revenue bills and restricting appropriations unauthorized by "Law"—U.S. Const. art. I, sec. 7, para. 1; ibid., sec. 9, para. 7—and the long Anglo-American tradition of lower-house control over the purse. On the special House role in raising armies, we should likewise attend to the automatic sunset rule of art. I, sec. 8, para. 12, geared to constitutional calendar of biannual House elections. (Madison himself noted this linkage; *Annals,* 5:492.) Similar reasons of structure and history would seem to support an indispensable House role in the war-declaring power more generally. (On this view, a treaty might commit Americans to wage war under certain specified conditions, but FDR could not properly have gone to the Senate on December 8, 1941, and asked that body to ratify an Anglo-American treaty formally declaring war on Japan.) On the need for a House vote before a federal criminal sanction can be imposed, cf. *United States v. Hudson & Goodwin,* 11 U.S. (7 Cranch) 32 (1812). This case and its particular connection to the constitutional role of the House are discussed in Akhil Reed Amar, *The Bill of Rights: Creation and Reconstruction* (1998), 102, 344 n. 85.

39. On the Jeffersonian position, see Yoo, "Globalism and the Constitution," 2083–84; Corwin, *President,* 195, 216. Yoo himself seeks to revive a similar position; see Yoo, "Rejoinder," 2224.

40. *Farrand's Records,* 2:297–98.

41. Ibid., 392–94. See also ibid., 538 (Wilson).

42. Ibid., 393.

43. As made clear by the illuminating debate between Professors Yoo and Flaherty, see n. 36 above.

44. *Elliot's Debates,* 2:506–07 (Wilson), 3:510 (Corbin) (emphasis added), 3:515 (Madison). Madison reiterated this view in the House in the course of the Jay Treaty affair; see *Annals,* 5:488 (Mar. 10, 1796).

45. *Elliot's Debates,* 4:246. Cf. ibid., 128 (Iredell). For discussions of the issue in South Carolina, see ibid., 267, 271, 277–79 (J. Rutledge, Lowndes, and C. C. Pinckney).

46. See generally Ruth Wedgwood, "The Revolutionary Martyrdom of Jonathan Robbins," *Yale LJ* 100 (1990): 229; Yoo, "Globalism and the Constitution," 2091.

47. See *Farrand's Records,* 1:123 (King), 2:89 (Randolph), 90 (Gorham), 476 (Madison).

48. See, for example, Charles Beard, *An Economic Interpretation of the Constitution* (1913; reprint, 1986), 237–52; Jackson Turner Main, *The Antifederalists: Critics of the Constitution, 1781–1788* (1961), 249; Charles W. Roll, Jr., "We, Some of the People: Apportionment in the Thirteen State Conventions Ratifying the Constitution," *J. of Am. Hist.* 56 (1969): 21. Some of these accounts tend to overstate their case by playing down an important temporal dimension. Anti-Federalist-leaning delegates in certain close states were often elected at a time when voters did not know that the Constitution would clear the nine-state bar and would thus go into effect elsewhere. But by the time the delegates in many of these states met, ratifications elsewhere had made clear that the Constitution probably or definitely would go into effect. Had the voters been able to revote with this information in mind, they might very well have drifted toward the Federalists—as did many of the Anti-Federalist-leaning convention delegates who may well have thus been faithful rather than faithless agents of the voters who sent them.

49. Because each town was guaranteed one delegate, rural Anti-Federalists enjoyed, in the words of one scholar, "a major advantage over Federalists, whose strength lay in the more densely settled parts of the state." Richard D.

Brown, "Shays's Rebellion and the Ratification of the Federal Constitution in Massachusetts," in Richard Beeman et al., eds., *Beyond Confederation: Origins of the Constitution and American National Identity* (1987), 113, 123 n. 28.

50. The number nine emerged very early on at Philadelphia. When Wilson first floated the idea of partial union at the outset of the convention's second week, Charles Pinckney promptly suggested that "nine States" should suffice. *Farrand's Records,* 1:123. Many weeks later, Randolph, in returning to the number nine, reminded his colleagues that it was "a number made familiar by the constitution of the existing Congress." Ibid., 2:469. See also *Elliot's Debates,* 3:28 (Randolph: "Nine states therefore seem to be a most proper number").

51. Thus, Gouverneur Morris found no takers for his suggestion that Article VII should be drafted in "a twofold way, so as to provide for the event of the ratifying States being contiguous which would render a smaller number sufficient, and the event of their being dispersed, which wd require a greater number." *Farrand's Records,* 2:468.

9: Making Amends

1. It also bears note that several of the veterans of 1789 still in Congress a decade later had not served continuously. For additional data on, and analysis of, early congressional turnover, see the sources cited in Chapter 2, n. 4.

2. For Madison's advocacy of the "No State shall" amendment, see *Annals,* 1:452–55, 784 (June 8 and Aug. 17, 1789). For the House passage of this proposal as amendment number fourteen, see *Senate Journal,* 1:64 (Aug. 24, 1789).

3. See Madison to George Eve, Jan. 2, 1789, in Madison, *Papers,* 11:405 ("it is my sincere opinion that the Constitution ought to be revised, and that the first Congress meeting under it, ought to prepare and recommend to the States for ratification, the most satisfactory provisions for all essential rights").

4. *Elliot's Debates,* 3:37.

5. Ibid., 2:413–14 (New York convention circular letter).

6. *Annals,* 1:446, 462, 466 (June 8, 1789) (Page, Gerry, and Sumter). For similar expressions of concern, see Jefferson to Washington, Nov./Dec. 4, 1788, in Jefferson, *Papers,* 14:328; Madison to Jefferson, Dec. 8, 1788, in Madison, *Papers,* 11:382–83; Jefferson to William Carmichael, Dec. 25, 1788, in Jefferson, *Papers,* 14:385; Madison to George Eve, Jan. 2, 1789, in Madison, *Papers,* 11:405. See generally Edward P. Smith, "The Movement Towards a Second Constitutional Convention in 1788," in J. Franklin Jameson, ed., *Essays in the Constitutional History of the United States in the Formative Period, 1775–1789* (1889), 46–115; Kenneth R. Bowling, " 'A Tub to the Whale': The Founding Fathers and Adoption of the Federal Bill of Rights," *J. of the Early Republic* 8 (1988): 223; Paul Finkelman, "James Madison and the Bill of Rights: A Reluctant Paternity," *Supreme Court Rev.* (1990): 301.

7. In the 1798 case of *Hollingsworth v. Virginia,* 3 U.S. (3 Dall.) 378, the Court

endorsed the permissibility of the practice that had already taken root, under which proposed amendments were not submitted to the president for his signature or veto. Two main theories have been offered to support this result. Some have argued that the two-thirds rule of Article V should be read as creating an implied exception to the usual rule of presentment set forth in Article I, section 7. On this view, since any proposed amendment has already achieved a two-thirds vote of each house, presentment is unnecessary. Others have argued, more directly, that Article V created its own separate higher-lawmaking track above and beyond the presentment-clause rules for ordinary Article I lawmaking. On this view, Article V did not envisage any role for a presidential signature or veto in the case of an amendment proposal emerging from a duly called proposing convention; and an amendment proposal made by Congress should stand on the same footing. In 1861, James Buchanan added his name to the Corwin Amendment (which was never ratified), and four years later Abraham Lincoln appended his own signature to the Thirteenth Amendment. On February 7, 1865, the Senate resolved that Lincoln's signature had been unnecessary and "should not constitute a precedent for the future." *CG,* 38–2:629–31. See generally Herman Ames, *The Proposed Amendments to the Constitution of the United States* (1896), 295–96.

8. *Annals,* 1:449 (June 8, 1789). See also Jefferson to Washington, Nov./Dec. 4, 1788, in Jefferson, *Papers,* 14:328; Madison to Jefferson, Dec. 8, 1788, in Madison, *Papers,* 11:382–83.

9. *Annals,* 1:463, 755 (Gerry, June 8 and Aug. 14, 1789), 948 (Sept. 24, 1789).

10. For more discussion and documentation, see Amar, *Bill of Rights,* 32–41.

11. *Annals,* 1:790 (Aug. 18, 1789). Cf. Articles of Confederation, Article II: "Each state retains its sovereignty, freedom and independence, and every Power, Jurisdiction and right, which is not by this confederation *expressly* delegated to the United States, in Congress assembled" (emphasis added).

12. Of course, the eventual firstness of the First Amendment—and thus the firstness of this sentence—cannot be said to be part of Congress's original plan. What ultimately became the First Amendment was originally third on Congress's list, and became first only when Congress's first two amendments fell by the wayside in the initial round of ratifications.

13. Cf. *Aymette v. State,* 21 Tenn. (2 Hum.) 154, 161 (1840), where the Tennessee Supreme Court declared that the "bear arms" phrase had "a military sense, and no other. . . . A man in the pursuit of deer, elk and buffaloes, might carry his rifle every day, for forty years, and, yet, it would never be said of him, that he had *borne arms.*" My claim is not that no one at the Founding ever used the phrase "bear arms" outside the military context, but rather that such usages were rare in law and legal literature—the proverbial linguistic exceptions that proved the rule and illustrated the elasticity and metaphoric nature of language generally. For the most prominent nonmilitary use at the Founding, see "The Address and Reasons of Dissent of the Minority of the Conven-

tion of Pennsylvania to Their Constituents," in *Storing's Anti-Fed.,* 3:145, 151 (affirming a right of the people "to bear arms for the defence of themselves and their own state, or the United States, *or for the purpose of killing game*") (emphasis added).

14. For the early draft, see *Senate Journal,* 1:63–64 (Aug. 25, 1789). For state constitutions, see the citations and discussion in Amar, *Bill of Rights,* 332 n. 33.

15. *Senate Journal,* 1:63 (Aug. 25, 1789).

16. *Annals,* 1:453 (June 8, 1789).

17. The full development of a proper approach to unenumerated rights must await another day, as I explain in the closing paragraphs of the Postscript; see p. 477.

18. Declarations of the Stamp Act Congress, Oct. 19, 1765, arts. VII–VIII; *JCC,* 1:69 (Oct. 14, 1774), 2:145 (July 6, 1775); Declaration of Independence (1776) (condemning "mock trial," deprivations of "trial by jury" and overseas trials); Va. Const.(1776), Declaration of Rights, secs. 8, 11 ("ancient" and "sacred"); N.J. Const. (1776), arts. XXII, XXIII ("inestimable" and "unrepealable"); Pa. Const. (1776), Declaration of Rights, arts. IX, XI ("sacred"); Del. Const. (1776), Declaration of Rights, secs. 13, 14 ("great[]"); Md. Const. (1776), Declaration of Rights, arts. III, XIX, XXI; N.C. Const. (1776), Declaration of Rights, arts. IX, XIV ("sacred and inviolable"); N.Y. Const. (1777), arts. XIII, XLI ("inviolate forever"); Ga. Const. (1777), arts. XL–XLIII, XLV, LXI ("inviolate forever"); S.C. Const. (1778), art. XLI; Mass. Const. (1780), pt. I, arts. XII, XV ("sacred"); N.H. Const. (1784), pt. I, arts. XVI, XX ("sacred"); *JCC,* 32:340 (July 13, 1787).

19. See, e.g., *Dimick v. Schiedt,* 293 U.S. 474, 475 (1935).

20. Act of Apr. 30, 1790, ch. 9, sec. 29, 1 Stat. 112, 118–19.

21. On confrontation, see, e.g., Va. Const. (1776), Declaration of Rights, sec. 8; Pa. Const. (1776), Declaration of Rights, art. IX; Del. Const. (1776), Declaration of Rights, sec. 14; Md. Const. (1776), Declaration of Rights, art. XIX; N.C. Const. (1776), Declaration of Rights, art. VII; Mass. Const. (1780), pt. I, art. XII; N.H. Const. (1784), pt. I, art. XV. See also *Blackstone's Comm.,* 3:* 373. In addition, an important English treason statute of 1661 had given all treason defendants a right to be brought "face to face" with the requisite "two lawful and credible Witnesses upon Oath." 13 Car. 2, ch. 1, sec. 5. On speedy trials, see, e.g., the previously cited sections of the Virginia, Pennsylvania, Delaware, and Maryland Constitutions. An antecedent of the speedy-trial idea may be found in the English Habeas Corpus Act of 1679, 31 Car. 2, ch. 2, which addressed, among other things, various problems associated with pretrial detention.

22. In addition to the sections of the Virginia, Pennsylvania, North Carolina, Massachusetts, and New Hampshire Constitutions cited in the preceding note, see Del. Const. (1776), sec. 15; Md. Const. (1776), art. XX.

23. 2 U.S. (2 Dall.) 419 (1793). Elsewhere, I have presented a more detailed dis-

cussion of this case and the amendment it triggered. See Akhil Reed Amar, "Of Sovereignty and Federalism," *Yale LJ* 96 (1987): 1425, 1466–92.

24. Judiciary Act of 1789, ch. 20, sec. 13, 1 Stat. 73, 80–81.

25. Ibid., sec. 34, 1 Stat. 73, 92.

26. In later chapters, we shall study all three occasions: the Fourteenth Amendment's repudiation of Taney's lead opinion in *Dred Scott v. Sanford,* 60 U.S. (19 How.) 393 (1857); the Sixteenth Amendment's pointed reversal of *Pollock v. Farmers' Loan & Trust Co.,* 158 U.S. 601 (1895); and the Twenty-sixth Amendment's overturning of the result in *Oregon v. Mitchell,* 400 U.S. 112 (1970).

27. Some scholars have wondered whether this language—"that no State shall be liable to be made a party defendant in any of the Judicial Courts established or to be established under the authority of the United States, at the suit of any person or persons, citizens or foreigners, or of any body politic or corporate whether within or without the United States"—was formally introduced in Congress. Nevertheless, all scholars are agreed that this language was floating around Congress, thereby proving what should be obvious in any event: If the Eleventh Amendment framers had sought to immunize states broadly—even in federal question cases—they surely knew how to say so. For more discussion of this proposal, compare Charles Warren, *The Supreme Court in United States History* (1922), 1:101, and William A. Fletcher, "The Diversity Explanation of the Eleventh Amendment: A Reply to Critics," *U. of Chicago LR* 56 (1989): 1261, 1269 n. 45, with John J. Gibbons, "The Eleventh Amendment and State Sovereign Immunity: A Reinterpretation," *Columbia LR* 83 (1983): 1889, 1926 n. 186.

28. No federal jurisdiction existed over a state-law breach-of-contract suit brought by a Georgian against Georgia. Thus, the matter would be decided by state courts, which recognized Georgia's substantive state-law defense.

29. At first glance, it might be thought that the amendment's text literally barred any lawsuit brought by a citizen of one state against another state, even one based on a federal question. But this hasty reading misses the way in which the Eleventh Amendment was worded to mesh with the textual gears of Article III itself. In Chapter 6, n. 52, we saw how the Article III language giving the Supreme Court original jurisdiction in cases "in which a State shall be Party" referred only to those lawsuits where Article III jurisdiction existed *because* a state was a party. Likewise, the Eleventh Amendment language abolishing jurisdiction in lawsuits brought by a citizen of one state against another state referred only to lawsuits where Article III jurisdiction had been given *because* of that very party alignment. For more discussion, see Akhil Reed Amar, "*Marbury,* Section 13, and the Original Jurisdiction of the Supreme Court," *U. of Chicago LR* 56 (1989): 443, 488–98.

In the early 1800s, various senators unsuccessfully proposed a constitutional amendment whose language precisely tracked the Eleventh Amendment. Under the proposal, "the judicial power of the United States shall not be construed to extend to controversies between . . . citizens of different States." *Annals,* 14:53 (Breckinridge, Feb. 8, 1805), 15:68 (Maclay, Jan. 22, 1806), 16:76 (Clay, Feb. 20, 1807). Yet Breckinridge et al. plainly aimed only to remove state-law controversies where Article III jurisdiction existed *because* a lawsuit involved citizens of diverse states; where a diversity suit also involved a federal question or admiralty issue, Article III courts would continue to hear such first-tier cases under the Breckinridge/Maclay/Clay plan. Ibid., 216 (Elliot, Dec. 26, 1806). The same interpretive approach sensibly applied to the analogous words of the Eleventh Amendment.

30. See *Blackstone's Comm.,* 3:*23; *Marbury v. Madison,* 5 U.S. (1 Cranch) 137, 163–63 (1803); *Federalist* No. 43.

31. For the modern Court's approach, see generally *Seminole Tribe v. Florida,* 517 U.S. 44 (1996). Four justices have sharply dissented from this approach. See ibid., 76–100 (Stevens, J., dissenting), 100–85 (Souter, J., dissenting, joined by Ginsburg and Breyer, JJ.). Most legal scholars have tended to side with the dissenters. A great deal of this scholarship (including my own) is analyzed and synthesized in Justice Souter's comprehensive dissent.

32. Act of Mar. 1, 1792, ch. 8, sec. 12, 1 Stat. 239, 241.

33. Madison to Jefferson, Jan. 10, 1801, in Madison, *Papers,* 17:454.

34. Such is the intriguing speculation (accompanied by interesting bits of evidence) put forth in Bruce Ackerman's book-in-progress, *America on the Brink.* The 1801 essay itself, entitled "The Presidential Knot" and appearing over the pseudonym "Horatius," was printed in two newspapers in the Washington area—on January 2 in the *Alexandria Advertiser* and four days later in the *Washington Federalist.* Though the essay did not specifically name the secretary of state, it did call for a revision of the 1792 Act with a legislatively designated cabinet officer to replace the Senate president pro tempore atop the line of succession.

35. See Neal R. Peirce and Lawrence D. Longley, *The People's President: The Electoral College in American History and the Direct Vote Alternative* (1981), 247. In 1800, ten states chose electors legislatively, five had popular elections of electors, and one used a mixed system. In 1804, six states used the legislative method and eleven states opted for popular elections. Some backsliding occurred during the (rather tame) elections of 1808–1820; in 1824, six states chose electors via the legislature, seventeen via popular elections, and one via a mixed system.

36. See Milton Lomask, *Aaron Burr* (1979), 332. Special thanks to Rick Brookhiser for bringing this material to my attention.

37. Louis Clinton Hatch, *A History of the Vice Presidency of the United States of America* (1934), 71. Martin Van Buren—who later was elected president in his own right—might be thought an exception to Hatch's generalization.

38. Lolabel House, *Twelfth Amendment of the Constitution of the United States* (1901), 50 (unpublished Ph.D. dissertation, U. of Pennsylvania); Tadahisa

Kuroda, *The Origins of the Twelfth Amendment: The Electoral College in the Early Republic, 1787–1804* (1994), 172.

39. The only large state unrepresented in the pre-1804 cabinet was North Carolina, and the only small state which was represented was Georgia.

40. On state-winner-take-all, see also Jefferson to Monroe, Jan. 12, 1800, in Jefferson, *Writings* (Ford), 7:401–2.

41. On Delaware, see House, *Twelfth Amendment,* 58–59; Kuroda, *Origins of the Twelfth,* 158. For an earlier similar expression of the Rhode Island legislature, see ibid., 109. Both House and Kuroda also document the small-state objections in Congress itself; and for still more on these objections, see David P. Currie, "The Twelfth Amendment," in David E. Kyvig, ed., *Unintended Consequences of Constitutional Amendment* (2003), 73–109; Garry Wills, *"Negro President": Jefferson and the Slave Power* (2003), 106–13.

42. See, e.g., *Annals,* 13:157 (Jackson, Dec. 2, 1803), 704–5, 722–23 (Gregg, Campbell, Dec. 8, 1803).

43. Albert F. Simpson, "The Political Significance of Slave Representation, 1787–1821," *J. of Southern Hist.* 7 (1941), 315, 325 n. 40. The next direct tax would not be levied until 1813, and it, too, would be a small one; see ibid. For an example of a Northerner in 1788 who was fooled by the T-word, see *Elliot's Debates,* 2:39 (Nasson). For a prominent reminder of the limited role that direct taxes were expected to play at the Founding, see *Federalist* No. 12.

44. *Boston Mercury and New-England Palladium,* Jan. 20, 1801, quoted in Simpson, "Political Significance," 322. Similar statements appeared in Boston's *Columbian Centinel* on Dec. 24, 1800; in the *Philadelphia Gazette & Daily Advertiser* on Dec. 31, 1800, and Jan. 2, 1801; in Philadelphia's *Gazette of the United States* on Jan. 2, 1801; and in the *Palladium* (again) on Feb. 27, 1801. See generally Wills, *"Negro President"*; Ackerman, *America on the Brink.*

45. *Annals,* 11:1290 (Dana, May 1, 1802), 13:536–38 (Hastings and Thatcher, Oct. 28, 1803).

46. Ibid., 155 (Dec. 2, 1803). For an extended version of Plumer's speech, taken from his own papers, see *William Plumer's Memorandum of Proceedings in the United States Senate, 1803–1807,* ed. Everett S. Brown (1923), 46–73. See esp. ibid., 67: "Why should the four states of Maryland, Virginia, North & South Carolina be entitled for their slaves to more than thirteen Electors & Representatives, while all the wealth of New England does not give them a single vote, even for the choice of one of those officers?"

47. Alan P. Grimes, *Democracy and the Amendments to the Constitution* (1978; reprint, 1987), 25.

10: A New Birth of Freedom

1. Though Lincoln penned these words after 1858—in 1864, to be precise—he immediately added that "I can not remember when I did not so think, and feel." Lincoln to Albert G. Hodges, Apr. 4, 1864.

2. Fourth Debate, Sept. 18, 1858, Charleston.

3. See William M. Wiecek, *The Sources of Antislavery Constitutionalism* (1977), 50–51, 89–90; David Brion Davis, *In the Image of God: Religion, Moral Values, and Our Heritage of Slavery* (2001), 200–1.

4. Dwight Lowell Dumond, *The Secession Movement, 1860–61* (1931), 131; Michael J. Dubin, *United States Congressional Elections, 1788–1997: The Official Results of the 1st through 105th Congresses* (1998), 187–93. Ackerman draws on Dumond's estimates but misstates the House size as 228. Bruce Ackerman, *We the People: Transformations* (1998), 448 n. 6. The correct number is 237 (not counting Kansas).

5. In its entirety, it read as follows: "No amendment shall be made to the Constitution which will authorize or give to Congress the power to abolish or interfere, within any State, with the domestic institutions thereof, including that of persons held to labor or service by the laws of said State." Joint Resolution of Mar. 2, 1861, 12 Stat. 251.

6. On grammar, what did the words "authorize or" add, except confusion? Didn't "with" belong between "interfere" and "within"? On euphemism, note the use of the classic Article IV circumlocution "Person[s] held to Service or Labour."

7. *CG,* 37–1:243 (July 24, 1861).

8. Joint Resolution of Apr. 10, 1862, 12 Stat. 617; Act of Apr. 16, 1862, 12 Stat. 376.

9. For the territories, see Act of June 19, 1862, 12 Stat. 432. On confiscation, see Act of Aug. 6, 1861, 12 Stat. 319; Act of July 17, 1862, 12 Stat. 589.

10. Eric Foner, *Reconstruction: America's Unfinished Revolution, 1863–1877* (1988), 8.

11. New Jersey, which had voted no in March 1865, later repented and voted yes in January 1866—after the amendment had become valid, thanks to ratifications elsewhere.

12. One of the characters at the emotional heart of *Uncle Tom's Cabin,* the fictional slave Eliza Harris, was a woman, as were many of the real-life slaves whose narratives captured the imagination of the antislavery movement. On various noneconomic forms of slavery, servitude, and degradation targeted by the Abolition Amendment, see Akhil Reed Amar and Daniel Widawsky, "Child Abuse as Slavery: A Thirteenth Amendment Response to *DeShaney,*" *Harvard LR* 105 (1992): 1359.

13. For an argument that this "taking" was nevertheless not a "using" and thus properly lay beyond the scope of the Fifth Amendment just-compensation clause, see Jed Rubenfeld, "Usings," *Yale LJ* 102 (1993): 1077.

14. For the economic figures, see David Brion Davis, *Challenging the Boundaries of Slavery* (2003), 76.

15. *McCulloch v. Maryland,* 17 U.S. (4 Wheat.) 316, 404–5, 421 (1819).

16. *CG,* 39–1:474 (Trumbull, Jan. 29, 1866).

17. Ibid., 322 (Jan. 19, 1866).
18. Ibid., 1095 (Feb. 28, 1866) (emphasis added).
19. Ackerman, *Transformations,* 99–119, 207–34. Ackerman also plays up the fact that although Ohio and New Jersey purported to rescind their ratifications of the Fourteenth Amendment, Secretary of State Seward, under pressure from Congress, counted New Jersey and Ohio as yes votes in an apparently official ratification tally issued by the Secretary on July 28, 1868. Ibid., 112, 233–34. In Chapter 12 we shall see good reasons for permitting rescission until the three-quarters bar is cleared (at which point the ratification process stops and the amendment becomes valid). Under a proper approach, Ohio and New Jersey should not have been counted as yes votes, but thanks to ratifications by Alabama and Georgia in mid-July 1868, the rescission issue was moot by July 28: Even without the two rescinding states, the magic twenty-eight out of thirty-seven total states had indeed said yes when Seward issued his final proclamation, which did in fact properly count both Alabama and Georgia as yes votes. See Proclamation of Andrew Johnson, July 27, 1868, 15 Stat. 708; Certification of William H. Seward, July 28, 1868, 15 Stat. 708–11, esp. 711. While aware of these mid-July ratifications, Ackerman ignores the mootness issue. *Transformations,* 445 n. 35, 469 n. 85.
20. Ackerman, *Transformations,* 100, 109, 111. In particular, Ackerman points to the decisive victories achieved by reformers in the Northern congressional elections in 1866 and their general national triumph in congressional and presidential elections in 1868.
21. David P. Currie, "The Twelfth Amendment," in David E. Kyvig, ed., *Unintended Consequences of Constitutional Amendment* (2000), 73, 89–94; Tadahisa Kuroda, *The Origins of the Twelfth Amendment* (1994), 143–46, 158–59.
22. The true-blue ratification tally rises to twenty if we count Tennessee, which was in the process of being readmitted to Congress; see n. 35 below. Two more states, including the newly admitted Nebraska, would add their yes votes before midsummer 1867. (On this view, Ohio's and New Jersey's purported rescissions of their ratifications in early 1868 came too late—*after* the amendment had been duly ratified; cf. n. 19 above.)
23. See Ackerman, *Transformations,* 150–57.
24. Indeed, Sumner himself described a true-blue-only approach to Article V as one best fitting "both its letter and its spirit." *CG,* 39–1:2 (Dec. 4, 1865). Ackerman himself quotes this passage; see *Transformations,* 150.
25. *CG,* 39–1:2 (Sumner, Dec. 4, 1865).
26. Unless of course one adopted a true-blue-only approach, in which case, as we have seen, all the Reconstruction Amendments passed easily.
27. As a matter of general causation principles pervasive in American law, certain illegalities have traditionally been treated as harmless error in situations where the illegalities did not prejudicially affect the outcome. To recast the point in the language of standing doctrine, only those wrongly excluded—

free blacks—were entitled to complain about their exclusion from the vote on the Thirteenth Amendment, yet none of these blacks were in fact complaining about the yes votes cast by all-white governments.

28. Ackerman, *Transformations,* 113.

29. For the classic legal case exemplifying a principle that a person should not generally profit from his own wrongdoing, see *Riggs v. Palmer,* 115 N.Y. 506 (1889). For extensive evidence and analysis showing that nineteenth-century Congresses did in fact—and justifiably—judge contested elections in the fashion I am now elaborating and defending, see Josh Chafetz, "Democracy's Privileged Few: Legislative Privilege and Democratic Norms in the British and American Constitutions" (unpublished D.Phil. dissertation, Oxford Univ., 2004).

30. See *Texas v. White,* 74 U.S. (7 Wall.) 700, 733 (1869). See generally John Harrison, "The Lawfulness of the Reconstruction Amendments," *U. of Chicago LR* 68 (2001): 375. Ackerman does not discuss the "de facto" doctrine.

31. *Luther v. Borden,* 48 U.S. (7 How.) 1, 42 (1849). In its famous 1869 decision in *Texas v. White,* the Supreme Court prominently quoted this passage in *Luther* to provide context for the seating decisions made and Reconstruction laws passed by the Thirty-ninth and Fortieth Congresses—decisions and laws that were not under direct review in *White* itself. See *White,* 74 U.S. at 730–33.

32. *CG,* 38–1:2898–99 (Sumner, June 13, 1864), 38–2:588 (Sumner, Feb. 4, 1865), 39–1:2 (Sumner, Dec. 4, 1865), 74 (Stevens, Dec. 18, 1865), 684 (Sumner, Feb. 6, 1866), 919 (Broomall, Feb. 19, 1866), 39–2:7 (Sumner, Dec. 4, 1866), 192 (Sumner and Wilson, Dec. 19, 1866), 255 (Pike, Jan. 3, 1867), 288 (Spalding, Jan. 5, 1867), 501–5 (Bingham, Jan. 16, 1867), 814 (Cullom, Jan. 28, 1867), 1182 (Blaine, Feb. 12, 1867), 1365 (Howard, Feb. 15, 1867), 1392–93 (Stewart and Sumner, Feb. 15, 1867), 39–2:App. 176 (Banks, Feb. 9, 1867), 40–1:App. 28 (Lawrence, July 20, 1867), 40–2:453 (Sumner, Jan. 11, 1868), 1928 (Colfax, Mar. 17, 1868). For Ackerman's account of Bingham's later decision to move beyond this true-blue-only approach, see *Transformations,* 195–97. But Ackerman fails to discuss Bingham's still later reembrace of this approach; see *CG,* 40–2:475 (Jan. 13, 1868); Joseph B. James, *The Ratification of the Fourteenth Amendment* (1984), 278–79, 282–83.

For other invocations of *Luther,* see, e.g., *CG,* 39–1:145 (Shellabarger, Jan. 8, 1866), 40–2:957 (Williams, Feb. 4, 1868), 3630–31 (Trumbull, July 1, 1868), 3912 (Conkling, July 10, 1868). Although Ackerman has argued for a narrow reading of the key passage of *Luther*—see *Transformations,* 442–44 n. 23—this narrow reading scants other language in the opinon. See, e.g., *Luther,* 48 U.S. 45 ("Undoubtedly, if the President in exercising this power shall fall into error, or invade the rights of the people of the State, it would be in the power of Congress to apply the proper remedy"). See also *Texas v. White,* 74 U.S. 730 ("the power to carry into effect the clause of guaranty is primarily a legislative power, and resides in Congress"). For further evidence of congressional primacy in the facts that gave rise to *Luther,* and in the opinon itself, see William M. Wiecek, *The Guarantee Clause of the U.S. Constitution* (1972), 105; Charles O. Lerche, Jr., "The Guarantee Clause in Constitutional Law," *Western Political Qtly.* 2 (1949): 358, 362.

33. See David M. Potter, *The Impending Crisis: 1848–1861* (1976), 386–88; Michael Kent Curtis, *Free Speech, "The People's Darling Privilege,"* (2000), 273–76.

34. Lincoln's more famous remarks at Gettysburg would of course reiterate and refine these themes. Note also Lincoln's treatment of "republic" and "democracy" as basically synonymous.

35. First Reconstruction Act of Mar. 2, 1867, sec. 5, 14 Stat. 428, 429. As my phrase "eventually came to be hammered out" is designed to suggest, I am necessarily glossing over much of the complexity, confusion, and contradiction that characterized the Reconstruction deliberations. My focus is on what Congress as a whole ultimately did, and on which statements made in the cacophony best justify these deeds from a legal point of view. For a fascinating blow-by-blow account, see Michael Les Benedict, *A Compromise of Principle: Congressional Republicans and Reconstruction, 1863–1869* (1974). See also Ackerman's engrossing narrative.

In June 1866, Congress did readmit Tennessee without imposing a requirement of black suffrage on that state, which had the lowest percentage of blacks in the Confederacy and which had ratified the Fourteenth Amendment with alacrity. See Joint Resolution Restoring Tennessee to her Relations to the Union, July 24, 1866, 14 Stat. 364. The state itself adopted black suffrage in January 1867—several weeks before black suffrage was ultimately imposed by Congress on the other ex-rebel states; see Foner, *Reconstruction,* 271.

36. *CG,* 39–1:1006–1011 (Clarke, Feb. 24, 1866), 1630 (Hart, Mar. 24, 1866), 2880–83 (Ashley, May 29, 1866), 2947 (Wilson, June 4, 1866), 39–2:350–51 (Broomall, Jan. 8, 1867).

37. Ibid., 39–1:2 (Sumner, Dec. 4, 1865) (no ex-Confederate state "can be accepted as republican, where large masses of citizens who have been always loyal to the United States are excluded from the elective franchise, and especially where the wounded soldier of the Union, with all his kindred and race, and also the kindred of others whose bones whiten the battle-fields where they died for their country, are thrust away from the polls"); 1230–31 (Sumner, Mar. 7, 1866) ("According to the definition of a slave, he has no will of his own, and can give no 'consent' to government. Therefore he was not considered as belonging to the 'body-politic.' . . . When the slaves of our country became 'citizens' they took their place in the 'body-politic' as a component part of the 'people' "); 40–1:958 (Williams, Feb. 4, 1868) ("State government[s] which tolerate[d] slavery" were "recognized by the [Founding] fathers"

as "republican in form" but none of these states permanently excluded "one half . . . or even one third" of its "free male citizens"); 40–2:1957 (Broomall, Mar. 18, 1868) ("Bad as the system of human slavery was, it might in theory coexist with a republican form of government. None but freemen can constitute the political element of any state").

38. Ackerman, *Transformations,* 105.

39. As Ackerman himself explains elsewhere in his account; see ibid., 130–35.

40. See Wiecek, *Guarantee Clause,* 191, 200 ("Disfranchising half the [adult free male] population of a state was qualitatively as well as quantitatively different from disfranchising 5 per cent or less. . . . [Many Republicans came to accept] the idea that republican government was impossible where a large minority of a state's citizens were disfranchised. The guarantee clause did not necessarily require the enfranchisement of all Negroes everywhere, but it forbade their wholesale proscription where they were numerous").

41. *CG,* 39–1:674–87, esp. 683, 685 (Feb. 6, 1866). See also ibid., 684 (pouring contempt on "the argument that, since certain States of the North have disfranchised the few colored persons within their borders, the United States are so far constrained by this example that they cannot protect the millions of freedmen in the rebel States from disfranchisement"). For an earlier statement of this principle by Sumner, see ibid., 2 (Dec. 4, 1865) ("no government of a State recently in rebellion can be accepted as republican, where large masses of citizens, who have always been loyal to the United States are excluded from the elective franchise").

42. Ibid., 40–2:958 (Feb. 4, 1868).

43. Ibid., 39–1:406 (Eliot, Jan. 24, 1866), 1627 (Buckland, Mar. 24, 1866), 39–2:351 (Broomall, Jan. 8, 1867), see also 39–1:1836–37 (Lawrence, Apr. 7, 1866), 40–2:1956 (Broomall, Mar. 18, 1868).

44. Ackerman himself labels the quantitative argument "convoluted," but fails to say why. *Transformations,* 107. He also suggests that the quantitative theory was inconsistent with section 2 of the Fourteenth Amendment. How so? The quantitative theory did not require black suffrage everywhere or universal free male suffrage in every state. Neither did section 2. So where is the inconsistency? Ackerman apparently reads section 2 as validating *all* black disenfranchisements, both large and small, so long as a state was willing to pay the apportionment penalty. On this reading, the Fourteenth Amendment itself might well seem to be inconsistent with an absolute demand of Southern black suffrage. But a more complete account of what the Fourteenth Amendment said and did contradicts Ackerman's apparent reading. Section 2 suggested that *some* disenfranchisements—for example, the sorts of smallish voting exclusions generally in place in the North—might well be permissible, so long as states paid the apportionment penalty. But in the South, where black masses bulked large, federal Reconstruction statutes *required* black suffrage as a condition of reentry, and indeed as a fundamen-

tal condition that had to be honored even after an ex-rebel state had been readmitted. These statutes—the very statutes that also required ex-rebel-state ratification of the Fourteenth Amendment as a further condition for readmission—were inextricably part of the very process of amendment and are thus indeed part of the Fourteenth Amendment itself. See First Reconstruction Act of Mar. 2, 1867, 14 Stat. 428; An Act to Admit the State of Arkansas to Representation in Congress, June 22, 1868, 15 Stat. 72; An Act to Admit the States of North Carolina, South Carolina, Louisiana, Georgia, Alabama, and Florida, to Representation in Congress, June 25, 1868, 15 Stat. 73. It should also be noted that section 2 ranged beyond race and dealt with disenfranchisements that were formally race-neutral. In fact, nowhere did section 2 *explicitly* authorize Southern (or even Northern, for that matter) race-based suffrage laws, as had earlier proposed amendment language that men like Sumner blocked for that very reason. Section 2 thus supplemented the Reconstruction Republicans' quantitative theory of republican government and in no way contradicted or displaced it: The republican-government clause (as read by leading congressmen) absolutely *prohibited* disenfranchisements occurring on a *massive* scale, while section 2 merely *penalized* disenfranchisements operating on a *limited* scale. To see the point one final way, imagine that in 1869 Delaware tried to restrict the franchise to a single man and vested that man (and thereafter his eldest male heir) with all government power. Suppose further that Delaware cheerfully accepted the section 2 apportionment penalty—zero, in this case, given that the state would continue to get one representative. Surely nothing in the text or logic of section 2 would exempt Delaware's monarchial regime from invalidation under the republican-government clause: *Section 2 left preexisting republican-government-clause requirements entirely undiminished.* Note that nothing in my argument implies that the Fourteenth Amendment *itself* created any right to vote. It did not; see pp. 391–92.

45. See Foner, *Reconstruction,* 195.
46. See, e.g., *CG,* 39–1:379–80 (Brooks, Jan. 23, 1866), 2767 (Reverdy Johnson, May 23, 1866). For a moderate Republican playing the gender card against his more expansive colleagues, see, e.g., ibid., 704 (Fessenden, Feb. 7, 1866).
47. Ibid., 177 (Jan. 10, 1866).
48. Women did, however, vote in school elections in Kentucky and Kansas; see Aileen Kraditor, *The Ideas of the Woman Suffrage Movement, 1890–1920* (rev. ed. 1971), 3.
49. See, e.g., *CG,* 38–1:2243 (Howe, May 12, 1864) ("Females send their votes to the ballot-box by their husbands or other male friends. . . . We [men] go there to carry votes. We are instructed to carry them before we leave home"); 39–1:410 (Bromwell, Jan. 24, 1866) ("Ladies are part of the family with most of us. The head of the family does the voting for the family. But . . . the negro is not even of the white family [and] is of a different race and [is] so

treated. . . . You do not associate with him; you do not affiliate with him; . . . you do not sympathize with him."); 411 (Cook, Jan. 24, 1866) (Women and children "are represented, in the true sense of that word, by their fathers and brothers. The man who represents them does so really and practically, and not by legal fiction, like the man who represents 'three fifths of all other persons' "); 705 (Fessenden, Feb. 7, 1866) ("I have received considerable support from some of them [the ladies], not exactly in the way of voting, but in influencing voters"); 2962 (Poland, June 5, 1866) ("The theory is that the fathers, brothers, husbands, and sons to whom the right of suffrage is given will in its exercise be as watchful of the rights and interests of their wives, sisters, and children who do not vote as of their own"); 3035 (Henderson, June 8, 1866) (the ballot "is not given to the woman, because it is not needed for her security. Her interests are best protected by father, husband, and brother"); 39–2:56 (Williams, Dec. 11, 1866) ("to extend the right of suffrage to the negroes in this country I think is necessary for their protection; but to extend the right of suffrage to women, in my judgment, is not necessary for their protection. . . . Sons defend and protect the reputation and rights of their mothers; husbands defend and protect the reputation and rights of their wives; brothers . . . of their sisters"); 63 (Wade, Dec. 11, 1866) ("there is not the same pressing necessity for allowing females as there is for allowing the colored people to vote; because the ladies of the land are not under the ban of a hostile race grinding them to powder. They are in high fellowship with those who do govern, who, to a great extent, act as their agents, their friends, promoting their interests in every vote they give"); 66 (Frelinghuysen, Dec. 11, 1866) ("the women of America vote by faithful and true representatives, their husbands, their brothers, their sons. . . . There is a vast difference between the situation of the colored citizen and the women of America"); 307 (Sherman, Jan. 7, 1867) ("So far as the families, the women and children, are concerned, we know that they are represented by their husbands, by their parents, by their brothers, by those who are connected with them by domestic ties; but so far as the black people of this District are concerned, we knew that the white people generally were hostile to them").

Professor Ackerman seems wholly unaware of these and other congressional speeches on the gender/race distinction. He claims that the virtual-representation "line of thought was not powerfully developed in the *Congressional Globe,*" although he does point to a single speech made by Representative John Broomall on Jan. 8, 1867. *Transformations,* 441 n. 16. In that speech, Broomall defined a republican government as one "in which the rulers are chosen by the suffrages of the people, and in which every citizen may either exercise the right of suffrage himself or have it exercised for him by some one who may be fairly considered as representing his interests by reason of legal, social, or family relations to him." Broomall continued as follows: "Under this definition, if the right of suffrage be exercised by all the adult males, the women and children may be considered as mediately represented in the government, and hence the form would be republican. But it would meet the requirements of the definition much better if the right of suffrage were extended to all adults without regard to sex; and I am ready to advocate this extension whenever the women of America shall believe themselves unfairly treated by this mediate representation and shall demand the right of suffrage for themselves." *CG*, 39–2:350–51 (Jan. 8, 1867). For Broomall's later remarks in a similar vein, see ibid., 40–2:1956–57 (Mar. 18, 1868).

50. For an example of attentiveness to the uneven distribution of blacks within a given state, see ibid., 40–2:3090–91 (Farnsworth, June 12, 1868). For attention to the uneven distribution of women across states (as distinct from within them), see ibid., 39–1:411 (Cook, Jan. 24, 1866).

51. Ibid., 39–2:40 (Morrill, Dec. 10, 1866) ("the ballot is the inseparable concomitant of the bayonet. Those who practice the one must be prepared to exercise the other. To introduce woman at the polls is to enroll her in the militia").

52. For acknowledgments of this linkage, see, e.g., ibid., 39–1:1072 (Nye, Feb. 28, 1866), 1617 (Moulton, Mar. 24, 1866), 1621 (Myers, Mar. 24, 1866), 1629 (Hart, Mar. 24, 1866), 1838–39 (Clarke, Mar. 26, 1866), 41–2:1254 (Morton, Feb. 14, 1870).

53. See, e.g., ibid., 39–1:2767 (Howard, May 23, 1866) ("this amendment is so drawn as to make it the political interest of the once slaveholding States to admit their colored population to the right of suffrage. . . . It holds out the same penalty to Massachusetts as to South Carolina").

54. This need for a credible (nonrepealable, federally enforceable) signal helps answer Ackerman's repeated objection (*Transformations,* 111, 197–98, 231) that Congress's demand for ratification was improper overkill in light of other conditions Congress had successfully imposed. For Andrew Johnson's earlier emphasis on the need for ex-Confederate governments to ratify the *Thirteenth* Amendment as a credible signal of their contrition and sincerity, see ibid., 143, 146, 152, 205. See also Eric L. McKitrick, *Andrew Johnson and Reconstruction* (1960), 92, 176, 182, 200, 256; Foner, *Reconstruction,* 179, 276; Benedict, *A Compromise,* 127, 142, 156.

Note also that in 1867 Congress initially implied that ex-rebel states would be readmitted only after the Fourteenth Amendment had become part of the Constitution. Here, too, fear of a Southern double-cross—insincere state ratifications followed by readmission and purported repeals prior to the Fourteenth's final enactment—would seem to be at work. But in June 1868—when ratification of the Fourteenth Amendment by three-quarters of the states seemed imminent—Congress ultimately chose simply to require that each ex-rebel state *itself* ratify. On Tennessee's prior admission after its prompt ratification, see n. 35 above.

55. On the legal doubts surrounding any attempted federal imposition of a fundamental condition of state nonrepealability, see n. 101 below.

56. Edward McPherson, *The Political History of the United States of America During the Period of Reconstruction* (1875), 107–09. For a slightly different tally, see McKitrick, *Andrew Johnson,* 178–79.

57. It is worth noting that Congress formally required ex-gray states to ratify only after the Fourteenth Amendment had won ratification in more than three-fourths of the true-blue states.

58. Joint Resolution of Feb. 8, 1865, 13 Stat. 567. For some of the background behind this resolution, see, e.g., *CG,* 38–2:551–52 (Trumbull, Feb. 2, 1865), 584 (Lane, Feb. 3, 1865), 40–2:954–55 (Williams and Buckalew, Feb. 4, 1868).

59. Last Public Address, Apr. 11, 1865. For emphasis on Lincoln's tactical and theoretical flexibility in this address and more generally, see McKitrick, *Andrew Johnson,* 103–08.

60. Ackerman, *Transformations,* 113–15.

61. The quotation here is from Lincoln's July 4, 1861, Address, a more extensive excerpt of which appears earlier in this chapter; see pp. 372–73.

62. *CG,* 39–1:2 (Sumner, Dec. 4, 1866).

63. Ackerman, *Transformations,* 113–15. In fairness, Ackerman does note in passing that differences existed between Sumner's lapsed-state/de-facto-territory approach and Thaddeus Stevens's more extreme "conquered province" theory. Ibid., 113 & 445 n. 37. But Ackerman then declares that the two approaches "had the same implications" for the Article V issues at hand, and he proceeds to treat the two interchangeably, dismissing both as resting on "secessionist" logic and asserting that "Sumner and Stevens seemed to be saying the rebels were right: the Constitution had not created an indissoluble Union." Ibid., 113–15. Yet the very scholarship that Ackerman cites at this point makes clear that Sumner emphatically rejected secessionist logic: See McKitrick, *Andrew Johnson,* 110 ("Constitutionally, he [Sumner] argued, it was impossible to remove United States territory from the jurisdiction of the federal government"); William Dunning, *Essays on the Civil War and Reconstruction* (1898), 105, 108 ("Sumner's famous theory" held that "the territory of the extinct commonwealth belongs irrevocably to the United States . . . [and that] the people of the South, upon submission to the national forces, became entitled to the rights of United States citizens"). See also John W. Burgess, *Reconstruction and the Constitution* (1909), 60–61 (Sumner, Shellabarger, and "the great mass" of congressional Republicans "were not able to accept Mr. Stevens's view of the temporary validity of secession." On their view, "secession was a nullity legally from the beginning, and could not take the territory occupied by the 'States' attempting it, or the people inhabiting that territory, out of the Union, or from under the rightful jurisdiction of the United States Government and Constitution, for one instant").

64. Special Session Address, July 4, 1861, quoted more extensively in Chapter 7, p. 275.

65. The metaphor derives from Charles Sumner, who described the republican-government clause as "like a sleeping giant in the Constitution, never until this recent war awakened, but now it comes forward with a giant's power." *CG,* 40–1:614 (July 12, 1867).

66. The Reconstruction Congress gave the national military a leading role in overseeing Southern Reconstruction and facilitating Southern ratification of the Fourteenth Amendment. See, e.g., the First Reconstruction Act (also known as the Military Reconstruction Act) of Mar. 2, 1867, 14 Stat. 428; Supplementary Reconstruction Act of Mar. 23, 1867, 15 Stat. 2. For general discussion of these acts and of the military's role, see Benedict, *A Compromise,* 223–43; Foner, *Life and Writings,* 271–77, 307–8, 438; Kenneth M. Stampp, *The Era of Reconstruction, 1865–1877* (1965),144–47; James, *Ratification,* 210–11.

   For a clever argument that the text of the Fourteenth Amendment—in its first sentence, nationalizing American citizenship—did indeed in effect rewrite the intricate Article I, section 8 matrix governing armies and militias, see David Yassky, "The Second Amendment: Structure, History, and Constitutional Change," *Michigan LR* 99 (2000): 588, 638–42. Without more, the amendment's terse first sentence, which said nothing specifically about armies and militias, would seem too slight to bear all the weight Yassky places on it as a comprehensive rewriting of the military system laid out in great detail in Article I. Yassky points to no specific historical evidence in which Reconstruction Republicans linked the first sentence to army/militia issues (such as conscription). Indeed, he concedes that "congressional debates on the Fourteenth Amendment give no indication that it was expected to alter the Constitution's military structure." Ibid., 642. But perhaps Yassky here concedes too much. As I see it, the very *enactment process* of the Fourteenth Amendment was itself a visible signal to the American people that the central army's role vis-à-vis local militias was being constitutionally redefined.

67. *Op. Att'y Gen.,* 10:382 (1862).

68. Act of Apr. 9, 1866, 14 Stat. 27.

69. *Gibson v. Mississippi,* 162 U.S. 565, 591 (1896).

70. *Dred Scott v. Sanford,* 60 U.S. (19 How.) 393, 407 (1857).

71. *Civil Rights Cases,* 109 U.S. 3, 46 (1883). Harlan took care to point out that the Court had upheld proslavery laws operating on private actors in *Prigg,* notwithstanding any explicit enforcement clause and indeed in the teeth of an Article IV text that spoke only of states and thus had no true counterpart to the Fourteenth Amendment's more expansive first sentence.

72. To the extent that some persons might be born with a particular sexual orientation, laws that targeted orientation and status pure and simple would

also seem to run afoul of the core principle. See generally *Romer v. Evans,* 517 U.S. 620 (1995); Akhil Reed Amar, "Attainder and Amendment 2: *Romer's* Rightness," *Michigan LR* 95 (1996): 203.

73. Jefferson to Roger C. Weightman, June 24, 1826, in Jefferson, *Writings,* 10:391–92. Jefferson here borrowed from the English leveler Richard Rumbold.

74. See Pa. Const (1776), Declaration of Rights, art. I; Vt. Const. (1777), ch. I, art. I; Mass. Const. (1780), pt. I, art. I; N.H. Const. (1784), pt. I, art. I. See also Wiecek, *Guarantee Clause,* 156 (discussing an 1838 speech by the influential antislavery theorist Alvan Stewart elaborating on the ideal of "equality at birth").

75. For Madison's proto–Fourteenth Amendment as it passed the House, see *Senate Journal* 1:64 (Aug. 24, 1789).

76. *Dred Scott v. Sanford,* 60 U.S. (19 How.) 393, 417, 449 (1857).

77. 32 U.S. (7 Pet.) 243 (1833).

78. *CG,* 39–1:1088–94, 1291–93 (Feb. 28 and Mar. 9, 1866). Note that these two speeches occurred in the span of ten days, not six weeks as I mistakenly reported in Akhil Reed Amar, *The Bill of Rights: Creation and Reconstruction* (1998), 183.

79. *New York Times,* Mar. 1, 1866, 5 (summarizing Bingham's speech of Feb. 28, which begins at *CG,* 39–1:1088). Bingham's pamphlet was published by the *Congressional Globe* office.

80. *CG,* 39–1:2765–66 (May 23, 1866).

81. Ibid., 1090 (Bingham, Feb. 28, 1866), 1292 (Bingham, Mar. 9, 1866), 2756–66 (Howard, May 23, 1866).

82. On the possible differences between the first eight amendments and the last two, see Amar, *Bill of Rights,* 180, 215–30.

83. Act of July 16, 1866, 14 Stat. 173, 176 (emphasis added).

84. Act of Feb. 10, 1855, 10 Stat. 604.

85. The Court read the relevant clauses in just this way in *Minor v. Happersett,* 88 U.S. (21 Wall.) 162 (1875).

86. For a long list of cites, see Amar, *Bill of Rights,* 217 n. *.

87. *CG,* 39–1:356–57 (Conkling, Jan. 22, 1866).

88. On white bigotry, see, e.g., ibid., 704 (Fessenden, Feb. 7, 1866) ("What can pass? If we report a [black-suffrage amendment] is there the slightest probability that it will be adopted by the States and become a part of the Constitution of the United States? It is perfectly evident that there could be no hope of that description"). The five equal-suffrage states in 1865 were Maine, New Hampshire, Vermont, Massachusetts, and Rhode Island. Equal-suffrage measures went down to defeat in Connecticut, Wisconsin, and Minnesota in 1865, and thereafter in Kansas, Ohio, New York, and Minnesota again. Foner, *Reconstruction,* 223, 315.

89. See, e.g., *CG,* 39–1:141 (Blaine, Jan. 8, 1866) ("Basing representation on

voters—unless Congress should be empowered to define their qualifications—would tend to cheapen suffrage everywhere. There would be an unseemly scramble in all the States during each decade to increase by every means the numbers of voters"); 357 (Conkling, Jan. 22, 1866) ("One state might let women and minors vote"); 705 (Fessenden, Feb. 7, 1866) ("perhaps the result might be an unseemly race between States to increase their political power by increasing the number of their voters").

90. On school suffrage, see the (slightly varying) accounts in Kraditor, *Ideas,* 3; Alexander Keyssar, *The Right to Vote: The Contested History of Democracy in the United States* (2000), 186, 399.

91. For early expositions of the point, see *CG,* 39–1:141 (Blaine, Jan. 8, 1866), 357 (Conkling, Jan. 22, 1866). For a later reminder, see ibid., 2767 (Howard, May 23, 1866).

92. In addition to remarks cited above in nn. 89 and 91, see, e.g., ibid., 141 (Blaine and Stevens, Jan. 8, 1866) (discussing "disparity of men and women" in New England); 379–80 (Brooks and Stevens, Jan. 23, 1866), 705 (Fessenden, Feb. 7, 1866) ("the newer the State is, the greater is its proportion of males over twenty-one years of age"). See also Joseph B. James, *The Framing of the Fourteenth Amendment* (1956), 23.

93. On Lucy Stone and other feminist supporters of the Reconstruction Amendments, see Eleanor Flexner, *Century of Struggle: The Woman's Rights Movement in the United States* (rev. ed. 1975), 147–48; Kraditor, *Ideas,* 2–3; Sara M. Evans, *Born for Liberty* (1989), 122. On feminists' general embrace of section 1 of the Fourteenth Amendment, see *HWS,* 2:315. On Stanton, see Ellen Carol Dubois, *Feminism and Suffrage* (1978), 61 (quoting Stanton to Gerrit Smith, Jan. 1, 1866).

94. *HWS,* 2:171–72 (emphasis deleted).

95. See *CG,* 39–1:380 (Jan. 23, 1866).

96. According to Professor John Harrison, "States had residence requirements, literacy requirements, property qualifications, and a few other regulations of the vote, and it wasn't clear which qualified for the section 2 penalty. If a restriction did, it wasn't always clear how to apply that conclusion. For example, some states required that voters be paid up on their taxes; what was the status of someone who was in arrears when the census taker came around but might pay up and become eligible before election day? And there were massive problems in gathering the information. If the Rhode Island property qualifications counted as a denial, how were the census enumerators to determine who was denied the vote? Were they supposed to go to the property tax rolls? ... The results of the 9th census included [limited] information, which virtually everyone concerned seems to have agreed was unreliable and indeed arbitrary." Harrison to ARA (by e-mail), Feb. 25, 2004.

97. Lincoln to Michael Hahn, Mar. 13, 1865; Lincoln to James Wadsworth, circa Jan. 1864; Last Public Address, Apr. 11, 1865.

98. *CG,* 39–1:2 (Dec. 4, 1865) (emphasis added).

99. See, e.g., ibid., 707 (Feb. 7, 1866).

100. Two years earlier, Tennessee had been readmitted to reward the state's prompt ratification of the Fourteenth Amendment at a time when no other ex-Confederate state showed any similar inclination; see n. 35 above. Note also that Georgia's readmission occurred only in the House; for more details, see Benedict, *A Compromise,* 325–36; Dunning, *Essays,* 237–47.

101. Although the congressional statutes readmitting seven ex-Confederate states in 1868 purported to impose upon them a "fundamental condition" prohibiting future disenfranchisements, many in and out of Congress expressed serious doubts about the constitutionality of these conditions, and about their practical enforceability. See An Act to Admit the State of Arkansas to Representation in Congress, June 22, 1868, 15 Stat. 72; An Act to Admit the States of North Carolina, South Carolina, Louisiana, Georgia, Alabama, and Florida, to Representation in Congress, June 25, 1868, 15 Stat. 73. For doubts about the status of these conditions, see Earl M. Maltz, *Civil Rights, the Constitution, and Congress, 1863–69* (1990), 124–28, 138–41, 143; Benedict, *A Compromise,* 318–22.

102. On Grant, see William Gillette, *The Right to Vote: Politics and the Passage of the Fifteenth Amendment* (1965), 79.

103. Cf. James, *Ratification,* 121 ("many in the North wanted rights and votes to be recognized in the South in order to induce people of that race [blacks] to stay there, or even to return there"). In the antebellum era, Iowa, Illinois, Indiana, and Oregon had each purported to bar the entry of free blacks from sister states. See Foner, *Reconstruction,* 26.

104. *Plessy v. Ferguson,* 163 U.S. 537, 555 (1896).

105. For an earlier statement by Charles Sumner illustrating this inherently integrationist vision, see *CG,* 42–2:242 (Dec. 20, 1871) ("we have had in this Chamber a colored Senator from Mississippi, but according to [segregationist ideology] we should have set him apart by himself; he should not have sat with his brother Senators").

106. *Plessy,* 163 U.S. at 561. On the link in Harlan's mind between the Fifteenth Amendment and jury service, see *Neal v. Delaware,* 103 U.S. 370, 389 (1881) (Harlan, J.). In both *Plessy* and *Neal,* Harlan echoed themes that were common even among conservative Reconstruction Republicans in the 1860s. See, e.g., *CG,* 39–1:704 (Fessenden, Feb. 7, 1866) ("a voter is an officer, not in the same degree, perhaps, but as much so in substance as the man who enters the jury box, as any one who holds an office"). See also Dunning, *Essays,* 159 ("It seemed axiomatic . . . that, if the freedmen were qualified to vote, they were qualified for jury service"). Early drafts of the Fifteenth Amendment had explicitly encompassed an equal right to "hold office," but this language disappeared in a joint House-Senate committee in part because one key committee member thought that the additional words were not merely unneces-

sary but counterproductive. On his view, the inclusion of this clause wrongly implied that the equal "right to vote" language *itself* did not encompass an equal right to serve in government. In the preceding months, Georgia had been readmitted to Congress after promising to let blacks vote, and had then excluded blacks from its legislature. In response, Congress insisted that Georgia had broken its word: As leading Republicans saw it, voting eligibility presumptively encompassed all other political rights unless otherwise specified. For much more elaboration and documentation, see Vikram David Amar, "Jury Service as Political Participation Akin to Voting," *Cornell LR* 80 (1995): 203.

11: PROGRESSIVE REFORMS

1. *Chisholm v. Georgia,* 2 U.S. (2 Dall.) 419 (1793); *Dred Scott v. Sanford,* 60 U.S. (19 How.) 393 (1857).
2. Tariff Act of Aug. 15, 1894, ch. 349, secs. 27–37, 28 Stat. 509, 553–61.
3. *Pollock v. Farmers' Loan & Trust Co.,* 158 U.S. 601 (1895). Full disclosure: The theory relied upon by the *Pollock* Court—that a tax on rental income was constitutionally equivalent to a direct tax on the land itself—has been said to have been developed by Charles F. Southmayd, the man for whom the Yale University chair I now hold was named. Needless to say, Mr. Southmayd would probably not have agreed with my analysis of *Pollock* or of the underlying constitutional questions at issue in that case. For discussion of the link between Mr. Southmayd and the *Pollock* theory, see Boris I. Bittker and Lawrence Lokken, *Federal Taxation of Income, Estates, and Gifts* (2d ed. 1989), 1:17 n. 20, sec. 1.2.2. It also bears mention that Professor Bittker himself once held the Southmayd Chair.
4. *Pollock,* 158 U.S. 684 (Harlan, J., dissenting).
5. *Farrand's Records,* 2:350.
6. Several plausible tests for drawing the direct/indirect line might be deduced from the relevant Founding materials. First, "direct" taxes might simply be limited to capitations—that is, to head taxes that levied a fee on each person simply by dint of his being a person. Textually, such a head tax was "direct" in the sense that it could not be avoided (short of death itself). By contrast, an indirect "duty" on an imported good might be avoided simply by not buying the taxed good. Along this axis, an income tax, which came into play only when income had been generated, could indeed be avoided. For example, a person could refrain from making new income and could instead live off savings or the income of others. Measured by a simple textual test of avoidability, income taxes would thus be indirect. Cf. *Federalist* No. 21. Historically, capitations were indeed the paradigm Founding-era example of a direct tax. The text of the Constitution confirms this status in its reference to "Capitation, *or other* direct, Tax." Many Founders probably also swept land taxes into the direct-tax category. Thanks in no small part to the experience under the Arti-

cles of Confederation, head taxes and land taxes had become linked in many minds. The Articles had tried to apportion taxes among states based on the value of land within each state. When assessment issues arose, a head-count proxy for land values—counting slaves at three-fifths—emerged as the compromise. Because this three-fifths approach was the precise one that the Constitution's direct-tax clause required, it helped cement an understandable connection in many people's minds between head counts (apportionments/ censuses), head taxes (capitations), and land taxes. Of course, the main purpose of the direct/indirect line at the Founding was to prohibit Congress from imposing burdensome head taxes on slaves—taxes that masters would be obliged to pay and that might enable the new federal government to destroy slavery via the tax power. But this main purpose had been rendered moot by the Emancipation Amendment, and thus it, too, offered no support for the *Pollock* result.

Several subsidiary purposes also underlay the direct/indirect line, but these also argued against *Pollock*. First, some taxes—on heads or on the assessed value of land—could sensibly be pegged to decennial census enumerations in which persons could be counted and lands assessed. On this functional view, land taxes and head taxes should be treated as "direct" precisely because these taxes meshed with a workable census. But other taxes— duties on imports or sales-tax excises—would have nothing to do with any sort of workable census measurements and were thus sensibly viewed as "indirect." Under this test, income taxes plainly fell on the non-census side of the line. (The very fact that the "direct"-tax clauses themselves mentioned the words "Census" and "Enumeration" invited functional integration of these concepts.) Yet another Founding-era concern about direct taxes was that a person might not have the cash to pay such a tax. This was obviously true of a head tax, and also true of a land tax in the Founding era's cash-poor agrarian society. To oblige a person to sell all or part of his family homestead in order to pay a land tax was to impose a special harshness on him that did not exist for other taxes like excises and imposts, in which the very transactions themselves occurred only when money was changing hands, a fraction of which could go to the government. Similarly, a tax not on land but on *income* generated by the land—or on other income being generated—would not involve the hardships of head taxes or direct land taxes. On this view, the development of a cash economy in the years after the Founding also argued against an expansive reading of directness. Thus, it would be outlandish today to treat wealth taxes or consumption taxes as "direct" taxes requiring state-by-state apportionment. For a different view, see Eric M. Jensen, "The Apportionment of 'Direct Taxes': Are Consumption Taxes Constitutional?" *Columbia LR* 97 (1997): 2334, 2393–97.

7. See, e.g., *Hylton v. United States,* 3 U.S. (3 Dall.) 171, 174 (Chase, J.), 181–83 (Iredell, J.) (1796).

8. 102 U.S. 586, 601–2 (1881). For an earlier statement that income taxes were not direct taxes, see *Scholey v. Rew,* 90 U.S. (23 Wall.) 331, 346–47 (1874).

9. Eric Kades, "Drawing the Line Between Taxes and Takings: The Continuous Burdens Principle, and its Broader Application," *Northwestern U. LR* 97 (2002): 189, 209–10.

10. Act of Mar. 3, 1865, 13 Stat. 469, 479; Tariff Act of Aug. 15, 1894, ch. 349, sects. 27–37, 28 Stat. 509, 553–61; Alan P. Grimes, *Democracy and the Amendments to the Constitution* (1978; reprint, 1987), 68–69; Kades, "Drawing the Line," 210–11.

11. Emphasis added.

12. Act of Oct. 3, 1913, 38 Stat. 166 (1913); Sharon Nantell, "A Cultural Perspective on American Tax Policy," *Chapman LR* 2 (1999): 33, 50.

13. *Brushaber v. Union Pac. R.R.,* 240 U.S. 1, 25 (1916).

14. Don E. Fehrenbacher, *Prelude to Greatness: Lincoln in the 1850's* (1962), 48–49; George H. Haynes, *The Senate of the United States: Its History and Practice* (1938), 1:99. For discussion of some precursors of, even if not full-blown precedents for, the Lincoln-Douglas model, see William H. Riker, "The Senate and American Federalism," *APSR* 49 (1955): 452, 463–64.

15. Fehrenbacher, *Prelude,* 114–20.

16. Riker, "Senate," 466.

17. 1909 Or. Laws 15; Riker, "Senate," 466–67. Although Riker and others have described the 1908 Oregon law as a state constitutional provision, it would appear that it was presented to voters as a *statutory* initiative.

18. George H. Haynes, *The Election of Senators* (1909), 36–50, 62–63.

19. For a statistical analysis suggesting that the amendment did somewhat reduce the number of extremely wealthy senators and senators who were younger members of political dynasties, see Sara Brandes Crook and John R. Hibbing, "A Not-so-distant Mirror: The 17th Amendment and Congressional Change," *APSR* 91 (1997): 845, 846–48.

20. In the thirty years before the Direct Senate Election Amendment, Lucius Lamar, Howell Jackson, and Edward White all came to the Court with Senate experience, as did George Sutherland, Hugo Black, and James Byrnes in the next thirty years.

21. My tally omits Millard Fillmore, Gerald Ford, and George H. W. Bush, who as vice presidents did serve in (by presiding over) the Senate. Note also that Garfield had been elected to the Senate but never served. For additional data on how representatives seeking the presidency have fared much worse in the post–Seventeenth Amendment world, see Robert L. Peabody, Norman J. Ornstein, and David W. Rohde, "The United States Senate as a Presidential Incubator: Many Are Called but Few Are Chosen," *Political Science Qtly.* 91 (1976): 237, 244.

22. Between Washington and Lincoln, the only presidents who spent no time in the Senate were Madison, Polk, and Taylor. Between Grant and Harding,

the only presidents who spent no time in governorships were Garfield, Arthur, Harrison, and Taft. Note also that from 1804 through 1860, "all but five of the twenty-four major party [presidential] nominees (excluding the renomination of incumbent presidents) had had some prior service in the United States Senate." Ibid., 241.

23. Of the ten presidents from Grant through Wilson, only Arthur (as VP), Harrison, and TR (as VP) had served in the Senate. (As previously noted, Garfield was tapped for the Senate but did not serve.) Of the next ten presidents—Harding through Ford—all but Hoover, FDR, and Eisenhower had Senate experience (Coolidge and Ford only as VPs). If we focus only on elected presidents, Arthur and Ford drop out of the analysis, making Lincoln the first elected president in the tally and Carter the last.

For other recent efforts to measure traffic on the road between the Senate and the White House, see Robert L. Peabody et al., "United States Senate"; David R. Mayhew, *America's Congress* (2000), 153–57; Barry C. Burden, "United States Senators as Presidential Candidates," *Political Science Qtly.* 117 (2002): 81.

24. Pre-amendment vice presidents from Wheeler through Marshall included ex-senators Hendricks and Fairbanks. Among the next ten—Coolidge through Humphrey—Curtis, Truman, Barkley, Nixon, Johnson, and Humphrey had all served as senators. Among Democratic Party nominees, only Ferraro in 1984 was not a current or former senator. (In 1972, Senator Eagleton later withdrew from the ticket, to be replaced by Shriver, who had never served in the Senate.) The complete list of Democratic VP nominees, beginning in 1944: Truman, Barkley, Sparkman, Kefauver, Johnson, Humphrey, Muskie, Eagleton/Shriver, Mondale, Ferraro, Bentsen, Gore, Lieberman, and Edwards. Cf. Robert L. Peabody et al., "United States Senate," 239 n. 4, 245.

25. Act of June 2, 1851.

26. Grimes, *Democracy and Amendments,* 84–85.

27. See generally Alan P. Grimes, *The Puritan Ethic and Woman Suffrage* (1967), 115 ("Between 1914 and 1917, seven western states adopted prohibition; all of them were woman suffrage states").

28. Various official federal publications report that Connecticut ratified the Prohibition Amendment on May 6, 1919; other official tallies omit Connecticut. State archives reveal that on May 6, Connecticut *failed* to ratify; see *Connecticut Senate Journal* (1919), 1191 (Report of Committee of Conference on S.J. Res. No. 56). National Archive records likewise count Connecticut as a nonratifier. Special thanks to Lisa Chan for uncovering these materials.

29. A thirty-eighth state—Montana—said yes in 1934.

30. Everett S. Brown, "The Ratification of the Twenty-fifth Amendment," *APSR* 29 (1935): 1005, 1010; David E. Kyvig, *Explicit and Authentic Acts: Amending the U.S. Constitution, 1776–1995* (1996), 283–85.

31. See David E. Kyvig, *Repealing National Prohibition* (2d ed. 2000), 21.

32. See *Cong. Rec.,* 55:5666 (Aug. 1, 1917), 76:4231 (Feb. 13, 1933). Grimes, *Democracy and Amendments,* 112, reports that seventeen senators voted for both Prohibition and its repeal, while Kyvig, *Repealing,* 172, counts only thirteen. The accurate number would appear to be fifteen, namely, Senators Ashurst, Fletcher, Hale, Johnson (Ca.), Kendrick, King, McKellar, McNary, Pittman, Robinson (Ark.), Smith (S.C.), Swanson, Trammell, Walsh (Mont.), and Watson. In two other cases, involving Alabama's Bankhead and Wisconsin's La Follette, senatorial sons had replaced senatorial fathers with the same first and last names, perhaps leading Grimes to overcount. (Elsewhere on the same page, Grimes apparently conflates two different senators named Reed.) Conversely, the source on which Kyvig relies simply overlooked Kendrick and McKellar. Note, finally, that at least eight senators who voted for repeal had previously voted for Prohibition as House members, namely, Barkley, Byrnes, Connally, Dill, Harrison, Hayden, Hull, and White. If these eight are added to the other fifteen, we find that nearly one-third of the senatorial yes votes for the Repeal Amendment came from legislators who had switched sides—not counting any senators who might have previously supported Prohibition in their state legislatures.

33. *HWS,* 3:727. Wyoming also moved to protect various economic rights of married women and promised equal pay for female teachers; see ibid., 728.

34. See ibid., 730 ("The favorite argument . . . and by far the most effective, was this: it [the woman-suffrage law] would prove a great advertisement . . . and attract attention to . . . the territory"); Eleanor Flexner, *Century of Struggle, The Woman's Rights Movement in the United States* (1959, rev. ed. 1975), 160 (Western "women gained in prestige by their very scarcity"); Grimes, *Puritan Ethic,* 58 ("Women were a scarce commodity in Wyoming. It may be conjectured that the legislature resorted to special inducements to help alleviate this shortage, granting privileges in much the same manner in which states have historically sought to attract businesses by offering them special benefits"); T. A. Larson, "Woman Suffrage in Western America," *Utah Hist. Qtly.* 38 (1970): 7, 9–10 (quoting the 1869 testimony of Professor J. K. H. Willcox before the federal House Committee on Territories; according to Willcox—a suffrage advocate—letting women vote in the West would encourage emigration from "the overcrowded East" and would reduce the Western gender imbalance); 12 (quoting editorial in Cheyenne's leading newspaper: "We now expect at once quite an immigration of ladies to Wyoming. We say to them all, come on"); John D. W. Guice, *The Rocky Mountain Bench: The Territorial Supreme Courts of Colorado, Montana, and Wyoming, 1861–1890* (1972), 131 ("the territory desperately needed immigrants, particularly the feminine variety"); Beverly Beeton, *Women Vote in the West: The Woman Suffrage Movement, 1869–1896* (1986), 1 ("The completion of the [transcontinental] railroad had linked Wyoming with the East, and many citizens of the newly

organized territory were seeking a way to draw attention and hopefully attract settlers to the area"); 4 (discussing particular desire to "attract women to the territory"); 116, 119 (discussing the notable, if lesser, role that such arguments appeared to play in Idaho).

35. For example, when Wyoming extended the suffrage to women in 1860–70, men in the territory outnumbered women six to one. Grimes, *Puritan Ethic,* 24, 53; Beeton, *Women Vote,* 4.

36. *HWS,* 6:752–53; *Encyclopedia Britannica* (11th ed. 1910), N:626 ("New Zealand"); Australian Bureau of Statistics, *Census of 1901* (online "1901 Australian snapshot").

37. It need not be shown that Northern black-suffrage rules did in fact prevent a mass migration of freedmen or that Western woman-suffrage rules did in fact prompt a large flow of females. Even if the hopes and fears of mass migrations eventually proved illusory, these hopes and fears alone could suffice to generate important results in America's federal system.

38. *HWS,* 3:75–97; Flexner, *Century of Struggle,* 176–77. On Stanton's role alongside Anthony's in drafting the proposal, see Ellen Carole Dubois, *Woman Suffrage and Women's Rights* (1998), 225.

39. See Beeton, *Women Vote,* 116.

40. Carrie Chapman Catt and Nettie Rogers Shuler, *Woman Suffrage and Politics* (1923), 107; Flexner, *Century of Struggle,* 150, 176.

41. Of the eleven states with woman suffrage before 1915, nine had initiative and referendum; conversely, of the eleven states with recall, eight embraced woman suffrage. Grimes, *Puritan Ethic,* 101.

42. Alexander Keyssar, *The Right to Vote: The Contested History of Democracy in the United States* (2000), 401.

43. The six holdouts were Idaho's Senator Borah, New York's Senator Wadsworth (on whom see n. 45 below), Michigan's Representative Doremus, and New York Representatives Dunn, Riordan, and Sanders. Congressmen from presidential-suffrage-only states also overwhelmingly supported the Nineteenth Amendment, by a combined vote of 142 to 10, as compared with an even split among congressmen from nonsuffrage states, 102 of whom supported the amendment and 99 of whom opposed it.

44. Keyssar, *Right to Vote,* 213–14.

45. Similarly, New York woman suffragists targeted Senator James Wolcott Wadsworth, Jr., who had been an uncompromising foe of the amendment. In 1926, Wadsworth was finally defeated, in a contest in which former suffragists played a prominent role. See Martin L. Fausold, *James W. Wadsworth, Jr.: The Gentleman from New York* (1975), 127, 131, 192–95. Later, however, Wadsworth was repeatedly elected to the House. Also, in several other states, foes of the amendment, such as Idaho Senator William Borah, continued to win repeated Senate reelection even after women became part of the electorates to which they had to account.

46. Address to the Senate, Sept. 30, 1918, in *The Papers of Woodrow Wilson,* Arthur S. Link, ed., (1985), 51:158–61. See also Wilson's statement of Jan. 9, 1918, in ibid., 45:545.

47. *Cong. Rec.,* 58:618 (June 4, 1919). For similar statements by other Southern leaders, see Grimes, *Puritan Ethic,* 126–27.

48. In the current case law, see, e.g., *Taylor v. Louisiana,* 419 U.S. 522 (1975); *Duren v. Missouri,* 439 U.S. 357 (1979); *Powers v. Ohio,* 499 U.S. 400 (1991); *J.E.B. v. Alabama,* 511 U.S. 127 (1994). For discussion of how these cases mesh with the letter and spirit of the voting rights amendments, see Vikram David Amar, "Jury Service as Political Participation Akin to Voting," *Cornell LR* 80 (1995): 203; Vikram David Amar and Alan Brownstein, "The Hybrid Nature of Political Rights," *Stanford LR* 50 (1998): 915.

49. Civil Rights Act of Mar. 1, 1875, ch. 114, sec. 4, 18 Stat. 335, 336 (currently codified as amended at 18 U.S.C. 243). Note that various aspects of this law were held invalid by the Supreme Court in 1883, but not its provisions regarding jury trial, which remain on the books to this day. For more on this law, see Chapter 10, footnote on pp. 400–401.

50. "Suffrage Wins in Senate; Now Goes to States," *New York Times,* June 5, 1919; *HWS,* 2:687–88 (quoting Susan B. Anthony's protest against a June 1873 conviction for her unlawful effort to vote in 1872: "Had your honor submitted my case to the jury, as was clearly your duty, even then I should have had just cause of protest, for not one of those men was my peer; . . . a commoner of England, tried before a jury of lords, would have far less cause to complain than should I, a woman, tried before a jury of men. . . . No disenfranchised person is entitled to sit upon a jury, and no woman is entitled to the franchise").

51. For Progressive-era state court decisions holding women eligible to serve in juries and/or hold certain other public offices as a result of their state/federal constitutional right to vote by itself or in tandem with prior state laws or customs, see, e.g., *Parus v. Dist. Court,* 174 P. 706 (Nev. 1918); *Rose v. Sullivan,* 185 P. 562 (Mont. 1919); *People v. Barltz,* 180 N.W. 423 (Mich. 1920); *Opinion of the Justices,* 113 A. 614 (Me. 1921); *Commonwealth v. Maxwell,* 114 A. 825 (Pa. 1921); *State v. Walker,* 185 N.W. 619, 626 (Iowa 1921); *Opinion of the Justices,* 135 N.E. 173 (Mass. 1922); *Preston v. Roberts,* 110 S.E. 586 (N.C. 1922); *Dickson v. Strickland,* 265 S.W. 1012, 1023 (Tex. 1924); *Palmer v. State,* 150 N.E. 917, 918–19 (Ind. 1926); *Opinion of the Justices,* 139 A. 180 (N.H. 1927); *Browning v. State,* 165 N.E. 566, 567 (Ohio 1929). For more narrow readings in the early 1920s, see, e.g., *In re Opinion of the Justices,* 130 N.E. 685 (Mass. 1921); *Harper v. State,* 234 S.W. 909 (Tex. Crim. App. 1921); State v. Mittle, 113 S.E. 335 (S.C. 1922); *State v. Bray,* 95 So. 417 (La. 1923); *State v. Kelly,* 229 P. 659 (Idaho 1924); *People ex rel. Fyfe v. Barnett,* 150 N.E. 290, 291 (Ill. 1925). For broad recognition by state legislatures of the spirit of the Nineteenth Amendment and counterpart state-constitutional provisions, see, e.g., *Ex*

parte Mana, 172 P. 986 (Cal. 1918); *Opinion of the Justices,* 113 A. 614 (Me. 1921); *State v. James,* 114 A. 553 (N.J. 1921); 10 *Op. Att'y Gen.* (Wis.) 15,369 (1921); Act of July 15, 1921, ch. 529, 1921 Wis. Laws 869 (codified at Wis. Stat. sec. 6.015) (1921); *State v. Rosenberg,* 192 N.W. 194 (Minn. 1923). For one particularly interesting state-legislative response, see *State v. Chase,* 211 P. 920 (Ore. 1922) (discussing 1921 statute providing for women jurors, allowing women to automatically exempt themselves from jury duty, and requiring that in certain cases "at least one-half of the jury shall be women"). All told, women sat on juries in roughly half the states in the early 1920s. See J. Stanley Lemons, *The Woman Citizen: Social Feminism in the 1920s* (1973), 69–70 (listing Idaho, Kansas, Michigan, Nevada, Utah, Washington, California, Indiana, Iowa, Ohio, Delaware, Kentucky, Pennsylvania, New Jersey, Arkansas, Louisiana, Maine, Minnesota, North Dakota, Oregon, and Wisconsin; to this list we should add Montana, while noting the later complications in Idaho in the *Kelly* case). Cf. Elizabeth M. Sheridan, "Women and Jury Service," *A.B.A.J.* 11 (1925): 792 (women eligible for juries in twenty-two of the forty-eight states). By 1953, women served as jurors in forty-three of the forty-eight states, and by 1968, all the states had joined the bandwagon. Alabama, South Carolina, and Mississippi were the last holdouts; see *Hoyt v. Florida,* 368 U.S. 57, 62 n. 5 (1961). In general, the ex-Confederacy lagged behind the rest of the nation. In the state-by-state struggle for jury rights, as in the earlier crusade for voting rights, reformers worked the ratchet well, steadily winning new states while generally preventing antifeminists from undoing past feminist victories. See generally Shirley S. Abrahamson, "Justice and Juror," *Georgia LR* 20 (1986): 257, 262–76 (1986); *State v. Sanders,* 163 S.E. 2d 220, 224–25 (S.C. 1968); *State v. White,* 214 So. 2d 467 (Miss. 1968).

52. It is of course possible to imagine constitutionally sound juror-eligibility rules that go beyond voter-eligibility rules. For example, English-language literacy is nowadays not a general qualification for voting—non–English speakers can follow current events in non-English-language media—but jurors may well need to understand English in order to follow (English-language) courtroom testimony and judicial instructions, and to deliberate with other (English-speaking) jurors. My argument here is thus not that juror-eligibility rules must in every single instance be identical with voter-eligibility rules. Rather, I am suggesting a more modest principle: Whenever a constitutional norm prohibits voting discrimination on a particular basis—race or sex, for example—jury rules that exclude persons on this basis are suspect. In no case can such a jury rule prevail unless it is based on a rationale wholly consistent with the excluded group's status as full and equal participants in American democracy.

    In one of the first post–Anthony Amendment cases to reach the Supreme Court, *Adkins v. Children's Hospital,* 261 U.S. 525, 553 (1923), the justices explicitly relied on the amendment as a conclusive legal recognition that women could think for themselves. On the basis of this fact, the Court struck down paternalistic legislation that it had previously upheld. For a provocative meditation on *Adkins* and on the underappreciated scope of the Nineteenth Amendment more generally, see Reva B. Siegel, "She the People: The Nineteenth Amendment, Sex Equality, Federalism, and the Family," *Harvard LR* 115 (2001): 947.

53. See Chapter 10, footnote on pp. 400–401, and sources cited therein.

54. In 1920 itself, twenty-three states elected women to the legislature or some other government post, and several other states had previously done so. Lemons, *Woman Citizen,* 68. Today, virtually all state and federal positions are formally open to women as well as men.

55. On the clear intent to give the incoming Congress the power to resolve electoral-college misfires, see H.R. Rep. No. 345, 72d Cong., 1st Sess., 2, 3 (Feb. 2, 1932).

56. For discussion of the Twenty-fifth Amendment's extension of the Twentieth Amendment's language on this issue, see Chapter 12, n. 34.

57. Act of June 2, 1924, ch. 233, 43 Stat. 253. On the reservation-Indian gap in the Fourteenth Amendment's guarantee of birthright citizenship, see Chapter 10, p. 381. For discussion of the double-edged nature of the 1924 approach, see, e.g., Joseph William Singer, "The Stranger Who Resides with You: Ironies of Asian-American and American Indian Legal History," *Boston College LR* 40 (1998): 171–74; Robert N. Clinton, "There is No Federal Supremacy Clause for Indian Tribes," *Arizona State LJ* 34 (2002): 113, 246–52. For a more emphatically negative view, see Robert B. Porter, "The Demise of the Ongwehoweh and the Rise of the Native Americans: Redressing the Genocidal Act of Forcing American Citizenship Upon Indigenous Peoples," *Harvard Blackletter LJ* 15 (1999): 107.

12: MODERN MOVES

1. See Chapter 4, p. 146.

2. At the 1880 party convention, Grant led the field for most of the voting, only to lose to dark horse James Garfield on the thirty-sixth ballot.

3. TR quotes are from Edward S. Corwin, *The President: Office and Powers, 1787–1957* (4th rev. ed. 1957), 35–36; cf. *The New York Times,* Feb. 18, 1912, 12. See also Richard B. Bernstein with Jerome Agel, *Amending America* (1993), 157–58.

4. Washington to the Marquis de Lafayette, Apr. 28, 1788, in Washington, *Writings,* 29:479; Jefferson to John Taylor, Jan. 6, 1805, in Jefferson, *Writings* (Ford), 8:339; Corwin, *President,* 333.

5. Corwin, *President,* 36, 335.

6. The partial-term issue had also arisen the 1920s, when Calvin Coolidge became president more than halfway into Warren Harding's term. Coolidge was elected once in his own right, in 1924, and declined to seek reelection.

For the suggestion that Coolidge would have welcomed an unsolicited renomination in 1928, see ibid., 36, 335–36.

7. Note the analogy between these transition rules and the starting-date-delay provision of the Prohibition Amendment.

8. Some scholars and pundits—most notably, Bruce Peabody and Scott Gant—have contended that such gambits remain constitutionally permissible. But this seems doubtful in light of the letter and spirit of the Twelfth Amendment: "No person constitutionally ineligible to the office of President shall be eligible to that of Vice-President." Peabody and Gant effectively treat the Twelfth's command as beside the point. On their view, although a two-term incumbent cannot be again *elected* to the presidency, he is nonetheless *eligible* and therefore also eligible to be vice president. Bruce G. Peabody and Scott E. Gant, "The Twice and Future President: Constitutional Interstices and the Twenty-second Amendment," *Minnesota LR* 83 (1999): 565, 619–20. But this reading slights the facts that the words "eligible" and "electable" spring from the same Latin root, and that standard dictionaries have long included "electable" as one of the standard definitions of "eligible." See, e.g., *OED* entry on "eligible." Given these facts, it would seem that a two-term incumbent is "ineligible" to the presidency (within the meaning of the Twelfth Amendment) precisely because he is made *unelectable* to that office (by the Twenty-second)—and is thus barred (by the Twelfth) from being elected to the vice presidency in the first place. The Twenty-second's retroactivity rules would seem to confirm this reading of the Twelfth. These rules applied not only to a past incumbent who might in the future be "elected" president but also to one who might thenceforth "act[] as President"—paradigmatically, by being elected vice president and then moving back into the Oval Office via death, disability, or resignation.

9. Arguably, this scenario might differ from the case of an elected vice president because no offending presidential or vice-presidential "election"—as distinct from a mere "nominat[ion]" and "confirmation" under the Twenty-fifth Amendment—has occurred. The Twenty-fifth Amendment is discussed more generally on pp. 449–53.

10. In this scenario, the eligibility rule of the Twelfth Amendment, discussed in n. 8 above, simply does not apply. On the other hand, the current succession law, 3 U.S.C. 19 (e), excludes from the line of succession any officer who is not "eligible to the office of President under the Constitution" and thus would seem to raise similar issues.

11. Andrew Johnson, it must be remembered, was president only because of one man's bullet as opposed to all men's ballots.

12. For a powerful meditation on the special difficulties confronted by presidents who begin in the shadow of their predecessor patrons, see Stephen Skowronek, *The Politics Presidents Make: Leadership from John Adams to Bill Clinton* (rev. ed. 1997).

13. Of the thirty-two vice presidents elected between the amendments, only five went on to run for president on a major-party ticket: Van Buren, Breckinridge, TR, Coolidge, and Truman. Seven of eleven modern vice presidents have gone on to win their party's nomination for the presidency: Nixon, LBJ, Humphrey, Ford, Mondale, G. H. W. Bush, and Gore (as opposed to Agnew, Rockefeller, Quayle, and Cheney). Van Buren, Breckinridge, Nixon, Humphrey, Ford, G. H. W. Bush, and Gore all led their parties while retiring presidents (or in Ford's case, a resigned president—Nixon) looked on.

14. For general background on the District, see Don E. Fehrenbacher, *The Slaveholding Republic: An Account of the United States Government's Relations to Slavery* (2001), 49–88; Garry Wills, *"Negro President": Jefferson and the Slave Power* (2003), 200–14; Eric Foner, *Reconstruction: America's Unfinished Revolution* (1988), 240, 272, 355; Bernstein, *Amending*, 143–48; Stanley Elkins and Eric McKitrick, *The Age of Federalism* (1993), 133–34, 155–208. See also Act of Jan. 8, 1867, 14 Stat. 375; Act of June 20, 1874, ch. 337, 18 Stat. 116.

15. See generally Mary L. Dudziak, *Cold War Civil Rights: Race and the Image of American Democracy* (2000).

16. On the geostrategic significance of Alaska and Hawaii, see, e.g., the Democratic Party Platform of 1952: "By virtue of their strategic geographical locations, Alaska and Hawaii are vital bastions in the Pacific. . . . We, therefore, urge immediate statehood for these two territories."

17. Had Negroes voted for Dewey in the same two-to-one ratio by which they instead favored Truman, the Republican would have won. Michael J. Klarman, *From Jim Crow to Civil Rights* (2004), 181. Democratic black votes proved especially important in California, Illinois, and Ohio. William Gillette, *The Right to Vote: Politics and the Passage of the Fifteenth Amendment* (1965), 10.

18. Joint Resolution of Aug. 22, 1978, 92 Stat. 3795.

19. Act of Sept. 22, 1970, 84 Stat. 848.

20. Act of Dec. 24, 1973, 87 Stat. 774.

21. As late as 1960, it was not clear that every serious presidential candidate had to participate in the primary process. LBJ, for example, sat out the primaries in the hope that he could amass enough convention delegates from non-primary states, or from states where the primary had been won by a local favorite son. On the increasing significance of presidential primaries, see James W. Ceaser, *Presidential Selection: Theory and Development* (1979). On issues of race discrimination in Southern primaries, see the "White Primary Cases" of *Nixon v. Herndon,* 273 U.S. 536 (1927); *Nixon v. Condon,* 286 U.S. 73 (1932); *Smith v. Allwright,* 321 U.S. 649 (1944); *Terry v. Adams,* 345 U.S. 461 (1953).

22. The five were Alabama, Arkansas, Mississippi, Texas, and Virginia. *USCCAN* 89–1:2437, 2451 (1965 House Rep. 439 on H.R. 6400). Some parts of Vermont used poll taxes in connection with local elections. Ibid. See generally Alan P.

Grimes, *Democracy and the Amendments to the Constitution* (1978; reprint, 1987), 126–27, 131, 134; Alexander Keyssar, *The Right to Vote: The Contested History of Democracy in the United States* (2000), 229, 259.

23. Act of Aug. 6, 1965, sec. 10, 79 Stat. 437, 442. For the current version, see 42 U.S.C. 1973h.

24. *Harman v. Forssenius,* 380 U.S. 528, 543 (1965).

25. Keyssar, *Right to Vote,* 264.

26. Texas's LBJ, Georgia's Carter, and Arkansas's Clinton all ran well among black voters in every region. Texas's George H. W. Bush placed Clarence Thomas on the Supreme Court and Texas's George W. Bush named Colin Powell and, later, Condoleezza Rice, secretary of state. Only two elected presidents from 1964 through 2000 came from outside the South: Nixon and Reagan. (Ford, never elected, is omitted from this tally.) In the pre-1964 database, note that Wilson, born and raised in Dixie, ran as a New Jerseyan.

27. Similarly, in Congress, the great majority of no votes on the Anti–Poll Tax Amendment came from lawmakers representing current and former poll-tax-suffrage states—or to put the matter slightly differently, from Southern lawmakers. See Grimes, *Democracy and Amendments,* 126, 132, 135.

28. 400 U.S. 112 (1970).

29. *Mitchell,* 400 U.S. 213 n. 90 (Harlan, J., concurring in part and dissenting in part).

30. *Lowering the Voting Age to 18: Hearings Before the Subcomm. on Constitutional Amendments of the Sen. Judiciary Comm.,* 90th Cong., 2d Sess. 23 (1968) (Oliver).

31. The first state to lower the voting age to eighteen was Georgia, which did so in the midst of World War II—in 1943, to be precise, after Congress in 1942 lowered the draft age to eighteen. Keyssar, *Right to Vote,* 278.

32. As with earlier amendments extending the right to "vote," the Twenty-sixth should be applied to the right to *vote on juries:* Young adults should not be excluded from jury service or subject to age-based peremptory challenges. (Similarly, the Anti–Poll Tax Amendment should protect the right of the poor to vote and serve equally on federal juries; and since the principles of this Amendment and a more general "right to vote" properly apply to state elections, the same principles should apply to state jury service.) While the Supreme Court has begun to recognize important links between jury service and the voting rights amendments, it has yet to follow this logic to its final conclusion. For more, see sources cited in Chapter 11, n. 48.

33. Similarly, most Revolutionary-era state constitutions, with the conspicuous exception of South Carolina's, featured succession rules in which the "powers" of the top executive office, but not the "office" itself, would be transferred.

34. This language extended a principle that had been enunciated earlier by the Lame Duck Amendment, which had provided that in the event "the presi-

dent elect shall have died [in the transition period], the Vice President elect shall *become* President." By contrast, in other cases where the president-elect was not available for immediate service but might later become available, "the Vice President elect shall *act as* President" (emphasis added).

35. On the ad hoc Eisenhower-Nixon arrangement, see John D. Feerick, *From Failing Hands: The Story of Presidential Succession* (1965), 228–29; John D. Feerick, *The Twenty-Fifth Amendment: Its Complete History and Applications* (rev. ed. 1992), 55–56.

36. Precisely because of the indispensability of the vice president, Congress would do well to provide by statute for a framework to determine the existence of any possible vice-presidential disability. Otherwise, the Twenty-fifth Amendment's careful clockwork may well jam up in a later presidential-disability scenario. A sensible statute would give the next person in the line of succession—ideally, a cabinet officer—the same triggering role in determining vice-presidential disability that the amendment gives to the VP in triggering a determination of presidential disability.

37. See Chapter 4, pp. 170–73. The Presidential Succession Act of 1947 is currently codified at 3 U.S.C. 19.

38. In order to conform with the Article I, section 6 incompatibility clause, the 1947 statute requires a legislative leader to resign from Congress before assuming duties as acting president. This requirement makes it awkward for a president undergoing a temporary disability—say, planned surgery—to hand power over to the speaker of the House for a few days. Why would the speaker (or Senate president pro tempore) give up his position for so short an expected stint as acting president? The problem is further complicated because if the speaker and Senate president pro tempore decline to resign, the secretary of state would then become acting president, but would, under the statute, be subject at any later time to being bumped out of the Oval Office if either top legislator changes his mind—as might happen if, say, the presidential disability unexpectedly lengthens. The bumping provision creates terrible incentives for political gamesmanship. It is also unconstitutional. Article II says that a statutory successor shall act as president *"until the Disability be removed."* By what right can Congress instead declare that a statutory successor shall act as president *until some other suitor wants the job?*

39. For more discussion of these issues, see the sources cited in Chapter 4, n. 110.

40. The most emphatic proponent of this view is Professor Ackerman. See Bruce Ackerman, *We the People: Transformations* (1998), 490–91 n. 1. For a forceful rebuttal, see Michael S. Paulsen, "A General Theory of Article V: The Constitutional Lessons of the Twenty-seventh Amendment," *Yale LJ* 103 (1993): 677.

41. *Cong. Rec.,* 138:S6948 (Senate vote on S. Con. Res. 120, May 20, 1992), H3505 (House vote on H. Con. Res. 320, May 20, 1992); Richard L. Berke, "Congress Backs 27th Amendment," *New York Times,* May 21, 1992, p. 26.

42. In seeking to prevent possible abuses by electorally repudiated lawmakers, the 1789 proposal anticipated—and the 1992 ratification echoed—the spirit of the intervening Twentieth Amendment, which also, in its own way, sought to limit mischievous lame ducks.

43. Foner, *Reconstruction,* 523. As Foner explains, many factors were at work in the election of 1874.

44. *Dillon v. Gloss,* 256 U.S. 368 (1921). The *Dillon* case is discussed below, in n. 49.

45. See Chapter 10, n. 19. Note also that New York ratified the Fifteenth Amendment in April 1869 and then rescinded this ratification in January 1870, well before the needed twenty-eight (out of thirty-seven total) states had said yes. By early February 1870, twenty-seven other states had said yes, and two more states said yes by mid-February. Thus, as with the Fourteenth Amendment, the Fifteenth cleared the Article V bar without any need to count rescinding states as yes votes.

46. Ohio ratified the Fifteenth in January 1870 after having rejected it in April 1869; Arkansas approved the Sixteenth in April 1911 after having disapproved it in January of that year; and Idaho said yes to the Twenty-second Amendment in January 1951 after having said no to it two years earlier.

47. As the master of its amendment proposals, Congress is also free to insert sunset clauses in the proposals themselves. As we saw in Chapter 11, p. 417, several amendments, beginning with the Eighteenth, have contained in their texts provisos effectively requiring ratification within seven years.

48. Such a resolution would not require the president's signature; presidents play no formal role in the Article V amendment process. See Chapter 9, n. 7.

49. Although *Dillon v. Gloss* suggested that amendment proposals must lapse at some point, this suggestion occurred against a general backdrop in which the last-in-time rule was not clearly understood. In fact, leading scholars in the *Dillon* era asserted that a yes vote could not be rescinded at any later moment; see Herman Ames, *The Proposed Amendments to the Constitution of the United States* (1896), 300. Given this backdrop, *Dillon*'s dicta would have worked to limit the perversity of the ratification ratchet. But once it becomes clear that the last-in-time rule should apply, there is much less need to read sunset rules into Article V, à la *Dillon.* In any event, *Dillon*'s legal status today is doubtful, thanks to the later case of *Coleman v. Miller,* 307 U.S. 433 (1939), where the Court pointedly declined to declare that a proposed amendment had lapsed due to the excess passage of time. Some members of the *Coleman* Court appeared to think that the Reconstruction Amendment process had established in practice that Congress would be the sole ex post judge of ratification timing issues. But a narrower and sounder reading of the Reconstruction precedent is that Congress is properly the judge of state republicanism, insofar as that issue bears on Article V. On this narrower view, Congress is not neces-

sarily the judge of all other Article V issues. Cf. *CG,* 39–2:501–05 (Bingham, Jan. 16, 1867).

Another interesting question that case law leaves open: If Congress has placed a sunset proviso not in the amendment text itself, but rather in *the enacting resolution* accompanying a proposed amendment, is a later Congress free to extend this sunset without thereby wiping the ratification slate clean? This issue famously arose in the context of the proposed Equal Rights Amendment. For analysis, see generally Paulsen, "General Theory."

50. *Annals,* 1:735 (Madison, Aug. 13, 1789); *Elliot's Debates,* 1:325 (S.C.), 331 (N.Y.), 4:246 (N.C.).

51. For important reminders that at the statutory and state constitutional levels, and at the level of actual practice, the story of American suffrage has not been so dramatically unidirectional, see Keyssar, *Right to Vote,* and Rogers M. Smith, *Civic Ideals: Conflicting Visions of Citizenship in U.S. History* (1997).

52. *Annals,* 1:735 (Aug. 13, 1789). See generally Edward Hartnett, "A 'Uniform and Entire' Constitution; or, What if Madison Had Won?" *Constitutional Commentary* 15 (1988): 251.

53. *Annals,* 1:735 (Aug. 13, 1789).

54. Ibid., 737.

POSTSCRIPT

1. See generally Bruce Ackerman, *We the People: Foundations* (1991), 3–33, 230–322; Bruce Ackerman, "The New Separation of Powers," *Harvard LR* 113 (2000): 633; Robert A. Dahl, *How Democratic Is the American Constitution?* (2001); Edmund S. Morgan, *Inventing the People: The Rise of Popular Sovereignty in England and America* (1988).

2. Among the many fine Philadelphia stories now in print, my favorite is Christopher Collier and James Lincoln Collier, *Decision in Philadelphia: The Constitutional Convention of 1787* (1986).

3. And also in the Founders' lives. For instance, in Jack Rakove's engaging biography, *James Madison and the Creation of the American Republic* (2d ed. 2002), the author is at pains to tell the reader that Madison was personally kind to his slaves. Ibid., 213. I should think the far more important point to stress is that Madison *failed to free them.* Regardless of how "exemplary" (Rakove's word) Madison was as a master, what security would Madison's slaves—and their children—have upon the master's death? What if he fell into financial distress during his life? Cf. ibid., 208 (Madison "felt he had no choice, and in a transaction that pained him deeply, he sold a number of slaves to a kinsman").

4. *Marbury v. Madison,* 5 U.S. (1 Cranch) 137, 176–77 (1803); *Martin v. Hunter's Lessee,* 14 U.S. (1 Wheat.) 304, 324–25 (1816); *McCulloch v. Maryland,* 17 U.S. (4 Wheat.) 316, 402–5 (1819). In Lincoln's First Inaugural Address, the refer-

ence to the Preamble's "more perfect Union" was explicit; at Gettysburg, Lincoln's allusion was more subtle, playing on the grand "We the People" phraseology in a passage that also recalled *McCulloch*'s musings on the Preamble; 17 U.S. 404–5 ("The government of the Union . . . is, emphatically, and truly, a government of the people. In form and in substance it emanates from them. Its powers are granted by them, and are to be exercised directly on them, and for their benefit").

5. See Gordon S. Wood, "Slaves in the Family," *The New York Times,* Dec. 14, 2003, Book Review, 10; Garry Wills, "Letter to the Editor," *The New York Times,* Dec. 28, 2003, Book Review, 4.

6. 198 U.S. 45 (1905). For Ackerman's account of this case, see his *Foundations,* 63–66, 100–3.

7. In addition to *Lochner* itself, see *Coppage v. Kansas,* 236 U.S. 1, 17–18 (1915), in which the *Lochner*-era Court condemned legislative efforts to level "inequalities of fortune." For what it's worth, my reading of *Lochner* is the orthodox one. For similar readings, see, e.g., Laurence H. Tribe, "The Supreme Court, 1972 Term — Foreword: Toward a Model of Roles in the Due Process of Life and Law," *Harvard LR* 87 (1973): 1, 6–7, 12–13; Cass R. Sunstein, "*Lochner*'s Legacy," *Columbia LR* 87 (1987): 873; Jed Rubenfeld, "The Anti-Antidiscrimination Agenda," *Yale LJ* 111(2002): 1114.

8. The only textual amendment to be ratified under FDR was the Twenty-first, repealing Prohibition.

Acknowledgments

For research assistance, fact-checking, editorial input, and overall good cheer, I owe a great debt to my students, both graduate and undergraduate. I am especially grateful for the friendship and assistance of Josh Bendor, Manuel Berrélez, Nola Breglio, Todd Brewster, Ashlie Case, Josh Chafetz, Lisa Chan, Olivia Choe, Ileana Ciobanu, Davon Collins, Brett Edkins, Taniyah Eyer, Sarah Griswold, Josh Hawley, Allon Kedem, Daniel Korobkin, Ariel Lavinbuk, Jon Lewinsohn, Marcelino Pantoja, Nick Parrillo, Jaynie Randall, Brian Rodkey, Peter Shindel, Matt Spence, Jake Sullivan, Bart Szewczyk, Felix Valenzuela, Caroline Wilson, Evan Young, and Jenny Xueni Zhang.

Among my colleagues, I have benefited enormously from conversations with Bruce Ackerman, Ian Ayres, Jack Balkin, Stuart Benjamin, Boris Bittker, Linc Caplan, Stephen Carter, Robert Dahl, David B. Davis, Noah Feldman, Rob Harrison, John Langbein, David Mayhew, Edmund Morgan, Jeff Powell, Jed Rubenfeld, Peter Schuck, Reva Siegel, and Stephen Skowronek. Over the years, three extraordinary deans—Guido Calabresi, Tony Kronman, and Harold Koh—have given me unstinting financial and moral support. Outside the walls of the academy, Paul R. Johnson and Jon Blue have been particularly faithful readers and dear friends.

In the world of book publishing, my literary agents, Glen Hartley and Lynn Chu, have helped me write a book that is both more intellectually ambitious and, I hope, more publicly accessible than the project that I originally envisioned when I came to their office to seek their counsel. For all their support and advice, I am grateful. At Random House, working with the legendary editor Bob Loomis has been a dream come true for me. Every one of the many pieces of advice he has offered has been pure gold.

My deepest debt is to my family. Thanks, Mom and Dad, (big) Vik, Arun, and Chris for your moral support. Thanks, (little) Vik, Kara, and Sara, for your merrymaking and mischief making. Most of all, thanks, Vinita—for everything.

Illustration Credits

Chapter 1, page 3: *The Pennsylvania Packet, and Daily Advertiser* (September 19, 1787). Courtesy National Constitution Center, Philadelphia.

Chapter 2, page 55: *Earliest Known Photograph of the United States Capitol* (1846). Photo by John Plumbe, Jr. Courtesy Library of Congress.

Chapter 3, page 99: *The United States Senate, A.D. 1850.* Drawing by Peter Frederick Rothermel; engraving by Robert Whitechurch, 1855. Courtesy Library of Congress.

Chapter 4, page 129: *The Washington Family* (1789–96). Painting by Edward Savage. Image copyright © 2004 by Board of Trustees, National Gallery of Art, Washingon, D.C. Courtesy Andrew W. Mellon Collection.

Chapter 5, page 175: *King Andrew the First* (1833). Courtesy Library of Congress.

Chapter 6, page 205: *John Marshall* (1808). Engraving by J. H. E. Whitney after an 1808 crayon drawing by Charles B. J. F. de Saint Memin. Copyright © 1889 by Thomas Marshall Smith. Courtesy Library of Congress.

Chapter 7, page 247: *JOIN, or DIE* (May 9, 1754). Drawing by Ben Franklin, originally published in *The Pennsylvania Gazette*. Courtesy Library of Congress.

Chapter 8, page 283: *The Eleventh Pillar* (August 2, 1788). Originally published in *The Massachusetts Centinel*. Courtesy Library of Congress.

Chapter 9, page 313: *The Presidential Elections of 1796 and 1800.* Courtesy Images of American Political History.

Chapter 10, page 349: *"Shall I Trust These Men, And Not This Man?"* (August 5, 1865). Drawing by Thomas Nast, originally published in *Harper's Weekly*. Courtesy Library of Congresss and HarpWeek, LLC.

Chapter 11, page 403: *Woman Suffrage Parade, May 6, 1912.* Courtesy Library of Congress.

Chapter 12, page 431: *March on Washington, August 28, 1963.* Photo by Warren K. Leffler. Courtesy Library of Congress and U.S. News & World Report, Inc.

Index

Page numbers in *italics* refer to illustrations.

About the Author

AKHIL REED AMAR graduated from Yale College and Yale Law School, and has been a member of the Yale Law School faculty since 1985. He is the author of *The Bill of Rights: Creation and Reconstruction* and has written widely on constitutional issues for *The New York Times, The Washington Post,* and the *Los Angeles Times.* He lives in Woodbridge, Connecticut, with his wife and three children.

About the Type

This book was set in Granjon, a modern recutting of a typeface produced under the direction of George W. Jones, who based Granjon's design upon the letter forms of Claude Garamond (1480–1561). The name was given to the typeface as a tribute to the typographic designer Robert Granjon.